W Stewart Barrow
Edinburgh, 1984

THE SOCIAL AND ECONOMIC DEVELOPMENT OF SCOTLAND

BEFORE 1603

CAITHNESS
LEWIS
L. Broom
ROSS
Tain
Moray Firth
N. UIST
KINTAIL
SKYE
Raasay
Elgin
BUCHAN
Inverness
MORAY
BADENOCH
S. UIST
MAR
Aberdee
Barra
MEARNS
LOCHABER
ATHOLE
Brechin
Montrose
Coll
ANGUS
Arbroath
Tiree
BREADALBANE
Dundee
L. Etive
MULL
STRATHEARN
Perth
Firth of Tay
Iona
LORNE
St Andrews
MENTEITH
FIFE
Crail
Anstruther
Scarba
L. Fyne
COWAL
Kirkcaldy
Colonsay
LENNOX
Stirling
Burntisland
Firth of Forth
JURA
Dunbar
Leith
Dumbarton
Linlithgow
Edinburgh
Glasgow
Haddington
Renfrew
LOTHIANS
MERSE
ISLAY
BUTE
CUNNINGHAM
Gigha
TWEEDDALE
KINTYRE
Irvine
Kelso
ARRAN
KYLE
TEVIOTDALE
Jedburgh
Firth of Clyde
Ayr
CARRICK
NITHSDALE
ANNANDALE
Dumfries
ENGLAND
IRELAND
GALLOWAY
Solway Firth
Land over 600 Feet above Sea Level
Copyright
John Bartholomew & Son, Ltd. Edinbur

THE SOCIAL AND ECONOMIC DEVELOPMENT OF SCOTLAND

BEFORE 1603

BY

I. F. GRANT

AUTHOR OF
"EVERYDAY LIFE ON AN OLD HIGHLAND FARM

GREENWOOD PRESS, PUBLISHERS
WESTPORT, CONNECTICUT

Originally published in 1930
by Oliver and Boyd, Edinburgh and London

First Greenwood Reprinting 1971

Library of Congress Catalogue Card Number 72-114533

SBN 8371-4804-9

Printed in the United States of America

FOREWORD

THE writer would like to take this opportunity of thanking Mr J. R. N. Macphail, K.C., Dr Marguerite Wood, Dr H. W. Meikle, and Principal J. F. Rees, to whose learning and wisdom her book is in many ways deeply indebted. One of the greatest joys in her pleasant task of trying to write a summary of early Scots social and industrial history has been the helpfulness and kindness she has met with from those with greater expert knowledge than her own: Professor R. K. Hannay, Dr Annie E. Cameron; Mr W. Angus of H.M. Register House, Edinburgh; Mr Thomas Innes of Learney, Mr A. O. Curle, Dr Mary T. Rankin, Dr Charles Malcolm; Mr J. Robb, Secretary to the Carnegie Trustees of the Universities of Scotland; Mr F. J. Cox of the London Library, and Mr Joseph Davidson of the National Library of Scotland.

In ploughing yet one more furrow in the field of Scots history, the writer has been constantly indebted, not only to the work of those who are labouring there at the present time, but to the workers of the past—especially to the editors, and, above all, to the indexers who have done so much to make the ancient records and chartularies available to the ordinary reader; and, even more, to the scribes of long ago, who so laboriously and racily recorded the doings of their own day to our infinite benefit. To all these, past and present, the writer would like to say " thank you "; and if by this, her so generalized book, she can tempt any Scot to hew a little upon his or her own account in those most fascinating quarries, the original sources of our native history, she will feel well satisfied with the result of her labours.

CONTENTS

SECTION I

CHAPTER I

CHAPTER II

CHAPTER III

CHAPTER IV

SECTION II

CHAPTER I

CHAPTER II

CHAPTER III

CHAPTER IV

CHAPTER V

CHAPTER VI

CHAPTER VII

CHAPTER VIII

CHAPTER IX

CHAPTER X

PRELIMINARY

ALTHOUGH clearly cut boundaries cannot be drawn, Scots economic history falls into certain very definitely marked periods. In the twilight of history there was a period dominated by Gaelic types of social organization. This was followed, in the eleventh century, by a period in which the feudal ideas that were spreading themselves all over Western Europe became current, and in which Scotland made her own adjustments to a system of social organization that was largely uniform with that of other neighbouring countries. This period of the early Middle Ages was one of intense organizing activity ; the framework of the national institutions, that were to last for centuries, was then built up. From the fourteenth to the sixteenth century, the condition of the country was curiously static. The social framework that had been created was elaborated and modified, but was not fundamentally changed. In most essentials Scotland was still in the feudal period, whilst England was undergoing the great adjustments of Tudor times. The seventeenth, eighteenth, and nineteenth centuries, which fall outside the scope of the present work, saw the struggle between the older forms of social and industrial organization and the new ; the desperate fight that Scotland made to attain prosperity ; and her final emergence as one of the great industrial peoples of the world.

From the purely economic point of view the later periods are undoubtedly of greater importance. The story of the great clash of traditions and interests ; that of the long series of efforts and failures and of ultimate successes, possess a dramatic quality by reason of their intensity. Nevertheless, the study of the earlier periods also has its value and its especial interest. It is impossible to appreciate the changes that were made unless one realizes what went before. All that pertains to the land is under the influence of very ancient things : the organization of the countryside, the layout of holdings; most important of all, the attitude of country-folk to the rights of possession—all have their origins in the misty past. It is surely the filial duty of all Scots of the present day to know something of that curious process of fusion between the Norman, the Angle, the Gael, and those dimmer ancestors who went before, to which modern Scotland owes its individuality and the character of its people. Then the study of economic history is peculiarly helpful to anyone who is interested in the more general history of the country, especially in the troublous and complicated times of the fourteenth, fifteenth, and sixteenth centuries. It has often been said that the history of England describes the growth of her institutions, whereas the history of Scotland is merely a succession of episodes. It is for this reason that much of the political history of Scotland, in spite of its picturesque and lurid details, possesses a certain sameness. Economic history shows one of the main motives—the absolute need of the possession of land—and deals with the outward circumstances—an uncertainty of tenure, and a constantly wavering balance of power between the Crown and certain factions of the nobles—which again and again, and with but minor variations, tended to produce the same results. Lastly, when we come to the sixteenth century, the period when the great intellectual awakening of the Renaissance was vitalizing the life of Western Europe, and when an intensification of religious and polemical fervour was manifesting itself in the Old Religion as well as in the New, the very negativeness of Scots industrial progress is of especial interest. It was not in the mellowing times of prosperity but under the most adverse material circumstances that the Scots took their full and fair share in the great European movements of that age. When we read of the meagre shifts, the rather pitiful ostentation, the very humble means of those forebears of ours who lived in those most unspacious days, may they move us neither to scorn, nor to pity, nor to a feeling of smug superiority, but to a realization of the fact that the relative ease with which the material wealth of a people can be computed bears no ratio whatsoever to its importance in the greater scheme of life, and that of nations it may be as truly said as of men, that they do not live by bread alone.

SECTION I

"Too often we allow ourselves to suppose that, could we but get back to the beginning, we should find that all was intelligible and should then be able to watch the process whereby simple ideas were smothered under subtleties and technicalities. But it is not so. Simplicity is the outcome of technical subtlety; it is the goal not the starting-point. As we go backwards the familiar outlines become blurred; the ideas become fluid, and instead of the simple we find the indefinite."—F. W. MAITLAND, *Domesday Book and Beyond*, p. 9.

CHAPTER I

PART I. BEFORE HISTORY

We can study the economic history of Scotland only so far back as the dates of the material upon which we can work allow us to do so, but the economic life of the people stretches back for centuries beyond such artificial limits. Flint arrow-heads are picked up in most parts of Scotland, and therefore in regions that are far from flint-bearing soil—grain, which is not an indigenous plant, has been found there in connection with bronze age and even neolithic remains [1]—a prehistoric dug-out discovered in the present city of Glasgow had a hole plugged with cork.[2] Such examples of local and foreign exchanges could be multiplied almost indefinitely; for instance, a bronze balance beam, evidently belonging to a pedlar, was picked up near the Moray Firth, and with it a Mercian coin of the eighth century.[3]

Our unstoried predecessors had made their great discoveries, discoveries even more epoch-making than the harnessing of steam or of electricity. They had learned to light fires, to build dwellings, to work metals, to domesticate animals, to weave fabrics. By the time that they come within the ken of the twilight of history they had advanced to a considerable degree of specialization. The stones with mysterious symbols carved upon them, that are a feature of very early Christian Scotland,

[1] E. Cecil Curwin, " Prehistoric Agriculture in Britain," in *Antiquity* (1917), vol. i, p. 261.

[2] S. Smiles, *Industrial Biographies*, p. 4.

[3] J. Anderson, *Scotland in Early Christian Times*, vol. ii, p. 23. Another example of the early exchange of goods comes from the excavations at Traprain Law by A. O. Curle. Pottery and glass of the distinctive type made in Gaul and on the Rhine and dating from after the fourth century, when the Romans withdrew from Scotland, were found there. *Proc. Soc. Antiq. Scot.*, 1916, p. 139.

were the work of special masons,[1] the exquisitely wrought brooches, also typical of the period, are much more obviously the work of very skilful craftsmen ; in Saint Andamnan's *Life of Saint Columba* sailors are mentioned many times, also fishermen ; and, more than once, a smith.

The study of such vestiges of the social life of the people in Scotland in the times of prehistory, and in the shadowy period which followed, and which lasted, in Scotland, down to the eleventh century, is a special branch of knowledge and falls outside the scope of this book. There are, however, two points that should be stressed. In the first place, there is the merely negative fact that we have no evidence to suggest that the Gaels who came over to Scotland managed to build up a state of society in any way approaching the old Irish civilization, from which they were an offshoot. We have nothing to compare in quality with the gold work of the Irish, with their voluminous code of laws, with their early literature, or with that supreme masterpiece, the *Book of Kells*. There are merely indications that a much ruder form of the same Celtic civilization did exist. Let us, for instance, take that lovely Irish thing, Cael's song about the house of Cridhe, his sweetheart.[2] The house was full of men, women, and boys who rendered her perfect service, and whose mantles were none of them " pale and smooth," i.e. worn to a gloss, and of minstrels and musicians. There was abundance of crystal vats and of exquisite goblets of ruddy gold and polished horn. The dun itself was built with lime ; it measured a hundred feet from one angle of it to another, and the roof was of blue and yellow birds' wings. Before it was an apple tree, dropping four apples at a time into a vat of princely bronze. Cridhe's own bower, by the lochside, was made of silver and yellow gold, and its ridgy roof was thatched with crimson birds' wings. Its door-posts were green hued, and silver was the lintel above. Men heavily wounded might fall asleep at the sound of the warbling of the fairy birds in the eaves. Within were a gold-covered chair and a gold-covered bed set with gems,

[1] J. Anderson, *Scotland in Early Christian Times*, vol. ii, p. 230. An inscription, partly Celtic, partly Scandinavian, found in the Isle of Man reads : " Malbrigd, son of Athacan the Smith, erected this cross for his soul; but his kinsman Gaut made it and all in Man."

[2] Translation from Standish O'Grady, *Silva Gadelica*, p. 101.

and yet another bed wrought of gold and of silver and with tent-like curtains, " having the appearance of the foxgloves flower and running upon slender copper rods." In the ballads of mediaeval times preserved in the *Book of the Dean of Lismore*, and the folk tales and poems diligently collected in Lord Archibald Campbell's *Waifs and Strays of Gaelic Tradition*, and in the collection called *Leabhar na Feinne*, by Campbell, we have nothing at all to compare with this as an artist's dream of a house, merely a scattered phrase here and there, such as the description of a house with green door-posts, and a truly Gaelic love of the colour yellow, to show that the ruder makers and singers of decaying epics in Scotland still drew inspiration from the old flowering of their civilization in Erin. The point is of more than archaeological interest, for our estimate of the value of the feudal civilization of the middle ages largely depends upon the degree of civilization that it displaced. We have abundance of material to prove that a Celtic culture existed in Scotland until the eleventh century, but there is nothing to show that it had reached at all a high degree of organization or that it was capable of doing so.

The other point is of even greater importance. It is commonplace knowledge that, before David I and his dynasty introduced feudalism into Scotland, all land, at least north of the Forth, was held under a tribal system, but one is rather too apt to leave the matter there. The phrase " tribal system " automatically calls up a definite conception of organic development. One imagines the patriarch passing into the wilderness—the increase of his progeny and of his stock—a gradual localizing in their wanderings after pasture and game—the beginnings of the cultivation of the tribal lands—a system of communal agriculture, and, perhaps later, a temporary allotment of shares in the common land—the allocation of individual shares to the ruler, the priest, the judge—the enslavement of captives and malefactors, even of the poorest tribesmen—the emergence of right to the private ownership of land. Such is the commonly accepted idea of the story of the evolution of a tribe, and there is good evidence that the inhabitants of Scotland themselves, or their closest kindred, went through most of these stages.[1] It

[1] The folk tales and sagas of Ireland concerning the Gadheal, of which many translations exist—Lady Gregory, *Gods and Fighting Men*; A.

is, however, rather important to remember that they cannot have been lived through by the same tribes, for waves upon waves of immigrants must have come to our shores. The anthropologists can prove from our present day physical characteristics that we are a very mixed people.[1] Archaeologists reach the same conclusions from the examination of the prehistoric remains of Scotland.[2] The story of such racial conflicts has come down to us in some of our fairy tales.[3] The classical writers, who give us our first glimpse of the people of Scotland, also notice the presence of different races.

Certainly, in times that are dimly known to history, the whole of our country has changed hands.[4] Besides lesser adjustments, such as the obliteration of the British kingdom in Strath Clyde, the Angles invaded the north-east coast of England and carried their conquest right up to the Firth of Forth. In other parts of Scotland the Picts—that mysterious people whose race has never been authoritatively determined—were dominated

Douglas Hyde, *A Literary History of Ireland*; Standish O'Grady, *Silva Gadelica*, etc.—describe a sparsely populated country, where land was largely unallotted and where men lived to a great extent by hunting, and upon acorns and honey. In St Andamnan's *Life of St Columba* (Dr Reeves' translation), p. 63, poor folk also lived largely by the chase, and wealth was estimated by cattle and not by land or money (pp. 50, 51). Julius Caesar, describing Southern Britain, writes of coastwise tribes that grew corn and of inland tribes that were mainly hunters and herdsmen. The Welsh laws show tribal organization and common family possession at a later date. Cf. J. E. Lloyd, *History of Wales*, vol. i, p. 284. G. H. Orpen, *Ireland under the Normans*, vol. i, p. 24, shows how largely the organization of the Kingdoms of Ireland was theoretic.

[1] J. Beddoe, *Races of Britain*, pp. 26, 42, 43, 368, 387.

D. A. Mackenzie, *Ancient Man in Britain*, ch. xi.

T. H. Bryce, "Certain Points in Scottish Ethnology," in *Scottish Hist. Review*, ii, p. 275.

John Brownless, *Origin and Details of Racial Types in Scotland* (pamphlet). Published for the Henderson Trust by Oliver and Boyd.

[2] R. Munro, *Prehistoric Scotland*, Conclusion, p. 442 *et seq.*

T. H. Bryce, Papers Before the British Association, Oxford, 1926; Glasgow, 1928.

[3] See J. F. Campbell, *West Highland Popular Tales.*

Sir J. Rhys, *Celtic Folklore.*

Campbell, *Waifs and Strays of Celtic Tradition*, for examples.

[4] P. Hume Brown, *History of Scotland*, vol. i, chs. ii and iii, gives summary of the changes and a map.

by the Scots, whose latest and recorded occupation of Argyle took place in the ninth century, and lost their language and national individuality, and, it is only reasonable to assume, the greater part of their land to the newcomers. In the North and West the Vikings began their incursions in the ninth century, and gradually obtained possession of the Hebrides, the Orkney and Shetland Islands, and the more fertile parts of Sutherland and Caithness.[1]

All the early sources of history describe a welter of fighting while these territorial changes were adjusting themselves,[2] and as the Picts themselves, to judge from the *notitiae* in the *Book of Deer*, as well as the peoples who supplanted them, had reached a stage of social development when some at least of the land was privately owned and slaves were held,[3] there is surely more

[1] W. F. Skene, *Celtic Scotland*, vol. i, p. 396, gives a map of the Scandinavian possessions in the tenth century.

Canon J. Macleod, "Norsemen in the Hebrides," *Scottish Hist. Review*, vol. 22, 1924–5, p. 42, stresses fact that Norsemen conquered land and founded new ruling families.

[2] A. O. Anderson, *Early Sources of Scots History*, has a complete collection of them.

J. Robertson, *Scotland under her Early Kings*, vol. i, gives them in narrative form.

[3] Commentaries on Early Irish Laws by Joyce and by Prof. Macmillan.

T. P. Ellis, *Welsh Tribal Law and Customs in the Middle Ages.*

Scandinavian Sagas, such as the Orkneyinga and Burnt Njal. Translations are available. See also article by F. Storer Clouston, *Scottish Hist. Review* vol. 16, pp. 22-23.

For general summary, see J. Mackinnon, *Constitutional History of Scotland*, p. 16 onwards.

In dealing with "Celtic System," Cosmo Innes and Skene have built up their theories on *Notitiae* in *Book of Deer*, 565–1100.

Sir Archibald Lawrie in *Early Scottish Charters*, p. 220, states as his personal opinion that "the value of these *notitiae* has been exaggerated. The account of the foundation of Aberdour and Deer is a picturesque tradition written nearly 600 years later than the time of St Columba. The rest is little more than a list of donations of lands to an unnamed Church of St Drostan. There is little to fix the date of any of them. The record is meagre. It is not safe to draw from it conclusions as to the state of the people and of the Church in Scotland prior to the twelfth century."

Lawrie doubts if there was a Columban Monastery at Deer. Considers that it was impossible that if it survived from the time of St Columba to David I no notice of it should have survived.

Lawrie considers that the *Notitiae* "may have been written by an Irishman, one of the secular clergy living at Aberdour or Deer in the twelfth

than a strong probability that conquered land fell to the share of the hero who led the victors and that conquered people became a landless, probably a servile class.[1] Most likely what happened in the Highlands in historic times—the evolution of a clan organization among the kindred of the head of the family, and the manufacture of a nominal kinship with the ruling family by some of the original occupiers of the soil—also occurred in earlier times, but the result cannot have had the organic completeness of a tribal system that had grown up from the beginning. Nor was there a time of peaceful consolidation in which social organization would have had favourable opportunities for development. The provinces into which Scotland was divided in the ninth, tenth, and eleventh centuries seem to have been vexed by many warfares among themselves, with the king of all Scotland, and with the Norsemen and the Angles. How far their mormaers or leaders achieved the continuity of tribal family leadership there is nothing to show. It is at least suggestive that, according to *The Scots Peerage*, in the twelfth century, two out of the seven—Fife and Athol—had mormaers who were probably descendants of Malcolm Canmore himself.[2]

We have a twelfth-century account of what went on in the South-West, and it was probably worse but not very different from what happened in other parts. David I, the great organizer, wished to restore the ancient church lands to the see of Glasgow. He consulted the wise men and elders of Cumbria, who made inquisition and reported to him that [3] the line of bishops founded by Kentigern came to an end and " various

century, who may have collected the traditions of grants of lands to Drostan's churches, writing in Irish and using titles—Mormaer and Toisech—known in Ireland.

[1] When the Scots first took possession of Dalriada the references suggest clan rather than tribal ownership.

A. O. Anderson, *Early Sources of Scottish History*, vol. i, pp. ciii, civ, 1, 2, 148.

W. F. Skene, *Chronicle of Picts and Scots*, pp. 308-314.

In Ireland, according to tradition, the victorious Gauls enslaved the original inhabitants, the Firbolg. One clan of slaves was said to be their descendants. W. F. Skene, *Celtic Scotland*, vol. iii, p. 139.

[2] See vol. iv, p. 2 ; vol. i, p. 415.

[3] The Translation is from W. F. Skene, *Celtic Scotland*, iii, p. 23.

seditions and insurrections rising all around not only destroyed the church and its possessions, but, laying waste the whole country, delivered its inhabitants into exile. Then, also, all good being exterminated, after a considerable interval of time different tribes of different nationalities pouring in from different parts inhabited the deserted country, but being of separate race, speaking a dissimilar language, and living after different fashion, not easily agreeing among themselves, they maintained paganism rather than the cultivation of the faith." Until David himself, as Prince of Cumbria, " corrected their obscene and wicked contagion and bridled their contumelious contumacy with nobleness of soul and inflexible severity."

Fate has indeed conspired to obliterate any organization that the Scots may have introduced when they dominated the Picts, for those parts of the country which in after years were the least affected by the feudalizing process—the Northern and Western Highlands and Islands—are also those where the Norsemen effected a certain degree of settlement, and certainly for a time held the overlordship of the land.

Tribal, or perhaps it would be more correct to say, clannish, the method of landholding in early Scotland doubtless was. This form of social structure is inherent in the Celtic culture, which was then predominant over the greater part of the country. The point that I am anxious to make is that the word "system," if it conveys any idea of a settled, organized, uniform condition of affairs, is rather a misleading one. The matter is of some importance when one comes to deal with the Norman penetration, the history of the Highlands right down to the middle of the eighteenth century, perhaps down to the present day, and the whole development of agriculture and rural organization.

Part II. Outlines of History

The period covered by the reigns of Malcolm III, and by those of his direct descendants, i.e. from 1057 to 1286, is a very definite and important epoch in the economic and social history of Scotland. It is a period of development and change. The materials for tracing some of its movements are far more plentiful than were those relating to earlier times; but in others the process of evolution is almost entirely mysterious. Like a snowfall in springtime that vanishes in a night, the old order fades away and the student becomes aware of a new world, with only a vestige here and there—often curiously significant of the essential contours of the landscape—to remind him of a vanished phase.

It is perhaps worth while to summarize the political history of the times. When Malcolm III, surnamed Canmore, secured the throne of his father, the kingdom of Scotland was very loosely knit together—it might almost be likened to a bundle of unassorted fragments. As late as the seventh century the present country of Scotland was possessed by four inimical nations—the Picts to the North and the East, the Scots on the West Coast, the Angles encroaching upon the South-East, and the Britons in the South-West—in the words of their contemporary historian, the Venerable Bede, each studying divine truths in its own native tongue,[1] and, as we may gather from other sources, all of them fighting each other like wild cats. In addition, there were Calatria and Manann, covering rather the same ground as the modern counties of Stirling and Linlithgow, which were occupied by a mixed population of Angles, Picts, and Britons, and were a battle-ground for the rival peoples; and Galloway, possessed by a race long known as Picts, but whose connection with the rest of the old Pictish nation is uncertain.[2]

The centuries that followed saw a gradual fusion of these rival races. The Scots conquered the Picts, pushed back the advancing Anglian invaders on the South-East, and secured the ruined remains of the old British kingdom of Strath Clyde, and much territory to the south of it. There were, however, forces of disintegration as well as of consolidation at work. The various provinces of the united Scot-dominated country had a wild, independent identity of their own; Moray and the Mearns, especially, were most formidable subject states. The raids of the Vikings, which began in the ninth century, developed into a more permanent occupation of almost all the islands, Western and Northern, and of much of the coastwise

[1] Bede's *Ecclesiastical History*, L. Stevenson's Translation, vol. ii, p. 309.

[2] P. Hume Brown, *History of Scotland*, vol. i, ch. ii, p. 10, gives a helpful summary of the position.

and arable land on the adjacent part of the mainland.[1] Twelve out of the seventeen Scots kings who were Malcolm Canmore's predecessors were killed, either by the Norsemen or by their own insurgent subjects, and it was indeed a period of constant battle and sudden death, although the clouds were somewhat lightened during the prosperous reign of Macbeth, the usurper (1040–57).

By birth, and by early circumstances, Malcolm III (Canmore) was destined to introduce fresh influences into Scotland. He was the son of Duncan, Macbeth's victim, but, according to Boece, his mother was the daughter of Siward, the Anglian Earl of Northumberland, and he spent his years of exile in England. His father-in-law, Siward, was the enemy of Macbeth, and it was probably with Anglian aid that Malcolm finally overcame Macbeth and his heir and secured the kingdom. Until he came to the throne the heart of Scotland had lain to the North of the Forth, in the wide and fertile straths about the head of the Firth of Tay; but Malcolm's interests were turned towards the South, and he made five desperate attempts[2] to extend his frontiers beyond the lightly held Lothians.

By his second marriage, which took place in 1068, his leanings towards the South were intensified. Edgar Atheling, with his mother and two sisters, had taken refuge in Scotland after an unsuccessful attempt to reconquer Yorkshire, and Malcolm, urged by love and policy, married one of the Saxon princesses. Thanks to the biography written by Turgot, her confessor, Queen Margaret is one of the earliest names in Scots history that conveys to us a sense of personality—of an actual human entity.[3] The immediate result of the marriage, Malcolm's support of the Atheling's cause, ended in failure and was evanescent, but Margaret's dominating influence, inflexibly exercised towards bringing the Church in Scotland

[1] J. Robertson, *Early Scottish Kings*, vol. i, gives a very full account of the period.

A. O. Anderson, *Early Sources of Scottish History*, vol. i, has a complete and carefully annotated collection of all contemporary references to Scots History.

[2] P. Hume Brown, *History of Scotland*, vol. i, p. 56.

[3] St Columba, thanks to his biography by St Andamnan, and to a much lesser degree St Ninian, whose life is told at second hand by St Aildred, are the only two previous examples.

into much closer touch with that of Rome, and towards Southernizing the manners and customs of her husband's court and nobility, produced a permanent effect upon Scotland, the more so because it was strenuously carried on by her sons—who were all deeply influenced by her—and by their successors.

Turgot, in his intimate account of the queen's life, graphically, though probably with exaggeration, describes the economic effects of her racial and ecclesiastical policy. In order to provide objects that "appertained to the dignity of the divine service," the queen turned her chamber into " a workshop of sacred art, in which copes for the cantors, chasubles, stoles, altar-clothes, together with other priestly vestments and church ornaments of an admirable beauty, were always to be seen, either already made, or in course of preparation." These works being entrusted to " certain women of noble birth and approved gravity of manner . . ." [1]

Of the court, Turgot rather grandiloquently writes : " The queen, a noble gem of royal race, much more enobled the splendour of her husband's kingly magnificence, and contributed no little glory and grandure to the entire nobility of the realm and their retainers. It was due to her that the merchants who came by land and sea, by various countries, brought along with them for sale different kinds of precious wares which, until then, were unknown in Scotland. And it was at her instigation that the natives of Scotland purchased from these traders clothing of various colours, with ornaments to wear, so that from this period, through her suggestion, new costumes of different fashions were adopted, the elegance of which made the wearers appear like a new race of beings."

Turgot goes on to describe how Margaret organized the king's entourage, arranged that " persons of a higher position should be appointed for the king's service, a large number of whom were to accompany him in state whenever he either walked or rode abroad " ; and how she added to the sumptuousness of the clothing and equipage of the court.[2]

After Malcolm Canmore's death there was an attempted Gaelic revival, and there followed four years of struggle between Donald Bane, the brother of Malcolm, whom the " Scots chose as king," and Duncan, Malcolm's eldest son by an earlier wife,

[1] Turgot, *Life of St Margaret*, tr., Wm. Forbes Leith, p. 30. [2] *Ibid.* p. 40.

who was residing at the English court when his father died, and who was supported by a force of "English and French." Eventually the Atheling, in command of an army supplied by William Rufus, invaded Scotland and established Edgar, the son of Malcolm III and of Margaret, upon the throne.[1]

In 1107 Edgar died and was succeeded by his brother, Alexander I, surnamed the Fierce, who became king of Scotland to the North of the Forth and of part of the Lothians, Edgar, however, made David, a younger brother, heir to the rest of his possessions, which included Strath Clyde, the rest of the Lothians, and the greater part of what is now Cumberland and Northumberland. David assumed the title of Prince of Cumbria. In 1124 he succeeded Alexander, and became king of all Scotland. His reign is one of the most momentous in all Scots history. In it the policy ushered in by Malcolm and Margaret assumed its greatest activity. He is the founder of many of the institutions upon which Scotland's existence as a civilized community is based. In 1153 he died and was succeeded by his grandson, Malcolm IV, known as the Maiden, a delicate youth, who reigned twelve years. He was followed by his brother, William I, surnamed "the Lyon," who reigned till 1214. He was succeeded by his son, Alexander II, 1214–49, and by his grandson, Alexander III, who reigned from 1249 till 1286. And, as Hume Brown writes: "The period of seventy-two years covered by the reigns of Alexander II and Alexander III, is the golden age of Scottish History." [2]

Two directions taken by the general policy of these kings may be briefly indicated here. Like Malcolm Canmore, his five successors were all very wishful to extend the southern border of Scotland. Their energies were largely absorbed in trying to make good their claims to the Principality of Cumbria, but what successes they had were very transient, and both David I and William the Lyon were heavily defeated in 1138 and 1174 respectively; and the capture of William and his acknowledgement of the overlordship involved his country in deep humilia-

[1] R. S. Rait, *Making of Scotland*, pp. 17-18, gives a helpful summary of this very complicated episode, and quotes from the *Anglo-Saxon Chronicle*. The passages in inverted commas in my paragraph are taken from his fuller extracts.

[2] P. Hume Brown, *History of Scotland*, vol. i, p. 110.

tion, and was an important point in the English claims which caused the devastating Wars of Independence a hundred years later. For the time being, however, by the statesmanship of Richard I, and at great financial sacrifice to Scotland, a settlement was reached that lasted until after the death of Alexander III in the reign of Edward I of England, and the Scots frontier was fixed much where it is now (with the notable exception of Berwick), and the English claims to suzerainty were temporarily laid aside. The reigns of the two Alexanders differed from those of their predecessors in being entirely peaceful so far as the South was concerned.

The other line of policy pursued by this group of kings which calls for a brief mention is their determination to unify the subordinate provinces of their dominion. It was only after prolonged and constantly renewed struggles that the more outlying districts, especially Galloway, Moray (which included the present county of Inverness), and the districts partially occupied by the Norsemen were finally subdued. There were constant rebellions—that of 1160 was especially serious—and both Malcolm the Maiden and William the Lyon, are said to have systematically "planted" the province of Moray with more loyal adherents from the South. Alexander II and Alexander III completed its subjugation and were able to carry the process of consolidating their sovereignty over the semi-Scandinavian lords of the West much further. Finally, in 1263, after an unsuccessful expedition against Scotland by Haco, King of Norway, the whole of the Western Isles were formally ceded to Scotland, and, but for the Orkneys and Shetlands, and with the additional possession of Berwick, the boundaries of the kingdom of Scotland were complete and as they are at present.

The whole period is noteworthy for the close connection that existed between Scotland and England. David, William, and all three Alexanders were married to English, or rather Anglo-Norman, women,[1] and by right of these wives, as well as in compensation for their claims on Cumbria, they all held

[1] Several Scots princesses were also married to Englishmen, notably David I's elder sister "the Good Queen Maud," who had a great influence upon him when he came to the English Court as a youth. At one time he styled himself, "Earl David, brother of the Queen of the English." Cosmo Innes, *Scotland in the Middle Ages*, p. 87.

wide possessions in England as private subjects of the king of England. This was especially the case with David I, who, during his wife's lifetime, held the earldoms of Northampton and Huntingdon, with scattered possessions that even lay as far south as Tottenham.[1] Many of their great nobles, such as the de Bruces, de Morevilles, de Umphravilles, Paganis, de Braosa, likewise had possessions on both sides of the border, and owed allegiance to both the kings of England and of Scotland,[2] a position which was to lead to far-reaching complications. In the intervals of the earlier wars, and during the peaceful reigns of the two last Alexanders, the kings of Scotland—as relations of the king of England, as great English landowners, and, during the period of William's humiliation as a vassal monarch—often visited England and even went to Normandy. In the case of some of the great landholders of Scotland, the connection was even closer, and their homes, so far as a mediaeval baron had a home, were rather in England than in Scotland. This close connection with England had very deep effects upon the social structure of Scotland, but it would not be correct to think that Scotland was merely copying an established state of affairs in England. On the contrary, both countries were changing and developing very quickly, and because of the bonds between them their progress was nearly simultaneous and was closely analogous.

In point of economic development England and Scotland were more on a par in the twelfth century than they were for centuries afterwards. As Sir William Ashley points out: "Till nearly the end of the fourteenth century England was a purely agricultural country . . . entirely dependent on importation from abroad" for goods of finer quality, and only exporting raw products, "and of these by far the most important was the agricultural product, wool."[3] It was undoubtedly a period of expanding commercial life in England, and, whatever their origin, it saw the definite beginnings of mediaeval burgh organization, and of gilds and of hanses. Scotland, as will be shown

[1] Sir Archibald Lawrie, *Early Scottish Charters*, p. 306.

[2] *Ibid.* pp. 273, 307, 309.

[3] W. J. Ashley, *An Introduction to English Economic History and Theory*, Part I, p. 5. See also W. Cunningham, *Growth of Industry and Commerce*, p. 2.

later, was also advancing, step by step, along similar, though not identical lines. The great officers of the court and the king's household were instituted in both countries during this period. A system of fiscal administration was built up in England and Scotland almost simultaneously. Certain forms of law in Scotland were largely modelled on those in England. The feudal system not only took its rise in both countries during this period, but it was mainly supported in each by the Norman barons—in many cases by the same families and even the same individuals.

PART III. THE NORMANS

It is now time to consider the actual social development of Scotland. It was proceeding rapidly in many directions. It is perhaps most convenient to begin with the gradual feudalization of the kingdom. In England, by the end of the Saxon period, strong feudalizing tendencies had manifested themselves. The theory that the king was universal landowner, and that the great men held of him and owed him military service, was developing, and large numbers of lesser free men had, by commendation, placed themselves in dependence on a lord. Such a state of social organization had spread to the Anglian Lothians, which were only finally secured by Scotland in 1018.[1] The influence of these Saxon approximations to the theories underlying feudalism was extended by Queen Margaret, who, as we have seen, energetically remodelled her husband's court, and by the Saxons and Angles who were the chosen associates of her son King Edgar.[2]

With the accession of Alexander I, and, in an intensified degree, with that of David I, the predominating influence was not Saxon but Norman. As Professor Hume Brown says,[3] " the dominating fact of the period is the extensive assignment

[1] D. J. Mackinnon, *Constitutional History of Scotland*, vol. i, pp. 59-60.

[2] W. F. Skene, *Celtic Scotland*, vol. i, p. 438.

Cosmo Innes considered that the examination of early Scots charters showed " that so early at least as the reign of Malcolm IV the Crown was held to be the origin of all real property. Royal confirmations occur so frequently after that period, that we cannot avoid the conclusion that they were considered necessary for the completion of titles." Cosmo Innes, *Sketches of Early Scottish History*, p. 205.

[3] P. Hume Brown, *History of Scotland*, vol. i, p. 88.

of lands within the bounds of Scotland to men of Norman, Saxon, or Danish extraction," but the Normans certainly got the lion's share. At the assembly that acknowledged the sovereignty of the Maid of Norway (in 1283), out of thirteen earls and twenty-four barons, four earls and eighteen barons were Norman,[1] and of the rest few can have been without some strain of Norman blood. It is not possible to quote exact figures showing the actual proportion of the more fertile lands of Scotland held by Normans, or the exact number of the newcomers ; but there is abundance of evidence that they gradually obtained at least overlordship over a greater part of the lands of Scotland. The proportion of donors of land with Norman names that are preserved in the Abbey chartularies is astonishing. In the *Statistical Accounts of Scotland*, in parish after parish, one finds that the ancient lords of the land were Norman. Apart from a good many names of doubtful origin, J. Coutts, in *The Norman Invasion of Scotland*, claims nearly a hundred present-day Scots surnames as of Norman origin. Many of the newcomers founded different branches in many counties ; such were the Roses, the de Frisels, and the Comyns. Evidence of Norman landholders is to be found all over Scotland, in the fertile Lothians in large numbers, in the South-West, especially in Ayrshire and Renfrew, holding the fertile valleys among the Border hills, in Fife, in the seaboard lowlands of the Mearns and Aberdeenshire, in the Laighlands of Moray, and in the straths of Perthshire—holding the veins of richer valleyland that penetrate into what are now purely Highland districts—in Badenoch, Glen Lyon, and the Aird.[2] In some cases the possessions of a single Norman family were enormous. David I granted Walter Fitzalan, the

[1] P. Hume Brown, *History of Scotland*, vol. i, p. 128.

[2] Illustrations of such Norman holdings are very numerous and have never been systematically collected. The following are only a few examples of Norman penetration. J. Wilkie, *History of Fife*, p. 270, gives the names of 14 local landowners of Norman descent. The Introduction by C. E. Chisholm Batten to *Beauly Priory* (*Grampian Club*) gives an excellent picture of Norman penetration and inter-relations in the North. The Olifards and de Maynes held lands in Glenlyon and Fortingal in Perthshire—as inaccessible and Highland a district as one can imagine. A. Stewart, *A Highland Parish*, pp. 11 and 75. See also C. Sanford Terry's interesting genealogical tables in his *History of Scotland*: III, Bruce of Carrick—IV,

Steward, a third part of Bute, and what are now the parishes of Legerwood in Berwickshire, Innerwick in Haddington, Dundonald, Sorn, Mauchline, and Muirkirk in Ayrshire, and practically the whole of Renfrewshire.[1] The Bruces, de Morvilles, Comyns, Durwards, etc., were also great landowners.

Needless to say, the Normans never conquered Scotland by force of arms, as they conquered England. They owed their great acquisitions of land primarily to the favour of the Crown, but they actually obtained them in many ways. Some were gained through the forfeitures of rebels, as in the case of Moray, which was "planted" by Malcolm IV and by William, and which furnished a patrimony for the Bissets, Roses, Le Chiens, de Moravias (not originally Normans), and others. Some were granted lands that had reverted to the King, a very common thing in those uncertain times, as histories of early peerages show. Most commonly of all the Normans' lands were acquired by the "commendable method of marriage" with the heiresses or widows of the native nobility. In this way a cadet of the family of de Mowbray, originally de Albini, married the daughter of Earl Waltheof of Dunbar,[2] the Earldom of Angus passed to the de Umphravilles,[3] the Comyns secured the Earldom of Buchan and also Menteith for a time, though it afterwards fell to the Stewards, Durward secured temporary possession of Athol.[4] In one way and another the Normans thus gained a predominant position in Scotland. The matter is not merely one of genealogical interest, for their influence was a very formative one.

It is not difficult to understand why our native kings, largely of Norman blood themselves, should have made these

House of Stewart—XVI, Comyns of Badenoch—XVIII, Comyns of Buchan. Andrew Lang points out that the Ragman's Roll relating to all the districts between Perth and Elgin only has six possibly Celtic names. *Scottish Hist. Review*, vol. vi, p. 325.

[1] C. Innes, *Scotland in the Middle Ages*, pp. 203-204, gives a more detailed list.

[2] J. Coutts, *The Norman Invasion of Scotland*, 120.

[3] W. F. Skene, *Celtic Scotland*, iii, p. 288.

[4] *Ibid.* p. 290. C. Sanford Terry's tables: IV, House of Stewart—XI, Ancient Earls of Angus—XIV, Ancient Earls of Athol—XVIII, Comyns of Buchan—XXVII, Ancient Earls of Menteith, etc.

W. F. Skene, *Celtic Scotland*, iii, pp. 287-290, describes the Normanizing of four out of the seven ancient earldoms of Scotland.

sweeping introductions of the new race into Scotland. The Normans of the eleventh and twelfth centuries were .congenial and fascinating companions for the able, ambitious, enterprising descendants of Malcolm and Margaret. They were members of the proudest and most successful race in Europe—they were, as one of them said, infeft with victory. Their arms, their methods of fighting, their system of military and social organization, were " the newest things " in Europe. Renowned as they were as soldiers and as organizers, they were extremely useful to the kings of Scotland in the latter's efforts to extend their frontiers and to exert their dominion over insubordinate provinces.[1]

Now that gunpowder has annihilated the old methods of warfare, it requires an effort of imagination to visualize the enormous prestige that the mail-clad knight enjoyed during the Middle Ages. One has to go back to contemporary accounts of ancient wars, especially those written by eye-witnesses, to gain any idea of it. Luckily such accounts have survived—Froissart's immortal history, the *Scalachronica*, an account of the Scots Wars of Independence, by Sir Thomas Gray of Heton, a knight who actually took part in much of the fighting, and the rather indifferent Norman-French poem by de Fantosme, who was with the English forces during William the Lyon's raid into England and his capture, have all been translated and are easily accessible.[2] The subject of the Norman infiltration into Scotland is so vastly important that two examples may be quoted out of the considerable store of contemporary or almost contemporary accounts to show how invaluable the Norman knights were to the kings of Scotland.

When one of the many Scots revolts broke out, Alexander I was at Invergowry, " with ane honest cowrt "—as we know from the names of the witnesses to his charters, he was sur-

[1] G. H. Orpen, *Ireland under the Normans*, vol. ii, p. 324, shows the effect of the Normans' " instinct for organized rule " in Ireland. In after years the Irish districts were known as the " land of war," and those that were Normanized as the " land of peace."

[2] There are several editions of Froissart.

The *Scalachronica* was translated and annotated by Sir Herbert Maxwell.

Jordan de Fantosme's poem is published by the *Surtees Society*, and, with a translation, in the *Church Historians of England* series.

rounded by Normans. Suddenly he was attacked by " a multitude of Scottis men " (another version has " Ylis men "),

> in entent for to sla the King :
> Bot of ther come he gat wittering.
> He had nocht with him than him by
> Bot his awne Court solemply.
> Bot yet he esunterit thaim in by,
> And put thaim to the ware suthly.

He chased them through the Highlands, to the Stockford, the crossing of the Beauly river, a place of the greatest strategical importance in the history of the North. There they prepared to make a stand, but when he and his followers rode up :

> Off his cummyn thai were agast
> And turnyt all the bak and fled.
> Oure the watter thai thaim sped.

At the Stockford the Beauly is a tidal river, and

> the se withe a gret sprynge
> At the Stokfurde made stoppynge,

as if "to let him for to ryde." Alexander, however, and his mounted court "rode our" the ford at the height of the tide, and the rebels again broke,

> Eftyr thaim he fast hym spede,
> whil he our tuk thaim at the last
> And tuk and slew thaim, or he past
> out of that lande, that few he left
> To tak on hand sic purpose eft.
> Fra that day his legis all
> Oyssit hym alexander the Fers to calle.

It is entirely typical of the period that, in commemoration of his victory, he founded the abbey of Scone with English canons and endowed them with

> . . . ornamentis,
> Jowellis, bukis and westimentis.[1]

We must remember that so late as the '45 Highlanders had a superstitious dread of encountering mounted troops. The

[1] Androw of Wyntoun, *Orygynale Cronykil*, Book VII, ch. v, l. 620.

armour-clad followers of Alexander must have seemed to the ancient Scots to be terrible as a vision of the devastating forces of the Apocalypse.

In the Scots king's contests with the feudalized forces of England, it was essential to have troops of a similar type. The Battle of the Standard (1138) has been generously treated in the old chronicles, and it gives a wonderfully illuminating picture of the relations of the different elements in the Scots forces. According to Richard of Hexham, "that wicked army was composed of Normans, Germans, English, of Northumbrians and Cumbrians, of [men of] Teviotdale and Lothian, of Picts who are commonly called Galwegians, and of Scots."[1] The king of England was fighting in France, and David I was opposed by a hastily collected force of northern barons. Many of these had possessions in both countries, and their allegiance was divided. Robert de Bruce (the ancestor of the patriot king), in the name of these Normans, tried to dissuade David from fighting. No doubt the long peroration which Aildred of Rievaulx here inserts is of his own composition, but he was giving the arguments that he would expect the Norman to use; in fact the gist of it may well be genuine. He makes de Bruce say: "Against whom dost thou bear arms today and lead this huge army? Against the English, truly, and the Normans. O king are not these they with whom thou hast ever found useful council and ready help, and willing obedience besides? Since when, my lord, I ask thee hast thou found such faith in the Scots that thou dost with such confidence divest and deprive thyself and thine of the council of the English, the help of the Normans, as if the Scots would suffice alone for thee even against the Scots. . . ."

De Bruce goes on to remind David of the services of the Normans in restoring the line of Malcolm Canmore, when Donald, his brother, with Gaelic support, seized the crown, how they supported David himself in securing his separate Cumbrian principality during the lifetime of Alexander I, and how they came to his assistance when he besought their aid against a formidable rebellion in Moray: ". . . how joyful, how eager, how willing to help, how ready for the danger came Walter

[1] A. O. Anderson, *Scots Annals in English Chronicles*, p. 181. Quotation from Richard of Hexham, *Chronicles of Stephen.*

Espec and very many other nobles of the English to meet thee at Carlisle ; how many ships they prepared, how they made war, with what forces they made defence ; how they terrified all thy enemies, until they took Malcolm himself, surrendered to them : . . . So did the fear of us . . . by quenching all hope of success remove the presumption to rebel." [1]

David, with his strangely mongrel hosts, was determined to fight. Dissension and rivalry, however, broke out about the ordering of his battle array. The king wished to set those Normans who still remained with him—he had about 200 mail-clad knights—in the van, but the Galwegians claimed that position as their right. The Normans harped upon the inferiority of unarmoured troops; the Galwegians and Malise, Earl of Strathearn, who was bitterly anti-Norman, denied it. Finally the king gave way. His ill-assorted army was drawn up, each nationality apart:—the men of Galloway in the van—the knights, the men of Teviotdale and the Cumbrians under Prince Henry, the king's son—the men of Lothian, the men of Lorn and the Islanders in another division—the king with a bodyguard of English and Norman knights with the Scots and the men of Moray.

The English army was grouped round a great wooden platform, containing the Host and the most precious relics in Northern England set high on the mast of a ship. The archers were tellingly disposed, but the armoured men, who were dismounted, were so placed that they would bear the brunt of the attack : " shield was joined to shield, side was pressed to side ; lances were raised with pennons unfurled, hauberks glittered in the brilliance of the sun."

It was now time for the gallant Picts to make good their claim to the vanguard. " Naked and almost unarmed," they " advanced against columns mailed and thus invulnerable," and Aildred exults that " when the frailty of the Scots lances was mocked by the denseness of iron and wood they drew their swords, attempted to contend at close quarters." For three hours the men of Galloway kept up the hopeless struggle.

[1] Aildred of Rievaulx. A. O. Anderson, *Scots Annals in English Chronicles*, p. 193. Malcolm M'Heth, " heir of his father's hatred and persecution," was the leader of the revolt. For the rest of this description Anderson's translation and collection is used ; see pp. 197-199, 201, 203, 204, 207, 208.

They could not break the formation of the men in armour, and the archers who had been scattered among the knights "wounded and transfixed these truly unarmed men." At last the Galwegians lost heart and turned, and, further demoralized by a false report of the king's death, the whole Scots army broke and fled, in spite of a minor success achieved by Prince Henry and the knights under him.

The retreat was disastrous : " For the English and the Scots and the Picts and the rest of the barbarians, wherever they chanced to meet one another, whichever of them were in greater force either slaughtered or wounded the others, or at the least robbed them ; and thus by the just judgement of God they were oppressed as much by their own men as by strangers."

The different portions of Scotland's motley forces showed the same hostility to each other again after the capture of William the Lyon, and there is very definite evidence that some of the Gaelic revolts were mainly inspired by anti-Norman feeling. For instance the Galwegians, hating the rule of the Normans, who had married the heiresses of their last native ruler, asked Alexander II to take the inheritance into his own hands, but the king would not go against the organization that his family had created; in the words of the *Melrose Chronicle*, he was " too just to do this," and " the Galwegians were angry above measure." They rebelled, and it took two campaigns to subdue them. One of the chroniclers, Walter of Coventry, of the time of Edward I, declared that " The Kings of Scotland pride themselves on being French in race and in manner of life, in speech and in culture. They have reduced the Scots to utter slavery, and they admit none but Frenchmen to their friendship and their service." [1]

Walter was rather overstressing his facts, and, considering how greatly favoured were the Normans, it is very remarkable, not that there were traces of anti-Norman feeling, but that there was so little of it. The explanation seems to lie in the fact that, so far as the nobility and men of position were concerned, a process of welding and of fusion was going on at the same time. The newcomers were setting the fashions, and the natives and

[1] R. S. Rait, *The Making of Scotland*, pp. 41-43, 55, 63, quotes the evidence that old references give of this. *Book of Pluscardine* (1461–96), *Chronicle of Melrose* (contemporary).

the earlier Anglian invaders tended rather to assimilate the ways and manners of life of the Normans than to oppose them. For instance we find the Frenchified prefix " de " being assumed by families of Saxon stock, such as the de Laverdaes.[1] Intermarriage among the different races also was so general that long before the end of the period the whole nobility must have become about equally mongrel. The successors of that very Malise Strathearn, who championed the privileges of the Galwegians at the Battle of the Standard, soon acquired an admixture of Norman blood, held their lands by charter and adopted a coat of arms.[2] Even in the case of the revolts against Alexander and his successors there was no real trial of strength between the old native lords and the intruders. In the case of those risings that Walter of Coventry attributes to anti-Norman feeling, the kings of Scotland were supported by some of their Scots subjects. In the Moray rebellion of 1214–15 Alexander II was accompanied by several of the native earls, and he subdued another rising, with the aid of Ferquhard, the Earl of Ross.[3] It is significant that during the intrigues and faction struggles that took place during the minority and after the death of Alexander III there was no racial cleavage and that no anti-Norman party was formed.

PART IV. THE FEUDALIZING OF SCOTLAND

The all-pervasive influence of the Normans upon Scotland has never been fully traced out, though abundant evidences of it still remain ; the surviving buildings of the time are a case in point.[4] In a generalized account, however, only the most essential changes that the Normans brought about, and those

[1] J Coutts, *The Norman Invasion of Scotland.*

[2] This family showed more hostility to the Normans than any other. Ferteth, successor to Malise, led a revolt against Malcolm IV, and his race were the patrons of the Keledei, a religious order peculiar to the ancient Gaelic Church. Yet Gilbert Earl of Strathearn, who succeeded in 1171, " took charters for his lands ; practised the usages of knightly heraldry ; connected himself with Norman families by marriage " (Cosmo Innes, *Sketches of Early Scotch History*, p. 205).

The genealogical tables in C. Sanford Terry's *History of Scotland* show in a convincing way the hybridization of the Scots nobility.

[3] R. S. Rait, *Relations between England and Scotland*, p. 209.

See also the Earldom of Ross in *The Scots Peerage.*

[4] C. Innes, *Scotland in the Middle Ages*, p. 294, gives a list of Norman buildings. When the characteristic " Early English " style was introduced

most directly affecting the economic life of the nation, can even be touched upon.

In the first place, Scotland became to a very large extent organized upon the feudal system. The definitely feudal theory that all land was held of the king, and that it was granted to his vassals in return for specified services was generally accepted.[1] In the words of a great authority upon early Scots tenures, the Scots charters, even so early as the time of David I "exceedingly resemble, I may say they entirely coincide with, those of a parallel date in England. They consist of a grant by the king, . . . to an individual and his heirs of certain lands described, and they specify a reddendo, or a certain amount of military service. There is nothing to distinguish these early charters from those of Norman England, or, indeed, of any strictly feudal kingdom."[2]

Feudal tenure thus became general over a great part of Scotland. It was not confined merely to the Norman newcomers—the native landholders also received confirmation of their possessions in terms of the new tenure. The Earl of Menteith had his lands confirmed by charter in 1213, the Earldom of Mar, though the earliest charters extant are spurious, was probably feudalized about 1171; Athol received a charter towards the end of the twelfth century. The Earl of Fife, the greatest of them all, also had his right to his lands confirmed by royal charter.[3] Nor was this the only characteristic of the great

it was rapidly copied in Scotland, even in Highland districts. Examples occur in Argyleshire and Ross-shire almost contemporary with English buildings of this type. C. E. Chisholm Batten, *Beauly Priory*, p. 82.

[1] Sir John Skene's "Translation" of the *Regiam Majestatem*, ch. i. "King Malcolm gave and distributed all his lands of the Realm of Scotland amongst his men. And reserved na thing in propertie to himselfe, bot the royal dignitie, and the Mute-hill in the towne of Scone. And all his barons gave and granted to him, the wards and relief of the hiere of ilk Baron, quhen he sould happen to deceis, for the King's sustentation."

This transaction is entirely mythical. W. F. Skene's note to Fordoun (*Historians of Scotland Series*), p. 414.

[2] C. Innes, *Scotland in the Middle Ages*, pp. 200-201. He quotes a charter by David I granting Annandale to Bruce with the same customs by which Bruce held his lands in Cumberland.

[3] For Menteith, see *Scots Peerage*, vol. vi, p. 126.

For Mar, see *Scots Peerage*, vol. v, p. 568.

For Athol, see *Scots Peerage*, vol. i, p. 415. *A.P.S.* vol. i, p. 387.

For Fife, see J. Mackintosh, *History of Civilization in Scotland*, vol. i, p. 225; quotes Nat. MSS., Part I, No. 50.

vassals of the Crown. They, in their turn, tended to feudalize their possessions. Thus Malcolm, Earl of Fife (1228), granted a charter to Richard, son of Andree de Lintune, for certain lands in return for the service of one knight,[1] and, in a charter attributed to the time of David I, Waldeve, son of Gospatric, Earl of Dunbar, granted the lands of Dundas to Helias, son of Huctred for half the service of a knight.[2]

The feudalization of the landholding system of Scotland, which the Normans so largely helped to bring about, was one of the most important features of the period. Its effects can be traced all through the course of the history of Scotland, right down to the present day. The Normans, however, also played a determining part in bringing about many other changes.

Part V. The Organization of Scotland as a Feudal State

The Scots kings of the twelfth and thirteenth centuries were, nearly all of them, great organizers. Some of them were energetic law-makers, especially William the Lyon, who was greatly influenced by the Anglo-Norman jurist, de Glanville. The authenticity and date of many of these early laws of Scotland have been contested, but the general tendency of the various codes and individual laws is unmistakable. It is towards the regulation of an orderly, feudal type of kingdom. The privileges and obligations of those who held land of the king or of his feudatories, the laws of succession, which insisted upon the principle of primogeniture, all these, and many other characteristic features of feudal law were worked out. In the words of the old jurist, Lord Kames, feudal law " was brought to a considerable degree of perfection in Scotland." [3]

This was the great and essential achievement of the laws of

[1] *Scottish Historical Review*, vol. viii, p. 222.

[2] C. Innes. *Scotland in the Middle Ages*. p. 202.

[3] Lord Kames, " On the Introduction of Feudal Law into Scotland," in *Essays upon Subjects concerning British Antiquities*. See also J. Dalrymple, *Essays towards a General History of Feudal Property in Great Britain*.

See also C. Innes, Preface to vol. i, *A.P.S.*, and G. Neilson, *Trial by Combat*, p. 82.

the period, but it was only gradually reached. Only slowly were existing codes of laws, the special customs of separate districts, such as the Lothians and Galloway, superseded. In fact, the process was not quite complete by the fourteenth century. The curious " law that is callyt clarémathan," attributed to William the Lyon,[1] is a good example of how uniformity was gradually evolved out of chaos. The law apparently applied to stolen cattle that had passed into the hands of a third party. It ordered that if such cattle were claimed by the original owner, they were to be brought to " that stede in ilke schirefdome qhar the King David statud and stablyst catal chalangyt to be brocht "—within fifteen days, but an extra month was allowed to anyone dwelling in Moray, Ross, Caithness, Argyle or Kintyre. If the accused person wished to produce a " warrand " that lived in that part of Argyle pertaining to Moray and would not go there himself, he might apply to the sheriff of Inverness to send one of the king's sergeands or one of his own " to se that all rycht be done till hym "—" after the assise of the land." If the "warrand" refused to go with the sergeand, the latter was to order the man's lord to " ger hym cum wyth hym." And if the lord refused he forfeited to the king a hundred kye " if he hes sa mekil in gudis," or his body should be in the king's will. If the " warrand " refused to go, he also forfeited three times the value of the challenged cattle. If the accused called upon a man dwelling in Argyle that pertains to Scotland to be his " warrand " he was to apply to the Earl of Athole or the Abbot of Glendochir to send men with him, and to the Earl of Menteith if the "warrand" was in Cowal or Kintyre. All who lived " beyhond Forth, as in Lothyane or in Galloway," were to answer " the chalangeouris of Scotlande " at the Brig of Stirling, and *vice versa.*

This active line of kings also organized the administration of the country. Malcolm III and Alexander I appointed the great officers of state, the Chamberlain, the Constable, and the Chancellor, but David I carried the work very much further. In his reign the Chamberlain was not only a court official, but entrusted with very important duties of supervision over the Royal Burghs. It was David who created the office of Justiciar,

[1] *A.P.S.* vol. i, p. 50.

the supreme judge under the king, who travelled about Scotland administering justice. It was also David who began to parcel the country out under sheriffs, each of whom was in general charge of a given district.

The office of sheriff was an innovation, intended to replace the more ancient organization of mairs, toisechs, brehons, judices, etc. The transformation was only gradual; for many years the two systems worked side by side in different districts, and two of the older officials, the mair and the judex, were embodied in the new organization, and continued to fulfil offices that gradually declined in importance, till the mair became a comparatively minor official, and the judex deteriorated into the Dempster of the seventeenth and eighteenth centuries. The earliest sheriff bore the Anglian name of Cospatric, and he held office in what is now Roxburghshire. It is known that David appointed several more during his reign who resided at Scone, Berwick, Stirling, Clackmannan, and Perth. During the twelfth and thirteenth centuries sheriffs were also appointed at Aberdeen, Banff, Edinburgh, Haddington, Forfar, Lanark, Linlithgow, Kincardine, Selkirk, Peebles, Ayr, Nairn, Inverness, some of the Fifeshire towns, Elgin, Forres, Dumbarton, Dumfries, Kinross, Wigtown, Cromarty, and for the districts of Skye, Lorn, and Kintyre. The process, on the whole, began in the more settled districts of the South-East and was extended. The territorial unit over which the sheriff presided was the shire. This was an integral part of the old Saxon organization, but it was an innovation in Scotland, created as part of the new system of administration, though the duties of the sheriff himself were largely modelled upon those of Norman officials. It was only slowly that David's successors built up and adjusted the organization of the shires, and Edinburgh absorbed Haddington and Linlithgow, the sheriffdom of Fife emerged from the fusion of lesser sheriffdoms, etc. It was not until the fourteenth and fifteenth centuries that the whole country was covered; and sheriffs were appointed for Renfrew, Bute, the Isles, the Separate Northern Counties, etc.[1]

Mr. W. Dickinson suggests that the sheriffs and the shires were originally intended to form an organization dealing with

[1] W. C. Dickinson, *Sheriff Court Book of Fife* (*Scottish History Society*), pp. lxiii, lxvi, lxvii, lxviii, 347-368.

the whole administrative work of the country upon a uniform system. The defences of the kingdom, the maintenance of order and the administration of justice, the economic organization of the country—the holding of fairs, the institution of certain monopolies in connection with the original Royal burghs, even the payment of the royal church dues—all seem to have been planned to fit into such an administrative design. In its entirety the project was never quite fulfilled. The powers of the nobles interfered with the original scope of the sheriffs' duties, the development of the country led to more Royal Burghs being formed, etc.; nevertheless the powers of the sheriffs were very wide, and the organization of the country that was brought about was an important advance.[1]

The sheriff resided at the royal castle at the *Caput Comitatus*, and thus formed the focal point for the administrative activities of his district. His military duties were important. He was responsible for the keeping of these castles in repair, for the holding of wappenschawings for the purpose of exercising the fencible men of the district, for seeing that the local barons produced their proper quota of men for military service, and for leading the men of the sheriffdom in the field. His had been originally intended to be the most important court of justice under that of the Justiciar, both in civil and criminal cases, although the powers granted to lords of regality interfered with his jurisdiction. Free-holders and barons, though they had the rights of holding their own courts, were obliged to render a specified number of suits at those of the sheriff, and he had considerable powers of supervision over their lesser courts. There is evidence that the system of holding the head courts at fixed dates at the capital of the shire, and the lesser courts held in different districts of the sheriffdom, was gradually built up, and so also was the practice of appointing sheriff deputes.[2]

The sheriff was also responsible for the administrative work of his district. His court dealt with such matters as the service

[1] W. C. Dickinson, *Sheriff Court Book of Fife*, pp. 365-370, 381-385.

[2] *Ibid.* p. xi for residence of sheriff; p. 325 for civil jurisdiction; p. 335 for criminal jurisdiction; p. xxv onwards for organization of sheriff courts.

See also C. A. Malcolm, *Scottish Hist. Review*, vol. xx, p. 131.

of brieves of inquest—the claims made by an heir to succeed to his father's estates—the allocation of the land that should provide payment of a widow's terce, the appointment of curators to a minor, if this had not been done by will, etc. He was responsible for the capture of outlaws, and, in later times, such work as the administration of the Sumptuary Laws, the punishment of beggars. Sometimes the fixing of prices, and many other matters, fell to his lot. He did the executive work for the justiciar's courts, issued summonses, made arrests when the person to be arrested was too powerful for the coroner to tackle, collected the fines and other dues.[1]

The sheriff was also the local fiscal unit. He was required to collect the money dues and produce in kind of the Crown lands, the payments due from the feudal casualties of ward, marriage, and relief, as well as the fines and escheats of the justiciar's court and of his own. He also had to furnish the chamberlain with an account of all that he received. And on the other hand he had to disburse and account for the money spent upon the miscellaneous expenses of the king's household when he visited the sheriffdom; upon the upkeep and repair of the royal castles and manors, and for the defence of the country; the pensions, salaries, gifts, and ecclesiastical dues with which the Crown possessions were charged; and to hand over the balance to the chamberlain. He also had considerable dealings with the Royal Burghs.[2]

David I began to organize the collection and disbursement of the royal income, which was also the revenue of the state. It was mainly drawn from feudal casualties—a very fluctuating source of income; from tolls and customs; from the burgh ferms; and from the annual reddendos of the thaneages; from the fines and escheats levied in the royal courts of justice—the second largest source of revenue—and, most important of all, from the Crown lands. Figures relating to the king's income survive for 1264. In that year the chamberlain received £5413, of which £2893 was derived from Crown lands. Taxation was only " an extraordinary source of income to which the

[1] W. C. Dickinson, *Sheriff Court Book of Fife*, pp. 339-343, xxxix, xli, xlv, xlvii.

[2] This paragraph and the next are based on G. Burnett, *Introduction to Vol. I, Exchequer Rolls.*

king was not expected to have recourse except on the occasion of great national emergencies." [1]

David I planned his fiscal organization upon the same lines as that of his contemporary, Henry I, although the Scots system was simpler, and at this period there was no treasurer, and the procedure at the audits was different. Annual audits were held, presided over by the great officers of the state, and some of the other leading men, always including churchmen. Even so early as the twelfth and thirteenth centuries "the rolls contain many indications, in both text and marginal notes, of the care with which the audit was habitually conducted, and the accuracy aimed at. Charges were often disallowed on grounds which were explained. Sometimes the auditors objected to a charge as insufficiently vouched for, or remarked that it seemed right, but "could not be passed without a regular warrant; or they added a memorandum for further enquiry, or for a reference to the king." Nevertheless, they contain many mistakes in addition, due, no doubt, to the cumbrous Roman numerals that were used.[2] David I also standardized the weights and measures, and introduced a Scots coinage.

In all this busy state-building work of the Scots kings, the men who helped to shape and to carry out the royal policy were mainly Normans. In a list of sheriffs and of other officials who made returns in 1263–66 more than two-thirds of the names are either Norman or Normanized.[3] The greater officers of the state were also mainly Norman, and how closely they were associated with their royal masters can easily be seen by noticing how often they acted as witnesses of charters.[4]

Part VI. The Influence of the Normans on Scots Social Life

In many other ways the development of the Scoto-Norman nobility had very important, though less fundamental, effects upon the general growth of the country. They must have

[1] G. Burnett, *Introduction to Vol I, Exchequer Rolls*, p. xxxiv.
Sir James H. Ramsay, *Revenue of the Kings of England*, vol. i, p. 26, ch. ii, p. 39, ch. iii.

[2] *Exchequer Rolls*, vol. i, pp. xxxiii, xxxv-xxxix.

[3] *Ibid.* p. xliii.

[4] Cf. Sir Archibald Lawrie's very full collection.

deeply influenced its trade, for they and the churchmen were the main consumers of the choicer goods that seem to have been imported, even in that non-luxurious age. Margaret, as we have seen, had set the fashion for foreign things, and the court and nobility of Scotland throughout the period were closely in touch with England, and had some connection with the continent, and their tastes must have been thoroughly cosmopolitan. The break with older traditions of native art, if these had managed to survive the gruelling years from the sixth to the tenth centuries, was complete, except in remoter districts; and Scotland was destined to build up new styles of her own, founded upon examples more akin with her changed type of civilization. Nevertheless, for centuries, Scots people were to continue to import all the choicer manufactured goods that they could afford from abroad.

The domestic arrangements of the greater Scots lords were no doubt like those of their fellows to the south of the Border. In those days the produce of his land was remitted to the overlord in uncommuted form. As its carriage was very difficult, the question of providing himself and his retainers with adequate maintenance was a pressing one, even for a great one of the earth, and the magnate and his entourage were obliged to be constantly on the move from one part of his dominions to another, to consume the produce on the spot. It does not sound a very comfortable kind of existence, but we have several contemporary and minute descriptions of the life of a typical great lord in England during the twelfth century.[1] It must have been much more the case in Scotland, a land less fertile, more mountainous, and giving scope for larger retinues of armed followers. This fact explains the constant wanderings of the kings and their families, which are vouched for by the *Exchequer Rolls*, and it may have been the reason why the greatest lords were willing to undertake the offices of justiciar and of chamberlain, involving, as they did, constant perambulations through Scotland. This wandering life of the greater lords, moving from one part of the country to another (for their possessions

[1] William Cunningham, *Growth of Industry and Commerce*, vol. i, pp. 241, 245.

Mary Bateson, *Mediaeval England*, pp. 116, 168, quotations from Walter of Henley and Grosteste.

were very scattered), must have done much to break down local variations and to bring about the growing homogeneousness of the Lowlands. It probably is of real importance that absentee landlordism was not among the many ills that afflicted early mediaeval Scotland.

Castle building was another feature of the age in which the Norman feudalizing influence can be traced. It is difficult to realize the immense importance of castles in the days before powerful artillery was invented—not only as a means of national defence, but for maintaining law and order. The early mediaeval Scots kings were energetic builders; by means of castles they consolidated their hold upon the conquered provinces, and they made castles an integral part of the organization of the sheriffdoms.[1] The greater vassals of the Crown followed their lead, and so thickly was the east coast land of Scotland dotted with castles and monasteries that, when Edward I made his expedition up to Elgin in 1292, in going and in coming, he only had to sleep in a tent once.[2]

It is beyond the scope of a treatise such as this to embark upon a discussion of the moral worth of the Normans as compared with the Gaels, whom they so largely supplanted. They were of mixed origin, and yet they consistently displayed the attributes of ability, efficiency, courage, and greed. They were a race of mercenaries with many adopted fatherlands. Although many people think otherwise, yet perhaps, on the whole, in Scotland, they may be said to have justified their existence.[3]

Part VII. The Church

Closely associated with the changes that were being wrought in the aristocracy of the country were those that were being brought about in the personnel and organization of the Church. Organized religion had suffered severely during the troubled times that lasted from the eighth to the tenth centuries, especially

[1] C. Innes, *Scotland in the Middle Ages*, p. xxi.
Exchequer Rolls, vol. i, p. xlix.

[2] P. Hume Brown, *Early Travellers to Scotland*, p. 2.

[3] The attitudes of J. Mackintosh, *History of Civilization in Scotland*, vol. i, and of the Duke of Argyle, *Scotland as it was and is*, are amusingly different with regard to the value of the Normans' influence in Scotland.

by the incursions of the Vikings, and the differences that existed between the Pictish and the Scottish Churches were an added source of weakness.[1] It would be a controversial and not a helpful task to try to estimate the condition of the Church before the reign of Malcolm Canmore, when his queen devoted all her energies to bringing the Church of her husband's country into exact conformity with the practices of the Western Church.[2]

The Church continued to develop throughout our period. In politics the question of the independence of the Church in Scotland and of the claims of the Archbishop of York was a burning one, and the boundaries of the national Church were gradually consolidated so as to follow the line of the frontier, itself only definitely fixed during the period.[3] The period also saw the arrival in Scotland of one after another of the newly founded religious orders. We are not here concerned with their spiritual labours, but the coming of these monks and canons is definitely important in the economic history of Scotland because of the social effects that they produced. One of the paradoxes of the age was that the development of individual nations, which was typical of the times, was so largely achieved by theories and agencies that were cosmopolitan. It was the period of the great development of the monastic spirit throughout Western Europe. The movement affected seculars as well as regulars, and one new order after another was founded, expanded during its vigorous youth, and eventually penetrated into Scotland.

The Benedictines had come to England during Saxon times, and were brought to Dunfermline by Margaret. They were followed by the Augustinians, or Black Canons, a strongly missionary body, the Premonstratensians or White Canons, the Cluniacs, the Cistercians, famous as agriculturalists, and the Carthusians. All these orders acquired foundations in Scotland. The Friars came rather later.[4]

[1] W. F. Skene, *Celtic Scotland*, vol. ii, describes the period.

[2] Sir Archibald Lawrie, *Early Scots Charters*, p. 323.

[3] During the early part of the period the Lothians were mainly within the region influenced by the strong Church centre at Durham.

[4] This is not at all an exhaustive list. Refs., see a list compiled in 1272 of monastic possessions quoted by W. F. Skene, *Celtic Scotland*, ii, p. 510. Sir Archibald Lawrie, *Early Scots Charters*, pp. 372, 376, 379, 387.

In many cases the first monks and canons were brought from England ; Alexander I settled Scone with Augustinians from Nostel in Yorkshire, and David I founded his Cistercian monastery at Melrose with monks from Rievalle, also in Yorkshire.[1] In the case of the Isle of May, the abbey was granted to the Cluniac foundation at Reading, and remained under its control for years.[2] But sometimes the monks were brought directly from abroad. David I himself visited Tiron and persuaded twelve monks to come back with him to found an abbey at Selkirk ;[3] and, rather earlier, the Canons Regular at Stirling were brought from Arras.[4] Some of these religious houses in Scotland were organized as parts of the province of their order in England, others were directly governed by the mother house abroad ; in either case, considerable coming and going was involved.

The organization of the state church was also carried out during our period, on lines similar to that of the other branches of the Western Church.[5] Tithes were imposed ; bishoprics were established and endowed with adequate lands—the Gaelic bishops appear not to have been diocesan ; Scotland was divided into parishes ;[6] the Keledei, the monastic foundations belonging to the old Gaelic Church, were gradually eliminated. And, all the while that this was going on, there was a gradual increase in the Norman and Normanized names among the great churchmen.[7] Yet here again the fact must be stressed that the Norman penetration did not create a permanent political party. In the Wars of Independence no section of the com-

[1] Sir Archibald Lawrie, *Early Scots Charters*, pp. 28 and 376. *Scottish Hist. Review*, vol. vii, 1909–10, pp. 4 and 141.

[2] *Ibid.* p. 387. The ritual and constitution of Elgin Cathedral was modelled on that of Lincoln, *Registrum Moraviense*, p. 649.

[3] *Ibid.* p. 451.

[4] *Ibid.* p. 401.

[5] Bishop Bowden, "The Parish Church," *Scottish Hist. Review*, vol. vii, 1909–10, p. 218.

[6] See article by J. Wilson, *Scottish Hist. Review*, vol. viii, p. 172, 1910–11.

[7] For international organization of Church, *Scottish Hist. Review*, vol. viii, pp. 172-175, vol. ix, p. 5. See, for instance, the charter of 1125 given by Lawrie on p. 326. Out of five bishops only one had a Gaelic name. See also the list of bishops of St Andrews. J. Wilkie, *Fife*, p. 197.

munity deserved better of their country than the churchmen, who urged the people to fight for the excommunicated Robert the Bruce as in a holy war, and whose manifesto of the rights of Scotland rings down the centuries like a silver trumpet blast.

It is, however, the great extent of the Church's possessions that most concerns the student of economic history. Scotland was not unique in her munificence to the Church at this time, she was only taking part in a general European movement. In England, for instance, twenty-six Benedictine monasteries were founded during the reigns of William I and II.[1] Nevertheless, Scotland probably made larger benefactions to the Church in proportion to her total wealth and area of arable land. It is certain that Church lands played a more important part in her economic development and in her history than was the case in England.

The generosity of David I, the "sair sanct," to the Church has become a by-word, but it was a characteristic of his family and of their nobles. Before the twelfth century Scotland had only one bishopric, that of St Andrews. Alexander II added Dunkeld and Moray; David I restored Glasgow while still Prince of Cumbria, and then created Brechin, Dunblane, Caithness, Ross, Aberdeen, and perhaps restored Galloway. His monastic establishments also far outpassed those of his predecessors. He founded or enriched Holyrood, the Isle of May, Newbattle, Kelso, Melrose, and Berwick; Selkirk, Jedburgh, and Glasgow, in the Lothians and the South; Cambuskenneth and Stirling north of the Forth, and Urquhard and Kinloss in turbulent Moray. His son David, Earl of Huntingdon, founded Lindores; his constant companion, Hugh de Moreville, enriched Dryburgh and Kilwinning. Earl Gospatric, of Anglian stock, founded Eccles; and Fergus of Galloway restored Whitherne. His successors were also generous, especially William the Lyon, who had a particular affection for Arbroath and dowered it richly. The Earl of Angus and eighteen other magnates also made donations to this monastery.[2] Altogether twenty abbeys and

[1] W. Ashley, *Growth of Industry and Commerce*. The part played by the Church in the Norman penetration of Wales is shown in J. E. Lloyd, *History of Wales*, vol. ii, pp. 443, 447.

[2] C. Innes, *Sketches of Early Scottish History*, p. 146.

priories were founded by the kings of Malcolm Canmore's line,[1] and their nobles were equally generous.

These religious houses were very unequally dowered, but, in every case, their possessions included very much more than the monastery and surrounding farm lands. Among the donations they received were fishings, salt-pans—Newbattle had at least eight of these,[2]—a mansura or toft in one or perhaps three or four of the Royal Burghs, tithes of brushwood, of the skins of beasts killed for the royal table, on the royal dues on ships, freedom from tolls, regular payments settled on the burgh fermes, a share of the royal dues from whole shires, and large pieces of land, scattered far and wide over the country. Dunfermline, for instance, received twenty-three royal gifts of land, and Scone had thirty-three ploughgates in eight different localities.[3] According to figures, as early as 1274 declared to be out of date and very much below the actual wealth of the Church, the value of the lands of the Church in Scotland were £18,662;[4] at this time the whole royal revenue only amounted to £5413 per annum.

No doubt there was adequate reason why David I, that exceptionally able king, and his kindred should have poured such largesse upon the Church. Apart from all considerations of piety—and they were a very devout family—the Church was undoubtedly extremely useful to the rulers of such a country as Scotland then was. In the first place, she was a warm supporter of the prerogatives of the Crown. In the old chronicles many a vigorous phrase reminds us that so long as the king was careful to give the Church the dues which she claimed, and not to interfere with her prerogatives, the pens of the monkish chroniclers were whole-heartedly devoted to his service, asserting his rights, praising his virtues, anathematizing his enemies and his rebellious subjects. Secondly, the churchmen were peace-

[1] J. Mackinnon, *Constitutional History of Scotland*, p. 161.

[2] Sir A. Lawrie, *Early Scottish Charters*, p. 387.

[3] Records of ecclesiastical gifts abound. In Lawrie's exhaustive collection of charters, see especially pp. 61, 116, 69, 326, 296, 74, 204, 287, etc.; in the chartularies of the different abbeys, etc., in the case of dues from the *Exchequer Rolls*, see vol. i, p. xcii, for a complete list.

[4] *Statuta Ecclesiae Scoticanae*, p. lxv.

D. Masson, Introd., *Register and Privy Council* (second series), vol. i, p. cvii, for the most exhaustive list of Church possessions in Scotland.

able, docile, and, above all, wealth-producing subjects, skilful farmers and flockmasters themselves, and in some ways more enlightened superiors than the great lords.[1] Thus the Church must have been especially useful as a civilizing and organizing agency in those districts where the royal power was only gradually being established, Moray, the South-West, and the North. For instance, in 1140, five monks were established at Dornoch, and David I founded a bishopric of Caithness. The work of organization and feudalization of the newly appointed bishop has been traced out from surviving records. For a long time, owing to the invasions of the Norsemen, Caithness and Sutherland had virtually ceased to be a part of the kingdom of Scotland, and were still very lightly held. The civil power was mainly in the hands of the descendants of the Norse Jarls, though the more ancient Pictish possessors, perhaps with an admixture from the Gaelic conquerors, still occupied the central plateau. Churches of Columban or Pictish foundation also still existed in the district. The bishop was a member of the great family of de Moravia—probably of Flemish origin, but which had become thoroughly absorbed into the Scoto-Norman aristocracy. He proceeded to parcel out some of the great lands, with which the king had endowed him, to cadets of his own people, upon feudal tenures, besides organizing the district into parishes, etc. Elgin is a later example. Twenty-three canons were attached to the Cathedral, spending half the year in residence there and half the year serving their county parishes. The constitution of Elgin was largely based on that of Lincoln Cathedral.[2]

PART VIII. THE BLENDING OF NORMAN AND GAELIC INFLUENCES

The feudalization of Scotland, however, was by no means a simple and uniform process, and the scope of the movement was limited. It is now time to consider some of the complexities

[1] Especially in commuting feudal services for fixed reddendos.

[2] See J. Gray, *Sutherland and Caithness in Saga-time*.

J. Gray, "Boundaries of Estates in Caithness Diocese," *Scottish Hist. Review*, vol. xx, 1922–23.

C. Innes, *Ancient Laws and Customs of the Burghs of Scotland*, p. lxv.

of the situation. It is impossible to give a slight yet general picture of the past that is even approximately correct for two good reasons. We are only able to use the material that from its nature is capable of surviving to our own day. Of this kind, formal legal charters that convey the right to possess something are pre-eminent, and, in trying to classify even these poor remains, we tend to evolve a generalized, orderly statement, that necessarily gives a wrong idea of the groping, hand-to-mouth, piecemeal organization of a state of society that was primitive, developing rapidly but very unevenly, deficient in means of communication, and largely illiterate. The feudalization of land-holding in Scotland is well attested by her code of laws, and by the surviving charters, but it would be the greatest possible mistake to imagine that the mass of Scots people were thereby transformed ; or that the system was imposed upon the general organization of the people, as a complete and totally separate thing, like the crust upon a pie ; or that the feudal system itself worked out in practice upon a neatly classified and tidily uniform plan.

The usual services due from a military holding—ward, marriage, and relief—were stereotyped, and they were often dismissed in the phrase "services used and wont," *pro servitio suo servitium debitum et consuetum*.[1] And the Knight's Fee, in which land was so often granted, represented, no doubt, an area of land that was expected to supply a definite standard of maintenance. Upon this organization of the land the defence of the country depended, but many other conditions were inserted into individual charters. A money payment might be required—land might be practically given away as a reward for services or benefits—for a rose, a pair of gloves, or some trifling task. Scott has immortalized such a tenure in his inimitable description of the Baron of Bradwardine and the bootjack.[2] Mr. R. L. Jones, after an exhaustive enquiry into those ancient Scots tenures in which a reddendo was paid, has come to the conclusion that: "The variety and confusion of tenure previous to the Feu-farm Act of 1457 has

[1] Cosmo Innes, *Scotch Legal Antiquities*, pp. 36, 62-63.

[2] In *Waverley*. On the less exalted plane of sober history Cosmo Innes has compiled a rather amusing list of these nominal services. *Scotch Legal Antiquities*, pp. 64-68.

never been fully appreciated. Every possible combination of lease and ward and blench-farm holding seems to have been adopted." [1]

Nor were the Normans and the feudal system imposed *en bloc* upon the native nobility. The Normans never conquered Scotland. A good many charters of the time of David I which still survive have been collected and annotated in a work of monumental thoroughness.[2] By comparing the names of the witnesses one can gather a good deal of information about the state of society during what is perhaps the most formative period in Scots history.

The king nearly always had about him the small group of men whose names appear over and over again, and who were evidently his chosen friends and colleagues. Among these men were Robert de Bruce, Hugo de Morville, Robertus Corbet, Galfridus Ridel, and Engaine de Berengarius, who were certainly, or almost certainly, of Norman extraction. But Alwyn Mac Arkil was also a favourite—his name appears as witness on eighteen documents—and although his origin has been disputed, he certainly was not a Norman.[3]

The charters were granted whilst the king, in the course of his wandering life, was in many different parts of the country, and it is evident that considerable numbers of the older nobility still resided in their own districts, and that the king held court among them. A charter given at Ercildoun in 1140 has, among its list of witnesses, a large proportion of Anglian names.[4] Again, when David visited Glasgow in 1136, a charter was witnessed by several Normans, including William Comyn, the chancellor; but also by Malise, the most purely native of the earls; by Fergus, who was one of the leaders in a Gaelic revival which will be dealt with later on; the names of eight witnesses who follow also appear to be Gaelic, and there is one which

[1] Mr R. L. Jones, Carnegie Research Student. (Quoted by the courtesy and with the permission of the Carnegie Research Trust, from the essay submitted to them.)

[2] Sir Archibald Lawrie, *Early Scottish Charters*.

[3] He is thought to have been created Earl of Lennox. Sir William Fraser and others believe that he was of Northumbrian descent. W. F. Skene considers that he was of "Celtic" (Gaelic or Pictish ?) origin, and the *Scots Peerage* inclines to this view.

[4] Sir Archibald Lawrie, *Early Scottish Charters*, p. 107.

suggests the survival of a representative of the yet more ancient British inhabitants of the district.[1] Then, in 1150, a charter that gave the monks of Holyrood certain rights in the Highlands—viz. half the tithes of Argyle—was witnessed by seven men with Normanized names and six with names that are evidently Gaelic.

In Strathearn, which was ruled over by a family of partly Normanized Gaelic earls, right down to the thirteenth century, not only the rural population but almost all the landowners were Gaels.[2]

There are many other examples of the same mixture of society, and two documents give an interesting picture of the survival of purely Gaelic centres. A quarrel arose in 1128 between the Keledei of St Serf, who numbered six (and who were named Duftah, priest and abbot; Sarran, son of Sodelm; Eugenius, monk; Dodinalde, nephew of Leod; Morchat, an Irishman; and Cathan) and Sir Robert Burgonensis. The case was tried by Constantine, Earl of Fife; Macbeath, Thane of Falleland; Dufegal filium Mocche, described as *senex justus et venerabilis*; and Meldionneth filium Macludath, *judicem bonum et discretum*. Sentence was given for the Keledei.[3] There is also a *notitia* in the *Book of Deer*, dated 1131, in which Gartnait, son of Cainech and Ete, daughter of Gillemichel, make a grant of land to the Church. The ten witnesses, all of whom have Celtic names, include Nectan, Bishop of Aberdeen; Ruadri, the Mormaer of Mar, i.e. the ancient Pictish and Gaelic noble whose title was afterwards changed into that of Earl; Matadin the Brehon—the ancient Gaelic title for a judge; and Domongart, the Ferlegin or Man of Learning, one of the principal officials in a Columban Monastery.[4] On the other

[1] Sir Archibald Lawrie, *Early Scottish Charters*, pp. 85 and 340.

[2] Sir A. Lawrie, *Scottish Hist. Review*, vol. v, p. 444.

[3] Sir A. Lawrie, *Early Scottish Charters*, p. 66.

[4] The *notitiae* of the *Book of Deer* have been printed several times, for instance, in A. O. Anderson's *Early Sources of Scottish History*. The Brehon and the Mormaer are well-known officials. The Ferlegin is mentioned in the ancient Laws of Ireland and as one of the principal ecclesiastics at Iona. See W. F. Skene, *Celtic Scotland*, vol. ii, pp. 248, 59, 360, 414. Strathearn was another district where Gaelic landowners predominated at the beginning of the thirteenth century. See Sir A. Lawrie, *Scottish Hist. Review*, vol. v, p. 444.

hand, practically every name in the early Rose deeds is Norman.[1]

As time went on the fusion proceeded further and further. Angles continued to hold lands in districts where the great lord was a Norman, for instance, the de Lavirdaes, said to be Saxon, still held their lands in Lauderdale, though the de Morevilles had become the most powerful landowners in the district. The parish of Dalmeny was occupied in the twelfth century by one Angle and two Normans.[2] Norman overlords would probably tend to have Normans as their principal vassals, as the de Hodelms held Hoddom in Dumfriesshire of the Bruces of Annandale, but there are many exceptions. For instance, de Moreville, the companion of William the Lyon, granted land heritably to Edulf, a Saxon, in 1170, for the service of one knight. He also gave land to a natural daughter and her husband, Malcolm;[3] and among the names of his greater vassals were de Pollok and Haig, for both of which a non-Norman origin has been claimed.[4] In Caithness and Sutherland, Norse, Gael, Norman, and Normanized Flemings all had land.

Another manifestation of the fusing and welding that was going on can be seen in the thanages, a curious, not purely feudal type of holding that was evolved on the east coast of Scotland. W. F. Skene has made a careful study of them. And although it is thought that his list is not exhaustive, he has traced sixty-three, and he points out that they are nearly all grouped in certain areas.[5] Six of them formed " a belt of thanages extending from the River Nairn to the Spey," along the coastal land, and on the foot-hills. One covered the lower part of Strathspey. Farther south, in Buchan and Mar, there were eleven, and three up Deeside. In Kincardineshire there were seven, covering three-quarters of the coastwise area. Farther south the thanages were smaller and more interspersed with purely feudal holdings. There were fifteen in Angus and Fife and the adjoining

[1] The Rose Charters have been published and edited by C. Innes, and there are a good many early ones.

[2] *Second Statistical Account*, vol. ii, pp. 94-96.

[3] J. W. Buchan, *Peeblesshire*, vol. ii, pp. 445, 450.

[4] J. Coutts, *Norman Conquest of Scotland*, p. 118.

[5] W. F. Skene, *Celtic Scotland*, vol. iii, p. 242 onwards. See also W. C. Dickinson, *Sheriff Court of Fife*, p. 375.

districts. In Perthshire there were some in the wide lowland straths, and others among the hills, even on Loch Tay and in Athole. They generally consisted of from four to six *davochs* of land. Skene points out that practically all of them were situated " in those eastern districts which formed originally the seat of Pictish tribes, and afterwards fell under the dynasty of kings of a Scottish race." (He considers that the thanages of Dingwall and Callendar were altogether exceptional.) They were nearly all held directly of the king, and were regarded as part of the royal domain. They paid an annual money rent, and also the Gaelic dues of *Cain* and *Waytinga* = *Conveth*, but rendered no military service. There was considerable variation in the status of the men who held them. Some seem to have been perpetual tenants, others removable at will. Sometimes they were rather stewards than occupiers.[1] Even by the twelfth century some of the thanages had been feudalized, but more than half of them survived into the fourteenth.[2]

They form an interesting survival from the past. They may have had some connection with Pictish times. They may have been evolved by the conquering Gael. Possibly, as their name implies, some Saxon influence may have helped to shape them under Malcolm III—though the Scots thanes, the English thanes, and the Anglic thegns were certainly different things. Eventually, we find them fitted into the land system of a country that was rapidly becoming feudalized.[3]

The officials connected with the thanages were also interesting survivals. W. F. Skene equates the words thane and toisech or tosheador, the Gaelic titles for chief and for coroner or steward.[4] For instance, when the lands of Urquhart, in the Black Isle, were granted to the Thane of Cawdor in 1475, the inhabitants, who were at that time still Gaelic-speaking, renamed Urquhart Ferintosh, or the Toisechs land. The word

[1] *Registrum Moraviense*, p. xxviii.

[2] The charter granting two of them to Walter de Lesly is given in W. F. Skene's notes on *Fordoun*, vol. i, p. 414.

[3] R. R. Reid, " Barony and Thanage," *English Historical Review*, vol. xxxv, p. 180.

[4] W. F. Skene, *Celtic Scotland*, vol. iii, 278. The survival of the double duties of the toshach or tosheador are elaborately worked out by W. F. Skene. For duties of Crownar, see Sir John Skene, *Regiam Majestatem*, p. 8.

tosheador, meaning coroner, was widely found in the Highlands upon Crown lands.[1] Another word, either representing a lesser official of the older society or the tosheador fallen from his higher estate, also appears. In the laws attributed to William the Lyon it is ordered that a citation must be made by the serjeand of the coroner or tosordereh or other summoner. Traces of it are found down to the fifteenth century, generally in connection with the east coast districts, and it seems to have been more or less the equivalent of the sergeant or mair of fee—another office of Celtic origin—which was the usual title of a rural officer of mediaeval Scotland. Sir John Skene mentions the word tosheoderache in his sixteenth century treatise *De Verborum Significatione*.[2] It has long since passed away, but its equivalent, the word mair, was still used for an official on Hebridean estates in the middle of the nineteenth century.

The feudal system may be truly said to have been woven into the social fabric of Scotland. Many are the interesting examples of the gradual incorporation of new and old ways of life. The curious variety of land measures that were in use down till recent times is a case in point; and in considering land measures it may not be out of place to remind ourselves that early methods of mensuration were primitive, and that the area of a given piece of land was largely estimated according to the maintenance that it was supposed to supply.[3] In Northern England, at the time of the Conquest, the *Oxgate* and *Ploughgate*, Latinized into the *Bovata* and *Carrucata*, were the typical land measures. Probably the Angles used them when they occupied the south-east of Scotland. In any case they are the measures almost invariably used in early Scots charters. In Lawrie's collection the southern word *virgate* only appears twice. One may, therefore, fairly say that they had become the

[1] W. F. Skene, *Notes in Fordoun's Chronicle*, vol. ii, p. 459.

[2] W. F. Skene, *Celtic Scotland*, vol. iii, 279-281, for five or six examples of the office or its lands.

[3] In Saxon times in England Vinogradoff says that hides and carrucates did not represent a definite number of shares in the common land. *Growth of the Manor*, p. 152.

In the parish of Moy, so late as 1792, "land is not let by the acre but by the piece, or lump," *First Statistical Account*, vol. viii, p. 507. For an Aberdeenshire example see *First Statistical Account*, vol. xix, p. 290.

standardized unit of land measurement in all the more settled parts of Scotland.[1]

During the fourteenth and fifteenth centuries the *Oxgate* and *Ploughgate*, the *Bovate* and *Carrucate*, were constantly mentioned in connection with land in the Lothians, in the Merse and Teviotdale, and also in Banff and Inverness-shire.[2] One might call them the official land measurements, and they were definitely equated with the units upon which taxation was levied. By an Act of Sederunt of 1585 it was declared that "an *oxengate* or *oxgate* contains thirteen acres, four *oxgates* a *twenty shilling land*, eight *oxengates* a *forty shilling land*." Sir John Skene is quite definite that the area of the *oxgate* and the *bovata* "suld conteine thretene aicker." Two *oxgates* represented a *husbandland*, a common measurement, though it does not appear in the earlier charters; and four *husbandlands* made the *ploughgate* of 104 acres, which were equivalent to the *forty shilling land* upon which the taxation and the parliamentary representation of the country came to be based.[3]

On the East Coast another land measurement of older origin has been fitted in with these denominations of southern origin. The *Davoch* appears constantly in early Gaelic entries in the *Book of Deer*,[4] but it is only mentioned twice in the two feudal codes of laws, the *Regiam Majestatem* and the *Quoniam Attachamenta*,[5] and it is not very common in charters previous to the thirteenth century. Then it again came into increasingly

[1] The English *carrucate* represented 120 acres, that of Scotland 104, but Scots acres were larger and the total area was similar. Sir A. Lawrie, *Early Scottish Charters*, p. 257.

[2] C. Innes, *Scotch Legal Antiquities*, p. 270.

[3] Jamieson's *Dictionary* has an excellent collection of references.

C. Innes, *Scotch Legal Antiquities*, p. 283, quotes a legal decision that an oxgate = 13 acres = £1 land.

Antiquities of Aberdeen and Banff, vol. iv, p. 690, there is an example of an oxgate of twenty acres.

For the intricacies of the meaning of the Forty Shilling Land of the Old Extent, which is traditionally based upon a valuation of the time of Alexander III, the best, indeed the only reference, is the learned dissertation by T. Thomson in the Cranstoun *v.* Gibson case. *Session Papers, 2nd Division, 6th Jan.* 1816.

[4] A. O. Anderson, *Early Sources of Scots History*, ii, p. 180.

[5] *Regiam Majestatem*, cap. iv, 17.

Quoniam Attachamenta, c. 223.

common use in documents until at least the sixteenth century. In the East Coast and Lothian arrangement of *oxgates* and *ploughgates* it nearly always represented four *ploughgates*.[1] It seems to have often been the unit of a barony.

The *davoch*, however, also appears in the Central Highlands and Islands, where land was generally divided into *Merklands*,[2] subdivided into *Pennylands*.[3] W. F. Skene points out " the Davoch was the old Celtic unit, combined in the Eastern districts with the Saxon denominations, and in the Western with the Norwegian." [4] But the matter shows the complicated and mixed state of affairs, for we have references that equate the *davoch* with the *tierunga*, an obsolete land measure of the Western Highlands, and which definitely prove that they both consisted of twenty pennylands.[5] The *tierunga* was also divided into six *merklands*; [6] but we learn from other references that the *merkland* was said to be the same size as the husbandland [7]—of which there were eight in a *davoch*. Furthermore, the commonest rentals all over the Highlands, and in many other parts of Scotland, throughout the fourteenth, fifteenth, and sixteenth centuries are for 33s. 4d., 16s. 8d., and 8s. 4d., and less commonly for 50s. and 25s.[8] The figure

[1] Jamieson's *Dictionary* gives illustrations.

C. Innes, *Scotch Legal Antiquities*, p. 272, quotes a series of documents in which half a Davoch and two ploughgates are used alternatively to describe the extent of the same land.

[2] Merklands, however, were not peculiar to the Highlands. Much of the land of Kelso Abbey was held in *merklands* in a 1567 Rental. *Liber de Calchou*, p. 321.

[3] Cf. "Records of Dunstaffnage, 1502–1609," *Scottish Hist. Review*, vol. viii, p. 109.

[4] W. F. Skene, *Notes on Fordoun's History of Scotland*, vol. ii, p. 450.

[5] *Ibid.* Quotations from *Origines Parochialis.*

" The Davoch called in Scotts a Terung of Yllera," vol. ii, p. 374; " the ten pennylands of Moilachunry and the ten of Moillockinais called a Davoch," vol. ii, p. 829.

[6] " An old Tiree Rental of the Year 1662," *Scottish Hist. Review*, vol. ix, p. 343. By the nineteenth century the merkland had become a most variable measure, differing in neighbouring townships, *First Statistical Account*, vol. v, p. 195; vol. xii, p. 580.

[7] Sir John Skene, *De Verb. Sig.*

Agricultural Survey of Argyllshire, p. 33.

[8] Cf. *Crown Rentals, Exchequer Rolls*, vol. x, p. 634. Larger units, such as £3 : 6 : 8 (=2 × 33s. 4d.) and £6 : 13 : 4 (=4 × 33s. 4d.), are also common.

33s. 4d. does not fit in with the pound or merk, and its fractions, which are ÷2÷2, do not correspond with the divisions of the *ploughgate*, *husbandland*, and *oxgate*, which are ÷4÷2. Cosmo Innes, working on a sixteenth century rental of the Isles, noticed that there were a few ten *merkland* holdings; these divided into four would make two and a half *merkland* holdings, which would correspond with the 33s. 4d. of the rentals—for the Scots merk was 13s. 4d.—which, multiplied by two and a half, would make 33s. 4d.[1]

F. W. L. Thomas, from similar sources, has compiled the following table:—

1 davoch	= 20d. land	= 10 merks	= 133s. 4d.	= 1	*Tirunga.*
$\frac{1}{4}$,,	= 5d. ,,	= $2\frac{1}{2}$,,	= 33s. 4d.	= 1	*Ceathramh.*
$\frac{1}{8}$,,	= $2\frac{1}{2}$d. ,,	= $1\frac{1}{4}$,,	= 16s. 8d.	= 1	*Ochdamh.*
$\frac{1}{16}$,,	= $1\frac{1}{4}$d. ,,	= $\frac{5}{8}$,,	= 8s. 4d.	= 1	*Leothas.*
$\frac{1}{32}$,,	= $\frac{5}{8}$d. ,,	= $\frac{5}{16}$,,	= 4s. 2d.	= 1	*Cota-ban.*
$\frac{1}{64}$,,	= $\frac{5}{16}$d. ,,	= $\frac{5}{32}$,,	= 2s. 1d.	= 1	*Dha Sgillin.*

He points out that in the North the *davoch* was often regarded as = one instead of four ploughs.[2]

Although the size of the divisions in such a system would be different, it is rather curious that the multiples should be the same as those of the Lowland system, as evolved in the fifteenth century from the original *bovate* and *carrucate*.

2 oxgates = 1 husbandland.	2 8s. 4d. lands = 1 16s. 8d. land.
4 husbandlands = 1 ploughgate.	4 16s. 8d. lands = 1 33s. 4d. land.
4 ploughgates = 1 davoch.	4 33s. 4d. lands = 1 ten merk land.

There were several other old land measures of Pictish, Gaelic, and Scandinavian origin—*raths*, *bals*, *pettes*, *örelands*, *farthinglands*, etc.—but they are less important. So much vague and perhaps tiresome detail has been given regarding land measurements, because these exemplify so well the process that went on in every branch of the national life; the building up of a new system which incorporated fragments of older ones, and the strange persistence of more ancient things that survived, dumb and recessive, and yet part and parcel of the life-stream of the race.[3]

Fortunately the Scots law and its intricacies lie beyond the

[1] C. Innes, *Scotch Legal Antiquities*, p. 278.

[2] F. W. L. Thomas, *Proc. Soc. Antiqu.* (*Scot.*), vol. xx, p. 200.

[3] G. H. Orpen, *Ireland under the Normans*, vol. ii, p. 110, shows dual character of early Irish land measures.

scope of this book, but it is just worth while noting that many of the laws of Malcolm Canmore's successors show the same phenomena of general feudalizing tendencies modified by deep-seated Gaelic survivals and influences. For instance, G. Neilson considers that " compurgation was the prominent characteristic of the native Scotch system before Norman influence brought in the duel." [1] And there are many evidences of the existence of both systems, side by side, in our early laws and charters. Then the Scoto-Normans, developing their methods of administration of justice on similar lines with those of the rest of Western Europe, gradually learned a better way of deciding the innocence or the guilt of an accused person than either of these, and the *visnet* or trial by jury was introduced. In this great reform it is satisfactory to know that Scotland was slightly ahead of England.[2] A far less important but very picturesque example is the law relating to the killing of a *househound*. The old Gaelic saga-cycle of *Cuchullin* must have been first told in Scotland in the days when the small colony of Scots in Dalriada were still but a lesser branch of their parent tribe in Ireland. One of the first feats of the hero as a " wee boy " was to defend himself when he was attacked by a great hound. " Nor was it to carve the boy decently as for a feast that he was minded, but at one gulp to swallow him down." [3] Cuchullin killed the hound with his hurley ball, but Culann, the " good smith and artificer " who owned it, complained to the king. Cuchullin himself, however, decided the matter and condemned himself to keep ward and watch over the smith's possessions for a year and a day, so that he should have time to procure and train another hound. It was thus that the hero earned for himself the name of *Cu Chulainn* or *Culann's hound*. No doubt the story typifies some forgotten law or custom of the Gael. It is very curious to find among the *Assisi Regis David* a law that if anyone slays another man's *househound* through " villany," either " he sal wak upon that mannis myddin for a twelf moneth and a day," or be responsible for all damage done to his goods during that time.[4]

Of course such a law must soon have become obsolete and is of no intrinsic importance. Nevertheless, it does show the

[1] G. Neilson, *Trial by Combat*, p. 78.

[2] C. Innes, *Scotch Legal Antiquities*, p. 213.

[3] Eleanor Hull, *Cuchullin Saga*, p. 140.

[4] *A.P.S.* vol. i, p. 13.

lingering survival of the old in the new. Probably it was also due to this surviving Gaelic influence, and that the Normans were guests merely, not conquerors, that although there was in Scotland a comprehensive code of Forest Laws, attributed to the reign of William the Lyon, yet they were milder and their jurisdiction was less wide than were the corresponding laws of England.

These lingering Gaelic survivals are important, because they show that the period was one of gradual transition; and because, when proof exists of a fusion of ideas in some directions, it justifies us in searching for similar influences in the general social life of the people, where they are subtler and less easy to trace, but are of far greater importance.

In the case of all land not held by noble tenure, the old Gaelic services remained in general use until they were commuted for money payments. This is important, for it suggests that the actual arrangement of the estates and of the farms upon them, and perhaps the methods of agriculture, were not necessarily much altered. These services were the military duties of *Feacht* or internal service and *Sluagad* or external service, afterwards known as *Scotch Service*; *Cain* or *Can*, a fixed amount of the produce of the land; and a due variously known as *Coigny*, *Conveth*, *Waytinga*, *Sorryn*, or *Cuddiche*, a specified amount of entertainment to be given to the overlord when he visited his vassals.[1]

These were the dues paid by the ancient Scots when they came to Dalriada from Ireland. At a gathering held at Drumceatt in Ireland in 575, which was attended by Aedh, King of Ireland, the sub-kings, the heads of tribes, and the principal clergy—including Saint Columba—the question of the independence of Dalriada and the proper assignment of its dues was discussed, and the following judgement was given. The men of Dalriada were to pay: "Their fecht and their sloged with the men of Erin always, for there is sloged with territories always; their cain and their cobach with the men of Alban, or their sea-gathering only with the men of Alban, but all beyond that with the men of Erin." [2]

[1] W. F. Skene, *Celtic Scotland*, vol. iii, pp. 308, 232. J. R. N. Macphail, *Highland Papers*, vol. ii (second series), *Scottish Hist. Soc.* p. 227.

[2] From the context it would appear that the decision was that the *cain* and *cobach* were to be paid to their own chiefs, the other dues to the chiefs

These services are mentioned all over Scotland, in Argyllshire and Aberdeenshire, in Badenoch, Moray, in Strathearn and in other parts of Perthshire, in Fifeshire, Kincardineshire, Cunningham, Carrick, Kyle, etc., etc., everywhere, in fact, with one exception—the Lothians.[1] They also survived till comparatively late times. The word "Scotch Service" was still occasionally used in the sixteenth century. "Coigny" and its cognate words only persisted in certain districts—in Galloway, in the fourteenth century, and, as "cuddiche," in the Western Islands till even the eighteenth century. But "cain" or "can"[2] —the last vestiges of which, in the dues known as "kain hens," survived in some rural districts into the nineteenth century—became an integral part of the revenue system of mediaeval Scotland. It regularly appears in the *Exchequer Rolls*, not only in the returns from the Crown lands, but it was levied on wool and hides[3] exported from the burghs; and the royal dues on trading ships in the days of David I, Malcolm IV, and William the Lyon were known as their can.[4]

The story of the Keledei is another good example of the adjustments and fusions of the period. They were monastic foundations of the Gaelic Church, and it has been suggested that they lived under a rule somewhat like that of the canons regular of the rest of Western Christendom.[5] Under Malcolm Canmore and his elder sons they were encouraged; Malcolm and Margaret gave the lands of Balchristen to the Keledei of Loch Leven.[6] About the middle of the twelfth century they were established at St Andrews, Dunkeld, Dunblane, and Brechin, and had many other scattered foundations such as Loch Leven and Monymusk.[7] David I, however, disliked their variations

of their parent clan in Ireland. The passage is an extract from the *Lebar Breac*, tr. A. O. Anderson, *Early Sources of Scottish History*, vol. i, p. 84.

[1] Cf. W. F. Skene, *Celtic Scotland*, vol. iii, p. 227. The terms are very common in old Scots documents.

[2] W. F. Skene, *Celtic Scotland*, vol. iii, p. 233.
Exchequer Rolls, vol. xiii, p. clxxxvi.

[3] *A.P.S.* vol. i, p. 361.

[4] Sir Archibald Lawrie, *Early Scottish Charters*, pp. 162, 296. It was evidently regarded as synonymous with tolls and dues; see charter of 1147 to the monks of May.

[5] W. F. Skene, *Celtic Scotland*, vol. ii, p. 277.

[6] Sir Archibald Lawrie, *Early Scottish Charters*, p. 7.

[7] Cosmo Innes, *Scotland in the Middle Ages*, p. xxvii.

from the standardized monasticism of Latin Christianity and tried to stamp them out. The monastery at Loch Leven was handed over to regular canons, and the king ordered that those of the Keledei who refused to conform to the rule of the new community were to be ejected.[1] The community at Kilrimont was more considerately treated: they were only to be transferred, with their possessions, to the prior and canons of St Andrews if they gave their own consent. If they refused to do this, they were to be allowed to continue in possession for their own lifetimes; but, as each vacancy occurred, it was to be filled up by a regular canon. In spite of this, however, they put up a tough fight for their old rights and were still in existence as late as 1309.[2]

It has been suggested that it was from definitely pro-Gaelic motives that Malise, Earl of Strathearn—who had showed himself so strongly anti-Norman at the Battle of the Standard—placed Keledei at Dunblane, the bishopric that he founded. But other Gaelic nobles showed no predilection for the old order. The Lord of the Isles, the son of the great Somerled, who re-established the rule of Gaeldom in the Western Highlands, founded a monastery of Black Monks at Iona in 1203, and also a convent of Black Nuns, and he placed Grey Friars—other references say Cistercians—at Saddel, in Kintyre.[3] Malcolm, Earl of Fife, founded two Cistercian monasteries, one at Culross in 1216 and the other at North Berwick, and also a Dominican monastery at Cupar.[4] On the other hand, the last Provost of the Keledei at St Andrews, who was a great champion of the failing community, was William Comyn, brother of the Earl of Buchan, and there were other Scoto-Norman names among the brethren.[5] By the thirteenth century, however, the Keledei had almost died out, and we hear of them no more.

By far the most important of all the Gaelic institutions that survived was the clan. The clan organization, as apart from the tribe, had already developed in ancient Ireland, and was one of the institutions that the Gaels brought with them to Dalriada, although it probably also existed already in Alba among the

[1] Sir Archibald Lawrie, *Early Scottish Charters*, p. 187.
[2] *Ibid.*
[3] Cosmo Innes, *Scotland in the Middle Ages*, p. 109.
[4] W. F. Skene, *Celtic Scotland*, vol. ii, p. 413.
[5] J. Wilkie, *History of Fife*, pp. 114-171.

Picts and other ancient inhabitants. In Aberdeenshire, in a district where a Gaelic social group lingered for a long time, the word clan is mentioned in a Gaelic document so late as 1135;[1] but with the exception of the Law of Clan Macduff, the word appears in no official document of this period. It was ignored, although its living organization was so strong that features of it are found surviving in districts that had been feudalized; in 1372, for instance, Robert II confirmed a charter granting to the Earls of Carrick that they should be *caput totius progeniei*.[2] The Gaelic revival in the Highlands will be dealt with elsewhere; but it is very significant that under propitious circumstances the clan organization should have sprung up in other parts of Scotland, and, notably, in the largely Anglian Borders. In 1587, one of many laws dealing with the disorderly subjects of the Borders and Highlands mentions "the Clans that have Captains, Chiefs and Chieftains, on whom they depend . . . as well on the Borders as in the Highlands."[3]

Even where the word clan was never used, the Scots responded, to an unusual degree, to what was the primary bond in the clan, that of kinship. All through the troublous later history of Scotland, the great followings of the nobles, formed of gentlemen of their name and kin, played a distinctive part, and in every ancient rent-roll or chartulary of a noble house, younger brothers, and humble cousins to the *n*th degree, are to be found established upon the land as wadsetters, tacksmen, or kindly tenants. As we shall see, feudalism survived in Scotland when it had become a worn-out institution in all neighbouring countries. It would be interesting to know how largely it did so, because in Scotland, more than elsewhere, into the purely feudal relationship had crept something of the greater warmth and fervour of the simpler and more ancient bond of union of the clan.

The Middle Ages were the days of pageantry. It was by symbols and outward show that the man in the street learned his civics and his politics, besides a great many other things. It is therefore historically meet that this chapter should end with

[1] Sir Archibald Lawrie, *Early Scottish Charters*, p. 84 (*The Book of Deer*).

[2] Cosmo Innes, *Scotland in the Middle Ages*, p. 74.

[3] *A.P.S.* vol. iii, p. 496.

a description of the coronation of Alexander III, the last king of Malcolm Canmore's happy line. One sees in the ceremonial a curious mingling of the conventional coronation rites of Christian Europe with something far older, which also had its survival in the ceremonial attending the inauguration of the ancient Lords of the Isles—when, according to the custom of the Gael, the new Chief stood upon a particular stone in his ancient heritage of Islay, and, swinging his sword to the four quarters of the compass, asserted his sovereignty.[1]

The incident, however, is even more significant. The old Gaelic theory that descent was computed from the founder of the race and not from the last deceased possessor, and that brothers, therefore, had a stronger claim than sons, had utterly passed away, so far as the royal line of Scotland was concerned. The last example of it was when the Gaels tried to put Donald Bane, the brother of Malcolm Canmore, upon the throne. So forgotten was the practice that, after Alexander III's death and that of the little Maid of Norway, when there was the momentous difficulty in deciding upon the rightful heir, such a claim was but very tentatively made by one of the claimants as a secondary consideration, and was brushed aside without serious consideration. The feudal principle of primogeniture had been absolutely accepted as the law of the land. And yet, as we shall see, a wraith-like Gaelic sentiment still lived on, part of the mental heritage of the so greatly transformed people of Scotland.

Alexander II had died when his heir was still a child, and the kingdom was rent by factions, led, one of them, by the Durward, and the other by Walter Comyn, Earl of Menteith—both of them of Anglo-Norman descent. There was much wrangling as to whether the boy king's coronation should take place at once or be delayed until he was knighted. Comyn, who had " always loved King Alexander of pious memory, now deceased, and this boy also for his father's sake," prevented the dangerous delay, and, surrounded by his Scoto-Norman nobles, the child

[1] An Irish stone with two footprints carved on it is preserved in the National Museum, Dublin. There is a Highland example in the Museum of Inverness. See *Red Book of Clan Ranald.* Also, Sir Walter Scott's account of the succession of the Chief in *The Fair Maid of Perth.* A. Carmichael in *Ortha nan Gadheal*, p. 323, has collected much of the lore upon this subject.

was crowned at Scone. The Stone of Destiny was " decked with silken clothes inwoven with gold " so that it formed a royal throne, and, sitting upon it, the boy was consecrated king, as was meet, by the Bishop of St Andrews. " So the king sat down upon the royal throne—that is, the stone—while the earls and other nobles, on bended knees, strewed their garments under his feet, before the stone. Now this stone is reverently kept in that same monastery, for the consecration of the Kings of Albania ; and no king was ever wont to reign in Scotland unless he had first, on receiving the name of king, sat upon this stone at Scone, which, by the kings of old, had been appointed the capital of Albania. But, lo ! when all was over, a Highland Scot suddenly fell on his knees before the throne, and, bowing his head, hailed the king in his mother-tongue, saying these words in Scottish : 'Benach de Re Albanne Alexander, Mac-Alexander, MacWeyliam, MacHenri, MacDavid '—and, reciting it thus, he read off, even unto the end, the pedigree of the Kings of Scots." [1]

[1] *Chronicle of Fordoun*, vol. ii, p. 389 (Historians of Scotland Series).

CHAPTER II

Part I. The Evolution of the Lowlander

Having in some sort disposed of the Scoto-Norman nobles and officials, the way is now cleared for the consideration of the most interesting and important change that the twelfth and thirteenth centuries wrought in Scotland—the evolution of the Lowlander.

Before the coming of the Normans, a Gaelic civilization was dominant over the greater part of Scotland. The exceptions were the parts where Norsemen had settled, and, much more important, the district of the Lothians. This district had been occupied by Anglian colonists for some five hundred years, although there had been constant fighting for the sovereignty of the territory, which had been finally secured by the kings of Scotland. This Lothian kingdom was but a pendicle of the rest of Scotland, mainly occupying the southern shores of the Firth of Forth. Even there the older inhabitants do not seem to have been completely exterminated, for Gaelic names appear among Lothian serfs in historic times and the proportion of non-Anglian place-names is far higher than in Northern England. All over the rest of the mainland, including the south-west, and in the Western Isles, save for the fugitive influence of the Norsemen, the people were of Gaelic and Pictish stock and were Gaelic-speaking. Nine-tenths of the older place-names in what are now the Lowlands are either Gaelic or Pictish.[1] During the reign of Malcolm Canmore, Gaelic was the national language. In the momentous meeting between Queen Margaret and the bishops, the king acted as interpreter, because he "knew the English language quite as well as his own."[2]

[1] R. S. Rait, *Making of Scotland*, p. xvi.

[2] W. Forbes Leith, Trans. of Turgot's *Life of St Margaret*, p. 45.

For a long time the Lowlanders seem to have retained the tradition of their Gaelic-speaking descent. Hector Boece, in his *Scotorum Regni Descriptio*, writes: "Those of us who live on the borders of England have forsaken our mother-tongue and learned English, being driven thereto by wars and commerce. But the Highlanders remain just as they were in the time of Malcolm Canmore in whose days we began to adopt English." And John Major, after describing the difference between the Highlanders and the Lowlanders, that had become so clearly marked in his own days of the sixteenth century, adds that "most of us spoke Irish a short time ago." Moreover, Gaelic continued to be spoken at a much later date than this in districts that are now purely Lowland. Sir Thomas Craig, who was the contemporary of James VI, wrote: "I myself remember the time when the inhabitants of the shires of Stirling and Dumbarton spoke pure Gaelic"—and there were many other similar survivals.[1]

Nor is there any evidence that a large displacement of the population took place. The only possible exception, what Fordoun calls the "planting" of the province of Moray, is generally considered merely to refer to the sweeping introduction of new feudal superiors into the district.[2] Even this was not very effective, for in the reigns of the two next kings there were serious revolts in Moray in favour of the old family of mormaers.

In spite of all the changes that the country underwent, there is an unbroken continuity in many of its folk traditions. Fairy tales may seem to be strange subjects for an economic history, yet it is only in such by-ways that we can find any material at all for a study of that obscure subject, the social life of the people of Scotland in early times. It is a striking fact that the fairy lore of the Lowlands and of the Highlands is very similar, although there is a wide gulf between that of Scotland and England. The character of the rather sinister Good Folk is similar in the folk-tales of both the Highlands and the Lowlands.

[1] R. S. Rait, *Making of Scotland*, pp. 34, 64-65, Appendix A.
R. S. Rait, *Relations between England and Scotland*, p. xxviii.

[2] Fordoun's account, vol. ii, p. 252, in Historians of Scotland Series.
R. S. Rait, *Relations between England and Scotland*, pp. xxii, 208.

Kelpies are common to both; so are the rites of divination practised at Hallowe'en; and the ceremonies connected with the cutting and keeping of the "klyock sheaf" at harvest. Scots folklore abounds with such parallels.[1] Nor are they modern importations, for Major, writing in the sixteenth century, mentions the "brobne" (i.e. brownie, so familiar in Highland tales) as a superstition of the Lothians.[2] Contrariwise, Scotland has few dragon myths, whereas it is a common theme of local stories in England.

Nor was the people's traditional attachment to their old Holy Places broken. The moot-hills, known in Gaelic as "Tom Void," were, according to local traditions, the hillocks where the druids gave justice; and, in many districts, the baronial and even the burgh courts were still held there. There are also instances of mediaeval courts being held at standing stones.[3] The Register of the Bishopric of Moray records a stormy interview that took place in 1380 between the Bishop and Alexander Stewart, the son of Robert II, the infamous "Wolf of Badenoch." The Wolf, as Lord of Badenoch, was holding his court at the "Standand Stanys of the Rathe of Kyngusy," and he had ordered the landholders of the district to produce their title-deeds in accordance with the feudal law of the land, when the Bishop appeared, and, standing outside the circle of stones, shouted to him that he had no right of jurisdiction over the episcopal tenants, and that he, the Bishop, defied him. To give the end of the story, the Wolf ignored the Bishop, and pro-

[1] W. Bonser, *Folklore*, Sept. 1926.

J. Wilkie, *History of Fife*, p. 21, for Fifeshire examples of well-worship, sacredness of the rowan-tree, kelpies, Hallowe'en rites.

Jamieson's *Dictionary* for general account of Hallowe'en rites.

T. Pennant, *First Tour, 1769*, p. 156, for contemporary Banffshire beliefs in holy wells, sacredness of rowan-tree, divination by cabbage stalks, etc.

J. M. Macpherson, paper read before British Association, Glasgow, 1928, *Primitive Beliefs in the North-East of Scotland.*

[2] J. Major, Introduction to *History of Greater Britain*, published by Scottish History Society, p. xxx.

[3] G. Neilson, *Trial by Combat*, p. 117. Examples cited, the Skeat and the Loch Maben Stane.

D. Murray, *Early Burgh Organization*, p. 25. Examples cited, Baronial Court held in 1468, "Apud la Graystane de Cluny"; Court held by King's Justiciar, 1349, at the Stone Circle at Rane, Aberdeenshire.

ceeded with his court, but, by the following day, his blood had cooled and he gave way But he never seems to have forgiven the Bishop and the sequel was the burning of Elgin Cathedral a few years later.[1] Another old record tells how the Prior of St Andrews held his pleas on Thursday next after the feast of St Scholastica the Virgin, in the year of grace 1264. The court was held near the great stone by the vicar's house at Dull, and, in the presence of Sir Mauricius and Sir Richard, canons, and of Sir Thomas, vicar, Kolin, son of Anegus, the soutar, did homage to the prior as his liegeman. And the names of nine of those present are recorded, all of them Gaels, including Duncan the clerk, named Makmunthir, Ewayn the Doomster, and Makrath the priest.[2] Could there be a more perfect mingling of new and old ? The present writer knows of no less than four churches that have megalithic remains enclosed within their churchyards, and one of them happens to be in the "planted" province of Moray.

The old Gaelic seasons which divided the year into two, Beltane and Samhain, also were preserved, especially Beltane. In 1456 the courts of justice in Ettrick Forest were held at Beltane and All-Hallows; right down till the seventeenth century the great civic festival of Peebles—the annual horse race for the silver bell—was held at Beltane. James VI uses the term in his instructions to his financial advisers, "the Octavians."[3] Again, one of the most typical foods of the people, oatcakes, baked on a girdle, were, in the Middle Ages, common to the Highlands and the Lowlands.[4] Similar examples of identical folk customs might be multiplied indefinitely. On the other hand, there is no evidence that at all suggests that the lesser folk, Pictish and Gaelic, were removed from the soil they had tilled from generation to generation. The names of only a small proportion of such humbler people have come down to us, but, among these, Gaelic names very largely predominate. The tenacity with which the humbler folk continued to occupy

[1] *Registrum Moraviense*, p. 183.

[2] C. Innes, *Scotch Legal Antiquities*.

[3] *Exchequer Rolls*, vol. iv, p. cxvii.
Register of the Privy Council, vol. v, p. 759.
J. W. Buchan, *Peeblesshire*, vol. ii, p. 41.

[4] P. Hume Brown, *Early Travellers in Scotland*, p. 9.
J. Major, *History of Greater Britain*, p. 11.

even conquered territories can be traced in many countries. Ireland is a case in point.[1]

If, however, we accept this position, we are faced with the almost insoluble problem of how the Lowlanders became Lowland. When a Scots literature arose, in the fifteenth century, the language of the people had become a strongly individualized Anglian dialect. The change, however, went far deeper than that. In the accounts of the Battle of the Standard, and in other contemporary documents,[2] the contingents from the more purely Gaelic parts of the kingdom were known as Scots, as opposed to the Normans, Angles, men of Teviotdale, etc.; but, by the end of our period, a new conception was beginning to arise. The word Scots was acquiring its modern, national meaning, while the districts least affected by the innovation that had come about had become known as the Highlands. A definite change had taken place in the type of national culture, but the alteration was even yet more fundamental; we may fairly class it with those mutations by which new species are created For it was in these potent twelfth and thirteenth centuries that a new and very strongly individualized race appeared and began the arduous course of its evolution.

It is of course possible to trace certain channels through which a strongly Anglicizing influence was brought to bear upon Scotland. In the first place, there was a certain immigration of Anglo-Saxons at the time of Malcolm Canmore and immediately afterwards, though we cannot formulate even the most general guess at its extent. Some came with the Atheling and his family; there were a certain number of refugees when William the Conqueror ravaged the north of England, though, as Professor Rait points out, it was not at that time very populous, and William is reported to have massacred large numbers of the existing inhabitants.[3] There were also a number of Saxon slaves in Scotland, carried off in Malcolm Canmore's southern campaigns.[4]

[1] J. Mills, "Norman Settlement in Leinster," *Proc. Royal Soc. Antiquaries of Ireland*, 5th series, vol. iv, p. 161.

G. H. Orpen, *Ireland under the Normans*, vol. ii, p. 329.

[2] Cf. "The Terms of the Proclamations by the different Scots Kings," W. F. Skene, *Celtic Scotland*, vol. i, p. 458.

[3] R. S. Rait, *Making of Scotland*, p. xv.

[4] *Turgot's Life of St Margaret.* Translated by W. Forbes Leith, p. 57. Cf. in *Registrum Vetus de Aberbrothoc*, p. 74.

The Norman incursion also probably brought certain Saxon influences to bear on Scotland. They came to Scotland through England. As we know, in England, the Normans gradually became Anglicized, and, as the connection between the nobility of the two countries was very close, this tendency must have had its effect on both sides of the Border. One sees this influence, for instance, in the stylistic language of the charters: the grants of soc, sac, tol, them, and infangthef and outfangthef.[1] It may very well have been that the Anglo-Norman feudal lords brought Saxon reeves and other followers with them, when they received grants of land in Scotland. The king had a *praepositus* at Dunfermline, in 1130, named Swain, who may have been such a one.[2]

The increase in the importance of the burghs also brought a good many English to Scotland. William of Newburgh, the contemporary of Edward I, says that the towns and burghs of Scotland were inhabited by Englishmen. This, however, must be taken with considerable reserve, for a list of Aberdeen burgesses of 1406 shows a large proportion of Gaelic names.[3]

But probably the greatest factor in the evolution of Lowland Scotland was the increasing importance of the Lothians. The Lothians had been overrun by Angles, and had been held by them, and although an understratum of the original inhabitants remained, yet a definite Anglian settlement had been established in the south-east of Scotland. The Livingstones, who held the same land for generations, had Anglian ancestors;[4] the Balfours, Lauders, and Swintons were also of Anglian origin, and there are a number more. In some cases a place-name has perpetuated the memory of an old Anglian settler; Crake, Kyd, Molk, and Orm are such.[5] These Anglian settlers brought with them, and retained for a long time, their own code of laws and their social organization—nowhere else in Scotland are thegns and drengs mentioned.[6]

With the consolidation of the kingdom the rich land of the

[1] C. Innes, *Scotch Legal Antiquities*, p. 37.
[2] Sir Archibald Lawrie, *Early Scottish Charters*, p. 70.
[3] R. S. Rait, *The Making of Scotland*, pp. 31 and 66.
[4] Sir Archibald Lawrie, *Early Scottish Charters*, p. 331.
[5] C. Innes, *Scotland in the Middle Ages*, pp. 80, 88-89.
J. Coutts, *The Norman Invasion*, p. 94, gives examples.
[6] Sir Archibald Lawrie, *Early Scottish Charters*, p. 270.

Anglian colonization gained more and more relative importance. The ancient heart of the Gaelic kingdom was in Perthshire. Malcolm Canmore seems to have lived a good deal at Dunfermline. Although none of his direct descendants really made Edinburgh the capital of Scotland, they were all much in the Southern Lowlands. Berwick was by far the most important of their cities; the hill country behind it was the greatest wool-producing district—the source of Scotland's most important export; the Lothians must always have been pre-eminent as agricultural land; many of the most influential Anglo-Norman families secured possession south of the Forth.

This differentiation of the Lowlander, although the process was so silently accomplished that scarcely a clue remains by which we can trace it out, is, without doubt, the most vital occurrence of all in those epoch-making centuries. It is a strange fact that the most dominant section of the present-day people of Scotland, the one which is at once the most prosperous and that which has exerted the most powerful influence over the destinies of the nation and which has made the greatest contributions to the progress of mankind, should have been so largely democratic in its development—that it should have taken form so largely through the influence of the lesser folk, even of captives and of conquered people, exerted over their seeming superiors; and that the race which gave this dominant section its language and much of its type of civilization should not have been the Gael, though once he conquered a larger area of Scotland than any other people, nor the Viking, though he raided her the most successfully, nor yet the Norman, though he finally secured by far the larger share of possession and power in this land of his adoption, but the Angles, who in England were eventually largely dominated by the Saxons of the South, and who in Scotland had been finally conquered by the Gael.

Part II. The Absence of the Manorial System in Scotland

Although materials are scanty, it is at least clear that during this period the rural development of Scotland followed markedly different lines to that of England. So much more is known about

England,[1] however, that it is perhaps easiest to indicate in outline the growth of the manorial system in that country and then to try to work out some of our national individualities. In England there had been a gradual tendency towards feudal and manorial ideas during the later part of the Saxon period. This approximation was suddenly crystallized by the Domesday survey following the Norman Conquest. "The Norman commissioners classified the rural population, which had consisted of many layers of rank, claiming status upon a variety of reasons, upon the clear-cut definitions formulated in connection with their own system of land organization." They " made an attempt to put the people engaged in rural occupations, as villains, bordarii, and cotters, on one side, and the people entirely or mainly free from these occupations on the other." [2] During the reigns of the Norman and Plantagenet kings the process of organization and of reduction to certain clearly defined grades continued. In the case of the land, " The elements of the manor were . . . all elaborated in the course of former periods, but their social formation was by no means uniformly constituted or generally prevalent all over England." The degree of subjection of their people to their superior varied, in the time of Edward the Confessor, " from mere commendation of free villages to different protectors, to the settlement of colonii and slaves by the lord on the soil of his estate." Even in 1086, the date of Domesday, the manors " were as yet ungainly combinations, usually straggling over the fields of many scattered townships, creations of haphazard possession as well as of economic union." With this material the Normans built up their manorial system, so that, as Vinogradoff says, " When we compare these shades of subjection to the well rounded, compact manors of the Hundred Rolls, we are struck by the progress made by unification and subjection." [3] He divides the feudalizing process into two periods. The first one was covered by the reigns of William I and his successors, including Henry I, and it was marked by the clash between " the principles introduced by the Conqueror and earlier traditions," and the gradual establishment of the manor. The second period, which lasted

[1] See the works of Rowntree, Maitland, Round, Vinogradoff.

[2] Vinogradoff, *The Growth of the Manor*, pp. 213-216.

[3] *Ibid.* p. 299. This is an abridged version of a longer paragraph.

from Henry II to Edward I, was characterized by the growth of the central jurisdiction and the formation of the common law.[1]

In Scotland the antecedents were entirely different. It is dangerous to generalize from the few fragments of information which have come down to us regarding the state of society that existed during the tremendous conflicts of the period of racial organization. Probably things were only uniform in being all more or less piecemeal. There was, however, one very essential point of similarity about the different races: probably in the case of the Picts, quite certainly in the case of the Gaels, the Scandinavians and the Angles, a state of society had been evolved in which there were three definite grades—a class holding certain rights over the land (it would be dangerous to use the term land-owning in relation to a period so unknown and so radically different to our own); a class of independent freemen; and a class of tillers of the soil, a servile class. In practice, of course, there must have been infinite gradations, variations, and exceptions. Although, as we have seen, the Angles exerted an extraordinarily prepotent effect upon the language and culture of the people of Scotland, and though their type of social organization probably approximated to the English foundation upon which the Normans built up the English manorial system, yet it is necessary to remember that the period during which they could have exerted much influence outside the Lothians was quite a short one—only between the reigns of Malcolm Canmore and Alexander I—and that the Anglo-Saxon approximations to the manor, even in the south, were not universal and showed an almost endless variety of variations from what became the definite type of later times. How far any vestiges of tribal land-holding survived in the Lowlands it is, unfortunately, impossible to say. There is no evidence of its existence.

Imposed upon a state of society that must remain little more than x to the student of its history was the influence of the Normans, with their very clearly cut feudal theories. Two points about these theories deserve special attention. In the first place, they indoctrinated the kings of Scotland with their own particular ideas of land-ownership. Vinogradoff has described the effect of the Norman feudal theories upon the

[1] Vinogradoff, *The Growth of the Manor*, p. 291.

rural communities of England: "The legal theory of land ownership undergoes a complete transformation. Instead of treating the rights of the several dwellers and cultivators of the locality as originally independent and combining through mutual agreement, or as derived from an original communal ownership, the legal theory of the feudal states treats them as derived from a private and exclusive ownership of land." According to each Norman conqueror, "the freeholders of the manor are his tenants, and their possession of land, though guaranteed in every way, resolves itself into a hereditary feoffment. As for the unfree tenants, they have no rights in the eye of the law but to follow customs by the suffrance of the lord; their possession, so far as it exists within the manor, is included in the proprietary rights of the lord. Such is the feudal theory clearly formulated by Norman courts and Norman law writers. . . ."[1] The reciprocal rights of the villein, as evolved in Plantagenet common law, and which finally developed into the English tenure of copyholding, had no place in the original Normans' scheme of society.

Another point in the Normans' views of ownership was their theory that the lord absolutely possessed the whole of the waste—which, it must be remembered, was of great importance to early communities, for it furnished them with a large part of their pasturage, their firing, their building materials, and with means to enlarge the arable when population pressed upon them. Although, in practice, the tenants were allowed to continue to make use of the waste, and, in the subsequent development of English laws, to make good their claim to certain rights in it, nevertheless, the lord's right to its exclusive ownership was clearly stated in early charters and upon occasion asserted.[2]

In Scotland the Normans' *influence* deeply permeated the whole conception of their rights among the land-holding classes, and also the legal doctrines. Charters, by which land came more and more to be held, clearly show the claims that the new lord of the soil was entitled to make. Cosmo Innes has summarized the items usually included in a Scots grant of free barony of the feudal period.[3] The baron was to hold in free

[1] Vinogradoff, *The Growth of the Manor*, p. 308. [2] *Ibid.* p. 311.

[3] Cosmo Innes, *Scots Legal Antiquities*, p. 42 onwards.

barony, by all the right marches and bounds—"*in boscis et planis*," planum probably meaning arable land—"*in pratis et pascuis*," pratum meaning hay-meadow—"*in viis et semitis*," not so generally granted, and giving the right of excluding other persons from using the roads and paths, "*in moris et maresiis*" = moors and marshes, "*in aquis et stagnis*" = running water and ponds, "*in vivariis*" = fish-ponds, and also, sometimes, parks for game—"*cum brucis et brueriis*"—with brushwood and heaths, "*cum petariis et turbariis*" = places where peats and turves are cut; rights to salt-pans, coal-pits, quarries, and the right to cut broom. Rights of huntings, hawkings, and fishings, though implied in the grant of barony, were also often specially stated. "*In molendinis*," generally with "*cum multuris et sequelis*," was "one of the oldest adjuncts of a barony," a valuable right for the lord and a heavy burden on the peasantry: for it meant the exclusive right to have mills, the right to impose multures or dues for grinding corn, and to "astrict" or bind the tenants to bring their corn to a particular mill.

The lord's rights over the inhabitants of the land were asserted in the following clauses: "*Cum tenentibus, tenandriis*," with tenants and tenandries, which apparently applied to the lord's rights over the free tenants, and almost invariably included certain service dues—harvest work, the obligation to go messages and to convey goods, road labour; "*Cum bondiis et bondegiis*" = with bondmen and their services, and "*Cum nativis*" or "*cum hominibus*," that is, with serfs or natives.[1]

It would be safe to say that this Norman theory of the individual ownership of land (always, of course, acknowledging that it was only held of the king and that it was granted for certain services) was the generally accepted view in those districts of mediæval Scotland where the king's writ ran—a region that seldom covered the whole extent of Scotland, but which included the most populous, fertile, and influential portions of the kingdom. On the other hand, the Normans were not in a position to work out their theories in Scotland as they did in England. The drastic standardization that took place in England when the Domesday survey was compiled had no counterpart over the border. Nor were subsequent developments at all parallel.

[1] Cosmo Innes, *Scots Legal Antiquities*, p. 30 onwards.

In England, Vinogradoff has traced out a considerable development after Domesday, not only in the consolidation of the manors and their organization as social and political units in the national body,[1] but in the position of the groups of people who lived upon them. Intermediate classes tended to disappear and the status of the numerous groups was not only more clearly defined but was altered.

The most important of all these groups was that of the villeins. At the time of Domesday the status attached to this term was indefinite. It meant little more than the member of a township community.[2] By the time of Magna Carta, King's Writs, Bracton, and Common Law there had been a great change. Various classes, including slaves, servile labourers, and free ceorls, had been gradually amalgamated into the one great class of villeins.[3] This class occupied an intermediate position between a freeman and a slave: for in the eye of the law he was in relation to other people practically a freeman, but in relation to his own lord he was virtually a slave.[4] Meanwhile, however, a great body of custom was being built up, which eventually secured to the villein the security of copyhold. Even in the early days, Vinogradoff points out that his position in the manorial courts " is anything but an abject and rightless one ; a body of customary law is evolved in all these local tribunals which keeps in close touch with the development of the canon law, and paves the way towards the ultimate recognition of the binding character of customs." [5] J. R. Green in the *History of the English People* summarizes the position, not only of the villein, but of the landless cottager. " The possession of his little homestead with the ground around it, the privilege of turning out his cattle on the waste of the manor, passed quietly and insensibly from mere indulgences that could be granted or withdrawn at a lord's caprice into rights that could be pleaded at law. The number of teams, the fines, the reliefs, the services that a lord could claim, at first a mere matter of oral tradition, came to be entered on the court rolls of the manor, a copy of which became the title-deed of the villein. It was to this that he owed the name of ' copyholder,' which at

[1] Vinogradoff, *The Growth of the Manor*, p. 307.

[2] *Ibid.* p. 339.

[3] *Ibid.* p. 313.

[4] *Ibid.* p. 344.

[5] *Ibid.* p. 439.

a later time superseded his older title. Disputes were settled by a reference to this roll, or, on oral evidence of the customs at issue, by a social arrangement which was eminently characteristic of the English spirit of compromise, generally secured a fair adjustment of the claims of villein and lord. It was the duty of the lord's bailiff to exact their due services from the villeins, but his coadjutor in this office, the reeve or foreman of the manor, was chosen by the tenants themselves and acted as representative of their interests and rights." In the words of a law of Edward IV, "the tenant by the custom is as well inheritor, to have his land according to the custom as he which hath a freehold." [1]

In Scotland, manors were not organized to anything like the same degree. The very word, so common in England as part of the name of a large house, is not found with us. Manors are only very occasionally mentioned in contemporary writings. The word hardly occurs in the laws of the period. In the *Regiam Majestatem*, the most English of all the codes, it only appears twice, in one case in connection with the very unfeudal custom of dividing land among several heirs. In the case of certain socmen the *messuagio capitalis* was to go to the eldest son.[2]

Moreover, in Scotland, the common law, which did so much to develop the relationships of the manor in England, did not exist. J. R. N. Macphail has pointed out that "the lines upon which the formation of English law proceeded" is "in sharp contrast with the course followed in" Scotland. "The loss of all the old Scots national records on which Edward I could lay his felonous hands has occasioned enormous difficulties to students of our legal history. But this seems clear: that from early times the local tribunals in Scotland held their own, while in England the king's judges gradually obtained control of litigation. In this way the decision of those judges, noted, referred to, followed as precedents or obeyed as authorities, contributed greatly to the building up of that common law which they proposed only to administer and expound; whereas in Scotland the local courts went their own independent ways and their deter-

[1] W. Ashley, *An Introduction to English Economic History and Theory*, p. 40.

[2] *Regiam Majestatem*, ix, 24 and 25. (See *A.P.S.* vol. i.)

minations were of little, if any, interest to others than the actual parties to the suit."[1] In the words of D. Murray: "The common law which bulks so largely in jurisprudence had almost no place in Scotland: the law of the land was the law administered in the local courts, and when something of the nature of a Court of Appeal came to be established, it administered the same law and did not attempt to supersede it or to explain it away."[2]

The very word which seems to suggest a similarity with the English institutions attached to the manor really emphasizes the difference between the two countries. A "commonty" in Scotland was not a common, but a piece of land belonging to more than one proprietor, the boundaries of their several shares being undemarcated. It could be divided up among these proprietors if they all wished this, without any formality. Even when all were not agreed, the matter was dealt with in the courts. On the other hand, in England an Act of Parliament is necessary for the division of a common. In Scotland all land was owned by the king or held of him and there was no "waste." (Commonties where the ownership was joint, moreover, were not nearly so usual as joint lease-holdings.[3])

The social condition of Scotland made the institution of the manor, with its long-settled customary interrelations, an impossibility. Perhaps an illustration of what happened to certain actual lands that were held in common, itself a rare thing in Scotland apart from burgh land, will best illustrate this very important point.[4] The burgh of Peebles was an ancient one. "Having been a royal burgh long before the date of the first charter" (given by James II), "it is not possible to state definitely the lands which were originally granted to the burgesses." Among the lands, however, that have been definitely traced as in the possession of the town, the widely differing stories of five are worthy of notice. Walthamshope appears in none of the charters. In 1262 there was a lawsuit which upheld the burgh's claim to have peat-cutting rights there—in Scots words, "a

[1] J. R. N. Macphail, "Review of Year Book Series of Selden Society," vol. viii, in *Juridical Review*, 1914.

[2] D. Murray, *Early Burgh Organization*, p. 580.

[3] For an early example, see Sir James Ramsay, *Bamff Charters*, p. 61. The formalities were so slight that such transactions are often barely recorded.

[4] J. W. Buchan, *History of Peebles*, vol. ii, chapter beginning p. 219.

servitude." Four hundred years later, in 1663–64, a Hay of Haystoun obtained a "declarator" against the burgh that the Moss belonged to him. No details survive of the cause of this action; probably the council had been putting forward a claim to more than the right of peat-cutting. Finally, Haystoun gave the burgh another piece of land in exchange for the servitude on Walthamshope, but of the land thus secured in exchange no further mention whatsoever is made. It was lost to the burgh. The proceeding seems to be, at least, casual.

Four other pieces of land—Cademuir with Common Struther, Hamilton Hill, Venlaw, Glentress—appear in all the charters, and the wording that confirms their possession to the town is almost identical. Yet the town council never claimed more than pasture rights on Glentress and claimed property in the three others. The result of these claims was curiously different.

Cademuir, in the words of the 1518 charter, had been held "sen the first infeftment of our said burgh." In 1456 the town council decided to "soum" it to the burgesses, i.e. let the grazing rights for a certain proportion of beasts. In 1484 John of Gledstanes claimed Cademuir. The matter was not settled till 1506, and there was fighting in the law-courts and upon the actual ground—in the latter several persons were killed. Eventually the burgh retained possession. During these troublous times the land was sometimes soumed and sometimes let out in separate pieces. About 1605 the letting was more carefully organized and "the practice began of feuing soums of ground on Cademuir to the inhabitants on condition that these soums were annexed as a pertinent to a tenement of land in the burgh."

From 1625 there was a struggle for the sole occupation of Cademuir with Scott of Hundleshope. Scott had obtained a royal charter in 1618, which granted him a commonty and common-pasture on Cademuir. Once more there was fighting on the land and in the courts, but once more the burgh remained in possession. In 1655 the burgh bought some adjacent land from Scott of Hundleshope for 7750 merks. The money was raised by inducing those burgesses who held burgh tenements to pay £50 in return for a permanent right to a soum upon Cademuir and the new land. It is significant that in fresh trouble that arose with Scott over the payment of the teinds, the burgesses who had paid for the soums were alluded to as "heritors"—a Scots word almost the equivalent of proprietor. By the eighteenth century it was acknowledged that those burgesses who had advanced the purchase price of the new land had become virtual proprietors not only of that ground but of the rest of Cademuir. The title to the land, however, remained in the name of the town council, and they paid for the herds and their houses and the minister's stipend. In return they drew the "lamb teind and the teind of the ground when in tillage."

In the middle of the eighteenth century some of the 280 heritors of Cademuir wished to sell the land; others objected. The town council sought legal advice with regard to the position, but, unfortunately, the opinion has not been preserved. In any case, the lands were let for seven years and the heritors drew the rent. In 1786 the Provost made a formal protest and pointed out that Cademuir had been illegally acquired for one-tenth of its value. The burgh still retained the right of refusing to infeft anyone who had acquired a soum on the hill unless it were conveyed with a tenement in the burgh. The town council also refused to allow the heritors to sell their land. In 1793 they offered to buy back the soums at a twenty-five years' purchase, but by 1808 they were trying to sell the sixteen soums they had thus acquired to Campbell of Hallyards. There was, however, an obstacle. The Cademuir heritors had gradually and by tacit consent been acquiring claims on the other burghal commons. The burgh refused to admit these unfounded demands.

In 1830 Campbell, who had acquired 130½ soums, wished for a charter giving him the title to them, so that he might sell them. He was willing to give up the claims to the other commons. The town council, however, would only grant a charter to the whole of the heritors of Cademuir. The rest of the heritors were willing to buy such a charter, but insisted that their other claims should be recognized. This the town council refused. Eventually, the matter was settled by the whole of the heritors buying a charter for all that they claimed, but at an enhanced price, and they resold the lands for over £11,000. The transaction was one of private arrangement. No Act of Parliament was required.

Hamilton Hill was sometimes let in severalty and sometimes grazed as a common by the beasts of the burgesses. In the seventeenth century there began to be trouble. Lauder, the neighbouring laird, had often grazed his beasts there. In 1610 he secured a Crown charter which included Hamilton Hill, whereupon the burgh obtained a renewal of their general charter. A lawsuit followed, and Lauder tried to impugn the validity of the burgh charter, but failed to do so. There continued, however, to be trouble with Lauder, and with Burnett, who succeeded him, until 1653, although, apparently, the burgh upheld their rights. For a time the grazing of the hill was let to the burgesses by roup, then the matter lapsed—probably the grazings were no longer required.

Then Murray of Cringletie made claims to the land, and in 1714, in order to assert their rights, the town had the hill ploughed up. Cringletie assaulted one of the burgh herds and the townsfolk retaliated. In the good old way, a battle was simultaneously waged in Edinburgh by lawyers' tongues and with the stout right arms of the disputants upon the spot. The town council reduced the burgh mails that were due from one burgess who was dangerously wounded by Cringletie. In 1717 the lawsuit ended. It was held that the charters "imported only a servitude and not a property in the lands of Hamildoune." "The theory underlying this decision seems to be that 'common pasturage,' the expression used in the charter, only gave to the community a right of pasturage and not of property, and although they possessed the hill for centuries, that was of no avail against a competitor who produced a charter containing a grant of the lands in property. If that was sound, then the [town] council never had any right of property in Cademuir and Venlaw, although they soumed them, and the soum-holders finally sold them." Three years later, the burgh, in right of the servitude, wished to open a quarry on Hamilton Hill. Cringletie objected, and there was a lawsuit. The Court found that the burgh had no rights to let the pasture to drovers, to dig slates, etc., for sale, or to "set their right of pasturage separate from the dominant tenement." The Cademuir heritors paid one-quarter of the costs of this action.

The early history of Venlaw also includes the attempts of a rapacious neighbour. It was soumed out among the burgesses early in the seventeenth century. About 1763 it was let in separate holdings, and the sixteen or seventeen soum-holders received the rent, the burgh had the title, and the generality of burgesses drew their water supply from the hill, quarried stone, and bleached clothes there. In 1792, Sir Ludovic Grant, who had bought up all the soums, asked the burgh for a charter which should include the neighbouring lands of Pilmuir, which was granted, but only after a furious debate in the town council, in which the whole question of the legality of the soums, which were only founded on a servitude, and the position of Pilmuir, which had only gradually and officially been included with Venlaw, were discussed. Surely this summary of what happened to five pieces of land belonging to one smallish burgh gives a fairly clear idea of how impossible was the establishment of a manorial *system* in Scotland. It is probably more convincing than many pages of generalized statements.

PART III. THE STATUS OF THE COUNTRY-FOLK

In Scotland, also, the status of the occupiers of the soil developed on totally different lines from those followed in England. At the beginning of the period the position was not radically different. In the social organizations of all the earlier people of Scotland there were two types of non-freemen, who seem to have corresponded with the slave and gebur of the late Saxon period, and with the serf and villein of the Norman organization. There was the same tendency towards superiority and subjection. "For every word in the early Saxon language which designates any due or fine or exaction of a rude and unwritten Feudalism some corresponding word is to be found in the various dialects of the Celtic language which prevailed over Ireland, Wales, and Scotland."[1] The ancient *Leges inter Brettos et Scotos*, the earliest of our surviving laws, which goes back to unknown antiquity, gives the *cro* and *kelchyn*—the composition for killing or wounding various grades of persons. There are versions in Latin, French, and Scotch, and the only grade lower than a thane is rendered the *carl*, *vileyn* or *rusticus*, showing that the generality of the people were in a very humble position.

[1] Vinogradoff, *The Growth of the Manor*, pp. 25 and 232.
W. F. Skene, *Celtic Scotland*, iii, p. 232.
Duke of Argyle, *Scotland as it was and is*, p. 85.

During the earlier part of our period a variety of lesser people are mentioned, *drengs*, in the Lothians, *herdmanni* and *gresmanni*, mentioned with *bonde*, all in one charter of the middle of the twelfth century relating to Eccles.[1] These terms disappear, and it is impossible to hazard a guess at the exact status that they represented. There were, however, most definitely slaves, generally called *nativi* or *bondi*, and sometimes *neyfs* and *cumlaws*. The chartularies of most of the abbeys contain several records of the sale or transference of such people —David I, for instance, grants Kagewin, Gillepatrick, and Ulchil for ever to the church of Holy Trinity at Dunfermline; about the time of William the Lyon, the Earl of Dunbar gives to Kelso Abbey, "Halden, William, his brother, and their children and following"; and in the same reign, Richard de Moreville sells to Henry Saint Clair, "Edmund, son of Bonde, and Gillemichael his brother, their sons and daughter, and the whole progeny descended from them," for three merks. The Prior of Coldingham bought from Adam of Lesser Riston, "Turkil Hog and his sons and daughters" for three merks of silver, which sum had been given to Adam in his "great want" of the money of the house of Coldingham. Coldingham also bought six more families of nativi, two of them from Henry de Prendergeste.[2] The number of such transactions in this southern priory is, however, exceptional. There were also serfs in the North; for instance, in a composition between Walter Comyn, Earl of Buchan, and the Bishop of Moray, relating to Badenoch (the upper valley of the Spey), an agreement was made about services and customs due from certain lands, and "*De nativis autem ita convenit inter predictum episcopum et Walterum quod Episcopus et successores sui habebunt omnes clericos et duos laycos, scilicet Gyllemallouvik Macgeeigelle et Sythack Macmallon, hos autem clericos et laycos nativos habebit episcopus Moraviensis et successores sui cum cattallis suis et possessionibus omnibus.*"[3] And there is a curious contract, dated 1222, between the Priory of St Andrews and one of their thralls, Gillemor Scolgo of Tarland (Tarland is a parish in Aberdeenshire. In the Middle

[1] Sir Archibald C. Lawrie, *Early Scottish Charters*, pp. 270 and 403. Date 1147–50.

[2] T. Johnston, *History of the Working Classes in Scotland*, p. 13.

[3] *Registrum Episcopatus Moraviensis*, No. 76, p. 82.

Ages St Andrews owned a great deal of land there.) Gillemor was to be allowed to remain with Sir James, son of the deceased Malcolm, Earl of Mar, during the pleasure of the convent.[1] The names of these serfs were generally Gaelic or Anglian in the south-east and Gaelic in the north, but among the serfs and their families bought by Coldingham are the Norman names of Roger Fitzwalter, Walter and Mabel.

It is certain that serfs existed and that they were a valuable form of property. The right to reclaim fugitive nativi is to be found in every surviving collection of charters of the period.[2] It is, however, much more difficult to decide how large a proportion of the population were serfs and to what extent the organization of the larger estates depended upon slave labour. There is too little material available for us to draw any definite conclusion. A passage from the Chronicle of Lanercost says that when Alexander III had crossed the ferry, on his fatal ride to Kinghorn, he ordered the master of the royal salt-pans to provide him " with a couple of bondmen, to go afoot as guides to the way," [3] as if they were quite usual (the position of workers employed at salt-pans however, in later years at any rate, was exceptional). On the other hand we have a list of the serfs belonging to the Abbey of Dunfermline just before the beginning of Baliol's reign. The list gives seventeen names, and shows that some of the families had been serfs for three or four generations. It was a most exhaustive list, for it included one serf from the " shire of Rerays " and two who belonged to the abbey's dependent house at Kinloss in Morayshire. A rent-roll of the abbey lands in the sixteenth century, which includes most of the places from which the serfs came (with the exception of the two in Morayshire, and also, apparently, the Rerayshire one), shows that at that time there were thirty-seven agricultural holdings at these places, not including mills. This seems to show that the serfs can only have supplied a very small part of the labour required for the cultivation of the land,[4] but sweeping generalizations cannot be made from such meagre evidence.

[1] *Liber Cartarum St Andrae*, p. xxxvi.

[2] C. Innes, *Scotch Legal Antiquities*, pp. 25 and 213.

[3] *Chronicle of Lanercost*, tr. by Sir H. Maxwell. *Scottish Hist. Review*, vol. vi, 1904, p. 186.

[4] *Reg. Dunfermline*, pp. 220 and 425.

The ancient laws of Scotland are vague and contradictory with regard to the status of the serfs. It is significant that in the *Regiam Majestatem* and the *Quoniam Attachamenta*, both codes of laws largely based upon or influenced by those of England, we get a clearly cut definition. Bondmen might be "born bondmen" or "natural natives," the descendants of slaves; or the descendants of three generations of "strangers" who had occupied servile land; or freemen who, in order to secure the maintenance of a great and potent lord, had become his bondmen. In the first two cases the lord who wished to reclaim them as his natives had to prove their descent, in the third case he had to produce evidence that the man had formally and voluntarily enslaved himself. In these codes the class of *adscripti*, or non-freemen bound to the soil, is also fully described.[1] In the *Regiam*, moreover, we find two general terms applied to the cultivators of the soil, viz.: *husbandi*, used in contradistinction to *liberi homines*, in a clause stating that the former was liable to herezelda and not the latter—and *rusticus* used in the same way = the *rusticus* must submit to ordeal by water, the freeman to that of iron, etc.[2] Such laws are compatible with the systematic English classification of serfs, villeins, and free cultivators.

In the purely Scots laws there is considerable confusion of thought and ambiguity. In the *Leges Quatuor Burgorum*, the Scots burgh laws attributed to the reign of David I, a variety of words are used for country-folk. In a law freeing any serf who can purchase a tenement in a burgh and hold it unchallenged for a year and a day, the word used is *nativus* in the Scots version "*bonde*."[3] A similar law regarding villeins was common to almost every English burgh. There are several laws[4] relating to country-folk in which the terms used are *forinsecus*, *rure manentem*, and *oplandensen*, rendered in Scots as "*uplandismen*," and which deal with the "poinding" of goods supposed to be stolen, the recovery of debts, etc.[5] Another law relates to the

[1] *Quon. Attach.*, *A.P.S.* vol. i, supplement, cap. 37. See also Sir John Skene's translation of the *Regiam Majestatem*, xxxix and xv.
Also *Regiam Majestatem*, *A.P.S.* vol. i, Ap. I, p. 244.

[2] *Regiam Majestatem*, *A.P.S.* i, Ap. I, cap. iv, viii, ix, x, xi.

[3] *Leges Quatuor Burgorum*, p. 26.

[4] *Ibid.* p. 62.

[5] *Ibid.* pp. 21, 25, 26.

rusticus, in Scots "*churl*," who owns property in a burgh.[1] The very nature of these laws shows that such country-folk cannot have been slaves ; in the case of the rusticus owning property, he cannot even have been a semi-servile villein, yet the Latin terms, in their generally accepted meaning, imply a servile status.[2]

Turning to the general laws of the land—David's statutes only state that a freeman may, of his own will, give up his freedom in open court, but that he cannot in like manner recover it.[3] Dating from the reign of William the Lyon there is a precept concerning the collection of tithes in Moray. If a *villanus* or *rusticus* (used interchangeably), refuses to pay his tithes, either the thane or his lord, if he has one, must collect them from him. If the thane or lord neglects to do so or retains the tithe, he is to be fined eight cows by the sheriff, and, failing him, by the justiciar.[4] Another law directed that anyone who did not give up a fugitive *nativus*, when he was claimed by his lord or his lord's bailiff, should be fined. In the Forest Laws, attributed to William, the fines for trespass were to be less for the king's *bondi* or *nativi*, in the Scots version "*bonds*," than for burgesses or for other people in general.[5] Two laws of this reign refer to agricultural workers as a class as *husbandi*, Scots "*husbandmen*." Thus justice was ordered to be done equally to poor and rich, especially to clerics and husbandmen, and churchmen were not to be husbandmen, shepherds, or merchants.[6] (It is rather interesting to note that in the *Regiam* they might not be bondmen. The agreement between the Bishop of Moray and the Earl of Buchan regarding the serfs and clerics of Strathspey shows that even in those organizing days Scots laws often represented aspirations, not realities.) The laws of William's reign show that there was an unfree class, but there is nothing that clearly indicates whether a great, partially free group, like the villeins of England, was being evolved, or whether the Scots bondmen were a small and slave-like class, like the earlier English *neyfs*. It must always be remembered that there was

[1] *Leges Quatuor Burgorum*, p. 23.

[2] C. C. Martin, *Record Interpreter*. *Rusticus* = used as the opposite to liberi in the twelfth century. *Villanus* = a villein, a bondman. *Manentes* = attached to the soil.

[3] *A.P.S.* vol. i, p. 9.

[4] *Reg. Epis. Moraviensis*, p. 5.

[5] *A.P.S.* vol. i, p. 59.

[6] *A.P.S.* vol. i, pp. 60, 61.

no vital distinction between liberty and slavery, such as existed, for instance, in the eighteenth-century American plantations, and. freedom and liberty had many meanings. According to another law the son of a chaplain should answer as a " freeman " so long as his father was in life, but should lose his freedom after his father's death. And the sons of merchants should be in like case, unless, after their father's death, they should be merchants.[1]

In the next reign all the lesser folk are generally legislated for *en masse*. In 1214,[2] Alexander II decreed that " ilke bondman that was wonnand in stedis and in tounis "—in Latin the word is *rusticus*—are to begin to plough and sow for their own profit with all their study and might, beginning fifteen days before the Purification. Anyone who has more than four cattle must take land of his lord and plough and sow it for his own sustenance, and those who have less than five cattle and cannot plough shall dig the land with their hands and feet to sustain themselves. Those who have oxen shall sell to those who have land to plough and sow, and any earl or vassal of the king in whose lands they dwell, and who will not allow them to do so, shall be fined eight cattle. If he holds of an earl he must pay the same fine to the earl. Any *servus*, rendered " *servandman*," " *husbandman* " and " *bondman*," who refuses to obey is to be fined a cow and a sheep by his own superior. The terms of this statute suggest that the population was in a servile or semi-servile state, like that of the English villeins. Another act, passed in 1220 after a " hosting " summoned to Inverness to put down one of the northern rebellions, made regulations for enforcing military service, and three classes of the population were recognized : thanes holding of earls whose fines were to go to the king ; bishops, abbots, barons, knights, and all holding of the king, whose fines were also to go to him ; and *carles*, whose fine of a cow and a sheep were to be divided between the king and the thane or knight who was their lord, unless they had been absent by leave of the latter, when the whole forfeit went to the king.[3] But in a third law of Alexander II it is stated that a lord may only become security for certain people, viz.—" his legeman or kind born bondman or wonnand on his lands or of

[1] *A.P.S.* vol. i, p. 58.

[2] *A.P.S.* vol. i, p. 67.

[3] *A.P.S.* vol. i, p. 68.

his samel "—*homo suus legius aut nativus aut in sua terra manens aut de familia sua*,[1] which clearly implies several grades in the rural community.

In the unclassified laws attributed to the period there is a good deal of legislation regarding lesser folk. A *churl* or *bondman* might not take part in an assize. By another law: "An thryll man may haf nan heritage"; even his son by a freewoman might not inherit his mother's property: "The wyff deis may the sone recouer the heritage? Nay he sal nocht forby that he was gottyn wyth that throllys body at is dede." Such statutes imply great servility. A churl, however, could plead in certain cases where a free woman might not. An act ordering everyone to buy and sell at the fair held within his own sheriffdom is to apply to all who hold land, to free tenants as well as to *rustici qui sunt manentes*. Manentes is commonly applied to tenants bound to the land.[2]

These rather ambiguous laws were not moulded into something definite by the decisions of the judges who administered them, for Scotland had nothing similar to the English Common Law, and "the local courts went their own independent ways," their decisions "of little, if any, interest to others than the actual parties to the suit."[3] It is significant that two of the greatest authorities on Scots law are not in agreement in their description of the status of serfs in Scotland. Stair, writing of the term *adscripta glebae*, says, "Such are the English villeins; but in Scotland there is no such thing." Whereas Erskine, after defining the Roman term *adscripti*, adds "much like to these were our ancient nativi, or bondmen; who could not, indeed, be sold by their masters but in most other respects resembled the Roman servi, for they had nothing which they could call their own."[4]

In the charters, writs for recovering fugitives, and writs of manumission, *servus* and *nativus*, which in England would mean the different grades of slave and villein, are used inter-

[1] *A.P.S.* vol. i, p. 69.

[2] *A.P.S.* vol. i, pp. 357, 365; *Regiam Majestatem*, ii, 2, iv, 2. For meaning of word, see Glossary, C. C. Martin's *Record Interpreter*.

[3] J. R. N. Macphail, *Juridical Review*, 1914, p. 235. Also D. Murray, *Early Burgh Organization*, p. 580.

[4] These passages are quoted by Sheriff Scott Moncrieff in an article on "Slavery in Scotland," *Trans. Banffshire Field Club*, 1882, p. 24.

changeably—*servus* and *nativus homo noster*, but Cosmo Innes points out that the terms *nativi sui* and *nativi de terra sua* possibly refer to these two different degrees of servitude. He quotes from the Kelso Chartulary two grants of slaves which also postulate these two distinct grades. In the earlier one Earl Waldev of Dunbar gives the abbey "Halden and his brother William, and all their children and all their descendants." In the other, Andrew Fraser grants the lands of Gordun with two crofts held by Adam of the Hog and John, son of Lethe, in the days of Alysie de Gordun, "with Adam of the Hog, himself, my native, with all his following." [1] A very late document, in which the language is merely formal, implies, perhaps, a difference that had really existed: in 1392 when the abbey lands of Paisley were erected into a barony, the charter contained the words *cum bondis, bondagiis, nativis et eorum sequelis*.[2] The legal position of the tillers of the soil, however, in such a country as eleventh, twelfth, and thirteenth century Scotland must necessarily represent merely an abstraction. In practice, by the end of the period, the rural workers had attained an entirely different position to those of England. There was no large semi-servile class such as the English villeins. They had imperceptibly passed into free-men, whether tenants, sub-tenants, or cottars, and even humbler individuals depending upon the cottars, but, apart from the rather shadowy rights of the "kindly tenants," they were able to acquire no claims to the land. There was in Scotland no equivalent to the English "copy-holders." The position in Scotland was also different to that in Wales, where tribal or at least family group land-holding survived, and in Ireland, where in some districts tribal land-holding to some extent survived, but where, for the greater part, the conquering Normans were able to introduce a manorial system.[3]

Part IV. Feudalism in Practice in Relation to the Country-Folk

Nevertheless Scotland was not a modern but a feudal country, and the relations of the lords of the soil and the lesser folk were part of the all-pervasive social system of the country.

[1] Cosmo Innes, *Scotch Legal Antiquities*, pp. 52 and 231-232.

[2] *Registrum de Passelet*, p. 91 (A.D. 1392).

[3] G. H. Orpen, *Ireland under the Normans*, vol. i, pp. 110-111.

The technical status of the land-workers probably did not feature so largely in the consciousness of contemporary folk as we are apt to imagine, when we approach the subject from the point of view of the twentieth century. The lord and his vassals were interdependent in many ways. The lesser folk were not merely his chattels and the appendages of his lands, but they were his retainers, the source from which he drew the military following which he, in his turn, was obliged to furnish to his own surperior. He and they were both links in the chain of mutual services that made up the feudal system. Although the theoretic relationship varied in the case of the free socman and the unfree villein, in certain essentials they were both the commended vassals of a lord.[1] They both gave suit in his court, they both claimed his protection. In the relationship between a lord and his people, the economic, social, political, and judicial aspects are but different sides of a connection that was far deeper, vaguer, and more general. In actual daily life, especially in those rather hand-to-mouth days, the fact that there was this general connection, and the sentiments that it involved, were of far greater importance than the actual degree of servitude or liberty. In Scotland the function of the feudal superior as military organizer, fiscal unit, and as part of the machinery for administering law and order was definitely recognized, although there was little organization such as the English manors. The relationship between the lord and vassal was an essential part of the whole structure of society. The general feudal maxim *nulle terre sans seigneur* had its Scots counterpart in the law of David I entitled *De homine invento sine domino*, wherein it was statute that if any man be found within the kingdom "that hes no propir lord," he must find one within fifteen days or be fined eight cows and his body be "at the King's behuffe." [2] In the case of royal demesne land the principle was the same, and the thanes, sheriffs, and other officials were the substitutes of the king.

The old charters constantly refer to the men belonging to a superior or to certain land. Lands might be granted to an abbey with their men and their services, or with the services which implied the men ; rights of pasturage might be given to

[1] Vinogradoff, *The Growth of the Manor*, p. 26.

[2] *A.P.S.* vol. i, *Assise Regis David*, p. xviii.

the abbot or other superior and his men, etc.[1] It is not possible to tell whether the relationship implied in such documents involved servile tenure, but it is the very fact that such a relationship existed that is of permanent importance, and, fortunately, a vivid description of it has survived. In 1320, on the Feast of St Peter, an inquest was held at Logie concerning the liberties of the men of Tweeddale who belonged to the Abbot of Dunfermline. The following claims were dealt with :

Firstly, the abbot's men sought to have a bailiff, appointed by the abbot, but of their own race, who should repledge them from more oppressive lay-courts to the abbot's court. To that the assize of inquest made answer that such a bailiff should be given them, not of fee, but of usage.

Secondly, they demanded that if any one of their race fell into poverty or helpless old age, he should have support from the monastery. To this the jury replied that the abbey was not bound to do this as of right, but from affection, because they were its men.

Thirdly, the men demanded that if any of their race slew a man or committed any crime for which he had to seek sanctuary, if he should come to Dunfermline, that he should be sustained as long as he stayed there at the expense of the monastery. To which it was answered that the abbey would do as much for a stranger, and therefore much more for a man of their own and of the race of the claimants.

Fourthly, they claimed that if any of their race committed homicide and incurred a fine therefor, the abbey should be bound to contribute twelve merks thereto. To which the jury answered that they had never heard such a thing in all the days of their lives—*nunquam tale quid omnibus diebus vitae suae audierunt*.[2]

In this reference there is nothing to show the status of the abbot's men, or to define their economic relationship with the abbey. The questions at issue were the benefits due to them by their superior. The point is of enormous importance, for it explains why the feudal system was able to survive and continue to be a living force in Scotland without anything analogous to

[1] To take one chartulary only, see *Liber Cartarum St Andreae*, pp. 40, 44, 286, 252, 277, 282.

[2] C. Innes's translation, *Scotland in the Middle Ages*, p. 143.

the organization of the English manor, with its carefully graded folk.

PART V. THE ECONOMIC RELATIONSHIP

Another relationship, however, was growing up between the superior and the cultivators of the soil—that of landlord and tenant: in itself a mere *cash nexus*, and yet capable of being fitted in with some of the special features of feudalism. The development of the firmour or rent-paying farmer did not suddenly create a new class, for already there were many grades of men between the humblest tillers of the soil and the knights and the free tenants holding of knight's fee. The socman originally belonged to the old Saxon system, yet he is found in the old Scots laws, holding of a feudal lord and yet retaining the distinctive customs of the division of inheritance and of wardship by the nearest of kin.[1] In all the chartularies small pieces of land held by individuals of a superior are constantly mentioned. Some of these landholders were probably socmen, some were possibly of a superior type of the servile grade, some perhaps were tenants on short leases or tenants at will. For instance, in a rental of the Abbey of Kelso, dated 1290, there were nineteen separate holdings which paid rent and in which no services were specified. Two of them consisted of two carucates, six of one carucate, there were also two half-carucates, one holding of 30 acres, one bovate and six smaller holdings, and also one holding giving rent and services.[2] Such folk, whatever their exact status, came definitely between the cultivators of joint farms or of granges and the knights, barons, etc.

This most important rental, moreover, shows that a further development was taking place. The husbandmen, apparently joint cultivators, had lately had their service dues and payments in kind commuted for money rents, and the cottagers gave rent and boon work, but not weekly work.

The word " tenant " applied to lesser folk definitely begins to emerge during the period. We find, for instance, in a law of Alexander II that the line of social cleavage is drawn between (*a*) the knight and free tenant of knight's fee on the

[1] Sir John Skene, *Translation* of the *Regiam Majestatem*, p. 58, cap. xxi, and p. 72, cap. xlvii.

[2] *Liber de Calchou*, vol. ii, p. 455.

one side and (*b*) the "malaris of carls borne and they that are of foul kin or any other that has no free tenement"—*sed firmarii de rusticis nati vel qui in vili prosapia fuerint seu rustici vel aliqui alii qui liberum tenementum non habent*—on the other. But in one of the fragmentary laws we learn that a "fermour" having a "malar" might only sub-let during his own lease, and there is a very similar act in the Laws of the Four Burghs. By another of the fragmentary laws the "malar" (=*firmarius*) was to be punished for putting guld—a kind of weed—into the land "as he that ledes ane host in the kingis lands or the barounis"; whereas the "natiff man" or "bonde" (=*nativus*) is to pay his lord a sheep for every plant and also must clean the land of the guld.[1] These acts, taken together, suggest that definite classes of farmers, sub-tenants, and bondmen existed simultaneously; but it is now our task to trace out a change and development, showing that the classes of servile husbandmen and bondmen were becoming merged into that of tenants, and that the latter were growing up as an integral part of the feudal system of social organization of Scotland.

It is rather significant to find the penalty imposed on natives who grew guld in the law last quoted, i.e. the fine of a sheep was inflicted on tenants who had marigold plants on their land at Cupar.[2] In Sir John Skene's (1609) version of the *Regiam Majestatem* and of the *Quoniam attachamenta*, which he calls the *Laws of the Barons*, he almost invariably uses the words "tennents or vassals" for rural workers and the word "maister" quite often in place of landlord. There is, for instance, the interesting account of the aids and subsidies that a feudatory may ask of "his men or tennents." Skene says he is entitled to contributions towards his own payment of "relief," and to payments at the time of the knighting of his eldest son or the marriage of his eldest daughter, but he says that it is doubtful whether he may compel them to help him in his personal "deadly feuds" or at the marriage of his younger daughters: "Some men thinks, that the overlord may not compel or distrenzie his men or tennents to this effect; bot as they please, to do of their awin free will." Skene, however, considers that

[1] *A.P.S.* vol. i, *Fragmenta Collecta*, pp. 369, 387.

[2] Rogers, *Social Life in Scotland*, p. 198.

he has this power, because he has the general right to distrain them "according to the reasonable custom of his court, without the King's precept: and poynde their cattell and moveable gudes, apprehended within their lands for making payment to him of sic helps."[1] Another act gives a suggestion of another aspect of the old social organization: "Gif any dwelles upon land perteining to ane frie man, and as ane husbandman haldes lands of him, and he happin to deceis, his maister sall haue the best caver, or beast of this cattell, provyding that the husbandman did haue of him the aught part of ane dawche of land or mair." Men with less were not liable to this payment.[2] Herezelde was an old servile due, and it was still a burning grievance to tenants in the sixteenth century. In the same way, service dues tended to be done, as time went on, by free tenants instead of by servile dependants. According to one of the fragmentary laws attributed to our period, a lord might rightfully resume the land of a tenant if he died without heirs, or from his heirs under certain conditions, or if he committed a murder and fled the country, or if he alienated his lands, or if he did not fulfil his *services*.[3] In many parts of Scotland services were still exacted from sub-tenants at the end of the eighteenth century, and, occasionally, they were still to be found in the middle of the nineteenth century.[4]

It is, however, unsafe to generalize about a state of society in so fluid a condition as was that of Scotland in the eleventh and twelfth centuries. The examples of the rural organization of the times are too few to furnish the material for a picture of national conditions. Nevertheless, they do show what actually happened at the time in a few localities. An early document is illustrative of conditions where serfs and two other classes of country folk existed. This, perhaps, was not unlike the state of English society of the Domesday period, before the manors and the villeins had been organized. It is dated about 1147–50, and is the text of an agreement between the Bishop of St Andrews and the Abbot of Dunfermline regarding the Parish

[1] Sir John Skene, *Regiam Majestatem*, cap. lxxiii, p. 87, a passage founded on Glanville and a law of Robert I.

[2] *Ibid. Quon. Attach.* cap. xxiii.

[3] *A.P.S.* vol. i, *Fragmenta Collecta*, p. 369.

[4] *Second Statistical Account*, Caithness, pp. 40 and 147

Church of Eccles and the chapel in Stirling Castle, made in the presence of the king and his barons : " The King's barons unanimously held it proved that on the day on which King Alexander caused the chapel to be dedicated, he gifted and granted to it the tithes of his demesne lands within the jurisdiction of Stirling, whether these demesne lands increased or decreased, that the parish church ought to have all the tithes which come from *herdmanni* and *bondi* and *gresmanni*, with the other rights which the church ought to have ; that the bodies of those who die, whether they be serfs—*mancipi*—of the demesne or of the parish, shall lie in the parish churchyard, with the things which dead bodies ought to have with them in the church, unless by chance a burgess die there suddenly ; that if the demesne lands increase, by cultivation or by breaking them up for the first time, the chapel shall have the tithe, if the lands of other men of the parish increase, the parish church shall have the tithes, and if the number of men in the demesne increase, the chapel shall have their tithes, and also those of all the men who cultivate the demesne ; that the parish church shall have the bodies of those who dwell in the demesne ; and if on the lands which were not demesne, houses shall increase, the parish shall have their tithe, and shall render to these men the rites of Christianity in seemly burial." [1]

To contrast with this early agreement, the chartulary of Kelso gives a most interesting picture of the general arrangement of a great estate in 1290.[2] The monks had several stretches of sheep and cattle walk, a number of separate properties let for a money rent (as already stated), certain lands attached to the parochial churches in their gift, and smaller parcels allotted to the shepherds, millers, etc., employed upon

[1] A. C. Lawrie, *Early Scottish Charters*, p. 148.

[2] *Liber de Calchou*, vol. ii, p. 455. For comparison it is interesting to note that, according to Cato, a Roman domain of 60, 75, or 150 acres was cultivated by 10, 12, or 16 slaves. See Fustel de Coulanges, *Origin of Property in Land*, p. 9. J. Mills, in his careful study of the Manor of Finglas (Ireland) in the fourteenth century, points out that the customary services were insufficient to till the demesne, and that hired labour must have been employed, probably that of the cottars who are always found near the demesne. "Tenants and Agriculture near Dublin in the Fourteenth Century," *Proc. Royal Soc. Antiq. of Ireland*, 5th series, vol. i, part I, pp. 57, 61.

the abbey estates. They also had fourteen granges, with groups of cottages attached to them, and also sometimes with individual holdings let in severalty, and sometimes with groups of "husband-lands" tilled by "husbandmen," one presumes in common. There were mills and brewhouses also connected with these granges. There was, therefore, a great variety in the means of the men who lived on the lands at Kelso.

By a fortunate chance, the roll includes a list of the services that the husbandmen had lately rendered but which had been commuted, and it states that they had also previously held their stock under "stuht" or "steelbow" tenure—that is to say, let to them by their superior along with the land. The rental is therefore an example of the trend towards the modern condition of tenancy.

The rent roll is also very suggestive as to the working of a mediaeval Scots estate. It is hard to see how the lesser cottagers can have lived unless they had employment from the abbey, for there were no considerable rural industries at the time. On the other hand, the commutation of the husbandmen's labour dues would increase the need for labour. I have tabulated the number of ploughs worked on the granges, of the cottagers, their rental, acreage and service dues, and those of the husbandmen (see pp. 88-89).

The term plough means the acreage ploughed up in a winter as well as the actual implement, and, as this varied in different parts of the country and at different periods, it cannot be computed for Kelso. The monks had 29½ ploughs, besides 50 acres. They also had 74 cottagers not actually upon the granges, exclusive of those who worked Faudon and were probably fully occupied, and 110 cottagers upon the demesne land, which would give an average of over 6 cottagers to each plough. Compared to Maitland's analysis of the Domesday estates, this is a fairly high proportion. It does not seem possible that a large stock of serf labour could also be employed. The status of the cottagers and husbandmen themselves is not given, and there is nothing to show whether they were bondmen, villeins of the English type, or free tenants, though from another entry in the chartulary it is known that the Barony of Bolden rendered military service and provided a captain and thirty bowmen. The rental is valuable because it stresses the fact that whatever their theoretic connection, the superior and the occupier of the land were essentially landlord and tenant, farmer and farm-worker. Another example, taken from the same chartulary, brings home the same fact. About 1160, the abbot granted half a carucate of land in Meddleham to "his man Hosbern," he having become his man and agreed to pay 8s. yearly. Did this mean that Hosbern had become the abbot's bondman according to the formulae given in the *Regiam Majestatem*? If so, he seems to have made a poor bargain, for 8s. was a considerable rent for such a holding. Whatever the terms of his agreement were, his value to the abbey was surely as a rent-payer—in other words, as a tenant.[1]

The foregoing examples do not show if the cottagers and husbandmen had fixity of tenure. An almost contemporary reference shows an estate let to tenants at will. According to a somewhat salacious tale in the *Chronicle of Lanercost*, a certain Sir Robert of Robertstone owned land in Annandale "which he let in farm to the inhabitants thereof." The tenants, "waxing lewd through their wealth," gave way to gross immorality and "would frequently replenish the archdeacon's purse, and, by repeating the offence, were almost continuously upon his roll." The landlord, on this account, could not get his rents, and told them that if the rents were too high they could be reduced—if the land were not worth cultivating, it could be restored to him; but on discovering the real state of the case, he declared: "I make this law among you, that any man who commits adultery shall relinquish my land forthwith." The tenants thereupon reformed themselves, and, devoting themselves to agriculture, were no longer upon the archdeacon's roll and were able to pay their rent. The archdeacon, furious at losing his dues, remonstrated with the landlord for his interference. Whereupon Sir Robert retorted: "I make a rule about my lands, not about offences."[2]

The next example comes from rather later than the actual period under review. It is almost the earliest written lease in Scotland, and is dated 1312. It is between the Abbot of Scone and two gentlemen of the name of De Hay del Leys and relates

[1] Maitland, *Domesday Book and Beyond*, p. 26.

[2] Translation by Sir Herbert Maxwell, *Scottish Hist. Review*, vol. vi, p. 29.

RENT ROLL OF KELSO

Granges in Demesne.	Ploughs worked on Granges.	Groups of Cottages.	Cottages on the Demesne.	Acreage of Cottages.	Rental of Cottages.	Yearly Work of Cottagers.	Husband-lands.	Rent.	Labour Dues.	Holdings held Separately.
Reveden .	5	..	19	Not stated	1/- (in case of 10)	6 days each; also help at sheep shearing	8	Not stated	..	½ plough-gate
Hauden .	1	..	..	..	..	..	..	..	..	..
Sprouston .	2	..	6	1½ in case of 5 of these	3/-	6 days each	..	..	..	1 oxgate
Colpinhopis .	2	..	..	..	..	..	..	..	..	..
Molle . .	50 acres	..	14	Not stated	2/-	6 days each	..	..	..	..
Ileshow . .	2	..	..	..	..	..	..	..	..	..
..	..	Faudon	(21 cottage	rs cultivate	the grange	of Faudon	and pay £	10 p.a.)		..
Wittemer .	2	..	7	1 (one cottage without land)	From 1/6 to 5/-	9 days each and sheep washing	10	6/-	Labour dues *commuted*. 5 days reaping, 1 of these with 2 men—certain "carriages"—to till 1½ acres of *Newton* every year—1 day's sheep washing—1 day's corn carrying	..
Witelaw. .	3	..	18	Not stated	1/6 to 2/-	6 days each	..	..	..	1 plough-land

..	..	Town of Bolden 36	..	Total acreage—12½ acres and 1 rood	Total rent, 55/8	9 days each	28	6/8	Labour dues *commuted* as above	..
Selkirk abbatis	1½	..	16	Total—10 acres	1/- and 2/-	9 days each	15 (each consists of an oxgate)	6/8	Labour dues *commuted* as above	30 acres 4 acres
..	..	Town of Medilham 11	..	Total—9 acres	1/6	9 days each	27	11/-	Labour dues *commuted* as above	2 husbandlands in 1 holding
Newton . .	7	..	..	..	..	..	..	..	..	..
..	..	Clarilaw 21	..	3 acres, less a rood pasture for 2 cows	None	2 bolls of meal & seed—Town of *Newton*	..	..	..	..
Malcarueston	2	..	12	1 toft and ½ an acre pasture for 2 cows	Some 1/6, some 4/-	9 days each	..	..	..	..
..	..	Gordon 6	..	1½ acres	None	9 days carrying peats	..	..	..	2 separate holdings
Spertilden .	2	..	16 or more cottages for their servants and their shepherds	..	..	..	..	..	..	..

to certain lands in Perthshire. It is for thirty years and in the eighteenth century would have been called an "improving lease." The rent was as follows:

First year	2 merks	
Second year	2 ,,	
Third year	3 ,,	
Fourth year	4 ,,	
Fifth year	5 ,,	
Sixth year	6 ,,	This rent was to continue for six years, until the twelfth year.
Thirteenth year . . .	8 ,,	This rent was to continue for eight years, until the twentieth year.
Twenty-first year . . .	10 ,,	This rent was to continue for ten years, until the end of the lease.

The tenants were to grind their corn at the abbey mill. They were to pay a multure of one twenty-fourth of the value of the corn, but "their men and their husbandmen and their cottars" were to pay one sixteenth. They were to do suit at the abbey court three times a year, at the three head pleas; and their "husbandmen" were to do suit at all the pleas of the abbot's court. But "if disputes trivial and not grave shall arise among the men of the said Edmund, William and the heirs of the said William, they shall decide and correct them among themselves; but if there shall be greater differences, and pertaining to the lordship, such ought to be reserved for the court of the Lord Abbot and there justly to be determined." The tenants were to render "the forensic service." The abbey retained joint rights of pasturage and turbary.

The tenants were to build competent buildings for themselves and their husbandmen, and were to leave them in proper condition at the end of the lease. The abbey itself held the lands of the Crown by no fixed tenure, and a clause was inserted to the effect that if the king should revoke the gift, the Hays, with their husbandmen, should quit without having to pay the rent of the year of their quitting.[1]

[1] Original in *Liber de Scone*, p. 104.
Translation by Duke of Argyle, *Scotland as it is and was*, p. 96.

In the lease the usual word employed for the lesser folk was *husbandus*. In the clause about the multures, the *cottari* of the *husbandi* are mentioned. The Hays were to deal with the minor quarrels of " their men "—*homines*. But in the clause regarding the abbey rights to common pasture, which perhaps safeguarded the provisions of an old charter, the terms are *husbandi* and *nativi*, and another scribe has thought it necessary to add a gloss, giving the meaning of *nativi* as " inborn men."

It is interesting that the land granted in this lease had been previously let to smaller tenants, for the Hays were to hold it with all the pertinents and marches " with which husbandmen were wont to hold the same land to farm " (=rent). In this lease we have a curious mingling of the old and the new. Many of its provisions might well apply to the leases granted to " tacksmen " of the seventeenth century, who farmed their land with the help of sub-tenants.

In this example the sub-tenants cannot have had permanent possession. They may have held their land from the Hays upon short leases, they may have been their tenants at will. But in other cases the country folk had a long connection with the soil. The witnesses at a trial in connection with the claims to some land by Paisley Abbey had all lived in the same parish all their lives, though whether because they had customary rights or had merely never been disturbed, there is nothing to say.[1] Sometimes such customary rights were undoubtedly recognized. The chartulary of Inchaffray records that " Colmin, the liegeman of the master and brethren shall not be removed from the lands—nor may he be unjustly burdened—but shall be treated kindly." [2] Colmin was therefore " a kindly tenant," a form of tenure that, in later times at least, had many varying meanings. What it exactly represented, or how prevalent it was, seems to be impossible to find out. Kindly tenants were most often met with upon the Church lands of the south-west, or at least they were most successful there in converting their tenures into out-and-out ownership. In the bishopric of Glasgow there was a local customary law, ascribed to St Mungo (St Kentigern), by which the widow of a Church tenant was entitled to the liferent of the lands owned by her husband at his death, which received

[1] *Registrum de Passelet*, Introduction.

[2] *Chartulary of Inchaffray*, p. 244 (*circ.* A.D. 1266).

effect in the civil courts.[1] All holders of Church land, even in early times, however, had not such rights. In the middle of the twelfth century there was a lawsuit between the Bishop of St Andrews and the Laird of Arbuthnot, over conflicting rights they both claimed in the Kirkton. In the course of the evidence it appeared that this had been occupied by the mysterious class of Church tenants known as "scologs," who owed dues both to the bishop and to the lay lord superior. These scologs the Laird of Arbuthnot had proceeded to remove, in order that he might till the land himself, apparently without any formality whatsoever. The cause of the suit was not the rights of the "scologs" but those of the bishop. An Aberdeenshire inquest of 1387 also shows the indeterminate rights of Church tenants, and also concerns "scologs." The good men and true of the country swore that it was the custom, when any scolog upon the Church lands of Ellon died, that his heir should be entered into his lands by the bailiff without giving seizin and certain other formalities. It was, however, proved that in one case, at least, seizin had been given, and the bishop claimed it. The point was not a relevant one to the actual dispute at issue, and no decision seems to have been come to. This case is only one example of the complete difference between England, with its carefully preserved customary law, and Scotland, where records and decisions had so little aftereffect.[2]

During the latter part of the period there must have been a general and gradual decline in serfdom, though no contemporary record notices the change. It has been pointed out that the disorganization caused by the Wars of Independence, and the very independent line taken by many of the country folk, who, of their own free will, chose to fight for the national leaders, helped to make the final break; but previously there must have been a long-drawn-out change in the economic conditions responsible for serfdom or liberty, for it is very

[1] J. Carmont, "The Kindly Tenants of Lochmaben," *Juridical Review*, vol. xxi, 1909, p. 321.

J. W. Buchan, *Peeblesshire*, vol. ii, p. 454.

"Ecclesiastical Antiquities of Scotland," *Quarterly Review*, vol. 72, pp. 369, 396.

[2] *Spalding Club Miscellany*, vol. v, pp. 56, 63, 58.

significant that not one single protest from those having vested interests in serfdom can be discovered. In the fourteenth century there are a few traces of the waning system. In the reign of Robert the Bruce an assize found that "Ada, the son of Adam, was not the king's native bondman; but might transport himself, his children and their goods, whithersoever he chose, without question from anyone," and David II manumitted three bondmen. In 1364 the Bishop of Moray proved the servility of a serf in the Sheriff Court—the last occasion upon which the old procedure was put into force.[1] When the Chamberlain paid his periodic visits of inspection to the royal burghs during the reign of Robert I, he was still directed to ask if there were any bondmen (=*nativi*) of the king hiding within the burgh; but by the end of the century this question had been dispensed with.[2] In charters the old terms lingered on, but their language is so largely stylistic that they are probably of little account.[3]

Cosmo Innes calls the freeing of the serfs in Scotland "that great, peaceful, silent revolution which has never found its way into the pages of our histories," and points out that when, in 1778, a negro slave who had been brought to Scotland claimed his freedom, "the fifteen judges of Scotland had forgotten that our laws had ever admitted of slavery."[4] There are concrete reasons why Scotland should have freed her peasantry long before England, without any struggles or formalities, so in-

[1] J. Robertson, *Deliciae Literariae*, pp. 261-264.
Registrum Episcopatus Moraviensis, p. 143.

[2] *Ancient Laws of the Burghs* (Scottish Burgh Record Society), p. 19.
For dates, see J. D. Marwick, *Edinburgh Gilds and Crafts*, p. 3.

[3] For instance, W. F. Skene, *Celtic Scotland*, vol. iii, p. 273, quotes a charter of 1502 from the Earl of Athole containing the words, "*bondmen, bondages, native men and their issue.*" Skene, however, points out that in the sixteenth century the term native men was used in the Highlands to denote men of the lowest class. *Ibid.* p. 320.

For examples of the stylistic use of terms in charters, see Cosmo Innes, *Scotch Legal Antiquities*, p. 53.

There is an interesting example of a change in the wording in charters relating to the barony of Murthil. In 1388 the Chapter of Aberdeen let it with hawkings, huntings, fishings, and with serfs, bondages, natives and their issue. In a lease dated 1420 the serfs, etc., were omitted. See D. Murray, *Early Burgh Organization.*

[4] Cosmo Innes, *Scotch Legal Antiquities*, p. 159.

stinctively, in fact, that no one seems to have noticed that she was doing so. The absence of the systematized organization of the manor was, no doubt, partly responsible, and so was the growing importance of the economic relationship of landlord and tenant between the superior of the land and those who tilled it. But more fundamental forces were also at work. In England the sturdy Anglo-Saxon ended the feudalizing efforts of the Normans by a compromise that produced a fixity of rights and of obligations; but the proud Scot, lacking the Englishman's gift for constructive compromise, secured his bare but almost complete liberty. It would take more than a merely economic history to try to answer why.

Part VI. The Happiness of the People

It is not easy to come to any decision as to whether the people were worse or better off than in later times. The population was probably smaller, so that they had more land at their disposal. Under the strong and fortunate kings of Canmore's line the country was better governed than in later periods, although there were two long minorities, during which there were risings, faction fights and general oppression. An obvious but very important point to keep in mind is that in these so primitive times an organisation such as the feudal system was of advantage to everyone: and that, because there were obligations and benefits upon both sides, and because the services the different classes rendered to each other were essential ones, therefore it worked with some degree of efficiency.

Even in this period, so often called the "golden age" of Scots history, the times were very lawless,[1] and a lord's protection was really valuable to his people in the unpoliced land of Scotland. The superior's protection was sometimes exercised in ways that seem a little strange to modern ideas of justice. For instance, in a case tried in 1233, the men occupying certain lands claimed by the Abbey of Paisley said that they were quit of all temporal services, but were "always defended by the Church and in the Church courts against all men." They were, of course, alluding to the exercise of the superior's

[1] *A.P.S.* i, p. 60, Act ordering people not to "truble othir mennis landis."

right to repledge men to his own court; but the closer the feudal tie, the less such jurisdictions can have made for impartiality.[1]

Theoretically the feudal magnate had wide powers, but for their execution he was dependent upon his vassals, for it was from them that his following was recruited for war-time service and peace-time feuds, and it was by them that his land, the great source of his wealth, was tilled. Money was scarce, farming was poor, produce had to be largely consumed upon the spot. The barons could not have supported large followings of mercenaries with which to enforce the working of their estates as if they were slave plantations.[2] The garrisons of the royal castles were very small; during the national scare caused by Haco's invasion, when the whole seaboard was put into a state of defence, the royal castle of Innuery was garrisoned by eight men, and the watchmen employed at Stirling for three weeks cost 35s.[3] It was only by the most careful organization of their great estates that the twenty, fifty, and, very exceptionally, the hundred monks who went to form the monastic establishments were supported. This sheerly economic limitation upon the authority of the barons, who could only enforce their powers upon their vassals by means of the latter's support, helps to explain why most of the working arrangements of estates during the Middle Ages, in spite of the high theoretical power of the lords, partook so largely of the nature of a bargain.

The relationship between the lord and his vassals, however, had other aspects besides the purely materialistic one, and there was a very real sense of moral obligation upon both sides. A sense of loyalty ran through the relationships of the feudal system. Thus, it is not uncommon to find lands given to the Church for the benefit of the soul of the donor's feudal superior, as well as for those of his own family and for his own; and in a thirteenth-century code of regulations regarding the rights of sanctuary, homicides and those who have broken their fealty to their feudal lords are classified among the worst type of

[1] Quoted by Cosmo Innes, *Scotland in the Middle Ages*, p. 214.

[2] See Miss Bateson's account of a similar development on an English manor, *Medieval England*, p. 10.

[3] *Exchequer Rolls*, i, p. liv.

malefactors.[1] And, on the other side, although examples of abominable oppression have come down to us,[2] yet the king and the nobles who were his companions in law-making very fully acknowledged their obligation to protect the humble folk. In the *Regiam Majestatem* it is declared that a villein is freed if he is tried for life and limb and his lord will not go pledge for him; [3] and, by a law of Alexander II, lords may do battle in ordeal by combat for their *rustici*, or appoint someone to do so, " because the body of a tenant and all his goods ought by right to be in his lord's protection." [4] The Scots *Regiam Majestatem* varies from the codes of Glanville in declaring that ordeal by combat may not be used to prove or disprove a man's liberty.[5] Finest of all is the spirit of a law of David I, that gives the king's special protection to " pur folk and waik." If such people are robbed and will swear to their loss upon the altar, the goods taken from them must be restored as if they were the king's own possessions that had been stolen, and he who took from them by " stark hand " must pay a forfeit to the king.[6]

PART VII. AGRICULTURE

It is rather tantalizing that so little can be deduced about the early cultivation of Scotland. Almost nothing was written about Scots methods of farming until the end of the eighteenth century, when a flood of literature appeared. By that time an extraordinarily uniform system of cultivation is described as existing, or having existed in the past, all over Scotland—in the Lothians, the South-West, the Eastern Lowlands, and the Highlands—although, the more one actually comes to investigate the agriculture of individual farms or small districts, the more variations one discovers.[7] Under this system the land

[1] Cf. C. Rogers, *Rental Book of the Abbey of Cupar* (Grampian Club), vol. i, pp. ix, xi.

See article by Bishop Dowden, *Scottish Hist. Review*, vol. vii, 1909–10, p. 230.

[2] See, for instance, J. Edwards' article on " The Templars in Scotland," *Scottish Hist. Review*, vol. v, p. 17.

[3] *Regiam Majestatem*, vol. ii, and vol. i, p. 245.

[4] *A.P.S.* i, Alex. ii, cap. viii.

[5] G. Neilson, *Trial by Combat*, p. 109.

[6] *A.P.S.* i, p. 12.

[7] *Report of the Commission on Types of Rural Settlement, Union Géographique*, 1928, p. 102.

was divided into "infield" and "outfield." The infield was the best land or that nearest the farm. It was held in common, in intermixed strips, or, in the Scots phrase, "run-rig." It received the whole manure of the farm, and was under constant crops of barley or bear or oats. Wheat was little grown, but in certain districts, evidently as an improvement, a crop of peas or beans was sometimes taken from infield land. The outfield was most of the time treated as pasture. But a proportion of it was ploughed up from time to time and was cropped continuously so long as it would bear anything; it was then allowed to go derelict, and another piece was taken into cultivation. The only method of manuring the outfield was by "tathing," i.e. folding the animals upon it. At anyrate, by the eighteenth century the Lothians outfield land was managed rather more carefully.

Closely associated with this method of agriculture was a group system of farm organization. The typical group homestead consisted of a ploughgate occupied by eight tenants, each owning an eighth part, i.e. an oxgate, and contributing an animal to the common plough. This arrangement, as we have seen, was worked into the land measures of mediaeval Scotland, and there are a good many examples of farms actually lent to eight tenants; there are, however, also a great many quite early examples where this exact subdivision has not been followed or has been lost.

It is rather important to remind any student of English field systems that the change in the layout of Scots agricultural holdings is probably far greater than is the case south of the Tweed. In the nineteenth century we have the introduction of tile drainage and subsoil ploughing, which has entirely altered the layout of many Eastern and Southern farms; and among the so ancient-looking crofter settlements of the North-West and of the Islands the extended use of potatoes and the greatly increased population have changed things far more than one is inclined to allow for. In many parts of Scotland the demand for cereals during the Napoleonic wars also altered the disposition of the land. During the eighteenth century there were even more sweeping changes. The "agricultural revolution" replaced group farms by single houses, and scattered patches of infield and outfield cultivation by rectangular fields, under regular shift cultivation, throughout the greater part of Scotland. Rather later, the "clearances" due to the sheep-farming movement even more drastically disturbed the more purely Highland districts. The people were moved from their farm groups to the newly formed crofter villages, with their rows of cottages and strips of individual holdings, which now seem so typical of the North-West. The sweeping changes introduced into Scots' village life must also be allowed for, but is dealt with more conveniently under the burghs.

But long before these changes, the rural communities of Scotland were by no means in a stable condition. During the fifteenth and sixteenth centuries the tacksman system was developing, and the introduction of feu, the new form of tenure, caused considerable displacement of the lesser folk. Population was also increasing, and not only was there subdivision of holdings, but there was a considerable change from pastoral to arable farming. There is evidence that this change was still actually taking place during the industrial developments of the sixteenth and seventeenth centuries, but it must have been going on to an even greater extent in earlier times, especially in inland and hilly districts. In the period we are now dealing with, some of the laws suggest that the people were being drawn from a pastoral life. There is, for instance, the law by Alexander II which has already been quoted, and which orders all rustics "living in stedis and tounis to begin to plough fifteen days before the Feast of the Purification," for their own profit and with all their study and might; and that those who have more than a plough team of cattle are to sell to those who have not, and those who have less shall dig with their hands and feet to maintain themselves"—perhaps very much as the crofters of some West Highland districts do at the present day with their primitive *càs chrom*, or foot-ploughs.[1] Another law forbade barons and freeholders to keep great herds of sheep to the wasting of men's lands, and ordered them to live upon their own lands, rents and farms.[2] The country folk of St Columba's day who lived by hunting and cattle-keeping, the considerable stress laid upon the agricultural labours of the monks of Iona,

[1] *A.P.S.* i, p. 67. The *càs chrom* is still in common use at Applecross and on Loch Broom.

[2] *Ibid.* William, cap. xxxvii.

and the miracles in connection with sowing, reaping, and folding cattle which are attributed to St Ninian and St Ternan, all suggest that agriculture was only making its way into many parts of Scotland in the eighth century, although the *notitiae* of the *Book of Deer* show that it was established among the Picts of Buchan at that time.

What we should look for in Scots agriculture is a gradually evolved system, in process of development during the great changes of the historic period, rather than a cut-and-dried "Celtic system," such as certain writers have postulated.[1] It is very significant to find that in all cases where the holdings upon a given piece of land can be compared at different dates, a very considerable alteration can be seen to have taken place, but, unfortunately, such instances are few and far between.[2]

Nevertheless, on the other hand, until the eighteenth century, there was no clear-cut break between the old and the new. *Cain* and *Conveth*, the Gaelic dues, were in many cases still levied down to the fifteenth century or later, and the estates were managed by the same type of official. The Gaelic Tosheachdor and Mair were equated with the mediaeval sergeant, and the word mair, especially, continued in general use in Scotland till the sixteenth century. In the Outer Hebrides—that land of ancient survivals—it lasted till the nineteenth century.[3]

Scots rural life has been little studied and the interesting variations in local tools have never been worked out. In many parts of Lewis it is customary to build the houses and steadings in long rows, joined end to end and even side to side (these are not to be confused with such eighteenth-century villages as Plockton and Loch Carron on the mainland).[4] But the most primitive settlements on some of the other islands and on the

[1] S. Gray, *English Field Systems*.

[2] For example, see W. F. Skene, *Celtic Scotland*, vol. iii, p. 259, for the changes that took place in the lands of Arbuthnot. See also p. 258 of present book for examples of Short Tenures.

[3] W. F. Skene, *Celtic Scotland*, vol. iii, p. 280. *Exchequer Rolls*, vol. iv, p. 593; v, pp. 59, 462, 472, 479. Ten mairs are mentioned in this reference.

[4] W. F. Skene, *Celtic Scotland*, vol. iii, p. 392. This trait is still common among the less modernized townships.

mainland are of the unorganized cluster type, exactly like the pitiful little stone heaps that tell of the evictions in Sutherland, and like those to be found in Perthshire and other Highland districts—and like a particularly graphic description of an old settlement in the *Statistical Account* for Angus. The variation that existed in the old ploughs and methods of yoking—there were at least four [1]—may be largely accounted for by differences in soil or the surface of the land, but other causes may have been in operation. It was customary in parts of the Highlands for a man to lead the plough teams, walking backwards in front of them and singing to them or calling to them. Several writers have noticed this custom in Eastern and Central Inverness-shire. Although the resemblance may be due merely to chance and not to some deep racial affinity, it is rather strange to find that this was also the Welsh custom.[2] It is curious to find that the same primitive type of flail was used in Ireland, the Orkneys, Lewis, and Norway, and that the word for flail in Gaelic should be *suist*, in Erse should be almost identical, and in Norwegian should be *thust*; whereas a different type of flail is found in Perthshire, Glenlivet, Cumberland, and Durham, which, in its turn, differs from the kind used in other parts of England, including the neighbouring county of Yorkshire.[3] It might be possible to build up a theory of the evolution of Scots agriculture from such sources that would connect it with racial or cultural distributions, but so far the attempt has not been made.

On the other hand, the custom of making the rigs run vertically down the slopes instead of across them, which is very definitely characteristic of nearly all the traces of old Scots agriculture in the Highlands and Lowlands, on the West Coast and on the East, is in marked contrast with the practice further south. It has been pointed out that the strip lynchets commonly found in Yorkshire, Westmorland, Cumberland, Durham, Northumberland and a few places in Lancashire and Derbyshire generally run parallel with the contours, and, in steeper

[1] The "twal ousen plough," the plough with four beasts harnessed abreast, the plough preceded by a ristle, the single-stilted plough.

[2] J. E. Lloyd, *History of Wales*, vol. i, p. 295.

[3] See article by Dr. Allison, *Archaeologia Aeliana*, Second Series, vol. ii, p. 94. The present writer has seen a flail of the Irish-Orkney-Norwegian type in use in Lewis.

places, often have masonry to support their outer edges. By means of excavations, mapping, the collection of field names, correlation with Domesday survey, etc., A. Raistrick and S. E. Chapman have come to the conclusion " that the strip lynchets of the North of England preserve to us the actual common fields of the Anglian settlers of the seventh and ninth centuries."[1] This being so, it is interesting to note that the few places in Scotland where these horizontal lynchets are to be found, such as Dunsappie, Dunsyre, and Romanno, are all in or near the Lothians. (These are not to be confused with the short " lazy-beds " of the North-West.) Most of these are in high-lying sites, where there was little inducement to continue agriculture were lower situations made available by drainage or clearing of forests; but it seems to be impossible to tell their age, and whether similar horizontal ridges existed elsewhere and were obliterated by the vertical ridges which were almost universal in Scotland, and which continued to be used until the agricultural revolution. It at least shows that Scots agricultural practice was not introduced *en bloc* from the Anglian settlers.

The various features of the Scots system of agriculture, group cultivation, outfield, and the sending of the flocks to the hills in the summer, are none of them, in themselves, unique. They are all primitive features, common to more than one of the peoples who helped to colonize Scotland. The group settlement with intermixed strips of cultivation is a case in point. The Irish *Bailé*, enshrined in the common Gaelic prefix *Bal*; the Anglian and Saxon *Hams* and *Tuns*, common in the South-East of Scotland; and the Danish *Bys*, occasionally found in the South-West, were all evolved because of the early peoples' sheer need for mutual protection and for mutual help in managing the clumsy tools and fenceless land of the period. The system of cultivating land in mixed strips is a rational method in cases where there is communal cultivation, where the agriculturists are so primitive in their technique that they cannot ameliorate the natural variety of the soil—cannot drain wet patches or

[1] A. Raistrick and S. E. Chapman, " Lynchet Groups of Upper Wharfedale," *Antiquity*, June 1924, p. 181. The writers were stressing the difference between the strip lynchets and the small rectangular enclosures of the Iron Age.

sweeten sour ones, etc.—and where they are so dependent upon crops of their own rearing that they dare not risk having all their corn upon an exceptionally wet or dry piece of land.[1]

Outfield, the practice of ploughing up the land, cropping it till it becomes exhausted and then allowing it to go back to the wild, is an even more primitive form of cultivation. It was an early German process—Tacitus describes it: "The German community takes up a tract of land in shifting possession, according to the number of its husbandmen. The land so occupied is then allotted among the members in proportion to their rank, the extent of open ground making the process a simple one. The arable allotments are shifted yearly, and there is unallotted land to spare."[2] Curiously enough, the same cultivation was practised by the eighteenth-century settlers of Northern America. Adam Smith quotes from the account of a Swedish traveller of 1749: "They make scarce any manure for their cornfields—but when one piece of ground has been exhausted by continued cropping they clear and cultivate another piece of fresh land; and when that is exhausted proceed to a third. Their cattle are allowed to wander through the woods and other uncultivated grounds, where they are half-starved." Adam Smith himself points out that it is "a system of husbandry not unlike that which still continues to take place in so many parts of Scotland."[3]

This system of movable cultivation, so like the outfield of Scots agriculture, seems to have been an Anglian custom. In 1632 the isle of Axholme was "cavelled out," i.e. divided by lot,[4] and, until 1847, the lands of North Middleton, in Northumberland, were cultivated in the following way: "The general rule of cultivating and managing the lands within the township

[1] In the only Scots township still under run-rig that is known to the writer, the need for having a share of the wet and the dry land, in order to make sure of getting something of a harvest, was given as the main reason for the continuance of the system. W. F. Skene notices the same thing, and says that, in his practical experience in the Outer Isles, run-rig tenants did better in very wet or very dry years than did many of those with separate crofts (*Celtic Scotland*, vol. iii, p. 385).

[2] F. Pollock, *Land Laws*, p. 181, for translation. See also Dr. Giles, *Cambridge Ancient History*, vol. ii, p. 37.

[3] Adam Smith, *Wealth of Nations* (edited by E. Cannan), p. 222.

[4] See *Murray's Dictionary*, under *Cavel.*

has been for the proprietors or the tenants to meet together and determine how much and what particular parts of the land shall be in tillage, how much and what parts in meadow, and how much and what parts in pasture; and they then divide and set out the tillage and meadow land amongst themselves in proportion to the number of farms or parts of farms to which they are respectively entitled within the township, and the pasture lands are stinted in the proportion of twenty stints to each farm." [1] The Welsh were also in the habit of breaking in, by common consent, a certain portion of the tribal land every year, and of then letting it go out of cultivation.[2] As the most primitive method of agriculture, it may have been the custom among the Gaels and, for aught we know, among the Picts. In the Outer Hebrides, the place least likely to exhibit purely Anglian survivals, a similar system existed in 1884. In the Iocar district of South Uist there were eighty-eight crofts, divided into four sections of twenty-two each. The constables of the four groups balloted for the land that was to be taken into cultivation, which was changed every three years. Each of the four portions was divided into rigs, or *imirean*, among the landholders, who occupied the same ones for the three years. At the end of that time fresh ground was broken in as before. In North Uist run-rig was still practised in the townships of Hosta and Caolas Paipal and the island of Heisgeir. In all these places the system had survived a break in continuity, for they had each been let to single tenants at one time. The system of cultivation is thus described: "About Hallowtide—in Gaelic 'Samhuin'—the tenants of the islands meet for *Nabac* (neighbourliness). Probably the only thing to be done at the neighbourly conference is to decide upon the piece of ground to be broken up for cultivation. This foregone conclusion decided, the men proceed at dawn of day to divide the ground. The land to be divided is called Scat, Clar, or Loeb." The constable having divided the land into portions, and shares having been set aside for the herdman and the maintenance of the poor, lots ("crann") were cast for the "imirean" or rigs. "This arrangement of land lasts for three years, at the end of

[1] Article by F. W. Dendy, *Archaeologia Aeliana,* New Series, vol. xvi, p. 138.

[2] F. Seebohm, *Customary Acres and their Historical Significance*, p. 5.

which time the ground is let out under grazings as before and new ground broken in." [1]

Such an arrangement was not the same as the typical Scots division of infield, outfield, and pasture. Was it a local peculiarity of Uist or the survival of the general custom of one of the component races that went to make the modern Highlander? The only Highland township where a system of intermixed strip cultivation is kept up that is known to the writer is situated on the west coast of Ross-shire, almost within sight of Lewis. The strips are permanently allotted to the different cultivators and are under constant crop. There is no outfield. It is therefore an example of the one-field system. From this isolated example it is impossible to say whether it was derived from a system of reallotment, such as we have described, gradually changing to permanent possession of the best land, or whether it was regarded as "infield" land, and that, owing to soil-conditions or other reasons, outfield land was dispensed with. From the look of the land in this district and also in many parts of Lewis, it would certainly appear that such was the case.

It must be remembered that the "infield" of the old Scots system was virtually a form of one-field cultivation, and that, where land can stand such treatment, or where there is enough manure, perpetual tillage is the most obvious method of cultivating it. Examples of one-field cultivation are to be met with all over Europe where the soil conditions permit, quite regardless of the race of the cultivators.[2]

No student of agricultural history seems to have recorded whether the Irish practised infield and outfield. Agricultural conditions, even in early days, seem to have been very different.[3] In West Meath, so late as the eighteenth century, lots were cast for the arable land. A contemporary writer says that the pasturage of the town-land was held in common. The arable appears to have been held under an open-field system of some kind, but it "was divided among the members of the community with

[1] *Crofter Commission*, 1884 (P. P. xxxii), pp. 461-466. See evidence by C. Carmichael.

W. F. Skene, *Celtic Scotland*, vol. iii, p. 378.

[2] Report of the Commission on the *Types of Rural Settlement, Union Geographique International*, 1928, p. 36. Article by S. Harris.

[3] P. W. Joyce, *Social History of Ancient Ireland*, p. 264.

the most extraordinary nicety. The whole field was divided into plots of an acre, half an acre, or quarter of an acre, measured with a rope. These plots were then grouped into as many shares as there were ploughs in the town-land. The utmost care was taken by joining together, in one share, plots, good and bad, from different quarters of the field, that the shares might be of exactly equal value. Then came the distribution: a number of stones or sods of turf, equal in number to the shares into which the land had been divided, were placed in a row on the ground. Then each man entitled to a share placed in a hat, in view of all the others, some distinguishing article—a bit of stick, a pebble, a scrap of iron, a rag, a flower, etc. Then a child or a stranger was called upon to draw these lots. He, taking the several articles from the hat, placed them, one by one, on the stones representing the divisions of the land."[1] In parts of Inverness-shire, so late as the eighteenth century, it was the custom to cast lots for the infield land.[2]

The custom of allotting land by lot has been cited as *the* distinguishing feature of the "Celtic field system." It certainly accorded well with the clannish spirit of the Gael; and, till quite recent times, the shares of a peat face, the portions of a road to be repaired by the individual members of a township, and similar advantages or duties, were, in the Outer Isles, assigned by the casting of lots. But we have seen that it was also an Anglian custom. The Scots word for a lot was a *Cavel* or *Kavel*, which was also an Anglian term, and both Jamieson and Murray derive it from the Norse. It was in constant use in the Lowlands in mediaeval and later times. By the laws of the burghs the burgesses and gild-brethren were ordered to cast cavels for their shares in communal purchases. About 1478 a case of "caveling and deling" came before the Lords of the Council. In 1551–52 it was proposed by the Privy Council of Scotland that England and Scotland should divide the debatable land by the casting of "cavillis." In 1578 a portion of the burgh lands of Glasgow was divided into separate holdings, and cavils

[1] J. Mill, "Tenants and Agriculture near Dublin in the Fourteenth Century," *Proc. Royal Soc. Antiquaries of Ireland*, 5th Series, vol. i, Part I, p. 57.

[2] T. Robertson, *Report on the Agriculture of the County of Inverness*, p. 335.

were cast for them. Until 1536–37 the burgh lands of Edinburgh were annually allocated by lot.[1]

Certain lesser features of the Scots agricultural system are primitive rather than peculiar to any one race. The custom of sending live stock up to the hills in the summer, for instance, was due to geographical conditions, combined with scarcity of winter feeding, and is still done in Switzerland and Norway. In Scotland, long before the eighteenth century, the practice of going to the shealings in summer had become confined to the Highlands. Yet traditions of the custom still survived in a lowland district of Aberdeenshire, and in early times it was the practice in many other parts of Scotland, such as Peeblesshire. In Haddingtonshire the parishes all consist of portions of low ground and hill pasture, suggesting an arrangement due to the agricultural methods of the people, and the word shealing is found in many place-names — Luckysheal, Popelsheal, Outsheal, etc.[2]

The custom of letting stock with the land, which died out upon the lands of Kelso Abbey about 1290, was called " Stuht " in that chartulary, a word which Cosmo Innes derives from the Saxon. In later times the custom was very usual in the Highlands. It survives to the present day in the South-West, the tenant being known as a "bower." It is the same as the French *métayer* system.[3]

The derivation of words is a dangerous guide, but the Scots term for intermixed strips—*run-rig*—has been claimed by some authorities as a derivation from the Gaelic word *Roinn-ruith*. This, however, was an uncommon word, and *Mor-earann* was almost invariably used. Moreover, it does not seem to have had any connection with the component parts of the system.

[1] *Acta Dominorum Concilii*, vol. i, p. 61.
Register Privy Council, vol. i, p. 122.
D. Murray, *Early Burgh Organization*, pp. 125-126.

[2] *Second Statistical Account*, vol. xii, p. 840.
J. W. Buchan, *Peeblesshire*, vol. ii, p. 242.
Gazetteer, under heading of Haddington.

[3] For Stuht see Introduction to *Liber de Calchou*, vol. i, p. xxxi.
C. Innes, *Scotch Legal Antiquities*, p. 265.
By the courtesy of A. M. MacEwan, Esq., the writer has been allowed to see a manuscript account-book of the eighteenth century, showing extensive use of the system in the Highlands.

The Gaelic for rig is *Iomair* (though nowadays, at least, *Fiann-agan*, which properly means " lazy-bed," is generally used, and arable land is *Fearann-grainsich*). In the Lowlands, on the contrary, rig is a common word; run-rig seems a natural derivative with its counterpart of run-dale, a dale being a larger piece of land (the word dale itself, however, is derived from the Gaelic *dal*, a field). Might it not therefore be that *Roinn-ruith* was derived from the Anglian rather than the other way about? In hazarding such an opinion, the writer, however, is venturing to disagree with very considerable authorities.[1] There are, moreover, no Gaelic words that exactly correspond with " in-field " and " out-field." The nearest terms appear to be *talamh treabhta*=ploughed land, and *talamh ban*=fallow land.

What theory, then, can be put forward for the origin of the typical Scots system of agriculture? It would seem at least certain that several different influences were brought to bear upon it, and that many of its features are those that any race might evolve in its early struggles to cultivate the soil. For historical reasons, great weight must be given to the Anglian influences. In language and general culture, as we have seen, the people of the Lothians exercised a preponderating influence over the rest of Scotland. Moreover, the typical Scots features of infield and outfield are to be traced in the Lothians as much as in other parts of Scotland. They cannot have been taken over from the Gaels, like some of the place-names, by the Angles when they over-ran the country, for at that time the Gaels themselves seem to have practised little agriculture (although the grants in the *Book of Deer* show that the Picts were more advanced). The arrangement of the rigs, however, shows that Scots agriculture of later times was not purely Anglian.

The valuable report of the *Commission de l'habitat rurale*, published by the *Union Géographique*, clearly shows that the presence of a one-field, two-field or three-field system largely depends upon the productivity of the soil, altogether apart from the race of the cultivators. In most parts of Scotland and along

[1] According to Sir Herbert Maxwell and A. W. Johnston, the word *Run-rig* is of Gaelic origin. See *Scottish Hist. Review*, vol. xiii, p. 207. For Gaelic agricultural terms, see W. F. Skene, *Celtic Scotland*, vol. iii, p. 278.

the " Celtic fringe " of England, where outfield is also found, there is a great deal of hilly country, with fertile lower ground and cultivation pushed up on to the more accessible slopes above, a terrain which would be particularly suitable for this dual method of cultivation.

In Scotland itself we also get very unsettled social conditions, with an absence of the settled and elaborated organization of the English manor, which made possible the orderly " nucleated " village disposed round its age-old village green, and with its well regulated two or three field system.[1] The present writer ventures upon the suggestion that the Scots system of agriculture, which combines the two most primitive types of agriculture —temporary intakes from the waste, and constant tillage—was largely due to this absence of the organization of the manor, allied to a type of country that was unsuitable for the extended use of perpetual tillage (i.e. the one-field system) and to certain facts in the earlier history of the country, viz. the fusion of races—Angles, Gaels, Picts, and Normans—in different stages of development, and a primitive state of rural society and, presumably, of agriculture, crystallized by the sudden introduction of a comparatively advanced type of social organization with the introduction of the feudalizing influences of the Normans.[2]

[1] In those parts of Ireland where the Normans, as conquerors, were able to impose the organization of the manor, it is rather striking also to find instances of a three-field system : cf. J. Mills, " Tenants and Agriculture near Dublin in the Fourteenth Century," *Proc. Royal Soc. Antiquaries of Ireland*, 5th Series, vol. i, Part I, p. 60.

[2] F. Seebohm, *Customary Acres and their Historical Importance*, p. 62, in his equation of the ploughgate and carrucate suggests such a sudden transition.

CHAPTER III

PART I. THE GENERAL ECONOMIC POSITION

THESE potent centuries saw the laying of the foundations of so much of the structure of our normal social life that it is not easy to realize that, at the same time, they were very primitive ages. Contemporary documents abound with little incidents that are wholly charming and picturesque by reason of their almost pastoral simplicity. David I, Scotland's greatest organizer, was accessible to all classes: *ut sacros, vel miles, vel monachus, vel dives, vel pauper, vel cives, vel peregrinus, vel negociator, vel rusticus.*[1] This king, who did so much to build up the Scots system of law administration, would himself, when starting for a hunt, dismount to do justice to poor suppliants—or, at least, so his panegyrist tells us. Such was the fashion among virtuous kings of the Middle Ages—the same kind of stories are told about St Lewis of France—but it is significant that it was highly commended at the time, and would be unthinkable in later days. The old charters—the symbols of the radical changes in land tenure that David and his kinsmen introduced—often inform us that the kings had personally perambulated the marches of the lands that they were donating, passing from weathered stone to meandering burn or ancient bush, as earlier folk had done before them, ever since, in the misty past, men had carved permanent abiding places for themselves out of the wild.[2] In the same way, although in fixing national weights and measures David made a considerable advance, these

[1] St Aildred, *Vitae Antiquae Sanctorum, Eulogium Davidis*, pp. 443, 444.

[2] Sir Archibald Lawrie, *Early Scottish Charters*, pp. 73, 112, 113, 117, etc. Cf. "*Quas ego cum probis hominibus meis perambulari feci.*"

See J. W. Buchan, *Peebles*, vol. ii, p. 241, for a picturesque description of a march line.

weights and measures were in themselves extraordinarily primitive. They were generally calculated by the simplest means. The inch, for instance, was to consist either of three grains of bear set end to end or of the width of a man's thumb, but three men were to be used for the calculation, "that is to say, a mekill man and a man of measurabill stater and of a lytill man." [1]

Such incidents are not merely attractive: they help to create something of a mental picture of times that were extraordinarily unlike our own. The feudal idea of the apportionment of land and rank in return for services was actually in force—dignities, for instance, were territorial and not personal.[2] They lapsed when services could not be rendered, as during the nonage of a minor; and could be sold with the land from which they were derived. The whole theory of personal rights to property in land was very different from that of the present day. There were no police, a very small civil service, no standing army, no regular taxes. The administration and defence of the country depended upon the working of the feudal system, which was based on a particular form of land tenure. Scotland was very incompletely united; so late as the reign of William the Lyon, the Lothians had their own code of laws. She had no real capital. The meetings of fifty General Councils previous to the fourteenth century have been recorded. Only ten of them were held at Edinburgh, whilst fourteen were held either at Perth or Scone and six at Stirling.

Nowhere is the contrast between the early Middle Ages and the present day more obvious than in the affairs of the towns. Everyone must realize the enormous outward contrast between the cliff-like street frontages and teeming traffic of a modern city and the small huddle of thatched houses of mediaeval times, set haphazardwise beside the natural haven or the castle or the great religious house that was its chief *raison d'être*. The difference, however, is more fundamental than a mere question of size or of the organization of civic amenities. Land in those days was the main source of wealth. In the Lord Chamberlain's account for 1264 the total amount of the royal revenue that passed through his hands was £5413. Of this

[1] *A.P.S.* vol. i, p. 309.

[2] W. L. Mathieson, *Scottish Hist. Review*, vol. vi, p. 51.
J. H. Stevenson, *Scottish Hist. Review*, vol. ii, p. 41.

sum, £2893 came from Crown lands, including thanage dues; the rest was made up of all other sources of royal income, fines, escheats, casualties, etc., as well as burghal dues.[1] In England, in 1169–1170, the total Crown revenue was £23,535, to which the counties contributed £10,529 and the boroughs £1990.[2] So late as the sixteenth century the Scots burghs only paid one-fifth of the periodic "aids" levied upon the wealth of the country.[3]

It would seem anomalous to attempt to write an economic history of early Scotland and not to devote a special section to industry and commerce: nevertheless, if one may indulge in a paradox, the most striking thing about industry and commerce during this period is their relative unimportance. This was a feature of the age. As T. W. Ashley says, England "till nearly the end of the fourteenth century was a purely agricultural country. Such manufactures as it possessed were entirely for consumption within the land; and for goods of finer qualities it was dependent on importation from abroad. The only articles of export were the raw products of the country, and of these by far the most important was the agricultural product, wool. To understand, therefore, the life of rural England during this period is to understand nine-tenths of its economic activity."[4] The same is certainly true of Scotland.[5] The country folk themselves mainly lived by local agriculture, and, in addition, furnished the main exports of the country, wool, hides, herrings and salmon. The folk of the burghs merely exported these and imported commodities and manufactured goods. Their own little industries—cloth and leather goods were made—probably merely supplied local needs. In any case, neither industry nor commerce sufficed to maintain even the embryonic Scots burghs, for they were largely, perhaps mainly, agricultural

[1] *Exchequer Rolls*, vol. i, p. xlvii.

[2] Sir James H. Ramsay, *Revenue of the Kings of England*, vol. i, p. 106.

[3] Sir Archibald Lawrie, in *Annals of the Reigns of Malcolm and William, Kings of Scotland*, p. 375, convincingly disposes of Bower's statement in the *Scotichronicon* that the burghs, in 1211, contributed three-fifths of a royal inquisition.

[4] Sir William Ashley, *Introduction to English Economic History*, vol. i, p. 30.

W. Cunningham, *Growth of Industry and Commerce*, vol. i, p. 2.

[5] C. Innes, *Scotland in the Middle Ages*, pp. 229-230.

communities. In their charters all the Scots burghs received considerable grants of land, which the burgesses cultivated. Thus a twelfth-century charter to Ayr states that for every full toft a burgess " shall have six acres of land which they shall have clear of underwood, within the aforesaid pennyworths of land, with a view to making their profit from them." [1] The burgesses' bestial and holdings are copiously legislated for in the old Laws of the Four Burghs and in the individual affairs of every single burgh. Even the Edinburgh burgesses were much taken up with their agricultural affairs down to the sixteenth century. In smaller burghs agriculture was a mainstay till much later; D. Murray has shown how the very pattern of the old burghal rigs can be traced right through the ground plan of Glasgow.[2]

Although, as we shall see, a certain amount of foreign trade existed, it is important to bear in mind how very small, both actually and relatively, was the trading community. A charter by Alexander I, dated 1124, gives a good idea of the very small scale of the commerce of the British Isles. Addressing all the merchants of England, *omnibus mercatoribus Angliae*, he announces that he has granted the can and custom of one ship to the church of the Holy Trinity at Scone; and grants his peace to those who desire to bring that ship with its cargo up to Scone, and freedom from all customs save those of the prior.[3]

Many of the articles of trade of this early time were the results of special conditions rather different from our own. Salt was an absolute necessity in the mediaeval world, when people lived on salted meat for five months in the year.[4] Spice was also required to make this fare palatable. Iron was not mined in Great Britain and was expensive and valuable. Fish was much eaten all over Europe during the fasts of the Church. " The use of fur-lined clothes was necessitated by the mediaeval custom of living exposed to the weather." Even villeins wore it, and a fur coverlet was included in the outfit of a

[1] A. Ballard, *British Borough Charters*, vol. i, p. 52.

[2] *Leges Quatuor Burgorum*, cap. cii, lxxxiv, etc.
D. Murray, *Burgh Organization in Scotland*, p. 103.

[3] Sir Archibald Lawrie, *Early Scottish Charters*, p. 43.

[4] Sir William Ashley, *Introduction to English Economic History*, vol. i, p. 35.

novice at Ely.[1] Leather was also more widely used. It was probably often employed where we should use metal, and it was much used for clothing. In bad years, at least, the larger communities were not self-supporting in the way of agricultural products, and from time to time many of the great abbeys of Scotland obtained temporary permission from the King of England to buy corn in Ireland. Moreover, private merchants seem to have shipped a good deal of corn and beans from England.[2]

An important Scots import, even at this so early period, was wine, which apparently was sometimes directly shipped from France to Scotland and sometimes from English ports.[3] The Scots, moreover, seem to have imported large quantities of manufactured goods. The *Assisa de Tolloneis* (attributed to David I) gives a long list of imports, though one cannot tell how far this list of dutiable articles really represented the actual trade of the country. It included iron, in bundles of gads; madder, woad, and brazil for dyeing; teazels for raising the nap of cloth; mercury, spices, pepper, comyn, alum, ginger, almonds, figs, and raisins, all packed in bales; thread for making nets, and linen thread, deals, and knives—these three last articles apparently in large quantities; wax and soap in kists and "schrynes;" cooking pots—"pannys of battry"—cauldrons, locks; onions and garlic; honey, wine, oil and salt, apparently by the shipload.[4] The land was, on the whole, flourishing; and the kings, the lords, and the great churchmen, in their constant comings and goings to the South, no doubt had to keep up appearances. It may be that Wyntoun was not exaggerating when he described the princely seisin by which Alexander I gave the canons of St Andrews possession of the wide lands of the "bares rayke." His "cumly sted of Araby,"

Sadelyd and brydelyd costlykly,
Wyth his armrys off Turky,
That pryncys than oysid generaly,
And chesyd mast for thare delyte,

[1] M. Bateson, *Mediaeval England*, pp. 258, 333.

[2] J. Bain, *Calendar of Documents relating to Scotland*, vol. i (1108–1272), p. xlvi, quotes eleven examples. See also Nos. 907, 937, 1044, 876-877, etc.

[3] *Ibid.* Nos. 858, 800-803, 935, 1044.

[4] *Assisa de Tolloneis* and *Custuma Portuum* are printed in *A.P.S.* vol. i.

was led up to the High Altar, and there he presented it as the symbol of his greater gift.

The main Scots exports consisted of wool, hides and skins, salmon, herring and other fish, especially wool, hides and skins, and salmon, which are many times alluded to as the cargoes of Scots ships.[1] Of these, wool was undoubtedly the most valuable export. It was sometimes sent directly abroad, but much of it was imported into England; for instance in 1242, when the King of England seized all warlike stores at Yarmouth, Dunwich, and other places, it was reported that Scots wool was worth 3 merks the sack and English wool 4 merks. At Dunwich, 41 sacks of Scots wool were seized, and also 10 lasts and 15 daikers of Scots hides, including deer, roe, and goat skins. At Yarmouth, besides hides and skins, 25 sacks of Scots wool were seized, but this was apparently not all the Scots wool at Yarmouth.[2]

A large proportion of the wool seems to have come from the great flocks of the abbeys of the Southern uplands. Kelso Abbey alone had nearly 7000 sheep, and in succeeding centuries "Forest" wool still had a great reputation.[3]

But it was also exported from the North. A case which occupied a great deal of attention about 1304–5 will give some idea of the nature of the trade. A merchant of St Omer, on behalf of himself and three fellow-citizens, went to Moray and bought 32 sacks of wool, valued at 60s. per sack; 3 sacks of lambskins, worth 2 merks per sack; 36 daikers of hides, worth 11s. per daiker; lard in a little pipe, and 3 "packells" of deerskins. There followed private and national calamity. The merchant of St Omer was drowned at sea. In the course of the Wars of Independence, the goods, which had been stored at Pluscardine Priory, were seized by the agents of Edward I as part of the possessions of that Scots patriot the Bishop of Moray. Eventually they were taken by sea from Elgin to Aberdeen, and from Aberdeen to Berwick, at a cost of £12 5s. 4d., including the

[1] J. Bain, *Calendar of Documents relating to Scotland*, vol. i (1108–1272), Nos. 1042, 1051, 907.

Ibid. vol. ii, Nos. 9-10-20 (1273), 74 (1276), p. 440 (1304–5), 1639.

[2] *Ibid.* vol. i, Nos. 1594, 1599.

[3] *Liber de Calchou*, vol. i, p. xxxiii.

Ledger of Andrew Haliburton, p. lxvi.

expenses of a valet in charge of the goods for 60 days at a cost of 4d. per diem. At Berwick the surviving St Omer merchants made formal claim to them, and an inquest of twelve burgesses of Berwick, in the presence of the Chancellor of England, sat upon the matter, but the result of their deliberations has not been recorded.[1] Salmon fisheries were most valuable possessions. They figure in many charters. Even in comparatively remote districts the salmon were caught and preserved. The Priory of Beauly, in Inverness-shire, and that of Ardchattan, on Loch Etive in Argyllshire, both had an annual income of about £200 in the thirteenth century, and in both cases this was principally derived from salmon fisheries and teinds of salmon fishings. Preserved salmon were a very important article of diet. When Edward I came to Scotland, early in the fourteenth century, large amounts were used for his entertainment.[2] Fish of all kinds was much eaten in the early Middle Ages. The Laws of the Four Burghs have most careful directions regarding its price, condition, and place of sale. But Scotland had no monopoly of its preparation. Sir John de Drokensford, who in 1304 expected to have to entertain the king all Lent at St Andrews, wrote a pressing appeal to a friend to send him salt haddocks and cod from Newcastle, eels (salted) from the Borders, and to buy any "porpoys" and "laumprees de Nantes" that he can.[3] Nevertheless, much fish besides salmon seems to have been exported. Herring were fished for in the Firths of Forth and Clyde, and at this so early period they generally seem to have been dried, not barrelled. In 1299–1300 it is amusing to come across an allusion to red herring (*Aleci Rubei*) among the king's stores at Berwick, though there is nothing to say where they were prepared.[4] "Aberdeen fish," whatever that might mean, is also men-

[1] J. Bain, *Calendar of Documents relating to Scotland*, vol. ii, No. 1639, and pp. 440, 443-444.

[2] Sir Archibald Lawrie, *Early Scottish Charters*, pp. 86, 27, 157, 408, 83, 120, 419, 27, 117, 2, 134, 365, etc.

C. E. Chisholm Batten, *Beauly Priory* (Grampian Club), pp. 149, 165.

J. Bain, *Calendar of Documents relating to Scotland*, vol. ii, Nos. 1557, 1591.

[3] J. Bain, *Calendar of Documents relating to Scotland*, vol. ii, No. 1458.

[4] A. M. Samuel, *The Herring*, pp. 61, 62, 71.

J. Bain, *Calendar of Documents relating to Scotland*, vol. ii, No. 1180.

tioned.[1] Fishings and fish were definitely important as a source of revenue, saleable commodities and items of diet, and allusion to them is very frequent in contemporary documents.

Native cloth-making was unimportant from the commercial point of view; not for hundreds of years and only after a long struggle was Scotland to achieve any success as a maker of woollen fabrics. The manufacture is, however, interesting as an indication of the degree of specialization that had been reached. Two types of cloth were made in Scotland—the rough white or grey cloth which was the usual dress of the country folk till the eighteenth century, and which the poorer burgesses wore,[2] and the better-finished cloth, dyed, fulled, and sheared, which was the object of a special monopoly granted to the burgesses.[3] Combers, shearers, fullers and dyers, as well as weavers, were employed in making this relatively well-finished article. In leather-working there was also some degree of specialization. Tanners, shoemakers, glovemakers, and lorrimers are mentioned, but this trade also was evidently merely a local one.

There was, moreover, another important home-product, although it was never an article of export—coal. The grant of coal heughs in their charters and the carrying of coals as a service due are mentioned, during our period, in several of the abbey chartularies.[4] Such coal-workings can only have been very primitive, and peat and, in favoured places, wood were the usual fuels. Nevertheless, coal was regularly used in certain districts. The purchase of coal, always in small amounts—sometimes sixpence or fourpence worth—constantly appears in the expenses of the English army of occupation during the Wars of Independence, at Glasgow, Linlithgow, Dunipace (in Stirlingshire), and Edinburgh. In some cases the coal may have been used as fuel for the garrisons and workmen employed by the English, but in many entries the coal is stated to be for the use of the smith.[5]

Such was the state of industry and commerce. As we shall

[1] J. Bain, *Calendar of Documents relating to Scotland*, vol. ii, No. 1884.

[2] *Leges Quatuor Burgorum*, cap. lvi.

[3] *Ibid.* cap. xx.

[4] Cf. C. Rogers, *Rental Book of the Cistercian Abbey of Cupar Angus*, p. viii (Charter of Malcolm IV).

[5] J. Bain, *Calendar of Documents relating to Scotland*, vol. ii, No. 1271. *Ibid.* vol. iii, pp. 349, 351, 353, 355, 356.

see, many of the exclusive privileges of the merchants in the developing burghs were concerned with foreign trade. The burghal code had regulations regarding shipping and foreign merchants, and, from the same source, we know that Scots merchants also went " errandes beyhonde the sea." [1] (Perhaps this latter fact should be stressed, for, according to Boece, one of the Alexanders forbade Scots merchants from trading overseas because of the heavy losses incurred. If one of these able kings ever made such a law, it can only have been very temporarily in force.)

The main centres for foreign trade were upon the East Coast. Berwick seems to have been by far the most important town. Its customs in 1286 were said to amount to £2190. This, however, is probably an exaggeration, for in 1304–5 the English only received £119 6s. 11¼d. from the customs and issues of the courts of Berwick: the town, however, had suffered very severely in the meantime. Its main exports were wool and wool-fells, the produce of the great monasteries of the South-East—such as Kelso—and also hides. Its greater merchants must have been men of considerable substance. It is said that the wife of one of them, named Cnut the Opulent, was captured as she was returning from pilgrimage in one of her husband's ships, by Erlend, jarl of the Orkneys. Cnut took 100 marks of silver from his coffers, hired fourteen ships and gave chase. But the old chronicler does not say whether he succeeded in rescuing her.[2]

Other towns along the East Coast also enjoyed some foreign trade. David I, as we have seen, gave the canons of Holyrood a hundred shillings of the cans of ships trading to Perth, although he was careful to make provision for subsidizing the amount if the total dues did not come up to this figure. The names of some of the sixteen Scots burghs with sufficient foreign trade to require a " cocket " are interesting. They include such lesser burghs as St Andrews, Crail, Elgin, Inverness, Cromarty, and Dingwall.[3]

Probably the closest Scots trading relations down to the end of the thirteenth century were with England. As we have

[1] *Leges Quatuor Burgorum*, cap. xlv.

[2] J. Bain, *Calendar of Documents relating to Scotland*, vol. ii, p. 440. J. Scott, *History of Berwick*, pp. 13, 14.

[3] J. Bain, *Calendar of Documents relating to Scotland*, vol. ii, p. 441.

seen, the two countries were in intimate touch with each other, and the documents of the time show that there were a good many Scots merchants at Yarmouth, Lynn, and Dunwich. In 1242 the Mayor of Dunwich was an individual named Lucas le Scot. There was also some trade with other English ports, and, to judge from the sales of live stock and the frequent complaints of wool-smuggling, a considerable landward trade. In 1288–9, live stock belonging to Scotsmen in Yorkshire were seized to make satisfaction for a debt owed by the late King of Scotland; they included 11 horses, 40 head of cattle, 86 lambs and also sheep and swine, and were valued at £15 13s.[1]

There seems to have been a certain amount of Irish trade. Scots ships or merchants at Dublin and Drogheda are mentioned in English documents.[2] Of French trade we only learn incidentally, when ships passing between Dieppe and other French ports and Scotland called into English ports and got into trouble, or when they were wrecked or captured outside. Probably already the Scoto-Flemish trade was very considerable. In 1291 there was a street called "Scotland" in Bruges, and in Flanders the rich monasteries of the South-East disposed of much of their wool. A trade between Scotland and Lubeck seems also to have sprung up before the Wars of Independence.[3]

It is evident that the mariners of the time were not very ambitious sailors, and generally preferred to sail along the coast, so far as they could. French wine would be brought to Dieppe, thence shipped across to one of the South-Eastern towns of England, and so up the coast to Scotland. If the sea was difficult to navigate, the roads inland were almost as dangerous and far more toilsome, and so a great coastal trade seems to have flourished, stimulating the growth of towns whenever a convenient roadstead or haven gave anchorage or shelter to the little ships that plied to and fro along the coasts of Scotland.

In some respects foreign and coastal trade was carefully

[1] J. Bain, *Calendar of Documents relating to Scotland*, vol. i, Nos. 858, 876-877, 883-884, 880-883, 907, 932, 934, 1042, 1044, 1045, 1051, 1102-1103, 1588, 1086, 1594, 1599.

Ibid. vol. ii, Nos. 79, 151, p. 131; see also Nos. 718, 726, 736.

[2] J. Bain, *Calendar of Documents relating to Scotland*, vol. i, p. xlvii.

[3] T. A. Fischer, *Scots in Germany*, p. 1.

J. Bain, *Calendar of Documents relating to Scotland*, vol. i, Nos. 880, 883, 907.

organized. As we shall see, the royal burghs and their merchants probably received their special privileges largely to facilitate the collection of revenue, and the royal receipts from customs were systematically collected and accounted for. By the end of the period the system of stamping receipts for the customs with the "cocket" (a kind of stamp or seal) of each royal burgh had been introduced.[1]

Scotland does not seem to have had any important commercial treaties or trade agreements at this time,[2] apart from safe conducts to merchants trading abroad. Matters of dispute, due to the seizure of ships or goods, non-payment of debts, etc., were generally dealt with by the burgh authorities, but were often referred to the king. In both cases methods of redress were somewhat crude. If a burgess offended a stranger-town and his own authorities could not or would not redress the wrongs complained of, all those of his fellow-citizens or fellow-nationals whose person or goods were available were held responsible for his misdeeds and were seized. Thus, upon one occasion, we find the King of Scots and upon another the Justiciar of the Lothians being obliged to guarantee the payment of debts that Scotsmen owed the citizens of Bordeaux (at that time belonging to England), in order to secure the release of Scots shipping and merchandise that had been seized at Lynn as a security.[3] Such methods may seem haphazard and arbitrary, but in many of the cases embodied in the official correspondence between England and Scotland it can be seen that very careful and impartial enquiry was made into alleged wrongs, and that the King of England not only ordered restitution to be made in case of wrongful seizure, but insisted that his orders should be carried out.[4]

[1] J. Bain, *Calendar of Documents relating to Scotland*, vol. ii, p. 441.

[2] There were clauses for mutual trade protection in a treaty between Scotland and Wales in 1258. J. Bain, *Calendar of Documents relating to Scotland*, vol. i, p. 421.

[3] J. Bain, *Calendar of Documents relating to Scotland*, vol. i, Nos. 1694, 1768.

For other similar examples, see *ibid.* Nos. 1261, 2273, 1237, 1364.

Ibid. vol. ii, Nos. 252, 255, 264, 295, 297, 299, 353, 360, 359, 685, 686, 687-688 (these documents all relate to the same case).

[4] *Ibid.* vol. i, Nos. 1088, 2337, 883-884, 1051.

Ibid. vol. ii, Nos. 9-10-20, 74.

Although the thirteenth century has been called Scotland's Golden Age, it is not possible to estimate the degree of actual wealth that had been attained. Few figures are available, and, owing to the changed values of money, even these are not particularly helpful. The Panegyric of St Aildred and the statement that Berwick was a second Alexandria may be discounted as merely characteristic of mediaeval fervour and lack of restraint. A Scotland that was solely dependent upon the produce of her very patchy soil, and that had much the same difficult climate as at the present day, with far less efficient methods of agriculture and of distribution of supplies, can hardly have been very wealthy. As a matter of fact, her kings and nobles were often heavily in debt, and the gibes at the appearance of the Scots clergy who came to one of the continental church councils have survived with the usual vitality of ill-natured things.[1]

Nevertheless, her wealth was not inconsiderable. Alexander III gave the customs of Berwick as a pledge for the repayment of a debt of £2197 that he owed to a Gascony merchant.[2] Her prosperity was, moreover, increasing; the revenue derived from the papal taxation of her Church lands during the thirteenth century increased by about three-eighths, although this is partly accounted for by new donations to the Church and by the under-assessment of the first valuation, which made a second one necessary within fifty years.[3] Some indication of the relative wealth of Scotland and England is given by the fact that the value of their coinage was equal down to the thirteenth century, a ratio never again reached throughout the independent existence of Scotland. At the time of the Union, in 1707, when the Scots coinage was recalled, it only equalled one-twelfth of the value of similar English denominations.

The development of the country was, indeed, carried little, if any, further during the next four hundred years, for the valuation of the Church lands, made for the Pope, in 1275, by Boiamund Vicci (the well-known Bagimont's Roll), remained the

[1] C. Patrick, *Statutes of the Scottish Church*, p. xxix.

[2] *Exchequer Rolls*, vol. i, p. lxxxiii.

[3] This statement is based on the figures quoted by T. Thomson in the case of *Cranstoun v. Gibson, Court of Session, Second Division*, 1816.

basis upon which they were assessed right down till the seventeenth century.

It was in contrast with the dark days that followed that the times of Alexander II shone so goldenly, and that the wistful lines were written :

> Quhen Alysandyr oure Kyng wes dede,
> That Scotland led in luve and lé,*
> Away wes sons† off ale and brede,
> Off wyne and wax,‡ off gamyn and glé,
> Oure gold was changyd in to lede.
> Cryst, borne in to Virgynytie,
> Succoure Scotland and remede,
> That stad in hir pirplexyté.[1]

* Love and law. † Abundance. ‡ Wassail cake.

PART II. THE EARLY ORGANIZATION OF THE BURGHS

The development of the Scots burghs in the eleventh, twelfth, and thirteenth centuries is of great historical interest. Not only does their organization, like that of the towns of other countries in Western Europe, begin to assume prominence about this time, but it definitely manifests those distinctive national features that persisted for centuries and that deeply affected the whole social life of the country. Nevertheless, the interest is historical only, and the effects of the social structure of the old Scots burghs have almost entirely died away. The connection of the present and the past is not nearly such a living link as it is in the case of the country.

There had been towns in Scotland long before the eleventh century, especially in the district centring about the head of the Firth of Tay,[2] and by the time of David I they had evidently reached a considerable degree of development. The charter granted by that king to the canons of Holyrood, which gave them the right to found a burgh of their own, shows that Edinburgh had a market, and, in the clause especially entitling the burgesses of the church burgh to buy and sell there, it implies

[1] These hackneyed lines, quoted in almost every History of Scotland, appear in Wyntoun, but are attributed to an earlier date.

[2] W. F. Skene, *Celtic Scotland*, vol. i, pp. 70 and 369.
J. Mackinnon, *Constitutional History of Scotland*, p. 66.

that the men of Edinburgh were already inclined to assert their exclusive privileges.[1]

About this period there was a movement towards the development of towns throughout Western Europe.[2] No doubt it was largely due to the increase of trade and of intercourse between different lands, the national organization which was proceeding in almost all countries, and to a rising standard of luxury and refinement. This international impulse towards town development had far-reaching effects upon the organization of the Scots burghs. As one authority says, it was the influx of foreigners who "inoculated the infant communities with the corporate spirit, which so soon made them a power in the land."[3] Of these foreigners who came to Scotland, the Flemings were the most important. They formed a large element of the community in England,[4] but in Scotland they seem to have been even more numerous and influential. The sparse documents of the times furnish a considerable proportion of Flemish names.[5] They enjoyed royal favour, and Berowald, the progenitor of the Inneses, received grants of land. One hears of them as mercenaries fighting in William the Lyon's army, as a justiciar appointed for the Lothians, as burgesses in Perth, Berwick, Aberdeen and, especially, St Andrews, etc. Very significantly, when the Bishop of St Andrews founded his burgh, in 1144, the king gave him Mainardus the Fleming, his own burgess in Berwick, to be the first provost, evidently to organize the new community.[6] The common place-name of Flemington also marks the presence of many of these incomers.

In the charters of David I twelve towns are mentioned as *burgo meo*: Aberdeen, Berwick, Crail, Dunfermline, Edin-

[1] Sir Archibald Lawrie, *Early Scottish Charters*, p. 119.

[2] C. Innes, *Scotland in the Middle Ages*, pp. 150-155.

[3] *Scottish Hist. Review*, vol. xxi, p. 190.

[4] W. Cunningham, *Growth of Industry and Commerce*, pp. 186-190.

[5] Sir Archibald Lawrie, *Annals of the Reigns of Malcolm and William, Kings of Scotland*, pp. 137, 140.
Sir Archibald Lawrie, *Early Scottish Charters*, pp. 186, 133, 395.
Exchequer Rolls, vol. i, p. lvii.
Collections from Aberdeen and Banff (Spalding Club), pp. 547, 548.
Chartulary of St. Andrews, pp. 132, 139.
See also Index to Ragman's Roll (Bannatyne Club).
J. Davidson and A. Gray, *Scottish Staple at Veere*, pp. 4-5.

[6] Sir Archibald Lawrie, *Early Scottish Charters*, pp. 132, 395.

burgh, Elgin, Haddington, Inverkeithing, Linlithgow, Perth, Roxburgh, and Stirling. Peebles and Rutherglen are also alluded to as burghs in this reign.[1] William the Lyon and Alexander the Second and the Third added extensively to the list. About the same time certain church burghs were founded. St Andrews, Glasgow, Brechin and Dunblane were bishops' cities. Jedburgh, Kelso, Dunfermline, the Canongate, and Paisley owed superiority to monasteries. Two, at least, of the great lords also owned burghs: Renfrew belonged to the Steward and Lochmaben to the Lords of Annandale.[2]

The organization of the burghs did not appear full-fledged, but had to be built up slowly. The two codes of laws concerning the burghs, the *Leges Quatuor Burgorum* and the *Statutes of the Merchant Gild of Berwick*, though portions of them go back to the times of David I, bear evidence of having been gradually added to and evolved as the burghs grew in dignity and self-government.

David I did not grant individual burghal charters; the custom only became general under his grandson, William the Lyon. During the earlier part of our period the burgesses were valuable tenants to the Crown, but the privileges that they enjoyed were rather of favour than by right.[3] When the burgesses of Peebles had a lawsuit in the thirteenth century about the cutting of their peats on Walthamshope, they were merely spoken of as the king's men.[4] It was no idle form of speech when David described the burgesses of Edinburgh as *mei proprii burgenses*[5] in his charter to the canons of Holyrood. In that charter he gave the canons the right of founding a burgh, the burgesses of which should have equal rights of buying and selling within the burgh of Edinburgh with the burgesses of that city, thus ignoring what was in later times *the* most jealously-guarded of the burghal monopolies.[6]

[1] *A.P.S.* vol. i, p. 76.

[2] C. Innes, *Ancient Laws and Customs of the Burghs of Scotland*, p. xliii.

Exchequer Rolls, vol. i, p. lxxxi.

[3] Sir Archibald Lawrie, *Early Scottish Charters*, p. 314.

[4] J. W. Buchan, *Peeblesshire*, vol. ii, p. 219.

[5] Sir Archibald Lawrie, *Early Scottish Charters*, p. 119 (Charter to Canons of Holyrood).

[6] A. Ballard, *British Borough Charters*, vol. i, p. xliv.

The king was, in fact, the direct landlord of the burgesses of the royal burghs, and the individual rents were collected for him by his personal officials. He could give away houses and tofts within the burghs at will. For instance, in 1125, he granted the monks of Dunfermline dwellings in four of *burgi mei*, viz., Dunfermline, Stirling, Perth, and Edinburgh; and most other religious houses were granted dwellings in the principal burghs.[1] The Steward had a toft and twenty acres of land in each of the royal burghs.[2] In the same way Ada, widow of the son of David I, announces to *Praeposito meo et Burgensiis meis et omnibus probis hominibus meis de Hadigtunes Schyra* that she had given the church of Dunfermline a toft in *burgo meo de Hadingtona* in perpetuity.[3] Occasionally, when making such grants, the king gave exemption from watching and warding, or from payment of rent, which was the usual condition of burgage holdings. Thus, a toft in Berwick was given to the Prior of St Andrews, to be held exempt from custom, exaction, and toll.[4]

As the foregoing examples show, the tolls and can of the towns belonged directly to the king. He could grant exemption if he chose—as when he gave the monks of May the right to buy and sell throughout the kingdom without custom, exaction, or toll;[5] or he could give them away, as he often did. As already noted, David I gave the canons of Holyrood a hundred shillings of the " cans " of ships coming to Perth, and ordered that, if this sum were not realized, it should be made up out of the revenue drawn from Perth, Edinburgh, and Stirling.[6]

At this early stage of development the position of the individual burgess was a humble one. His status depended upon his possession of a burgage tenement—i.e. upon whether he was a Crown tenant or not, not upon any freedom bestowed upon him by the burghal community. The *Laws of the Four Burghs* bring this out very clearly.[7] No one might be made a burgess who could not do service to the king for at least a rood of land; even a churl living outside the burgh, if he had property

[1] Sir Archibald Lawrie, *Early Scottish Charters*, pp. 53, 57, 200, etc.

[2] C. Innes, *Scotland in the Middle Ages*, pp. 203-204.

[3] Sir Archibald Lawrie, *Early Scottish Charters*, p. 208.

[4] *Ibid.* pp. 314, 428.

[5] *Ibid.* p. 162 (*circ.* 1147).

[6] *Ibid.* pp. 86, 296.

[7] Sir William Ashley, *Introduction to English Economic History*, p. 80.

within it, had the rights of a burgess there.[1] One finds Maynard the Flambard, the king's own burgess, *proprius burgensius regis*, being given to the Bishop of St Andrews in alms—*in eleemosyna*—in order that he should be first provost of the bishop's new burgh. And Baldwin the Lorrimer, the king's "client," when he is given a toft in Perth in 1150, is granted the following privileges: He is only to be sued in the king's court and is to hold his land free of all services except *vigilia infra burgum et claustra burgi . . . reddendo . . .* I *turet et* II *colores*. He may also sell his house and toft when he wishes to leave the town.[2] But in the finally evolved code of the four burghs nothing is more carefully provided for than the personal liberty of the burgesses and their rights to devise their property according to their own burghal laws.

It was only slowly that the idea of the burgh as an entity, apart from the group of individual burgesses who composed it, grew up. A. Ballard has shown how vague were the terms of the grants of land in the early charters of Inverness and Ayr: "These ambiguities show that the draftsmen had scarcely begun to perceive that there was a difference between gifts to individuals and gifts to the respective bodies of burgesses, but their attempts to use the word burgh to signify the body of burgesses show that they were beginning to perceive this difference."[3]

While the burghs were in this early stage the officials in charge of them were merely the servants of the king, working under the chamberlain. They were generally known as the *praepositi*, nearly always in the plural, a word that in England, at least, is sometimes the equivalent of *reeve*, an officer of the manor, who acted as intermediary between the baron and his villeins, but who was himself a villein by birth.[4] But one also finds them described as *bedelli*, *ballivi*, or *aldermen*.[5] There are a good many royal charters addressed to the *praepositi* of a given burgh, generally announcing to them, or to them and the sheriff, that the king has given a toft within the burgh to such

[1] *Leges Quatuor Burgorum*, cap. xlix, xi.
A.P.S. vol. i, p. 357.

[2] Sir Archibald Lawrie, *Early Scottish Charters*, p. 200.

[3] A. Ballard, *British Borough Charters*, vol. i, p. c.

[4] W. Cunningham, *Growth of Industry and Commerce*, vol. i, p. 574.

[5] D. Murray, *Early Burgh Organization* (many references quoted).

and such a one, or ordering them to collect and bestow the sums he had granted to local churches and religious bodies out of the burgh ferms and customs. In a mandate to the king's *praepositus* at Dunfermline, he is ordered to make the tenants of the Church give what the royal tenants give and not to suffer them to omit paying their dues.[1] In the very early charters to Rutherglen we find the *praepositus* made responsible for collecting the royal tolls, and in the *Exchequer Rolls* it is the *ballivi* or *praepositi* who remit the money from the burghs to the royal exchequer [2]—rents, fines pertaining to the chamberlain's court, and the petty customs. In several laws he is spoken of as responsible for the king's prisoners within the burghs.[3] It was only gradually that—with the change in the status of the burghs—the town officials became representatives of the burghs and not of the king, and the modern provost and bailies emerged from the vaguer designation of *praepositi* and *ballivi*.[4] During the later part of our period the burghs began to acquire leases from the king in lieu of having their rents, petty customs, and the issues of their courts directly collected from them.[5] The advance from these temporary leases was rapid: by the end of the fourteenth century many of the burghs had obtained permanent feus. In Berwick, the mayor, bailiffs, and clerk were paid a salary until the reign of Alexander II, when the burgh was granted the revenues of the town in return for an annual rent to the Crown and these payments ceased. By the time of Edward I the citizens elected their mayor annually and he chose the four bailiffs.[6]

This instance shows that the emergence of the idea of the burgh as a corporate entity and of the view that the *praepositi*

[1] Sir Archibald Lawrie, *Early Scottish Charters*, pp. 57, 86, 71, 110, 200, 208, 334, etc.

[2] *Exchequer Rolls*, vol. i, pp. lxxxvi, 313, 410.

A. Ballard, *British Borough Charters*, vol. i, p. 179.

[3] *Exchequer Rolls*, vol. i, p. lvii. It was evidently by favour that the king in the charters to Perth and Aberdeen orders *his* ballivi to aid the citizens and to maintain their customs.

[4] Cf. J. D. Marwick, "Municipal Institutions of Scotland," *Scottish Hist. Review*, vol. i, p. 127.

D. Murray, *Early Burgh Organization*, p. 30.

[5] G. Burnett, *Introduction* to *Exchequer Rolls*, vol. i, p. lxxxvi.

[6] J. Scott, *History of Berwick*, pp. 245-246.

were representatives of the burgesses and not of the king were contemporary. According to one of the later statutes of the *Laws of the Four Burghs*, the *praepositi* were to be chosen yearly, " through the consaile of the gud men of the toune," and were to be men " lele and of gud fame." They were to swear fealty to the king and to the town, and that they would keep the customs of the town, " alsua thai sal suer nother for radnes na for lufe na for haterent na for cosynage na for tynsale of thair silver thai sal nocht spare to do rycht til all men." Lesser officials, the " criours " or " serjeands "—*precones*—were also to be chosen " communly be the consent of all the burges." Other statutes enacted that the " aldermen "—*praepositi*—were to choose the " lyners," the men entrusted with the demarcation of the boundaries of the burgesses' holdings, " at the sycht and be the consale of the communiti of the burgh ; " and that the " mare " or " alderman "—*superior illius burgi*—was to make twelve of the " lelest " and wisest burgesses swear to maintain the laws and customs of the burgh.[1] But how these elections were to be conducted, or the exact duties of the twelve leal men, are nowhere stated.

According to two of the later laws of the *Statutes of the Merchant Gild of Berwick*, probably dating from the end of the thirteenth century, " the community of Berwick shall be governed by twenty-four good men, of the better, more discreet, and more trustworthy of that burgh, thereto chosen, together with the mayor and four bailies. And whensoever the said twenty-four men are summoned to treat concerning the common business, he who comes not at the summons, before night shall give two shillings to the Gild." By the other statute it was ordained that " the mayor and baillies shall be chosen at the sight and by the consideration of the whole community. And if any controversy be in the election of the mayor or baillies, then their election shall be made by the oaths of twenty-four good men of the said burgh, elected to choose one person to rule the said community." [2] Such were the beginnings of the hierarchy of the Scots burghs, Provost, Bailies, Town Council, and Douzane. It is very significant that, as in these laws, none

[1] *Leges Quatuor Burgorum*, cap. lxx, lxxi, cv, cxii.

[2] *Statutes of the Merchant Gild of Berwick*, trans. by C. Innes, *Ancient Laws of the Scottish Burghs*, vol. i, pp. 80-81.

of the old burgh charters prescribe the constitution of government.[1] The extreme vagueness of the early provisions regarding the election of the burgh authorities and the special powers of the merchants are of historical importance. These facts explain why the struggles of succeeding centuries were necessary; and show that certain developments in later burghal administration were not so reactionary as they appear, and that they came about in the efforts to make an institution work that was indefinite and primitive rather than simple and democratic.

The Scots burghs were by no means unusually backward in their early relations with the Crown. In England, also, the burghers rose from being the king's individual tenants—those of Leicester only commuted their harvest labour dues to the king in 1190. The records of Carlisle show how long and bitter was the struggle in that town between the burghers and the sheriff, before the former were able to secure a lease of their rents, petty customs, and the issues of the courts. A mayor of Carlisle does not appear until 1292.[2]

Part III. The Burghs in relationship to the National Life

Before describing something of the life of the individual burghs as they became evolved into separate communities, it will be convenient to deal with their more national aspect. In their earliest days they were under direct royal control and the kings of Scotland fitted them so definitely into the general pattern of the national life that they retained certain characteristic features and fulfilled certain definite functions right down to the eighteenth century or later. As individual entities the burghs developed very much upon the lines of similar communities in other parts of Europe, but in these, their wider aspects—in relation to each other and to the nation as a whole—they showed features that were unique and peculiar to Scotland, and which deeply affected the whole social life of the country.

[1] C. Innes, *Ancient Laws of the Scottish Burghs*, p. xl.

[2] Sir William Ashley, *Growth of Industry and Commerce*, p. 213.

W. Nansen and R. S. Fergusson, *Some Municipal Records of the City of Carlisle*, pp. 4-5. (Published by the Cumberland and Westmorland Antiquarian and Archaeological Society.)

The kings of Scotland were very much interested in their burghs, and lived in them constantly. David I, for instance, can be traced by his charters at Aberdeen, Berwick—he was there at least five times—Dunfermline, where he was nine times; at Edinburgh, nine times; Peebles and Perth, four times (he had a house there); Roxburgh, six times; and Stirling, six times.[1] The burghs were very useful to the kings in many ways: in the first place, as stable centres in touch with Southern culture —in this they were rather like the monasteries—in those parts of the kingdom that were gradually being brought under the royal control. According to a later charter, Alexander II gave privileges to Dumbarton so that it should be a civilizing and protecting centre against "a lawless and wild kind of man dwelling in the neighbouring mountainous parts." [2]

The following special privileges were granted to the Northern burghs: William gave a charter to Perth and built a castle there. He also granted to Aberdeen, Moray, and all the districts north of the Mounth the right to have their "ansum" or hanse, when or where they pleased, as in the time of King David I. In addition, by another charter, the burgesses of Moray had the special privilege that their goods were only liable to seizure for their own debts (the seizure of the goods of a fellow-burgess in satisfaction for the debts of any merchant from the same town was a common mediaeval burghal custom). William gave two charters to Inverness. The goods of the burgesses were to be free of all tolls and customs. They were to have trading monopolies over a wide district; the lands called Burch were granted them for sustaining the town, and an agreement was made whereby, after the king had surrounded the town with a ditch, the burgesses should erect and maintain a palisade. In the second charter, the king granted Gaufridus Blundus and the other burgesses that they need fight no duels among themselves—that no one should challenge them to ordeal by combat—and that they should only have to produce half the number of compurgators and pay only half the forfeits

[1] Sir Archibald Lawrie, *Early Scottish Charters*, pp. 180, 50, 79, 85, 115, 187, 52, 53, 56, 66, 82, 97, 121, 123, 167, 55, 77, 110, 112, 114, 120, 123, 79, 46, 137, 43, 52, 72, 102, 65, 69, 86, 73, 83, 138, 188, 57, 42, 534, 97, 110, 151, 198.

[2] J. Irving, *History of Dumbartonshire*, vol. ii, p. 15 (Charter by James VI recapitulating one of Alexander II).

due from the burgesses of other towns. William and Alexander II also gave charters to Elgin.[1]

The burghs were in themselves useful sources of income to the king, for the burgesses paid rent for their tofts, and tolls and dues upon exports and imports, but they seem to have been deliberately used as collecting points in a wider national system. When David I planned the organization of the country under sheriffs, he seems to have intended to make the towns that had gathered themselves about the skirts of the royal castles the centre of the economic life of the surrounding districts, just as their military, fiscal, and judicial organization was to be concentrated in the hands of the royal officer dwelling in the *Caput Comitatus*. This at least would explain the monopoly of the right to hold fairs, to carry on certain industries, to trade in certain goods that was bestowed upon the earlier royal burghs.[2] The system was never evolved in its entirety, for more and more royal burghs were created, and the connection with the organization of the sheriffdoms was lost sight of. Nevertheless, the practice of using certain favoured persons and places as convenient points for the collection of revenue from the main resources of the country (which, as we have seen, were so largely rural) seems to have been carried into effect. At least, this would seem the most likely—indeed, almost the only possible—reason for the thorough and systematic policy of the kings in concentrating the export trade of the country into the hands of the merchants of the royal burghs, and in confining the local industries and the buying and selling of wide districts to the royal burgh situated within them.

The connection between burghal privileges and burghal payments is quite definitely stated. The charters to Perth and to Aberdeen, the basic charters upon which so many other Scots burgh charters are modelled, state that all who dwelt in the burghs and wished to be in community with the burgesses at market should also be in community in paying the royal aids.[3] This is a general feature in burgh organization, but the

[1] *A.P.S.* vol. i, pp. 77, 87, 79.
G. Gross, *The Gild Merchant*, p. 197.
J. Shaw, *History of Moray*, vol. iii, p. 60.

[2] W. C. Dickinson, *Sheriff Court Book of Fife* (Scottish History Society), p. 384.

[3] A. Ballard, *British Borough Charters*, vol. i, p. 109.

Scots kings went further and gave each of the royal burghs a complete monopoly of trade within a clearly defined district. As A. Ballard says: "It would not be difficult to draw a map of Scotland showing that the country was divided into a number of districts within each of which some specified Royal Burgh had the monopoly of trade." The monopolies were most sweeping and clearly stated. The matter so deeply affects the course of Scots economic history that it is perhaps worth while to quote the Aberdeen charter *in extenso*: "I firmly forbid any foreign merchant within the sheriffdom of Aberdeen from buying or selling anything except in my burgh of Aberdeen; but the foreign merchants shall come with their merchandise to my burgh of Aberdeen and shall there sell them and pay his penny. If any foreign merchant, in defiance of this my prohibition, is found in the sheriffdom of Aberdeen buying or selling anything, he shall be taken and detained till I declare my will concerning him. I also firmly forbid any foreign merchant from cutting in cloth for sale in my market of Aberdeen, except between Ascension Day and the Feast of St Peter's Chains, within which terms I will that they may cut their cloth for sale in the market of Aberdeen and there buy and sell cloth and other merchandise in common with my burgesses, as if they were my dominical burgesses, saving my rights." The monopoly, however, was carried much further, and affected local industries and crafts: "I forbid also that any keep any tavern in any town within the sheriffdom of Aberdeen except when a lord is knight of the town and residing in it, and then he shall have only one tavern. I also firmly forbid that anyone residing outside my burgh of Aberdeen in the sheriffdom of Aberdeen shall make any dyed or mixed cloth within the county of Aberdeen nor shall cause it to be made, except my burgesses of Aberdeen who are in the Gild Merchant and share with the burgesses in the payment of my aids, except those who have had their charter liberty before this date. Wherefore I firmly forbid that any in the sheriffdom of Aberdeen shall presume to make dyed or shorn cloth, on pain of my full forfeiture. If any dyed or shorn cloth should be made in spite of this prohibition, I order my sheriff of Aberdeen to take the cloth and deal with it according to the custom which was in the time of David my grandfather. I also forbid any foreigner without my burgh of Aberdeen from buying or selling hides or wool, except within my burgh of Aberdeen." The charter to Perth is almost identical; that to Inverness has the same clause forbidding the setting up of taverns and the making of cloth outside the burgh; Rutherglen has a clause forbidding the sale of anything that has not already been offered for sale in its own burghal market.[1] Glasgow and the Canongate are examples of church burghs securing some of these exclusive trading privileges.[2]

Sweeping monopolies were thus given during our period to Perth, Inverness, Aberdeen, Stirling, and Lanark, over their respective sheriffdoms. Ayr had a district; Inverkeithing had exclusive rights to levy tolls and to exercise burghal privileges from the water of Leven to the water of Devon. The district of Dumbarton was carefully defined and covered fourteen davochs.[3] Edinburgh had a district from Edgebucklin Brae to the water of Almond. The district controlled by Rutherglen included the little episcopal burgh of Glasgow and marched with the district apportioned to Ayr.[3]

So consistently was the principle that trade was to be concentrated in the burghs observed, that even the interests of those privileged classes, the nobles and the churchmen, were forced to give way to it. Prelates, earls, barons, and freeholders were only to sell and buy wool, skins, hides, and "sic like merchandise" through the merchants of the burghs within their sheriffdom. Another law ordered that all who held land, all free tenants as well as rustics who were "manentes," must buy and sell at the fair in their own sheriffdom.[4] The Abbot of Scone received special permission from Malcolm IV to have a smith, a leather-dresser, and a shoe-maker, who should have the same freedom as the burgesses of Perth; and William the Lyon gave the Abbey of Kelso the right that their men who dwelt in Kelso might sell fuel, timber, bread, flesh, and beer out of their windows except on the market day of Roxburgh.

[1] A. Ballard, *British Borough Charters*, p. 170.
[2] *Register of the Bishopric of Glasgow*, vol. ii, p. 608.
A. Ballard, *British Borough Charters*, vol. i, p. 87.
[3] J. Irving, *Book of Dumbarton*, vol. ii, p. 20.
D. Murray, *Early Burgh Organization*, pp. 44-45, 461.
C. Innes, *Ancient Laws of the Burghs of Scotland*, vol. i, p. xxxvii.
[4] *A.P.S.* vol. i, pp. 61, 365.

He did not give them a market.[1] Until the sixteenth century, Brechin was the only example of a non-burghal market in Scotland.[2] The royal burghs also enjoyed an almost complete monopoly of fairs.

These exclusive rights of the royal burghs were to be the cause of constant disputes and struggles until they lapsed in the eighteenth century. Sometimes unfree towns or clachans managed to defy them, but they are largely responsible for the lack of villages in Scotland until the late part of the eighteenth century, and for the fact that her rural industries were far inferior in quality and value to the great cloth-weaving industry of England, until almost that period.

The king's unifying policy manifested itself in many ways. The provisions of the royal charters were all very much alike; one might almost say that their pattern was standardized. The kings were generous in relieving the burgesses from the payment of tolls and customs, thus encouraging them to move about.[3] A national code of burgh law, the *Leges Quatuor Burgorum*, was current throughout Scotland,[4] and in this Scotland differed entirely from England, where each town had its own different constitution and code. The fact that the royal burghs were subject to an annual inspection by the chamberlain must also have tended to secure uniformity. Two searching questionnaires, prepared for his use and dating from the fourteenth century, show how thoroughly he was supposed to do his work. He was to enquire into the general conduct of the bailies: if they fulfilled their duties and did justice to rich and poor alike. He was to see that the regulations regarding the inspection of food and drink were carried out, to ensure that these were wholesome and sold at reasonable prices. The

[1] C. Innes, *Early Sketches of Scotch History*, p. 124.
A. Ballard, *Scottish Hist. Review*, vol. xiii, p. 18.

[2] A. Ballard, *Scottish Hist. Review*, vol. xiii, p. 18.

[3] *Ibid.*
See also *A.P.S.* vol. i, pp. 362, 356.

[4] The four burghs were Berwick, Edinburgh, Roxburgh, and Stirling. The code is attributed to David I.

C. Innes considers that it was " collected and sanctioned in his reign " rather than " altogether framed by him." See Preface, *A.P.S.* vol. i, p. 5.

M. Bateman, that the code consists of a nucleus of laws of the " first half of the twelfth century " to which other laws of many dates have been gathered.

rights of the king with regard to tolls, dues, multures, etc., were enquired into, and also the general burghal administration, the maintenance of law and order, the state of the defences, etc. He was also to see that the privileges of the burgesses in connection with strangers, "stallangers," and other outsiders were properly safeguarded.[1]

The chamberlain also presided over a unique and very interesting Scots burghal institution, the Court of the Four Burghs. Little is known about this court, but it "probably existed as an association to which application could be made by other burghs with regard to existing customs, and a court in which the laws were administered."[2] Burgesses certainly did possess the right of appeal to a higher tribunal from the burgh courts, and the dramatic procedure to be followed is carefully given in the Laws of the Four Burghs. The burgess could only make his challenge immediately after sentence had been pronounced, before he had turned away—"and he shall not turn the toes of his feet where his heels stood," is the expression used. The words of the challenge were to be: "This dome is fals, stynkand, and rottin in the self, and theirto I streik a borch and that I will prieff."[3] Very few records remain that refer to the work of the Court of the Four Burghs—one of them states that in 1295 "the worthy and noble burghs of Berwyk, Edinburgh, and Stirling . . . at the Abbey of the Haly Cros of Edinburgh" made a decree regarding the rights of succession of the heir of a burgess.[4]

The initiative for these measures, that tended so strongly towards uniformity among the Scots burghs, rested with the king, but the burghs themselves also manifested, even in these early days, a faculty for working together. Several scraps of inter-burghal correspondence of the thirteenth century have come down to us. Some of the burghs, for instance, seem to have been uncertain as to whether a burgess, when dying, had the right to bequeath his goods as he chose, and Perth, Lanark, and Aberdeen consulted "thar derrest freinds the burrow

[1] *A.P.S.* vol. i, p. 316.

[2] Th. Pagan (Th. Keith), *The Convention of the Royal Burghs*, p. 2.

[3] *A.P.S.* vol. i, *Fragmenta Collecta*, cap. 52.
M. Bateson, *Borough Customs*, vol. ii, p. 19.

[4] Th. Pagan (Th. Keith), *The Convention of the Royal Burghs*, pp. 10-11.

greffis and burges of Edinburgh." [1] This habit of co-operating together survived and developed among the burghs of Scotland long after the jurisdiction of the chamberlain had passed away and when most of the Laws of the Four Burghs had become obsolete. It was an important and characterisitc feature in Scots burghal history.

PART IV. THE GILD MERCHANT

Another salient feature of burghal life, which in Scotland developed upon individual lines, is the institution of the Gild Merchant. The charter to Aberdeen, which has already been quoted from, is typical of many others in the monopoly that it gave the royal burgh in the matter of dealing in merchandise. This limitation, however, came to be drawn much more narrowly, both by the laws of the land and the regulations of the burgesses themselves. King William decreed that the merchants of the realm were to have their Merchant Gild and to "joice"—*gaudeant*—" and possess the samyn, with liberty to by and sell in all placis within the boundis of the liberties of burghis sua that ilke ane be content with his awne libertie and that nane occupy or usurpe the libertie of another, that he be nocht convict and punischit in the chamerlane ayre as ane forestaller." [2] And according to another of his laws, merchants of the realm were to have their Gild Merchant with the liberty of buying and selling everywhere within the bounds of burghs. Merchant strangers were not to buy and sell outside the burgh, nor were they to cut cloth and offer it for sale, nor sell anything else by retail but only in gross, and that only within the burgh and to merchants of the burgh. Any merchant-strangers found guilty of breaking this law were to be arrested by the officers of the Gild and punished.[3]

Within the burghs themselves there was, therefore, a tendency towards a further monopoly. The Burgh Laws enacted that no dyer, shoemaker, or butcher might belong to the Gild Merchant unless he gave up working at his craft with his own

[1] *A.P.S.* vol. i, p. 169.
[2] *A.P.S.* vol. i, p. 362.
[3] *A.P.S.* vol. i, p. 383.
G. Gross, *Gild Merchant*, pp. 207, 213.

hands and only employed servants to work for him,[1] and in the typical charters to Perth and Aberdeen the prohibition was absolute and the burgesses were given the right to have their Merchant Gild, "except the fullers and weavers." The principle of demarcation that is manifested in these regulations was one that developed and became formalized as the organization of the burghal communities proceeded.[2] Five centuries of struggles and of attempted adjustment lay before the two classes, before equilibrium was at last reached in a virtual equality.

The Statutes of the Gild Merchant of Berwick have come down to us. They date from 1249 to about 1294. They were probably the model upon which the Gild regulations of other Scots towns were founded, and they certainly embody tendencies that persisted for hundreds of years among the Scots Gild Merchants. The main privilege of the Gild Merchant was definitely laid down. No one except a Gild brother or a stranger-merchant might buy hides, wool, or woolskins for purposes of reselling, and the stranger-merchant might have no lot or cavil with a Gild brother. No butcher might buy wool and hides unless he abjured his axe and swore that he would not lay his hand upon beasts. These early statutes thus secured for the merchants the monopoly of dealing in the most important articles of Scots commerce. In later times they also acquired the sole right of engaging in foreign trade and in retailing the most valuable of the imports—wine, etc. (They were extensively engaged in the wine trade at the time of the statutes, but no monopoly was claimed; perhaps it was understood.) The statutes also deal with the regulations of the Merchant Gild itself, the rate of contributions payable, the conduct of members at meetings, the provision for the maintenance of poor members and their burial, etc.[3] Such provisions one would expect to find, but the statutes also make most arbitrary rules regarding the craftsmen who worked upon the commodities of the merchant's special monopoly. Shoemakers were only to use hides

[1] *Leges Quatuor Burgorum*, cap. xcix.

See also article contributed by M. Wood, *Edinburgh, 1329–1929* (published in celebration of the sexcentenary of Edinburgh), p. 266.

[2] G. Gross, *Gild Merchant*, pp. 108-109, 212.

[3] *Statutes of the Gild Merchant of Berwick*, cap. xxiii, xxx, i, xvii, xxv, xl, xliv, xxxiii, xxxii, xxxiv, xxvi, xlix, xxvii, xxv, xxviii, xxix, xc, xxxiv, xlv, xli, xviii-xx, xl.

with horns and ears of equal length, and no tanner was to salt hides. No tanner or glover was to " make " wool or any skin between Whitsunday and Michaelmas, but must sell all skins as they were, under penalty of losing his craft for a year and a day. They seem to have had special charge of the buying and selling in the town. Laws against " regrating " and " forestalling " were given rather on the lines of statutes in the Laws of the Four Burghs, and it was provided that anyone could claim a share in a purchase of herrings if he needed them for his own consumption. There were also half a dozen rules concerning the sharing of bargains in hides and wool—the Gild's particular monopoly—and the dues on the carriage of wine were laid down. But the powerful Gild went much further. Their regulations about the election of the aldermen and the twenty-four good men have already been quoted. They also forbade burgesses to interrupt or to procure outsiders to plead for them in court, or to put dirt on the streets or market-place. Every burgess having £10 worth of goods was to keep a " seemly " horse, worth at least 40s., or pay a fine of 8s. to the Gild. Strange lepers were not to be admitted into the town; and handmills were only to be used in time of scarcity, and multures (in the case of the royal burghs, a royal due) were to be duly paid. No one was to conspire against the community; and anyone revealing the secrets of the Gild was to be banished for the first offence, for the second offence was to lose the liberty of the burgh for a year and a day, and for the third one was to lose the liberty of the burgh for his life and to be ineligible for the freedom of any other.

It has often been thought that the Gild Merchant actually absorbed the whole government of the town and that Gild membership and burgess-ship were equivalent. But Gross has collected a wealth of evidence to prove that this was not so in England, but that the Gild Merchant was primarily an association of traders with an important monopoly and very wide powers of regulation—" a very important but only a subsidiary part of the municipal administrative machinery." [1] In Scotland also it is clear that the Gild and the municipality were not synonymous. For instance, in the Gild's own laws, the dues of the Gild and of the bailies are distinguished, and two laws

[1] G. Gross, *Gild Merchant*, pp. 43, 63, 66, 69, 71.

about the sharing of bargains are specially limited to Gild brothers. In one of the questionnaires provided for the chamberlain, he is to require a list of the Gild brothers and of the other burgesses.[1]

Part V. Life in the Burghs

The famous Laws of the Four Burghs give us a pleasantly intimate picture of the life of the people in the little, early Scots towns. They were primitive folk—ordeal by battle was a recognized institution and the Laws of the Four Burghs deal with the subject. Two laws deal with fugitive serfs. There is a charming simplicity about the rule that the house and family of anyone going on pilgrimage are to be in the king's special peace, and a primitive ferocity in the enactment that the accuser shall be responsible for carrying out a sentence of death or mutilation or be himself liable to punishment.[2]

Although the constitution of the burghal authorities was very vague at this early period, their powers and duties were considerable. The burgh courts dealt with all cases, civil and criminal, that arose within their boundaries, saving the four pleas of the Crown. They could, of course, inflict the death penalty. These powers are great compared to those of a modern municipal corporation, but they are not surprising in those days of decentralized control, when every baron had his right of pit and gallows.

The burghs not only administered their own justice, they had their own procedure and methods. Unlike the church courts, the burghs were backward in adopting the visnet—a form of trial by jury—and preferred the older trial by compurgation, in which the innocence of the accused was established by the oaths of his friends as to his character. The Laws of the Four Burghs are most explicit about the administration of justice. Eighteen laws deal with the procedure of the courts—when they were to be held, the forms of trial, the penalties that might be inflicted, the conduct of the witnesses, etc.

[1] G. Gross, *Gild Merchant*, p. 207.
Statutes of the Gild Merchant of Berwick, cap. iii, xlviii, xli.
A.P.S. vol. i, p. 331.

[2] *Leges Quatuor Burgorum*, cap. xi, xii, xiii, xxii, xv, lxxxviii, lxxviii.
M. Bateson, *Borough Customs*, vol. i, p. 50.

The burgh laws also deal at length with a subject that is quite beyond the scope of modern civic jurisdiction, viz. the rights of the citizen to bequeath property, and, closely allied to it, the rights of married women over their own property. The wardship of a minor and the custody of his heritage and chattels were entrusted to his relations, a procedure entirely different from feudal custom. A clear definition was drawn between land acquired by purchase and land that had been inherited. The former might be left as the burgess liked, the latter had to go to his heirs; and if the burgess wished to sell it during his lifetime, he had to offer it first of all to these heirs. These distinctions are not found in ordinary Scots law. In addition, a burgess might divide any of his land, bought or inherited, among his children as he pleased. This also was a liberty not enjoyed by feudal charter-holders. These laws are perhaps survivals from the pre-feudal period, although, actually, in Scotland they do not seem to be directly so, but to be derived from the Norman burghs. Unlike many of the Scots statutes, which are merely pious resolutions, there is evidence that they were actually put into force, at least in some of the church burghs; and a correspondence between Perth, Lanark, Aberdeen, Edinburgh, and Newcastle about the rights of a burgess to bequeath his goods as he wished, and a conference between Berwick, Edinburgh, and Stirling, show how the laws of the burghs were partly built up by the burghs themselves, and how very large their powers of constructive interpretation gradually became.[1]

Perhaps this is a convenient point to make a digression and to point out how largely the Laws of the Four Burghs were derived from those of foreign towns, and how closely connected were the codes of the mediaeval cities of all nations. Ballard suggests that the restriction of trading rights in a given district to its burgh was of Saxon origin. It is not found in Normandy. One of the special freedoms granted by William to his burgesses is referred to as "the Law of Winchester," and the Laws of the

[1] D. B. Smith, "Scots Laws of Inheritance," *Scottish Hist. Review*, vol. xxi, p. 191.

Miscellany of the Spalding Club, v. pp. 50-51 (explanation of the term "Retrait Lignager," by P. Chalmers).

M. Bateman, *Borough Customs*, vol. ii, pp. xciv, cxiv, lxxxvii.

A.P.S. vol. i, pp. 169, 170, 171.

Four Burghs are admittedly founded on those of Newcastle-upon-Tyne.[1]

The Scots code, however, is also very like the laws of Preston, and these, in their turn, are more like the laws of Breteuil than any other English borough, although thirty-three of these show traces of the influence of this small Norman town.[2]

Besides more fundamental resemblances, however, it is rather interesting to see how often one burgh would take an individual law from another. For instance, a law, in the Laws of the Four Burghs, that a burgess in possession of land must not be forcibly ejected by a claimant until the case had been tried, is said to be " the assize of Newcastell," and goes on : " Wharfor it is asket of us burges of the Newcastell whether he that was first in possession sal recover his sesing befor that he answer till him that put him out. To that than ansuer we, . . ." It cannot be mere coincidence that the Laws of the Four Burghs and a Sandwich law of the fifteenth century have the same provision that a debtor may not be pulled off the horse that he is riding in order that it may be seized for debt. The Scots laws about the trespass of animals have clauses identical with those of Portsmouth and Exeter, and the valuing of the gage of distress is very similar in Scotland, Romney, and Nottingham. In the case of house property for which rent has not been paid for a year, there is a general agreement among the burgh codes that the landlord is entitled to resume possession. Winchester (1250) ordained that he might first take out the doors and window-frames of the house and present them at the burgh court, and that then, if the tenant did not pay up, he might take forcible possession. The Scots code, however, condemns the old custom of thus mutilating the house, and ordains that the landlord must visit his premises or land, accompanied by the beadle and by witnesses, and must take a sod or stone and present it at the next chief court, when the bailie is to put it in a bag and seal the latter and give it back to the landlord. The same procedure is to be repeated at the next two head courts, and at the fourth one, viz. in a year and

[1] A. Ballard, *British Borough Charters*, vol. i, p. lxvi.
A.P.S. vol. i, p. 163.
M. Bateson, *Borough Customs*, vol. i, p. l.

[2] A. Ballard, *English Historical Review*, vol. xxx, pp. 446, 454.

a day, the landlord can produce his bags, claim judgement, and be forcibly put in possession of his house or land.[1]

The Laws of the Four Burghs, however, have many original and characteristic laws of their own. For instance, if a burgess's house should go on fire and the fire should spread to neighbouring houses and do damage, he is not to be held liable, because " he ought not to be grieved or troubled in addition, for he is burdened with sorrow and heaviness enough." Or if a man is sued for money damages because he has beaten or otherwise injured another, and if he admits the wrong but opposes the amount of the damages, he may contest this matter. If, however, in the first place he denies the original assault and is proved guilty, he must pay up the whole of the damages demanded.[2] But such amusing little laws are only traps to lure the student of the old codes into dalliance.

In all these laws the status of the burgesses as freemen is clearly implied. In achieving this status they definitely made an advance during our period. One of the laws relating to possession states that " every burgess may give or sell his land of purchase and go freely whither he will." One has only to compare this act with the provisions of a charter granted by David I to Baldwin the Lorrimer, that has already been quoted, in which the right of selling his toft and leaving the town is specially granted, to realize the advance that was being made. This right to move about as he wished and (less often) to sell the land that he had acquired, is carefully included in a great many early English charters.[3] It is significant that it should require to be stated. The burgesses, moreover, are declared free of the servile dues of merchet and herezelde. Moreover, the townsfolk acquired well-safeguarded rights against imposition and interference by all outside powers. Many of the burghs were built close to royal castles, and it is specially laid down that the castellan may not " ryn in the town within a burges house " to seize swine, geese, piglets, or hens, but must

[1] *Leges Quatuor Burgorum*, cap. xcix.
M. Bateson, *Borough Customs*, vol. i, pp. 88, 301.

[2] *Ibid.* p. 165.

[3] *Leges Quatuor Burgorum*, cap. xxi.
M. Bateson, *Borough Customs*, vol. ii, p. 90 onwards.
Sir Archibald Lawrie, *Early Scottish Charters*, p. 200.

ask to be allowed to buy them. At Yule, Pasche, and Whitsunday, if the burgesses cannot or will not supply him, he may seize any of these creatures in the street, but must pay compensation. A burgess can only be required to lend the bailies of the castle forty pennyworth of goods for forty days, and if these are not repaid he is not to be forced to lend again. In the case of a quarrel between the burgesses and the men of the castle, if the men of the castle are the offenders, justice is to be done at the castle gates; if the burgesses are the accused party, law is to be asked within the burgh. Anyone dwelling in the burgh, if arrested by the king's bailies—*ballivis regis*—may not be taken out of the freedom of the burgh, nor to the castle; a king's sergeand may not summon a burgess within burgh if he is unaccompanied by a sergeand of the burgh. Even when burgesses were cited to appear before the king's court they could claim to have the matter dealt with in their own burgh court. The wide judicial powers of the burgh have been alluded to already. It was probably no mean advantage that all mutes and plaints were to be "endyt wythin burgh," and that even those falling to the Crown were to be tried by the justice within the burgh itself.[1] Nevertheless, the sheriff seems to have had certain powers within the burghs.

The position of the burgesses in relation to strangers coming to their burgh is also carefully defined. Most careful attention was paid to the relations between burgesses and the "upland men," or *rustici*, who might have dealings within the burghs. Eleven laws deal with the matter, and although the country-folk were certainly not rightless, the native burgesses were in a far stronger position, especially in their right to "poind" questionable goods without asking permission of the bailies—perhaps so that the erring rustic should not carry them off incontinently.[2] The same right was enforced in the case of a foreign merchant. But foreign merchants were in a strange position. They were viewed with grave suspicion by their hosts—no burgess might keep them for more than a night

[1] *Leges Quatuor Burgorum*, cap. cii, iv, xlvi, cxvii, cx, vi, lxi.

Merchet, due payable on the marriage of a daughter.

Herezelde, the best animal possessed by a vassal, due to the overlord at his death.

[2] *Leges Quatuor Burgorum*, cap. iii.

unless he were willing to go "borch" for them as lawful men. According to the statutes of the Gild, no Gild brother might have lot or cavil with one of them or trade with their money, under penalty of forty shillings—the heaviest fine imposed by the statutes of the Gild. The burgh laws repeat the royal mandate that a stranger-merchant was only to buy wool and hides from a burgess. Nevertheless, the strangers were by no means without protection. In a lawsuit between a burgess and a foreigner, the burgess had to have one foreigner among his compurgators and the foreigner one burgess. They were not to be penalized by inconvenient delays, for all quarrels between stranger-merchants and burgesses were to be judged before the third tide. In these laws one can trace the anxiety to do right that undoubtedly runs through so much contemporary legislation, but they were also the result of enlightened common sense. The chamberlain, in his ayre, was specially to enquire whether burgesses had mishandled any foreign merchants "to the damage of our Lord the King, and the manifest wrack of the communities of the burghs on account of herships of this kind." A human if not very heroic law at Dumbarton enacts that if disputes arose among foreign sailors the bailies were to see the king's tolls had been paid and then to send them to their ships, that "tane of the tother may get his right as he best may." [1]

One curious feature of the laws regarding foreign merchants is the principle of *withernan* or communal responsibility. The relations of foreign town with foreign town were largely individual and there was little possibility of adjusting differences, and it was widely held that any member of such a community visiting another was responsible for the debts that might have been contracted by any of his fellow-citizens. His goods might be seized until he made satisfaction, and it was left to him to secure restitution from the original offender through his own town. The Laws of the Four Burghs empowered the *praepositus* to seize the goods of foreign merchants in settlement of the debts of their fellow-citizens, an advance on more primitive legislation in other places which allowed private citizens

[1] *Leges Quatuor Burgorum*, cap. lxxxv, xvi, viii.
Statutes of the Gild Merchant, cap. xxiii, xxv.
J. Irving, *Book of Dumbarton*, vol. ii, p. 3.

to do so. A modified procedure existed even in the case of merchants from other Scots towns. A burgess was not to poind his neighbour, being a burgess of another burgh, unless he was actually the debtor or the borch, or unless the bailies (of the other town ?) would not do him justice, which God forbid.[1]

Unfortunately it is impossible to tell whether at this early period there were many heads of families in the burghs who did not possess the status of a burgess. On the other hand, the regulations with regard to the sale and preparation of food are more minute than anything else in the code. The weight, the price, the quality of bread and meat, and the quality of fish, the strength and price of ale, were all to be fixed, and careful provision was made for proper inspection. All foodstuffs were to be sold in the market or shown in the salesman's window, to prevent fraud. In the days of limited markets and deficient transport there was a very real danger that the market might be cornered. The burgh laws have very careful enactments against "regrating," i.e. buying to sell at a profit, and "forestalling," viz. buying up goods before they have been exposed for sale. The people's food was regarded as all-important. The enquiries prescribed in the chamberlain's ayre involved a most searching investigation as to whether the provisions of the burgh laws had been carried out. Any *praepositus* who neglected his duties in this respect was liable to severe punishment—his body and chattels were to be at the king's will. Both by the Laws of the Four Burghs and by the general law of the land, no town official might bake bread or keep a tavern.[2]

Provisions with regard to public health and sanitation were few. Lepers belonging to the town were to be supported in the spital and not to go into anyone's house. Swine were to be kept in styes or to be herded in the fields and were not to wander through the streets. The statutes of the Gild had really more to say upon this subject.[3] The burghs were to keep a watch by night and burgesses were to take their turn; and

[1] M. Bateman, *Borough Customs*, vol. i, p. 121.
Leges Quatuor Burgorum, cap. lxvii.

[2] *Leges Quatuor Burgorum*, cap. xix, xxxvi, ix, lxiii, lxiv, xix, lix.

[3] *Ibid.* cap. lviii, lxxxiv.

when wakened by the " wakstaff," they were to come forth, armed with two weapons, and to watch " wysly and bisily." Unless they had a reasonable excuse, burgesses were not to leave their tenements unbuilt upon, and provision was made for the careful " lyning " of the boundaries of the holdings.[1]

The burghs were evidently largely dominated by the exclusive merchants. The laws of the Gild, that only craftsmen who abjured their trade might become members of the Gild Merchant, and the restrictions upon shoemakers are repeated in the laws of the burghs. Kempsters—woolcombers—were not to live with upland men if there was work for them in the town; bakers might only employ three men.[2]

On the other hand, in many acts, brotherliness is enjoined between burgess and burgess. By their own statutes the exclusive Gild Merchants were obliged to share their bargains with each other, and they had their special duties towards the infirm, the old, and the dead of their own Gild. Moreover, ordinary burgesses had the right to share in their purchases of foodstuffs, so far as they required them for actual consumption. In the burgh laws, when a brother-burgess was arrested beyond the boundaries of the burgh, his friends were expected to go and be borch for him. The *Fragmenta* enact that burgesses must be pledge for each other up to three times or until they suffered loss. Bakers, brewers, and butchers had to supply their neighbours with goods so long as they had anything for sale; but if a neighbour did not pay, these tradesmen could distrain him for the money and were not obliged to supply him again.[3] The whole framework of civic life was built up upon the principle of " commoning." On the other hand, the exclusive little communities were not heavens upon earth. No doubt the closely crowded folk often had causes of difference and settled them with a typically mediaeval lack of restraint. The minute particulars regarding actions, civil and criminal, at least suggest this. Nevertheless, they successfully rubbed along, cheek-by-jowl, in iron-bound association, for over four hundred years of municipal protectionism.

It is dull work merely repeating the rather obscure and

[1] *Leges Quatuor Burgorum*, cap. lxxxi, xxvii, cxxix.
[2] *Ibid.* cap. xciv, xciii, ciii, lxi.
[3] *Ibid.* cap. li.

contradictory acts of the *Leges Quatuor Burgorum*. It is more profitable to try to build up a picture of the general life of the burgh, such as can be drawn by implication from the allusions to trades, the list of dues, etc. In the burgh harbours there were foreign ships, vessels used in a considerable coastal trade, and fishing-boats. From the landward side there was coming and going of carts and wains and of men carrying burdens. In the town, besides the burgesses and visiting uplandmen, there were stallangers, who set up their booths in the market-place, and *pipouderi*, peddling merchants, " having no certain dwelling-place in the sheriffdom, but being vagabond in the country." Mercers, glovemakers, tanners, shoemakers, fishermen, butchers, dyers, weavers, lorrimers, tailors, smiths, all plied their trades or offered their wares. If the burgh was near a castle, the garrison and, upon occasion, the castellan or the sheriff would visit the town. The religious of many orders were there, serving the numerous churches, or visiting the *mansura* that the kings had given them, and busy over the affairs of their great possessions. The lords and barons of the shire and their servants also came in, to buy supplies for their families and households, and to dispose of the surplus produce of their estates.

Every burgh had its market day, which was probably busy enough, but the great occasions were the fairs. The barons and lords—even the king himself—bought their luxuries there; and the runaway " bonde " could enjoy the fun and bustle and be immune from capture. Burgesses from other towns were there—attendance at a fair was a recognized excuse for non-attendance at a burghal court; mercers and stallangers set up their booths, both covered and uncovered, the dues a fat source of revenue for the burgh. All the trading restrictions upon the sale of worked wool, yarn, and silk were removed and hucksters might buy them and sell them again; the exclusive burgesses and the stallangers at this time only might go shares in a bargain. A special court was set up to deal with all cases of disorder, and careful rules were made about the reclaiming of stolen goods; but, once the "pece of the fayr was cryet," there was a relaxation of the restraints and limitation of everyday burghal life. No one was arrested except for breaking the peace of the fair, or if he was a traitor to the king or so grievous a misdoer that even " the gryth of haly kyrk " ought not to suffice him.[1]

To complete the picture, we know the actual plenishing possessed by an ordinary burgess, for the *Leges* give a list of chattels so necessary that they ought not to be separated from a burgess's house and land in a will. They include :

1 best burd (table) with trestles.
1 tablecloth.
1 towel.
1 basin.
1 laver.
1 best bed with sheets and " all the laif that tharto pertaines of clothes."
1 best feather bed or flock bed if there is no feather bed.
1 leyd (instrument used in brewing).
1 gylfat (used in fomenting the wort).
1 barrel.
1 cauldron.
1 kettle.
1 brander.
1 posnet, i.e. porringer.
1 chimney.
1 stop = pitcher.
1 cruk for hanging the pot over the fire.
1 kist.
1 schyrn = shearing hook.
1 plough.
1 wain.
1 cart.
1 char = waggon.
1 brasyn pot.
1 pan.
1 rostin iron.
1 girdle.
1 mortar and pestle.
1 masar.
1 dubblar = platter.
1 cop = cup.
12 spoons.
1 bench.
1 stool.
1 form.
1 ballance and weights.
1 spade. 1 axe.[2]

[1] *Exchequer Rolls*, vol. i, p. lii.
Leges Quatuor Burgorum, cap. xi, xcii, xxxvii, lxvi, liv, lxxxvi.
[2] C. Innes, *Ancient Laws of the Scottish Burghs*, cxvi.

From the provisions in the *Leges* with regard to the leaving of property we learn that the burgess had armour—sometimes more than one suit—and live stock. He sometimes owned ships or little boats. He could hold more than one house and tenement.[1] We are left with the picture of a man much engaged in agriculture, one whose hands could keep his head—occasionally a man of considerable substance. The old burghs must have been a miscellaneous assortment of dwellings. In Elgin there were mansions, edifices, huts (*habitacula*), and booths or bothies (*bothae*).[2] Would that the chroniclers had left us a description of the little Northern burghs themselves. We must rest content with a picture of Carlisle, the Border city, in the awful panoply of war :

Away goes King William with his great gathered host
Towards Carlisle the fair, the strong garrisoned city.

. . . .

The earls of Scotland lead the hated people
Who never had any repugnance to do fiendish things.
They make such progress, I know not what more to tell you,
That they could see Carlisle full of beauty ;
The sun illumines the walls and turrets.
He who has a merry banner, gladly displays it ;
And the trumpets sound in every rank :

. . . .

The King summons Roger and Adam to council,
Walter de Berkeley, who was one of his retainers :
Now behold, noble knights, much gentle preparation ;
You cannot count the white nor the red,
So many are the pennons dancing in the sun.[3]

[1] *Leges Quatuor Burgorum*, cap. xxiv.

[2] J. Shaw, *History of Moray*, vol. iii, p. 67.

[3] Jordan de Fantosme, *Chronicle* (Church Histories of England Series), p. 273.

CHAPTER IV

The State of the Highlands

So far our attention has been mainly directed towards the interaction of influences, new and old, that laid the foundation of the social organization of the South. The adjustment that was reached in the Highlands was markedly different, and it is now time to consider the little that can be deduced about what went on in the fastnesses of the hills.

At the beginning of the eleventh century Scotland was mainly under Gaelic dominance, and had its centre in Southern Perthshire. We have seen how largely the kingdom was transformed by Norman and Saxon influences and how the centre of gravity shifted southwards. At the beginning of our period the division between the Highlands and the Lowlands, as they were afterwards evolved, did not exist, for, save for the Lothians and the Norse spheres of influence, all Scotland was Gaelic. At the end of it the differentiation between them was evidently coming into being—it was an established thing during the Wars of Independence and became increasingly marked in the fifteenth century.

The pendulum has swung back, and once more it is not easy to realize how utter and how clean-cut was the dividing line between the Highlands and the Lowlands during the four hundred years between the fourteenth and eighteenth centuries. There was an old saying that the King of Scots had a town so long that one end of it did not understand the language of the other, which referred to the little burgh of Nairn, which lay at the very end of the Highland line. Scott, through the mouth of Bailie Nicol Jarvie, has left an incomparable picture of the mutual suspicion and dislike, the emphasized differences of tradition, language, and culture that kept the Highlander and the Lowlander apart.

It was not, however, the case that one part of Scotland was profoundly modified and the other remained entirely unchanged. All the old Gaelic provinces were gradually feudalized and their organization broken down or transformed. The Highland line cut through the old earldoms of Menteith, Strathearn, Angus, Mar, Buchan, and Moray.[1] It ran along the edge of the hill country, and it was determined by strategic and not historical considerations.

During the twelfth and thirteenth centuries, moreover, the Highlands were subjected to considerable feudalizing influences by the active and powerful Scots kings. Successive rebellions were crushed. Burghs were planted and encouraged in the North. By the end of the period a considerable part of the country had been covered by the new organization of sheriffdoms. The curious law about challenged cattle, that has already been quoted, shows how, piecemeal, the kings tried to enforce law and order. The feudal law of the land came to be applied in the Highlands as elsewhere, and the country itself was disposed of by feudal charters, identical with those by which other land was held. The Norman followers of the kings and the feudalized gentry of the South acquired a considerable footing in the glens and straths. Thus, the rule of the Comyns extended right across the Highlands, up the valley of the Spey, and in Lochaber. Many lesser families, Bissets, Roses, Le Chiens, etc., were planted round the Moray Firth. Many parts of Perthshire were feudalized, including the inaccessible districts of Fortingall and Glen Lyon, which were granted to a Norman baron. The most southern of the Western Isles became the patrimony of the Steward. To anticipate a little, in some cases the feudalizing process was repeated more than once: Badenoch, for instance, during the thirteenth, fourteenth, and fifteenth centuries was granted successively to the Comyn Earl of Buchan, to Randolph, Earl of Moray, and to Alexander Stewart, the son of Robert II.[2] Among these intruding Scoto-Norman families were the Chisholms, the Frasers, and several different branches of Stewarts.

Only the vaguest inferences can be drawn about the state

[1] W. F. Skene, *Celtic Scotland*, vol. iii, p. 285.

[2] A. Stewart, *A Highland Parish*, pp. 11, 75, 77.

J. Stevenson, *Documents Illustrative of History of Scotland*, ii, pp. 189-190

of the Gaelic society exposed to these feudalizing influences. Its organization was shattered in the extreme North and throughout the Western Isles and along that seaboard by the inroads and settlements of the Norsemen; all over the rest of the country by the transformation or extinction of the old system of mormaers and provinces. The larger units of social organization had therefore perished. Nevertheless, the people were tenacious in their allegiance to the old order of things. They rose again and again in support of the claimants to the heritage of their ancient rulers, and they preserved not only their language and their culture but their lesser group forms.

The clan was a feature of Gaelic organization that the Scots had brought with them from Ireland, although it may already have existed in Scotland among the Picts. At the beginning of our period it appears in the *Book of Deer* and in that curious institution the Law of Clan Macduff; but with the exception of the race of Somerled, the progenitors of Clan Donald, no group of insurgent Highlanders was sufficiently powerful, during the twelfth and thirteenth centuries, to be alluded to in any of the accounts of the rebellions given by the Southern chronicles. Nevertheless, the people preserved their clannish instincts. In fact, one cannot doubt that the nuclei of many of the clans were in existence, some of them clustered about the descendants of the old leaders of their race, some of them in process of formation, whenever natural leaders of men appeared. So strong and ingrained was the instinct that, as soon as favourable conditions arose, in the fourteenth and fifteenth centuries, a complete clan organization, covering a very large part of the Highlands, sprang up spontaneously, and embraced not only the native Gael but many of the families of the Norman incomers. Moreover, in the earlier period with which we are now dealing, the Gaels were able to bring about a considerable revival of their power.

Professor Brögger, in his Rhind Lectures of 1928, emphasized the fact, not perhaps sufficiently brought out by the purely Scots historian, that the diminution of the power of the Norsemen in Scotland was largely brought about by a decline in that of Norway herself. The local Gaels, however, were quick to profit by the weakness of their conqueror. All down the Western Coast of Scotland a hybrid race, known as the

Gall Gadheal, had been evolved. In Galloway, surviving place-names show that there was a permanent Scandinavian settlement among the Gaels, although, as Sir Herbert Maxwell points out, we are left to imagine whether the relations between the two races were those of overlord and tributary, or whether they merely became fellow-pirates. The Irish chronicler Macfirbis declares that these Southern Gaels renounced their baptism and had the customs of the Norsemen. They at least made common cause with them in their incursions upon the rest of Gaeldom. In the early eleventh century we find Galloway ruled over by Sigurd the Stout, Earl of Orkney, with a native prince, Malcolm, known in the sagas as the Earl Melkoff, as his resident lieutenant.[1]

During the reign of Malcolm Canmore, Galloway became definitely a part of Scotland. The Scandinavian culture now faded out as the Gaelic one became dominant. The share taken by the Galwegians in the Battle of the Standard has already been told. Their ruler at that time, who did not take part in the battle because he was in disgrace for a previous rebellion, was " one Fergus of the line of Galloway princes or native rulers," who had accompanied David I to England, and who had married there an Englishwoman, David's own sister-in-law. Fergus joined in two of the Gaelic rebellions, but for his churches and abbeys, of which he founded several, he brought monks from Prémontré, in Picardy, and from Yorkshire. He did not favour the keledei as did Malise of Strathearn, the protagonist of the rights of the Gaels at the Battle of the Standard.

The dynasty of Fergus lasted till 1234. It was able to hold its own against the kings of Scotland, and it was in close alliance with the kings of England. By these latter large tracts in Ireland were granted to the family, and Roland, Lord of Galloway, who had married an Anglo-Norman, held estates in Northampton, Huntingdon, and Bedford by right of his wife. His grandson also held English estates. The Lords of Galloway served the King of England in Ireland and on the Welsh marches. In 1187 they helped the King of Scotland to subdue a rising in Moray.

In 1234 this little Celtic principality came to an end. Alan, the last Lord of Galloway, died, leaving three daughters, all

[1] Sir Herbert Maxwell, *Dumfries and Galloway*, pp. 39, 41, 42, 45.

of them married to Anglo-Normans. The native gentry vainly asked the King of Scotland to become their direct lord or to appoint Thomas, the late lord's illegitimate son, to rule over them. When this was refused, they rose in rebellion and Alexander II was barely able to subdue them. The feudal rule of Scoto-Normans was then introduced.[1]

Farther north, in the Western Highlands, there was a more permanent revival of Gaelic power. Piratical Norsemen had made settlements upon either side of the Irish Channel, and in time the King of Norway asserted a certain amount of authority over them. How far the Norsemen modified the civilization of the older inhabitants is not known. It was natural that, coming as conquerors as they did, they should have had some influence over the possession of land. That they did so is almost certain from the fact that they introduced the land-measures of merklands, pennylands, etc. As in Galloway, a mixed people arose, known as Gall Gadheal. Some authorities have suggested that these were a settled people, others that they were merely pirates. In any case, the Scandinavians and the Gall Gadheal waxed in power and the Gaels declined, so that Dalriada, the cradle of Gaeldom in Alban, passed largely into the hands of the two former.

About the middle of the eleventh century a great Gaelic leader arose in the person of Somerled. His name is Scandinavian, and he has been held to be a Pict, a Gael, a Norseman, and a Gall Gadheal by different authorities. According to the seannachies of his own race, he was of the line of Colla Uais, whose stock, in the fourth century, had been the Gaelic colonists of Dalriada; and through Colla Uais, but more questionably, his descent is traced to Conn of the Hundred Battles, one of the great warrior kings of Ireland. This descent is accepted by the latest historians of Clan Donald. It was a living tradition of the clan when MacVurich, the bard, sang his people into the furious mood of battle before the Red Harlaw.[2]

[1] Sir Herbert Maxwell, *Dumfries and Galloway*, ch. iii.
Sir Archibald Lawrie, *Early Scottish Charters*, p. 346.
Sir Archibald Lawrie, *Annals of the Reigns of Malcolm and William, Kings of Scotland*, pp. 326, 346, 359, 371, 380-382.

[2] A. Macdonald, *Clan Donald*, vol. i, pp. 23-30.
See extracts from Book of Clanranald, printed as appendix to W. F. Skene, *Celtic Scotland*, vol. iii, p. 298, for the traditional descent of Somerled.

According to the traditional history of the Macdonalds, Gilledonnan, the grandfather of Somerled, had been driven out of his lands by the Norsemen early in the eleventh century. Gillebride, the father of the champion, after a vain attempt to recover them, lived as a fugitive, and so young Somerled had grown up. In the fighting between the men of Argyle and the Norsemen, which was again renewed, he was chosen to be their leader, by the MacInneses, who were a powerful group among the Gaels. The Gaels were once more defeated in a great fight, but Somerled and his men retired in good order; he continued the struggle, and, before another decisive battle, the whole of the Gaels, realizing the weakness of a leaderless host, chose him as their leader. He was victorious.

The rest of his reign is dimly known to authentic history. He called himself Regulus and Thane of Argyle. He fought with the Norse kinglets at that time established along the coasts of the Irish Channel, and he supported the revolts led by the claimants to the old Gaelic province of Moray. In 1164 there was serious trouble between Malcolm the Maiden, King of Scotland, and Somerled, and the latter, with 15,000 men and 64 galleys, sailed up the Firth of Clyde to Renfrew. There he either died or was assassinated, and his army melted away.

After Somerled's death, the Scandinavian King of Man resumed possession of much that Somerled had conquered from him—Man, Lewis, Harris, Barra, and Skye. Somerled's mainland possessions were divided among all his sons, but in addition his three sons by Ragenhildis, the daughter of the King of Man, received shares of the Southern Isles. Kintyre and Islay fell to Reginald; Mull, Coll, Tiree, and Jura probably fell to Dugall; Bute and other territories, including perhaps the Rough Bounds, extending from Ardnamurchan to Glenelg, presumably formed the share of Angus. One sees in this family distribution of lands a typically clannish arrangement. It was not tribal, for although Somerled had many followers, his possessions went to his sons. It was, however, in distinct contrast to the feudal custom of primogeniture.

Of the three branches, two waxed, one died out in the male line, and, through an heiress, some of its possessions were carried into the Scoto-Norman family of the Steward, who thus secured possession of Bute. Eventually one of the other branches also died out in the male line, and the marriage of the heiress brought back part of the lands to the line of Reginald of Islay. Reginald, at his death, had divided his lands between his two sons, and the branch of Garmoran was formed, but its possessions five generations later were once more carried by an heiress into the Islay branch. At the historic meeting of the Estates, in 1254, which recognized Alexander III's grand-daughter as the future Queen of Scotland, the family of Somerled were represented by three magnates of the West Coast, Alexander de Ergadia, Anegus filius Dovenalde, and Alanus filius Rotherici.[1] The Islay branch was the most powerful among these descendants. Reginald of Islay's grandson, Angus Mor, once more divided his lands among his sons, Alexander and Angus Og, who both took decisive parts in the War of Independence.

The family arrangements made among Somerled's descendants (only some of which have been alluded to) at this time were very complicated. There had been constant subdivisions, so that, in the words of the *History of Clan Donald*, " Oirthirghael and the Isles were now divided into a number of little principalities . . ." possessed by the descendants of Somerled. There seems, however, to have been a strong dynastic feeling, and by marriage arrangements some of the lands had come back and back to the senior branch of Islay. Meanwhile the strong clannish feeling that had rallied to the founders of the lordship of the Isles and of the great Clan Donald was also shown by other neighbouring families. The Clan Dougal, who were descendants and followers of the Lord of Lorn, had been founded. Another great Highland clan of the future, that of the Campbells, was also in process of development. A charter of the fourteenth century granted to Sir Neil Campbell (at that time head of the family), in the conventional terms of such feudal documents, " all the liberties and customs " that had belonged to his progenitor, Duncan Macdhuine. This Duncan is supposed to have flourished about A.D. 1200, but there is nothing to show whether he had received a fresh feudal grant as a newcomer or if it had been the acknowledgement of some older status as a native ruler.[2] The

[1] *A.P.S.* vol. i, p. 82.
[2] Duke of Argyll, *Scotland as it was and is*, pp. 57-58.
Article on Dukedom of Argyll in *Scots Peerage*.

same clannish feeling had developed among the descendants and following of the Scoto-Norman family of Stewart, which was also established in Lorn as the result of the marriage with the heiress of the line of Dugall, son of Somerled.

We do not know the relations that existed between these rising families and other inhabitants, for it must be remembered that the land that they dominated was not an empty one. The story of the Dalriadic Scots and the great following of Somerled proves that. It is interesting to find that the traditional history of the Macdonalds alludes to earlier inhabitants of the land. We are told that when Somerled began his career some people called Macinnes and Macgilvray were in occupation of Morvern, and that when he became Thane of Argyle the inhabitants all accepted him, except the Macphadins, who for a short time resisted him. A charter of Reginald, son of Somerled, speaks of his friends and men. According to the history of the Campbells of Craignish, the founder of this cadet branch was a son of Campbell of Lochawe, who, having been fostered by M'Eachern of Craignish, succeeded to his lands.[1] Neither of these histories can be claimed to be reliable accounts; nevertheless, they are illustrations of a general drift of early clan tradition that cannot be ignored, and it fits in perfectly with the ideas conveyed by the chronicles of the times. What is now the Highlands was inhabited by warlike peoples, who rose again and again in support of the families of their old mormaers, but there were no great clans sufficiently outstanding to have transmitted their names to the pages of the Lowland chronicles. There were, however, many social nuclei, some new, some old, round which the people rallied.

It may be said that the later part of our period, after the establishment of Somerled's race, was not one of peaceful consolidation on the West Coast. Besides internal troubles, the possession of the islands and peninsulas was in dispute between the Kings of Norway and of Scotland. When Alexander II enforced his authority over the mainland of Argyle, in 1221, he seems to have made a sweeping rearrangement of lands.

[1] "Manuscript History of the Macdonalds," *De Rebus Albanicis*, pp. 282-283. "Manuscript History of Craignish," *Miscellany of the Scottish History Society* (Third Series), iv, p. 204. Reg. de Pass. No. 125.

De kyng that yhere Argyle wan,
Dat rebell wes til hym befor than.
For wythe hys Ost thare in wes he
And Athe tuk of thare Fewte,
Wyth thare serwys and thare Homage,
Dat of hym wald hald thare Herytage.
But of the Ethchetys of the lave
To the Lordis of that land he gave.

Fordoun states that those who had offended the king too deeply fled, and that their lands were given to those who had followed the king into Argyle.[1]

In studying the agrarian problems of later times in the Highlands, this early period is an important one to bear in mind, for there is a tendency to regard the conditions that obtained in the later Middle Ages and in the post-mediaeval period as a cast-iron system that had been received intact from remote ages. The social organization of the Gael was, however, on the contrary, very fluid and adaptable, and was being actively developed during the times we are now dealing with and in the succeeding period.

From lack of all other material, the differentiation between the Highlander and the Lowlander can only be traced to the effects of the political history of the country. There were, however, other important factors at work. The Highland line, running as it did along the edge of the hill country, was obviously determined largely by strategic considerations, but its effect was to make a demarcation between the largely arable land of the Lowlands, which was coming more and more under tillage, and the mainly pastoral and cattle-raising country of the Highlands. The social conditions likely to be developed by a country predominantly lived in by herdsmen are obviously different to those of a country largely inhabited by agriculturists, and it is possible that in this economic fact we have the fundamental cause of the great social cleavage that became increasingly marked among the inhabitants of Scotland. It is an hypothesis that would explain many differences.

[1] W. F. Skene, *Highlanders of Scotland.* See especially the edition edited and amended by A. Macbain, p. 203.

SECTION II

FOREWORD

A ! fredom is ane nobile thing :
Fredom maes man to have liking ;
Fredom al solas to man gifis,
He lifis at es that frely lifis.
Ane nobile hart may haf nane es,
Na ellis nocht that may him ples,
Gif fredom falyle, for fre liking
Is yharnit our all othir thing.

JOHN BARBOUR, *The Brus* (flourished about 1357).

INTERLUDE

THE Wars of Independence, those episodes so vastly satisfying to Scots national pride, scarcely come within the purview of an economic history: yet the results of the double crisis were so far-reaching that it is necessary to remember the magnitude of the struggle. Edward I had awarded the Scots Crown to John Balliol; had subjected his nominee and, through him, the kingdom of Scotland to three years of piled-up humiliations; and, having goaded the proud nation into war in 1296, he had burnt and sacked Berwick and had overrun the country. Nine years of fighting and raiding followed, during which the Scots under Wallace and Moray, the patriot leaders, partially threw off the English yoke. In 1303–1304 Edward again overran the country, and proposed to govern it through his nephew, John of Brittany, who was to act as viceroy. In 1306 Bruce murdered the Comyn and began his desperate struggle against England. By 1309, from being merely a guerilla leader, he had acquired a formidable following and held practically the whole of the North of Scotland. In the long-drawn-out hostilities of the following years he gradually wrested nearly all the Lowland fortresses from the English. Bannockburn, in 1314, made him master of Scotland, but fighting, mostly to the south of the Borders, dragged on till 1327. In 1328, by the Treaty of Northampton, England acknowledged Scots independence. The later part of Bruce's reign, especially after 1323, was a period of reconstruction, but unfortunately a very short one, for the king died in 1329, leaving a child-heir, and, in 1330, Edward III assumed the personal rule of England.

Within a year trouble again arose between England and Scotland. The nobles who had been disinherited during the late war—the Comyns, Balliols, and others—tried to recover their lands and Edward III supported them, and the two countries drifted into war. There followed an ebb and flow of fighting, which culminated in Edward's decisive victory of Halidon Hill in 1333. The English now occupied as their own all Scotland south of the Forth and supported Edward Balliol's claims to the rest of the country. In 1336, Edward III burned and harried as far north as Elgin, and the little Scots king was sent to France for safety. Fortunately, after 1337, Edward III turned his main attention to his conquests in France, and the Scots were able, bit by bit, to win back their country. In 1341, David II, a youth of seventeen, returned from France.

To the student of social history the Wars of Independence are of great importance. Not only do they reveal the fact that Scotland had fused into a nation, but that she put up her heroic fight, not as a state feudally organized, but as a people of individual patriots. Until Bruce ended his long equivocations by incurring the inveterate animosity of Edward I, the great feudal lords—the men who held such wide estates upon "military tenure"—at best were indifferent leaders, by more than half were renegades.

The first great stand was made by William Wallace, a simple knight, and he "was joined by an immense number of Scots, for the community of the land followed him as their leader and chief. Moreover, all the followers of the magnates adhered to him; and as for the magnates themselves, they were with our king" (i.e. Edward), "but their heart was far from him."[1] And so it was right through the darkest days in both struggles, the main support of the Scots resistance was drawn from the people, fighting not as part of a feudal train but as self-determined patriots. It is very significant that the fact that Bruce was chosen by the *people* should be stressed so strongly in the magnificent declaration of the Scots clergy assembled at Dundee in 1309.

Unfortunately, the war did not end on a note of triumph with David II's return, for France was fighting for her life against England, and persuaded the Scots to make a diversion by continuing their own war. In 1343, David II was defeated and captured at Neville's Cross and, after some delay, peace

[1] Hemingburgh. Quoted by E. M. Barron, *Scots Wars of Independence*, p. 84.

was made and the king's ransom was fixed at 100,000 marks and he was allowed to return to his kingdom. The story of how the country, fresh from its life-and-death struggle, faced this heavy financial burden is pleasant reading. It is but an episode, and yet, perhaps, as example of the strong *national* feeling that had grown up, an outline may be included, even within the so-limited scope of this history.

The Scots Parliament lost no time in facing the problem. How vast it was can be seen from the fact that each of the annual payments in which the ransom was to be made, i.e. 10,000 marks, was nearly twice as much as the total revenue of the Crown, which in the rather palmy year of 1331 amounted to £3777. Four sources of revenue were exploited. The Crown was empowered to buy up all wool and wool-fells, at two-thirds of their market value, in order to resell them. In the first year £2000 was expended in such purchases. All past alienations of Crown lands were cancelled and all future alienations prohibited. Gifts of wards and escheats were not to be granted without careful consideration. It was characteristic of the weakness of the central authority and the undue power of the landed classes, which was to be the determining feature in the social life of the whole of the following period, that this measure was largely inoperative. The sheriffs were unable to enforce it to any large extent, and in 1367, when a stronger act of the same kind was passed, most of the occupiers of these lands were still in possession. The great customs which were levied on hides, wool, and wool-fells were trebled.[1]

Two annual payments of 10,000 marks were punctually made, and the Scots, meanwhile, tried to get foreign help to pay the ransom. Their hopes in this direction were destroyed when France, in whose quarrel they had really been fighting, made peace in 1360. They had other causes for disheartenment. The king whom they were ransoming at such high cost was utterly unworthy of his people. "An examination of the various accounts regarding the contribution" shows that although "the Estates had agreed to tax themselves so heavily

[1] Before this act the English and Scots customs on these goods were the same, i.e. ½ a mark on every sack of wool, and 1 mark on every cast of hides.—*Exchequer Rolls*, vol. ii, p. xli.

W. Cunningham, *Growth of Industry and Commerce*, p. 377.

for the ransom, the sums collected were mainly absorbed in David's private expenses." [1] Provoked beyond measure, four of the greatest nobles, Mar, Douglas, March, and the Steward, quarrelled with the king, and there was fighting. David, however, acted with vigour and decision, collected an army and forced his powerful subjects to submit.

Not only was the king extravagant; he had an unworthy love for the land of his captivity and all through his reign he was constantly going south, "with seemly court and weill farand," [2] to squander money in the brilliant company of Edward III, his country's enemy. In 1363, by which time the Scots payments were heavily in arrears, he sank lower still, and entered into agreement with Edward III that, in return for cancelling the debt, the English king or one of his sons should be made heir to the Scots throne. The Scots Parliament furiously repudiated the arrangement. In the words of the old chronicler:

> Til that said al his legis nay;
> Na thai consent wald be na way
> That ony Inglis mannys son
> In to that honoure sulde be done
> Or succede to bere the crowne
> Off Scotland in successione.
>
> . . . . .
>
> Qwhen this denyit was vttrely,
> The kynge was richt wa and angry;
> Bot his zarnynge nevertheles
> Denyit of al his legis was.[3]

Edward was very angry at the failure of this plan and demanded that the arrears of the ransom should be paid up instantly, on pain of immediate renewal of hostilities. The Scots had to send expensive embassies to the English Court and terms were at last arranged in 1345. The ransom was now fixed at £100,000—one-third more than the original figure—and was to be paid in annual instalments of £4000 within twenty-five years. Moreover, the English had the right of breaking the truce in four years' time, but in that case the ransom was to be 80,000 marks—that is, the original sum, less

[1] *Exchequer Rolls*, vol. ii, p. xlix.
[2] Wintoun, *Orygynale Chronkyl*, vol. vi, p. 242 (*Armour's edition*).
[3] *Ibid.* p. 253.

the two contributions that had actually been paid. This proviso gave Edward a useful handle wherewith to bargain. The Scots did not feel able to face a war, but when Edward suggested that, in order to secure peace, they should dismember the kingdom and acknowledge the suzerainty of England, they decided that they would rather pay off the whole debt by a kind of capital levy and ordered a valuation of the wealth of the kingdom to be made.

Meanwhile, the graceless king continued his extravagances and his trips to England, and, as an extra liability, married Margaret Logie, the greedy widow. The kingdom was rent by factions, for March, Douglas, and the Steward were bitter opponents of the queen. The Islands, Badenoch, Athole, Lochaber, and Ross-shire were virtually in a state of rebellion. The Northern lords, especially the Lord of the Isles, refused to pay customs, robbed the collectors, and would not obey summonses to attend Parliament. Even in the settled Lowlands there was resistance, and even by men of such standing as Sir Alexander Lindsay, one of the justiciars. Yet, in spite of all this, two of the annual payments under the new arrangement were made, a further law revoking alienations of Crown lands was passed, and the great customs were raised to four times their pre-ransom figures.

By 1369 the situation had become easier. Edward was busy over the project of a French war and wished to prolong the truce. He accepted 56,000 marks as the balance of the ransom, the annual payments were reduced by one-third, and it was agreed that half the rents of those parts of Scotland still held by the English should be given to the Scots. The Lord of the Isles was forced to submit. The king, however, went bankrupt in 1370 and spent £2421 in trying to divorce his wife. He died later in the year. The chamberlain's whole receipts for that year were £15,349, of which £2660 was reserved for the ransom, £4148 was spent in defraying the cost of embassies to England, France, and the Papal Court, and £966 was paid for one of the king's journeys to England.[1] During the first years of Robert II's reign the payments of the ransom were regularly made, but after 1377 they ceased, leaving a balance of 24,000 marks unpaid, and, although the English made

[1] *Exchequer Rolls*, vol. ii (*Burnett's Introduction*).

many protests and there was nearly war, it never was cleared off.[1] The actual payments of the instalments abound with picturesque detail. They took place in the Low Countries. The bullion was weighed out in the presence of the representatives of the English and the Scots.

The period of fighting had its deep effects upon the national life—some transient, some lasting. The material losses must have been enormous, for the struggle had been waged with great bitterness on both sides. Edward's brutal sack of Berwick, in the opening campaign, had set an evil standard. Both armies, in mediaeval fashion, had lived upon the land—in 1298, just before the Battle of Falkirk, the English army had been almost starved into a retreat—and the country had been systematically wasted by the Scots, as part of their tactics, and by the English in retaliation. Outstanding examples are Bruce's terrible "hership of Buchan," which Barbour describes so vividly, and the devastation wrought all about the head of the Firth of Tay by Edward III.[2] Here and there, valuations of actual properties showing complete ruination survive;[3] and how vast a sum of human misery is represented by the following national figures! Thomson has calculated that the temporal lands in the days of Alexander III were worth £50,000 and in 1366 scarcely £25,000. During about the same period the Church lands had declined from £16,000 to £10,000. The effects of the second phase of the war are more exactly seen from the chamberlain's accounts which survive:

	1331.			1341.		
Received from the sheriffs .	£1474	18	0½	£500	17	6
Ferms of the burghs . .	499	16	2½	318	8	4
Customs	1794	9	6¾	379	8	3¾
	£3769	3	9¾	£1198	4	1¾

[1] *Exchequer Rolls*, vol. iii, pp. lv and lxxi.

[2] *Wyntoun*, vol. vi, line 5561 (Barbour's edition).

[3] C. Innes, *Sketches of Early Scots History*, pp. 140, 196, gives examples. See also T. Thomson, *Cranstoun* v. *Gibson, Court of Session, Second Division*, 1816.

See also *Calendar of State Papers relating to Scotland* (First Series), vol. iii, Nos. 461, 245.

For examples of ruin in burghs and of exactions by both sides, see *ibid.* No. 68, p. 228.

In these figures the land has suffered heavily but the export trade even more.[1]

The present generation, which has lived through a great war, albeit one that was not fought upon our own soil, and is feeling the crippling effects of post-war depression, may well envy the Scots of the fourteenth century their resiliency. An individual example has survived. The Barony of Brade, near Edinburgh, had been fully cultivated, and, with its mill, had been worth forty merks in 1305. It was said to be only worth eight merks after the first part of the war, owing to the destruction that had been wrought. But, in an inquisition, the jury estimated that if the mill were rebuilt and the land recultivated and reinhabited, it would be worth twelve merks in two years, and fifteen merks in six years, and eighteen merks in the next year and so on.[2] During the immediate aftermath of the war, and whilst David II's ransom was being paid off, the country managed considerably to increase its live stock. Burnett has calculated that the exports of hides and wool were as follows:[3]

	1327.	1378.
Hides	8,861	44,559
Wool and wool-fells . .	1,450,485	1,473,586

No doubt it was the extreme simplicity of their economic organization, allied to their extraordinarily high spirit, that enabled the Scots to endure the harryings of the English, as they were to continue to endure them for two hundred years more.

[1] T. Thomson, in law paper in *Cranstoun v. Gibson, Session Papers, Second Division,* 1816.

Exchequer Rolls, vol. ii, p. clxv.

J. Bain, *Calendar of State Papers relating to Scotland,* vol. ii, shows how heavy was the drain of Scots money confiscated to England during the occupation of Scotland. Thus in 1304–5 the royal revenues of Scotland, or all that could be got of them, amounting to £1393 16s. 7¼d., were remitted to England. It is highly satisfactory that it cost Edward I £1794 6s. 2d. to secure them (p. 438 onwards). In the same two years the value of the possessions of loyal Scots to the south of the Forth confiscated by the English amounted to £668 4s. 2¾d., and in the following year to £206 3s. (pp. 423, 429).

H. T. Buckle, *History of Civilization in England,* p. 635, has collected many examples of the devastation worked by the English.

[2] T. Thomson, *Cranstoun v. Gibson, Session Papers, Second Division.*

[3] *Exchequer Rolls,* vol. ii, p. xci.

The simple raw products upon which they depended were easily driven away or replaced. They held their household goods—so few and so rude—very lightly. Froissart, writing with the utmost scorn, has left us a curious picture of utter poverty: lack of comfort among the rich, lack of productive crafts among the townsfolk, the lowest possible standard of living among the country-people, and yet allied to it a sturdy spirit of independence. When the French knights who had come to fight the English and who were used to the down-trodden peasantry of France, sent out their varlets to forage, the country-people resisted so fiercely that in a month a hundred Frenchmen were killed. When the Frenchmen rode through their corn instead of following the roads, the country-folk were furious, and not only demanded but secured satisfaction.[1]

In spite of liabilities and poverty, the reign of David II was one in which Scots arts developed. The luxurious king encouraged native metal-work, carving, and painting.[2] Full of the sense of her destiny, Scotland produced the first of her historians and "makars," to record her great struggles while their memories still were warm. Above all, it was one of the greatest building ages in Scotland, and those who are historically minded, as they marvel at the work of architect or craftsman in the churches and castles that survive, may look on these lovely fabrics as the vehicle of expression for the aspiring and eager spirit of Scotland in the period in which her national pride touched its very apex.

The Wars of Independence, however, had certain more lasting effects. The relationship with England was entirely changed: a period of bitter and unremitting animosity followed the struggle; and Scotland lost Berwick, her most valuable town, which changed hands repeatedly and finally became permanently English. Roxburgh, another of the Four Burghs, never recovered from the Border warfare and dwindled into nothingness. The powers of the nobles were very greatly increased owing to the sweeping confiscations and unlimited rewards that followed the war. (This important result can best be dealt with in the actual narrative of the following centuries.) The influence of war-time disorganization upon the freeing of

[1] P. Hume Brown, *Early Travellers to Scotland*, p. 10.
[2] *Exchequer Rolls*, vol. ii, p. cxiii.

the serfs has already been noticed. Finally the Royal Burghs considerably improved their status.

At a parliament held at Cambuskenneth in 1326 Robert the Bruce asked the Estates to grant him means to maintain his royal office and state owing to the dilapidation of the Crown revenues. Representatives of the royal burghs were present at this parliament for the first time, and they were also at a parliament held in the following year. And from this time onwards, they more and more definitely assumed their position as one of the component parts of the representative assembly of the nation. It was also about this time that individual burghs began to secure the very important advance of regular feus of their rents, issues of court, and petty customs, instead of short leases from the chamberlain. Edinburgh secured its feu in 1329, Dundee about 1360. Royal need for money and royal recompense for favours received or to come were probably at the root of both these important innovations.[1]

The Scots Wars of Independence ended what the people in later times regarded as the Golden Age of Scotland, and they left behind them legacies of unhappy conditions that were to cause suffering and weakness to Scotland for centuries. Superficially, they must appear to the student of economic and social history as an almost undiluted misfortune. I cannot but think, however, that this is a limited and short-sighted view It is an elementary calculation merely to compare the Scotland that had suffered certain misfortunes due to the war with a hypothetical Scotland which had suffered none of these things. It would be more accurate to compare her, mutilated but victorious, with what she might have been had she become a vassal kingdom to England. The tragic yet rather sordid history of Ireland gives at least a clue to what might have happened. England had many bitter lessons to learn before she was fit to become the mother of an empire, and, even upon the lowest, most materialistic, and purely economic grounds, Scotland may have done a better thing for herself in resisting her more powerful neighbour until at last she extorted a union upon terms of almost absolute equality. The matter, however,

[1] *A.P.S.* vol. ii, p. 115.
Cosmo Innes, *Ancient Laws and Customs of the Burghs of Scotland*, vol. i, pp. xii, xli.

is a far greater one than merely pounds, shillings, and pence or the mere amenities of life. The period that followed the Wars of Independence was a miserable one for Scotland, and yet it was in one sense the most formative in her whole history. This could hardly have been the case had she entered upon it as a beaten and servile nation.

Moreover, although the wars, by wasting the national resources and in strengthening the power of the nobles, very largely contributed to Scotland's poverty and unstable condition in the succeeding centuries, nevertheless they were only partially responsible. In spite of many efforts, it was not for over three more centuries that Scotland learnt to become a successful industrial people, and she was to exhibit a pitiful deficiency in the power of government and administration In 1318 the lords, barons, and free tenants had solemnly declared the objects for which Scotland fought : "While there exist a hundred of us, we will never submit to England. We fight—not for glory, wealth, or honour, but for that liberty which no virtuous man shall survive."[1] The miserable records of the social history of Scotland almost throughout her existence as a separate country were to show how little constructive use the Scots could make of this so dearly bought liberty.

[1] *A.P.S.* vol. ii, p. 114.

CHAPTER I

PART I. GENERALIZATIONS

THE arrangement of historical matter is so much more an art than a science that some explanation of why the next period has been carried from the end of the fourteenth century right down to 1603, the date of the Union of the Crowns, is called for. It is true that in many ways, especially in religion and politics, the sixteenth century marks a clear-cut break with the past. Yet, on the other hand, much that happened then, including the Reformation itself, is very largely the culmination of causes and effects that had long been in operation. The possession of the land is a most important factor in this chain of causation, and therefore economic history seems to make a valuable contribution in providing the connecting thread between the fragmentary and confused episodes of a complicated period.

Throughout our period Scotland was faced with the problem of how to govern herself, and was most strikingly unsuccessful in tackling it. The essential factor in the situation was the gross inefficiency of the feudal system. In the preceding centuries we have seen how the social organization of the kingdom was modelled and transformed upon feudal lines. F. Pollock, contrasting the two countries, says that feudalism was " deeply modified by circumstances peculiar to England. In Scotland the feudal system grew to its full development with little interference, if any, from legislation."[1] It is impossible to tell how the system might have worked had there been an uninterrupted line of kings of the mental calibre of the Canmore dynasty. It is common knowledge that this did not happen, and that, on the contrary, Scotland was now afflicted by a

[1] F. Pollock, *The Land Laws*, p. 2.

For transformation of the English feudal system, see W. Cunningham, *Growth of English Industry and Commerce, Modern Times*, Part I, p. 1.

combination of adverse circumstances which naturally tended to produce and enhance all disorder and poverty.

In the first place, there was inveterate hostility between England and Scotland. England had become the "auld enemy" instead of the neighbour with whom Scotland had sometimes quarrelled and often lived in friendship. France, another enemy of England, was now the chosen ally to which Scotland turned. Between 1377 and 1550, there was either tacit or open war between Scotland and England during fifty-two years, and, moreover, when there was not actual fighting, there were generally only rather precarious truces. Between 1360 and 1502 no real peace was made. On the Borders the fighting was even more frequent, and at sea there was constant warfare. This represented a very serious drag upon the country. Mediaeval campaigns were not nearly so costly as are modern ones. Nevertheless the *Exchequer Rolls* do record constant expenditure upon fortifications, the provisioning of castles, and ordinance. For instance, in 1496, when James IV agreed to help Perkin Warbeck to gain the English throne, the cost of the proposed expedition was assessed at 50,000 merks. Moreover the loss to the lieges who had to serve on military expeditions was very heavy. Perth paid £150 and Dundee £229 to be exempted from serving in a raid in 1495; and Edinburgh, in 1557, paid £12,000 to be exempted from the assault of Wark.[1] The drain of man-power, especially after the crushing defeats of Flodden, Pinkie, and Solway Moss, was very heavy; and the wastage of life in the constant savage raids must have been considerable. The destruction of property must have been incalculable: in 1555, for instance, owing to "weir, pest, and otheris cummeris," some of the burghs were impoverished and a new stent roll had to be drawn up.[2] Besides actual losses, there must have been a hampering feeling of insecurity at almost all times.

Geographically, Scotland was at a great disadvantage in the warfare with England. Edinburgh, now becoming her

[1] *Exchequer Rolls*, vol. xi, p. lix.
Accounts of the Lord High Treasurer, vol. i, p. ccxv.
J. D. Marwick, *Edinburgh Gilds and Crafts*, p. 89.

[2] Cf. Charter to Lochmaben, E. B. Rae, "Extracts from the Burgh Records of Lochmaben," *Dumfries and Galloway Scientific Society Transactions*, vol. xvii (1900–6), p. 105.

capital and her largest city, and the Lothians, her richest corn land, were within easy striking distance. Edinburgh was actually captured or besieged by the English four times during our period, and, whilst the intensive raiding of the middle of the sixteenth century was going on, there was an important shift of the economic life of the country across the Forth to the Fifeshire coast. The enmity of England encouraged the insubordination of the nobles and the separatist movement among the clans. The absolute need of fighting leaders, with their followers, undoubtedly was largely the cause of the survival of feudalism and was its main justification.

Another factor that contributed to the weakness of Scotland was the singular fatality that attended her kings. David II, Robert II, and Robert III were, all three for different reasons, most inferior kings. There followed five Jameses, Mary Queen of Scots, and James VI, all victims to a greater or less degree of the misfortunes that followed the unhappy house of Stewart. Between 1406 and 1528 there were no less than sixty years of virtual minority.

> Sum time the realme was reulit be Regentis,
> Sum time luftenantis, ledaris of the law;
> These rang sa mony inobientes
> That few or nane stude of ane other aw:
> Oppression did sa lowd hys bugle blaw
> That nane durst ride bot into feir of weir;
> Jok-apun-land that time did miss his meir.—LINDSAY.

Here, however, another factor besides mere ill-luck came into play. Robert II and Robert III were weak kings, but Robert III's very able brother, the Duke of Albany, during his regency could only manage the kingdom by encouraging the nobles, a course that merely increased the evil. James I and James III were killed by sections of their nobility. James V virtually died of a broken heart after the debacle of Solway Moss, due to the refusal of the nobles to fight under the leader whom the king had appointed. Mary of Lorraine, the queen-regent, was worn out by the troubles of her adopted country, intensified by the cataclysm of the Reformation. Mary Queen of Scots was forced to abdicate. Scotland was an almost unmanageable country, and for this the third unfortunate factor—the undue power of the nobles—was largely responsible.

PART II. THE POWER OF THE NOBLES

As we have seen, the Wars of Independence had brought about a large transference of land. Many old families were dispossessed, many new ones rose into power. Among these were the Douglases, who became a regular group: for besides the great possessions of the senior branch, the Douglases of Dalkeith owned Aberdour, much land in Fife, and the fortalice of Dalkeith; and there was also the Leswalt family.[1] Robert II, to provide for his large family, also made sweeping grants, and so the evil increased, as time went on, rather than was diminished.

A noticeable feature of these grants is not only the large area that was bestowed but the enormous powers that went with it. A grant of barony made the landowner the military leader of the men upon his estates, and their judge, with powers of life and death. A grant of regality went much further. It "took as much out of the Crown as the sovereign could give. It was, in fact, investing the grantee in the sovereignty of the territory, and it raised up those formidable jurisdictions which too often set the Crown at defiance" (Innes). With it generally went the right of levying and keeping the great customs within the burghs of regality. The Earls of Douglas had the fermes and customs of Kirkcudbright and Wigtown, their burghs of regality. Crawford, when he was made Duke of Montrose, was granted the fermes and customs of that burgh. The great spiritual lords had equal rights. The Bishops of Glasgow had the customs of Glasgow; Dunfermline Abbey received the fermes and customs of Dunfermline and Kirkcaldy; the Abbey of Arbroath received these dues from the burgh of that name, and so on.[2]

The great lords had their vassal barons, who held of them; their heralds or pursuivants; their council of retainers, very like a parliament;[3] and their armed followings. The Spanish

[1] *Exchequer Rolls*, vol. vi, p. cxi.
C. Innes, *Sketches of Early Scotch History*, p. 329.
[2] C. Innes, *Scotch Legal Antiquities*, pp. 40-49.
Article on *Crawford* in *Scots Peerage*.
D. Murray, *Early Burgh Organisation*, pp. 145-146, 404.
[3] *Exchequer Rolls*, vol. v, p. cv.

ambassador at the Court of James IV, who wrote a report upon Scotland, said that there were thirty-five great barons, some of them able to raise an individual following of five or six thousand men. As a matter of fact, the Lord of the Isles is supposed to have had 10,000 men at Harlaw. When James I went up to Inverness and executed very summary "justice" upon the Highlands chiefs who had convened to meet him there, those whom he executed and imprisoned are said to have had a total following of 70,000 to 80,000 men. Douglas at the time of his greatest power (*tempo* James II) had 30,000 to 40,000 fighting men. According to the probably more accurate estimates of the sixteenth century, Huntly and his allies had 6000 to 7000 men when he raided Linlithgow and checkmated the plan of carrying the infant Queen of Scots to England. Bothwell and Hume, on another occasion, had a thousand men each; Arran, when he was governor, had 7000 to 8000 men. Arran's household a few years later amounted to 264 persons.[1] The barons were assessed at three-tenths of the total wealth of the country, and when one remembers the political situation one can safely assume that this assessment was not unduly heavy.

All this power represented enormous local prestige. Leslie, writing of the great struggle between James III and Douglas, says: "Subiectes at this tyme war sa upprest with the Weiris . . . that few travellinge in the waye durst tell quhidder he wes the kingis man or the Erle of Douglas"; and during the dominance of another branch of the family, during the sixteenth century, Pitscottie wrote: "None at that time durst strive against a Douglas nor yet a Douglas man." An old rhyme tells of the power of Cassillis in the South-West:

Frae Wigton to the toon o' Ayr,
Port Patrick to the Cruives o' Cree,
Nae man need think to bide there
Unless he coort wi' Kennedy.

The local standing of the Gordons, Ogilvies, Lindsays, Hamiltons, and many other families was at least as great as that of the Kennedies.

[1] J. Major, *History of Greater Britain*, pp. 348, 558, 383.
Hamilton Papers, vol. i, p. 418, 424.
P. Hume Brown, *Early Travellers in Scotland*, p. 45.
Article on Hamilton in *Scots Peerage*.

Nor did these great lords each stand in isolation. By bonds of alliance and of " manrent " the lords and lairds, great and small, were bound together in groups and factions. All the great houses, Campbells, Kennedies, Douglases, etc., followed this custom. A very large collection of such deeds has been preserved among the Huntly documents. There are a hundred and seven of them, covering the period between 1444 and 1670. They show how completely the country was organized into factions. There are bands between the very great men—such as Huntly and Athol. These alliances were a most formidable menace to the Crown. Such an agreement between Douglas Crawford, and the Lord of the Isles (at that time Earl of Ross) drove the King of Scotland to desperation and brought the struggle between James II and the House of Douglas to a crisis. The Fleming, Kennedy, and Boyd compact of 1460 was almost as formidable.

Then there were " bonds of manrent," which always denoted an alliance between a superior and an inferior, between the greatest nobles and the men within their " sphere of interest." Thus the rich and powerful laird of Grant received six davochs of land from Huntly, and in return he and his heir became his " men and servandis." In this one corner of Scotland one finds the Grants, the Roses, the Mackintoshes, the Inneses, the Dunbars, etc., banded together with or against each other: one finds them banded with Huntly and with his principal rival, the Earl of Moray, in inextricable confusion. Sometimes the lesser gentry were bound to Huntly by grants of land; sometimes the promise of his protection was enough. For instance, John Leslie of Balquhain, the representative of an ancient and powerful house, in his agreement states that " forsamekle as my predecessouris, lardis of Balquhain, hes bene dependaris and servandis to the hous of Huntlye, and that the said George, now Marquess of Huntlye, is villing to except me, and use me in the place of my predicessouris," therefore he becomes the " leill, trew, efauld, and faithful man and servand to my said Lord Marquis." [1]

[1] *Miscellany of the Spalding Club*, iv, p. iii, liii.

Published collections of the family papers of the *Roses of Kilravock* and of the *Campbells of Cawdor*, both edited by C. Innes.

For Lord Boyd's *bonds of manrent*, see R. Chambers, *Domestic Annals of Scotland*, pp. 71-78. *Bonds of manrent* have sometimes been traced

A much closer union generally existed between the head of a great house and the cadet branches of his name. The rise of every great noble brought about the rise of his relations also. Whenever a family was able to establish itself for any length of time, it produced a crop of cadet branches, all usually devoted to the support of the head of the house. Even before the Wars of Independence, the great family of Comyn had planted younger sons right across Scotland, from Morayshire to Lochaber.[1] The long and bitter memory of the Gael has preserved the tale of their uprooting, after the fall of the greater Comyns, when the story of similar tragedies in the South has been forgotten. Ogilvies, Crichtons, Lindsays, Ramsays, Murrays, etc., all developed into all but clans. The great name of Douglas produced, one after another, three branches so formidable that, with the support of their kinsfolk, they overshadowed the power of the Throne. The house of Huntly, whose history is unusually well documented, and which has already been referred to, is an outstanding example. One sees how Aberdeenshire and Banffshire were dotted over with offshoot branches, occasionally given heritable possession but more often established by wadsets upon the family estates. When evil days fell upon the house of Huntly, after the rebellion against Queen Mary which ended in the defeat at Corrichie, and during the troubles with James VI which involved the battle of Glenlivet, when other allies fell away, the men of the name of Gordon were staunchly loyal to their house, even against their sovereign, and in many cases they suffered heavily for it. The story of the loyalty of the Homes of Wedderburn to the head of their house has been recorded. David Home of Wedderburn died in 1574 and his son wrote a panegyric upon him: "Not the least of his virtues" was said to be his love of the house of Home. Lord Home happened to be prejudiced against him,

to a servile origin. In the *Black Book of Taymouth*, p. 177, there are very humble examples, but in the fifteenth and sixteenth centuries such bonds were largely entered into by the gentry. For examples from the South-West, see Sir Herbert Maxwell, *Galloway and Dumfries*, p. 149.

In 1550 an ineffective act of the Scots Parliament was passed against bands and leagues.—*A.P.S.* vol. iii, p. 49.

[1] Such local traditions come from Strathspey, Moy, Nairn, Lochaber, and Darnaway.

but "he bore it patiently and never failed giving all due honour." Finally, when Lord Home was imprisoned by the Regent Morton, Wedderburn went to see him and obtained his release, and his staunch friendship won the heart of his chief. In the next generation, George Home of Wedderburn went to plead with Morton for the succeeding Lord Home, who had been forfeited. The regent pointed out that Wedderburn had received no friendship from Lord Home and was his next heir. But George Home instantly replied that Home was the head of his house, and that he was only doing what he was bound to do; that "if his chief should turn him out of the front door he would only come back through the back door." [1]

Part III. The Feudal Functions of the Nobles —Military Service

Such was the power of the great nobles. Moreover, they did not exist merely as private individuals, for they had important functions to perform, and their existence was woven into the very fabric of the feudal state. The most important duty involved by feudal tenure was military service. The recurrent wars with England, as well as the constant domestic troubles, made it absolutely essential that the kingdom should have adequate means of defence. For this it was dependent upon the man-power of the nation, who were liable to give military service between the ages of sixteen and sixty. The earlier kings employed no mercenaries at all, and when Mary of Lorraine proposed to introduce a paid army the outcry was so great that the project had to be abandoned.[2]

[1] The Indices of the *Exchequer Rolls*, the *Register of the Great Seal*, the *Register of the Privy Council* give some idea of the number of landholders of these names; see also that of Sir James Ramsay, *Bamff Charters*. For early examples of wadsets, see *ibid.* pp. 16 and 158.

R. Chambers, *Domestic Annals of Scotland*, vol. i, pp. 99, 120.

(A wadset, it should be noted, was an old Scots form of mortgage. In return for the loan of a sum of money the wadsetter was given the occupation and usufruct of a piece of land until the sum originally borrowed was repaid. It was a very common method of raising money among the landed gentry, and wadsets were often given to younger sons. In family arrangements the wadset would probably often represent the younger son's portion.)

[2] *Exchequer Rolls*, vol. xiii, p. clxxxviii.

Major describes the working of the system upon the Borders. When Scotland was invaded, "a working day of twelve hours would scarcely pass before her people were in conflict with the enemy. For the nearest chief gathers the neighbouring folk together, and at the first word of the presence of the foe, each man before mid-day is in arms, for he keeps his weapons about him, mounts his horse, makes for the enemy's position, and, whether in order of battle or not in order of battle, rushes on the foe." [1]

Such methods of defence, though spirited, would not commend themselves to a modern G.H.Q. staff. As a matter of fact, a certain degree of organization did exist, and it was dependent upon the feudal system. By their charters most of the freeholders were not only obliged to supply a certain quota of well-armed men but were responsible for bringing all the man-power upon their estates into the field. Thus, in a charter of 1509, the laird of Grant was bound to supply "a lance with its supports, viz. three sufficient horsemen, for each £10 of land, in time of war beyond the kingdom, along with all fencible persons." [2] A memorandum was drawn up by the English in 1547 of the forces of those lairds of Dumfriesshire who had sworn allegiance to them, and it shows how complete was the feudal organization of the country. Exclusive of the Border clans, it was estimated that thirty-nine gentlemen would be able to put 5000 men into the field, the individual followings varying from 1000 men to 27. Some of the best-known names of the district, to their honour, are absent from the list.[3] The sub-vassals of the greater feudatories of the Crown were responsible, in the same way, for local levies, and it was the custom to entrust the raising of the national army from wide districts to the great magnates and to appoint them as leaders. The connection between landholding and military service was the fundamental theory upon which the military organization of the nation was based.

[1] J. Major, *History of Greater Britain*, p. 29.

[2] *Exchequer Rolls*, vol. xiii, p. clxxxviii. The accounts of the Lord High Treasurer abound in allusions to missives sent to the Crown vassals summoning them to attend with their followings, cf. vol. x, pp. 368, 374, 380.

[3] Sir Herbert Maxwell, *Dumfries and Galloway*, p. 178.

The feudal form of military organization was not an efficient one. If the Crown were weak or unpopular, it largely failed to make the lieges perform their service, although afterwards they were often called to book and were obliged to pay fines. Moreover, too much depended upon the personal dispositions, abilities, and circumstances of the great landholders who were its mainstay. The report of an English spy, during the critical days of Mary's minority, is an excellent illustration: "Item, the Erll of Huntly's cuntry, his friends and tenants . . . are straightly commaunded to repair hither"—(i.e. to the siege of Haddington)—"to the warres. But . . . it is doubtful whether they come or not, bycause the Erll him self is prysoner." (He was captured by the English at Pinkie.)[1]

It was inevitable that where generalship was determined by hereditary rank some of the leaders should be indifferent. The utter incompetency of Hamilton at the Battle of Pinkie is one example. A more glaring one occurred in 1513, when the command of Scotland's promising navy was assumed not by Wood, her experienced and successful naval captain, but by the Lords Arran, Fleming, and Ross, and the fleet was first uselessly employed and then lost.[2]

When they were successful, feudal leaders rather tended to acquire more land in reward for their services than to earn their right to what they already possessed. The worst slur, however, upon the nobles of Scotland was the constant disloyalty that occurred, and which was rendered almost inevitable when sovereign power was so largely controlled by factions. From the days of Robert III onwards, there was scarcely a struggle in which one disgruntled Scots lord or more was not actively pro-English. This culminated in the shameful pact by which no less than seven Scots lords, who had been captured at Solway Moss, in return for their freedom, bound themselves to help Henry VIII in every way, open and secret, that lay in their power.[3]

Nevertheless, during the many royal minorities, Scotland was absolutely dependent upon the great feudatories to defend her against the "auld enemy" and to subdue the rebellions that

[1] *Hamilton Papers*, vol. ii, p. 618 (1548).
[2] *Exchequer Rolls*, vol. xiii, p. clxxxv.
[3] Hill Burton, *History of Scotland*, vol. iii, p. 190.

broke out from time to time, especially in the North. It was, for instance, by his services in breaking the power of Donald, Lord of the Isles, at the Battle of Harlaw, that the Stewart Earl of Mar, as thoroughgoing a rascal as ever disgraced his order, justified the favour that the Regent Albany had shown him. Moreover, when the nobles had a king really fit to lead them, they were magnificently loyal. Lindsay wrote, with truth, of the men who fought and died in a ring of steel about James IV at Flodden, "I never heard in tragede nor storie, at ane journaye so many nobles slain for the defence and lufe of their soverane." [1]

PART IV. THE FEUDAL FUNCTIONS OF THE NOBLES —ADMINISTRATIVE DUTIES

In a feudal state of society the great landowners naturally tended to become not only the military leaders but the principal administrative officers under the Crown. Their own feudal levies were employed to maintain law and order, and their powers were enormously increased. In moments of stress or of royal weakness, special commissions were granted, such as the sweeping "lieutenandry of the North" granted to Huntly in 1543.[2] His jurisdiction extended from the Mearns on the East Coast to the Western seaboard and included the whole of the North of Scotland, with the adjacent islands. Within these bounds he was entrusted with the government and defence of the lieges. He could raise armies and compel the lieges to join them. He was empowered to bear the royal banner and to make such statutes and ordinances, for the administration of justice and preservation of peace, as he thought necessary. He might invade the territories of those who rebelled against him, with fire and sword; imprison or execute them, seize their castles, and appoint constables for them; or, on the contrary, he might treat with them and receive them back into obedience. He held two royal castles and had in his own possession five more, besides many strong places owned by his friends and supporters.

During the sixteenth century the house of Argyle received about twenty-five commissions of this kind, of very varying

[1] P. Hume Brown, *History of Scotland*, vol. i, p. 336.
Twelve earls, 1 archbishop, 1 bishop, 2 abbots were killed at Flodden.

[2] *Miscellany of the Spalding Club*, vol. iv, p. lvi.

extent, most of them against the Highland clans, but others in connection with the Lothians, Merse, Teviotdale and Lauderdale, and with Paisley.[1]

The Wardenships of the East, Middle, and Western Marches were offices of a similar type. They were quite commonly given to some of the great Northern lords—Ross, Moray, Huntly, Argyle—partly perhaps because of their feudal power, perhaps partly in order to keep these powerful subjects away from their own great territories at critical times.

The activities of the great feudatories were nominally worked into the national organization for that administration of justice which the best of the Scots kings were carefully building up. In many instances they were appointed hereditary sheriffs [2] of the districts in which they held large possessions. In those cases where they were granted baronies and regalities the administration of the ordinary law was entrusted to them. In an economic history, however, it is important to remember that their position was due to their possession of land and the power that they derived from this possession. As a generalization, it might be said that they were not powerful because they were entrusted with the administration of the law, but that they were entrusted with the administration of the law because they were so powerful. It is startling to find how largely order was maintained not by the ordinary orderly administration of the law but by special commissions granted to landed magnates to be enforced by the sheer force of their feudal power. Between 1545 and 1550, 133 of these commissions were granted. About 1568–1579 they were even commoner.[3]

The most terrible forms of such private commissions were "letters of fire and sword." They emphasize the difference that exists between the ideas of common justice of sixteenth-century Scotland and of to-day. The following is only one example, not particularly glaring, among many. The Mackintoshes and certain other branches of Clan Chattan inhabited one of the more settled parts of the Highlands, for their lands extended almost to the southern shores of the Moray Firth, and

[1] *Historical Manuscripts Commission—Appendices to the Fourth Report*, p. 487 onwards. (A. and P. vol. xxxv, 1873.)

[2] W. C. Dickinson, *The Sheriff Court Book of Fife*, p. xxxv.

[3] *Exchequer Rolls*, vol. xviii; see Appendix; xx, p. lxiv.

the whole district had been to a considerable extent " planted " and feudalized in the period previous to the Wars of Independence. During the first half of the sixteenth century they were incessantly at feud with a neighbouring family of Ogilvies and with the Earl of Moray, and, in 1528, a proclamation was issued in the name of the Crown to the sheriffs of the six Northern sheriffdoms, to six neighbouring nobles, to two lairds and heads of clans, and to " all the freeholders, barons, captains of clans, and gentlemen " within the sheriffdoms of the North, commanding them " to pass at anys upon the Clanquhattan and invaid thame to thair uter destructioun be slauchter, byrning, drowning and uther wayis, and leif na creatur lewand of that clann except priestis, wemen and bairns." The women and bairns were to be exported to " Zealand." The execution of this terrible order was mainly undertaken by Moray, one of the most aggrieved parties, but although he succeeded in apprehending and executing a considerable number of its leading men, Clan Chattan was very far from being exterminated.[1]

It was of the very essence of feudalism that the superior of the land should be held responsible for the conduct of his vassals, and they, in their turn, for their lesser dependants. A sixteenth-century statute that every baron and freeholder must answer at justice ayres for his own men upon his own land, sums up this aspect of feudalism.[2] It is very significant to find that this theory, so far from dying out during the period now under review, was developed and systematized in some of the latest legislation of the sixteenth century. In the Privy Council minutes of the last quarter of the century there is frequent reference to a " general band," by which the landholding gentry of the country bound themselves to maintain good rule within their possessions. This band seems to have been in standing use and a copy has survived among the minutes for 1590. In this document " the earls, lords, barons, landed gentry and others " bound themselves " in all time coming " to " keep and cause to be kept good rule within our lands, lordships, tacks,

[1] A. M. Mackintosh, *Mackintoshes and Clan Chattan*, p. 99. The Earl of Moray was the illegitimate son of James IV. The touching story of the loyalty of the clan to its captain and of Moray's execution is most vividly told in Sir Robert Gordon's *History of Sutherland*, p. 100.

[2] *A.P.S.* vol. ii, p. 332.

steadings and balliaries." They undertook to deliver any criminal dwelling upon their lands up to justice ayres or to special diets of justice, and, if they failed to do this, to make themselves responsible for such crimes as he might have committed, according to a scale of fines appended to the band. Should the malefactor escape, they bound themselves to eject his family from his tack and to prevent him from ever returning to their land. They also bound themselves to " ryse tegidder with oure kin, friendis, tennentis, servandis and adherentis, and all that will do for us," to bring any persons who were rebels at the horn, or conspirators against the king, to justice, or to slay them, or to eject them from their lands.[1]

The general band was no dead letter. Landlords all over Scotland were constantly made to carry out the provisions, and were often punished for not doing so. Excuses, such as that the sheriff and not the landlord was responsible for the arrest of rebels, or that the provisions were only supposed to apply to the Highlands and Borders, were disallowed.[2] The responsibility of the chiefs and captains of clans in the Highlands and on the Borders, as well as that of landlords, was insisted upon in the systematic attempts that James VI and his advisers made to pacify these unruly districts, and lists of the chiefs and landholders were compiled and used ; and there is evidence that James was planning to make the general band and the responsibility of the landlords more effective in the Lowlands also. In 1590 a list had been made of all the landowners of twenty-two sheriffdoms, for the use of the Privy Council, although it was never completed for the whole of Scotland. (It is rather interesting to find that although it omits the sheriffdoms of Forfar, Kincardineshire, Aberdeenshire, Banffshire, Elginshire, Forres, Nairnshire, Inverness-shire, Ross-shire and Cromarty, Caithness and Sutherland, it contains 950 names.) [3]

The rights bestowed by grants of barony or regality were, moreover, very widely administrative as well as judicial. Without some sort of social machinery it would have been impossible

[1] *Register, Privy Council*, vol. iv, p. 787.

[2] *Ibid.* From vol. iii to vol. vi the *Register* is full of allusions to the *general band.* See especially, vol. iii, pp. 79, 262, 341, 319, 565 ; vol. iv, pp. 151-152 ; vol. v, pp. 279, 436 ; vol. vi, p. 221.

[3] *Ibid.* vol. iv, pp. lvi, 783-787.

for the rural districts to have been "run," for the terms of the vague and meagre acts of parliament to have been enforced, for the endless complications due to a communal system of agriculture to have been adjusted. A good many records of baron courts have survived to us from the seventeenth century, and they show that only a fraction of the time of the court was taken up with the crimes and peccadilloes of the country-folk. It is true that much of their energy is devoted to the extraction of the laird's rents, service dues, and other perquisites, but they are also much concerned with the settlement of dispute between tenants, the adjustment of the relations between the miller and the agricultural tenants, the appointment of birly men to adjudicate in dispute in the communal working of the joint farms, the preservation of wood, and the due enforcement of acts of parliament.[1] The fragmentary notices of the working of baron courts in the fifteenth and sixteenth centuries show that they then followed the same lines. Four minutes of the Baron Court of Longforgan, held at the moot-hill in the middle of the fourteenth century, have been preserved. In 1462 we find the Abbot of Cambuskenneth and his "forespeaker" appearing at the Baron Court of Tulchadum as plaintiff in a lawsuit about the ownership of certain lands. In the Baron Court Records of Glenurchy (preserved in the *Black Book of Taymouth*) we find important grazing regulations and many formal ordinances, often declared to be passed "with the consent and advice of the whole commons and tenants." The Cupar barony court prosecuted tenants for destroying wood, dealt with disputes over the joint tenants' shares in the holdings, and the remissness of one of the more considerable tenants; made most important regulations regarding the cultivation of the land, and indulged in even more paternal regulations. These matters, however, are more conveniently dealt with under agriculture and estate management.[2] That such a court was of real benefit to the

[1] Seventeenth-century records of Baron Court Books that are easily available are those of Stichil and Urie, both printed by the Scottish History Society.

[2] *Third Report, Commission on Ancient Manuscripts*, Appendix, p. 410.
Chartulary of Cambuskenneth (Grampian Club), p. 121.
Duke of Argyle, *Scotland as it was and is*, pp. 192, 202.
C. Rogers, *Social Life in Scotland*, vol. i, p. 196, 197, 198, 201.
Register of Cupar Abbey, p. 130, 137.

folk upon an estate can be seen from the formal complaint of the tenantry of Cupar Abbey, in 1540, when the Church's power was weakening, that they were being much troubled by being summoned before outside courts in matters that might easily and with less expense be dealt with by the bailiff court of the Abbey.[1]

On the royal estates the officials in charge, the chamberlain and his subordinates, etc., were entrusted with similar administrative work.[2]

PART V. THE INEFFICIENCY OF FEUDALISM AS AN ADMINISTRATIVE SYSTEM

The descriptions of the social life of Scotland during the fifteenth and the sixteenth centuries all show how completely ineffectual was the feudal system in maintaining an orderly state of society. The utter lawlessness of the kingdom, moreover, is not only the most convincing proof of the harmfulness of this system ; it is also a most important fact to bear in mind, when one attempts to study the institutions of Scotland. The student is invariably faced not merely with the problem of discovering what laws were passed or what forms the constitutions of various bodies took, but with the far more elusive one of deciding how far these laws were observed and to what extent such constitutions were liable to be overridden or ignored. The poverty of the country, which is the outstanding economic fact of the period now under review, must have been enormously aggravated and enhanced by the extraordinary social conditions of the times. It also had its effects upon the national revenue.[3]

All through our period general complaints of lawlessness are rife, and the accounts of grisly outrages, that shocked even

[1] *Chartulary of Cupar Abbey* (Grampian Club), p. 299.

[2] See almost every volume of the *Exchequer Rolls* from the middle of the fifteenth century for the accounts of these officials. Cf. vol. vii, pp. 463-464. For a commission of balliary, see vol. xvii, p. 763 (1538–9) Among the Mackintosh muniments there is a copy of the acts and statutes to be observed by the Crown tenants of Petty in 1563. Mackintosh was at that time acting as chamberlain for these lands.

[3] *Exchequer Rolls*, vol. xxi, p. lviii.

the hardened conscience of the time, abound. Parliament at the end of the fourteenth century was much taken up with the "grete and horrible destruccions, heryscheppis, brynyngs and slachters that ar sa commonly done throch all the kynrike." Next it was "deliveryt yt the mysgouernance of the Realme and the defaut of kepynge of the common law sulde be imput to the kynge and his officers." The king was urged to accuse his officers of the default of their duty before the council. A regent was appointed. The author of a little chronicle preserved in the chartulary of Moray, writing of these times, says: "In those days there was no law in Scotland; but the great man oppressed the poor man, and the whole kingdom was one den of thieves. Slaughters, robberies, fire-raisings and other crimes went unpunished, and justice was sent into banishment, beyond the kingdom's bounds."[1]

Throughout the fifteenth century parliament continued to make laws about the quieting of the kingdom, but except when a strong king was in power, they were quite ineffective. Bower, the contemporary of James II, was not merely writing "at large" in the following passage: "Confounded as we are with daily tyranny, oppressed with rapine, spoil, and tribulation. . . . The groans of the humble and the miseries of the poor, whom I myself who write this, have seen this very day in my own neighbourhood—stripped of their garments and inhumanely despoiled of their domestic utensils, constrain one to exclaim with him who says, 'I have seen the injuries which are done, the tears of the innocent, the helpless and the destitute, who cannot resist violence and have none to comfort them.' I have praised the dead more than the living, and happier than both have I esteemed the unborn, the sole strangers to the evils of this world." Henryson, the poet, is another contemporary who tells, again and again, of the appalling lawlessness of the times.[2]

In the sixteenth century things were probably worse than ever. Sir David Lindsay of the Mount, the unknown author of the *Complaynt of Scotlande*, Maitland of Lethington, and

[1] *A.P.S.* vol. ii, pp. 208, 210 (1398).
Chartulary of Moray, p. xxvi.
[2] *A.P.S.* vol. ii, pp. 5, 34, 51, 247.
Bower, *Scotichronicon*, vol. ii, p. 473.

many more of the " Makars " complain of the constant unrest and the hard lot of him whose hands could not keep his head. The spokesman of the people in the *Complaynt* roundly declares that he is left desolate without supply or defence among the hands of wrongous oppressors which profess themselves to be his brothers and defenders—" for i indure mair persecutions be them nor be the cruel veyr of ingland, for my takkis, steyding, and teyndis ar nocht alanarly tane fra me or ellis hychtit til ane onrasonabil price, bot as veil i am maid ane slaue of my body to ryn and rashe in arrage and carriage." In sober records of officialdom there is an abundance of evidence of the wildness of the times, in the numerous actions for the restoration of spuilzie and among the acts of the Lords of the Council. Bishop Leslie's comments on sixteenth-century Scotland, that " the realm " was " in sik deformitie, that justice appeirit rugitt vp be the rutes " was no exaggeration.[1]

Perhaps it takes a little imagination to realize how entirely normal to the whole of Scotland this state of affairs had become. The Highlands are commonly recognized not only as a home of lost causes but of utter insubordination. One is perhaps not surprised to find the king writing in 1527 that Macleod " duellis in ye Hieland where nane of ye officeris of ye law dar pas for fear of yair lyvis," or that the rights of mine and thine were chronically disregarded upon the Borders :

Off Liddisdail the common theifis
Sa peartlie steilis now and reifis,
  That nane may keip
Hors, nolt, nor schiep,
  Nor zit dar sleip
For thar mischeifis.

It is more important to remember that constant fighting and high-handed actions were everyday affairs in the Lowlands—churchmen fought hand-to-hand in Glasgow Cathedral; in the streets of Edinburgh there were numerous tuilzies and brawls.

[1] *The Complaynt of Scotlande* (1549) (Early English Text Society, p. 125).
J. Warrack, *Domestic Life in Scotland in the Sixteenth Century*, p. 3.
Bishop Leslie, *History of Scotland*, vol. ii, p. 207.

The best-known of them is the famous fight to Clear the Causeway of 1520, between the Hamiltons and the Douglases; but fatal brawls were quite common affairs in the capital between the gentry. In 1525 three hundred gentlemen had to obtain remissions for taking part in such an affray.[1] The records of Scotland teem with complaints of the murders and slaughters " universallie committit ower all partis of this realme." Sometimes rather surprising people indulged in open animosities. In a quarrel between the bailies of Perth and Bruce of Clackmannan, which arose because the former had arrested some of the latter's servants for not paying customs, the laird retaliated, whereupon the bailies destroyed his standing corn. The laird then seized and carried off the bailies, and the matter was brought before the Privy Council. That body decided that both parties had been in the wrong and imprisoned everybody. Lawless acts did not merely consist of sudden quarrels or of raids upon cattle or other movable goods. The Privy Council Records of the end of the sixteenth century are noteworthy for the number of cases in which land was forcibly seized and held for years, or where a more powerful neighbour made it impossible for anyone who was obnoxious to him to live upon his holdings at all. About 1578, one of the bailies of Edinburgh complained that he had bought land in the Lothians and that the laird of Dalhousie had interfered again and again with the servants he had sent to cultivate it. Dalhousie had killed three of them and had destroyed most of his work-beasts, so that at last he had given up cultivating it. Sometimes even the Crown tenants dared not till their lands, on account of the enmity of some neighbouring laird. The stories of the sufferings of helpless working folk and lone women make piteous reading; but one of the turbulent lairds, Gordon of Avochy, was a bit of a wag in the lengths to which he would go. Attended by a motley crew, including the miller and the cobbler, he kept the surrounding country-folk in terror for over twenty years, murdering, stealing, forcing them to perform unpaid services for him, and, as the height of insolence, tearing the wooden fittings out

[1] A. Bellesheim, *History of the Catholic Church of Scotland*, vol. i, p. 171. Sir Herbert Maxwell, *Dumfries and Galloway*, p. 167.

R. Chambers' *Domestic Annals of Scotland* abounds with lurid anecdotes of lawless doings, especially in the capital.

of their houses and forcing them to carry these themselves to his mansion-house.[1]

Two features of these lawless deeds require to be specially stressed. The misdeeds of lesser folk are buried in oblivion. One cannot tell how far they were criminals upon their own account, besides following law-breakers of a higher rank. Most of the teeming lists of the crimes that were sufficiently important to be recorded refer to men of some position. Sir Herbert Maxwell, in *Dumfries and Galloway*, gives a list of the cases tried before the justice ayres held in Kirkcudbright and Wigtown between 1507 and 1513. Lesser folk were dealt with by the sheriffs' and barons' courts and the cases nearly all concerned country gentlemen and their near relations. In a good many instances more than one crime was preferred against the same individual, but the charges include eight cases of theft and felony—often for very small amounts—and fourteen for oppression and violent actions against the lieges. One charge was for "taking and tearing the king's letters."[2] These are instances in which the accused were so unfortunate as to have been captured and brought to book. There were many individuals like the laird of Johnstone, who, with his sons, remained at the horn "for very wilfulness . . . ryden plainly in the country with jacks and spears, boastan the true men how he maintained Gebbie Johnstone at Powden, fugitive frae the laws for stealing and fire-raising." The Privy Council, who considered the case, merely ordered the laird to obey them in future and to make his peace.[3]

A second noteworthy feature about the lawlessness of the times is the way in which the central authority often accepted or condoned entirely illegal acts. Among many examples the following is very glaring. In 1454, John Carruthers, who had been appointed keeper of Lochmaben Castle by royal warrant, was ejected by the laird of Johnstone, who in a private quarrel took forcible possession of the royal castle. The king allowed him to retain it and even paid him the

[1] See especially *Register, Privy Council*, vol. iii, pp. lxxvii, 109; vol. iv, p. 660; vol. v, pp. 6-8 (1592–3); vol. vi, pp. 283, 319, 501 (1601–2).
Exchequer Rolls, vol. xi, p. xliv, xlvii.

[2] Sir Herbert Maxwell, *Dumfries and Galloway*, p. 155.

[3] *Register, Privy Council*, vol. i, p. xxiii.

fee due as its keeper. A very similar case occurred at Urquhart Castle.[1]

The lawlessness of the country is plainly shown by the type of law cases. During the sixteenth century "no form of action was so much in use as that of spuilzie, whereby redress was sought for violent or wrongful taking away of movable property," and the form of the law itself was even affected. Assythments and "letters of slains," which were a device to prevent violent reprisals for wrongs already committed, were a "familiar part of Scots law." The taking of "lawburrows" or surety to prevent feuds and trouble was a very common precaution. The Records of the Privy Council sometimes consist of page after page consecutively taken up with the passing of acts of caution. As Hill Burton sagely points out, the prevalence of the arrangement of such pacts of guarantee and suretyship for the preservation of peace conveys "the impression of a turbulent people, likely to suffer from each other's violent propensities." [2]

Part VI. Reasons for the Inefficiency of Feudalism

It must be remembered that feudalism, as a system, was to blame for the lawless state of the country and not the characters or lack of abilities of the actual individuals who were in power. The lords and the Government were by no means regardless of the duty that the hereditary administrators of justice owed the lieges. An act of parliament of 1496 ordered all barons and freeholders to send their sons to the schools, so that they might learn Latin and law. Although complaints of the slowness and venality of Scots justice abounded, the examination of the working of an individual institution, such as the sheriff court of Fife (and the hereditary sheriffs were invariably of the greater landlords), shows that on the whole, although the methods were clumsy, justice was impartially administered, and that the

[1] *Exchequer Rolls*, vol. v, p. cviii.

[2] *Acts of the Lords of the Council in Secret Causes*, vol. i, Preface by G. Neilson, pp. lxix, lxx.

Register of the Privy Council, vol. ii, Preface by J. Hill Burton, p. xxiii; vol. vi (1599–1604), pp. 609-660.

local gentry showed commendable public spirit in serving upon juries.[1]

Nevertheless, the feudal system was intrinsically an unsuitable organization to serve for the administration of justice. The local great lord was sometimes the aggrieved party, or the aggrieved party might very often be one of his vassals, in which case all the lesser loyalties of the age would incline him to support his own follower. If the offender were one of his men the case was even worse, and if the great man himself were in the wrong it was almost hopeless. Even where he justified his appointment by his efficiency—as Huntly and Argyle, acting as they did as buffers between the wilder Highlands and the Lowlands, may be said to have done—it was almost inevitable that he should add to his power both by the grants of land that were required to keep him active and by the opportunities for self-aggrandisement that his great offices gave him.[2] Moreover, when malefactors were sufficiently powerful to be beyond the ordinary arm of the law, it was only by force of arms that they could be brought under control. It was impossible, in such instances, to apportion the punishment according to principles of abstract justice. The following is only an illustration of what was liable to happen.

In 1491, Sir Alexander of Lochalsh, the nephew of the Lord of the Isles, helped by sections of Clan Mackintosh and of the Roses, ravaged the Black Isle (to the north of the Moray Firth) and was finally beaten back by the Mackenzies. The Mackenzies proceeded to raid the Crown lands of Ardmannoch, held for Huntly by the Roses of Kilravock and also those of Monro of Foulis. Huntly, the lieutenant of the North, was the kinsman of the Roses, and he gave commission to the chief of Mackintosh, whose son had been among the original insurgents, Grant of Freuchie, Kilravock, and others, with their followers to the number of two thousand, to proceed against the Mackenzies "for divers other herships, slaughters, and spulzies committed on the King's poor lieges and tenants in the lordship of Ardmannoch." Rose of Kilravock and the Mackintoshes

[1] *A.P.S.* vol. ii, p. 238.

W. C. Dickinson, *Sheriff Court Book of Fife*, pp. ciii, civ, cv, 390.

[2] Cf. Huntly and Argyle. The articles on these titles in the *Scots Peerage* give a summary of the lands they acquired.

carried out this commission, but unfortunately they exceeded it and also ravaged the lands of Urquhart, sheriff of Cromarty, which had already suffered at the hands of Alexander of Lochalsh. The sheriff appealed to the law and they were sentenced to pay him 800 merks in compensation. Quite characteristically, the matter was adjusted by the marriage of Rose's son and Urquhart's daughter, the lady bringing her husband a remission for these damages instead of a dowry.[1]

Feudalism not only failed to perform the duties for which the whole system was built up, but, from its very nature, it almost inevitably created and caused much of the lawlessness and troublousness of the times. The armed power of the great lords overshadowed that of the officers of the Crown. Acts were constantly passed ordering that no one should come to court with a multitude of folk nor with armies, or limiting the retinues that were to be brought to courts of justice, "becaus there hes bene grete Inconvenietis and truble wrocht in the cuntre be grete personnis throw convocatioun of the Kingis lieges at courtis and gadderingis."[2] In 1474, for instance, the king wrote to the Earl of Buchan and Lord Oliphant ordering them to stay their master for the court of Forfar. They disobeyed and bloodshed followed.[3] Such were not mere incidents. The undue power of the nobles prevented the increase of centralized authority, such as took place in England, especially during the Tudor period; it was, therefore, a fundamental factor in the development, or rather the lack of development, of Scotland.

Besides preventing the growth of the powers of the Crown, feudalism produced a constant state of petty civil war in Scotland. The right to carry on private quarrels was one which feudal nobles assumed in all countries where they were strong enough to do so. John Major, writing of contemporary Scotland of the sixteenth century, says: "If two nobles of equal

[1] C. Innes, *Roses of Kilravock*, p. 170.
A. M. Mackintosh, *Mackintoshes and Clan Chattan*, p. 90.
Macfarlane's Genealogical Collections (Scottish History Society), vol. ii, p. 379.

[2] *A.P.S.* vol. ii, p. 332.
W. C. Dickinson, *The Sheriff Court Book of Fife*, p. xxix.

[3] James Mackintosh, *The History of Civilization in Scotland*, vol. i, p. 353.

rank happen to be very near neighbours, quarrels and even shedding of blood are a common thing between them; and their very retainers cannot meet without strife."[1] Or as the modern historian points out, feuds in a state of feudal society were "as natural as trade competition at the present day."[2] The history of Scotland teems with instances of fights between great magnates. In 1478 there were serious feuds going on between the Earl of Buchan and the Earl of Erroll, the Master of Crawford and Lord Glamis, Lord Caerlaverock and the laird of Drumlanrig. There was also a fight going on that involved Caithness, Ross, and Sutherland; and there were, in addition, minor troubles in other parts of the country. During the sixteenth century these open feuds among the nobility continued. In 1569, in a quarrel between Lords Oliphant and Caithness, there was a pitched battle round the market cross of Wick, and, about the same time, the Earl of Mar and Lord Oliphant were fighting together in Clackmannanshire.[3]

In a state of feudal society grown out of hand, government by faction was inevitable. Leslie's account of the dissensions during the time when the rivalry between Margaret Tudor and Angus was at its height might have been written about any one of the seven minorities of the period. "The Realm was now in sik distress, al drew to factiounes and pairties, sum to defend the Quene, sum the nobilitie, al studiet to thair particular proffet, outher occupieng his nychtbours landis with force, or his nychtbouris gudes wrangouslie, how euer he could."[4]

It was to the credit of James VI that he should have made determined efforts to stamp out the feuds among his nobles. In 1595 he resolved to end the disorders that were "shaking loose the commonweal," and he summoned the principals of all the feuds that were at the moment going on to appear before him, with strictly limited retinues. No less than thirty-three nobles and lairds were thus called upon to appear. Three years later the Privy Council was convened "for removing of the present feedis that aboundis within this realm," and to

[1] J. Major, *History of Greater Britain* (Scottish History Society), p. 48.

[2] P. Hume Brown, "Scottish Nobility and their part in the National History," *Scottish Hist. Review*, vol. iii, p. 161.

[3] *Register, Privy Council*, vol. ii, pp. 37, 40, 660.

[4] Bishop Leslie, *History of Scotland*, vol. ii, p. 155.

devise means by which the "inveterat and dampnable custume of the saidis heynous crymes be ruitted out and altogether supprest." Feuds were methodically classified into three categories and detailed regulations were made for settling them, and during the rest of his reign James continued to make and enforce such orders.[1] Fate was upon his side, and with the Union of the Crowns his hands were greatly strengthened.

Until the very end of the sixteenth century, therefore, Scotland was in a constant state of civil war on account of these feuds; and in order to hold his own in such a state of society, it was absolutely necessary for a noble to increase his following as much as he could. It was essential that in order to secure followers he should, on his side, bestow protection. This double reciprocal obligation was strongly recognized. As Professor Hume Brown says: "The root of all the mischief was that a feudal lord was responsible for the life and goods of every dweller on his domain. An unavenged injury to any person or thing, however indirectly connected with him, was at once a personal insult and a derogation from his authority. If he could not defend those who looked to him for protection, the very reason for his existence was at an end." [2] The defence of their vassals and dependents was a constant cause of the outbreak of quarrel between one great noble and another. The opportunities were endless, for, as we have seen, not only were the magnates' possessions very great but, by means of bonds of manrent, their influence spread in ramifications over very wide districts. In the fifteenth century such a cause of quarrel precipitated a war with England. In revenge for the murder of one of his serving-men, the Earl of March "gathered his lieges together," attacked Roxburgh—then in the hands of the English—and slew every male person in the burgh. The English retaliated, and war broke out.[3]

[1] *Register, Privy Council*, vol. vi, pp. 248-249, 462, 585.

[2] P. Hume Brown, "Scottish Nobility and their part in the National History," *Scottish Hist. Review*, vol. iii, p. 161.

R. Chambers, *Domestic Annals of Scotland*, p. 311, gives an example.

[3] J. Major, *History of Greater Britain* (Scottish History Society), p. 310.

A better-known and very stirring exploit was the rescue of Kinmont Willie from Carlisle Castle by his overlord, the laird of Buccleuch, in 1596. —R. Chambers, *Domestic Annals of Scotland*, p. 269.

The evils of a constant state of civil war are obvious. Not only was the development of the country generally retarded, but the tenants of those lords who got the worst of any of the constant broils suffered severely. The lot of men living upon the land of a freeholder who was not strong enough to defend them must have been a very hard one. It was, for instance, the high-handed action of Douglas against Colville of Ochiltree and his tenants that provoked the first clash with James II. The many cases in which recompense for spuilzie is granted narrate the great booty swept off from the tenants of the complaining lord or laird. The double spuilzie of Urquhart, already described, is only one example of quite a number that directly or indirectly concerned even that one district. In the *Register of the Privy Council* of the sixteenth century there are many cases in which the wrongs of the poor tenants, suffering through the inability of their lord to defend them, are narrated. *The Diurnal of Occurrents* describes a raid that took place in 1570 upon the lands of the Hamiltons by members of the opposing factions. Four hundred cattle, 600 sheep and other animals were carried off from the unfortunate tenants. Their lamentations were great enough to " make ane stane-hearted man to greet and bewail. But cry what they wald cry, and lament as they pleasit, there was nane that obtained comfort at " the " unmerciful hands " of the raiders.[1] At times even the Crown tenants were victims. In 1459 the king's poor tenants, malars, and inhabitants upon his proper lands made lamentable and many complaints because of the wrongful exactions of the neighbouring gentry, and an act of parliament was passed for their protection.[2] One cannot help wondering if it were as effective as the more drastic measures of the nobles.

[1] For examples, see Sir Herbert Maxwell, *Dumfries and Galloway*, p. 128.

R. Chambers, *Domestic Annals of Scotland*, p. 71.

Among many instances in the *Register of the Privy Council*, see vol. iv, pp. 37-40.

The published papers on *The Roses of Kilravock* (C. Innes), *The Chiefs of Grant* (Sir William Fraser), and *Huntly* (Spalding Club) give a general idea of the raids endured even in one district. There are inventories of the damage done to the tenants.

[2] *A.P.S.* vol. ii, p. 22.

PART VII. SOCIAL BENEFITS DUE TO THE FEUDAL SYSTEM

Nevertheless, the survival of the feudal system had its good sides. The entire personnel of the Scots nobility cannot be dismissed in the terms of Dame Scotia's bitter reproach : " Thou art the special cause of my reuyne, for thou and thy sect that professes you to be nobilis ande gentill men, there is nocht ane sperk of nobilnes nor gentrice among the maist part of you," [1] nor in Thomas Carlyle's swingeing generalization—" a selfish, ferocious, unprincipled set of hyenas." No doubt, in such an unsettled state of society, certain unlovely characteristics best secured and preserved high position and worldly gear. Nevertheless, badly as the feudal system worked, function it did, and Scotland continued to exist as a sovereign power, even through her many minorities and in spite of the enmity of her more powerful neighbour, England.

In their relations with the Crown the nobles undoubtedly kept the central authority weak. It must, however, be remembered that in the state of development of Scotland in the fifteenth and sixteenth centuries the only alternative to faction rule was the absolute power of the Throne, which, unless her kings had been both fortunate and able, would probably have been quite as unpropitious for the nation and might have been far more demoralizing. The story of the burghs will show how impossible was genuine democratic government and how corrupt and inefficient was the electoral machinery there devised. Nor can it be said that the king was always right and that the great lords were always wrong in opposing him. The nobles who refused to carry out the anti-English and unduly pro-French policy of the Crown, and to invade England in 1522 at the wish of the Regent Albany, in 1542 at the behest of James V, and in 1557 at the desire of Mary of Lorraine, were probably more useful to their country than the heroic group who fought and died with James IV at Flodden.

It is to the honour of the Scots nobility that, great as were their powers, they did not take occasion to introduce vexatious class legislation. Hill Burton has pointed out that : " Of the

[1] *The Complaynt of Scotlande* (Anon., sixteenth century), p. 139.

multitudinous exemptions from the obligations binding on common men, which made up the privilege of the peerage in England, there seems to be no trace in Scotland." Landed men and freeholders were tried by juries of their own class, but titled men had no special rights in this respect and could claim no exemption from imprisonment for debt until matters were equalized between the two countries at the Union.[1] Unlike almost every other country of Europe, in Scotland there were no peasant revolts or risings against the feudal form of government. In truth, it must in fairness be admitted that such a form of social organization accorded very well with the natural pugnacity and clannishness of the Scots.

It is this natural affinity between the national characteristics of the people and the form of government and social organization that made the feudal system in a strange sense a truly popular one. In a case such as Scotland, where government by great nobles was accepted by the people, there were strong democratic elements in the relationship between feudal superior and vassal. As has been noted, the power of the nobles prevented the Crown from becoming absolute, and it also, in a paradoxical way, preserved the liberties of the people. Every noble and laird in the constant struggles that went on was dependent upon the support not only of the phalanx of cadets of his house but upon that of the lesser folk who formed the rank and file of his train, and these in turn were dependent on his protection. Although there were instances of black oppression by the landowning classes upon their own tenants,[2] yet the position of the Scots farmer, as John Major has sketched it, is rather a proud one: "They keep a horse and weapons of war, and are ready to take part in his quarrel, be it just or unjust, with any powerful lord, if they only have a liking for him, and with him if need be, to fight to the death." [3] Although the social framework of Scotland was built up upon the relationship of those who owned the land and those who occupied it, yet, owing to the very wildness and troublousness of the times, an element of idealism and of mutual loyalty, a sense of mutual

[1] Hill Burton, *History of Scotland*, vol. iii, p. 389.

[2] T. Johnston, *History of the Working Classes in Scotland*, p. 27.
J. Edwards, "Templars in Scotland," *Scottish Hist. Review*, vol. v, p. 7.

[3] J. Major, *History of Greater Britain* (Scottish History Society), p. 47.

obligation, entered into and largely dominated this purely economic relationship. It is true that such loyalties were but lesser ones, and that it is well for Scotland that they have been merged into a greater loyalty to the State. Nevertheless, they were honourable and manly, and although the constant condition of warfare, internal and external, caused great suffering to the people, yet such misfortunes were neither humiliating nor debasing; and if they helped to preserve the lesser folk from descending into a state of servility, they were not endured in vain. These troublous centuries, as many historians have pointed out, were the period when the people of Scotland most developed their own clearly marked individuality.

The benefits conferred by feudalism were not merely due to virtues inherent in the system: for although it affected the characteristics of the people, yet the temperament of the people also reacted upon the system. A people so self-respecting and independent as are the Scots could only have developed where there were fine elements in the relationship between lord and vassal, such as certainly existed between the warlike nobles of Scotland and their devoted retainers. On the other hand, it is not enough to say that good came out of evil, in the preservation, or rather the accentuation, of the people's individual independence, through the civil misfortunes of Scotland—as if this happy result were a, so to speak, machine-made product of Providence. In other countries the feudal system in many cases was very far from producing such a result. It was because the sturdy Scots were never abject under the duress of circumstances; because, if lawless and violent, they were also loyal to the obligations of their position, to their comrades, and to the authority that they accepted, that the feudal period in Scotland, although it was a time of arrested material development, wrought no degradation or permanent harm to the race.

Part VIII. Development and Decline of Feudalism

The position of the lords and barons of Scotland during the fifteenth and sixteenth centuries was by no means a static one. The sweeping forfeitures of the Wars of Independence, and the great changes among the landholders that then took place, rendered the feudal abstraction, that all land was owned by the king and was granted to his followers in return for certain services, a literal fact in a very large number of cases. During the earlier part of this period the feudal system was still developing. The thanages, those hybrid holdings of the transition period, finally disappeared. David II, in one year, granted three of them to Walter Leslie upon feudal tenure, and fourteen of them had been feudalized by the end of the fifteenth century. Even the thanage of Cawdor, where the name last survived, was virtually held by feudal tenure after 1475.[1]

In the fifteenth century the system reached its completest and most logical development. James I reintroduced the important feudal casualty of "Recognition," and although he failed to force the freeholders to produce all title-deeds, many of the acts of the period, that deal with the intricacies of land-holding and of the casualties due from land, were very markedly feudal in character.[2] The fifteenth century, however, also saw the rise of an important non-feudal practice. The custom of feuing of land, a new form of land tenure that produced such far-reaching results that it must be dealt with separately, began to be introduced. By the sixteenth century the influence of the Roman Law and of continental practice had begun deeply to influence the theories of the Scots lawyers, and although the law of the land remained predominantly feudal, its interpretation was becoming considerably changed.[3]

A very definite change also took place with regard to the basis upon which a title was held, and the idea of a purely "territorial peerage," in which duties and titles were definitely attached to the possession of certain lands, was gradually altered into that of a personal dignity; although the present conception of a peerage "of blood descent" was becoming generally accepted, the change was only very gradual, and the older idea lingered on to a limited degree even until the Union

[1] W. F. Skene, *Celtic Scotland*, vol. iii, p. 246.

[2] H. B. King, *Short History of Feudalism in Scotland*, pp. 59, 74. For the text of the act ordering all who held land of the king to produce their charters, with its assumption of absolute possession of the land by the Crown, see *A.P.S.* vol. ii, p. 4 (A.D. 1424).

[3] D. B. Smith, *Scottish Hist. Review*, vol. xii, p. 271.

of 1707.[1] The different political status of the nobles and the lesser barons was also gradually evolved.[2] Moreover, there was a considerable alteration in the manners and customs of the nobility. Towards the end of the century a greater desire for the amenities and luxuries of life and an increased ability to use the produce of their great estates, not merely on the spot, where they were only suitable for the sustenance of mediaeval retainers, but as exchangeable commodities capable of supplying the refinements of high living, were being shown.[3] A law of 1581 declares that: Forasmuch as of late there is "croppin in" among some noblemen, prelates, barons, and gentlemen, being of good livings, great abuse contrair the honour of the realm and different from the honest frugality of their forbears, passing to burghs, towns, clachans, and alehouses with their households . . . wherefore scaithful and shameful inconveniences daily falls out to the offence of God, defrauding of the poor of their alms, slander of the country, and hurt of the authors, the nobility were therefore ordered to live at home with their families, for the setting forward of policy and decoration of their said dwelling-places, the supporting of the poor with alms, and the entertaining of friendship with their neighbours, under pain of a fine rising to 500 merks.[4]

The tendency cannot have been very marked, for Fynes Moryson, an Englishman who visited Scotland about 1598, although he was entertained after their best manner, specially noticed that the Scots gentry used "no Art of Cookery or furniture of household stuffe, but rather rude neglect of both." He further noticed that the Scots lived in factions and were therefore obliged "to keep many followers, and so consumed their revenue of victuals, living in some want of money." Such statements of the household expenses of great nobles and of their revenues as have come down to us certainly bear this out.

[1] J. H. Stevenson, "Sketch of the Scottish Peerage," *Scottish Hist. Review*, vol. ii, p. 1.

W. Law Mathieson, *Scottish Hist. Review*, vol. iv, p. 51.

C. Innes, *Scottish Legal Antiquities*, p. 73.

Exchequer Rolls, vol. xii, p. xxxiii.

[2] R. S. Rait, "Parliamentary Representation in Scotland," *Scottish Hist. Review*, vol. xii, p. 117.

[3] P. Hume Brown, *Scotland in the Time of Queen Mary*, pp. 76, 181-184.

[4] *A.P.S.* vol. iii, p. 222.

In 1590 the food consumed by the household of Campbell of Glenurchy was as follows:

364 bolls of meal.
207 bolls of malt.
90 beeves (more than two-thirds of them eaten unsalted).
20 swine.
200 sheep.
424 salmon.
15,000 herring.
30 doz. hand fish.
325 stone of cheese.
49 ,, butter.
26 doz. loaves of wheaten bread.
3¼ bolls of wheat flour.
1 sugar loaf and only very small amounts of spices and sweetmeats.

The Lord Lovat who died in 1631 used weekly in his household:

7 bolls of malt.
7 ,, meal.
1 boll of flour.

He used ninety beeves annually, besides venison, fish, poultry, kids, lambs, and game in great profusion. But he also exported salmon and imported spices, sugar, and wines from France.

The Huntly rent roll of the very early seventeenth century shows how largely, even at the end of our period, revenue derived from land was paid in kind. The money rental amounted to £3819, but 4498 bolls of grain were received, 167 head of cattle, 799 sheep and lambs, 5592 head of poultry of different kinds, enormous quantities of eggs, and also cheese, butter, linen, and peats.[1]

Nevertheless, the Scots nobles' increased desire for the same elegancies that their peers of other nations enjoyed is an important point, for it emphasized the relatively increasing poverty of the upper classes of Scotland compared to those living elsewhere. The land was becoming more and more insufficient for the provision of the rising standard of living that they required. This can be seen very clearly in the case of the king by means of the *Exchequer Rolls* and the *Lord High Treasurer's Accounts*,

[1] P. Hume Brown, *Early Travellers to Scotland*, p. 88.

R. Chambers, *Domestic Annals of Scotland*, vol. i, pp. 208-209, 319. The information is collected from C. Innes, *Black Book of Taymouth*, and Anderson, *History of the Frasers*, also *Spalding Club Miscellany*, vol. iv.

but it was also the case with the lords and barons. From the very beginning of our period they were much in touch with the courts of other nations—the tournament fought on London Bridge between Sir David Lindsay and Lord Welles in 1390 is only one picturesque episode among many details of the comings and goings of the Scots nobles. At the beginning of the period, when agricultural produce was the main source of wealth, Scotland was less well dowered than other countries. At the end of the sixteenth century, when commerce and manufactures were making England and France rich, but when Scotland was still at the more primitive stage in her economic development, the contrast must have been much more glaring.

The poverty of the Scots nobles can be gauged by the smallness of the bribes that tempted them from their loyalty. In 1543 Henry VIII tried to induce the "Assured Lords" to continue their traitorous allegiance to himself with £1000, of which Glencairn and Cassillis got £400. The great Angus obsequiously asked Henry for £1000, and Arran, the governor, accepted that amount in "most thankfull parte." Eventually an advance of £1500 changed the entire policy of the Assured Lords.[1] The rapacity of the nobles in demanding large grassums from their tenants, in securing Church lands, and in feuing their land can probably be largely accounted for, even if it cannot be excused, by their extreme need for money. Financial stringency was the prevailing condition of the affairs of all classes in Scotland, from the highest downwards, during our period.

In spite of certain modifications, Scotland remained, in all practical essentials, a feudal country. Sir Thomas Craig might complain that the system had been "twisted from its old symmetry" by alien economic developments, by the intricate relations of debtor and creditor, by the intervention of non-feudal tribunals, and by the application of doctrines of "possession and usufruct borrowed from the civil law,"[2] yet, in spite of this, the feudalism of Scotland at the end of the sixteenth century is still an outstanding fact, influencing the whole tenor of her social life and sharply differentiating her from England. During the following century—the seventeenth—the practical power of feudalism was profoundly modified,

[1] *Hamilton Papers*, vol. i, Nos. 364, 435, 443; vol. ii, No. 164.
[2] D. B. Smith, *Scottish Hist. Review*, vol. xii, p. 271.

but Lord Stair, writing at its very end, could still pronounce wardholding to be the prevailing Scots tenure : " It is the most proper feudal right we have ; and therefore wherever the holding appeareth not, or is unclear, there wardholding is understood." It was not until 1747 that this tenure was abolished, and with it not only the essential military service but also the casualty of recognition, so that the superior's consent before the sale of a vassal's lands was no longer required.

After dealing with these developments and modifications in the status of the ruling classes, one is tempted to pass on to the evolution of the Scots parliament and that of the system of the administration of justice. In a single book, however, such a general survey is impossible. Professor Rait and Professor Hannay have dealt exhaustively with the former. The latter is largely a matter for technical experts. Moreover, the development of the nicely adjusted machinery for the making and administration of the law, during the fifteenth and sixteenth centuries, is unfortunately to a great extent of merely theoretical interest—so largely was the legislature merely the quiescent mouthpiece of the faction in power, so ineffective was the administration of the law by ordinary channels, so lacking were the Scots throughout the whole period in any development of the power of actually and practically governing themselves.

Part IX. Feudalism as Part of the Fiscal System of the Nation

Something has been said with regard to the functions performed by the feudal magnate as military leader, keeper of the public peace, and local administrator of the law, but yet another important rôle that he filled must be mentioned. He was an important unit in the fiscal organization of the country. Don Pedro de Ayala, in a passage that is quoted later, estimated that about two-fifths of the royal income was derived from feudal casualties. This is probably an exaggeration, but the feudal dues were an important source of revenue. Not only were they a welcome addition to the general receipts, but they were sometimes earmarked for special purposes. In 1578–1579, in Lord Herries' report upon the defences of the Borders, he proposes

[1] Stair's *Institutes*, vol. ii, 3, 31.

that the house of Annand be be sum casualtie bildit again," nd he advised the repair of the defences of Lochmaben Castle y the same means.[1]

These casualties of ward, relief, marriage, etc., were an regular and fluctuating source of revenue, and the uncer-ainty of when the heavy payments would fall upon an estate as not only a disadvantage to the superior who received them, ut to the vassal who had to make them.[2] It was largely the iconvenience of the feudal casualties that rendered the new enure of the feu so acceptable both to the granter and to the ecipient. For this reason it is important to bear in mind the act of the financial obligations that were involved even in a ase of pure wardholding.

Part X. The Effect of Landholding upon the History of the Period

Feudalism was a system of national organization built up pon the holding of land. Largely upon this account, the history f the country, the relations of the Crown, the Church, and the obility were profoundly affected by the question of the actual ossession of land. This economic fact is profoundly illumin-ting, for it shows that because of certain given factors the ame results were repeated over and over again, with only ninor variations, in the kaleidoscopic politics of the Scotland f the period. It must always be remembered that the posses-ion of land was the supreme good. It was the main source of he national wealth ; it supplied the man-power upon which epended not only political power but security of possessions nd even of life and limb. From the times of the Wars of ndependence the equilibrium of landholding in Scotland was ipset, and the balance leant too far now in one direction, now in nother. The cause of most of the troubles was quite unlike hat which brought about the rebellions of the mormaers in the ays of the old Gaelic kingdom before the reign of Malcolm Canmore. There was little or no trace of any movement to ound independent provinces or principalities. The only excep-ions are the attitude of the Lord of the Isles and perhaps that

[1] *Register, Privy Council*, vol. iii, p. 81.

[2] Cf. Sir James Ramsay, *Bamff Charters and Papers*, pp. 53, 58.

of the earlier Douglas family. In both these cases the roya authority was completely asserted. The fundamental cause c trouble was the fact that the ownership of land became s largely mixed up with the question of politics, and was th reward and stimulus of faction. One may perhaps, withou impropriety, draw a parallel with the intrigues and struggle of vested interests which produced so much instability in th days of mercantilism and protection: when trade, in its turr had become the object of political gerrymandering.

Perhaps a general sketch of the national finances of the time may be allowed, to illustrate the supreme importance of lan and the poverty of the Crown. During our period the organiza tion of the collection and disbursement of the revenue wa carried rather further than in the preceding centuries, espec ally by James I,[1] but it was most inefficient, especially durin the troubled years of the sixteenth century.

In the case of the burgh fermes there was little opportunit for evasion. Of the collection of the great customs, which wer entrusted to the "customers," generally local burgesses, it impossible to judge. In the case of the land dues, instances d survive which show that Drummond's name for the revenu officers—"caterpillars of the state"—was sometimes we deserved. For instance, during the minority of the Earl c Buchan in the early sixteenth century, the estates were of cours liable to the casualty of ward, and the revenues were collecte for the Crown by an official receiver. The revenues fro Buchan's Forfarshire estates brought in £247 per annum, an after discharging all liabilities, the Exchequer at first receive £167; but year by year, although the revenue must hav remained the same, the surplus that was remitted became le and less, in spite of the fact that the young heir only had £1 a year spent upon him—until, in 1513, at the end of the war ship, the Crown only received £9 surplus from these estate and the receiver was £109 in arrears in money rents, beside owing rents in kind.[2]

The method of using these revenues was still very primitiv The king and court were still largely in the habit of movin

[1] *Exchequer Rolls*, vol. iv, p. xciii; vol. i, p. 5. For organization David I, see *A.P.S.* vol. ii, pp. 86-87.

[2] *Exchequer Rolls*, vol. xiii, pp. cxii, cxlix.

bout, in order to consume the produce upon the spot. This ustom especially struck Don Pedro de Ayala, the Spanish mbassador, who visited Scotland early in the sixteenth century.[1] In addition, goods—fish, cloth, etc.—were often requisitioned directly from the burghs in lieu of ferme, and ensions and rewards generally took the form of a grant of a iece of Crown land, either in perpetuity or in liferent, or of an nnual payment made directly from the rents of such land. The *Exchequer Rolls* abound with such entries.[2] In 1483, Andrew Wood received a charter for Largo, which he had reviously held on lease, as the reward for his sea victory over he English. The man who found Bruce's sword, which had een dropped by James III at the battle of Sauchieburn, and he messenger who brought James II the news of the birth of n heir, received grants of land, etc., etc.[3]

Don Pedro de Ayala sent an elaborate account of the Scots evenues to the king of Spain. The *Exchequer Rolls* show hat he exaggerated some of the amounts, but the proportions re suggestive. He gives the following figures :

Revenue from arable and pasture land .	40,000 ducats.	
,, the customs . . .	28,000 ,,	
,, fines and escheats . .	25,000 ,,	at least.
,, wardships . . .	20,000 ,,	

These figures bring out the relative unimportance of the ommerce of the country as a source of revenue, the value of the eudal dues, and, above all, the importance of the Crown lands.

We do not know the exact extent of the lands possessed by he Scots kings before the Wars of Independence. They were ertainly very large. Robert the Bruce came into lands dilapidated in value, but enormous accessions of territory passed hrough his hands. He, however, gave very many of these away. During the reign of Robert II, the first Stewart king, he dilapidation of the Crown lands went on apace. He had o provide for " a multitude of children of either sex," legitimate and illegitimate, and throughout his reign the following arrangements were made :

[1] P. Hume Brown, *Early Travellers to Scotland*, p. 46.

[2] See also *Lord High Treasurer's Accounts*, vol. i, p. xv.

[3] *Exchequer Rolls*, vol. v, p. lxxxix ; vol. x, p. xli ; vol. ix, p. xxxix.

The second son was provided for by being married to th Countess of Fife, and leaving no direct heir, the earldom passed by special arrangement to Albany.

The third son was made Duke of Albany, received man lands, and succeeded to the earldom of Fife.

The fourth son was created Earl of Buchan and received a grant of the lordship of Badenoch and also of lands in Banffshire, Sutherlandshire, Athole, Fife, Galloway, etc He left no legitimate descendants.

Two more sons received the earldoms of Strathearn and o Athole, and also many grants of fermes and of annuities also the wardship of the son of Mercer, a rich merchan of Perth. In addition, eight daughters and eight more sons were provided for.[1]

Owing to a rather fortunate mortality, only a few of thes royal scions transmitted heirs, but during the futile reigns o Robert II himself and of his successor, Robert III, the power of the next surviving son, the Duke of Albany, waxed greate and greater. During his regency for James I his income wa as follows: from his earldoms of Menteith and Fife, £1200 from his various offices at least £1400—altogether £2600. A few years later an account shows that the whole royal incom only amounted to £3323.[2]

Not only were the Crown lands given away, the receipt from the customs also fell off. It became the practice, durin the reigns of the two last Roberts and during Albany's regency to grant annuities to the most powerful nobles out of the burg customs—to reward them for services rendered and to try t retain their loyalty. Robert II granted, for instance, 250 merk to the Earl of March from the customs of Haddington, and als 200 merks to the son of the Earl of Douglas. During the reig of Robert III no less than thirty-eight persons were receivin money in this way.[3]

Moreover, large sums were also lost by the failure of grea folks to pay custom themselves, either by royal permission o without it. In this way Albany exported the whole of the woo and the hides of his earldoms of Fife and Menteith free of duty

[1] *Exchequer Rolls*, vol. iv, p. clvii.

[2] *Ibid.* vol. iv, p. li.

[3] *Ibid.* vol. iii, pp. lviii, lxxxiii.

and Douglas and some of the great churchmen were not behind him. Some of the wilder spirits, including the Duke of Rothesay (Robert III's elder son), did not hesitate to take by force. During the captivity of James I, which followed the death of Robert III, things became worse, and such robbing was continual. To take the Earl of Douglas alone, between 1406 and 1422 he made constant inroads upon the customs of Edinburgh and Linlithgow. During the first three years he took £100, in 1409 he took £708 from Edinburgh, and his extortions increased until 1414, when he took £1339, and 1418, when he seized £1254.[1]

In 1424, James I returned from captivity. The story of his capture and of the non-payment of his ransom throws so vivid a light upon the standards of public probity of the times that it may perhaps be briefly told here. In 1406 the ship which was taking him as a youth to complete his education in France was captured by the English, although there was a truce at the time between the two countries. The large sum which the Scots were required to pay for his restoration was euphemistically called his "expenses." It is not wonderful that the king and his people, when he at last regained his liberty, should have been unwilling to disburse the money, but there is a lack of moral sense that can almost be called robust in the manner in which they completely ignored their solemn obligations.

The sum was to be paid off in half-yearly instalments in six years, and a large number of hostages, including Moray, Crawford, and other nobles, were sent to England until it should be paid. A tax of one shilling in the pound was imposed, to be levied in two years, which it was hoped would cover four of the half-yearly instalments. In the first year 40,000 nobles were raised, of which 16,800 was paid to England and the rest appropriated by the king and the officials. No further sums were remitted to England; and the luckless hostages were left to languish in captivity, until some ransomed themselves, some escaped, and the rest died.[2] The root of the contrast between present-day standards and those of mediaeval Scotland lies in the fact that *credit*, used in the sense in which it maintains the whole economic organization of the present time, did not then

[1] *Exchequer Rolls*, vol. iii, pp. lxxv, lxxxix; vol. iv, pp. lvii, lix, lxxxii.
[2] *Ibid.* vol. iv, pp. cxxx, cxxxv.

exist. No little advance has been made in standards of probity as well as in financial organization.

As soon as James I got back to his kingdom, in 1424, he made his strong hand felt in many directions. He was the first of the abler kings of Scotland to make the boast that he would make the bush keep the cow, and "in his time there was no noble who dared to raise his sword against another; to his orders, written or spoken, every man alike yielded obedience."[1] He at once swept away nearly all the annuities levied on the great customs, and the robberies ceased. In 1420 the amount of the customs for *two* years was £4400. In 1424 the amount for *one* year was almost exactly the same sum. During the rest of his reign the customs averaged £5000.[2]

The king, however, was eager for more money. He introduced a good many new taxes, the income from which was inconsiderable; augmented his income by trading in wool, hides, and salted salmon in the royal ships; and, perhaps for political as well as for personal reasons, he greatly increased the Crown lands, at the expense of certain of his nobles.[3]

By the attainder of Albany and of his family he secured the earldoms of Fife and Menteith. The Earl of Lennox was executed—it is not known for what cause—and his estates were annexed to the Crown. In 1427, James dispossessed the young Earl of Strathearn, his cousin, upon the pretext that the earldom was a male fief; gave it to his uncle, the Earl of Fife, and, in exchange, gave Strathearn the less valuable earldom of Menteith. He then got rid of him by sending him to England as a hostage, and kept the rents of Menteith in his own hands. The father of the Earl of March had been a traitor, but Albany, whilst acting as regent, had restored him, and his son, the existing earl, had always been loyal. In 1434, James arrested him and seized his lands, upon pretext that Albany had exceeded his powers in pardoning a traitor. He also took possession of the earldom of Mar in 1426.[4]

The story of this title and of its estates is so striking an example of the looseness with which the individual held land

[1] J. Major, *History of Greater Britain*, p. 367.

[2] *Exchequer Rolls*, vol. iv, pp. xciii, cxxv.

[3] *Ibid.* vol. iv, pp. cxxv, cxxxiv, cxliv, cxlv.

[4] *Ibid.* vol. iv, pp. cxv, cxvii.

in Scotland that it may be told here very briefly. It was inherited by an heiress in 1388, who married Sir Malcolm Drummond. Sir Malcolm was done to death, it is supposed by a certain Alexander Stewart, illegitimate son of the Wolf of Badenoch, who has already figured in these pages. In any case, young Alexander besieged the widowed Countess of Mar in her castle of Kildrummy, captured her, and forced her to marry him and to resign to him her earldom. He lived to marry two other wives, to defeat the Lord of the Isles at Red Harlaw, and to gain great distinction as a soldier in France. The Regent Albany gave him a charter securing the earldom to his illegitimate son—an act of injustice, for there was a lawful heir to the late countess. However, the son predeceased Alexander Stewart, and, as already stated, James took possession of the earldom. In 1435, Sir Robert Erskine, the representative of the rightful heir, tried to secure the earldom, but, after lawsuits that lasted twenty years, and after it had practically been acknowledged that the Erskine claim was valid, the Crown refused to give up the lands. In spite of this, the Erskines continued to serve their kings loyally. One head of the family was killed at Flodden, another was the companion of James V. Eventually Mary Queen of Scots righted the wrong, and granted the earldom to John, sixth Lord Erskine.[1]

James I was murdered in 1437, and the country endured a long and troubled minority. James had considerably strengthened the Crown and had extinguished the power of Albany's successors, but the growing power of the Douglas family, in the South, was now an increasing menace, and so, to a less extent, was that of the Lord of the Isles (at this time also Earl of Ross) in the North and North-West. In addition two new families, the Livingstones and the Crichtons, became formidable and the country was vexed by their rivalries and quarrels. The *Exchequer Rolls* bear record of the exactions and arbitrary deeds of each party as it came into power.[2]

When James II at last assumed control he was involved in a life-and-death struggle with the Douglas family. At this time they held the earldoms of Angus, Moray, and Ormond, besides the earldom of Douglas and its great appendages. By assassination and by considerably drawn-out civil war the

[1] See *Scots Peerage*.

[2] *Exchequer Rolls*, vol. v, p. xlix.

Douglases were completely subdued by 1455. Although the faction who had supported the king also received gifts—Sir James Crichton, son of the chancellor, was made Earl of Moray, and Sir George Crichton was made Earl of Caithness, besides receiving lands in Caithness, Annandale, and the Lothians—nevertheless, the greatest beneficiary was the Crown.[1]

The Crown rents for 1451–1457 are given in detail in the *Exchequer Rolls* and make illuminating reading. The totals are as follow:

	£	s.	d.	
Lennox . . .	£216	11	10	acquired in 1425 by James I.
Ardmannoch, Duffus	330	9	0	acquired in 1455 by James II, from the Douglases, except for £20 of old Crown land.
Moray . . .	345	2	11	acquired in 1455 by James II, from the Douglases, except for £20 of old Crown land.
Lands on Dee and Spey . . .	93	0	0	mostly acquired in 1426 by James I.
Mar . . .	396	10	0	annexed 1329 by James I.
Galloway . .	751	3	4	acquired 1455 by James II, from the Douglases.
Bute and Arran .	198	17	2	old Stewart patrimony.
Carrick . . .	25	3	4	only held temporarily.
Three thanages .	142	0	8	old Crown land.
Brechin . .	133	12	8	annexed 1437 after James I's murder.
Lands in Perthshire	518	7	2	some old Crown land, some acquired in 1437 after James I's murder.
Athole . . .	139	0	0	acquired in 1437 after James I's murder.
Strathearn . .	147	6	5	acquired by James I.
Menteith . .	351	12	8	acquired in 1426 by James I.
Fife . . .	560	12	7	acquired in 1425 by James I.
Stirling . . .	184	19	0	mostly old Crown land, but the actual holdings much altered from time to time.[2]
Linlithgow . .	140	17	8	
Edinburgh . .	78	2	8	
	£4753	9	1	

From this list it can be seen that out of the total, £1765 was acquired by James I, at least £500 was added by the forfeitures that followed his murder, and £1386 was added to the Crown lands at the fall of the Douglases. These figures bring out well the "pull-devil, pull-baker" attitude of the King of Scots and his nobles for the land, the source of wealth and power.

[1] *Exchequer Rolls*, vol. v, pp. cxv, civ. [2] *Ibid.* vol. vi, p. lxxiv onwards.

The next minority, that of James III, again saw faction struggles, the three most powerful men being Lord Fleming, Lord Kennedy, and Sir Alexander Boyd. They eventually made a pact together, but Boyd gained the most substantial advantages. He married the king's sister and became Earl of Arran, and also received extensive estates on the mainland, in three counties, including Stewarton, Turnberry, Caverton, Teling, and Brichty; all this was in addition to the lands he inherited from his father. He also was given valuable wards in Aberdeenshire in lieu of the dowry of 1000 merks he had been promised with the princess, and was made sheriff of Wigtown and of Arran and Steward of Kirkcudbright. His relations also received emoluments. His prosperity was short-lived. In 1469, James III, having assumed control, ruined the family and took possession of the whole of their estates, both those inherited and those recently acquired, including the earldom of Arran, which passed, with the princess, to her second husband, Lord Hamilton.[1]

James III was a money-loving king. Like others of his race he was not above trading his wool and hides for wine and saltpetre, and his ships were several times sent to France and Flanders upon commercial expeditions. He managed to amass a great treasure of gold and silver, and, by good luck as well as by good management, the Crown lands were increased. Arran, it is true, was permanently lost, but Orkney was gained by marriage, and Ross by forfeiture, and Bothwell. The latter, however, was only held for a short time. Very full accounts of the royal revenue about this time have survived. In 1471 it was made up as follows :

Crown lands	£10,600
Great customs	3,300
Sheriffdoms	1,720
Burgh fermes	760
	£16,380 [2]

James III quarrelled with his brothers and with a section of his nobility. There were several acute struggles and eventu-

[1] *Exchequer Rolls*, vol. vii, p. lxi ; vol. viii, p. xliv.

[2] *Ibid.* vol. viii, pp. 254, 391, 465, 547, 380 ; vol. ix, p. lxviii. *A.P.S.* vol. ii, p. 230.

ally he was murdered. During the minority of the new king, James IV, the nobles who had made him the figurehead in their quarrel rose into greater power, but, for reasons of expediency, the followers of the old king were only dispossessed to a limited extent. Grants of land and offices of profit were freely distributed. For instance, Stirling of Keir, who was suspected of being the actual murderer of the late king, was given a large sum of money, a new charter to his land, and additional property; but the families whose profit was outstandingly greatest were the Homes and the Hepburns. The head of the house of Home was made Great Chamberlain, Warden of the East Marches, Bailie of Ettrick Forest, Keeper of Newark Castle, Keeper of Stirling Castle, Ranger of the Ward of Yarrow, Steward of the Earldom of March, guardian of the king's younger brother, the Earl of Mar, and large portions of Ettrick Forest were let to him on advantageous terms. His brother was made Master of the King's Wardrobe with an annuity of 20 merks from Cockburn and certain lands in the Merse. His three uncles all became possessors by lease or feu-charter of lands in Merse, Ettrick Forest, and Stewarton free of rent; in addition, one of them received a share of the estates forfeited by the supporters of the late king and another was made the king's butler. Yet another Home kinsman was made chamberlain of Stirling and Strathearn. Such was the typically clannish constitution of the great Lowland families. The list of donations made to the Hepburns is almost as long. Among other grants, the head of the family was made Earl of Bothwell. Five of his relations were also given appointments.[1]

The early part of James IV's reign once more saw the diminution of revenue. One of the sources of trouble was the rebellious conduct of the Macdonalds. Much of Ross was laid waste, and the fermes of Inverness, which had been sacked by the Macdonalds again and again, were heavily in arrears. By 1492, £375 0s. 8d. was owed by the burgh, and a composition of £35 13s. 4d., less than 2s. in the £1, had to be accepted. When James came into power he was obliged to lead eight expeditions, some of them of considerable size, into the Highlands and Islands before he could establish law and order there. The result was an increase in the area of the Crown lands—though

[1] *Exchequer Rolls*, vol. x, pp. xli, xlii, xliv.

it was not one that brought in much revenue. Islay, Tiree, and Kintyre came into the hands of the king. The rest of the lands of the Lords of the Isles, now forfeited, in 1500 were entrusted to a commission consisting of Argyle, Campbell of Glenurchy, and four others, and were to be let on short leases; there was, however, constant and serious trouble. It was due to this very disturbed state of the Western Highlands that two powerful houses—Huntly and Argyle—now emerged into far greater prominence and received grants of land and royal support, so that their territories should form barriers between the wilder Highlands and the Lowlands. (The *Scots Peerage* gives a list of their lands.) It was James's policy to use them to "daunton" and hold the Western Highlanders in check whilst he involved himself zestfully in the game of international politics. In 1500, Argyle was made lieutenant-general in the Islands. Two years later the letting of the king's lands in Lochaber and Mamore was entrusted to him and to Huntly, and in 1506–1507 the same policy was repeated. Huntly received such increases of land to his already considerable estates that they extended from Aberdeenshire through the hill country to the upper waters of the Spey and to the West Coast lands of Lochaber.[1]

Besides the doubtful blessing of owning West Highland property, James IV was able in other directions to add considerably to his lands. When his brother entered the Church, the lands of Ross, Ardmannoch, Brechin, and Novar, which had been granted to him by James III, reverted to the Crown. The lands of the earldom of Buchan and those of Lord Haliburton were held in ward for a considerable time, and, later in the reign, the earldom of Sutherland, worth £250 per annum, was also in ward for five years. The royal lands at this time (about 1507) consisted of the earldoms of Fife, Strathearn, Menteith, Moray, Ross, and Orkney and Shetland, the greater part of Mar, and some of the richest lands on the Borders, formerly held by the Douglases. During the earlier part of his reign the customs averaged £3106 12s. 4¾d., nearly £200 less than they had done in the reign of James III. Moreover, James IV was seriously straitened for money and, upon occasion, had to borrow from his nobles. The salaries of his household and of

[1] *Exchequer Rolls*, vol. x, pp. lvii, lix, lx, lxiv, lxv, lxvii; vol. xi, p. lvii; vol. xii, pp. xxxii, lxiv, lxv, lxi.

that of his queen, the Tudor princess, amounted to £646 per annum, and the accounts of the Lord High Treasurer abound with descriptions of the colourful apparel of the king and of his entourage.[1]

James IV had in full measure the fascination and the faults of his race. He was killed at Flodden in 1513, the victim of his own bad generalship, and the flower of his nobility fell with him. The country was now once more plunged into the miseries of a minority, and the revenues suffered. Ross and Ardmannoch were disturbed by raids and feuds and brought in a much-reduced rental. Nothing at all was received from Kintyre between 1511 and 1522, for the same causes. Stirling and Linlithgowshire, part of the earldom of March, and Ettrick Forest were in the hands of the queen-mother as her dowry, and so utterly inefficient was the administration of these that the queen complained that she only received £18 out of Ettrick Forest, which should have given her £2781. "The rest was spent in fees of officials or remitted to the tenants, or allowed to the accountant himself on account of failure in rents." The three rich wards that had fallen to the Crown during the preceding reign had all lapsed, and the revenues of the earldom of Moray were now also lost, because the illegitimate son of James IV, to whom it had been granted, reached his majority in 1515. The country had to undergo sixteen years of chaos, perhaps worse than anything that had occurred in the preceding minorities.[2]

The powerful houses of Huntly and Argyle increased their own local spheres of interest, but took no part in the faction struggles of the South. Among the principal leaders who contended for power were the queen-mother, who enjoyed the added prestige of being Henry VIII's sister, and the Duke of Albany—a descendant of James II, whose ancestor had fled to France, and who was more of a Frenchman than a Scot. After the death of James V's little brother, Albany was the next heir. Albany, though in many ways he deserved well of Scotland, was an expensive visitor; during the three brief visits that he paid to the country, his household expenses amounted to £700

[1] *Exchequer Rolls*, vol. xiii, pp. xlviii, li.
Accounts of the Lord High Treasurer, vol. i, pp. xcvii, clxxviii.
[2] *Exchequer Rolls*, vol. xiv, pp. cxiii, xxii-xxiii.

per month. The two most influential nobles were the Hamilton Earl of Arran, whose family had begun to be powerful when it succeeded the Boyd Earl of Arran during the reign of James III, and the Earl of Angus, descended from one of the cadet branches of the family of Douglas, which had escaped the ruin that had befallen the rest of the name. The Homes, also, were still very powerful.[1]

The tangled course of affairs gradually resolved itself into a duel between Angus and Arran, and ended with the triumph of the former about 1523. By that year Angus had driven all his principal opponents out of the country or into hiding. The person of the young king and the most important strong places were in his hands, and he was able to concentrate the administration of affairs into the hands of his own family. He himself was an auditor of the Exchequer and also the Chancellor ; his uncle, Douglas of Kilspindie, was Treasurer, Custumar-General for Scotland, an auditor of the Exchequer, and Provost of Edinburgh. Three more Douglases had places at court, and Kilspindie and a Douglas burgess of Edinburgh were exempted from paying customs. As Pitscottie bitterly wrote: "None at that time durst strive against a Douglas nor yet a Douglas man."[2]

The state of the country under this Douglas administration was deplorable. The Borders were in a state of exceptionally great confusion. Orkney and Shetland were wasted by the English and by the Sinclairs. In 1525, 1527, and 1529 the Highlanders made incursions into Strathearn. The yield of the customs was reduced by many grants to individuals to export their goods free. In 1526 a special tax had to be levied upon the burghs.[3]

In 1529, James V at last escaped from the vassalage in which Angus had held him, and set to work to re-establish the Crown revenues. By the forfeiture of Angus, large parts of his estates came into the hands of the Crown, and, by the same means, James secured Glamis, East Wemyss, and Avondale. By setting the West Highland lands upon favourable terms he antagonized Argyle, who had been fishing in troubled waters there, but he increased the revenue from (?) to £494. The death of

[1] *Exchequer Rolls*, vol. xiii, p. lxxiv ; vol. xiv, p. xcii.

[2] *Ibid.* vol. xv, p. xlviii. [3] *Ibid.* vol. xv, pp. lxviii, lxix, lxvii, lxxi.

the queen-mother restored to him the lands of her dowry, and by the arbitrary exercise of his power he appropriated the lands of Liddesdale, belonging to Bothwell, and certain lands of Huntly and Moray. He also, to the annoyance of Henry VIII, made money as a flockmaster. Henry sent his ambassador to remonstrate with his nephew of Scotland because he compromised his kingly dignity by gathering into his hands " numbers of sheep and other such vile and mean things in respect of his estate, being the livings of poor men, therewith to increase his revenue." It has been estimated that James's flocks and herds brought him in 2000 merks per annum.[1]

But James was, indeed, a desperately poor man. The revenues of his country were utterly insufficient to support him in the style of his colleagues, the far richer kings of France and of England. In 1525 the comptroller had protested that the expenses of the king's household could not be met out of his revenue. A year later the treasurer's accounts showed a deficit of £3704. In 1528 the comptroller's deficit was over £2000, and " so pressing was the need of money that on November 9, 1528, we read of escheats being actually granted before culprits were convicted." Four years later the comptroller's accounts showed that his deficit had grown to £5500 and the treasurer's accounts were also in a thoroughly unsound condition.[2]

The inadequacy of the Crown revenues of Scotland forms an important clue to the complicated course of ordinary Scots internal politics. This inadequacy was now increasing, for the Scots kings were becoming ambitious to play a wider rôle, and at the same time, owing to the increase of wealth in other countries, Scotland was becoming relatively poorer and poorer. Meanwhile the need of the king for money was involving far more decisive and fundamental issues. There was another great source of wealth in Scotland besides the land and the small burgh customs and fermes. It is now time to carry our minds back once more to the beginning of our period and to consider the history of the great possessions of the Church.

[1] *Exchequer Rolls*, vol. xvii, pp. xli, lii, lv, and 641.

[2] D. Murray Rose, *Revenue of the Scottish Crown*, p. xxx.

R. K. Hannay, "On the Church Lands at the Reformation," *Scottish Hist. Review*, vol. xvi.

CHAPTER II

POLITICAL REACTIONS ON CHURCH LANDS

THE twelfth and thirteenth centuries had seen the establishment of a large Church patrimony in Scotland. With the exception of certain collegiate churches, founded during the fifteenth century, she had practically attained her maximum material development before the Wars of Independence.[1]

It is now time to trace the gradual swing back of the pendulum, so far as the great religious crisis in Scotland affects the main stream of the economic life of the nation. The fifteenth century was definitely a period of decadence in the vigour of the material side of church life.[2] The first four Jameses, like all but two of the sovereigns of their race, were devout and active churchmen, but, owing to their vigorous, strongly nationalist policy and to their extreme need for money, they took active steps to increase their rights of control over preferment to the greater benefices of the Church, and to curtail the drain of Scots money to Rome that was involved by the Pope's claims to appoint as well as to confirm the appointment of churchmen in Scotland.

The point at issue was a serious matter. The right of the Popes to appoint as well as to confirm was not generally conceded. Usually bishops were elected by their cathedral chapters and abbots by their monks, but the Pope's undisputed right of confirming the appointments involved the payment of money fees and " many of the best preferments were bestowed at Avignon or Rome, and it was the custom of aspiring clerks to resort thither in great numbers, to try what love or money could accomplish." The power of the Pope was on the increase;

[1] Cosmo Innes, *Scotch Legal Antiquities*, pp. 200-201.

[2] A. MacEwan, *History of the Church of Scotland*, p. 357.

at one time no less than five bishops-elect were in attendance at the Roman court for several years, while their bishoprics remained vacant at home.[1]

James I immediately passed two acts forbidding any clerk to purchase any pension out of any benefice, secular or religious, and obliging him to prove to his ordinary that he had good cause before leaving the country. He was to take an oath that he would not be guilty of barratry. The same line of policy was adopted by James's successors, and four more acts of parliament with the same object were passed during the fifteenth century.[2]

Unfortunately, immediate material considerations entirely inspired this legislation. The spiritual efficiency of the Church is not once mentioned in the correspondence that relates to it, and the Crown, having to some extent secured control over the appointments to the benefices of the Church, broke its own laws. In the reign of James III two acts were passed, one forbidding the clergy to try to secure appointments to Scots benefices from Rome, the other confirming the right of the clergy to elect their own dignitaries. But within two years the king had overridden the choice of the monks of Dunfermline and secured the papal confirmation for his own nominee to the abbacy.[3]

Many authorities are agreed that this was a turning-point in the ecclesiastical history of Scotland. W. Law Mathieson, writing of the year 1473, says: " From this year down to the Reformation, a period of nearly ninety years, the wealth of the Church was at the mercy of the king and of all who could obtain his favour. The worst features of the new system, for James' innovation soon became the regular usage, was not the mere extinction of electoral freedom, though the clergy loudly complained of this, but the bringing in of a new race of prelates, men of merely secular ambition, whose manner of life savoured little of the clerical calling. Henceforward the court, and not the chapter or the cloister, was the true centre of ecclesiastical life." [4] The writings of the time bear ample evidence to the

[1] John Cunningham, *Church History of Scotland*, vol. i, p. 187.

[2] A crime almost equivalent to simony.

A. MacEwan, *History of the Church of Scotland*, pp. 345-353.

[3] A. MacEwan, *History of the Church of Scotland*, p. 354.

[4] W. Law Mathieson, *Politics and Religion in Scotland, 1550–1695*, p. 26. See also J. Cunningham, *Church History of Scotland*, p. 200.

effects. Winzet in his *Tractates*, the author of the *Diurnal of Occurrents*, the poet Dunbar, and many others comment upon it. Bishop Leslie, the supporter of Mary Queen of Scots, declared: "Than ceissit all religious and godlye myndis and deidis; quhairwith the secularis and temporal men . . . fell fra all devocioun and godlynes to the warkis of wikednes, quhairof daylie mekill evill did increase." But actual proof is accessible in the correspondence between the young Archbishop of St Andrews with his father, James IV, and Bishop Panter, his former tutor.[1]

In the depression and confusion of James V's minority matters became worse. There were constant and costly appeals to Rome by those who exercised the authority of the Crown, as well as by the ecclesiastics, when this was convenient. The lesser churchmen were among the worst sufferers, for the higher ones came to regard the incomes of their benefices as their private property, whilst the unfortunate communities were often reduced to great poverty. A glaring example of the extent to which politics had invaded Church preferment is seen in the struggle for the appointment of an archbishop of St Andrews, in 1513. There were three candidates, nominated respectively by the queen-mother (Margaret Tudor), the chapter of the cathedral, and by the Pope. Douglas, who was supported by the queen, seized the castle of St Andrews. Hepburn, who had been nominated by the chapter, collected his followers, took the castle by assault and garrisoned it. Forman, the papal nominee, had secured the support of Lord Home by bestowing the vacant priory of Coldingham upon him. Home raised 10,000 men, but Hepburn held the castle so stoutly that eventually a compromise was made.[2]

The Regent Albany was at the time in temporary authority (the semi-French Albany whose expensive household has been noted), and a general distribution of benefices was undertaken "to mitigat the myndes of the nobilitie." Forman received

[1] Bp. Leslie and the *Diurnal of Occurrents* are quoted by W. Law Mathieson, pp. 4 and 40. See also pp. 15, 29.

The poems of Dunbar are published by the Scots Text Society; see especially pp. 81 and 205.

For correspondence of Archbishop of St Andrews, see *Exchequer Rolls*, vol. xiii, p. lxxxviii.

[2] A. MacEwan, *History of the Church of Scotland*, p. 363.

the disputed archbishopric of St Andrews and also the Abbey of Dunfermline, which was to be held *in commendam*. Hepburn was to be allowed an annual pension of 1000 merks out of these benefices, and his brother was made Bishop of Moray. About the same time a Gordon kinsman received the bishopric of Aberdeen, a Hamilton the abbacy of Kilwinning. Beaton, Archbishop of Glasgow, received the abbacy of Arbroath, but was to pay a pension to Forman; and an Ogilvie got the Abbey of Dryburgh. They received these benefices "to ilk ane as he was noble, nocht conform to his vertue,"[1] and so the evil continued.

The main cause for this most disastrous policy was the great and disproportionate wealth of the Church. As Major, one of the profoundest historians of his time, says: "Behold what may happen to the religion from the possession of great wealth. By open flattery the sons of our worthless nobility get the governance of convents *in commendam* . . . they covet these ample revenues, not for the good help they might render to their brethren but solely for the high positions that these places offer, that they may have the direction of them, and out of them may fill their own pockets."[2]

In this passage Major alludes to a yet further development in the dilapidation of Church lands. The process was not merely by the intrusion of unsuitable persons, for Church benefices were often bestowed *in commendam*, that is, in trust or stewardship. This practice had been originally only a temporary arrangement for the performance of the duties of the benefice and the management of the revenues during a vacancy. Then the system had been carried a step further, and a favourite ecclesiastic was given a plurality of livings, or the income of a poor living was augmented by such a grant and it was made for the life of the holder. For instance, the Bishop of Orkney in 1540–1558 had the abbacy of Kinloss and the priorship of Beauly *in commendam*. The Bishop of Moray in 1535 had the

[1] Bp. Leslie, *History of Scotland*, vol. ii, pp. 162-164 (Br. Text Society). The actual fighting for St Andrews was not unique. There were also "incidents" in the struggle for the bishopric of Aberdeen. For further examples of the intrusion of royal favourites and of pluralities, see *Exchequer Rolls*, vol. xiii, pp. cxlix, clii. See also *Register of Dunfermline*, pp. xv-xvii; Bellesheim, *History of the Catholic Church in Scotland*, vol. ii, p. 322.

[2] J. Major, *History of Greater Britain*, pp. 136-137.

abbacy of Scone, a scion of the house of Gordon held the bishopric of the Isles and the abbacy of Inchaffray, etc. The institution was then yet further abused, and ecclesiastical appointments were conferred on laymen of position and family. Three of James V's natural sons were given valuable benefices whilst they were still children. The powerful family of Hamilton was able to place two scions in the abbacies of Paisley and Arbroath. So glaring did the evil become, that "of the twenty abbots and priors that sat in the Parliament that effected the Reformation fourteen were commendators."[1]

Cardinal Sermoneta, in 1556, wrote to the Pope that the clergy of Scotland far surpassed the laity in "the wealth and abundance of their resources." The Church lands, in fact, were assessed, in all mid-sixteenth century taxation, at one-half of the whole national contributions. It has been estimated that this great wealth was divided in the following proportions :

Income of 200 abbeys, monasteries, and convents	£220,618	15	0
" the archbishops, bishoprics, and cathedral chapters	33,765	11	0
" collegiate churches	5,350	0	0
" hospitals, etc.	18,000	0	0
" tithes, dues, etc.	50,000	0	0

Another estimate puts the total wealth of the Church at £250,000. There were about 3000 clergy and members of religious communities in Scotland.[2]

The position of the Church, moreover, was one of great weakness. Partly, no doubt, she suffered through the fightings

[1] D. Masson, *Introduction to the Register of the Privy Council of Scotland*, vol. i (Second Series), p. cvii.

C. Innes, *Sketches of Scotch History*, p. 217.

J. Cunningham, *Church History of Scotland*, p. 270.

Bishop Forman, who was notorious as an ecclesiastical place-hunter, is said to have worn as his heraldic arms "a chevron between three fishes haurient" = a heraldic term for sucking in air (C. E. Chisholm Batten, *Beauly Priory*, p. 169).

[2] D. Hay Fleming, "Influence of the Reformation," *Scottish Hist. Review*, vol. xv, p. 5.

W. Law Mathieson, *Politics and Religion in Scotland*, p. 27.

T. Thomson, paper in *Cranstoun v. Gibson, Law Papers, Court of Session, Second Division*, 1816.

Bellesheim, *History of the Catholic Church in Scotland*, vol. ii, p. 312.

J. Cunningham, *History of the Church of Scotland*, p. 384.

and extreme lawlessness of the times. In the Highlands, during the dynastic struggles between the descendants of Somerled, the Church was reduced to a very low ebb.[1] On the Borders, during the constant fightings and raidings of the sixteenth century, the great abbeys suffered severely. One finds the monks of Kelso petitioning, in 1517, that an abbot might be appointed who could defend them with the sword.[2] But one has only to compare the prestige of the Church in earlier times, when she was able to enforce respect for her territories from the most powerful nobles, to see how great a change had taken place by the sixteenth century. In Scotland, to a far greater degree than elsewhere, the Church had lost the support of the laity. This is a matter altogether apart from the questions of dogma which were agitated in the Reformation. The abuses that had crept in were deplored by the best of the Church party and by so orthodox a son of the Church as James V.[3]

The subject is obviously a difficult one to deal with in a work such as the present, and yet social and economic issues are so largely involved that it cannot be ignored. Much of the decay was due to the appointment of unsuitable persons to the rich Church benefices,[4] and this, in its turn, was due to the disproportionate wealth of the Church. As Bellenden, Archdeacon of Aberdeen, the continuator of Boece's Chronicle, writes: " If

[1] See dispensation for marriage between John, Lord of the Isles, and Amie Macruarie, 1337, *Scottish Hist. Review*, vol. viii, p. 348.

[2] A. MacEwan, *History of the Church of Scotland*, p. 409.

[3] *A.P.S.* vol. ii, p. 370 (1541).

Statuta Ecclesiae Scoticanae, pp. 146-179.

See also such writings as the *Complaynt of Scotlande* (Anon., 1549); Lindsay's *Satire of the Three Estates*, which was performed in public before James V and his court; the poems of Dunbar, who was really devout; etc. The episode of *The Beggar's Summons* (1559), though a piece of political propaganda, also showed how public opinion was trending.

For a favourable account of the Ancient Church, see M. E. C. Walcott's *Ancient Church of Scotland*. On p. 10 he gives a list of the learned, able, and virtuous churchmen she had produced; and in an appendix a list of the hospitals and other charitable institutions that she had set up and maintained. See also A. Bellesheim, *History of the Catholic Church of Scotland*, vol. ii, pp. 327, 417.

[4] This is very definitely the opinion of A. Bellesheim, *History of the Catholic Church of Scotland*; cf. vol. ii, pp. 96, 252, 322.

King David had considered the manners and nourishing of devout religion, he had neither built the churches with such magnificence nor endowed them with such riches. For the superfluities of churches (now as they are used) are not only occasion to evil prelates to rage in most insolent and corrupt life, but one sicker net to draw all manner of gold and silver out of this realm to Rome, to their continual promotion."[1]

The conduct of the king and the nobles towards the Church is but another manifestation of the land-hunger that, as we have seen, was complicating the political history of Scotland. Their extreme need for money was to prove a determining factor in the more material development of the Scots Reformation. When James V threw off the Douglas yoke in 1528 the financial condition of the Crown was deplorable. Nevertheless, he was extravagant by nature, and the aggressive policy of Henry VIII made expenditure upon military defences a necessity. It was small wonder that his councillors, and afterwards he himself, should turn longing eyes towards the "great and many" lands his ancestors had given the Church.[2]

The Church, however, was wise in her generation, and she retained the king's allegiance by subsidies, which saved his quite genuine allegiance to the Old Faith from the imposition of a breaking strain.[3] During 1530 there were negotiations with Rome, and the Pope, influenced by the general state of Europe as well as the critical condition of Scotland, eventually issued a bull in which he agreed to grant James financial help. It was, he stated in the bull, his policy to maintain the churchmen's immunity from secular exactions, but, owing to the inadequacy of lay resources and the urgency of the need, which involved the safety of the faith, he would ask the clergy to bear a share of the burden. He imposed a tax of three-tenths on all ecclesiastical incomings during the next three years.[4]

Two months later he granted James V yet further help. In another bull he stated that the king was anxious to establish a

[1] Quoted by M. E. C. Walcott, *Ancient Church of Scotland*, p. 19.

[2] Quotation from letter by James V. to Rome, 1536, quoted by J. Cunningham, *Church History of Scotland*, p. 228.

[3] R. K. Hannay, *Scottish Hist. Review*, vol. xv, pp. 35-36.

[4] *Ibid.* p. 36.

There had been a precedent in 1528: the prelates had paid £892 into the Treasury.—*Exchequer Rolls*, vol. xv, p. 455.

college for the administration of civil justice, but that he had not the means. The interest of the clergy in civil order was not less than that of other subjects, and he therefore ordered all prelates to contribute an annual sum of 10,000 ducats for the purpose, so long as James and his successors remained loyal to the faith.[1]

It was a fact that improved provision for the administration of justice was urgently needed, but the sum that the Pope had granted was four or five times greater than what was required for the purpose. James himself put the matter quite plainly. He wrote to the Lords of the Council that: "Our prelatis givis us certain contributioun to be expendit and varit to our neccesaries and honour royal . . . quhilk our mynd is nocht to waisit nor spend in any sort but as effiris to our kinglie honor and for necessite of the samyne."[2] The Scots churchmen, however, managed to negotiate rather better terms for themselves with the king. In 1534–35 a permanent settlement was made, whereby a yearly sum of £1400 was to be payable out of the benefices, towards the support of the College of Justice, and the king was to enjoy the casualties of the temporalities of the prelates for a year, whenever they fell vacant, with the right of nominating the successors. In addition, the prelates bound themselves to supply a sum of £72,000 Scots, to be paid in four years.[3]

These transactions were to have very deep and lasting effects upon the course of Scots history. In the first place, they greatly accelerated the process of the feuing of land—the most important rural development of our period. Professor Hannay traces out how the feuing of the lands of Lesmahagow by Kelso Abbey was the direct result of this taxation, and this was only one case among many. The question of feuing, however, will be dealt with later. In the second place, the payments from the Church had their immediate effects upon the policy of James V. Parliament passed laws strongly affirming the allegiance of Scotland to the Church of Rome and a considerable persecution

[1] R. K. Hannay, "On the Foundation of the College of Justice," *Scottish Hist. Review*, vol. xv, p. 36.

[2] *Ibid.* p. 38.

[3] R. K. Hannay, "A Study in Reformation History," *Scottish Hist. Review*, vol. xxiii, pp. 25, 41.

followed. When Henry VIII, in 1534, 1535, and 1540, feeling himself unpleasantly isolated in his policy, tried to induce the needy James V to throw in his lot with him and to enrich himself by breaking with Rome and seizing the lands of the Church, the Scots king was not to be moved.[1] His bent towards a policy that was anti-Reformation and anti-English and pro-Roman and pro-French was very definitely strengthened by his two French marriages and by the personal influence of those great churchmen the Beatons, uncle and nephew. During the last shadowed years of his reign, unbearably pressed for money, it was to the proscription of those of his nobles who were suspected of leanings towards the Reformed faith rather than to the confiscation of Church lands that his mind apparently turned. The *débâcle* of Solway Moss, which broke the failing king's heart, was the outcome of his policy. Always bearing in mind that a considerable agrarian change was proceeding all the time, as the result of the taxation of the Church lands, it is perhaps most convenient to continue a sketch of the politico-economic history of the period.

[1] J. Cunningham, *Church History of Scotland*, pp. 233-234.

CHAPTER III

The Political Background

In the last chapter the influence of current politics upon the possessions of the Church had, of necessity, to be alluded to. Before considering the great agrarian effects of the Reformation and of the events that led up to it, it is essential that the general state of the country should be taken more fully into account. Throughout the whole period between the fourteenth and the end of the sixteenth centuries Scotland had a most troublous career, and her affairs were infinitely complicated by the numerous minorities of her sovereigns and by her relations with England. The greater part of the sixteenth century saw a very crescendo of internal woes and external troubles.

In 1542, at Solway Moss, the Scots army turned and fled from the English, James V died, and Scotland was called upon to endure the worst, or almost the worst, of the many minorities. The country was not only vexed by the rivalries of Beaton, Hamilton, Angus, Mary of Lorraine, Lennox, and other great personages, but it also became the object of larger contentions. In the great European struggles of the sixteenth century those bitter rivals the English and the French contended for the adherence of Scotland, and even vaster issues were at stake and religion became mixed up with politics in the struggle of the Reformation. It is not necessary to trace out the tangle of separate and yet closely interwoven threads of policy that were spun by the principal leaders—Mary of Lorraine and Beaton, France, and the supporters of the Old Faith generally upon the one side; Angus and the Assured Lords, England, and the Protestants upon the other; Hamilton and Lennox wavering amid vaster issues as personal considerations swayed them—countless warring and jarring forces conglomerated into one great dissension.

The economic effects of such a period of stress were considerable, and mainly account for the general backwardness of the country. It was largely because Scotland enjoyed nothing analogous to the Tudor period of English history, with its consolidation and advance in prosperity and industrial and commercial affairs, that her development in the seventeenth century was so different. In justice to our forebears, we must allow for the state of the times in which they lived when we comment upon the poverty and backwardness of the country; the primitive state of many of its institutions and of its industrial organization; and on the survival of the feudal spirit.

A mere catalogue of some of the worst things that happened gives a better picture of the political state of the country than pages of generalizations. Some of the leaders were not backward in making hay during the brief sunshine of their interludes of dominance. Hamilton (afterwards Arran) did so to a disgraceful degree, although Beaton's honesty was above reproach, and Mary of Lorraine was unique among the sovereigns of Scotland, in that, although she was severely hampered by poverty, she defrayed the whole of her personal expenses. Helped by a grant of two years' taxation upon Church lands, from the Pope, she even pulled together the national finances, so that in 1558 the treasurer had a small balance upon the right side.[1]

Far worse than the personal perquisitions of the faction in power, in its effect upon the condition of the nation, was the utter lawlessness that resulted from a state of almost chronic civil disturbance. The party temporarily in power had little surplus time or strength for enforcing the maintenance of law and order, or for securing the proper collection of the revenue. Leslie tells how, while the queen-mother and Arran were struggling for the regency, contentious people, hoping to escape punishment, began to call to remembrance old injuries. In Edinburgh, in the one year of 1555, the Carrs killed the laird of Buccleuch, the son of Lord Ruthven killed a gentleman, and Lord Sempill attacked Lord Crichton.[2]

[1] R. K. Hannay, "Church Lands at the Reformation," *Scottish Hist. Review*, vol. xvi, pp. 57, 60.

A. Cameron, *Scottish Correspondence of Mary of Lorraine* (Scottish History Society), p. xiii.

[2] Bishop Leslie, *History of Scotland*, vol. ii, p. 351.

Meanwhile Scotland was the victim of international politics.[1] Henry VIII was trying to bludgeon her into an abject alliance with England; and France, for selfish reasons, was encouraging her to resist. Immediately after the *débâcle* of Solway Moss, and with the traitorous help of the Assured Lords, Henry had tried to arrange a peace that would have included the marriage of the baby Queen of Scots and his son Prince Edward, and which would thus have led to the eventual union of the kingdoms—but upon very unequal terms. Having failed to carry his point, he renewed the war, and, in one expedition alone, Leith was sacked and burnt and all its shipping destroyed. Edinburgh was next attacked, and, after street fighting, it was fired in three or four places. An eye-witness has left a circumstantial account of the damage in *The Late Expedicioun in Scotlande*: "The nexte mornynge very erly we began where we lefte, and continued burnynge all that daye and the two dayes nexte ensuinge contynvally, so that neyther within ye wawles, nor in the suburbes, was lefte any one house vnbrent, besydes the innumerable botyes, spoyles and pillages that our souldyours brought fro thense, not withstandyng habundance whiche was consumed with fyer." [2]

At the same time the country was devastated to within six miles of Stirling. Kinghorn, part of Pittenweem, Burntisland (all in Fifeshire) were burnt by the fleet, and also Queensferry; while the land forces, on their march home, destroyed Musselburgh, Preston, Seton, Haddington, and Dunbar, and as many peels, houses, and villages as could be "conveniently reached." In other raids Jedburgh and Coldingham were burnt, and an official return of "Exployts don upon the Scots" gives a list of the harrying and burning of 192 "towns, towers, stedes, barnikyns, parysche churches, bastell houses" in addition and in other districts. All this was done in one year.

During 1545 there were constant raids. Another official return gives the names of 287 "fortresses, abbeys, frere-houses, market townes, villages, townes and places brent, raced and cast downe.

[1] See, for an example, *Exchequer Rolls*, vol. xviii, p. lxxi.

[2] *The Late Expedicioun in Scotlande*, printed in Dalyell's *Fragments of Scots History*, p. 7.

" Whereof are—

In monasteries and frear-houses	7
In castells, townes and piles	16
In market townes	5
In villagies	243
In mylnes	13
In spytells and hospitalls	3"

These include the abbeys of Kelso, Melrose with the town, Dryburgh with thirteen or fourteen hamlets, Jedburgh with its town and surrounding villages, and Eccles. The corn was standing at the time and the English methodically set fire to it.[1] Figures survive of the loss to the revenue. For five years all fermes had to be remitted to Jedburgh ; Lauder, also, yielded no fermes and Newhaven no customs ; for years the returns from Dunbar were greatly reduced. But the sufferings of the people and the setback to prosperity can only be imagined.

All this happened when there was almost a state of civil war between the French party, which was dominant at the time, and the pro-English party—Glencairn, Angus, Lennox and Cassillis—followed by an extraordinary *volte-face* in which Mary of Lorraine and Angus, with the rest of the Douglases, were allied together against the Hamiltons (Arran) and Cardinal Beaton. Rival parliaments were summoned and the English envoys did not know which party to treat with as representing the Government of Scotland. To crown all, two subsidies, amounting to £42,000, had to be voted in that year.[2]

The following year the English, who had continued to occupy Coldingham, ravaged the Borders. The Scots, under Angus, achieved the victory of Ancrum Moor and received some help from France; but, in the autumn, the English took a frightful revenge. In an expedition on the Eastern Marches they burnt the abbeys of Kelso, Melrose, Dryburgh, Roxburgh, and Coldingham. In the South-West, Henry VIII tampered with Lord Maxwell, who gave up the castles of Caerlaverock, Lochmaben, and Threave, but these were recaptured by the Scots. Rather farther north he engineered a rising, in which

[1] D. Hay Fleming, *The Reformation in Scotland*, pp. 331-333. These references are but instances of the damage done. See also *Hamilton Papers*, vol. i, Nos. lxix, cxi, xciv.

[2] Paper by T. Thomson, *Cranstoun* v. *Gibson*.

the Highlanders of the West co-operated with Lennox and Glencairn and the castle of Dumbarton was captured, but that also was quickly regained.

In 1546 there was a lull in the fighting, but some idea of the weakness of the kingdom may be gained from the fact that when Cardinal Beaton was murdered, his assassins and their supporters, 150 persons in all, were able to hold out for two years in the castle of St Andrews in spite of the utmost endeavours of the ruling party in Scotland, and were finally captured by the French.

In 1547 the Protector Somerset, continuing Henry's policy, invaded Scotland once more. He inflicted a crushing defeat on the main forces of Scotland at Pinkie, a few miles to the south of Edinburgh, overran the country as far as the Firth of Tay, burnt Leith, and, most significant move, permanently occupied Haddington, the richest corn-growing centre in Scotland and only seventeen miles from the capital. There was also a raid on the Western Borders. 1548 was a dark year for Scotland; the English continued to hold Haddington and ravaged the country round it. Dalkeith Castle, Musselburgh, and Dunbar were burnt, and the English were able to boast that they had "under assurance the greater part to Edinburgh and beyond." The French sent help, but this was countered by a fresh English invasion. At last, in 1549, the French and Scots were able to drive out the English, who evacuated Haddington in November of that year, after holding it for eighteen months. About this time the country was called upon to raise a further subsidy of £35,000.[1] These operations are only the most considerable ones. There were constant raids upon the Borders and a state of war existed continuously upon the high seas—a very serious thing for Scotland, for, in order to reach the Low Countries, where her main trading centre was situated, her ships had to run the gauntlet of the whole coast-line of Eastern England.

In 1550 Scotland was included in the Anglo-French treaty of Boulogne. The rivalries between the two countries, however, did not cease with the end of actual hostilities. In the spheres of diplomacy and of politics there was a continuance

[1] I am indebted to a manuscript note by Professor Hannay for the correct date of this subsidy.

of high tension, which produced a general instability throughout the rest of the period.

Meanwhile, with the growing power of the new religion, a far more fundamental struggle was approaching its crisis. It is fascinating to work out the curious ramifications, large and small, of the great change—the effect of the very marked mental activity that accompanied the Reformation, for instance, upon the newly developing printing trade and upon the importation of books. "The Reformation may be said to have founded the book trade in Scotland," and of the three hundred books that were printed there during the sixteenth century, only thirty-four had appeared before the Reformation (although this must have also been due not to religious preoccupation but to the fact that printing was everywhere becoming more general by the middle of the century).[1] The effect of the law of 1579, that every householder with more than 300 merks yearly rent and all substantious yeomen and burgesses worth £500 in land or goods must have a Bible and Psalm-book in their mother tongue, can be imagined: for this was not one of the acts that were merely dead letters—at least, according to John Knox, "then mycht have bene seen the Byble lying almaist apoun euerie gentelmannis table." The queer mingling of religion and politics in the English dealings with Scotland also stimulated the book trade. When Henry VIII tampered with the loyalty of the Scots lords, he was careful, in every shameful pact, to insert a clause that the traitors should cause the Word of God to be taught and preached in their countries, and it was suggested to Arran that "it were not amiss to let slip amongst the people the Bible and the New Testament in English," and the English offered to supply him with quantities of these books. Later on, the English ambassador reported that there was a keen demand for Bibles and New Testaments in Scotland, and that "a cartload of them would be bought there."[2]

Their adherence to the Old Faith or the New is an interest-

[1] M. A. Bald, "Vernacular Books imported into Scotland," 1500–1625, *Scottish Hist. Review*, vol. xxiii, p. 266.

W. Law Mathieson, *Religion and Politics*, p. 208.

C. Rogers, *Social Life in Scotland*, vol. i, p. 392, gives a general sketch of early Scots printing.

[2] *Letters and Papers, Foreign and Domestic: Henry VIII*, vol. xix, Part I, Nos. 243, 522, 779; vol. xviii, Part I, Nos. 157, 214.

ing index of the development of independent thought among different sections of the community. In the towns an ardour for Reform was a symbol of the rising influence of the merchant-folk.[1] Leith was one of the earliest towns to declare for the Reformation. Perth was a staunch adherent. Dundee, however, was the chiefest supporter of the new doctrines. The "gude and godlie ballates" were produced there, and, in 1547, Bibles were in great demand. "The fervour of Dundee, reflected more or less in all the eastern seaports, found many converts among the gentry of Forfar, Kincardine, Fife, and Lothian." Killigrew's well-known dictum, "I see the noblemen's great credit decay in that country"—(Scotland)—"and the barons, boroughs and such-like take more upon them,"[2] has been constantly quoted, and no doubt it is true that the Reformation was partly a stimulus to and partly a result of the greater powers exerted by the merchants, the middle classes, of Scotland. Nevertheless, feudalism also had a great deal of influence upon the spread of the New Faith. As Cunningham, in his *Church History*, has pointed out, it was the support of the lords to the Reformation that was the decisive factor. It was monarchical in England and baronial in Scotland. Moreover the main support among the country-folk came from those districts of the West where Argyle and Glencairn were powerful, and from Fifeshire, which was under the influence of Lord Lindsay, the Earl of Rothes, and Lord James Stuart. Contrariwise, the great Gordon estates remained definitely pro-Roman with the Huntly family; and Carrick, under one Lord Cassillis, who was a Reformer, supported the Reformation, and under the next one, who was opposed to it, reverted to the Old Faith.[3] The effects, direct and indirect, of the Reformation, however, are innumerable, and in this single book only those which were most purely economic and most lasting can be even indicated.

Meanwhile, the national finances continued to go from bad to worse. Yet another subsidy of £20,000 was imposed in 1554.[4] In 1556 the Lords Auditors of the Exchequer calculated that the royal lands—still the most important source of the

[1] W. Law Mathieson, *Politics and Religion in Scotland*, p. 200.
[2] *Calendar of Foreign Papers*, 1572–74, No. 634.
[3] J. Cunningham, *History of the Church of Scotland*, pp. 351, 352, 353.
[4] T. Thomson, Law Papers, *Cranstoun* v. *Gibson*.

national revenue—only brought in £15,522, or with grassums and victual £17,515.[1] Allowing for depreciation, this probably represented a smaller sum than the income of James IV, and it was wholly inadequate to maintain the standard of living of sixteenth-century royalty. A tax of £4000 was levied in 1556 and in the following year £15,000 was required, but the latter sum was to provide for the expenses of the sovereign's wedding, which had always been the occasion of an extra levy.

In 1560 came the final armed clash between the supporters of the Old Religion and the New. The Treaty of Edinburgh, which Hume Brown has named the " central point " in Scots history,[2] was arranged by the French and English Commissioners. Religion is not mentioned in this document, but it left the Reformers in power and they were not slow to carry out their wishes. The Estates met. The Confession of Faith was produced and approved. The old religion was swept away.

The religious questions dealt with at this momentous parliament are not our affair. The allocation of the great possessions that still remained to the Church, however, was a by no means unimportant side issue, and very greatly concerns the student of economic history. The thorough-going Reformers, with John Knox as their most influential leader, were for transferring the whole of the revenues of the Old Church to the New, and in the first *Book of Discipline*, produced in 1560, they sketched out a scheme in which these resources should be employed for the maintenance of an adequate ministry, for the provision of education, and for the support of the poor. They were, however, in a minority. The Reformation had been carried through largely by the support of a large section of the nobility, and it was the nobility who had most benefited by the distribution of Church lands. Not unnaturally, they were opposed to the new scheme. The matter was thrashed out at a General Convocation of the Estates in Edinburgh. Representatives of the Old Church (which included a large number of commendators) made the proposal that one-fourth of the

[1] D. Murray Rose, *Revenues of the Scottish Crown.*

[2] P. Hume Brown, *History of Scotland*, vol. ii, p. 69.

The actual amount in 1562 was £73,880 from the thirds of benefices, of which £24,231 was allotted to the Church.—J. Cunningham, *History of the Church in Scotland*, p. 384.

Church benefices be surrendered to the Crown, and that the remaining three-fourths be left to the present incumbents. Eventually, in 1561–2, it was agreed that one-third of the revenues of the Church should be confiscated and divided between the needs of the Crown and the Protestant Church, and that two-thirds should be left with the " auld possessouris " during their lives.[1] This arrangement, which John Knox stigmatized as " two-thirds to the Devil and one-third between God and the Devil," virtually remained in force during the following twenty-six years—till 1587.[2] (In fact, so far as the very inadequate provision for the New Church went, it virtually remained in force until the seventeenth century.) The interests of the higher prelates and of the commendators were thus safeguarded, but no provision was made for the unfortunate rank and file of the Old Church, who were reduced to beggary, although Mary Queen of Scots, straitened as were her own means, did something to relieve them. The financial position of the new ministry, as their numbers slowly increased, was very little, if anything, better. Politically, the compromise cannot have been without effect. Staunch supporter of Rome as Mary was, she was also partly financially dependent upon the fruits of the Reformation.

The brief and tragic story of Mary's actual reign in Scotland is about the most often told episode in the whole life-story of the nation. All but one out of the five Jameses had given their country an interlude of comparatively stable government during their short-lived days of power. With Mary it was otherwise. The financial state of the country was as bad as ever—in 1564 the treasurer's deficit was £32,698, by next year over £10,000 had been added to the debt. By 1569, a year after her abdication, it was £60,000. The exchange with England had dropped to £6 Scots to the £1 sterling.[3] The country was in a state of uncertainty and suspense, for its future religion, with enormous political complications, trembled in the balance. Factions were strong at court and there were plots, counter-plots, alarums, and excursions. Murray rose into

[1] D. Masson, *Introduction, Register of the Privy Council*, Second Series, vol. i, p. cxvii.

[2] *Ibid.* p. cxviii, cxix.

[3] R. K. Hannay, *Scottish Hist. Review*, vol. xvi, p. 61; also vol. xv, p. 36.

power, fell, rose again, and finally broke with Mary. Bothwell's extraordinary career is part of the poignant fabric of Scotland's best-known love story. Huntly and his house were suddenly ruined and then were restored. The Hamiltons pursued their usual self-interested and wavering line of policy. There were no less than four campaigns during the seven years of Mary's personal reign—the expedition against Huntly, the Run-about Raid, the struggle which ended with the *débâcle* of Carberry Hill, and the Battle of Langside, from which Mary fled to England.

In 1568, after Mary's abdication, there followed twenty years of the actual and virtual minority of James VI. Thirteen of these years were occupied by four successive regencies: the regency of the Earl of Moray, the king's half-uncle, terminated by his assassination after three years; a year's regency by the king's grandfather, the Earl of Lennox, who was killed during a sortie from Edinburgh; the regency of the Earl of Mar, which lasted for about a year, when he died, worn out; and the regency of the Earl of Morton, which lasted till 1575, when he was displaced, but, by a *coup d'état*, regained his power and retained it in a sort of premiership till 1580, when he was executed. During the first fifteen years of this minority there was a strong pro-Marian party in Scotland, civil war was continuously imminent, and disorders broke out several times. Several nobles were forfeited. After the assassination of Moray, the first regent, the country was without a leader for five months, because the Estates were so profoundly divided among themselves that they were unable to appoint anyone. The Marian party at this time were so strong that Elizabeth intervened and sent an army to Edinburgh. There were raids and counter-raids in the North, and, owing to trouble on the Borders, the English burned down Dumfries. By 1571, "the haill realm of Scotland was sae divided in factions, that it was hard for any peaceable man as he rode out the hie way, to profess himself openly either to be a favourer of the king or queen. All the people were casten sae lowse, and were become of sic dissolute minds and actions, that nane was in account but he that wuld either kill or rieve his neighbour."[1] In that year civil war was

[1] *Historie of King James the Saxt*, quoted by R. Chambers, *Domestic Annals of Scotland*, p. 72.

begun in earnest. The castle and town of Edinburgh were held for the queen. The king's forces occupied Leith and besieged the capital, and fighting went on all over what is now the pleasant land of the Lothians and the suburbs of Edinburgh. In a desperate raid by the queen's supporters upon Stirling, Lennox, the governor, was killed. At the same time there was also fighting in Aberdeenshire. The attacks on Edinburgh continued fifteen months, till August 1572, when England and France arranged a truce which lasted till the end of the year. Mar was now dead and had been succeeded by Morton. When the fighting was resumed, Edinburgh itself was in the hands of the king's party, though the castle was still held for the queen, and the town suffered severely from the fire of the castle guns. In May, English artillery was sent up to bombard the castle, and it surrendered after a siege of two years and one month. The power of the Marian party was now broken. So greatly did the capital suffer during these troubles that the Privy Council actually resolved that a Royal Proclamation should be made urging all "habill" men to go abroad and enlist as soldiers, and that the other citizens should remove themselves and their dependants to the country on account of the hunger, dearth, and scarcity of victuals in Edinburgh.[1]

The execution of Morton, in 1580, brought no period of stable, autocratic rule to Scotland, for, to quote Professor Masson, "there followed (on the ordinary principle of alternate hold of the helm by one political party for a while and by the antagonistic party for another while) a series of haphazard Cabal Governments, describable neither as Regencies nor as Premierships."[2] From 1580 till August 1582 Scotland was governed jointly by two very new grandees: Esmé Stuart, a fascinating French cousin of the king's upon the Lennox side of his lineage, who had been granted the earldom of Lennox, which was afterwards made into a dukedom; and Captain James Stewart of Ochiltree, by an irony of fate John Knox's brother-in-law, who had secured the earldom of Arran during the eclipse of the Hamilton family. From 1582 to 1583 the Earl of Gowrie and a faction with strong Presbyterian sym-

[1] *Register, Privy Council*, vol. ii, p. 184.

[2] D. Masson, *Introduction, Register of the Privy Council*, Second Series, vol. i, p. cxix.

pathies were in power, followed by two years' anti-Presbyterian government by James Stewart, Earl of Arran, who had eclipsed his former colleague Lennox. In 1587, what Professor Masson terms a "coalition Government" came into power, consisting of members of the faction that had sympathized with Lord Ruthven, Hamiltons, and others; while Stewart, who for a short time had been Earl of Arran, retired into private life.

Many of these changes of party were accomplished with violence, and the period saw more than its full share of the transfer of lands and powers. There was the fall of the Hamiltons, brought about by Morton. The fall of Morton, brought about by Esmé Stuart, Lord d'Aubigny, and by Captain James Stewart, the son of Lord Ochiltree. The rise of Esmé Stuart has been described; he also received the commendatorship of the abbey of Arbroath. The rise of Stewart (of Ochiltree) has also been mentioned; he was made Earl of Arran upon a pretended relationship to the Hamiltons. The fall of the new Lennox (d'Aubigny) was followed by that of his opponent, the Lord of Gowrie.

It is not wonderful that throughout a period of such changes the country should have reached a very nadir of lawlessness. Commissions of Justiciary were very frequent. The rendering of the customs, etc., was uncertain; during the fighting Queen Mary's supporters collected them when they could, and the accounts of the revenue are very much disordered.[1]

Meanwhile, the financial position was unsatisfactory. The treasury deficit grew steadily:

In 1564 it was £32,696.
,, 1569 ,, 60,500.
,, 1583 ,, 67,000.

Constant recourse had to be made to taxation to supplement the resources that had become so insufficient, and the following subsidies were levied:

1580 . . .	£40,000	0	0	
1584 . . .	20,000	0	0	
1586 . . .	15,000	0	0	
1588 . . .	100,000	0	0	This was for James' marriage.
1593 . . .	100,000	0	0	
1597 . . .	133,332	13	4	

[1] *Exchequer Rolls*, vol. xx, pp. lvii, lix, lx, lxiv.

In 1574–75 the Crown was said to be "inabill upoun the present rentis thairof to sustein evin now the estait of our soverane lord and public chargies of the realme, meikle les to beir out his majesteis estait and expensis at his mair mature and perfyte aige." In 1587 no less than fourteen acts were passed bearing upon the king's property and income. In one of them the king was said to have been brought into great debt by the negligence of his officers, partly by not inbringing of his highness' patrimony and rents in due time, partly by the disponing and setting of the same untimeously and unthriftily. Therefore the Crown lands were to be wadsetted to the amount of £1000 annually.[1] In 1596, owing to the king's extreme poverty, eight Commissioners of the Exchequer, known as the Octavians, were appointed to collect and administer the royal revenue, and they effected a considerable improvement.

Meanwhile, the division of the Church lands that had been made in Queen Mary's reign (one-third between the ministers and the Crown, and two-thirds to the old possessors) came in for revision. By this time—about 1587—the bulk of the two-thirds left in the hands of the prelates and abbots for their lifetime had lapsed to the Crown, as they gradually died off, and most of the abbeys had been given *in commendam* to those courtiers and faction leaders who happened to be in power at the moment. No doubt this was done for a purpose. The writer of the *Diurnal of Occurrents* notices in 1570 the "greedy and insatiable appetite for benefices," and says that "there was none brought under the king's obedience but for reward either given or promised."

These commendations might also be likened to a sort of medium of exchange in the struggle for power. Stuarts of all degrees of kinship to the king or to his two Stuart favourites, Hamiltons, Douglases, members of the great families of Gordon, Campbell, Kennedy, and Home, all received commendatorships. Many of these desirable prizes changed hands many times over during that period of uncertain tenure of life and power—Arbroath no less than six times, Paisley five times,

[1] *A.P.S.* vol. iii, p. 456. In spite of the fact that the income of the Crown was considerably increased owing to the "annuals" = certain payments to religious houses which had lapsed to the Crown when they were destroyed (*Exchequer Rolls*, vol xix, p. lviii).

Dunfermline five times, Pittenweem four times, Kelso four times, St Andrews three times. The effect upon the development of such property can be imagined. In all there were forty-six commendatories.[1]

In the case of the second important section of the benefice-holders, the archbishops and bishops, the same wholesale transfers had not been carried out, but a new device, the institution of what were commonly called *tulchan* bishops, was introduced. The tulchan was a stuffed calf which the country-people used to put in front of a cow to make her give her milk when she had been separated from her own calf. The archbishopric of St Andrews had fallen to the share of the Earl of Morton and, after his fall, to the Duke of Lennox, and a series of tulchans had been appointed. Glasgow, somewhat docked of its revenues, a large share of which had gone to Mar and Morton whilst they were in power, had passed to Lennox, who appointed a Mr Keith as bishop under an agreement that he should have £1000 Scots annually and certain dues paid in kind, and that the rest of the revenues should go to Lennox and his heirs. The bishopric was afterwards bestowed upon a layman. Much the same melancholy tale can be told of the rest of the bishoprics—Dunkeld was held by a layman; Brechin, Ross, Orkney, Argyle, and the Isles by tulchans or virtual tulchans; Caithness was vacant, and had been much dilapidated by the late bishop;[2] Galloway had been bequeathed by one bishop to his son.

The status and continuance of bishoprics in the Church was a matter of violent political struggle during the period. It varied as the parties supporting the Kirk or the king gained and lost power. It was, in fact, a very storm-centre in the war of mingled polemics and politics which afflicted Scotland at this time, and which it is, fortunately, not our lot to unravel. So matters had dragged on until 1578.

There was yet one more important class of Church property, i.e. the teinds, whose value was estimated by one authority at about one-fourth of the rents of all the lands of the kingdom.

[1] D. Masson, *Introduction to the Register of the Privy Council*, Second Series, vol. i, p. cxx, for full list. See also *Register of Dunfermline*, p. xvii; *Liber de Calchou*, vol. i, p. xvi.

[2] D. Masson, *Register, Privy Council*, vol. i (Second Series), p. cxxix.

Although the post-Reformation Church of Scotland claimed the whole patrimony of the Old Church, she especially stressed her right to these dues. The arrangement by which the Church shared one-third of the revenues of the Old Church with the Crown was regarded as a temporary measure. Fairly early in the struggle, in 1567, the pro-Protestant party, led by the Regent Moray, had admitted this. An ordinance of the Privy Council had been passed safeguarding the Church's share of the third, but stating that this was only to be operative "aye and quhill the Kirk come into full possession of her proper patrimony, quhilk is the teinds." [1]

It is not possible to tell here of the ups and downs of Church finance, of how the collection and disbursement of the half of the third varied under different régimes, or of the organization and growth of the new Kirk. She was not able to make good her claims to the teinds, which lapsed to the Crown with other Church property and were given away or leased out in the same way.

The problem of the teinds had already become a complex one before the Reformation, for the practice had grown up of *annexing* or *appropriating* parishes to the monasteries, bishoprics, etc., who exercised the patronage, drew the teinds and made their own arrangements for the performance of the spiritual offices of the parish by a *vicar* or *curate*. Professor Masson estimated that "between 600 and 700 of all the 900 or 1000 parish churches of Scotland had been so annexed or appropriated to the larger ecclesiastical establishments, leaving only about 260 as independent parsonages." The practice of leasing the right to collect the teinds of the appropriated parishes to tacksmen of the teinds had also become very common. With the piecemeal allocation of Church property at the Reformation the complexities of the ownership and collection of the teinds were increased and became a burning grievance. "Property rights were very obscure and disputes were constantly arising, leading to litigation in the law-courts and armed struggles on the ground. The proclamations of the period frequently refer to the annual leading of the teinds as an occasion of illegal convocation in arms." [2]

[1] D. Masson, *Register, Privy Council*, vol. i (Second Series), p. cxii.
A. Birnie, *A Short History of the Scottish Teinds*, p. 35.

[2] *Ibid.* p. 38.
D. Masson, *Register, Privy Council*, vol. i (Second Series), pp. cxiii, cxvi.

In 1578 a most important act was passed for the annexation of the temporalities of the Church. In its preamble it was stated that because all the lands and revenues "disponit of auld" to abbeys, monasteries, and the clergy had originally been Crown or national property, and because the possession of these revenues was neither necessary nor profitable to the Reformed Church, and because the Crown had been so impoverished by these large gifts that it had been obliged to levy heavy taxation, therefore the whole of the lands and possessions of the clergy, regular and secular, were to be declared re-annexed to the Crown, and to be at its disposal for all time coming, subject to certain very important exceptions. These included lands already erected into temporal lordships, which included five abbacies and a considerable amount of other land; certain classes of Church property—the manses and glebes of parish ministers, the castles, etc., of bishops; all lands and revenues devoted to hospitals, colleges, schools, and, most important, the teinds. These latter were not formally annexed to the Crown, and were left in the unsatisfactory and chaotic state that they had drifted into. (Not till 1617 was the matter dealt with at all. The subsequent history of the teinds was to have important bearings upon the general political history of Scotland.) The act, however, had given the king the whole of the Old Church lands belonging to the secular as well as the regular clergy, the temporalities as well as the bishoprics. He was specially given the power to feu out his new possessions, and he also continued the process of erecting temporal lordships from such lands, which had begun before the act was passed and which had been confirmed by it.[1] Maitland, in his *Historie of James the Saxt*, describes the whole transaction. He says: "that it war necessar that the temporal lands of the prelaceis sould be annexed to the Crown to enriche the same, which was then at small rent. And he considderit weill that offers wald be maid be every possessour, wha wald bestow layrge money to obtene the gift thareof to him self heretablie, and that the king was frank in granting lands as he mycht be persuaded, being facile of his nature; and thareby he thught to make gayne of a part of the offerris to be maid, as it fell owt indeid." [2]

[1] D. Masson, *Register, Privy Council*, vol. i (Second Series), pp. cxxxv, cxxxvi, cxxxvii.

[2] Quoted by R. K. Hannay, *Scottish Hist. Review*, vol. xvi, p. 71.

CHAPTER IV

Part I. Lack of Security of Tenure under Feudal System

We have seen how the question of the possession of the land affected the general history of Scotland during this period. It is now time to consider some of the more purely practical and economic aspects of landholding during the fourteenth, fifteenth, and sixteenth centuries.

Feudalism was in a sense a system of land nationalization, for it was founded upon the theory that all land belonged to the king, who granted portions of it to individual subjects in return for their services to the State. During the period we are now studying this was no empty abstraction. Land was constantly reverting to the Crown and being re-granted. The general circumstances of the time combined to make a practical reality of the theorizings of contemporary jurists. Life was uncertain and short; the infant mortality was heavy, so that heirs often failed to survive; the individuals who struggled to maturity seldom seem to have enjoyed the span of the Psalmist. Moreover, when charters were very newly granted, the usual proviso limiting inheritance to the direct descendants of the recipient—to the heirs of his body—circumscribed the descent within narrow limits. During the period before the Wars of Independence, the chartulary of Melrose shows that the old line of the Lords of Galloway, of Carrick, and of March, and the De Morvilles all died out. They were succeeded by the Fitz Ranulphs and De Soulis, and by branches of the Grahams and the Douglases, who also died out. The chartulary of Arbroath shows the same sweeping changes among the gentry of Fife.[1] Probably much the same thing will be found to be the case in most districts, if their remote past is investigated.

[1] C. Innes, *Sketches of Early Scottish History*, pp. 41, 171.

The changes and chances of this transient life in ancient Scotland were much augmented by the exigencies of her stormy political history. The Wars of Independence profoundly affected the landowning class. " You will find, I think," wrote Cosmo Innes, " that the greatest number of charters of King Robert I proceeded on forfeiture." Sometimes in these charters the clause appears of *que proprius fuerunt A.B. inimici nostri*, some merely mention that the lands belonged to a Baliol or a Comyn as a sufficient explanation of the fact that they were in the king's hands.[1]

During the next three hundred years, land was constantly changing hands as the Crown waxed or waned in strength. The actions of the kings, even in arbitrarily confiscating land, cannot be considered as purely lawless, for according to feudal theories they were but resuming their own. They proceeded in no hole-and-corner manner, for as almost all of them assumed sovereign powers his parliament passed an act regarding the alienation of lands and movable goods in prejudice of the Crown, and revoking the grants that had been made during the king's minority. James II passed such an act in 1437, and James IV in 1488, which revoked all the grants lately made by his father; and again, in 1503, there was a revocation of all donations hurting the Crown and the Holy Kirk. In 1535, James V secured a particularly sweeping act, which included the revocation of grants of feu-farm. In 1587, James VI caused a general revocation of all alienations made during his minority to be passed.[2]

The power of the Crown to give away land led to awkward predicaments, when, as happened several times, the king gave away the same land more than once. There was, for instance, the case of Castlehill and Stocket Wood, which was held by the burgesses of Aberdeen under a charter of 1494, but which was re-granted to Andrew of Blairtown. The matter was referred to the Lords of the Secret Council, who upheld the first charter.[3]

Under the Scots feudal system, land was constantly changing hands in accordance with the exigencies of the political situation.

[1] C. Innes, *Scotch Legal Antiquities*, p. 39.

[2] *A.P.S.* vol. ii, pp. 31, 113, 211, 357; vol. iii, pp. 228 (*especially interesting*), p. 439.

[3] *Exchequer Rolls*, vol. xi, p. xxxii.

A few examples culled at random from the *Scots Peerage* will show how temporary was the hold of many of the great landowners upon their possessions. The title of Earl of Athol was derived from the more ancient Gaelic one of mormaer. Its holders during the eleventh century appear to have been descendants of a brother of Malcolm Canmore. It then passed with an heiress to the Strathbogie family, which descended from a cadet of the family of the Earl of Fife. It remained in their hands for four lives. It was forfeited in 1314 A Campbell held it for a short time, but his line died out with his son. There was an interregnum when it was claimed by both Douglas, who had received a grant of it, and Strathbogie, during the second period of the Wars of Independence. Robert II granted it to a Stewart (his son) and this family held it for two lives. It was forfeited in 1341 The king held it till 1460, when he granted it to another Stewart (his brother). This line died out in 1595. It was then granted to a Stewart " of the same house," whose line held it for two lives and beyond the end of our period, and died out in 1626.

Buchan, another of the old Gaelic provinces, had been held by the Comyns. It was forfeited in 1314. The title was revived about 1382 and was bestowed upon the fourth son of Robert II when he married the Countess of Ross, who had come into possession of most of its ancient lands. On his death it passed to his elder brother, the Duke of Albany, who bestowed it upon his sons, first John, then Robert. The house of Albany was ruined and Robert seems quietly to have abandoned his claims to Buchan and other lands that he had received. In 1469 it was granted to another Stewart, not directly of the royal house, and was held for three lives. In 1574 it passed, through an heiress, to a Douglas; its further vicissitudes fall outside our period.

The earldom of Moray was owned by an even greater succession of different families.

The Hamilton family, though it had considerable tenacity, is a good example of the ups and downs that beset the great ones of the earth. The first successful member was a supporter of the Douglases and his lands were made into a barony in 1450. The family was not involved in the Douglas ruin, and in 1503 the head of the family was made Earl of Arran in virtue of his marriage with the king's sister. On the fall of Angus it received some of the Douglas lands. The second (Hamilton) Earl of Arran was regent during Mary Queen of Scots' minority and was made Duke of Châtelherault in 1548, when he was forced to give this position up. Later he was imprisoned for opposing Mary's marriage to Darnley, but was afterwards her strongest supporter. The third earl was insane, but his brother, Lord John Hamilton, took his place and was made commendator of Inchaffray and of Arbroath. In 1579 the Hamilton estates were forfeited and bestowed on James Stewart (of Ochiltree). In 1585, having seized the king, Hamilton displaced Stewart and was restored to the estates, and was made keeper of Dumbarton with a pension of 550 merks. In 1597, Lord John received liferent of Arbroath. In 1599 he was made Marquis of Hamilton, Earl of Arran. As a contrast, the Crawford peerage, which was created in 1398, descended from father to son, with ups and downs: for the family took its full share in the troublous deeds of the times, right through our period. And the same is the case with Huntly and Argyle.

Although the lesser barons were not so liable to forfeiture as the great lords, they also were insecure. The cadets and other supporters of a great family tended to fall and rise with it. Drummonds fell with the De Soulis, and were "art and part" in the second Douglas ruin. The unfortunate estate of Strathgartney is an extreme example of the insecurity of tenure of the times. The families of Logie and Menteith both desired to possess it, and, between 1320 and 1364, it changed hands between them no less than four times, according as the fortunes of Margaret, David's paramour and afterwards his wife, and those of her opponents waxed and waned.[1]

Part II. Kindly Tenants

The matter is of importance, not only because of the lairds themselves, but because the same conditions must have affected the smaller folk. In Scotland, where the manorial system never became established, and where customary law had no legal force as in England, there was no exact equivalent to the English tenure of copyholding. There was, however, a form

[1] *Exchequer Rolls*, xiv, p. xxxv; vol. ii, p. lvi. *A.P.S.*, xii, p. 556.

of holding which bore a strong resemblance to it in its earlier stages before custom had become legally binding. Kindly tenants seem to have existed all over Scotland, but the exact meaning of the term—the status of such tenants, whether they were generally considerable farmers or were only quite humble folk, and also the proportion that they bore to the rest of the population—is obscure. Little more is known about them than in the period preceding the Wars of Independence.[1] If one were to judge by the complaints made in their name during the feuing period, they would seem to have been numerous; but these documents were trying to make a case, and their statements must to some extent be discounted as due to the vigour of expression and over-emphasis that is characteristic of many documents of the period.

Various meanings are given to the word. In *Jamieson's Dictionary* the term is defined as "a name given to those tenants whose ancestors have long resided on the same land." But in a lease of Gorgie, near Edinburgh, a family is described as *kindly tenants* who had only occupied the lands for two generations.[2] There is, however, evidence that it was used more and more loosely as the feuing system, to be described later on, interfered with the kindly tenancies. Altogether apart from the introduction of feuing, however, it would seem that the security of this tenure varied in different parts of the country and upon different types of estate. Upon the estates of the earldom of Moray, on the North-east Coast, there is an example where their rights merely seem to have depended upon good feeling. In the seventeenth century there was a quarrel between Clan Chattan and Moray, because the latter had dispossessed certain kindly tenants of his who were members of the clan, but who lived in the comparatively Lowland district of Croy (kindly tenancies were less usual in the Highlands). The old account tells how these "began to call to mind how James, Earl of Moray, their master, had casten them out of their kindly possessions whilke past memory of man their predecessors and they had kept for small duty, but for their faithful service, and planted in their places, for payment of a greater duty, a number

[1] See Section I.

[2] J. Smith, "Lands of Gorgie," *Proc. Society of Antiquaries* [*Scots*], 1928, p. 274.

of strangers and feeble persons, unable to serve the earl, their master, as they could have done, by which means these gentlemen were brought through necessity to great misery." [1] The only remedy that is recorded is that of armed retaliation by the clan. On the other hand, "kindness" certainly had strong moral if not legal claims. In other parts of the country examples exist of the sale of kindly rights, and even of an action between rivals as to who had the best "kindness." [2] As one authority says: "In the west country many rentallers were termed heritable proprietors; and several of their rentals have appeared in court, not only granted to the tenants, their heirs and successors, but in the words of resignation, viz. *in perpetuam remanentiam*. Their widows succeeded and their sons were received. In course of time these rentallers would certainly have created a tenure of their own like their brethren the copyholders of England. The rentallers of Scotland, however, were overtaken in their progress by a fatal revolution, which the copyholders in England entirely escaped"—i.e. the dispersal of the Church lands and the introduction of feu-farming.[3]

When one comes to examine the Diocesan Registers of Glasgow, however, where such tenancies would be most likely to abound, and which contain a list of the transmission of all the holdings on the bishop's lands between 1510 and 1553, one is struck by the vagueness of the position. The entries nearly always state that the new holder is "rentallit" with the consent of the old one. Thus, for instance, to quote a typical entry: "Williame Thomsone rentallit in Xs. Xd. worth of land of Achinnarne, of the consent of his fader, Jhone Thomsone, to bruik efter his faderis decis and his moderis: he suld pay X merkis." [4] In this entry, as in many others, it will be noted (*a*)

[1] John Spalding, *History of the Troubles and Memorable Transactions in Scotland* (Bannatyne Club), p. 1.

[2] *Register, Privy Council*, vol. i, pp. xxxii, 428-429.

[3] W. Ross, *Lectures on the Practice of the Law of Scotland*, vol. ii, quotes a legal decision "that a man being rentalled in the King's rental, of any lands and possession, and deceases, leavand behind him wife and bairns, the bairns ought to be rentalled, and the wife should bruik the same for all the days of her life-time . . . but to have no power to put anyone else in the rental."

[4] J. Bain and C. Rogers, *Diocesan Register of Glasgow*, vol. i, p. 42 (A.D. 1510).

that the new holder is rentalled in an undemarcated share of a farm: how such joint holdings were managed—in separate strips, or by periodic re-allotment—is nowhere explained; (*b*) that a grassum is paid by the new tenant to the bishop. This grassum was generally ten or twelve times the amount of the assessed rent, but was sometimes not exacted. Generally the holdings went from husband to wife, from father or widowed mother to son, or from parents to daughter, the son-in-law in such cases being generally jointly rentalled in the holdings. But it was not uncommon for a holding to pass from a holder of one surname to that of another. (This cannot always be accounted for by the practice of calling a woman by her maiden name: for instance, on pp. 48-49—A.D. 1514—out of twelve transfers of holdings, no less than six, all originally held by *men*, went to rentallers of a different surname.) In such cases we do not, as a rule, know how the transfer was made. In 1553, however, it is definitely stated that Jonat Aitken, with the consent of her husband, had sold her right and kindness to 10s. worth of the lands of Carstairs to Thomas Summervel, and the latter is duly rentalled in the lands. Summervel had already "copt the kindness" of another piece of land from another woman.[1]

It is evident that holdings generally went to the nearest heir, and there is one instance of a disputed succession. An undated letter "To my Maister, the Person of Carstaris," runs:

"Maister, I commend my service hertlie to zow. Pleis zou to wit thar is ane barne, callit Robe Jonston, rentallit in XI pennevorth of land in the Towne of Carstaris, quhilk is now liand seik lik to de. Alan Johnston in Ravinstruthir is this barnis fader brother, and quhen his brother decessit, left the barne to him. The barnis moder was sib to Andro Clerkson, and was last possessour of this pece lande, and at hir latter hour left hir kyndnes of the samyn to Andro Clerkson, faillande hir barne; and now the barne is bot aucht or nyne zeir auld, and has left his kyndnes and gude will to Alan Johnston. Quharfor he hes causyt me wryte to zour m. to se gif zhe ma of gude zele resaif him tennent, and he sall cum incontinent with the money efferande tharto, and content zour m. by the rentell for zour

[1] J. Bain and C. Rogers, *Diocesan Register of Glasgow*, v. i, p. 200.

gude wyll, and zour ansuer agane and lat na man wit herof quhat zhe ma do hereintill. . . ."[1] Apparently Johnson got the land; at least he was, for a time, a tenant in Carstairs.

In another entry we find this man or a namesake granting consent to the transfer of a holding to a man named Mowat, although, from another entry, we know that he had a son who was rentalled in other parts of his land.[2]

Moreover, it is not at all clear how absolute were the rights of the rentallers to their lands. The widow of a rentaller seems to have been invariably allowed to retain her husband's holding during her lifetime.[3] Nevertheless, it is evident that there was a rule that upon remarriage she should forfeit the holding, for special permission was sometimes given allowing her to retain it "nochtwithstandyng our statutis in the contra."[4] On another occasion two new tenants were received with the consent of the present owner, but upon condition that they should pay their rents. Another holding came into the bishop's hands owing to the execution of its present holder. There are two instances in which tenants were removed. Thus, in 1507, Thomas Kelso was to be expelled from his holding "on account of his demerits," and we have an account of the procedure. The Serjeand, accompanied by witnesses, went to warn him, but the door and the windows were shut in their faces. The Serjeand then shouted his warning and left a cross affixed to the door; and at the next bailiff court the Chancellor warned Kelso to go, and imposed a penalty for every day he did not do so.[5]

Most of the rentallers appear to have been quite humble folk, but there were about eighteen or nineteen lairds, or relations of lairds, and rich burgesses of Glasgow who held land of the bishop.[6]

It may be noted that one interesting survival, the kindly tenants of Lochmaben, was exceptional. These tenants, who were specially favoured in memory of their services in the days of Robert the Bruce, held their specific rights, which included

[1] J. Bain and C. Rogers, *Diocesan Register of Glasgow*, v. i, p. 55.
[2] *Ibid.* pp. 54, 59.
[3] Cf. *ibid.* pp. 50-51, etc.
[4] Cf. *ibid.* p. 113, etc.
[5] *Ibid.* p. 81; a somewhat similar condition on pp. 80, 136, 436. See also p. 57.
[6] *Ibid.* pp. 27, 32.

that of alienating their land, by special charters, which were from time to time renewed.[1]

Perhaps it is safest to consider kindly tenancies not so much as a definite category of holding but as a manifestation of the general tendency of the slow-moving age to admit, formally or informally, the son's right to the position occupied by his father. Feudal services were bound up with the possession of land and the latter was hereditary, but, although the sheriffdoms nearly all became hereditary, no general rule was evolved that all sheriffdoms must be heritable ones. Among the burgesses, it was usual for a son to follow his father's trade, and, as the custom of buying the " freedom " to work grew up, he was definitely entitled to acquire it upon specially easy terms. In rural districts there are examples of hereditary mairs upon private estates, and there are even instances, in the sixteenth century, of the infeftment of the hereditary blacksmith of the lordship of Brechin and of a hereditary porter at Cupar Abbey.[2]

Part III. Tenants and Leases

Kindly tenants, however, only formed a part of the agricultural population, and it is now time to consider the condition of the generality of the folk who laboured the ground. It will be remembered that in Scotland their revolution was different to that of the English peasantry. We have seen the emergence of a class that was personally free, but that had no rights upon the land.[3]

The mythical account of the institution of feudalism has already been quoted.[4] W. F. Skene has pointed out that in Fordoun's fourteenth-century version we have what was really a picture of the state of society in his own day. After declaring that of old the king had possessed all the land and had given it out in portions to his followers, he continues : " Of these he granted to each one as much as he pleased, either on lease by the year as tillers of the ground, or for ten or twenty years, or

[1] J. Carmont, " Kindlie Tenants of Lochmaben," *Juridical Review*, vol. xxi, p. 321.

Exchequer Rolls, vol. xiv, p. cxxv.

[2] W. Macgill, *Old Ross-shire*, vol. i, pp. 6, 7, 110.

Spalding Club Miscellany, v, pp. 25, 291.

C. Rogers, *Rental Book of Cupar Abbey*, p. xli.

[3] See Chapter II, Parts II, III, IV, V.

[4] See p. 25 *n*.

in liferent with remainder to one or two lives, as free and kindly tenants, and to some likewise, though few, in perpetuity, as knights, thanes, and chiefs—not, however, so freely, but that each of them paid a certain annual feu-duty to their lord and king." [1] This passage most plainly implies that the lesser folk had no fixity of tenure. They were merely tenants in the modern sense, and it is as tenants that they are generally mentioned. For instance, in an order of 1556, for making a retour for taxation, a list was to be made of "the names of Friehalderis and fewaris, tennentes and parochiaris of everie parochin, alsweill of craftismen as utheres, and cotteris, inhabitantis of this realme." [2]

More considerable tenants, sometimes probably kindly tenants, sometimes very much resembling the tacksmen of a rather later period, often the predecessors of the feu-farmers, are to be found in most rentals—for instance, the total rental of the earldom of Sutherland (which was in the hands of the Crown between 1508 and 1513) was £240 18s. 0d., and of this, £147 13s. 4d. was paid by six tenants.[3] The proportion of considerable tenants in this rental, however, seems to be exceptional; in all the rentals that have survived to us the proportion of very short leases is very high, although their actual duration varied.

In Mr R. Lowell Jones' essay for the Carnegie Research Foundation, which, by the great courtesy of the Trustees, the present writer has been allowed to read, there is a summary of the length of leases upon Church lands. At Cupar they were usually for five to seven years, but were sometimes longer: there is, for instance, a tack for nine years and a life lease. At Arbroath, small areas and tofts were "invariably" let for five years, but there are examples of larger pieces of land letting for seven years, and one for nine, one for thirteen, one for fifteen, and several for seventeen years. Leases for one life or for two are frequent. Other chartularies are not so rich in lease records,

[1] *Fordoun's Chronicle* (*Historians of Scotland Series*), vol. ii, p. 177 (Fordoun died *circ.* 1384).

[2] Quoted by T. Thomson, Law Paper, *Cranstoun* v. *Gibson*, *Court of Session*, *Second Division*, 1816.

[3] *Exchequer Rolls*, vol. xiii, p. cxli.
Spalding Club Miscellany, iii, p. 6 (1467).
Liber de Scon, No. 63, p. 40.

but those of St Giles, Inchaffray, and Coldingham "point to the same conclusion."[1]

Short leases continued right through the period. In the Register of Dunfermline there is a list of tenants and of their holdings during the second half of the sixteenth century and the beginning of the seventeenth, and, although two or three families appear to have held their shares of the farms right through the period, on the whole there were constant changes and even the proportions of the individual shares of the farms were often changed.[2]

In the only early example of a lay rental—that of the Honor of Morton, 1376—almost all the grants of land were for one year, the only exceptions being five for two years, six for three years, and one for four years.[3]

In the case of the Huntly rental of 1600, leases of five years are by far the commonest.[4] A sixteenth-century rental of Haddington, published in the *Scottish Historical Review*, shows that only in one case had the former and present owner the same surname.[5]

The *Exchequer Rolls* give a good many Crown rentals, especially after 1480. Until the end of the fifteenth century there were no leases in Bute, and the tenure is uncertain; but the other lands were all carefully let, and in granting these lands in lease, "the commissioners are generally empowered to grant leases for either three or five years; a three years' lease is the rule, and is often granted in anticipation when the existing lease has yet two years to run. Five years' leases prevailed in Galloway," but there were a few for seven or fifteen years. In the Strathgartney district all the twenty leases are for three years; and in Menteith, out of twenty-two leases, ten are for three years and one for five years.[6] In the rentals for 1513–1522,

[1] *Chartulary of Cupar*, Nos. 20, 48, 50, 32, 47, 35, 96.
Chartulary of Arbroath, Nos. 184, 191, 194, 209, 262, 246, 256, 252, 258, 263, 264, 265.

[2] This list appears as an appendix.

[3] This example is quoted from Mr. R. Lowell Jones' essay.

[4] *Spalding Club Miscellany*, iv.

[5] *Scottish Hist. Review*, vol. x, p. 377.

[6] Mr. R. Lowell Jones' analysis of figures given in vol. xii of the *Exchequer Rolls*. Quotation is from *Introduction* to Appendix, *Exchequer Rolls*, vol. ix.

the leases in Galloway are generally for three years, those in Fife for five years, but sometimes for six or seven years. Life leases also occur.[1] One finds the same short leases throughout the period.

Major, writing in the sixteenth century and accounting for the smallness of the Scots country-people's houses, gives as a reason that: "They have no permanent holdings, but hired only, or in lease for four or five years, at the pleasure of the lord of the soil; therefore do they not dare to build good homes, though stone abound; neither do they plant trees nor hedges for their orchards, nor do they dung the land; and this is no small loss and damage to the whole realm." Major goes on to urge longer leases.[2]

Nor did the early Scots tenants even enjoy the customary security of the present-day leaseless farmers of England. In the Register of Dunfermline, in the list of tenants and holdings already noted, the constant variation in the names is very striking. It was customary to demand a grassum, generally equal to a year's rent, at the outset of every lease,[3] and Dunbar, in his poem on "Discretion in Taking," tells what only too often happened:

Barownis takis fra the tennentis peure
All fruct that growes on the feure
In Mailis and garsomes raisit ouir hie,
And garnis thame beg fra dure to dure.

"The great fines on renewal of leases" were one of the most bitterly felt burdens of the lesser folk.[4] An act of parliament of 1469 states that the peace of holy days is greatly broken because of "punding for malis and annualis incasting and owtcasting of tenandis quhilkis makkis gret discenswine and causes oft tymes gret gadderings and dissordis vpoun the solempint days of witsonday and martynes," and therefore orders that these things be done three days after the festivals.[5] An act of

[1] *Exchequer Rolls*, vol. ix, p. xxxv; vol. xiv, p. xxxv.

[2] J. Major, *History of Greater Britain* (Scottish History Society), p. 31.

[3] *Exchequer Rolls*, vol. ix, Appendix.

[4] Cf. *Register, Privy Council*, vol. i, p. 177, for a case where a landlord "satisfied" a tenant for her "kindness" and was able to turn her out.

[5] J. Mackintosh, *History of Civilization in Scotland*, vol. ii, p. 238, for quotations.

nearly a hundred years later, of 1546, states that because there are great convocations made in the realm for putting and laying men forth of their tacks and steadings, and to resist the lords of the ground and their bailies and officers to lay them forth, which is the occasion of great trouble amongst our sovereign lady's lieges, therefore proclamation is to be made throughout the kingdom that no one take upon hand to make any convocation for putting and laying forth of tenants, but that it be done by their bailiffs and officers orderly and conform to the laws of the realm observed and kept in time past, and that no man of the tenants make any convocation or gathering for resistance of their lords or their bailiffs or officers.[1] A further act was passed in 1555 ordering the landlord to give the tenant fifty days' notice, and empowering him to receive the assistance of the sheriff if the tenant refused to go.[2] Leslie says that the former act was passed in order that "nane rin in harness as tha use to cast out the cuntrie-men." [3] All this seems to show that evictions were fairly common.

It is true that during our period certain acts were passed to increase the security of the country-folk. In 1400 an act was passed preventing tenants from being victimised for the debts of their superiors; they were only to be liable for the amount of rent that they paid. Another act of the same year forbade feudal superiors from resuming holdings except where they could show lawful cause for doing so. If tenants repledged their lands within forty days they were not to be evicted for a year and a day. This latter act seems to have gone the way of many enactments of the Scots Parliament, for in 1429 the king requested the barons not to remove *coloni* nor *husbandi* suddenly from their lands if they had leases.[4] A more important act followed about 1449 (passed by a parliament of James I): "It is ordained, for the safety and favour of the poor people that labour the ground, that they, and all others that have taken or shall take lands in times to come from Lords, and have times and years thereof, that, suppose the Lords sell or alienate these lands, the Takers shall remain with their tacks unto the ische ('expiry') of their times, into whosesoever hands these

[1] *A.P.S.* vol. ii, p. 98. [2] *A.P.S.* vol. ii, pp. 95, 476, 494.
[3] Bishop Leslie, *History of Scotland*, vol. ii, p. 359.
[4] *A.P.S.* vol. i, p. 213, vol. ii, p. 17.

lands come, for such male ('rent') as they took them for before."[1]

These acts seem to have given little security. In 1469, parliament enacted that on account of the great hardships and destructions of the king's commons and malars on lords' lands because their goods and cattle were seized in distress for their lord's debts, therefore, in future, only the year's rent that was due was to be taken by the lord's creditors and the rest of the debt obtained elsewhere. Again, in 1491, it was enacted that when lands changed hands by succession, ward, marriage, wadsetting, etc., the tenants, labourers, and inhabitants should " Remane vnput furth or Removit quhill the nixt terme of witsonday folowand," if they duly paid their rent, mails, duties, etc., to the new lord.[2]

A much later act, which should mainly be considered in connection with the feuing process, shows that the same insecurity continued to exist. It was passed in 1568, is very mutilated, nevertheless the general tenor is unmistakable. It decrees that: " Forasmuch as the common people and commons of this realm over all parts thereof in times past in good conscience have been removed from their native and kindly . . . steadings, Notwithstanding that they are aye ready to . . . used and wont therefore, wherethrough honest . . . and families are scaled and put to begging and a great number of beggars and poor ones gendered: And seeing that the ordo . . . of warning and removing is now most commonly used within this realm the mails and duties of lands heightened: The commons which are the greatest part of the people are and will be altogether made unable to serve in the wars. . . . Therefore it will be necessary to statute that no mailer, farmer or other occupier of lands, who pay their duties, shall be removed for the space of certain years, so that order may be taken for the relief of the poor and better forth setting of the Kings service."[3]

1 *A.P.S.* vol. ii, p. 35. According to an old custom, a tenant was given possession of a new holding by the presentation of a wand, and was given notice to quit by the breaking of a wand by the owner in his presence.

2 *Ibid.* vol. ii, pp. 96, 225.

3 *Ibid.* vol. iii, p. 45. For a mid-sixteenth century reference to the frequency of forcible ejectment of tenants, see *Register, Privy Council*, vol. i, p. 27.

This act formed a part of the adjustment of the hard lot of the tenants upon the secularised Church lands. It is interesting in showing that to a limited extent the moral claim of long tenancy was recognized, especially after the Church lands (where there seems to have been the greatest continuity of tenure) were brought into the possession of the nobles; but it made no great innovation in the status of the occupiers of the soil. Short lease tenancies continued to be the rule in Scotland for about two hundred years.

These acts have been quoted very fully because they show not merely that parliament endeavoured, unsuccessfully, to give the agriculturists a certain amount of protection, but that, in practice, they had no rights or security in the land whatsoever. Perhaps it is worth while tracing the development of some of the agricultural holdings possessed by Cupar Abbey, to show how fluid were the arrangements and how entirely different was the state of affairs to the accepted ideas of an English manor. Cupar has perforce been selected owing to the abundance of the material that survives, but it may be noted that the authorities there seem to have been enlightened agriculturists and considerate landlords.

There were several holdings leased by single tenants on the abbey lands. Thus, *Bucham* was invariably let on five years' leases to a single tenant, but between 1464 and 1511 there were four changes of the surname. *Eroly* was held by the same family throughout the period, generally upon life leases. *Adhory* was held by a single tenant, sometimes for five years, sometimes on a life lease. There was one change in the family ownership between 1464 and 1504. There are other similar cases.

Sometimes there were changes in the arrangements. *Murthly* was held by three joint tenants on five-year leases between 1464 and 1473, with one change of ownership. Then it passed to a single tenant. *Cragnevady*, on the other hand, first appears as a single tenancy, and in 1473 a life lease was granted. After 1475, however, it was divided into four parts, which appear to have been held without a lease. *Drumfolatyn* was sometimes held by an individual, but was afterwards divided into unequal shares among his relations.

Rather more common were holdings let to three, four, or

more joint tenants. *Syokis* was let in quarters, though for a short time one of these was subdivided and at one time a third share appears! One of the joint tenants had a life lease, the others had leases for five years. There were about half a dozen changes of ownership. *Campsie* was generally divided into four shares. *Pitlochry* was sometimes in four shares, at others two of these were subdivided. *Cotzyards* was sometimes divided into three unequal shares, sometimes into two, latterly into a half and two quarters. One family shared it for about twenty-five years, but it afterwards changed hands. *Muirtown* was sometimes divided into thirds, sometimes into quarters, rather perplexingly; latterly one tenant had one-half of it. The land was let for three years, six years, and on life leases. *Little Perth* was also constantly redivided. One-sixth shares, one-quarter shares, one-third shares (the most common), and one-half shares appear, and the tenants changed very often. *Balgreshach* was similarly treated between 1467 and 1501; sometimes there were five tenants, sometimes four, finally three. The shares were evidently very unequal and at times part of the holding was let off separately to cottars. Originally, *Balmyle* was shared by four tenants, and *Redfurdhalch* by three. In 1463 they were joined together and held by the same seven tenants; five of them each had a one-sixth share and two a one-twelfth. By 1473 there were eight joint tenants, but thereafter most of the holdings were one-sixths or were consolidated into one-thirds. *Cupar*, in 1457, was divided as follows: one-quarter by one tenant, two-quarter shares each held by two joint tenants, one-quarter share by three joint tenants (by eight tenants in all), upon five-year leases, but during this time there were two changes. By 1462 it was divided into sixths, each held by one, two, and even three joint tenants. By 1473 it was divided into three one-sixth shares and six one-twelfth shares, and most of the tenants appear to have been new. Life leases were granted, and in the lease it was ordered that the "town" should be divided up and lots cast. Six years later one of the tenants had secured one-third of the holding and a life lease with remainder to his wife and son. *Muirhouse of Kerso* was also more and more subdivided.

The story of the larger holdings is even more interesting. There were *Easter*, *Middle*, and *Wester Drummy*, their names suggestive of a previous division. *Easter Drummy*, in 1454, had first been consolidated into a single holding. It was afterwards subdivided into quarters and halves, and in 1514 a one-eighth share appears. *Middle Drummy* was first held by a widow and son, then by a single tenant, and was then, in 1489, divided between two tenants. *Wester Drummy* had previously been held by several tenants. In 1473 it was let in three unequal shares, and the most considerable tenant was made responsible for the conduct of the others and, should they give up or be turned out, for finding new ones.

The *Grange of Aberbrothny* was divided into one-sixths till 1462, when there were four one-sixth parts, two one-sixteenth parts, two one-twelfth parts, and one one-twenty-fourth part. It continued to be held in very small though somewhat changeful proportions; by 1473 there were ten one-twelfth parts and one one-sixth, but in 1480 there were only seven tenants. The tenants of these small portions, however, showed considerable tenacity. A good many life leases were given, and some of the families continued to occupy the land throughout the period.

Tullyfergus in 1438 was held on a life lease by a single tenant. It was then more and more subdivided until, in 1469, there were three one-quarter shares and two one-eighth shares. Further and more complicated subdivisions seem to have followed, for in 1470 an individual leased two one-thirds of one of the quarters. By the terms of the next lease, granted in 1474, the tenants made a new arrangement in the presence of the laird of Rattre and an official of the abbey. The holding was divided. The east half was apportioned into thirds, the west half into quarters; of these latter, one was held by a single tenant on a seven years' lease and three were held jointly by two tenants on a life lease. Under this arrangement some of the tenants were new and some old.

Grange of Kincrech was originally divided into thirds, but in 1475 a half appears and subsequently quarters. How the adjustments were made we do not know. There were few changes among the tenants and, from 1475, life leases, with remainders to wives and in some cases sons, were given. *Cupar Grange*, in complete contrast, was let to many tenants. In 1454 it was divided into two one-eighths, seven one-twelfth shares, and one one-sixth share; and the tenants seem to have continued to occupy it. In 1457 *Kethyk* was divided into ten one-twelfth parts and four one-twenty-fourth parts, but in 1464 it was let on a two years' lease to seven husbandmen, who, in addition to a low rent, were to supply sixteen score waggon-loads of divots—apparently for some special requirement of the abbey. "Moreover, if the said tenants shall propose to remain beyond the said term . . . they shall divide the *Grange* into just portions, and each shall thereafter, with domicile and cottar, maintain himself separately in his own part." By 1467 it was divided into eighths, held some singly, some jointly, and in 1473, in new lease, it was laid down that the Grange should be divided into three or four towns, to answer separately or as one, as the abbot pleases. Accordingly, by 1474, three new holdings appear: Kemphill (the east quarter of the old Kethyk) with seven tenants, some new, some old, all holding on life leases; Cothill, with four old tenants; and Chapeltown of Kethyk, with six tenants, all old ones. The west town of Kethyk continued to be known under the old name.

The Grange of Balbrogy was also subdivided. Previous to 1468 it had been held by sixteen husbandmen and sixteen cottars. But in that year one-half of it was leased to twenty-two tenants. "To ten of them a sixteenth part each, and twelve in pairs by the advice of the abbot, of whom six shall be husbandmen and other six cottars . . . and they shall divide the settings among themselves. . . ." About 1473 the rest of the Grange was broken up, the east half, "callet le Bernton," was let to four tenants, but in the following year was apparently again divided into Crunan and Arthurstane, let to five and seven tenants. About the same time other divisions appear: "the sixth part of the west half of Balbrogy, callit Middleton," let to two old tenants; Chapeltown of Balbrogy; Welton of Balbrogy.

In addition to these and several similar holdings, there were a good many very small pieces of land, and certain portions let "in cotterey," as holdings of an acre or two, to craftsmen and others. From these, during the period of the rent roll, was evolved the Burgh of Barony of Keithock in 1492.[1]

[1] These details are taken from the rental in the *Register of Cupar Abbey*, vol. i, beginning at p. 118. It is a task of some difficulty to distinguish between sons of old tenants and new-comers, since in many cases there was

From this rental it is evident that widows were generally, though not invariably, allowed to stay on, on their husband's holdings, or if they had more than one holding, upon one of them. Sons often succeeded fathers. Even where families moved about, from holding to holding, they often remained permanently upon the estate.[1]

The cottars and sub-tenants, where such existed, had far less security. The tenant of Adhory was allowed to "take in tenants and allot land to them to farm, and to dismiss them at will," and there are similar clauses in several other leases to considerable tenants; in one of them, one old tenant is specially exempted from such rights. Cottars who were not given yards for their kale and proper fuel rights by their husbandmen were also to be ejected.[2] It will be noticed, in the constant rearrangement of the holdings that took place, that sometimes formal agreements between the abbot and his tenants were entered in the new leases; once an oversman appointed by the abbot and the laird of Rattre were entrusted with the division. In some of the leases the joint tenants themselves carried out the re-division. In a dispute about a commonty shared by the tenants of Easter and Wester Drummy in 1553, the matter was referred to a duly fenced court. In most cases there is nothing to show whether it was a matter of private arrangement or if it were dealt with by the administrative machinery of the estate. It is at least clear that the process cannot have been toilsome or costly. Among the Protocols of the Bishopric of Glasgow we have an illustration of how the Earl of Lennox proceeded to divide up the common lands of his barony of Tarbolton in 1500. His procurator summoned all the tenants to appear upon a certain day "to see and hear the division made of the said

no real surname and the son of Thomas Johnson would be known as Robert Thomason, etc. At Cupar Grange there is a good example of the fluidity of the arrangements. At one of the periodic rearrangements, all the tenants were ordered to settle a cottar on the north part of the Grange in their first year, as the Lord Abbot might determine, and in the third year three of the tenants themselves were to go there (p. 139).

[1] This is well shown in C. Rogers' account of certain families in the *Introduction to the Register*, vol. i, p. xxxviii, xlii. It would appear that the holdings of Cambuskenneth Abbey were much altered about 1462; see *Chartulary of Cambuskenneth Abbey* (Grampian Club), p. 322.

[2] *Register of Cupar Abbey*, vol. i, pp. 123, 163, 169, 240.

common land," but Lennox was himself unable to be present. A meeting was apparently held three days later and Lennox signed a formal statement that he had duly met his tenants and had wished them to have a division of the common land. He further straightly prohibited them from occupying or working the common land until such a division be made, and cited them to meet again on a given day within a month, when division would be made by judges and arbiters chosen by both parties.[1]

The question of the fixity of tenure enjoyed by Scots tenants is of importance. It emphasizes the difference in the rural organization of England and Scotland. It is essential to an understanding of the feuing movement of the sixteenth century, and of the enclosure movement of the eighteenth and nineteenth centuries. Although the Scots agriculturists did not make good a formal claim to possession of the soil, as did the English under the manorial system, nevertheless, owing to the feudal exigencies of the landlords and to the innate force of character of the people, they certainly were by no means abject or rightless beings. One cannot tell what happened on the lands of the nobles, but it must be remembered that the well-intentioned though largely ineffective acts that sought to give the lesser folk protection were passed by a parliament in which the landowning interest was overwhelmingly predominant. In the case of the Crown lands, the rent rolls very often, although by no means invariably, have provisions that the new tenant shall not remove the sitting sub-tenants.[2] The regulations for the management of the royal estates, of which there are several examples in the *Exchequer Rolls*, prove that the welfare of the tenants and sub-tenants was carefully considered. The orders given to the commissioners entrusted with the letting of the Crown lands in Ross, Ardmannoch (Ross-shire), Trouterness (Skye), Strathdee and Cromar (both in Aberdeenshire), between 1539 and 1541, are particularly interesting:

" First, that ye provyde that all our saidis landis be sett to oure liegeis and tenentis occupiaris of the grund fer male and garssome as ye sall think expedient for oure proffitt, with sic

[1] *Register of Cupar Abbey*, vol. ii, p. 130.
Diocesan Register of Glasgow, vol. i, pp. 320-322.

[2] *Exchequer Rolls*, vol. xi, p. 413; vol. xii, p. 680; vol. xiii, p. cxxviii, etc.

conditiounis as thai sall be habill to serve ws alswele in were as pece.

"Item, becaus we ar informitt that ane grete parte of oure saidis landis and lordschippis ar in gentilmennis handis, parte of auld and parte of new, ye sal consider and se gyfe thai gentillmen hes other grete heretage or nocht; and gyfe thai have nocht, bot that thai and thare foirbearis hes levit upoun the saidis takkis in oure faderis tyme and utheris oure predecessouris, ye sall mak to thame takkis thareof, with this restrictioun, that thai have na mare nor thai may lauboure with thare awne pleuch and laubouris, and nocht to be sett to subtennentis; and quhat landis thai have that excedis, to sett the samyn to the tenentis occupiaris thareof, as ye sall think maist convenient for the wele of oure liegeis and oure proffitt.

"Item, as to oure landis sett to grete gentill men in oure les age that thai nor thare predicessouris had nevir of before, ye sall sett the samyn agane to the auld possessouris, and gyfe thai be sobir gentillmen and occupiis ane part of the saidis landis with thare awne gudis, and nane uthir man clames nycht thareto, ye sall sett that parte to thame and the remanent to the tennentis occupearis of the grund, gife thai will tak the samyn; and all uthire thingis ye sall do as ye think maist expedient, nocht with standing ony or quhat sumevir oure writtingis or takynnis to be send yow in the contrare, quhilkis we will that ye answuer nocht, quhilk salbe na caus to move ws to ony displeasure aganis yow."[1] In 1569 the Crown tenants of Ross-shire complained to the Privy Council of the illegal exactions of the baillie of Ardmannoch, and the case was investigated and the wrongs set right.[2]

The writers of the sixteenth century, though they paint a very dark picture of the lot of the country-folk, at least furnish evidence that this oppression was recognized as a serious wrong—a far better state of affairs than if it had been treated as a matter of course. Two acts of parliament specially enjoined that the plough-beasts of tenants were never to be destrained for debt, and the grievance of the inconsiderate taking of teinds was also legislated about.[3]

[1] *Exchequer Rolls*, vol. xvii, p. 663; vol. xviii, p. 374, gives another example.

[2] *Register, Privy Council*, vol. i, p. 672.

[3] *A.P.S.* vol. ii, p. 254; vol. iii, pp. 139, 217.

CHAPTER V

PART I. THE INTRODUCTION OF FEUING

OUR period, however, saw the evolution of another form of holding, quite distinct from the feudal fiefs, the tenancies for life, the farmers' very short leases, and the sub-tenants' more precarious holdings. This new tenure, the feu-holding, is peculiar to Scotland. Apart from legal technicalities regarding the degree of possession, the essence of feu-holding is that it is a heritable tenure, granted in return for a fixed and single rent and for certain casualties—it is therefore unlike the pure feudal conception of the tenure of land (such as a typical wardholding), where occupation is permitted in return for services and with far greater and more uncertain casualties. It also varies from the leasehold system, not only in the actual degree to which the land is possessed, but also because, under the latter, land is only granted for a limited and specified period.

Feuing is a development of the feudal system. Though superficially it resembles the older tenure of the thanages, there is no connection between them. The thanages died out, and meanwhile, but quite separately, feu-farming grew up. Nor is it directly derived from the long leases which existed during our period.

Even during the earliest period of feudalism in Scotland—covered by the preceding section of this history—the land-owners were not self-supporting to a barbarous degree. They inevitably required money instead of services or payments in kind for the provision of the amenities that even then were necessary to them. In the twelfth and thirteenth centuries land quite often was granted in return for a " reddendo " or money payment, but also generally in connection with some feudal service or casualty. In some cases the term " feudifirma " was actually applied to such holdings : for instance, it is used in an agreement in the chartulary of St Andrews, where the land of Calacman was held from the abbey in return for the payment of two silver marks, the king's service due from the lands, and for ward, relief, and other services, the prior being bound to defend the tenant against all men and women.[1]

There are a great many similar examples of this type of mixed tenure in the ecclesiastical chartularies. These are not only the contemporary documents that give a picture of early conditions, but they are also the places where feus are most likely to be found. The churchmen were in a better position to grant the permanent occupation of the land than the barons: they were not in such need of military service, for whenever possible they obtained grants of their land free from all customs and services; and they constantly required money, not only for the service of their houses but to meet the national calls made upon them and, most of all, the heavy expenses in Rome due to their constant struggles with neighbouring religious houses —they were very litigious people—and the acquisition of bulls from Rome whenever there was a change of abbot or bishop.[2]

Pure feu-farm holdings, however, apart from the burghs, first came into use in the fourteenth century. Mr R. Lowell Jones cites as the first complete example a charter of 1362, in which land was granted to a certain Alexander and his heirs in perpetual heritage " sine warda, relevio, secta curie seu maritagio preter tantum dictas marcas nobis nomine feodifirma et capitulo supradicto persolvendas ad terminos prenotatos."

[1] *Chartulary of St Andrews*, p. 398. For pre-fourteenth-century examples of tenure that are not quite pure feu-farm, see *Chartularies of Scone*, pp. 46, 49, *Dryburgh*, No. 19, *Inchaffray*, pp. 61-64. I am indebted to Mr R. Lowell Jones' essay for these examples. He considers that early feu-farm charters at *Kelso* were really wardholdings with the military service commuted.

[2] Mr R. Lowell Jones does not consider that this point has been sufficiently emphasized. He quotes as examples of such expenses, £200 borrowed by the bishop and chapter of Glasgow in 1279 "*pro arduiis negotiis in curia Romana promovendis*" (*Regis. Glasguense*, vol. i, pp. 193-194); also *Registrum de Aberbrothoc*, vol. ii, pp. 226-229. See also a papal bull of 1380 stating that the abbot and convent of Cambuskenneth had been alienating their property to laymen and clergymen, "to some in liferent, to others on long lease, and to some for ever," and charging the bishop of the diocese to revoke all such grants as he should find to have been illegally made (*Chartulary of Cambuskenneth*, p. 53).

Throughout this century the churchmen continued to extend their use of feu-farm tenure, to elaborate it and to make it more definite, and, finally, to attach conditions to it that were afterwards incorporated in the law of the land.

Meanwhile the tenure was also coming into use by the burghs. We have seen how the burgesses had at first merely paid rent as individuals for their tofts; the terms by which they held them must generally have resembled feus rather than leases, for, judging by the provisions of the Laws of the Four Burghs, heritable tenements were usual. The burghs then obtained short leases for the whole of the revenue due from them as corporate bodies. Finally, feus were acquired. Aberdeen obtained the first feu-charter for its burgh revenues in 1319 upon payment of £213 6s. 8d., and other burghs quickly followed suit.[1]

It was not until the middle of the fifteenth century that feuing began to come into operation upon the Crown lands, at a time when the vigorous policy of James I and James II had largely increased their extent. The lands of Bonfield and Ferryfield were feued to the community of Cupar in 1452, four years later the lands of Balcarres were feued to Robert Hunter, and a few more feus were given. In 1457 an act was passed declaring that it was speedful that the king begin and give an example to the lave, and that royal consent be given to those prelates, barons, and freeholders who could accord with their tenants upon the setting of their lands in feu-farm.[2] During the next year feus were given to three individuals, and in 1459 a number of feus were granted at Falkland and about nine elsewhere.[3] The names of the feuars were largely those of landed gentlemen, but one was a burgess of Cupar.

The wording of the act of 1457 suggests that feuing was being encouraged as an enlightened policy—it certainly was a lucrative one. So great were the evils of uncertain tenure and the inconvenience of the irregular feudal casualties that tenants and vassals were ready to pay handsomely to escape them.

[1] *Exchequer Rolls*, vol. i, p. lxxxvi.
A.P.S. vol. i, p. 478.
Sir Archibald Lawrie, *Early Scottish Charters*, pp. 85, 86, 132.

[2] *A.P.S.* vol. ii, p. 49.

[3] *Exchequer Rolls*, vol. xiii, p. cxvi; see also Index, vol. vi.

According to the rental of Falkland, £7 with victual rent was paid for the "villa" of Falkland and 15s. for some cottages before the feuing. The "villa" was feued in the same year for £20 and the six cottages for 50s., whilst the rest of the estate, which was not feued, paid the same rental that it had done before.

Burnett has extracted particulars from the rentals of Fife in 1508–9 showing the same thing :

1508. Pre-feuing.					1509. After Feuing.	
	Tenant.	Lease.	Rent.	Grassum.	Feu-holder.	Feu-duty.
Den Mill	L. Balfour	3 yrs.	£2 : 13 : 4	£2 : 13 : 4	Old tenant	£6 : 13 : 4. entry fee paic
Balcarres	Unstated	..	£6 : 13 : 4	Unstated	G. Creighton	£25 : 13 : 7. composition £30 to be pa on new infe ment
Balbuckie	A. Beaton	3 yrs.	£4 and a victual rent	£4	John Douglas of the King's wine cellar	£8 and rath less victu Entry £26 : 13 : 4
Le Casche	12 tenants	3 yrs.	£8 : 8 : 4 and victual rent	Unstated	2 brothers of Scott of Balweary*	£24 : 6 : 5 a same victu Entry £24 : 6 : 8

* The Scotts were ordered to continue the existing tenants in possession if they paid their rent

During the troubled reign of James III only seven feus were given, but under James IV, who was both energetic and hard up, the tenure came into common use.[2] In 1503 another act encouraging the king was passed "sua that it be not in diminution of his rental, gressoumes, nor uther dewteis." He was allowed to feu the lands he had annexed, but his successors were specifically excluded from this right. From 1509 feuing became more general on the Crown lands. Between 1508 and 1509 the whole of the stewartry of Fife—which had been previously let on three-year leases—was feued, also much of Menteith and Ettrick Forest,[3] and the process continued rapidly. In 1525, £190 18s. was paid in fees to the commissioners who let lands in feu-farm. About this time the annual payments made

[1] *Exchequer Rolls*, vol. xiii, p. cxix.
[2] *Ibid.* vol. xiii, p. cxii. [3] *Ibid.* vol. xiii, p. cxix.

upon feus that changed hands amounted to £268 19s. 5d. in one year only.[1] In 1527 a protest was made in parliament that the ratification of feus should not be allowed to hurt the king's patrimony.

As the sixteenth century drew towards its great central event, the establishment of the Reformation, the poverty of the king had not only the direct effect of encouraging the feuing of the Crown lands, but also indirectly, through the papal subsidies granted to James V and also to Mary of Guise, it had an effect in precipitating the feuing of the Church lands. Professor Hannay has shown the direct effect of the "Great Tax" imposed by Pope Clement, during the reign of James V, upon the feuing of Church lands. It brought about "the beginning of rapid dissolution in the landed property of the Church. In most unfortunate conditions, a tenure which had long been regarded with favour as conducing to the military and economic strength of the nation, was suddenly applied to the Kirk lands on an unprecedented scale and with unhappy results."[2] As the troubles of the country increased, towards the middle of the century, there was an ever-stronger incentive to feu. An unusually specious feu-charter of 1558–59, bestowing certain lands of the Abbey of Cupar upon a Thomas Kennedy, states that the grant was made in accordance with the acts of parliament for the erection of commodious dwellings, improvement of waste lands, planting of trees, and the construction of dovecots, gardens, and rabbit warrens: In order to provide tenants with arms and other requisites of war, for defence of the Kingdom of Scotland against the Old Enemy: *And also in consequence of sums of money paid by Kennedy "with glad hand and ready mind" towards the monastery's insupportable burdens, frequent taxations, manifold vexations, and in especial for his steady and thankful service rendered in defence of the community against the insults and dreadful threatenings of many lay princes and their subordinates in the Kingdom of Scotland.*[3] Even where lands were still let on lease the same tendency showed itself. Longer leases, often

[1] *Exchequer Rolls*, vol. xv, p. 129.

[2] R. K. Hannay, "A Study in Reformation History," *Scottish Hist. Review*, vol. xxiii, p. 30.

[3] *Register of Cupar Abbey*, vol. ii, p. 173.

for life, became commoner, but rents were raised and grassums and other extra payments appeared.[1]

Thus, as the years of Mary Queen of Scots' minority passed the Church was forced, by sheer necessity, to use her wealth more and more to maintain her political power, and to alienate her lands. Hitherto the feuing of Church lands had only been permitted after confirmation from Rome had been obtained for the individual feu, and great care was taken that the permanent interests of the Church were not damaged. Fortunately the whole proceedings in the case of the feuing of Drygrange by the Monastery of Melrose have been printed, so that one can follow out the elaborate process.[2] The authorities in Rome were now, however, forced to renounce this check and "to endow Beaton and his successor Hamilton with the power *a latere* which enabled them, without reference to Rome, to institute processes of confirmation" of such feu-charters.[3] Feuing proceeded apace throughout the whole period; even so early as 1545 a new rental book had to be made for the archbishopric of St Andrews.[4]

With the Reformation, the responsibility for confirming the feuing of the Church lands passed from the Church to the Crown; but before plunging into the consideration of the political problems that were involved, it is important that we try to form some sort of idea of the status of the feu-holders as a class.

PART II. THE STATUS OF THE FEU-FARMERS

Feuing was not a democratic movement. The payments which made it worth while to the superior to feu land were fairly heavy—Hamilton of Finnart paid £1550 for a feu of Lesmahago. Nevertheless, there were considerable numbers of people desiring land who were in a position to acquire it. The regulations for the letting of some of the Crown lands, which

[1] See *Register of Cupar*, vol. i, pp. 156, 157, 158, 163.

[2] G. Neilson, "Feuing of Drygrange from the Monastery of Melrose," *Scottish Hist. Review*, vol. vii, p. 355.

[3] R. K. Hannay, *Scottish Hist. Review*, vol. xxiii, p. 32.

[4] R. K. Hannay, Preface to *Rentale St Andrae* (Scottish History Society), p. xxviii.

have already been quoted from, show that the gentry were anxious to add to their estates; there were the younger sons of the landowners to be provided for;[1] the desire to establish a circle of cadet branches also inclined the heads of great houses to grant feus on their own lands or to obtain them from the secularized properties of the Church.[2] Churchmen of loose lives, especially just before the crash, often provided for their illegitimate children by means of feus. An outstanding example is Bishop Hepburn, "the great dilapidator of the See of Moray." He received the bishopric in 1535, and during the days both of the Old Faith and of the New he provided for his large family by feuing large portions of the lands of his diocese.[3] During the periods of faction rule, feus were often the reward of the kinsmen of the nobles in power. They were often granted to the officials about the court.[4] So great a personage as the treasurer got a feu in 1525. John Douglas "of the King's wine cellar" had a small one about 1509. There are a good many instances of burgesses, who probably had "made their pile," acquiring feus.[5]

Some of the feus were comparatively small—there is, for instance, the feu of a cotland;[6] but in the many instances when such small feus were acquired by a gentleman they probably rounded off an estate. In other cases feus were very large: the "lands and barony of Stratherne," for instance, were feued *en bloc*.[7] So little is known of the extent of the feuing movement, and so important is the bearing of the status of the feuars upon the whole subject, that a few examples may be quoted *in extenso*. The following is approximately a complete list of the persons receiving feus during the reign of James III:

[1] James Henderson, in *The Godly and Golden Book*, printed in *Calendar of Scottish Papers*, vol. i (1547–1563), p. 141, advises that younger children should have part of their parents' lands for life.

[2] *Black Book of Taymouth*, pp. 419, 422.

[3] See *Registrum Episcopatus Moraviensis*, p. xv. The chartulary contains a very complete list of his alienations.

See also W. Macgill, *Old Ross-shire*, pp. 6-7.

[4] *Exchequer Rolls*, vol. xiii, p. cxix.

[5] *Ibid.* vol. xviii. See rentals in Appendix.

[6] *Ibid.* vol. xiii, Appendix.

[7] *Ibid.* vol. xiii, p. cxix (1507).

Register Great Seal, Nos. 3088, 3105, 3130, 3135, 3155, 3156, 3177, 3180, 3193, 3238, 3244.

The sons of Robert Hunter, who succeeded their father in a large feu.
Gilbert *de* Johnstoun.
John Learmonth; from other entries he appears to have been a man of position.
Culquhoun of Luss, the head of an old and distinguished family. He received the important feu of Roseneath.
James Douglas, who received a large feu.
Andrew Wood, Scotland's great sea captain.[1]

A list of the duplicands and other dues falling vacant on feus and leases of Crown lands in one year, about 1542–56, shows the following facts. Sixteen *leases* were renewed, fifteen of them for five years, one for nine years, and the average rental (including the nine years' lease, which paid £90) was a little over £3 per annum. During the same period thirty-three *feus* paid fees on the succession of an heir or were created or re-feued. Among the names of the feuars there are eleven in a superior position, one knight, one burgess of Edinburgh, and nine persons who were either landholders or the sons of landholders. Of these latter, one had five feus, one had four feus, four had three feus each. The average rental of the 326 feus held by the knight, lairds, and burgess, counting the value of the plurality of feus held by some of them as a single unit, was over £53 10s. The average rental of the remaining nine feus, which were held by eight persons whose rank was uncertain and by a priest, was about £5 (some idea of the relation to acreage and value may be gained from the facts incidentally mentioned that a quarter of five bovates paid 25s., two and a half bovates paid £2 17s. 9d., and three and a half bovates paid £4 18s.).[2]

A rental of the bishopric of Moray of 1563 shows the following arrangement of leases and feus. The following lands were *leased*:

1 held jointly in six one-eighth parts and one one-fourth part.
1 ,, ,, four one-eighth parts and two one-quarter parts.
5 cottages.
1 held jointly in three one-quarter parts and 2 one-eighth parts.

[1] *Exchequer Rolls*, vol. xiii, p. cxvi.
[2] *Ibid.* vol. xviii, Appendix.

A mill and fishings, $\frac{3}{4}$ of a farm, and other pertinents	Held by Andrew Moncreiff and Elizabeth Innes. Moncreiff is a "good" name. Innes is that of one of the chief local landowning families. She had three holdings or parts of holdings.

1 holding held in severalty, name unknown.
1 ,, ,, ,,

1 holding leased by	Innes of Drainie, a gentleman who had five holdings or parts of holdings. The laird of Duffus.

1 holding held in severalty by an Innes.
1 ,, the laird of Innes, who had two other holdings.
1 ,, the provost of Forres.
5 very small pendicles.
2 crofts leased jointly by Innes of Drainie and another individual.
1 holding held jointly in four one-eighth parts, four one-twelfth parts, two one-sixteenth parts.
1 holding held jointly in one one-eighth part, two one-sixteenth parts, two one-fourth parts.
1 holding leased jointly in six one-eighth parts, one one-fourth part.
1 holding (small) held by two individuals.
1 ,, leased by Innes of Drainie.
1 ,, ,, Elizabeth Innes.
1 ,, ,, Innes of Drainie.
1 ,, ,, T. Innes, M.A., of Pethwick.
2 alehouses leased by Innes of Drainie.
1 holding leased by G. Mortimer and by seven joint tenants.
1 ,, ,, jointly in four one-quarter parts.
1 ,, ,, ,, ,, ,,
1 ,, ,, by Elizabeth Innes.
1 ,, ,, jointly in one one-quarter part, three one-eighth parts, three one-twelfth parts, one one-tenth part.
1 ,, ,, jointly in seven one-eighth parts, two one-sixteenth parts.
2 ,, ,, in irregular shares.
3 small holdings held severally.

The rest of the rental continues in much the same fashion. Among the gentry who leased land were the Sheriff of Moray, who was a Dunbar of Westfield; Comyn of Altyre, of an ancient and important local family; another landed Comyn, Kinnaird of Culbin, the lairds of Brodie and of Lethan, Brodie of Gartly, the Winchesters of Ardtrailzie, at that time a small landed family, and others.

In addition to these leases, the bishopric had the following *feus*: One held jointly by the Moncreiff already noted and Elizabeth Innes; one held by "Magister" J. Wood; two held by Alexander Ross, who is unknown; one by "Magister" Alexander Campbell, M.A.; three by the laird of Kilravock, and one by the laird of Cantray.

The whole of the Church lands in the barony of Keith were feued. Lord Huntly had two feus, and Innes of Drainie, the Lady Frendraught, two Ogilvies—at that time a very influential name in the district—and one Gordon (also an important name) had each one feu. The Church lands in the barony of Kinmyles, in the Fraser country, were set in five feus; Lord Lovat, the head of the clan, had three of them, and another Fraser one. The Church lands in the barony of Strathspey were feued to eight people. The laird of Grant had three feus, the laird of Ballindalloch had one, three other Grants had one each. The remaining one was held by a Gordon. The whole of the Church lands in the barony of Moy were feued by the laird of Mackintosh.[1]

Nevertheless on some of the Church lands this was not so. The lands of the Bishop of Glasgow were exceptional, owing to the practice of rentalling, and in an act passed in 1587, which ordered all persons holding leases or grants of Church lands to obtain renewals of them from the bishops, a special provision was made—"Our sovereign Lord, considering the feuars of the barony of Glasgow to be many in number, and the poverty of the maist part of them to be sik as they are not habile to furnish the ordinary charges for renewing their infeftments," therefore dispensed with this provision in the case of persons there who had obtained feus without diminution of the old rental and should be able to produce a ratification from the Bishop of Glasgow.[2] If one, however, takes the list of long leases (for nineteen years and for life) and of feus granted by Cupar Abbey between 1539 and 1559 the results are rather surprising. Nearly two hundred of such leases and tacks were

[1] *Register of Bishopric of Moray*, p. 433. See also *Book of the Roses of Kilravock*, pp. 211-213. I am indebted to Mr. Innes of Learney for genealogical information without which the list of names would be meaningless.

[2] J. Bain and C. Rogers, *Diocesan Register of Glasgow*, vol. i, pp. 30-31.

made. Of these, about sixty-five were for separate holdings or for fractions of holdings of not less than one-half. The remainder were for fractions of less than half a holding or for pendicles of less than ten acres. In seventy-five cases it appeared that the leaseholder or feuar was a new-comer. In four instances he was adding to an old holding, but in ninety-five cases he was only renewing his possessions. The proportion of new tenants was slightly higher among the larger holders.[1]

If one merely went by the formal rent rolls and the like, one would get little idea of the strange vicissitudes of feuing. A few incidents that happen to be recorded are probably typical of a great deal that went on that was "unknown to history." The obtaining of feus, like everything else, was influenced by the violent ups and downs of politics. In 1567 the Archbishop of St Andrews granted the lands of Cragfudy and Middlefudy, in Fife, to Grisel Semple and her son John Hamilton, a kinsman of Lord Hamilton. Before the feu was completed, the Hamiltons fell and a new Archbishop secured the feu for his son. Finally, with the restoration of the Hamiltons, the original feuars secured the feu upon payment of £200.[2] A curious manuscript, "Privit Historie off the Irvines of Kingcausie," describes how John Irvine of Achorthin and Gordon of Cluny contended for the feus of Midstrath and Marywell. "About this tym the Reformation was advancing here in Scotland," and Irvine, "being a zelous protestant, resolved he wold pay no more feu-duty to a popish bishop (for he held of the Bishop of Aberdeen). The Reformation not cuming in so quickly as he expected and Bishop Gordon being desyrous to curb the herisie (as he termed it) in the bud, disponed his right to Gordon of Cluny, who was his brother; and finding by the Charter from the Bishop to John that if two years' rent of the feu run unpayt his right was to fall, he brought down from his

[1] This list has been compiled from vol. ii of the *Register of Cupar Abbey.* It is only approximately correct. On the one hand, married women were often known by their maiden names, and apparent surnames were really only the father's Christian name with the suffix of "son." On the other, many of the holdings were evidently acquired as additional to others, and many of the tenants were really people of some considerable landed possession.

[2] R. K. Hannay, "On the Foundation of the College of Justice," *Scottish Hist. Review*, vol. xv, p. 65.

other lands of Glenlivat four hundreth highland men and laid a formall seidg to the house." Irvine was taken by surprise and could make no proper preparations for the defence of his property. However, he " immurde " himself and twenty men in the house, and, because the attack took place in July and the nights were " cleer," they were able to keep the Highlanders " at some distance." " In this posture they continued a fortnight's space and nyntine of the Highlandmen killed." However, when the latter saw from the slackening of the " besidged's " fire that their ammunition was spent, " the house being thatched with hether, they put combustable mater upon piks and cornforks and cam to the house calling to com out or otherwise they wold burn him to ashes and all that wer with him; qrupon he opened the doors and came out. Thay no sooner laid hands upon him than they put a rop about his neck and threatened to hang him over his own gate unless he wold dispon the heretable right to Cluny; which he chouse to doe rather than dy like a doge, and therby lost Midstrath and Marywell." It is a fortunate chance that the full story of this episode has been preserved. The record of the transfer from Irvine to Gordon appears as an ordinary entry, among many others, at the Register House.[1]

The local gentry were not, however, always anxious to feu their lands. The object of the Crown in feuing is attributed, quite bluntly, in the feu-charters to the desire for more money, and it was generally the Crown that took the initiative in feuing, not the occupiers who clamoured for feus. A commissioner or commissioners were appointed to feu the lands, and the sitting tenants were given priority of opportunity in securing a feu of their lands. Sometimes they could not or would not come to an agreement. In 1509 " Master James Henderson, advocat for our soverane lord, protesteit that sen the tennantis of the Erledome of Marche war summoned to this day to tak thair fewis and na man com to tak thaim, that thairfore the lordis mycht sett the saidis landis to other tennentis." [2] There is one amusing old tale which, if it be not exactly true, at least shows the attitude ascribed to the gentlemen feuars. John, tenth laird of Mackenzie, was a great favourite of Mary

[1] A copy of this manuscript history was kindly lent me by Mr Innes of Learney. See also *Reg. Epis. Aberdoniensis*, vol. i, pp. 445, 373.

[2] *Exchequer Rolls*, vol. xiii, pp. 649, 656.

of Lorraine, the queen-mother, but when he heard that she was sending up agents to report upon the Crown lands in Ross-shire with a view to feuing them, he made his plans. Whilst the other lairds of the county entertained the queen's emissaries to the best of their ability, Mackenzie fed them on the meat of an old bull coarsely dressed, saw to it that the fire smoked, and brought in his "great dogges" to eat and fight in the hall. The gentlemen thought that they "had gotten purgatorie," and gave the queen-regent such a pitiful account of Mackenzie's poverty that she granted him feus of his lands upon very much more moderate terms than anyone else.[1]

A petition laid before parliament in 1578 furnishes another example of the very undemocratic results that might follow the granting of feus. The Bishop of Dunblane—who had secured his benefice through the power of the Earl of Montrose—had "set" the temporal lands of the bishopric to Montrose, over the heads of the old tenants, who in the petition describe themselves as "the native tennentis and kyndlie possessouris" of the temporal lands of Dunblane. They were afraid of being removed from the lands which "thay be thair selffis and thair predicessouris haif possessit and bruikit as takkismen and tennentis to the said bishoprik and his predicessouris in all tymes bigane past memorie of man to quhome thay and thair predicessouris haif made sa thankfull payment of thair dewtie and otheris thair dew seruice That nether the present possessour of the benefice nor yit ony of his predecessouris haif gude caus or occasion To complene." If they are removed they declare that "ane thowsand of o^r^ souerane Lordis commonis and pure people will be put to vter heirschip and extreme beggartie besides the inlaik of o^r^ Soueranes seruice quhen as sa grite rowmes quhair vpon sa mony ar sustenit sal be reducit in the handis of ane particular man." And they ask that the feu be not confirmed. Parliament ordained that no charter was to be given till the Lords Commissioners deputed for the confirmation of feus had considered the matter, and that they were "to sie that the said kyndlie tennentis be satisfeit for thair kyndnes" before granting a feu-charter. Montrose objected to these conditions and brought the matter before parliament in 1579. He

[1] Applecross MSS. History of the Mackenzies (published in *Highland Papers*, vol. ii, Scottish History Society, p. 31).

complained that he had not been present at the proceedings of 1578, that the conditions were a breach of privileges that had already been granted to him, and that he was being treated exceptionally, "aganis all ordour usit in sic caisis and forme of all confirmatiounis of feud lands usit to be grantit be our soverane lord, the like quhair of was nevir usit aganis ony nobilman within this realme quha had gottin few of Kirklands."[1] Apparently, however, he did not succeed in obtaining the reversal of the previous enactment, and one hopes that the kindly tenants were left in occupation.

The poverty and stress of the period naturally produced anti-social conditions. The hardship of the older tenants, who were displaced by the feuars, was only one note in the great minor chord of misery that rings through so many contemporary descriptions of the country-folk. Lindsay of the Mount, who flourished during the reign of James V, noticed that the new tenure of feuing encouraged the dispossession of smaller tenants by those who were able to pay more, and he urged the clergy to let their lands in feu

> To men that labours with their hands,
> But nocht to ane gearking gentill man,
> That nether will he work nor can.[2]

He also sings of the sad case of those who are "plainlie harlit out be the haid and ar destroyit" by men who can "pay greit ferme, or lay thair steid."[3] Henryson declared that: "The worst wolves are lords that have lands as a loan from God and set them to mailliaris and rentallars" and then pick quarrels with these tenants in order to get a further gersum or fine on a fresh lease to new tenants.[4]

Maitland of Lethington, in his verses "Aganis Oppresioun of the Commounis" writes:

[1] *A.P.S.* iii, p. 111.

[2] Sir David Lindsay of the Mount, *Satire on the Three Estates* (Laing's Edition), lines 2575, 2695.

[3] T. Johnson, *History of the Working Classes in Scotland*, p. 42. He has a most bitter collection of extracts showing the wrongs that the people were called upon to endure.

[4] W. Law Mathieson, *Politics and Religion in Scotland, 1550–1695*, p. 31.

It is great petie for to sé
Hou the comouns of this cuntré
For thift and reif and plane oppressioun
Can na thing keip in thair possessioun :
Sum comouns that hes been weill stakit
Under Kirkmen ar now all wrakit
Sen that the teynd and the kirk landis
Came in grit temporale mennis handis.[1]

Labour, in the anonymous *Complaynt of Scotlande*, repines bitterly to Dame Scotia upon his sad plight and the cruelty of his brothers the nobles and the clergy:

Allace, quhou can i tak paciens considerand that ther can na thing be eikkyt to my persecutione bot cruel dede. i dee daly in ane transe throcht the necessite that i hef of the gudis that i van vitht my laybyrs. my cornis and my cattel ar reft fra me. i am exilit fra my takkis and fra my steddyngis. the malis and fermis of the grond that i laubyr is hychtit to sic ane price, that it is fors to me & vyf and bayrns to drynk vattir. the tendis of my cornis ar nocht alanerly hychtit abufe the fertilite that the grond maye bayr, bot as veil thai are tane furtht of my handis be my tirran brethir.

And to much the same effect his complaint continues through two pages, dwelling upon the hopelessness of obtaining redress, and, once more, on the question of evils of tenure and raised rents.[2]

Feuing was primarily undertaken as a method of increasing revenue. The cash nexus was predominant. This is quite clearly brought out in practically every act that has been quoted from, and also in others that related to feuing. For instance, one passed in 1540 encourages the king to feu because it will be "to the grett proffitt of his croun̄ swa the samin be maid in augmentatiounn of his rentale." The actual feu-charters of the period usually state in their preambles that the king is feuing his lands to augment his rents.[3]

There is, however, very definitely, another side to the picture.

[1] Quoted by T. Johnson, *History of the Working Classes in Scotland*, p. 45.

[2] *The Complaynt of Scotlande*, pp. 122-125, date *circ.* 1549 (published by Early English Text Society).

[3] See examples, *Exchequer Rolls*, vol. xv, pp. 265 and 313.

The reproaches of the " Makars " are a sign of grace and show that there was considerable tenderness of conscience at the time. The complaint by the tenants of the Earl of Montrose was, of course, a statement of their side of the case, and in considering this document, as well as many other acts of parliament of the times, it must be remembered that the official language of sixteenth-century Scotland was quite unfettered by the chaste restraint of the present-day bureaucratic style. History told by means of pithy extracts is very tempting to write, but it is apt to be misleading.

There is, moreover, evidence that the small tenants of the Crown were treated with a good deal of consideration. On one occasion, at least, they made good their possession of a feu. King's Barns, in Fifeshire, had been leased by joint tenants, but in 1509 it was feued to five individuals ; two of them were country gentlemen and one was a court official. Yet, by the following year, the original joint tenants had obtained the cancellation of the grant and had themselves secured the feu.[1] This seems to have been an exceptional case ; but it is fairly common, though not inevitable, to find that when a feu was given, the condition was made that the poor occupiers should not be removed during their lifetimes and whilst they paid their rent.[2] For instance, the twelve tenants of Le Casche, who had held the farm on a three-year lease, were safeguarded in this way when the farm was feued to the Scotts of Balweary in 1509. A few years later the tenants of Le Casche were given an allowance for the destruction of their corn by the king's order. In 1532 they received a chalder of the royal oats.[3] The tenants of Bute, the most ancient part of the Stewart patrimony, received feus in 1506 at the old rental.[4] In 1531, when the Lords Auditors passed an act that everyone on entering on a feu was to pay double duties in money and kind, the comptroller and auditors were specially permitted to " do favoris to the Kingis pur tenentis at haldis thaire landis in feu at thar enterers of the said victualis." [5]

[1] *Exchequer Rolls*, vol. xiii, p. cxxviii.
[2] *Ibid.* vol. xiii, p. cxxviii.
[3] *Ibid.* vol. xiii, p. cxix ; vol. xiv, see rental in Appendix ; vol. xvi, p. 551.
[4] *Ibid.* vol. xiii, p. cxix.
[5] *Ibid.* vol. xvi.

No information seems to be available as to what happened upon the lands of the great lords. The bond of feudal attachment which existed between the lords and their vassals on their own lands would not operate to the same degree with the tenants on the secularised Church lands, to which all the bitterest complaints relate. On the other hand, when one remembers the political situation during the reigns of Mary and James VI, one has to allow for the great power of the nobles and to give them a share of the credit for legislation that was at least well-intentioned if ineffectual. Moreover, it must be remembered that the screw was being applied to the poverty-stricken kingdom from the top downwards; that taxation, which fell directly upon the superior of the land, was becoming heavier and heavier; and that there was a natural tendency to pass on part of their burden to their vassals, and also to their tenants—though it was illegal to do the latter. During the latter part of the century there is evidence that the secularized Church lands were specially heavily assessed. It would be unfair to consider the relationship of the tenants of the Old Church lands and their new superiors without having some regard for the general situation of the kingdom. Nevertheless, in spite of some evidence of good intentions by the Crown and the nobles, the end of our period shows that political and economic forces, acting through the sheer pressure of individual self-interest, were too strong and that the process of squeezing out and dispossession continued.[1]

The last General Council of the Old Church, held in 1558–59, passed a statute forbidding the setting of the lands of kindly tenants over their heads. After the Reformation, however, the matter became a national affair, and the Crown, or those who ruled through it, had to assume responsibility. The legislation that followed was influenced by two dominant considerations: (*a*) to protect the tenants, and (*b*) to secure as much money as possible for the Crown by means of the compositions payable when feus were confirmed. On the one hand, acts in council were passed in 1561 and 1562–63, and also an act of parliament in 1563, that " hir hienes " (Mary of Lorraine) " hes statute and ordainit, that na kyndlie lauchfull possessour,

[1] T. Thomson, Law Papers, *Cranstoun v. Gibson, Court of Session, Second Division*, 1816.

tennent or occupyer of ony of the saidis kirk landis be removit fra thair kyndlie rowme, steiding or possessioun be the allegeit fewaris or takaris of the samin in lang takkis," except by special royal licence. This act was at first to last until 1564, but was then extended till 1566.[1] Matters, however, could not be kept in a state of fixity. The need for money was urgent, and a new authority had to take the place of the Church in confirming feus. In 1564 an act of parliament was passed empowering the Crown to grant confirmation of all feus of all Church land, and declaring that all infeftments granted since 1558–59 required such ratification (in return, of course, for a suitable payment). A special body of commissioners was appointed to examine each individual case upon its merits. Professor Hannay has pointed out that the commissioners followed no regular scale in fixing the composition to be paid to the Crown for the confirmations. "There were clearly several points to be considered. What was the date of infeftment? What was the character of the bargain? How much might the grantee be able or be prepared to pay? What of kindly tenants, and so on." He goes on to quote examples, showing the extreme variation of the ratio of the composition to the value of the feu. "Upon comparing the duty with the composition, in upwards of thirty cases it appeared that the latter was scarcely ever the exact multiple of the former. The approximate multiples varied . . . from ten to about one and a half." Between 1564 and 1566 these compositions brought in a sum of £9104, a very welcome addition to the extremely inadequate resources of the Scots Throne.[2]

The status of the kindly tenants and old possessors, moreover, remained a vexed question. They were certainly suffering, and in 1568 the proposal was made in parliament that it should be statute that no mailer, farmer, or other occupier of lands, who pay their duties, be removed for certain years, so that order may be taken for the relief of the poor and the better forthsetting of the king's service. The suggestion—the text of which is a good deal mutilated—was made: because the common people and commons of this realm over all parts

[1] R. K. Hannay, "A Study in Reformation History," *Scottish Hist. Review*, vol. xvi, p. 52.

[2] *Ibid.*

thereof have been removed from their native and kindly steadings and families have been scaled and put to beggary and a great number of beggars and poor ones gendered, and because the commons, which are the greatest part of the people, are and will be altogether made unable to serve in the wars, that therefore it should be statute that no mailer, farmer, or other occupier of lands, who pay their duties, be removed for certain years, so that order may be taken for the relief of the poor and the better forthsetting of the king's service.[1] Nothing, however, was done ; no doubt the poverty and unenlightened self-interest of the Crown and of the landlords were responsible. Meanwhile the status of the kindly tenants was left in a condition of extreme vagueness.

Many cases relating to the kindly tenants came before the Privy Council, and it is clear that to some extent their rights were recognized. Very often, when kindly tenants appealed against being evicted, an order was made that a local " court of kindness " should be appointed to examine their claims to be kindly tenants, and that they were not to be dispossessed should these claims be made good ; but unfortunately the definition of what constituted a " kindly tenant " is nowhere given by the Privy Council. There were, however, cases where, possibly for political reasons, the Privy Council did not interfere on behalf of the tenants. Even when the claims of the tenants were considered, it is by no means clear what title to the land the fact that they were kindly tenants was supposed to give them. In some cases they only claimed priority in the allocation of the feu of their land, but in many others it is stated that they claimed continued occupation; there is, however, nothing to show if this were for their lifetimes, or for that of their widow and sons as well, or for the family in perpetuity, although there seems to be a probability that it was merely for their lifetimes or was entirely indefinite.[2]

Meanwhile further legislation was required to enable the Crown to secure the compositions which made the feuing of the secularised Church lands so lucrative to it. The new feu-holders were not eager to pay up, and often preferred to dis-

[1] *A.P.S.* vol. iii, p. 45.

[2] *Register Privy Council*, vol. i, pp. 110, 432, 541, 558-559; vol. ii, pp. 432-433, 465, 467, 477, 590.

pense with the security of a royal confirmation of their feus. In 1578 and in 1584 acts were passed to hurry them up. It was enacted that in cases where more than one infeftment for the same feu was granted, that one which first received royal confirmation was to be recognized as valid, and all unconfirmed feus were to be submitted for confirmation within the year or under pain of the disposal of the lands by the Crown itself. The 1584 act also had a most important clause in favour of the " auld possessouris," stating that they might have their confirmations within a year at a fixed charge (viz. four times the maill or money rent and twice the ferme or victual rent), and that, if they offered for confirmation, they were not to be evicted and the land disposed to anyone else.[1] Although the scope of the act and its application are both obscure—for instance, according to the preamble, long tacks as well as feus required royal confirmation—yet it definitely gave the kindly tenants legislative consideration, although equally definitely it did not give them any absolute right of property.

The use of the term " kindly tenant " in contemporary documents seems to show that their position was rapidly becoming weaker and weaker, not only because their numbers were decreasing, but because their status was becoming more and more ill-defined. The *Register of the Privy Council* abounds with examples of the very loose use of the term. In 1578 the Earl of Lennox claimed to be the " Kindly Bailie " of the lordship and regality of Glasgow, and his claim was upheld. The Convention of Royal Burghs passed a rule that no occupier of the Common Good of the burghs was to interfere

[1] *A.P.S.* vol. iii, p. 351.

R. K. Hannay, "A Study in Reformation History," *Scottish Hist. Review*, vol. xvi, p. 70.

W. Ross, *Lectures on the Practice of Law of Scotland*, vol. ii, p. 480.

The story of the securing of the feu of Beauly Priory by Lord Lovat is an amusing illustration of the whole position and of the working of the acts of confirmation. Lovat is said to have paid the Prior of Beauly 13,500 merks for the feu. In 1584 it had not been confirmed, and he received word that Mackenzie of Kintail was going to Edinburgh to obtain a feu of the same land. Lovat took horse, and learned at Inverness that Mackenzie was actually on his way to Edinburgh, but " being better acquaint with the road " he managed by short cuts to get there a day before his rival and to secure the confirmation. (Quoted by C. E. Chisholm, *Beauly Priory*, p. 273. The Scottish History Society has printed the *Wardlaw Manuscript*.)

with the annual roupings under pretence of *kindness*, possession, or otherwise (although, at the same time, we come across an order that the " kindness " of lands is not to be bought and sold upon the Borders without the consent of the landlord, showing that in some cases the old tenure still carried real privileges). There are examples of kindly tenants with leases, and in 1582 two claims were made to " kindness," one (in Annandale) because the tenant had had occupation for a hundred years " by takkis and sufficient titillis," and the other (in Moray) because he had had heritable infeftment for over twenty-two years.[1] It is significant that although the claims of the kindly tenants occupy a very large proportion of the *Register of the Privy Council* throughout the third quarter of the sixteenth century, yet in the fourth quarter allusions to the word become few and far between. In the fifth volume of the *Register* (1592–1599), for instance, the word only appears four times. Probably claims to " kindly " possession were regarded as so shadowy that they were no longer considered worth fighting over.

PART III. THE RESULTS OF THE FEUING MOVEMENT

In the foregoing sketch of the feuing movement the status of the feuars has been somewhat stressed because it is often rather slurred over. The movement in no way produced a class analogous to the English yeomen. Had that been so, it would be puzzling to imagine how such a class afterwards completely disappeared. In country districts the feus were largely acquired by the great landholders to extend their estates and by lesser lairds who were of the same class and status as those who held their land by the older tenure of ward-holding. When wardholding was abolished, in 1746, practically the whole of the land of Scotland came to be held in feu-farm.

A computation of how much land was feued during the sixteenth century has never been made, but the area must have been very considerable. The feuing movement undoubtedly made for the unhappiness of large numbers of people, and it

[1] *Register, Privy Council*, vol. ii, pp. 697-698; vol. vi, pp. 368, 386, 391, 801.

Records of the Convention of Royal Burghs, vol. i, p. 303.

increased the gloom of the period of greatest mental stress that Scotland has been called upon to endure. It was, however, a movement that was almost bound to come during or after the decay of those social conditions that had produced the barons, with those armed followings that were the only means of ostentation that the unconvertible produce of their estates permitted them. It was probably, on the whole, a good thing that the movement came so early in the history of the Lowlands (a district that had suffered especially from this feature of mediaevalism). It had its counterpart in the Highland clearances which followed the decay of the clan system at the end of the eighteenth century, and in the English enclosure movement, so curiously retarded by the legalized customs of the manor.

It has been suggested that the spread of feuing prevented the kindly tenants from developing into a class with the same security of tenure as the English copyholders. Yet there seem to be fairly strong reasons that make this unlikely. The whole trend of the development of Scots law was against the recognition of customary tenures, and the kindly tenants had failed to make good their position in the centuries when conditions gave them the best opportunity for doing so.

The feuing movement was not an unmixed evil. It gave security of position to a large number of the lesser gentry—the number of landed families that date back to the obtaining of a feu must be very large; and, in view of the unsettled state of landholding in Scotland under pure feudalism, without any customary safeguards, this security was probably of national importance. Comparisons are odious, especially between classes, yet it is surely legitimate to say that the old stock of Scots gentry of the lesser sort is largely responsible at home and abroad—for the wanderings of its younger sons are proverbial—for a particular tradition of self-respecting pride in gentle birth combined with frugality and earnestness of living, that is not the least among the attributes of the people of Scotland.

CHAPTER VI

PART I. THE CONDITION OF AGRICULTURE

THE system of agriculture of our period was quite definitely the Infield and Outfield method which has already been described. The words themselves occur constantly in the writings of the times and of those of the following century.[1] Runrig was still the common method of cultivating the joint holdings.[2] As we have already seen, joint tenancies were very common, but joint ownerships—both in commonty and in holdings owned rig and rig about—also existed, for laws were passed relating to them in the following century. The actual ownership of intermixed strips, however, seems to have been an unusual method of holding land, for it is but seldom alluded to, apart from the commonties, which were almost entirely composed of land that was waste and therefore not worth demarcating, and are there-

[1] In a charter of 1611 by James VI to the burgh of Glasgow the common land of the burgesses is described as " terrae tam lie outfield quam infield, cultae quam incultae " (quoted by D. Murray, *Early Burgh Organisation*, p. 102). I am indebted to Mr W. Angus, of the Register House, for the following examples : *Infield* and *Outfield lands* occur in an *Instrument of Resignation* relating to the lands of *Randelstoun* in the lordship of Lowrestoun. See Register of Sasines for Edinb., Aug. 1606. Also *P.R.S.*, *Edinburgh*, vol. 13, fol. 336 B, June 1628 ; vol. 17, fol. 322 B, July 1631 ; vol. 18, fol. 147 A, Nov. 1631 ; vol. 19, fol. 52 A, May 1632 ; vol. 19, fol. 52 A, May 1632 ; vol. 19, fol. 137, June 1632 ; vol. 20, fol. 20, Oct. 1632.

Register, Privy Council, vol. v, p. 28, alludes to " fold dykes." These were used for folding animals at night on the outfield in order to manure parts of it.

[2] Murray's *Dictionary* quotes an example dated 1437 from the *Register of Dunfermline*.

The word is defined in Sir J. Balfour's *Practicks*.

See also Sir James Ramsay, *Bamff Charters*, p. 78 (1563), p. 128 (1586–87). In the second example the fourth part of a holding was granted as a feu to be held " by way of runrig."

See also *Register, Privy Council*, vol. iv, p. 503.

fore not of great importance.[1] Burgh commonties fall, of course, within a separate category.

It would be interesting to know how long the primitive system of periodically re-allotting the runrig strips survived in the Lowlands. Hebridean and Northumbrian examples of the nineteenth century have already been quoted,[2] and the practice was still carried on in some parts of the Highlands in the eighteenth century. In the Lowlands it was evidently the custom at one time, for the word cavel means both lot and rig, but by the fifteenth century there are cases which seem to show quite definitely that some of the burgh lands, at least, were being owned in severalty. The subdivision of some of the holdings owned by Cupar Abbey, especially the granges, rather imply a movement towards the holding of permanent shares in the farms. Thus, when Cupar Grange was repartitioned in 1473, it was ordained that " ilke man sal kepe his pairt of his malyn and his toft that his nichbur be nocht injuryt and the toun sal be partit gife nede be. . . ." Cotsyards was let in lease to two old tenants, " and tha sal pairt the toun in twa, gif it ma be; and gif it ma nocht, it sal be partyt in scheddis " (i.e. rigs ?). Occasionally the boundaries or the name of an individual tenant's share, within the holding, are mentioned.[3] On the other hand, in the leases that prescribed the sowing of wheat, peas, and bere, the tenants were ordered to sow them all together in one " sched," in order to keep the season of each of them " as timeously as is possible "—a most practical regulation.[4] The pasturage regulations show that the strips, whether permanently held or re-allotted, were in the open field.[5] It is a very striking fact that although runrig persisted for longer in the Highlands than elsewhere, there also this movement towards demarcated holdings was not only proceeding at the same time as in the South, but seems even to have advanced further. A lease dated 1568, of some lands of Beauly Priory, alludes to " ane pace of land callit John Clerks land " and " the croft callit Alexander Writhtis croft," and Lovat's feu-charter, confirmed in 1584, included Lie Mason's land, Johann Clerk's

[1] Cf. *Register Privy Council*, vol. vi, p. 224.

[2] See Chapter II, Part VII.

[3] *Register of Cupar Abbey*, vol. i, pp. 165, 172, 200.

[4] *Ibid.* pp. 172, 147, etc. [5] *Ibid.* p. 128.

land, M'Hucheon's croft, Dean James Pape's croft, Merschellis croft, M'Alesteris croft, then occupied by Sir David Dawson.[1]

Mansion-houses and larger farms certainly often had yards and "parks" (used, of course, in the old Scots sense of an enclosure) about them, for these are often alluded to in contemporary documents. The priory of Ardchattan, on the shores of remote Loch Etive, in 1602 had its offices, gardens, etc., "lying within the inner precinct or hedges of the priory." [2]

In the case of the joint farms, probably the rigs of the infield land, which were under constant cultivation, would tend to be permanently allotted to one occupier long before the shares of the outfield land, which was being constantly broken up and again allowed to go out of cultivation. As a matter of fact, during our period, Scotland must have been a comparatively empty land, and under the inefficient system of infield and outfield culture probably the farms shifted their principal lands about a good deal. An assize upon the rents of Drygrange (belonging to Melrose Abbey) tells its own tale. All the witnesses were emphatically in agreement with the sitting tenant, who was applying for papal confirmation of a feu. He stated that the previous tenant had originally paid ten merks, and that then: "Ye saidis Landis war reducit furth of wod and forest to telit landis quhilkis gaif sik playntie of cornis efter thai war telit and revin furth be quhilk occasioun ye said unquhile David was compelit for plentuousness of the ground at yat tyme to gif yairfor fyve chalderis of beir quhilkis thai micht wele pay salang as ye plentwisnes remanit with ye ground. And now sensyne ye saidis landis of Drigrange, be continvall vse and occupatoun yairof ar becumin to sik infertilitie and vnplentwisnes like as our landis of dornyk, galtounside, newsteid and vtheris are becumin to, quhairthrow our predecessouris and we behavit of necessitie to defalk large sowmes of ye victuall payit yairfor of befoir." This reason had been accepted and the rent reduced.[3]

[1] *Chartulary of Beauly Priory* (Grampian Club), pp. 254, 266.

[2] Cf. R. Chambers, *Domestic Annals of Scotland*, p. 358; *Chartulary of Beauly Priory* (Grampian Club), p. 155.

[3] G. Neilson, "Feuing of Drygrange," *Scottish Hist. Review*, vol. vii, p. 355.

For an example of new land being taken in, in Aberdeenshire, see Cosmo Innes, *Scotch Legal Antiquities*, p. 250.

Two foreigners who visited the country—Don Pedro de Ayala (early sixteenth century) and Estienne Perlin (1551)—were impressed by the inferiority of Scots agricultural methods. De Ayala said that the corn was good but that the land was not adequately cultivated; Perlin, that the arable land was indifferent and most of the country a desert. They both, however, were struck by the abundance of sheep and cattle.[1]

As a matter of fact, methods seem to have been much as they were in the eighteenth century. At Cupar, it was the custom to manure the infield before the barley crop, and the rule that calves might be kept in the young corn until 24th June has its parallel in quite enlightened advice in the early eighteenth century.[2]

Moreover there is evidence that the Scots Parliament pursued an enlightened policy in encouraging the planting of trees and improved agricultural methods. Apparently the growth of timber was its greatest concern, and three acts were passed ordering occupiers of land and farmers to plant. The law of 1454, for instance, orders that all freeholders, spiritual and temporal, in making their Whitsunday sets should statute and ordain that all the tenants plant woods and trees and make hedges and sow broom (which was much esteemed as a winter fodder), up to the faculty of their mailings in places convenient therefor, under such pain and unlaw as the baron or lord shall modify. The enforcement of the Government policy of afforestation in this case was thus to be part of the duties of the feudal landholder.[3] As time went on, the Government continued to try to improve the natural supplies. The Crown tenants of Fife were bound by special regulations to plant and preserve timber; and about the middle of the sixteenth century special orders were issued for the preservation of the woods of Inverness-shire, Aberdeenshire, Elgin, Banff, Nairn, and Forres. Among other regulations, it was ordained that bark (used for tanning) was not to be taken from standing trees, on account of the decay of the woods.[4] On Cupar lands, at least, these laws were by no means allowed to become a dead letter. The forests of the abbey

[1] P. Hume Brown, *Early Travellers to Scotland*, pp. 44, 73.

[2] *Register of Cupar Abbey*, vol. i, pp. xxix, 128.

[3] *A.P.S.* vol. ii, pp. 51, 343.

[4] *Register, Privy Council*, vol. i, p. 279; vol. iv, pp. 416-417.

were most carefully preserved, as one of the few surviving minutes of the bishop's court shows. Certain tenants were allowed rents upon moderate tacks in return for looking after them under the supervision of the foresters, and tenants were only allowed to take wood for building purposes under proper safeguards. Moreover, in most leases of 1468 and afterwards, the tenants were specially enjoined to plant ash trees and osiers. The provision was also contained in an ordinance by the abbot's court. In 1473 two men were entrusted with the making of a plantation (merica) for the abbey. It was to be enclosed and walled for as many years as were required for the trees to grow big enough not to be hurt by grazing cattle, and it was afterwards to be used as pasturage.[1] Unfortunately, all these efforts were not very effective. Most parts of Scotland were very deficient in trees. The imports of timber continued to be very heavy throughout our period and long afterwards.

The Planting Act of 1454 also enjoined the making of hedges for shelter, the sowing of broom for cattle fodder, and the sowing of wheat, peas, and beans; and other acts were passed to the same effect. The provision of winter fodder was one of *the* most serious problems of Scots agriculture until the agricultural revolution and the introduction of turnips and sown grass: for, unlike England, the country was very deficient in natural hay. The introduction of the sowing of peas and beans would have been a most important innovation had the idea been to use them as a substitute for a fallow. They were, however, only to be sown in small quantities: according to an act of 1427, every man who had eight oxen was to sow at least half a firlot of peas and forty beans,[2] and at Cupar, as we have seen, they were sown on a special rig. At Cupar, from 1460, most of the farmers, in their leases, were ordered to sow wheat and peas "in proportion to their corn sowing" or according to the "akkis of the parliament," and those of Aberbrothny were ordered to have a broom park.[3] The practice of growing peas and beans seems to have spread in certain districts. Bishop Leslie, writing in the sixteenth century, notices luxuriant crops

[1] *Register of Cupar Abbey*, vol. ii, p. xiii; vol. i, pp. xxx, 130, 141, 142, 163, 172, 185, 198, 212.

[2] *A.P.S.* ii, pp. 13, 343.

[3] *Register of Cupar Abbey*, vol. i, pp. 142, 164, 147.

of them about the Forth and the Tay, and according to an eighteenth-century writer they are said to have been grown in Stirlingshire " past memory of man." [1] In other districts, however, the good custom does not seem to have spread.

Another act of parliament dealing with agriculture, that was enforced at least at Cupar, is the older one against " guld." In many of the leases the tenants were bound to " wyn the land fra guld," in one case " ondir peyn of guld law." In 1479 a tenant had to pay 10s. for the foulness of the present year and give a special undertaking that in future his lands should be purged from guld twice yearly.[2]

The management of the pasture land was an important part of mediaeval agriculture. By the sixteenth century it was evidently the custom among some farmers to fence off a part temporarily, in order to preserve the grass, for allusions occur to " hained grass," such special pasturage being very valuable.[3] The management of the " parks " of Cupar Abbey, however, is even more interesting. The outfield, so characteristic of Scots agriculture, varied, at any rate by the eighteenth century, in different parts of the country, in the proportion it bore to the infield, in the number of years it lay under crop, and in its management (parts of Aberdeenshire and the Lothians had special ways of cultivating it). Much of such variation naturally depended on the conformation of the ground and the fertility of the soil. It is obvious that where there was much steep and sterile hillside, outfield would bear a large proportion to the infield, would only carry a few years of cropping, but would be continued long after the outfield in more favoured districts had been brought under the ordinary tillage of a modern farm.

It would be only natural to expect to find similar variations at earlier periods. Cupar Abbey lay in a naturally fertile and fairly level district where only a small proportion of the land can have been unsuitable for infield cultivation, and in the *Register* there is no actual allusion to outfield. The abbey " parks," however, are mentioned several times. The tenants of Cupar Grange were in particularly close touch with the abbey

[1] Ramsay of Ochtertyre, *Scotland and Scotsmen in the Eighteenth Century*, vol. ii, p. 196.

[2] *Register of Cupar Abbey*, vol. i, p. xxviii, pp. 144-228.

[3] *Register, Privy Council*, vol. vi, pp. 515, 802.

—they received all the stable manure and performed certain special services—and, under the supervision of the keeper of the abbey fields, they were obliged to fence and sow the parks either for a year or two years at a time " as the rede of the abbay ma suffyr," and " syn tha sal sufficiently hayn tham for pastur and feual to the plas." From another entry we know that the abbey beasts were to have the first grass of the newly hained enclosures, and that they were to be afterwards open to those of the tenants.[1] Such an arrangement in some ways resembles the ordinary Scots outfield and its primitive counterparts, but it is even more like very advanced English agricultural methods of the period, and the use of the word *haining* shows that the resemblance is not accidental.

Part II. Types of Rural Folk

The examples of holdings quoted so freely in previous chapters have shown how variable were the sizes of the holdings on Scots estates. Nevertheless both the farms and their tenants do fall into certain clearly defined groups. In fifteenth-century legislation there are allusions to the large farmer (every man having eight oxen was to sow a given quantity of peas and beans) and to the very small man—all men of simple estate that of reason should be labourers are to have half an ox in the plough or dig each work-day seven square feet of earth.[2] In other words, we have the ploughgate of eight oxgates, which might be termed the basic type of Scots holding whether occupied by a single farmer or by a group of joint tenants,[3] and the cottar, sub-tenant, mailer, or labourer.

The single tenant with a larger holding, and generally the possessor of a long lease, was fairly common. An act passed in 1524 to safeguard the interests of the dependants of the men who had been killed in a late war with England gives the status of such people. It enacted that the heirs of any " gentleman

[1] *Register of Cupar Abbey*, vol. i, pp. 139, 144.

[2] *A.P.S.* vol. ii, p. 8 (1424), p. 13 (1427).

[3] See, for instance, Cosmo Innes' analysis of the Forbes Rental of 1532, *Scotch Legal Antiquities*, p. 254. The lands of Arbuthnot were divided into 54 ploughgates at the end of the twelfth century (W. F. Skene, *Celtic Scotland*, vol. iii, p. 259).

unlandit or zemen " (=yeoman) who held tacks or steadings were to have security of tenure for five years.[1] Such " substantious " tenants were often younger members of neighbouring landed families, and they had sub-tenants. In the *Register of Cupar*, as we have seen, in several leases the tenant was given the right of installing and dismissing sub-tenants. The tenant of Murthly was empowered to hold his own courts for his sub-tenants, under the abbot's court. In some cases the principal joint tenant in a holding was responsible for finding the other tenants and had certain powers over them.[2] These are important developments, for they show that the " tacksman " system which was so general in the eighteenth century was an old-established institution.

The farms, however, were even more often held jointly by groups of tenants—all through the Crown Rentals, which are published as appendices to the *Exchequer Rolls*, from vol. xiii onwards, one finds these two types of holdings.[3] A husband-land, i.e. two oxgates, was a very common share for such a joint tenant, but in a sixteenth-century rental of the lands of the Abbey of Dunfermline a one-eighth or a one-sixteenth is the most usual size, although halfs and quarters are also common. By the end of the sixteenth century there is marked tendency of holdings on this estate to be less regularly divided and to be amalgamated. On the Gordon estates the usual size of farms was two ploughgates, divided among eight tenants.[4] In all these examples, however, there is also a large number of holdings of an irregular size.

The problem of how far the shares of the joint tenants were demarcated has been discussed under the heading of agriculture. On Cupar they seem to have paid their rent jointly. Sometimes, when a holding was rearranged, a set of fresh leases was given to all the tenants, but generally individual arrangements were made. Quite often, at Cupar, some of the joint tenants on a holding would have five-year leases, and

[1] *A.P.S.* vol. ii, p. 284.

[2] *Register of Cupar Abbey*, pp. 137, 163, 166, 169, 172, 197, 230.

[3] Also on the Honour of Morton and on the Church estates such as those already noticed in some detail. Joint tenancy was almost invariable among the rentallers on the lands of the Bishop of Glasgow.

[4] See Appendix to *Register of Dunfermline*.
The Gordon Rental is published in vol. iv, *The Spalding Club Miscellany*.

others for life. The position was further complicated by the fact that it was not unusual for a tenant to have more than one holding. Out of nearly 200 leases and feus granted by Cupar between 1539 and 1559, about thirty tenants had two holdings, about ten each had three, about eight each had four, and three individuals seem to have had five or six holdings apiece.[1] In the case of the estates of the Bishop of Glasgow and of the Abbey of Dunfermline it can be seen that the same thing had happened.

These joint farmers of a ploughgate or even of a husbandland employed a lower order of beings, their sub-tenants or cottars, to do much of the actual work upon the land, although, as Major tells us, they kept a diligent eye upon them.[2] The employment of such sub-tenants was a universal custom. One constantly finds allusion to them upon both Church and lay lands.[3] The tenure of such sub-tenants seems to have depended upon the will of the direct tenants, but some of the very small tenants holding directly of Cupar Abbey " in form of cottery " had life-leases.[4] On Cupar Abbey, at least, many regulations were made regarding the tenants' cottars. Their numbers were strictly limited. Tenants holding one-twelfth of Cupar were not to have more than two, and tenants holding one-eighth no more than three. The cottars themselves were forbidden to have " codrouchos "—apparently labourers of their own—under them. It was evidently customary to grant them rights to cut a specified supply of fuel, and the tenants on one holding were not to be allowed to keep them unless they gave them this and also yards for their kale. Their whole status was different to that of the smaller tenants, as may be seen from a clause in a lease to Balbrogy (1468): " Moreover, those cottars holding the middle ploughgate shall answer to the monastery in the law of husbandmen, but regarding fuel they shall stand as cottars." [5]

[1] *Register of Cupar Abbey*, vol. ii, list of feus and tacks granted, 1539–1559.

[2] J. Major, *History of Greater Britain* (Scottish History Society).

[3] Cf. *Register of Cupar*, Nos. 32, 67, etc.
Registrum Nigrum de Aberbrothoc, Nos. 63, 273.
Book of the Roses of Kilravock, p. 261.

[4] *Register of Cupar*, No. 219.

[5] *Register of Monastery of Cupar*, pp. 123, 129, 144, 176, 178, 235.

The steel-bow type of tenure, which was commuted at Kelso in the twelfth century, survived in many districts during the fourteenth, fifteenth, and sixteenth centuries.[1]

Part III. Estate Management

To manage such complex agricultural communities considerable estate organization was necessary. Something has been said of the importance of the barons' courts. There was also a system of estate officials. The *Exchequer Rolls*, in the accounts of the revenues and expenses of the Crown lands, give some indication of how estates were worked. For every larger district there was a chamberlain—sometimes a man of local standing, sometimes one of the numerous men of affairs employed upon the multifarious business of the king's court. Under him were mairs appointed to supervise smaller districts. This organization seems to have been the typical one, for it is to be found not only upon those lands that were the patrimony of the Crown, but on the estates that were from time to time forfeited or in ward. The Earldom of Moray is a good example.[2]

In some of the chartularies of the religious houses the information is fuller. The *Register of the Abbey of Cupar* is the best of all. There was the Regality Court, presided over by an Ogilvie, eventually by Lord Ogilvie as hereditary bailie, with a bailie-depute, and under it courts were held by sub-bailies in lesser districts.

For the administrative work of the estate there was the steward or "granger," held by successive members of the Rogers family, and under him the head forester, the "cunyngar" (keeper of the rabbit warren), and the superintendent of the fisheries. Other minor officials were the keeper of the cattle (which seems to have become a hereditary appointment), the flockmaster, the keeper of the abbey parks, and the five land officers who were responsible for seeing that the tenants fulfilled

[1] Cf. *Exchequer Rolls*, vol. vii, p. 464; vol. xii, pp. xlvii, 680, etc.

[2] Most of the information, conveyed incidentally as it is in the rendering of the accounts, can only be used by inference. In most volumes of the *Exchequer Rolls* it will be found included under the heading of "Chamberlain," and then cross-referenced under these officials' names.

the conditions of their leases, and who each had a separate district.[1]

To regulate the internal affairs of the joint holdings, "pundlers," who assessed the damage done by beasts straying in other people's crops or hainings and those of the abbey, etc., and "oversmen" were appointed, "according to the statutes of the abbey court that good neighbourhood be kept." Once the latter was, by the terms of the lease, to be appointed by the tenants themselves, but generally he was chosen by the abbot. The tenants of Nether Newton were ordered to have a weekly "byrlay court" for the common profit of the town and the correction of all faults.[2]

At Cupar a variety of regulations were made, either in the barons' court or in the leases. Some of these have been alluded to, such as planting, sowing peas and beans, the extirpation of guld. The proper casting of peats and divots, the pasturage of animals, which were to be kept out of the crops from June till after harvest, the reclamation of waste land, the limitation of the numbers of pigs to be kept by tenants and cottars, besides the proper rendering of the service dues, were all dealt with.[3]

Besides this, one gets an amusing picture of the rather paternal organization of the estate. Each of the tenants of Syokis was to lose his lease "if he shall not be sober and temperate, preserving more strictly a kindly intercourse with his neighbours and relatives." Others were to lose their lease "an he be vncorrigebil" in observing the orders regarding planting, guld, etc. Another family was to be "suet and gentill, and mak gud service to al that cummys without strubilance;" they were tenants of the "bait"—was this an inn? In a good many leases about 1503, tenants were not to grumble or complain about their lease, but were to "frely gif it our." The son of an old tenant in Drumfolatyn had the tack renewed and was "to keep the wood and be obedient to his mother." In 1474, tenants were ordered to be "honest" in their clothing and "wel beseyn" with jacks, splints, bows, arrows, swords

[1] C. Rogers, *Register of Cupar Abbey*, vol. i, pp. xxxv, xxxix, 139; vol. ii, p. xiv.

[2] *Ibid.* vol. i, pp. 147, 172, 176, 180, 230, 188.

[3] *Ibid.* vol. i, pp. 128, 129, 139, 144, 172, 178, etc.

and bucklers or axes to keep them in their persons and from scaith in their goods.[1]

There are instances of an enlightened policy. One tenant was forgiven arrears of rent "in hope of a good and better management." The "widow" of John Barber was allowed to keep on his land upon condition that he himself, after the sowing, should "freely depart from his wife and healthy children to a place which he should choose suitable to his infirmity," and never return or have communication with them. Was he a leper? [2]

Part IV. The Economic Organization of the Countryside

It is not difficult to realize individual differences between the present day and the past, but it is harder to grasp the all-pervading general spirit of an economic organization quite unlike our own. In the fifteenth and sixteenth centuries, as for long afterwards, farming was mainly for subsistence—for supplying directly the needs of the cultivators. The wheat which the tenants of Cupar were obliged to sow was too luxurious for their own use, and they did not sell it—by a special clause in their leases they exchanged it at the abbey for oats. Rents were invariably paid largely in kind all over Scotland, thus supplying the proprietor with the grain, meal, meat, poultry, cheese, butter, eggs he required. Sometimes, as we have seen, he moved about to consume these provisions; sometimes, with considerable difficulty (as the *Exchequer Rolls* show), they were conveyed to one of his principal residences. The system, however, went further. The tenants supplied services of various kinds. At Cupar Abbey, for instance, they cast and carried the peats, supplied reapers at harvest time; by the sixteenth century they wintered some of the landlords' cattle; they had to supply a given number of "short carriages," i.e. the carting of fuel, cheese, bent, etc., and of "long carriages," the carrying of lime, slates, coal, and other goods from a distance. Certain holdings had to sow the abbey parks and maintain the fences; others were responsible for a specially large

[1] C. Rogers, *Register of Cupar Abbey*, vol. i, pp. 154, 164-165, 194, 242, 253.

[2] *Ibid.* vol. i, pp. 145, 163.

quantity of peats. A tenant on a holding on Sandy Law had to carry sand for buildings; another tenant, as part of his services, had to maintain a sheep-cot; others to drain a marsh. Kethyk was let to seven husbandmen for two years, who were to supply sixteen score of waggon-loads of divots as part of their rent.[1]

From such arrangements it is but a step to find most of the abbey officials, the head forester, the cunyngar, the cattle-keeper, the porter, etc., receiving a holding as part of their wages. Or, further, to find that both the office and the occupation of the holding tended to become hereditary. The contracts between such employees and the abbey, however, were sometimes very complicated. The orchard of the Grange of Kerso was let to a tenant upon a life-lease at a rent of five merks. He was to put the orchard to all possible use in building houses and dykes, planting hedges and fruit trees, the latter the best that might be got. He was to have charge of the hainings, the stanks for fishes and eels, and the doo-cot. For all this he was to receive two bolls of meal and account for the produce, "and gyf the abbot chargis hym of hys froytis, fer the price he sal gif hym, an he wald sel yame in to the markat or alow him in his male." (Apparently he had to supply the abbey at current prices and kept the rest for his pains.) Such, at least, was the arrangement with a fowler employed to supply the monastery with game. Several leases deal with Campsy, where the four joint tenants had to help to look after the woods and were in charge of the fishings. They were to supply a boat and nets, but received £10 towards the cost. They were each to give the monastery thirty dozen of salmon, fresh or kippered, in the year, "according to their fortune," and they were not to sell, give away, or eat any that they caught until their tale was made up. If they could not catch the thirty dozen, they were to make up the deficiency with other fish.[2]

The craftsmen who were employed by the abbey were generally engaged by the year, though occasionally by the week. Sometimes they were engaged for longer, and sometimes they received a little land as part of their wages. A mason and his son engaged themselves to the abbey for their

[1] C. Rogers, *Register of Cupar Abbey*, vol. i, pp. xix, 119, 146, 207.

[2] *Ibid.* pp. 189, 200, 227, 248, 274.

lives for a 2½-acre croft, 6 merks wages yearly, and a daily allowance of food consisting of meat or fish, five short white cakes, and half a gallon of convent ale.[1] In a good many cases, even where they did not receive their crofts as part of their wages, the craftsmen were the abbey tenants. In five cases they bore their craft name as their surname—a man named Mason was a mason, etc., so that the trade had evidently become hereditary.

Part V. The Condition of the Rural Folk

In following out to their chronological end the happenings of the fifteenth and sixteenth centuries it is almost inevitable that a very misleading picture of the state of the people should be given. One sees them oppressed by their enemies of England and by the more fortunate and wealthy of their own countrymen—one realizes that they were at once the victims of the surviving feudal system and of the " cash nexus " that was gradually to take its place. Their method of gaining a livelihood from their small and precarious holdings was miserably inefficient. It is difficult not to imagine their plight as one of gloom and desperation; but, to their honour, it was not so.

Low and comfortless their ways of living certainly were, compared to contemporary European standards. Their houses were built without lime and with turf; the poorest ones had doors of hide, as Eneas Sylvius scornfully tells us. Froissart describes how the country seemed to be " ruined " after an English raid. But the country-folk, he says, made light of it, declaring that they had driven their cattle into the forests and that with six or eight stakes they would soon have new houses.[2] Eneas Sylvius wrote: " The common people are poor, and destitute of all refinement. They eat flesh and fish to repletion, and bread only as a dainty. The men are small in stature, bold and forward in temper." [3]

Almost all visitors to Scotland seem to have been struck in the same way by the low standard of living and by the high spirit of the people. John Major, who lived the greater

[1] C. Rogers, *Register of Cupar Abbey*, p. 309.
[2] P. Hume Brown, *Early Travellers to Scotland*, pp. 12-26.
[3] *Ibid.* p. 27.

part of his life abroad, agrees with them. He says he has observed that there is more outward elegance among the citizens of France than in those of Britain, but that among the country-folk there is more elegance in Britain than abroad. They try to rival the dress and arms of the lesser gentry; and if a noble strikes one of them, he returns the blow on the spot.[1] The farmers, he says, scorn the craftsmen and bring up their sons to live in the country and to follow war.

Not only was the general standard of comfort of the country-people low, but their means of maintaining it were most variable. In good years there seems to have been abundance of food. Estienne Perlin, already noted, says that Scotland was poor in gold and silver but rich in provisions; de Ayala, that there was abundance of meat and also of wool and hides; Eneas Sylvius, that the poor people ate meat and fish but little bread.[2] When one remembers the enormous export of hides and wool-fells that took place from Scotland during this period, one can indeed very well see that the stocks of meat and venison must have been very large—for it is unthinkable that the canny Scots allowed them to be wasted. At Cupar Abbey, meat (or on fast days, fish and extra strong ale) was given daily to the craftsmen who had their meals supplied by the community.[3]

Supplies were, however, most variable. Anyone who lives in Scotland must fully realize how deeply its difficult and very variable climate affects the produce of the ground—especially in hilly districts. But it takes a little thought to picture the state of the people after a bad harvest in the days when most folk lived upon their own produce and when transport was extremely defective. Even Berwick, a large town, with corn-lands near it, and with a considerable coastal trade, suffered the most violent fluctuations in the price of wheat. The following prices per "summa"(=quarter) have been worked out:

1248	2/-
1258	16/-
1287	1/- and 1/8
1301	30/- [4]

[1] John Major, *History of Greater Britain*, p. 47.
[2] P. Hume Brown, *Early Travellers to Scotland*, pp. 27, 43, 73.
[3] See following chapter. See *Register of Cupar Abbey*, vol. i, p. xxxiv.
[4] J. Scott, *History of Berwick*, p. 16.

What must the condition of the country-folk in more un-get-at-able places have been like, who needed the corn for seed and its straw for winter fodder?

The weather seems to have been at least as unkind as at present: from a small memorandum book, apparently kept by the parish priest at Taymouth, we learn that

> 1554 was a very stormy winter.
> 1563 a year of scarcity. A boll of meal was worth 5 merks = £3 6s. 8d
> 1564 a boll of meal was only 18s.
> 1571–2 a stormy winter.
> 1572 a year of scarcity. Meal sold at £2 3s. for a short time.[1]

How closely the fear of famine pressed upon the country may be seen from the large number of acts of parliament dealing with the subject that were passed. It is a fact that requires to be stressed if one indulges in comparisons between "the good old days" and the present. In 1449 two acts were passed to prevent "regrating" in time of dearth. In 1455 the amount of victual that might be held in time of dearth was limited—it was a "rationing" act. In 1526 no tallow was to be exported, on account of dearth. Nine years later there was another act dealing with dearth, and the eating of fish was encouraged. In 1540 the export of tallow was again forbidden. In 1551 it was enacted that wine and vivers should have their prices and quality fixed, because of dearth. Four years later the export of food and tallow was again forbidden, for fear of dearth. In 1567 it was enacted that no victuals were to be taken out of the kingdom, and more careful regulations to prevent this were made in 1578. In 1581 an act was passed ordering all earls, lords, barons, as well within regality as royalty, and their bailiffs to landward, and the provosts and baillies of all burghs and cities to fix the price on all stuff for the staunching of the dearth of victuals. In 1587, parliament was evidently thoroughly alarmed and four acts were passed. The ensuance of dearth was said to be due to the transporting of victuals by land and sea, and this was strictly forbidden—thus stopping certain valuable exports. Another act declared that it was due to the high and illegal impositions imposed on goods and victual coming to the markets, free ports and havens, and these were

[1] Cosmo Innes, *Sketches of Early Scotch History*, p. 353.

also forbidden. Horses were not to be kept on hard meat during the summer, the only exceptions being two for each earl or lord and one for each baron. An act of 1584 that meat was not to be eaten in Lent or on Wednesday, Friday, or Saturday was repeated. In 1592 it was forbidden to take nolt and sheep out of the country, because prices were thereby raised.[1] The prevention of dearth was one of the constant preoccupations of the Privy Council.

Nevertheless, in spite of all their hardships, the countryfolk managed to live a robustly cheerful life. When James V went wandering round the country, his expenditure included many payments to local singers and musicians, which shows that music lightened their lot. They had their Robin Hood plays and mumming.[2]

One of the most charming accounts of rural life is in the *Complaynt of Scotlande.* The writer in his allegorical wanderings comes to the seashore and describes the setting forth of a ship: ". . . the marynalis began to veynd the cabil, vytht mony loud cry. ande as ane cryit, al the laif cryit in that samyn tune, as it had bene ecco in ane hou heuch. and as it aperit to me, thai cryit thir vordis as eftir follouis: veyra veyra, veyra veyra. gentil gallandis, gentil gallandis. veynde i see hym, veynd i see hym. pourbossa, pourbossa. hail al and ane, hail al and ane. hail hym vp til vs, hail hym vp til vs." This was said as the anchor was being weighed, and other jingles were given for making the anchor fast and for hauling up the sails, a different one for each sail.

There is then a charming account of a group of shepherds, who, after putting their flocks to pasture, are sitting on a lea rig and eating their "refectioune," and making "greit cheir of euyrie sort of mylk," that is, butter, cheese, curds, etc. They had no bread "bot ry caikes and fustean skonnis maid of flour. Than after there disiune, tha began to talk with grit myrrynes that was rycht plesand to be hard." Then they danced together a great variety of country dances, all enumerated, and told each other tales.[3]

[1] *A.P.S.* vol. ii, pp. 36, 41, 314, 373, 378, 483, 495; vol. iii, pp. 40, 104, 225, 452, 453, 577.

[2] *Exchequer Rolls,* vol. vi, p. cxvi.

[3] *The Complaynt of Scotlande* (Early English Text Society), pp. 40-45.

One of the most attractive features of the times was the large part played by humble folk in the writings of the Scots "makars." It is surely most significant that James V, the King of the Commons, should have chosen to write so sympathetically of them. "The Gaberlunzie Man" describes the night's fortunes of a beggar man. "Peblis to the Play" tells how

> At Beltane quhen ilk bodie bownes
> To Peblis to the play.

The girls in their homely best; the coltish young men; the crowd of rustic folk, with the miller and the pedlar; the fun round the booths; the paying of the ale-house reckoning; the sound of the smacking kisses given when at last the company parted, all are described, and one is left with a vigorous picture of sturdy rustic jollity to set against the dark background of the period.

The king's third poem, "Chryst's Kirk on the Green," also describes rollicking country-folk at a fair, their courtships, a brawl, the scolding of the wives of the contending parties, and how the husbands beat them and all was well.

> Was nevir in Scotland hard nor sene
> Sic dansing nor deray,
> Nowthir at Falkland on the grene
> Nor Peblis at the play
> As wes of wowaris: as I were
> At Chryst kirk on ane day.
> Thair come our kitties * weschin clene
> Full gay
> At Chryst's kirk on the grene.

* Contemporary term for a young woman.

CHAPTER VII

PART I. THE ECONOMIC IMPORTANCE OF RURAL PRODUCE

THE preceding chapter has indicated how very important a part in the national economy was played by land—its political influence—and how largely the troubles of the period were caused by its inadequacy to maintain the upper classes of Scotland in the current style affected by their equals in other parts of Western Europe. The story of agrarian conditions in Scotland is of extreme importance, not only in relation to contemporary history, but because it still has a vital bearing upon the rural situation of the present day. The story of the burghs is of far less importance. In population, political weight, and in wealth they came far behind the country. Although important developments were beginning at the end of our period, the condition of the burghs was, on the whole, surprisingly static; nor does it seem to have had anything like the same formative influence upon later conditions. To this there is, perhaps, the one important exception of the burghal constitutions, which lasted until the Reform Act. This latter, however, is an example of clogging conservatism and not of creative influence

The proportion of the national taxation borne by the burghs remained almost constant:

1367	Extent (Thomson's estimate) . .	burghs' share	$\frac{1}{5}$
1471	Tax	,,	$\frac{1}{5}$
1481	,, ...	,,	$\frac{1}{5}$
1488	,, ...	,,	$\frac{1}{5}$
1554	,, ...	,,	$\frac{1}{6}$
1580	,, ...	,,	$\frac{1}{6}$
1584	,, ...	,,	$\frac{1}{6}$
1586	,, ...	,,	$\frac{1}{6}$
1587	Act of Parliament stating that burghs' share of taxation should remain at		$\frac{1}{6}$
1593	Tax	burghs' share	$\frac{1}{6}$
1597	,, ...	,,	$\frac{1}{6}$

The very complete returns for the royal revenue for 1471 have enabled Burnett to compile a table of the different sources from which it was derived in that year:

Crown lands	£10,600
Transmitted by the sheriffs	1,700
Customs	3,300
Burgh fermes	760
	£16,360

The more fragmentary returns of other years of the fifteenth century show that these proportions were not exceptional. Between 1479 and 1501 the customs averaged £3106 12s. 4¾d. per annum. Even at almost the end of the sixteenth century (1588), in spite of the fact that a considerable depreciation of the currency had taken place, the royal burghs leased the customs for £4000 and thirty tuns of wine.[1]

Even the burghs themselves, especially the smaller ones, were very largely dependent upon agriculture. Edinburgh had exceptionally scanty burgh lands, and yet they were a constant source of preoccupation to the burgh council even in the sixteenth century. The very lay-out of parts of modern Glasgow is affected by the old burgh lands that it covers. The burgh at one time had 1768 acres of arable, besides large commons and isolated crofts. Not only in the sixteenth century, but also in the seventeenth, many of the lesser burghs were largely agricultural communities, and the maintenance of their "common good," which consisted largely of land, was a matter of extreme importance to the burgesses. We have already seen how stoutly the burgh of Peebles struggled to maintain its possessions. The burgh records of Arbroath in the sixteenth century have many allusions to the common fields and pastures of the town; to the burgh "pundlar," who assessed the damage done by trespassing beasts, and to the common herd, who was ordered "to call forth the nolt ilk da at morne be four houris." In 1491 it was statute and ordained in plain court "be the balzes consall and hale communite of the said burght that thar yard dykis within burght in tyme cummyn be uphaldyn and maid

[1] *Exchequer Rolls*, vol. i, p. clxi; vol. vi, p. lxxiv; vol. ix, p. lxxvi. The account of Scots revenue for 1329 in the *Calendar of Documents relating to Scotland*, vol. iii, p. 313, gives very similar ratios.

sufficient fer the away haldyne and resistyne of incummand bestis that sall happyn to cum in our thar yard dykis for to ete draw out or destroye the cornis mowit or biggit kaill plantit and sett inwith thar yardis." Burgesses having insecure dykes to be fined and held responsible for the damage done by the "incummand bestis."[1]

The importance of agriculture in the internal economy of the individual burghs is largely a side issue, although one that is a striking index of the conditions of the times. It is, however, very essential to the consideration of the whole economic life of the period that the burghs should be viewed in a true perspective in regard to their share in trade and commerce—the national function that was pre-eminently their department. There are many reasons why students are apt not to take this wider view into account. The economic development of present-day Scotland is so largely based upon the *manufacture* of articles of commerce that it requires thought and imagination to realize a state of society that mainly depended upon raw agricultural products for its wealth. The general economic condition of England, and of many other western countries actually during the period under review, was changing from that of mainly agricultural to that of partially manufacturing countries. The balance of wealth production was shifting, and the whole organization of industry and of the towns was altering with it. It must be definitely borne in mind that Scotland was distinctly and markedly exceptional in the static condition of her economic development during the fourteenth, fifteenth, and sixteenth centuries. Finally, so complex, so much legislated about, and so interesting are the burgh organizations of the period—the merchant and craft gilds—that it is not always easy to remember how numerically small were these bodies, and that, both from the current economic and from the historical point of view, they were not of first-rate importance.

The fact cannot be too strongly stressed that the *main* and most important articles of trade throughout the period continued

[1] For information regarding the burgh lands of Edinburgh the writer is indebted to Dr Marguerite Wood, Archivist to the City of Edinburgh. For Glasgow, see D. Murray, *Early Burgh Organization*, pp. 79, 104, 113, 119.

G. Hay, *The Story of Arbroath*, pp. 112-114.

practically the same, and that they were rural products—and rather primitive ones at that. At the time of David II's ransom it will be remembered that the great custom was levied on wool, wool-fells, and hides,[1] evidently the most considerable items of trade on which to collect revenue. The fourteenth century saw the gradual increase in the export of hides. In 1327, 8861 hides were exported; by 1378–79 the number had increased to 44,559. Nevertheless, the customs derived from wool were still the more important. In 1378–79 the customs from wool brought in £7040 and those from hides £600.[2] Mr Burnett has worked out the proportionate value of the customs derived from the various burghs of Scotland, and they appear in the following order:

Hides.	*Wool.*
1. Edinburgh	1. Edinburgh
2. Linlithgow	2. Aberdeen
3. Aberdeen	3. Dundee
4-5. Dundee and Perth (equal)	4. Linlithgow
6. Inverness	5. Haddington
7. Stirling	6. Perth
8. St Andrews	7. North Berwick
	8. Montrose
	9. Dunbar
	10. St Andrews

About 1480–87 we are able to learn from a very full list of the customs, which by this time had been much extended, exactly what the main export trade of the country consisted of. The great customs, levied on wool and hides, brought in £2600, the principal burghs of export being:

Edinburgh	£1528
Aberdeen	366
Dundee	170
Haddington	162
Perth	67
St Andrews	47
Linlithgow	44
Cupar	32
Kirkcudbright	28

[1] *Exchequer Rolls*, vol. i, p. xcviii.

[2] *Ibid*. vol. i, pp. xci, lxxxviii. James I, when he was sent to France for education and was captured on the way by the English, sailed in a Danzig ship laden with wool, wool-fells, and hides. E. W. B. Balfour-Melville, *Scottish Hist. Review*, vol. xx, p. 46.

Stirling . . .	£23
Montrose . . .	19
Ayr	17
Inverness . . .	15

Customs on woollen cloth brought in £108, the principal ports of export being :

Leith	£50
Kirkcudbright . .	16
Dundee	9

The total value of the custom on furs was £37.

The total value of the custom on salmon was £310, and the following returns were made by individual burghs :

Aberdeen . . .	£137*
Banff	47
Perth	29
Elgin	15
Forres	15
Dundee	14
Montrose . . .	7
Stirling	6

* In spite of special privileges that only strangers exporting salmon should pay custom and that burgesses should be exempt.

The total value of the custom on herring was about £390.

During the latter part of James III's reign Edinburgh averaged £11. The West Country about 1479 brought in £180, but three years later the figure was £413.

The customs received on " mullones " (which Burnett thinks were dried cod) was £13, received from Edinburgh, Crail, and Montrose. The customs on salt amounted to £30, received from Preston and Dysart.[1]

It is interesting to contrast this list with a table of the Scots produce exported annually in 1614. According to the classification adopted in this list, the export of victual and vivers, including wheat, bere, and malt, oats, flour, bread, beef, and aquavitae, amounted to £37,653 ; that of hides to £66,630, which included £1830 of hart hides ; skins to £172,082, which included about £167,625 worth of skins of domestic animals, mostly sheep and lamb skins, with a few goats', and the balance of skins of roe-deer, rabbits, foxes, etc. ; commodities of land, which included :

[1] *Exchequer Rolls*, vol. ix, p. lxxi.

Wool	£51,870
Feathers . . .	1,324
Butter . . .	294
Lead ore . . .	20,000
Coal	25,232
	£375,085

(The addition is of the period. There may have been items that did not come under the headings given.)

Under the heading " Commodities that ar maid and wrocht in the countrie quhairby the people are set to labour," goods to the value of £169,097 are classified. Of these, the principal items are :

Small salt	£39,780
Cloth and plaiding	59,574
Linen cloth	11,550
Harden cloth	155
Linen yarn	33,331
Prick hose	10,755
Leather goods represented a total sum of .	13,929

The fisheries brought in a sum of £153,354, divided as follows :

Salmon	£47,208
Herring	99,760
Barrelled fish . . .	2,720
Fish in peale . . .	1,960
Fish oil	1,706[1]

If the figures of the whole list are analysed it will be seen that the share of produce that came directly from rural districts is overwhelmingly great.

The items grouped under " Victual and Vivers " are, with the partial exception of bread (£56), rural .	£37,597
Hides and skins are rural	238,712
" Commodities of the land " are rural to a greater degree than they would be at present, for the primitive coal mining can hardly have become a highly specialized trade, and the lead mines were for the most part in the most inaccessible places	375,085

[1] Printed as an Appendix to P. Hume Brown's *Scotland in the Time of Queen Mary*, p. 227. An exact comparison between this list and the one quoted previously is impossible, as one gives the value of the customs and the other of the goods.

In the case of woollen and linen cloth, stockings, and linen yarn, most of the raw material was produced in the country, and much of the manufacture was also a rural industry	£115,365
Salt was manufactured at many of the little burghs along the coast, but also in the country	39,780
In the case of the fishings, owing to the strict burghal monopolies, the greater part of the preparation of the fish was probably a burghal industry, the materials for which, salt and timber (for barrels), were imported. The fish themselves, the most valuable part of the product, were the harvest of the sea	..
In the case of the leather goods, the valuable raw material was produced in the country	13,929

Out of a total of £820,524, therefore, about £651,394 was produced in the rural districts, and £169,130, including manufactured goods and bread, consisted of goods the raw materials of which were rural, and which were even in some cases largely country trades. The remaining item, the fisheries, only partly an urban trade, amounted to £153,354.

One must not, however, run away with the idea that Scotland was an empty land of great flocks and herds—a sort of mediaeval Argentine; it was, on the contrary, a land mainly devoted to supporting a struggling population, the small surplus of produce being employed in supplying the luxuries of life to those who could afford them. The Gordon rent roll of 1600 (the estate returns of a great property that stretched right across Scotland and included the relatively productive lands of Aberdeenshire, the inland straths of Strathavon and Badenoch, and part of Lochaber on the West Coast) shows how small were the contributions of wool and hides from individual holdings—the land was evidently primarily devoted to subsistence farming.[1]

The transactions of a Scots merchant at Middleburg, whose account book for 1492–1503 has most fortunately survived, proves the same thing, The ledger of Andrew Halliburton contains nearly 100 accounts, and among his customers were William Scheves, Archbishop of St Andrews; the Duke of Ross, who succeeded him as archbishop; the Bishop of Aberdeen, and several merchants of good standing; but the consignments sent to him were comparatively small: two or three

[1] *Spalding Club Miscellany*, iv.

sekes of wool (=a measure weighing 680 lb.) or two or three hundred hides or skins were the usual consignments.[1]

The comparative smallness of Scots trade can be learnt from other sources. Guicciardini, in his description of the trade of Antwerp, states that from Scotland was brought a great quantity of sheep skins and rabbit skins, and much other fine peltry of different little beasts, especially marten skins; also large pearls, much inferior to those of the East. Into Scotland, because the people are poor, and because they are supplied for the most part from England and France, no great quantity of goods is sent from Antwerp: only some spices, some sugars, madder, some stuffs of silk, camlets, grograms and mohair, serges of different kinds, and mercers' wares. In his list of the main imports into Antwerp he mentions Germany (over 1,500,000 crowns), France (nearly as much), Spain (620,000 crowns), Portugal (over 100,000), England (12,000,000 crowns). But "Scotland and Ireland are placed in the same class with Barbary, and passed by as of too little importance to be mentioned in this calculation." [2]

PART II. THE HERRING FISHERIES

Before passing on to the import trade it will be convenient to consider some of these export industries. The preserving and exporting of herrings was important throughout the fifteenth and sixteenth centuries. Even in 1423 herrings were salted and barrelled and red herrings were made.[3] Their proper securing and preparation was the object of constant attention from the busy Scots parliament. From the fifteenth century onwards a series of acts were passed regulating the size and making of the barrels that they were to be packed in. An act of 1519 ordered that the barrels should be marked both by the cooper who made them and by the skipper in whose ship the herrings were caught, and inspectors were appointed to oversee the work.[4] The kind of salt that was to be used was also prescribed. Laws were passed regarding the nets that were to

[1] Preface by C. Innes, *Ledger of Andrew Haliburton*, p. lxv.
[2] *Ibid.* pp. xli, xlii.
[3] See taxes levied by James I—A. M. Samuel, *The Herring*, p. 86.
[4] J. Travers Jenkins, *The Herring and the Herring Fishery*, p. 68.

be used, the times when the fishermen were to go to the fisheries, the size of the ships themselves. In 1491, all those under twenty tons were forbidden to go to the fisheries, and it was the authorities' constant endeavour to encourage the use of the larger "busses" and to discourage the small boats. In 1474 certain lords, temporal and spiritual, and the authorities of the royal burghs were ordered to provide ships, busses, and boats, with all their pertinents; and another act, repeating these provisions, gave all sheriffs and bailies the power to force all idle men to work in these fishing busses. In making such regulations the Scots Parliament was but following the example of the Dutch, the most successful fishermen in Europe. Some of their other enactments were inspired by the economic theories of the age. There was, for instance, a short-lived act that forbade the lieges from exporting herrings, although strangers might come and buy them in Scotland. Several times it was enacted that the lieges must be fully supplied before herrings were exported.[1]

Herring were among the goods that might only be exported by the free merchant burgesses of the royal burghs. The nature of the merchants' exclusive rights is part of the internal history of the burghs of Scotland and will be dealt with later on. It may, however, be stated here that the herring trade was entirely confined to the merchant class of a certain number of burghs. These were fairly conveniently placed for the fisheries upon the East Coast, but on the west there was no royal burgh farther north than the Firth of Clyde—although, at the very end of the seventeenth century, it was proposed to create three, very largely with the object of developing the western fisheries. The number of acts that attempted to enforce this monopoly show how constantly it was evaded. Considerably over a dozen, especially referring to the monopoly of the herring trade, were passed altogether, and in most of them the western towns are specially mentioned.[2]

Throughout the fifteenth and sixteenth centuries, as in the

[1] J. Travers Jenkins, *The Herring and the Herring Fishery*, pp. 73-75, 69, 70-71.
A. M. Samuel, *The Herring*, p. 87; *A.P.S.* vol. i, pp. 179 (1487), 183, 235-237, 242, 345, etc.
D. Bremner, *The Industries of Scotland*, p. 513.

[2] *A.P.S.* vol. iii, pp. 224, 302, 375.

days before the Wars of Independence, herrings were fished for along the East Coast, and they were an important article of export from the large East Coast towns, Edinburgh, Dundee, and Aberdeen. They were, moreover, the foundation of the rising trade of Glasgow,[1] and the fisheries of the West Coast seem to have been in course of gradual development. In 1447 Loch Fyne was said to produce herrings in " mair plenti than ony seas of Albion." [2] By the end of the sixteenth century the Loch Broom fisheries were important.[3] One finds, for instance, a Dundee skipper trading six barrels of Loch Broom herrings in Germany.[4] The development of the fisheries of the Outer Hebrides was one of the new enterprises of the very late sixteenth century which are most conveniently considered by themselves.

The herring fisheries were the object of vigorous and successful competition by the Dutch. Even before the Wars of Independence the fishermen of the Low Countries had frequented Scots waters, and in the sixteenth century fishermen from Hamburg, Bremen, and Holland frequented the Shetland fisheries [5] and there was trouble from very early in the fifteenth century. In 1410 there was a quarrel over the Scots fishing grounds; and in the 1423 scale of customs the Scots were to pay 4s. on every last of barrels of salted herrings, and foreigners 6s.[6] In the sixteenth century there was more serious rivalry. Between 1532 and 1541 there was a fishery war with the Dutch. Robert Fogo, in command of several war vessels, captured a large number of Dutch fishing boats, In reprisal, the property of Scots merchants in Holland was seized. Finally, the Queen-Dowager of Hungary made peace between James V and Charles V.[7]

The Dutch were, indeed, becoming most formidable rivals. In the fifteenth century all cured herrings sent to Rome were known as " Flemish herrings," although most of them originally came from Britain. From the latter part of the fifteenth

[1] J. Clelland, *Annals of Glasgow*, vol. ii, p. 420.

[2] A. M. Samuel, *The Herring*, p. 86.

[3] The Loch Broom Fisheries are often mentioned in contemporary documents; cf. *A.P.S.* vol. iii, p. 452.

[4] *Compt Buik of David Wedderburne*, p. 55.

[5] *Reg. Privy Council*, ii, p. 658 (1577).

[6] A. M. Samuel, *The Herring*, pp. 85, 86.

[7] *Ibid.* p. 87.

century onwards the Dutch diligently improved the technique of their boat-building, their methods of fishing, and, above all, of their curing, and increased the size of their fishing fleets,[1] till they acquired a reputation for the excellence of their salted and cured herrings far greater than that of any other country; and by the seventeenth century they had largely ousted the Scots from their own fishing grounds. At the end of our period, at least, the Scots herring fishery was losing ground rather than gaining it.

PART III. THE SALMON FISHERIES

Cured and salted salmon were exported both from the burghs of the East Coast and of the West, but Aberdeen seems to have been the most important centre of the trade. Salmon was one of the main exports of the town. In November of 1484 the king wrote for twelve lasts of salmon, and the "consale" and community of the burgh answered very humbly that they could not supply him, as all the salmon of the year's fishery had been sold and sent to Flanders and other places.[2] In 1580, Aberdeen wrote to the Privy Council complaining of the infringement of its fishing rights by George Auchinleck of Balmanno. The town was declared to be very much impoverished, "seeing that without the industrie and commoditie of salmound na burgh nor inhabitant of burgh culd wiell be thair but desert solitude." It was added that, if the fisheries are taken from it, the burgh would be unable to pay its dues to the king.[3]

Although there can have been no sign as yet of any serious

[1] A. M. Samuel, *The Herring*, p. 86.

J. Travis Jenkins, *The Herring and the Herring Fishing*, p. 68.

[2] J. Clelland, *Annals of Glasgow*, vol. ii, p. 366. In 1420 a burgess of Glasgow was exporting cured and pickled salmon to France.

Spalding Club Miscellany, v, p. 28.

Register of Privy Council, vol. iii, p. 295.

[3] We learn from incidental notices that salmon were much exported from Aberdeen to London, and also from Leith and Montrose, during the fourteenth and fifteenth centuries. Between 1357 and 1509 there are 37 allusions to the salmon trade in the archives of the official correspondence between Scotland and England: cf. J. Bain, *Calendar of State Documents relating to Scotland*, vol. iii, Nos. 1061, 1078; vol. iv, Nos. 1437, 1124, etc. Sometimes English merchants came or sent to Scotland to buy the fish, at others they were shipped south by Scots merchants.

diminution of the supply in the salmon, the Scots were very much alive to the need for safeguarding this valuable industry. The parliaments of James I, II, IV, VI passed many acts for the proper observation of a close season, the protection of spent fish, and the prohibition of improper methods of fishing, and very heavy penalties were prescribed. Nearly as many acts were passed with regard to the proper barrelling of the salmon. By one of the evanescent acts of the Scots Parliament it was laid down that salmon were only to be sold for English money or in exchange for Gascony wine.[1] The export of salmon, like that of herring, was part of the monopoly of the merchants of the royal burghs.

Part IV. Salt, Coal, and Lead

Salt was an article both of export and import. The native salt made by the evaporation of salt water by means of coal fires was chiefly carried on at Prestonpans, and near Borrowstounness, Dysart, Culross, and Fordell, but salt-pans upon many other parts of the shores of the Firth of Forth are constantly mentioned—there were, for instance, twenty-three at Kirkcaldy and five at Wester Wemyss.

Unfortunately, the home-made salt was not suitable for curing fish, and therefore foreign salt had to be brought in. The attempt was made several times to produce a salt that would serve this purpose, but does not seem to have been successful. The salt trade was the object of much regulation by parliament and the Privy Council, their main intention being to secure an adequate home supply. The masters of the salt-pans, however, contended that it would not pay them to make salt unless they were allowed to export some of it. A system of price-fixing and of export by licence was then instituted, but the authorities complained bitterly of the evasions practised by the masters. Regulations were constantly being made, confirmed, or amended. At one time salt might only be exported if, in return, a certain amount of silver were brought back, and, at another time, only in exchange for timber.[2]

[1] L. Stewart, *Index to the Acts of the Parliament of Scotland*, summarizes these laws.

[2] *Register of the Privy Council*, vol. ii, pp. 265, 427, 442.
See also J. Davidson and A. Gray, *The Scottish Staple at Veere*, p. 65.

Of the mining of coal very little is recorded. It had already been worked in the period before the Wars of Independence, but the winning of it at that early period had merely been by quarrying the surface outcrops.[1] The treelessness of Scotland no doubt forced her people to realize something of the value of her greatest mineral outcrop sooner than did the English. The wonder tale of the traveller Eneas Sylvius, that in Scotland a curious kind of stone was given in alms to the poor, has often been quoted. In the sixteenth century two acts of parliament were passed forbidding the export of coal, because it was " decayand and growand skant daylie," and the Convention of the Royal Burghs endorsed this action and, in 1596, fined Dysart and Culross £100 each for disobeying the order. Rather earlier the Privy Council had made regulations fixing its price or prohibiting its export till all the lieges were supplied.[2]

As we have seen coal was used for smith-work as well as for fuel, and, at Dundee, it seems to have formed the object of a considerable coastal trade. There was a deacon of the coal trade there, who was ordered to keep a register of all the coal boats that arrived.[3] The coal teinds were of sufficient value to the monks of Cambuskenneth to make them take vigorous action to secure their due payment, and the use of the mineral appears often enough in the documents of the times to show that it was of considerable importance.[4] In 1592 a law was made that all persons maliciously setting coal heuchs on fire were to be punished as guilty of

[1] See a 1291 charter to Dunfermline Abbey, translated and printed in P. Chalmers, *Historical and Statistical Account of Dunfermline*, vol. i, p. 19.

[2] *A.P.S.* vol. ii, p. 543; vol. iii, pp. 147, 595.

P. Hume Brown, *Early Travellers in Scotland*, p. 61.

Th. Pagan, *Convention of Royal Burghs*, p. 154.

J. Mackintosh, *History of Civilization in Scotland*, vol. iii, p. 293. No doubt the fear of the exhaustion of coal supplies was not as absurd as it sounds, for the easily worked surface coal might well have been worked out, and there was no means of reaching the deeper seams.

[3] A. Warden, *Burgh Laws of Dundee*, pp. 42, 52, 115.

[4] *Chartulary of Cambuskenneth Abbey* (Grampian Club), p. 87.

Diocesan Register of Glasgow, vol. i, p. 27.

Calendar of Documents relating to Scotland, vol. iii, Nos. 210, 698, 813 (all fourteenth century); vol. iv, p. 459, No. 1186.

treason, and a miner was executed under this act.[1] The industry seems occasionally to have been carried on very profitably, or on a large scale, for the annual rental of the royal coal heuchs at Wallyford and Preston was estimated at 1100 merks in 1542. Nevertheless, it was not always lucrative, for in 1600 the king was said to be making nothing by the coal pits upon the annexed Church lands on account of the great expense of working them, and it was decided to let or feu them.[2] No doubt the best of the outcrops had by now been quarried out, and the Scots were faced with their long struggle to learn the technique of real mining. Sir George Bruce's famous mine, partly under the sea at Culross, dated from the very end of the sixteenth or from the early seventeenth century.

Although coal was a useful article of domestic consumption, even in 1624 it was not a very valuable item of export trade, for it brought in less than half the amount of the wool trade and only a little more than one-seventh the value of skins and hides. In Dundee the members of the Gild Merchant regarded coal as one of the articles included within their monopolies,[3] but during the sixteenth century it was never included in the general statements of the articles of trade in which merchants alone had the right to deal, and it was not one of the "staple goods."

Lead mining was important during the sixteenth century, and allusions to it are often made in contemporary documents. It was a capitalistic enterprise, and as a rule the mines were owned and worked by men of wealth and standing. The exploitation of the gold, silver, and lead of the country was carried on with vigour by James V, Mary of Lorraine, and James VI. It is, however, only an isolated incident, though a pleasant and interesting one, in the grey history of Scots economic development.[4]

[1] R. W. Cochran-Patrick, *Early Records relating to Mining in Scotland*, p. xlvi.

[2] J. Mackintosh, *History of Civilization in Scotland*, vol. ii, p. 286.

[3] A. Warden, *Burgh Laws of Dundee*, p. 115.

[4] R. W. Cochran-Patrick, in *Early Records relating to Mining in Scotland*, has collected all the available references to this subject and has written a valuable Preface.

PART V. THE CLOTH INDUSTRY

The manufacture of cloth had already fallen into two quite distinct categories before the Wars of Independence. There was the "made" cloth that had been sheared and dyed, which was made in the burghs for home consumption; and there was the rough plaiding which was woven and worn by the lesser folks, both in the burghs and in the country, and which was also exported in considerable quantities. Unlike the tweed made in the Highlands down to the present day, some at least of this country cloth was fulled, for waulk mills seem to have been fairly common.[1]

In 1497, when there was war between England and the Netherlands, the import of British cloth was forbidden, but the poor folk there made such a clamour to be allowed to buy cheap cloth from Ireland and Scotland that this had to be specially permitted.[2] In the sixteenth century the Scots cloths that were exported were said to be "coarse" and to "be narrow and shrinkle in the wetting."[3] The making of this rough cloth was considerably the most valuable manufacture that Scotland had, and, by the admission of the Convention of the Royal Burghs itself, it was almost entirely a rural one.[4]

There are certain slight indications that the cloth trade was especially active in the districts of Angus and the Mearns. According to a customs account of 1599, Dundee paid more upon the import dues levied on dyestuffs than any other town, and Montrose also imported a considerable amount. Cloth appears a good many times as items in the account book of a Dundee merchant that has been preserved. Sometimes it was sent to England and the Continent to be dyed and then brought back for use in Scotland.[5]

The making of both kinds of cloth was, like all other enterprises in Scotland, the object of legislative attention. During the reigns of James III and James V, acts of parliament were

[1] Cf. *Diocesan Register of Glasgow*, p. 75.
Register of Cupar Abbey, p. xvii (three waulk mills at least on Abbey lands).

[2] Quotation from Green, "Making of Ireland," *Scottish Hist. Review*, vol. vi, p. 103.

[3] P. Hume Brown, *Early Travellers to Scotland*, p. 87.

[4] *Register, Privy Council*, vol. vi, p. 309.

[5] *Compt Buik of David Wedderburne*, p. 79.

passed ordering how it was to be sold in order to prevent fraud; and the Convention of Royal Burghs persuaded the Privy Council to issue a similar order in the late sixteenth century.[1] Moreover, cloth was also affected by the Scots system of trade monopolies. In the twelfth century the royal burghs had received special rights in connection with the "made" cloth, and by the sixteenth century they seem to have tacitly assumed monopoly rights over all cloth offered for sale. The landward districts, however, were able to carry on this industry in spite of them.

At the very end of the sixteenth century the king and the Privy Council made an effort to improve the manufacture of "made" Scots cloth as part of the new policy then in vogue, but this will be more conveniently dealt with in connection with similar enterprises.

PART VI. THE LINEN INDUSTRY

All finer linens were imported into Scotland until long after the sixteenth century. There was, however, a certain amount of manufacture of the coarser kinds. In the Highlands, the saffron-dyed linen used for the *leiné chroich* was probably home-made, but possibly imported from Ireland. In the Lowlands but little is recorded of the industry that was to prove Scotland's mainstay in the penurious years of the seventeenth and early eighteenth centuries. Linen is mentioned in a list of custom dues that is probably contemporary with Bruce, but that consistently busybody institution, the Scots Parliament, forbore to make any regulations about it until 1573, when linen is mentioned in a list of goods that were not to be exported.[2]

The industry, however, was evidently quietly growing. Robert Henryson (1430–1506) describes it as a rural occupation.

> The lint ryped, the churle pulled the lyne,
> Ripled the bolls, and in beites it set:
> It steeped in the burne, and dryed syne,
> And with ane beittel knocked it and bet,
> Syne swyngled it weill, and heckled in the flet.
> His wife it span and twinde it into threed.[3]

[1] Th. Keith, "Influence of the Royal Burghs on the Economic History of Scotland before 1707," *Scottish Hist. Review*, vol. x, p. 256.

[2] R. W. Cochran-Patrick, *Mediaeval Scotland*, p. 41.

[3] C. Rogers, *Social Life in Scotland*, vol. iii, p. 378, quotes Henryson.

Such were the small beginnings of a great industry. By the seventeenth century the steeping of lint in running water had become an intolerable nuisance and was forbidden by an actively enforced law. The Records of the Privy Council several times allude to lone women who had little plots of lint,[1] and we learn indirectly, from a petition from the woollen weavers, that linen yarn made in Scotland was used in many kinds of cloth and was exported apparently for the same purpose.[2] Fynes Moryson, writing in 1598, said that the Eastern Scots carried into France coarse cloths, both linen and woollen, which were narrow and "shrinkled" in the wetting.[3] In the Compt Buik of David Wedderburne, a Dundee merchant of the late sixteenth and early seventeenth centuries, linen cloth and linen yarn are mentioned from time to time, and there are a few transactions such as the following: Alexander Rankyne, skipper, is entrusted with eighteen score and ten ells of bleached linen, packed in eighteen paper-covered parcels, which he is to sell "quhair he hapnit to mak mercat," and, with the proceeds, to buy gros-grain silk.[4] In 1614, linen yarn is given as the third most valuable item in the table of manufactured goods, and linen cloth as the fifth.[5]

Part VII. Scots Imports

In return for these exports Scotland was obliged to import not only large amounts of certain necessary materials which she herself was deficient in, such as iron, timber, and, in time of dearth, provisions, but also a large quantity of manufactured goods of better quality, to enable the rich to keep up the same standards as their equals in other countries—furniture, glass, fine cloth, silks, spices, and all the choicer manufactured goods. In addition, a certain amount of bullion had to be imported. It is the nature of these imports which most strongly marks the economic condition of the country.

Froissart writes: "There is neither iron to shoe horses nor

[1] Cf. *Register, Privy Council*, vol. vi, p. 268.

[2] *Ibid.* vol. vi, p. 520.

[3] P. Hume Brown, *Early Travellers to Scotland*, p. 87.

[4] *Compt Buik of David Wedderburne*, p. 79.

[5] P. Hume Brown, *Scotland in the Time of Queen Mary*, p. 227.

leather to make harness, saddles or bridles: all these things come ready-made from Flanders by sea; should these fail, there is none to be had in the country." [1] From this the advance during our period was very small. In 1587 the preamble of an act forbidding the export of wool declaims against "what costly, superfluous and unnecessary merchandis is commonly brought within this realm, and what profitable wares are carried furth of the same that aucht and suld pay custom," etc.[2]

Even in the period of poverty immediately after the Wars of Independence, the extravagant David II spent large sums in importing cloth of gold and coloured cloth, napery, spices, wines, oil, kitchen utensils, etc.[3] In the accounts of the Lord High Treasurer one gets an idea of the lovely and colourful clothes of the court during the fifteenth and sixteenth centuries. In 1495, for instance, the king's Easter outfit consisted of a "party" doublet (i.e. a doublet made in two colours) of crimson and black satin, a jacket of crimson velvet, and scarlet hose, a black grogar gown lined with fitch, and a riding gown of black velvet "begaryit" with crimson velvet.[4] Nor did the king alone go magnificently: his henchmen were dressed in different colours nearly every year. In 1474 they had gowns of green, doublets of camlet, and hose of black, while the yeomen had gowns of blue, doublets of white fustian, and hose of black, and the trumpeters had green gowns and white fustian doublets. In 1491 the court was largely dressed in "English" red and "English" green. Another year the favourite colours were "rowan tanny" and black.[5] The profusion of clothing was enormous: for instance, in one year the king possessed fifty-two gowns, forty-seven doublets, thirty-five bonnets and fifteen hats, besides hose, tippets, etc., in large quantities.[6] During their brief heyday of power, all the Stewarts seem to have loved to go very fine, but the high water-mark of ostentatious magnificence was reached when James V went over to France and bought a wedding outfit for his marriage with the sickly Madeleine.

[1] P. Hume Brown, *Early Travellers to Scotland*, p. 11.
[2] *Exchequer Rolls*, vol. xxi, p. lix.
[3] *Ibid.* vol. i, pp. cxiv, cxxxviii.
[4] *Accounts of the Lord High Treasurer*, vol. i, p. clxxiv.
[5] *Ibid.* vol. i, pp. clxxvii, clxxviii.
[6] *Ibid.* vol. i, p. clxxv.

The great lords were also very magnificent. Sir James Douglas of Dalkeith made a will in 1390 and disposed of three rings set with precious stones, two circlets of gold, a large quantity of silver plate, five suits of armour, and robes of cloth of gold, silk, and fur.[1]

The imports of the merchants of Edinburgh included fine woollens from England and finery from farther afield. One reads of a suit of "fulyie morte" satin, hose of "incarnat" silk, breeches made "after the Myllane fassoun," a mantle of the "Gascun fassoun," and "Romany violettis"—apparently a kind of purple satin from Rome.[2]

It is far more striking to find a profusion of costly foreign wares in the possession of some one of still lesser rank. A law-suit of 1542 has preserved a record of the furnishings of a certain parson of Stobo who died about that time. There is an inventory of his possessions—his great carven bed with its coloured curtains and golden tassels and its velvet coverlet, and all the rest of the sumptuous plenishings of his rooms; his golden chain and signet ring, and his fine clothes, mostly of red velvet, the cloak lined with marten sable.[3] The parson of Stobo was probably an exceptionally luxury-loving mortal, but the inventory of a Scots laird who seems to have been almost ascetic or miserly in his plenishings tells the same tale. He died in 1567. His waistcoat and gown were of "French black," his cloak of "Spanish black," he wore a pair of "Flanders" hose. His effects included a bed of "Baltic" timber with a "Flemish" coverlet. There was but one trencher, which was made of tin, and a good many tin vessels. In the paltry list of utensils was a pair of pepper querns."[4]

In the Ledger of Andrew Haliburton the actual process of the exchange of Scotland's raw materials for foreign wares can be seen; there are many transactions such as the following: a "steik" (piece) "of Rovane" (Rouen) "tanny . . . berterit with ane sek of woll," remitted by one of his correspondents in Scotland. Wool, salmon, hides are constantly being sold, and a miscellaneous assortment of articles remitted in exchange for

[1] C. Innes, *Sketches of Early Scottish History*, p. 332.
[2] D. Robertson and M. Wood, *Castle and Town*, p. 289.
[3] Warrack, *Domestic Life in Scotland in the Sixteenth Century*, p. 37.
[4] Sir James Ramsay, *Bamff Charters and Papers*, p. 56.

them—books, a tombstone, church vessels, a red altar frontal, wine, spices, comfits, much fine cloth, clothing, hats, napery, embroidery thread, a case for an horologe that had been sent back to be repaired, tiles for the floor, etc.[1]

The *Exchequer Rolls* show how James I sold his hides and wool to foreign merchants to the value of £900 in one year, and how he paid English and foreign merchants that brought him goods, partly in money, partly in salted salmon, which he himself bought and resold to them duty-free, and partly by giving them remissions of the wool impost. In about eight years he bought nearly £2000 worth of goods from two London merchants, over £800 from a Florentine and the same from a Genoese merchant, and nearly £3000 was spent on the king's furnishings in Flanders, in velvet, jewelry, cloth, wine, spices, ostrich feather, arras, etc.[2]

A ship bound for Scotland seized at Lynn in 1394 contained the following goods : 100 ells of canvas, more than ten swords, armour, "velan," a quantity of woollen cloth (more than two dozen pieces), linen cloth, wax, pepper, "crocum," zinzibre, brass pots, plates, ewers and basins, linen thread, wood, madder, wool-carding combs, white and black dyed wool, bridles, spurs, chests, gloves, hose, caps and hoods, shuttles for weaving, paper, parchment, red leather, keys and locks. The total value of this consignment amounted to £170.[3] At the very end of the sixteenth century the *Compt Buik of David Wedderburne* shows that the same sort of thing was still going on. There the actual accounts of a merchant show that the same primitive Scots produce, with but few additions, was being exchanged for comfits, sugar, oil, wine, onions, apples, timber, iron, cloth, dye-stuffs, silk and finery.[4]

Of the necessary imports the most important were wine, iron, and timber, and also, in time of scarcity, corn. The importance of the wine trade can be seen from the fact that an import duty upon it brought in £15,693 in 1590–91 and £10,378 in 1593.[5]

[1] C. Innes, *Preface, Ledger of Andrew Haliburton*, pp. xxi, lvi-lxii.
[2] *Exchequer Rolls*, vol. iv, pp. cxliv, cxlix.
[3] *Calendar of Documents relating to Scotland*, vol. iv, No. 426.
[4] *Compt Buik of David Wedderburne*, pp. 78-79.
[5] *Exchequer Rolls*, vol. xxii, p. xxxvi.
J. H. Burton, *The Scot Abroad*, p. 73.

Iron, apart from a very primitive working of bog ores, does not seem to have been mined or smelted in Scotland till much later. Although folks were ingenious in using substitutes, it formed an important item in many cargoes.[1] Something has already been said of the timber shortage in Scotland. The few existing forests were carefully preserved, and a grant of timber from one of them was a valuable gift. The import of Scandinavian wood had begun early. In 1335–36 "eastland boards" are alluded to in a building account. Something has also been said about famines, and the import of foodstuffs from abroad that had begun in an earlier period was still necessary from time to time. How dire must the need have been in 1589, when two applications were made to the English Government to import "certain quarters of musty, unsavoury, and very coarse wheat, which are not vendible in England."[2]

The customs returns for certain towns in 1599 give a good general idea of the relative values of the goods imported. These returns relate to Kirkcaldy (four months), customs £17 14s.; Dundee (one year and four months), customs £2579; Dysart (one year and four months), customs £315 2s.; Stirling (about a year and a half), customs £94 15s. 9d.; St Andrews (one year and four months), customs £342; Burntisland (one year and three months), customs £86 10s.; Ayr, Irvine, and Glasgow (one year and three months), £943 12s. 4d.; Crail, Anstruther, and Pittenweem (two and a half years), customs £409 5s. 1d.; Montrose (six months), customs £49 11s.[3] The total amounts arranged under different headings are as follows:

Iron	£697	15	8
Timber	591	7	4
Salt	295	8	0
Pitch and tar	273	11	6

[1] See also *Documents relating to Scotland*, vol. iv, p. 349, for allusion to Spanish iron.

C. Rogers, *Social Life in Scotland*, vol. i, p. 253.

[2] *Calendar of Papers relating to Scotland*, vol. iii, p. 349; vol. iv, No. 1815.

Calendar of State Papers relating to Scotland, 1587–1603 (the series edited by M. J. Thorpe), p. 565. See also *Documents relating to Scotland*, vol. iv, p. 452, Nos. 323, 668; *Calendar of State Papers relating to Scotland*, 1509–1587, p. 19.

[3] *Exchequer Rolls*, vol. xxii, p. 315.

	£	s.	d.
Tackle	£252	8	0
Flax, etc.	240	14	3
Groceries	162	10	2
Victual	159	2	4
Hemp	157	11	1
Dyestuffs	150	0	0
Cloth	148	8	6
Ashes	69	15	0
Silks, velvets, and ornaments . . .	52	16	10
Copper, brass, and steel	32	7	8
Cards (for cloth making ?). . . .	28	6	0
Soap	23	3	8
Beer and hops	19	9	0
Linen	17	18	0
Paper	17	1	0
Glass	10	0	0
Tinware, etc.	5	9	6
Hose	2	16	0
Playing cards and racket balls . . .	1	3	0

It is unfortunate that these returns do not include wine, which was taxed differently. It is also a pity that the returns for Leith and Edinburgh are not given. Nevertheless, even as they are, they are of great interest. The amount of timber imported must have been prodigious. The custom on the imports into Dundee was valued at £273 8s. 10d. This represented 12,324 deals, 70,751 spars of different kinds, 3700 "knappald," 14,000 "scowis," 26,200 "pipe staves," 314 wainscot and "Swedish boards." A considerable amount of cloth was imported, and some of it was designated "English," "Yorkshire," or "Kendal" cloth, although the import of English cloth was at the time prohibited by act of parliament.

The different goods were received at the ports in variable proportions. Glasgow and the other ports of the West imported no foreign cloth, groceries, or other luxuries except glass, paying £2 8s. custom, and spent a great deal on salt and tackle. Stirling and Dundee received most of the luxury goods. Stirling had 45 lb. of "scrotschettis and confeittis," 302 lb. of plumdammas, 518 lb. of raisins, 12 lb. of capers, a pair of silk stockings, 26 ells of "cramusie taffetie," besides "velvous pasmentis," "velvot," and "figourit stuf." Dundee imported 1100 lb. of licorice, much confeittis, 2695 lb. of plumdammas, sugar-candy, cloves, cinnamon, dates, almonds, figs; a hundred score and eighteen hats lined with taffetas, silk, and pasments; two hundred and twenty-five dozen buckles, 640 barrels of onions, 220 barrels of apples, playing cards, "1500 balls callit racket balls." The cargoes of ships that happen to be mentioned incidentally in a good many contemporary documents, although their variety is infinite, always show imports of much the same type, except that it is seldom that dyestuffs attain quite such prominence.[1]

Part VIII. Scots Foreign Trade

In the period before the Wars of Independence there had already been some Scots trade with the Netherlands. In the thirteenth century a street in Bruges had been called "Scotland," and in 1293 an agreement was made giving Scots travellers protection in Flanders.[2] There was also some trade with Germany, as a letter from William Wallace, dated 1297, proves. It is interesting as a link in economic history, but far more so, as one of the few documents actually bringing us into touch with the unsullied patriot, the loveliest character that Scotland's great hour of trial produced. It was written by Andrew Moray and William Wallace, the "leaders of the Scotch army" during their too brief triumph, and it is addressed: "To the prudent and discreet men, our good friends, the senate and the commoners of Lubeck and of Hamburgh, greeting and a continuous increase of sincere affection. We have been informed by trustworthy merchants of the said kingdom of Scotland, that you, on your own behalf, have been friendly and helpful in council and deed in all things and enterprises concerning us and our merchants, though our own merits do not occasion this. We are therefore the more beholden to you, and wishing to prove our gratitude in a worthy manner we ask you to make it known among your merchants that they can now have a safe access with their merchandise to all harbours

[1] J. H. Burton, *The Scot Abroad*, p. 72.
Register, Privy Council, vol. i, p. 308 (1564).
D. Robertson and M. Wood, *Tower and Town*, p. 285.
Compt Buik of David Wedderburne, pp. xxxiii, xliv.
[2] T. A. Fischer, *Scots in Germany*, p. 5.
Calendar of Documents relating to Scotland, vol. i, pp. 399-401.

of the kingdom of Scotland, because the kingdom of Scotland has, thanks be to God, by war been recovered from the power of the English." A postscript is added: "We also pray you to be good enough to further the business of John Burnet and John Frere, our merchants, just as you might wish that we should further the business of your merchants."[1]

Fynes Moryson, writing about 1598, gives a good general idea of Scots trade at the end of the sixteenth century. The Western Scots, he said, traded to Ireland. They exported salted herring, sea-coal, and aquavitae, and imported yarn, cows' hides, and silver. But the chief trade of the country (from the East Coast) was: to France, exporting coarse cloth, both woollen and linen, wool, skins, salt fish, and importing salt and wine; to Campveere in Zealand, exporting salt and skins, and importing corn; to Bordeaux, exporting cloths and skins, and importing wine, prunes, walnuts, and chestnuts; to the Baltic, exporting cloths and skins, and importing flax, hemp, iron, pitch, and tar; to England, exporting linen cloth, yarn, salt, and importing wheat, oats, and beans. The import of English cloth and the export of wool was forbidden at the time.[2] The reason for the import and export of salt has been already explained. The presence of chestnuts in a general list of this kind is due to the fact that they were a much more valuable article of trade when fruit and vegetables were scarce in Scotland. In an Inveraray account book, 600 were bought at one time and 1400 at another, and they also appear in other old account books.[3]

Fynes Moryson put the importance of Scots trade to different places in the following order: Campveere (the Low Countries), Bordeaux, the Baltic, England. Unfortunately, no figures survive that would enable one to form even an approximate estimate of the relative value of the trade with any of these countries. It is, however, clear that the trade with the Low Countries was far greater than that with any other nation. It will be remembered that Flanders and the Netherlands were great cloth-producing countries at the time, and that they formed the chief customer for the wool which was Scotland's main export. In

[1] T. A. Fischer, *Scots in Germany*, p. 3.
[2] P. Hume Brown, *Early Travellers in Scotland*, p. 85 onwards.
[3] I am indebted to Mr. A. O. Curle for this information.

1503 the King of England was obliged to reduce his duties on North of England wool because it could not be exported for profit "from the great plenty of Spanish and Scottish wools in the Flemish markets." The state correspondence between England and Scotland of the fourteenth century abounds with transactions regarding Scots or Flemish ships carrying wool from Scotland to the Low Countries. The proportion compared to other cargoes and destinations is very high. A large part of the wool was freighted from Leith, but cargoes from Perth and Inverness are also mentioned. It is not surprising that during the second phase of the Wars of Independence the English should have wished to interfere with this flourishing trade. The king wrote to the civic authorities of Bruges requiring them to abstain from countenancing Scots rebels. The burgomaster refused, because Flanders was open to the trade of all honest merchants.[1]

In addition to being a great consumer of wool, the Netherlands contained some of the great marts of Western Europe, where the commodities of many lands were assembled and redistributed. It was a thoroughly suitable market for the rest of Scotland's simple exports and for the strangely miscellaneous cargoes that she received back in exchange. It is probably a sign of the great importance of the Scots trade to the Low Countries that it was managed differently to all others, for it was regulated through a "staple port."

The idea of a staple port, so curious to modern conceptions of the proper methods of fostering trade, was quite in keeping with those of the fifteenth and early sixteenth centuries. From the days of Edward I, England also possessed a staple port. It was, however, mainly "a depot where goods were deposited so that tolls might be collected." "The object kept in view was the increase of revenue, rather than the privilege of merchants or the general welfare of the trade." It was directly controlled by the Crown. The Scots staple developed upon quite different lines. The customs on wool were collected at the ports of export. The staple port existed to some extent to protect Scots traders,

[1] *Calendar of Documents relating to Scotland,* vol. iv, No. 1732, for abatement of English duty, and vol. iii, No. 683, for the attempt to stop Scots wool trade. See also vol. iii, Nos. 471, 1451, 1514, 1518, 1524; vol. iv, Nos. 107, 108, 114, 163, 1014.

but its management was mainly in the hands of the burghs, acting through the Convention of Royal Burghs, a semi-official body consisting of the representatives of the governing class —the merchants—in the royal burghs, which was gradually developing during the fifteenth and sixteenth centuries, and whose attitude was one of rigid exclusiveness. In the words of Davidson and Gray, " The development of the nation's trade, or rather the prosperity of the merchant classes in the royal Burghs, was the object kept in view by the Convention, and any participation by unfreemen, by unfree burghs, or by foreign merchants was regarded as taking away some portion of that trade which, in the view of the Convention, was the right of the freemen of the free burghs." [1]

The idea that the establishment of a staple port meant that this port should enjoy a monopoly of the Scots trade was at first implied but was afterwards definitely stated in the agreements. But, like a good many other Scots enactments, it was by no means strictly obeyed. Davidson and Gray and Rooseboom have collected many gleanings that show that the Scots trade with other ports was considerable, especially with Bruges (which was but rarely the staple port) during the days of her greatest power. In return for the sole trading rights of the Scots, the staple port granted certain privileges, at first very similar to those usually given to foreigners in such commercial treaties. As our period, however, advanced and the conception of the staple port became more and more developed, these privileges were gradually added to and took a special form. In 1407, the Duke of Burgundy, besides promising liberty to trade and protection privileges similar to those contained in previous grants, gave the Scots the right of having certain commissioners to " prosecute, require, demand or defend the goods of these merchants and subjects, for and against all." These commissioners, however, had not the rank of judges, and it was apparently in the Flemish courts and by the laws of Flanders that the Scots were to be judged. It was only gradually that the office of conservator, who was appointed from Scotland, and who had full powers over the Scots community, grew up, and, with

[1] W. Cunningham, *Growth of English Industry and Commerce*, p. 311.

Davidson and Gray, *The Scottish Staple at Veere*, pp. 339-341.

it other civic rights and institutions which made the little Scots colony largely an autonomous entity in the Flemish port of their domicile.[1] The story of the staple, however, is one of innovation and development and can be most readily told in chronological order.

In the fourteenth century there had already been constant interchange of diplomatic communications between Scotland and Flanders and the Low Countries. Generally they were on good terms, but sometimes they quarrelled. The course of the little ups and downs of the trade shows how different were its conditions to those of the present day. In 1321 two burgesses, one of St. Andrews and one of Berwick, received " the freedom of coming, going, continuing and remaining anywhere " within the territories of the Earl of Holland " for the space of one year, void of all fear or disturbance, safe and free." More general grants of mutual privileges followed, but, in 1327, a Scots merchant in Middelburg was arrested for failure to pay his debts ; he escaped, and a general seizure of the goods of the Scots community in Middelburg was ordered. In reprisal, David II passed an act that similar measures should be taken against the Flemings in Scotland. In the following year two burgesses of the " quatre grosses villes de Escosse " were commissioned to settle differences, and so peace was established until the next tiff.[2] The end of the fifteenth century, however, saw the first emergence of the idea of a fixed staple port.

The closing years of the fifteenth century and the first quarter of the sixteenth had seen the decline of Bruges and the competition of three towns, Campveere, Middelburg, and Antwerp, for the staple and monopoly of Scots trade. The position of each of them offered certain different advantages, and they were ready to bid against each other in offering various special privileges in return for being made the staple port. For forty years the staple was moved from town to town or was in

[1] Davidson and Gray, *The Scottish Staple at Veere*, pp. 118, 121, 130, 136.

M. P. Rooseboom, *Scottish Staple in the Netherlands*, p. 6.

[2] For general summary, see Davidson and Gray, *Scottish Staple at Veere*, Part II, ch. i ; Rooseboom, *Scottish Staple in the Netherlands*, ch. i.

abeyance, and there were complications of many kinds. Both Scotland and the Netherlands were affected by the great duel between the kings of England and of France and the Emperor which was at the time being fought. In Scotland there were divergent policies. Negotiations were partly carried on by the Crown (and it will be remembered that during the minority of James V and even during his actual government there were constant alternations in the factions in power) and partly by individual towns, for the Convention of Royal Burghs was only in process of evolution. Even the policy of the burghs was not unanimous. Edinburgh was at times favourable to the establishment of the staple at Middelburg, and made a short-lived contract with Antwerp on behalf of herself and her "allies of the kingdom of Scotland," but she did not carry all the burghs with her. On the whole, the burghs were for a long time altogether opposed to a staple at all, and in 1526 they bought a royal permission to trade where they pleased. Nor was the affair a matter of straightforward policy. In its extreme poverty the Crown was anxious to make money out of the staple, and bribes were several times given or offered by the competing Flemish towns. In 1526, for instance, James, in consideration of a considerable gratuity from Middelburg, £2000 of which was to be paid to the comptroller to furnish the king's household, had concluded an agreement with that town. The burghs, however, with the exception of Edinburgh, were strongly opposed to the arrangement, and ordered their parliamentary commissioners to oppose it. A delay in the final ratification ensued, and James complained of this in the Privy Council, "becaus of necessity of money quhilk mon instantlye be providit." The royal household was in fact being maintained upon credit based upon the expectation of the Middelburg gratuity or upon a "gratitude" from the merchants to be paid in return for the annulment of the Middelburg agreement. Eventually the merchants had their way. Upon payment of £2000 they induced the king, upon a flimsy excuse, to disavow the agreement with Middelburg, and eventually, in 1531, the £1333 6s. 8d. already advanced by Middelburg was repaid. A fortnight after the agreement had been annulled or broken James was receiving 1000 merks and a present of plate from the lord of Campveere. It is not possible, within the compass of this single book, to unravel the whole complicated story of the negotiations with regard to the fixing of the staple. In 1541, however, the matter reached finality.[1]

In that year an agreement was made which fixed the staple at Campveere. The arrangement does not seem to have been altogether in accordance with the will of the burghs, who seem at this time to have more inclined towards Middelburg, nor to have been due to the greater privileges offered by the town—for at this time Antwerp seems to have been more generous in this respect—but to have been made in deference to the wishes of James V, who was influenced by the representations of the Duke of Burgundy, the overlord of Campveere. At Campveere the staple remained, except for two short interludes, for two and a half centuries.[2]

The privileges that the Duke of Burgundy gave the Scots at Veere included: A house, " commodious and convenient," to be provided rent free, with a garden for recreation, and a cistern for rain water with leaden pipes. (*b*) If Scots ships were robbed or spoiled the duke promised restitution. Buoys and beacons and, if necessary, free pilots were to be maintained at the ducal expense to guide the Scots " in the stream before our said town." Help was to be rendered at reasonable rates to those who were shipwrecked. (*c*) Room was to be made for them in the harbour as soon as they arrived. " Workmen, porters, and such-like" were to work for them at a specified rate of wages, and the hire of cellars for storing their goods was not to be raised. (*d*) Part of the church and a chaplain was to be provided for their spiritual needs. (*e*) They were to be protected against unfair exactions in the levying of customs. (*f*) Cases of dispute between Scot and Scot were to be decided by the conservator, but those between a Scot and a native of the town by the local judge " without any tedeous or long form of process." In the event of a lawsuit they were to have special protection and assistance.[3]

[1] Davidson and Gray, *Scottish Staple at Veere*, p. 143.
R. K. Hannay, *Shipping and the Staple* (Old Edinburgh Club), vol. ix, pp. 51-55, 68-69, 70.
M. P. Rooseboom, *Scottish Staple in the Netherlands*, p. 36.

[2] Davidson and Gray, *Scottish Staple at Veere*, pp. 161-163.

[3] M. P. Rooseboom, *Scottish Staple in the Netherlands*, p. 62.

The staple was hardly established at Veere, when Western Europe became involved in acute international troubles. The people of the Netherlands entered upon their heroic struggle with Spain, and Campveere became involved. At one time the Scots merchants were obliged to leave it. In the words of the commission appointed to re-establish the staple in 1578, it had " bene waguant and removit to syndrie places this tyme bypast, throwe the occasion of the ciuill tumultis, quhair vyth the maist pairte off Flanderis hes bene thir dyueris zeires occupiet to the hurt of mony."[1]

By the agreement signed in this year for the re-establishment of the staple, its organization was carried rather further and made more definite. The judicial powers of the conservator were considerably enlarged, and, in return, the Scots promised to take orders and not permit any of their ships with staple wares to visit any other port but Campveere. This was an important innovation. In an agreement of 1472 with Bruges, trade with other towns had been excluded, but in the arrangement made in 1526 by the Scots burghs the merchants secured royal endorsement of their right to go where they wished. Although " the very idea of the staple implied that the town chosen should enjoy a monopoly of Scottish trade—hitherto this condition had been understood rather than expressly declared" (Davidson and Gray). After the agreement of 1472, however, the enforcement of the staple monopoly was a question constantly before the Convention of Royal Burghs, and this led to constant reaffirmations of the principle that Scots ships should pass to Campveere and to no other port in the Low Countries.[2]

From 1575 onwards, the control of the staple port became stricter and stricter. In 1579 an act was passed to prevent individuals changing their nationality from Scots to Spanish, as it suited them, to evade or benefit by the regulations, and the Scots merchants were forced to form themselves into a corporation with entrance fee and oaths of allegiance. Anyone who did not join this organization was to be debarred from enjoying the privileges of the staple port and from trade with the members

[1] M. P. Rooseboom, *Scottish Staple in the Netherlands*, p. 89.
[2] *Ibid.* pp. 86, 97-103.
Davidson and Gray, *Scottish Staple at Veere*, pp. 131, 181-182.

of the Scots community,[1] and from time to time further regulations were made.

The definite establishment of the staple, however, only furnished occasion for the more vigorous exercise of powers which the Scots were always prone to use. The whole course of the trade with the Low Countries had offered scope for that passion for vexatious restriction which was such a feature of the enactments of all Scots legislative bodies. From the fifteenth century onwards laws were passed, were amplified by lesser authorities, and were actually enforced, regarding the whole way of life of the merchants — the time of year when they might sail or not sail, the number of voyages they might make in a year; that their clothing was to be that of men of substance; that they must sail with at least half a last of goods; that, whilst at Campveere, they must behave and sell their goods in a dignified and becoming manner.[2] The careful prohibitions and safeguards to prevent anyone who was not a merchant burgess of one of the Royal Burghs engaging in trade were even more elaborate, but also very much more important. For upon the system of privilege and special taxation the whole Scots fiscal system depended. It must, however, have been most harassing to the traders and most restrictive to the trade.[3]

In considering the Scots trade with the staple port one is hardly less surprised at the restrictions that individuals had to undergo than at the liberties that towns assumed when they conducted trade negotiations or concluded agreements with foreign cities. The status of the Convention of Royal Burghs, an assemblage established by no charter and yet fully accredited as the representative of such individual towns, is equally strange. The Conservator of the Privileges of the Scots Merchants also held an anomalous position. He acted as the king's ambassador in the Netherlands, but he was also the judge of, the spokesman for, the authority responsible for carrying out all regulations connected with the Scots colony at Campveere. The Crown and the Convention disagreed as to whether the latter ought to

[1] Davidson and Gray, *Scottish Staple at Veere*, pp. 182, 183.
[2] *Ibid.* pp. 28, 34-35.
M. P. Rooseboom, *Scottish Staple in the Netherlands*, p. 52.
[3] Davidson and Gray, *Scottish Staple at Veere*, pp. 28-29.

have any say in the election of this individual, but, once elected, he was definitely under the orders of the Convention in all routine matters and was obliged to report to them when they required his presence. But the intermingling of official, semi-official, and communal authority, without any very clear definition or constitution, was, after all, only thoroughly typical of the struggling, makeshift, but very vigorous organization of Scotland of the fifteenth and sixteenth centuries.

The importance of the trade between England and Scotland is impossible to estimate. It was liable to frequent interruptions, but, in more peaceful times, it always sprang up again. After the Wars of Independence the Truce of Calais (1348) reopened commercial intercourse between the two countries, and for some time afterwards Scots merchants were encouraged to come to England. In the troublous years that followed, whenever there was a truce between Scotland and England, the merchants of Scotland secured safe conducts to trade in England. Generally such safe conducts were for ships, which, incidentally, shows how largely all commerce was water-borne; but two Edinburgh merchants, in 1490, received permission to trade in England for a year, "on horsbak, or on fote, with pokke, male, or powgette." There were also a considerable number of Scotsmen living in England and of Englishmen in Scotland.[1] Even at a time of considerable international strain, such as 1546, when Henry VIII had temporarily paused in his terrible attacks upon Scotland, and was intriguing for the assassination of Cardinal Beaton, we

[1] *Exchequer Rolls*, vol. ii, p. xlv.

For Scots in England and English in Scotland, see *Calendar of Papers relating to Scotland*, vol. iv, p. xvii, Nos. 635, 512.

From this volume it will be seen that the trading licences were granted as follows:

Year	Number	Year	Number
1384	1	1459	1
1394	1	1464–68	24
1398	3	1468	1
1404–12	17	1470	1
1415	1	1473–76	14
1423–26	11	1479	1
1433–41	44	1484–86	5
1444–53	46	1490–99	19

See also No. 1558. Between 1357 and 1509 we learn of 49 Scotsmen naturalized as English subjects.

learn that Lord Borthwick had "sauld his woll to men that hes put it in Ingland like as all the merchandise and vittales on this side of the watter passes thair." It will be remembered that 1549 had seen the culmination of this campaign (the English were then in occupation of Haddington and had burned and pillaged as far as Dundee), yet in 1550 and 1551 no fewer than eighteen safe conducts were secured for Scots merchants who wished to trade in England.[1] As we have already seen, English cloth was imported and paid custom when the act forbidding its importation was still unrepealed. As a matter of fact, trade between the quarrelsome neighbour-states was inevitable: not only was the distance so much less than that dividing them from continental countries, but Scots wool was sure of a market in cloth-making England, and English cloth was welcome in Scotland with its lack of skill in the weaver craft. Even at a time when the import of these articles was forbidden, Fynes Moryson's list shows that there still remained a considerable number of exports and imports.

The Scots imports from France, which included most of the wine drunk in the country, must have been considerable. The Scots sailed directly to Bordeaux in the fifteenth and sixteenth centuries and brought the wine directly back to Scotland, but, in view of the close political alliance between the two countries, the Scots do not seem to have enjoyed very valuable commercial privileges.[2] In 1510, Francis I exempted them from the payment of customs in Normandy, and, about 1518, the Regent Albany did a great deal to foster Scoto-French trade. During the culmination of the struggle between England and France for the alliance of Scotland these privileges were confirmed (in 1554) and more were gained, for in 1558, when Mary Queen of Scots married the Dauphin, the Scots escaped all imposts levied on strangers. Seven years later the Scots were specially exempted from a new duty levied on wine exported at Bordeaux. By 1565, however, the whole political situation had changed. Although the Scots' privileges were nominally continued and

[1] A. Cameron, *Scottish Correspondence of Mary of Lorraine* (Scottish History Society), No. cxx.

M. J. Thorpe, *Calendar of State Papers relating to Scotland*, pp. 98-100.

[2] *Calendar of Documents relating to Scotland*, vol. iv, Nos. 962, 1372, 1380, 1424; *Calendar of State Papers relating to Scotland*, 1509–1589, p. 19.

were, indeed, confirmed in 1599, yet it was only by constant embassies from the Convention of Royal Burghs that exemption from new duties and from restrictive enactments was maintained.[1]

Such as they were, the Scots' privileges in France were dearly bought. This is not the place to discuss the question of the "Old Alliance" and its disastrous effect upon Anglo-Scots relations. In trade as well as in other ways, Scotland had to pay heavily for her rather one-sided friendship with France. A Scots document of 1524, containing instructions to an envoy to the French king, gives a contemporary account of what Scots merchants had to suffer. The envoy was to point out that: "Since war with the English began, our merchants are debarred from trade communication with England, Flanders, Spain and other realms. These realms were formerly allied with us or friendly; now, owing to our friendship, alliance and punctilious good faith with the French, we are suffering heavily. These many years past a very few of our merchantmen have succeeded in eluding the enemy ships and reaching France, the only country which professes to be friendly to us. Those who most recently braved the dangers of the sea and got through to France are being detained there an unusually long time. Our forbearance in the matter is too well known to make oral or written representations necessary: we have clearly before our minds how much we have endured for our friendship and alliance with France."[2]

In 1602, James VI, wishing to provide one of his courtiers with a salaried post, tried to have the French trade organized on the same lines as that of the Netherlands, in order to appoint him as "conservator." The Scots burghs, however, prevented this.

The Scots trade with Germany and the Baltic, as we have seen, had already begun before the fourteenth century. That there should be communication between the East Coast towns of Scotland and the shores of North-Western Europe was very natural. There was, however, a very clear-cut line of demarcation between the large numbers of Scots who permanently

[1] Th. Pagan, *Convention of Royal Burghs*, pp. 198-200.

[2] R. K. Hannay, *Shipping and the Staple*, 1515–1531, *Old Edinburgh Club*, vol. ix, p. 55.

emigrated from Scotland, became itinerant pedlars in Prussia and other adjacent lands, and, when they could, settled down there, and the Scots merchants who came to trade from their own country.[1]

During the fourteenth and fifteenth centuries, the trade with the North-Western Continent had to contend with many difficulties. The English kings displayed much malignant energy in trying to prevent it. Henry IV, for instance, wrote to the Master of the Teutonic Order asking him and his subjects to cease trading with the "rebellious" Scots altogether. The Master replied that the Order lived in peace with all Christians and could not forbid the King of Scotland from trading within its territories. In revenge, the English burnt a ship from Stralsund, "because it had traded with the enemy," and they constantly tried to interfere with Scots trade.[2]

Unfortunately, the Scots suffered much more through their own piratical propensities. All nations were addicted to this crime, but, with the Frisians, "the Scots seem to have enjoyed the worst reputation" (Fischer) and shipowners were constantly complaining of them. In 1412 the Diet of the Hanse Towns wished to interdict all commerce with Scotland on this account. Danzig and Stralsund disagreed, and finally only the import of wool and woollens was prohibited. But Scotland did not reform her ways, and, in 1415, all trade was forbidden by the Hanse; and it was not till 1436, after much negotiation, that this order was allowed to become a dead letter.[3] At other times the Scots merchants complained of high-handed action on the part of the continental authorities.

Subject to interruptions, however, the trade did definitely develop. About 1400, Scots merchants were beginning to settle in Danzig, and the Danzig merchants had agents in Edinburgh; and James II, later in the century, encouraged the trade and took the merchants of Bremen and Danzig under his protection. Fischer is of the opinion that about this time the Scots principally traded with Danzig—in 1474–76, twenty-four Scots ships entered Danzig harbour—but also with Königsberg,

[1] T. A. Fischer, *Scots in Prussia*, pp. 3-4, 13.
T. A. Fischer, *Scots in Germany*, p. 23.
[2] *Ibid.* pp. 4, 8-10.
[3] *Ibid.* pp. 5, 13-14.

Stralsund, Elbing, and Lübeck. There was also some trade with Hamburg, Bremen, Rostock, and Wismar. The main Scots trading ports were Leith and Aberdeen, but Perth, Dundee, and St Andrews had a considerable share of the trade, and it was a very general one; other towns, such as Inverness and Glasgow, are mentioned from time to time.[1] Trade negotiations were sometimes carried on by the king or by nobles who were in power, but largely by the individual burghs. The magistrates of Aberdeen, for instance, in 1489, wrote to Danzig saying that they were grieved that the ships from that town had been sailing for some time past to remoter parts of Scotland instead of to Aberdeen, and they declare themselves willing to indemnify the cloth merchant of Danzig who had suffered loss at Aberdeen on account of spurious money being given him in payment, if he will personally appear before them. The towns upon either side of the North Sea were constantly writing to each other upon such matters.[2]

In spite of interruptions and difficulties due to plague, wars, and pirates, the trade continued to flourish during the sixteenth century.[3] Fischer says that, by the end of the century, " in almost all the cities on the coast of Prussia, settlements of English and Scots merchants were now established." The colonies, however, can only have been comparatively small. In 1597, when careful inquiry was made, there were only fifteen Scots who were naturalized citizens of Danzig and nine other Scots residents. About the middle of the century the trade between Danzig and Aberdeen was greater than that of any other two ports, but that of Dundee and Danzig was also considerable. In the shipping returns of that city, which survive for eleven years between 1588 and 1612, there is record of fifty voyages made to Baltic ports. The return cargoes generally consisted of some of the following: iron, wood, pitch, tar, hemp, kettles, soap, salt, lint, beer, wax, rigging, grain, flour, glass, lead. During the famines of 1572 and 1595 the imports of grain became very large.[4]

[1] T. A. Fischer, *Scots in Germany*, pp. 7, 8, 10.
See also T. A. Fischer, *Scots in Prussia*, p. 10.

[2] T. A. Fischer, *Scots in Prussia*, pp. 7, 8, 9.

[3] *Register, Privy Council*, vol. v, has an unusual number of allusions to Danzig ships.

[4] T. A. Fischer, *Scots in Germany*, pp. 17, 18, 19-21, 24, 25, 27.
T. A. Fischer, *Scots in Prussia*, p. 17.

The Prussian and Northland trade was not only unregulated, it seems to have been carried on without any formal treaties: for, as Fischer points out, although the Scots constantly referred to mythical trading privileges that they declared had been conferred upon them, no evidence of such a grant can be found.[1]

The Scots, moreover, traded with other countries. Little is known of their Scandinavian trade, but it must have been considerable, especially with the Danish port of Grippiswald, and there was a commercial treaty with the Danes, granting reciprocal privileges.[2] The Scoto-Spanish trade benefited very much by the Anglo-Spanish War, which enabled the Scots to acquire a considerable carrying trade.[3] Unfortunately, later on, the General Assembly was able to secure the prohibition of all Scots trade with Spain upon religious grounds, though the Convention of Royal Burghs tried hard to delay the passing of the edict.

Many nationalities came to Edinburgh in pursuit of trade. The town council minutes mention " Lumbards," Frenchmen, Danes, merchants from Rotterdam and Campveere.[4]

PART IX. SCOTS TRADERS AND TRADING

Such is a general sketch of Scots foreign trade of the fifteenth and sixteenth centuries. Small in volume, circumscribed in scope it appears, beside the vast enterprises of to-day; yet it is of real historical importance that we visualize something of the difficulties and dangers that the hardy merchants and skippers encountered and overcame in the so primitive times we are dealing with. In order to realize something of the long-drawn-out struggle that lay in front of Scotland before she achieved commercial greatness, it is necessary to picture the

[1] T. A. Fischer, *Scots in Prussia*, p. 10.

[2] The connection between Scotland and Denmark seems to have been particularly close during the reign of Mary Queen of Scots. See *Register, Privy Council*, vol. xiv, pp. 183-184, 189, 190, 191, 252-253, 254, 266, and especially pp. 196-197 alluding to the Timber Trade and the "auld lig and conferatioun."

[3] Fynes Moryson. See P. Hume Brown, *Early Travellers to Scotland*, p. 87. For confirmation of Moryson's statement, see *Register, Privy Council*, (Second Series) vol. i, p. 303.

[4] I am obliged to Dr Marguerite Wood for this information.

conditions from which she raised herself. In times of industrial depression, such as the present, it is stimulating to call to mind the harder lot of those who have gone before us. Truly, it was not without good cause that foreign trade was known as the "Wild Adventure" in the Edinburgh town council minutes.[1]

The small ships of the time, sailing uncharted seas, were liable to great perils from storms, rocks, and shoals. In addition, the political situation greatly added to the danger of warfare at sea. During three-quarters of our period there was intermittent war with England. At sea, as on the Borders, hostilities were little affected by the truces that constantly intervened in the official war.[2] The history of the times tells of many exploits at sea against and by the Old Enemy. The line between piracy and national warfare was a very vague one. In the fourteenth century we have incidents such as the following. John Mercer, a burgess of Perth, a landowner and the richest man in Scotland, was captured by the English. In revenge, his son headed a fleet of Scots, Spanish, and French vessels and scoured the sea for English ships till he was eventually captured by a fleet commanded by a merchant of London.[3] At the end of the fifteenth century and the beginning of the sixteenth, there were the Bartons and Andrew Wood. They were Leith skippers who sometimes commanded royal ships and sometimes performed "gratuitous service" against the English, to the peril of their lives. Wood's two ships, the *Flower* and the *Yellow Caravel*, were famous. He became a laird and built a fortalice and a little burgh of barony with the labour of his

[1] The various collections of Scots State Papers are full of the notices of ships wrecked, foundered, and seized. Cf. *Calendar of Documents relating to Scotland*, vol. iv, Nos. 1115, 1047, 1303, 275, 23, 1265, 104, 1265, 462, 720, 1443, 381, 158, 164, 283, 490, 163, 350; Thorpe's (1509–89) Series, pp. 19, 27, 22, 29, 38, 62; after 1583 there are many complaints: p. 553 (1587) gives list of Scots goods pillaged.

[2] Davidson and Gray, *Scottish Staple at Veere*, p. 51.

D. Robertson and M. Wood, *Castle and Town*, p. 275.

[3] Cf. *Exchequer Rolls*, vol. i, p. xlii; vol. iii, pp. xlviii, xlix; vol. xv, p. lxvii.

P. Hume Brown, *History of Scotland*, vol. i, pp. 325, 331

For a similar episode in 1547, see M. J. Thorpe, *Calendar of State Papers relating to Scotland*, 1509–1587, p. 63.

English captives.[1] Such were outstanding examples, but contemporary accounts teem with allusions to the loss of ships and cargoes.

Besides the more or less continuous wars with England, Scots ships suffered from the Dutch, and Bishop Leslie tells how "sindre vailyant gentill men" did exploits against the "Holanderis quha had takin and spoilyeit divers Scottis ships and crewally had murdrest and cassin overburd the merchantis and passingeris being thairintill," and how Andrew Barton took many Dutch ships "and fillit certain pipis with the heidis of the Holanderis and send unto the King in Scotland for dew punishement and revenge of thair creultie."[2] In 1550, owing to the "gret enormities dayly done" to the lieges by the ships of Holland, Flushing, and other towns of the Netherlands, the warships of the realm were ordered to pass forth in warfare for staunching thereof. But the owners and master of each ship, before their departing, had to appear before the treasurer's clerk and find caution that they would do no scaith, harm, nor hurt to the friends, allies, and confederates of Scotland.[3] Neutrals, however, often suffered in such quarrels. And in the quarrelsome sixteenth century the Scots several times lost heavily in this way.[4]

Even in times of peace there was constant danger from pirates. In 1581 it was reported in Parliament that Inchcolm Island, situated in the Firth of Forth nearly opposite Edinburgh, had become "a receptacle of pirates," ever since the departure of the monks, but that it had now, happily, been feued.[5] Pirates swarmed along the coast of Fife. They seem to have frequented the waters round every considerable Scots port. They form the subject of constant complaints in the Records of the Privy Council.[6] The Convention of Royal Burghs upon one occasion complained to James VI that the ships of Dundee were pillaged

[1] *Exchequer Rolls*, vol. xiii, p. clxxix.
[2] Bishop Leslie, *History of Scotland*, vol. i, p. 74.
[3] *Register, Privy Council*, vol. i, p. 104.
[4] Cf. *Hamilton Papers*, vol. i, pp. lxx, lxxi, lxxii.
[5] *A.P.S.* vol. ii, p. 276.
[6] J. Wilkie, *History of Fife*, p. 608.

Register of the Privy Council, vol. i, pp. 236-237, 276, 289, 308, 431-432, 518, 658, 716; vol. ii, p. 223, etc.

T. A. Fischer, *Scots in Germany*, pp. 6, 13, 22, 27.

"gif thair war nother God in heavin nor we had a King on earth to complene to."[1]

A few of the pirates were men of position. The Earl of Bothwell, Mary Queen of Scots' evil genius, was afterwards a pirate, and so was a very undesirable Earl of Mar. Robert Barton, the comptroller, and other Scotsmen of position were, upon occasion, guilty of allowing their ships to be used for piracy. Burgh magistrates also sometimes turned pirate.[2]

The worst offenders, so far as the Scots were concerned, were undoubtedly the English. Unfortunately for the Scots, their trading routes to France and the Netherlands were peculiarly liable to attack from the Auld Enemy. Between 1569 and 1587 the Scots were despoiled of £20,717 worth of goods, of which £15,974 was unrestored.[3]

Many measures were adopted to check the nuisance. The king, the Convention of Royal Burghs, individual towns, such as Edinburgh, fitted out or planned to fit out expeditions against them. Edinburgh subsidized private sea captains to pursue the pirates, and even private adventurers against them were not unknown. A certain William Sibbet, in 1590, borrowed £200 on the security of his own lands in order to fit out a ship to chase pirates.[4] We have one rousing account by James Melville, minister of Anstruther, of how his parishioners dealt with the matter. "Ane of our crears" (a small ship with one mast), "returning from England, was beset by an English pirate, pillaged, and a very guid honest man of Anstruther slain therein. The whilk loon, coming pertly into the very road of Pittenweem, spulzied a ship lying therein, and misused the men thereof. This wrang could not be suffered by our men, lest they should be a common prey to sic limmers. Therefore, purchasing a commission, they riggit out a proper fly-boat, and every man encouraging another, made almaist the haill honest and best men in all the town go in her to the sea." They were away for eight or ten days, and came back "with all guid

[1] Th. Pagan, *Convention of Royal Burghs*, p. 160.

[2] T. A. Fischer, *Scots in Germany*, p. 5.

R. K. Hannay, *Shipping and the Staple* (Old Edinburgh Club), vol. ix, p. 56.

Register, Privy Council, vol. i, p. 716; vol. ii, p. 428.

[3] Th. Pagan, *Convention of Royal Burghs*, p. 159.

[4] D. Robertson and M. Wood, *Castle and Town*, p. 296.

tokens of joy, flags, streamers, and ensignies displayed, whom with great joy we recievit and went together to the kirk and praised God."

The captain, " a godly, wise, and stout man," told the story of their voyage. Joining forces with " their admiral, a great ship of St Andrews, weel riggit out by the burghs," they made every ship they foregathered with, of whatsoever nation, to strike and do homage to the King of Scotland, and explained their business and enquired of knaves and pirates. They had some little trouble " with a proud, stiff Englishman," but they " delashit " their nose-piece and, by a fortunate shot, brought down his mainsail. They sailed close to the shores of Suffolk, " and finds by Providence the loon, wha had newlins taken a crear of our awn toon, and was spulying her. How soon they spy ane coming warlike, the loons leave their prize, and run their ship on land, our fly-boat after, and almaist was on land with them ; yet, staying hard by, they delash their ordinance at the loons, and a number going a land, pursues and takes a half-dozen of them. . . ." At this point the local people, fearing a Spanish invasion, began to gather in haste, but the Scots were able to satisfy the justices of the peace, and were allowed to carry off their prize and prisoners. Two of the latter were hanged at the pier-head of Anstruther and the rest at St Andrews, and " ever since syne " the men of Anstruther were free from the attentions of English pirates.[1]

At other times direct reprisals upon the goods of merchants who happened to be of the same town, and to be accessible, were tried. On a large scale this was sometimes an effective measure. Edinburgh petitioned the Lords of the Council to restrain Barton and Fogo, whose ship had captured a Dutchman in time of peace, because " throw taking of the Hollandaris in tymes bypast thar has greit truble and scaithis cumyn becaus all merchandis in tym of pece shall put ther gier to the seye and under traist of pece sal be taken up be Hollanderis quhilkes lyis in ther hie way passand to France or Flanderis. . . ." [2]

Force, indeed, was often used to accelerate or assist the weak arm of the law. Some merchants of Edinburgh had lost

[1] R. Chambers, *Domestic Annals of Scotland*, vol. i, p. 176.

[2] R. K. Hannay, *Shipping and the Staple* (Old Edinburgh Club), vol. ix, p. 56.

£2300 through the piracy of the inhabitants of Northumberland, and although the English Court of Admiralty ordered the latter to pay up, they were so dilatory that the Scotsmen petitioned the Scots Privy Council that they should be paid out of the debts due from Scotsmen to Englishmen. We do not learn if this ingenious proposal was carried out or not.[1] In 1524 two Scots captains, Fogo and Barcar, seized three Dutch ships in Danish waters. The authorities of Copenhagen, on the representations of the injured Dutchmen, arrested the Scots; the latter, however, "contrar to thair faith and oblissing," sailed back to Scotland in their own ships. The Dutch then seized the next Scots ship that they could secure—the *Christopher*, laden with goods belonging to some men of St Andrews and Cupar Angus—as she rode at anchor in a Danish haven. They killed one of the crew, cleared the rest out, and disposed of the vessel and her cargo of silks, velvets, spices, and other goods. The owners of the *Christopher* brought an action before the Lords of the Council against Fogo and Barcar, and the King of Denmark wrote to James V urging that they should be punished as the original cause of the trouble. The two captains were ordered by the Lords of the Council to stand their trial in the Danish courts or to satisfy the owners of the *Christopher*. Our knowledge of the little episode ends while the culprits are still ingeniously trying to evade the order.[2] Such episodes might be multiplied indefinitely.

Nevertheless, lawless as were the High Seas, international trading relations were not in a state of absolute barbarism. Even in the fifteenth century, the sovereign often exerted himself to restrain his seafaring subjects and to redress wrongs. In 1430–31 the King of Scots empowered all the port authorities of England, Holland, Zealand, and Flanders to arrest five Scotsmen who were accused of plundering three English merchants. In the fifteenth century there are several instances in which the King of England made redress to Scots merchants. In 1435, for instance, thirteen merchants and four mariners of

[1] *Register, Privy Council*, vol. i, pp. 431-432 (1565).

[2] R. K. Hannay, *Shipping and the Staple* (Old Edinburgh Club), vol. ix, p. 60.

For a similar case, see *Calendar of Papers relating to Scotland* (First Series), vol. iv, No. 283.

Aberdeen complained that goods belonging to themselves and their masters and friends of Edinburgh and Aberdeen, to the value of £2250, had been plundered from two French ships during the truce; that the king and council had already ordered redress to be made to them according to the value of the cargo as shown by their "markes, lettres and paupires," but that many of these documents had been "embesaillez" when the ships were captured. The king, therefore, granted them safe conducts for witnesses—ten persons if they came by land and twenty if by sea—who should swear to the cargo or produce evidence of its value.[1]

The course of international law, however, occasionally erred in another manner. The ship of a venturesome Englishman was plundered in Loch Broom (Ross-shire), and the Edinburgh Town Council advised in the following words that compensation should be paid: "We haif concludit it salbe mair esie for our nichtbouris quhilkes was allegeit troublaris of Dowle, Inglisman, to give for cuting away of further troublis and entertaining of amitie alevein scoir ten pundis sterling money . . . albeit as we ar surelye informit his schip and haill guidis was nocht worth the soume abonewritten be far."[2]

Besides more direct methods, diplomacy was often tried, not by sovereign states but by individual towns. The burgh of Edinburgh, for instance, sent a burgess, with a letter from the Regent Morton and 900 merks to pay his expenses, to complain to Queen Elizabeth and her council. During the duration of this embassy the town refrained from all reprisals, and a certain Patrick Cranstoun complained that he had been appointed captain against the pirates, had missed a voyage upon this account, and had collected soldiers only to find that the expedition had had to be abandoned.[3]

By the second half of the sixteenth century pirates were coming to be considered common enemies, and their suppression a matter of national duty. The Scots Privy Council made an increasing effort to put down the evil and to obtain compensation for the sufferers, and the burghs supported it. Besides

[1] *Calendar of Documents relating to Scotland*, vol. iv, Nos. 164, 1115. See also Nos. 407-408, 720.

[2] D. Robertson and M. Wood, *Castle and Town*, pp. 293-294. See also, *Register, Privy Council*, vol. xiv, pp. 334, 336, 337.

[3] *Ibid.* p. 296.

taking active measures in fitting out ships to clear the seas, some of them individually forbade their citizens to buy captured goods —Edinburgh absolutely and on moral grounds; Aberdeen, unless by special consent of the bailies and town council, that the town might be kept in " a good bruit and name." [1]

Such a reform, however, could only come about very gradually; and so perilous were trading voyages, that the Convention of Royal Burghs decreed, in 1575–76, that: " In cais ony schippis be pilleit, the gudis saiff sall contribute scatt and loitt for the relief of the personis dampnyfeit, bayth schip and gudis according to thair wairing: . . . and the samyn ordour to be keipit anent the gudis casten for saiftie of lyfe and gudes upoun common consent." In the Edinburgh town council minutes there are two cases of scatt upon record. In one, the merchants complained " that ane greitt quantitie of thair guidis and merchandice in the said schip wes pilleit and reft the said voyage be certane Inglis pirats and siclyke," and the case dragged on for over four months before it was settled. In the other, a Leith ship sailing from Dieppe was forced to lighten her cargo on account of a stormy voyage.[2] Such were the very real perils of those of our ancestors who went down to the sea in ships.

Perhaps two more actual incidents may be included to show how disquieting was the calling of a " saillaris in merchandice." In one of the piracy cases in which Fogo was concerned, the wives and bairns of the merchants who had adventured in his ship complained bitterly to the Privy Council. The unfortunate merchants had embarked hoping to be conveyed to Danzig, but the master and the mariners, having captured a Dutch ship on the way there and wishing to dispose of her in Leith, found it more convenient to put into Copenhagen instead. The merchants went ashore there to sell their goods, but meanwhile Fogo, having heard that he was likely to be held to account, " past on burd and stall away be nycht" with the merchants' goods still on board; leaving them " on land, nocht ane penny in ther purs, to be adjourait and punyst for ther" (i.e. the master and mariners') " deidis and faltis." [3]

[1] Davidson and Gray, *Scottish Staple at Veere*, pp. 55-56.

[2] D. Robertson and M. Wood, *Castle and Town*, pp. 297-301.

[3] R. K. Hannay, *Shipping and the Staple* (Old Edinburgh Club), vol. ix, p. 58.

The perils of the sea overpast, the merchant arriving in foreign parts was received with grave suspicion by the natives. He was often forced to expiate the crimes and make good the obligations of any chance fellow-countryman. His movements were hampered. By two Scots acts of the fifteenth century, strangers were ordered to lodge at the principal town of the port (at Edinburgh, not at Leith), " to change no goods at sea " until they had been seen by the custumars and clerks of the coquet, and their hosts were to be surety for them that they paid all dues and customs. Such regulations were very usual. A petition by some Scots merchants to the civic authorities of Danzig, in 1597, gives a vivid picture of the position of foreigners. They wrote asking for the relaxation of an ordinance of the town that foreign indwellers there might not receive strangers as lodgers, and that only actual citizens might do so. The Scots complain that they had arrived with their ships and goods, through God's grace, for the fair, like other strangers, to attend their trade and gain their modest profit. The Scotsmen who were citizens of Danzig could not take them in, and none of the other Scotsmen who lived there were allowed to do so. " So that we wonder how different we find everything in this famous city from what we were told by our countrymen in our own country." They go on to say that they feel themselves " aggrieved " that strangers from the Netherlands and other places can use their own language in talking with the inhabitants, whereas they cannot. " Nor is it convenient for everybody to accommodate strangers not of their own race and tongue, especially when these must take their crews without distinction with them for their meals," and they describe what difficulties they had in procuring food, " our meals being very uncertain indeed." Some did their own cooking in the inns where they lodged, others lived entirely on board their ships. They earnestly beg that they may be allowed to board with some of their countrymen. The civic authorities made careful inquiry, but did not accede to the petition.[1]

Another difficulty was that of foreign coinages. In the *Compt Buik of D. Wedderburne* we learn that when he made one of his trading voyages he took seventeen different kinds of coin

[1] T. A. Fischer, *Scots in Prussia*, p. 14.
The acts of parliament alluded to were passed in 1488 and 1493.

with him. Sometimes merchants themselves or their belongings went abroad to sell their goods. William Carrebrie of Leith, a stout fourteenth-century merchant, had, one after another, six safe conducts, two of them for three years. One was for France, Brittany, Picardy, and Flanders. He also made a pilgrimage to Rome. At other times the skipper of the ship acted also as the supercargo. Goods were delivered to him and put on board the vessel, and he was instructed to sell them as well as he could, and to purchase other commodities, which he was either to sell at another port or bring back with him. He was generally a part owner of the ship. For instance, D. Wedderburne consigned a last of herrings to Peter Man, skipper, which the latter was to sell in whatever port he came to where the sale would be profitable. If he sold them in England, he was to lend the money he received for them on good security. If he sold them in France, he was to bring back Portuguese gold coin. If he sold them partly in France and partly in England, he was to spend the money on "lint hats with velvet about the brows," on two pieces of coloured fustian, and the balance upon dyestuffs. A rich merchant would sometimes own a whole cargo, but generally many merchants had shares. A sixteenth or a nineteenth share was quite common; cargoes were sometimes owned by as many as twenty-nine merchants. In a lawsuit about an Edinburgh ship, the cargo, which was worth £570 sterling, was shared by no less than forty-three persons.[1]

PART X. RELATIVE IMPORTANCE OF THE BURGH

The extraordinary smallness of sixteenth-century towns compared to those of to-day and the preponderance of wealth and population in country districts was not, of course, a peculiarity confined to Scotland. It is commonplace knowledge that everywhere population was much less than at present,

[1] *Compt Buik of David Wedderburne*, pp. xlv, xxxiv, 122, 140, 196-197. For examples of different coins, see *Extracts from Burgh Records of Edinburgh*, 1589–1603, p. 15; D. Robertson and M. Wood, *Castle and Town*, p. 300.

For Carrebrie, see Index, *Calendar of Documents relating to Scotland*, vol. iv. His contemporary, George of Fallawe, burgess of Edinburgh, was an even greater trader.

and that the proportion of rural to urban inhabitants was invariably greater. Ashley calculates that the population of England, about the time of Edward III, was about two and a half millions.[1] According to another authority there were only four towns in Europe in the fourteenth century with a population of over or about 100,000, viz., Palermo, Venice, Florence, and Paris. London had about 50,000 inhabitants, and Ghent, Bruges, Lubeck, and Hamburg, with whom the Scots traded so greatly, are classified among the towns having between 20,000 and 40,000 inhabitants.[2]

The smallness of the towns and their relative less importance compared to the countryside is, however, far more marked in the case of Scotland. Froissart declared that Edinburgh was "the Paris of Scotland," but he was only talking of her position as principal city, for he goes on to say that she was not so big as Valenciennes or Tournai and that she had 400 houses. He speaks of Dunfermline, Kelso, Dunbar, and Dalkeith as villages. Estienne Perlin, writing in 1551, says that Edinburgh was about the size of Pontoise; he mentions other "little towns."[3] The following estimates have been made regarding the population of Scotland and her burghs. About the middle of the second half of the fourteenth century the population was supposed to be about 470,000. In 1560 Edinburgh is said to have contained about 9000 souls, Glasgow 4500, and Aberdeen in 1572 about 2900. (These figures for the towns are calculated from the bills of mortality.)[4]

Actual figures of money are rather misleading taken by themselves, for the amount of the taxes and the value of the currency varied very much; it is, however, possible to compare the *relative* importance of the burghs, and although the following table shows certain violent fluctuations which could no doubt be explained by purely local events, it also gives a general idea of the trend of development. One sees, for instance, how the burghs belonging to the rich Lowlands suffered—Haddington, Linlithgow, even Stirling—from the great English invasions

[1] W. J. Ashley, *Introduction to English Economic History*, p. 112.
[2] M. V. Clarke, *Mediaeval City States*, p. 35.
[3] P. Hume Brown, *Early Travellers in Scotland*, pp. 10, 75.
[4] Chalmers' *Caledonia*, vol. v, p. 4. H. T. Buckle, *History of Civilization in England*, pp. 644, 645.

of the sixteenth century, and how, by the end of our period, they were recovering themselves. Edinburgh, protected from lesser incursions, and with her seaward trade, held her ground. At the same time the towns of Fife and Angus flourished. This is far more obvious if one considers column six especially. This represents the shares that the different towns took up of £98,000 which was collected as part of the tax voted in 1585 for James VI's marriage, and which was lent by the burghs at 10 per cent. It therefore represents a list of the burghs with money to spare, and the number of Fifeshire towns is striking. The two Anstruthers and the neighbouring burgh of Culross had only been made royal burghs in the reign of James V.

There were, moreover, two much more significant movements among the burghs. One was the definite emergence of Edinburgh as the capital of Scotland. This was of immediate as well as of lasting importance in Scots economic history. The other was the increasing size and wealth of Glasgow, which was to come to full fruition two hundred years later.

Edinburgh, at the beginning of our period, was less rich than Berwick. It is only during the fifteenth and sixteenth centuries that she made good her position as the real capital of the country. From 1508 onwards the annual audits were regularly held there instead of at different places, and James IV when he instituted his Daily Council for the Administration of Justice, arranged that it should be held in Edinburgh.

During the sixteenth century the burgh authorities of Edinburgh were often entrusted with a certain degree of power over other burghs; for instance, in 1500 the Court of the Four Burghs ordered Edinburgh to see that all royal burghs maintained the merchants' privileges. Edinburgh often took a leading part in negotiation with foreign towns and principalities—she did so in the case of the fixing of the staple. Her civic organization was generally in advance of that of other towns and was often copied: in 1552 the Convention of Royal Burghs ordered that all burgh elections should be held in the same way as those of Edinburgh; in the same year her scale of petty customs was also to be the standard throughout the Scots burghs. One finds the Aberdeen shoemakers and the Dundee weavers applying to their brother-craftsmen of Edinburgh for

Ref.: E.R. I. p. c. Great Customs, 1327.	Ref.: E.R. IX. lxxi. Great Customs, end of 15th Century.	Ref.: F. Warden, Burgh Laws, Dundee, p. 10. Tables of Contributions paid by Burgh, 1535.	Same Ref.: 1557.	Same Ref.: 1578.	Ex. R. v. XXII, 1585.	Warden. Burgh Laws of Dundee, p. 10. 1591.
1. Berwick	1. Edinburgh	1. Edinburgh	1. Edinburgh	1. Edinburgh	1. Edinburgh	1. Edinburgh
2. Edinburgh	2. Aberdeen	2. Dundee	2. Dundee	2. Dundee	2. Dundee	2. Dundee
3. Aberdeen	3. Dundee	3. Aberdeen	3. Aberdeen	3. Aberdeen	3. Perth	3. Aberdeen
4. Dundee	4. Haddington	4. Perth	4. Perth	4. Perth	4. Aberdeen	4. Perth
5. Perth	5. Perth	5. Haddington	5. *St Andrews*	5. *St Andrews*	5. **Glasgow**	5. **Glasgow**
6. Linlithgow	6. *St Andrews*	6. *St Andrews*	{ 6. Montrose	6. Ayr	6. *Dysart*	6. *St Andrews*
7. Cupar (Fife)	7. Linlithgow	{ 7. Montrose	{ 7. Cupar	7. Stirling	7. *Kirkcaldy*	7. *Dysart*
8. *Inverkeithing*	8. Cupar	{ 8. Cupar	8. Ayr	8. **Glasgow**	8. Haddington	{ 8. Stirling
9. Ayr	9. Kirkcudbright	9. Stirling	{ 9. **Glasgow**	9. Montrose	9. *Anstruther*	{ 9. Haddington
10. Stirling	10. Stirling	10. Ayr	{ 10. Dunfermline	10. Dumfries	10. *St Andrews*	{ 10. Ayr
Dumbarton } very small.	11. Montrose	11. **Glasgow**	11. Dumfries	11. Cupar	..	11. *Kirkcaldy*
Wigtown } very small.	12. Ayr	{ 12. Irvine	12. Inverness	12. Inverness	..	12. Dumfries
Kirkcudbright } very small.	13. Inverness	{ 13. Dumfries	13. Stirling	13. *Crail*	..	13. Inverness
..	14. *Inverkeithing*	{ 14. Brechin	14. Linlithgow	14. Brechin	..	14. Cupar
..	15. Dumbarton	15. Linlithgow	15. Haddington	15. *Dysart*	..	15. Montrose

The above table gives the principal Burghs of Scotland in the order of their importance at different periods. The type is arranged to show two noteworthy features: (*a*) the rise of **Glasgow**; (*b*) that of the Burghs on *the Southern Coast of Fife*.

copies of their regulations.[1] In 1526, owing to "the grete repair" to Edinburgh of the king, his lords, and many strangers, she was allowed to hold three weekly markets for the sale of meat and bread.[2] By that time she had far outstripped the other towns in wealth. In 1327 the great customs paid by Berwick amounted to £673, those of Edinburgh to £439, and those of the next important burgh—Aberdeen—to £349. By the end of the fifteenth century the customs of Edinburgh were £1528, those of Aberdeen, still the second largest contributor, £366. Owing to changes in taxation, these figures cannot be directly compared with each other, but the relative position of the two towns is most striking.[3] In 1585, at the time of the marriage tax which has already been quoted, the predominant position of Edinburgh is noticeable:

Edinburgh	took up	£40,000
Dundee	,,	20,000
Perth	,,	12,000
Aberdeen	,,	8,000
Glasgow	,,	4,000
Dysart	,,	4,000
Kirkcaldy	,,	4,000
Haddington	,,	2,000
Anstruther	,,	2,000
St Andrews	,,	2,000

The rise of Glasgow, which started life as an ecclesiastical and not as a royal burgh, was gradual. The table showing the importance of the different burghs shows that there was a steady rise in its wealth during the period, and also in that of several other western burghs. Nevertheless, in spite of this rise, the distribution of wealth was radically different from that of the present day. In 1526 a special tax was levied for permission to merchants to go abroad to trade with their ships as they pleased, and it was paid in the following manner:

Burghs north of the Forth	£876	15	2
Burghs south of the Forth	507	15	0
Edinburgh	572	15	0[4]

[1] J. D. Marwick, *Edinburgh Gilds and Crafts*, p. 57.
Records of the Convention of Royal Burghs, vol. i, pp. 2, 3.
E. Bain, *Merchant Gilds and Crafts*, p. 268.
A. Warden, *Burgh Laws of Dundee*, p. 512.

[2] *A.P.S.* vol. ii, p. 378.

[3] *Exchequer Rolls*, vol. i, p. c; vol. ix, p. lxxi. [4] *Ibid.* vol. xv, p. lxxi.

The great industrial belt that now stretches from the Forth to the Clyde did not then exist and Scotland's most important towns were dotted along the East Coast, and her main trade routes all lay towards the north-east.

It has already been suggested, in different sections, that commerce and industry were to some extent localized. Aberdeen was an especial centre for the Danzig trade; Aberdeen and Glasgow went in for fishing, Dundee for cloth-making—its imports of dyestuffs at the end of the sixteenth century were more than those of most of the other burghs put together. The lesser seaports, however, indulged in relatively a far greater share of direct foreign trade than at present.[1]

Part XI. The Policy of the Government

In dealing with the economic interests of the country, the policy of the central authority was consistently dominated by one leading idea. This main object was to foster abundant home supplies rather than to encourage the export trade. The regulations prohibiting and permitting the export of commodities are legion. Many are to be found among the acts of the Scots Parliament, but the enactments of the Privy Council are far more numerous. One of the first cares of the authorities was the provision of an adequate food supply. Three times, in 1526, 1540, and 1555, acts were passed prohibiting the export of tallow.[2] Foodstuffs were a valuable article of Scots trade, but again and again, in times of dearth, such export was forbidden. In 1535 no sheep or nolt were to be sent into England. The export of victual was forbidden in 1567, 1578, and 1589—in the latter year the shortage was attributed to the transporting of foodstuffs by land and sea; again in 1592 the taking of nolt and sheep out of the kingdom was prohibited because prices were thereby raised.[3] The Privy Council meanwhile watched the harvests from year to year, and its discussions upon the

[1] *Exchequer Rolls*, vol. xxiii, 315.
See also *Calendar of Documents relating to Scotland*, vol. iv, Nos. 163 (Inverness), 383 (Kirkcaldy); see also 1647 (Dumbarton), 1187 (Peebles).

[2] *A.P.S.* vol. iii, pp. 314, 378, 495.
See also J. Davidson and S. Gray, *Scottish Staple at Veere*, pp. 62-63.

[3] *A.P.S.* vol. ii, p. 346; vol. iii, pp. 40, 104, 452, 577.

measures to be taken to prevent dearth are manifold.[1] In good years, however, export was allowed as pious duty to humanity, but often under careful safeguard.[2] Nor were these acts allowed to be dead letters, like some of the other laws of Scotland. There are many instances where action was taken and where persons disobeying them were punished.[3] As we have seen, the export of coal was more than once forbidden, and in 1540, owing to the exorbitant prices charged for wine, salt, and timber, the town authorities were ordered to fix their prices at all ports where such commodities arrived.[4] The history of the period shows much oppression and much misgovernment, but it is at least clear that the authorities did consider themselves responsible for seeing that the people had food and other necessaries at reasonable prices, and that they did do their utmost to fulfil this duty.

We have seen that the Government bestowed much care upon the herring fisheries. Nevertheless, it was concerned about the adequacy of home supplies rather than the development of the export trade. In 1540 an act was passed that home needs were to be satisfied before herrings were exported, and this was followed by six more similar laws.[5] The home supplies of salt and of coal were carefully safeguarded.

Still more significant was the case of hides and skins, which were not only the most important articles of export of the country, but among those that particularly concerned the land-owning classes. In 1561 the Privy Council enacted that owing to the "sending away furth of this realm" of oxen and cow hides "in grit nowmer and quantite," the price of leather had risen so much that "the butis, schone, and uther apparalingis maid thairof, ar sauld sa dier that the pouer servandis, lauboraris, and utheris lieges of this realme ar and wil be thairby alluterly depauperat," and they therefore forbade the export of hides for three years. Unfortunately this ordinance is only an example among many of the goodwill but lack of power of the

[1] Cf. *Register of the Privy Council*, vol. i, pp. 114, 127, 137, 200, 232, 235, 334, 559, 571, 611.

[2] *Register, Privy Council*, vol. i, pp. 402, 571-572; vol. ii, p. 589.

[3] D. Robertson and M. Wood, *Tower and Town*, p. 288.

[4] *A.P.S.* vol. ii, p. 373.

[5] These acts were passed in 1573, 1579, 1584, 1587, 1600. See also *Register, Privy Council*, vol. iv, p. 123; vol. vi, p. 132.

Government. Three years later, in 1564, the Privy Council annulled this act, because their good intentions had been "frustrat and disapointed," "be craftie inventions and practices, alswell of the merchantis as of the craftismen." "For sum part of the merchantis evin immediatelie eftir the making of the act, and continesalie sensyne, hes nocht ceissit to salt and gaddir togidder the hydis, kepand thame in stoir, and sumpart be privy meanis obtenit licence for thair awin privat commoditie to transport hydis qhairof, althocht the licence did oftymes extend to a few nowmer, yit undir the cullour and pretence of that small liberite the saidis hydis wer cariet and stoin away in exceeding griet quantitie; and on the other part the craftismen, following thair awin commoditie, as it wer altogidder conspyrit, held thair grayth still at the auld derth, and the subjectis got na maner of ease nor relief be the said act, for quhilk caus chieflie the samyn wes maid and set furth. And by all this hir Majestie in the menetyme hes wantit and bene defraudit of hir dew custumes, quhilkis at the begynning, of guid-will fer the commoun weillis caus, hir Heines wes content to want; . . ."[1] The import of skins was again forbidden in 1592.[2] James VI, when imposing an impost on wine in 1601, elaborately explained that the policy of the Crown was to secure plenty in the necessaries of life for the lieges but to restrain drunkenness, and that if they insisted upon spending money upon superfluities, then this may well bring in some advantage to his Majesty. Even the grasping James had already proved himself as good as his word, for when the "Octavians" were appointed, at a time of particular financial stress in 1595–96, in the directions given to them it was laid down that they were to see that no licences for the export of forbidden goods (nearly all necessaries of life) be given until they were sure that the inhabitants of Scotland "being weill staiket, may spaire the same." These licences to export goods were, at the time, a valuable source of income to the Scots king.[3]

It was perhaps because of the same feeling, and because Scotland was so largely dependent upon foreign sources for many of her supplies, that, except for a duty of 2s. 6d. in the £1

[1] *Register, Privy Council*, vol. i, pp. 191, 288.
[2] J. Davidson and S. Gray, *Scottish Staple at Veere*, p. 66.
[3] *Register, Privy Council*, vol. vi, p. 205; vol. v, p. 759.

imposed on all English imports for a short time by James I,[1] no import duties were imposed in Scotland till 1597. In that year an act was passed levying a duty of 12d. in the £1 upon all such imports, and in the preamble it was stated that all foreign countries levied customs on goods brought into the country, and that Scotland was the only exception. Rather typically of Scots finance, the reason for imposing the duty was said to be to enable the king to maintain his princely estate.[2]

Certain other acts passed by the same parliament show a curious mingling of old and new ideas. The prohibition against the export of great coal was repeated, with drastic provisions for its enforcement. The importation of English cloth was prohibited, for the paternal reason that it was not so good as it appeared to be, and the old-fashioned one that it caused bullion to be sent out of the country. There was, however, probably another reason for this prohibition. By a third act, the export of wool was forbidden, except under licence, and woolworking strangers were ordered to be brought in. This marks the beginning of new ideas and new lines of policy, which were destined profoundly to affect the history of Scotland. Old conditions were, however, in some respects dominant. Dire as was the need of the Treasury at this time, lords, barons, and freeholders—the principal flockmasters—were specially allowed to export their wool free.[3]

It is perhaps rather a digression to point out that the restrictive fiscal policy of the end of the sixteenth century probably had a very considerable effect in breaking down the special monopolies of the royal burghs. As we have seen in the section dealing with the first institution of the privileged burghs, the sale of duty-paying articles of commerce was concentrated there. Revenue from this source could therefore be easily secured, and, as time went on, the whole machinery arranged for its collection was organized in relation to this trading monopoly.[4] When, at the end of the sixteenth century, new import duties

[1] *Exchequer Rolls*, vol. iv, p. cxxix.

[2] *A.P.S.* vol. iii, p. 136.

[3] *Ibid.* vol. iii, pp. 136, 138. As another example of the primitive economic ideas that still prevailed, an order of the Privy Council for suppressing "the haynous, pestiferous and intollerable cryme and sin" of usury may be noted (*Register, Privy Council*, vol. vi, p. 22).

[4] See Chapter III, Part III.

were imposed, the export of certain goods was forbidden except under special licence, and the customs were in many directions made more stringent; the unfree towns, where these goods had no right to go, but where there was no provision for the collection of the duties and the enforcement of the rules, had a considerable advantage. In 1599 complaint was made that the rules against the export of forbidden goods were being infringed by persons who preferred their private gain to that of the commonweal. Next year it was declared that in order to escape the customs stranger-merchants on their way to the royal burghs would dispose of much of their cargoes under colour of night at unfree ports where no custumar was; and that likewise merchants who were exporting goods, after their ships had left the free burghs and were lying in the roads, would receive uncustomed goods from non-free burghs. The Privy Council passed regulations to try to stop this; but, two years later, complaints were made that the same practices were still going on, and the Privy Council passed stringent orders that foreign ships were not to take any goods except coal and salt from sixteen ports, specifically named, and all lying along the northern and southern coasts of the Firth of Forth, under pain of confiscation. Merchants were specially forbidden from evading the customs by hiding articles that paid higher dues in bales that paid lesser ones; by concealing playing-cards, wool cards, combs, and other goods in packs of hides and lint; and by sending skins, hides, and other dutiable or forbidden exports by land to Berwick or other English ports.[1] The main struggle to break down the special rights of the royal burghs, and the rise of the non-free burghs, took place in the seventeenth century.

A policy of maintenance rather than of expansion underlies the constant acts passed by parliament and by the Privy Council that had the object of retaining or adding to the supply of bullion in the country. By an act of 1488, all merchants exporting wool, cloth, hides, or herrings—the most considerable articles of export—were to import a certain proportion of silver. By another act, strangers visiting the country were to take merchandise and not money out of it with them. In parliament after parliament the same sort of provisions were made. Some-

[1] *Register, Privy Council*, vol. vi, pp. 33, 85, 373, 375.

times the prohibitions were absolute, sometimes only a proportion of the bullion was to be brought in.[1] When one remembers that such were the current economic theories of the day, and that the unfortunate merchants were afflicted by the same regulations wherever they went, one is inclined to pity them heartily. They themselves pointed out how hardly such a law bore upon them. Fortunately for them, laws, in Scotland at least, were often more honoured in the breach than in the observance, and probably there was a good deal of evasion. In 1600, a stout Edinburgh merchant forcibly prevented the revenue officials from seizing some gold that he wished to export.[2]

The strongly conservative and vigorous action of parliament and the Privy Council with regard to price-fixing and the monopolies of the royal burghs, the Gild Merchants, and the Craft Associations are all more easily dealt with in the account of the actual institutions of the burghs. All through the period, right down to the very end of it, the policy that regulated trade was, in essentials, mediaeval. But, for the matter of that, in this it was quite contemporary with the very simple economic development of the country.

It is tempting to deal with cognate subjects, such as the fiscal machinery by which the customs were levied, and the whole question of the coinage. Where space is limited, however, some selection and elimination must be made, and these subjects have both been very fully treated by specialist writers —the former in the *Introductions to the Exchequer Rolls*, the latter by R. W. Cochran Patrick in *Early Records relating to Mining in Scotland.*

Subject to this line of dominant policy, the Scots kings and their parliaments were most energetic in trying to turn the resources of their country to account. The activities of James IV and V as flock-masters have already been noticed. The ledger of Andrew Haliburton shows how largely the great churchmen and nobles engaged in commerce, in order to dispose of the

[1] Cf. *Register, Privy Council,* vol. i, pp. 68, 85-96, 104, 212-213, 330.
J. Davidson and S. Gray, *Scottish Staple at Veere,* pp. 75-79, gives a summary of such legislation.

[2] *Extracts from the Burgh Records of Edinburgh,* 1589–1603, p. 235.
Register, Privy Council, vol. vi, p. 103.

revenues of their great estates. There was the same eagerness to exploit the mineral wealth of the country. Gold was found in 1513 at Crawford Moor, and a certain amount of the metal was successfully extracted. James V did still more to encourage the working of gold—which was one of his royal perquisites. Cochran Patrick considers that most of the gold coinage of his reign was minted from native metal. In 1526 a lease of all the mines of gold and silver in the country was given to several Germans and Dutchmen. Apparently they did not meet with much success, but in 1538–42, under new management, considerable finds of gold were made, and again in 1567; and from that time onwards licences to work the precious metal were given to several individuals. There was also some lead and a little silver mining.[1] The relative importance of these enterprises is small; they furnish, however, an interesting example of the energy of the Scots rulers, and of the ignorance of one age of the economic potentialities of the following ones. It is strange to compare the bulk of the records relating to gold with the little attention that was paid to coal—no one in the sixteenth century guessed at the wealth that was going to develop from the mere scratchings of the coal heuchs.

Meanwhile certain new industries were springing up, and the methods and machinery wherewith the Scots Parliament endeavoured to foster them mark the very substantial development that did take place at the end of this rather static period. It will therefore be more convenient to deal with them at the end of this section. Before, however, leaving trade and commerce and plunging into the story of the actual organization and social conditions of the burghs, it will be best to consider the question of Scots shipping.[2]

Part XII. Shipping

So dependent upon her overseas trade was Scotland, that the question of shipping was one of great importance. Ships were, of course, small, but the numbers that plied to and from Scotland seem to have been considerable. Between 1552 and

[1] See especially pp. xiii-xix, xxxiv, xxxv, xl.
[2] See Chapter VIII, Part VIII.

1566–67 the average number of ships calling at Leith, the port of Edinburgh, was between 81 and 82.[1] According to Dundee shipping lists, in 1581, 38 ships returned with cargoes; in 1582, 17; and in 1588, 69.[2] In addition to her foreign trade, coastwise shipping played an important rôle in the commercial organization of Scotland. Landward means of communication were so difficult, for reasons natural and political, that it was fortunate that the Scots coasts abounded with natural havens. Even so early as the fifteenth century the dues from the Northern Crown Lands, grain, barrelled fish, and even live stock, seem habitually to have been sent by sea.[3]

Scotland was very definitely a maritime nation, but it is more difficult to determine how far her wares were carried by native shipping. One comes across constant allusions to French, Dutch, Flemish, and German ships carrying goods to Scotland, but also to native ships, and there is but little information of the total numbers of either or of the proportion that they bore to each other. At a very early date—1330—Burnett estimates that at Aberdeen, Dundee, and Perth one-fifth of the exports that paid duty was carried by foreigners.[4]

In Scotland there does not seem to be evidence of that definite passion for maritime dominion that was so marked in England—what Cunningham calls the " one steady purpose " which ran " through the whole of the national life; so that despite the constitutional changes which England underwent, she still held the even tenour of her way towards maritime supremacy." [5] Nevertheless, shipping was the anxious care of the ablest rulers of Scotland. Robert I, in his last years, was interested in shipbuilding.[6] James I owned several ships, had a shipbuilding establishment at Leith, and built at least a barge and a little ship and repaired other vessels.[7]

[1] D. Robertson and M. Wood, *Castle and Town*, pp. 278-279. The returns for one year were omitted.

[2] See " Dundee Shipping Lists " published in the *Compt Buik of David Wedderburne*, p. 239 onwards.

[3] *Exchequer Rolls*, vol. i, p. cxvii; vol. xii, p. xxxvi.

[4] *Ibid.* vol. i, p. cxxxvi.

[5] W. Cunningham, *Growth of English Industry and Commerce, Modern Times*, Part I, p. 14.

[6] *Exchequer Rolls*, vol. i, p. cxxi.

[7] *Ibid.* vol. iv, pp. cxli, cxlii, 383.

Shipbuilding, however, made greater advances about the middle or the end of the fifteenth century, owing to the improvement in artillery. Vessels were required which could carry guns in their forecastles and resist shot by means of the thickness of their sides. From 1449 onwards Admirals of Scotland were appointed, although the post was generally held by some great lord and was probably largely titular.[1] James IV was deeply interested in shipbuilding. It was strictly enjoined by act of parliament in 1493 and 1503 upon all lords spiritual and temporal, and on the burghs, and the king vigorously practised what he preached. The *Exchequer Rolls* are full of entries recording his activities. The forests of Darnaway and Urquhart (Ross-shire) were felled to build his ships, and, in 1513, the Scots navy consisted of sixteen ships with tops, ten smaller craft, and sloops and barques. His greatest triumph was the building of the *Great St Michael*. She was 240 feet long and her side walls were ten feet high, and she carried a crew of 1000 men besides gunners and officers. Her armament consisted of "many cannons," besides "three hundred shot of small artillery," which included such deadly-sounding pieces as *battent falcons*, *pestilent serpentines*, and *double dogs*. She also carried hagbuts, culverins, cross-bows, and hand-bows.[2] She was the largest ship that had been built in Scotland. A French shipwright was engaged to build her and eighty French marines to sail her. One does not wonder at the king's pride in her, or that he boasted to the English ambassador that her array of ordnance was "more than ever the French brought to a siege"—a statement which the ambassador regarded as "a great crack." James visited her daily as she was a-building, arriving at the shipyard early in the morning and remaining till noon, after which he went home to dinner.[3]

The Scots navy, especially the *Great St Michael*, was of international importance. Both France and England wished to secure the aid of the Scots ships against her rival.[4] When the clash between England and Scotland eventually came, the

[1] *Exchequer Rolls*, vol. xiii, pp. clxxvii, clxxviii.

[2] *Ibid.* vol. xiii, pp. clxxxiii-clxxxv.

[3] *Calendar of Letters and Papers of Henry VIII*, vol. i, Part I, Nos. 1645, 1775.

[4] *Ibid.* Nos. 793, 1690, 1735.

immediate *casus belli* was the capture by the English of a Scots ship owned by one of the Bartons. During the war the share of the *Michael* and her twenty-one consorts was inglorious. Under the futile command of Hamilton, they frittered their energies away in an attack upon Ireland, and then sailed over to France; and, in the desolation and confusion after Flodden, the *Great St Michael* was sold to the French king for 40,000 francs of Tours. Nothing is known of what happened to the other vessels.[1]

The building of the *St Michael* was not the only shipbuilding enterprise of the second half of the fifteenth century, for it was a flourishing time for Scots maritime enterprise. Bishop Kennedy of St Andrews had built a great barge, at a cost of £10,000, before the king began the *Great Michael*, and Andrew Wood, the three Bartons, and William Brounhill all flourished at this time as sturdy sea-captains. The shipwright craft began to increase In the sixteenth century we hear of one Scots merchant ship of 100 tons and of another of 200 tons as if they were of no abnormal size, and of another with a crew of over 200 men.[2]

During the troublous years of the sixteenth century the records tell of no more royal shipbuilding. There was at times a considerable mercantile navy, but how far the Scots built and how far they bought their ships remains a matter for conjecture. In 1572, Killigrew, who seems to have been of rather an optimistic outlook, said that the Scots navy had been augmented " as it is a thing almost incredible," and that the Scots had " great traffic and favour at Ostend, and fourteen or fifteen sail there and fifty or sixty at Borcham." In 1596 there is an account of the fleet which brought wine from Bordeaux to Scotland. It consisted of four score sails or thereby, who were for the most part Scotsmen. All the ships sailed together in a fleet. But Fynes Moryson, who visited Scotland in 1598, considered that the Scots navy was small and inexperienced, but that since the Anglo-Spanish war it had begun to improve, as the Scots had secured a considerable amount of the carrying

[1] *Exchequer Rolls*, vol. xiii, p. clxxxvi.

[2] *Ibid.* pp. cv, clxxvii, clxxix-clxxxiii.

M. J. Thorpe, *Calendar of State Papers relating to Scotland, 1509–1589*, pp. 2, 62.

trade formerly done by the English.[1] From such shreds and patches of information it is impossible to work out any theory of the development or the decline of the Scots navy, or of its relative importance.

[1] See W. Law Mathieson, *Politics and Religion in Scotland, 1550–1695*, p. 202.

Register, Privy Council, vol. v, p. 537.

P. Hume Brown, *Early Travellers to Scotland*, p. 87.

In confirmation of carrying trade, see *Register of the Privy Council* (Second Series), vol. i, p. 363.

CHAPTER VIII

PART I. THE ROYAL BURGHS

THE ramifications of the different organizations that were evolved in connection with the Scots burghs are so closely interconnected that it is impossible to give even a sketch of the activities of one of them without mentioning all the rest. It is perhaps most profitable to approach these active little institutions from a very much generalized point of view.

The very definite organization of the Scots burghs is a point in which they were entirely different to the English towns. The three most characteristic features were: firstly, their demarcation into royal burghs, burghs of regality and of barony; secondly, the trade and craft monopoly which they exercised over large rural areas; and thirdly, the co-operation and uniformity that existed among the burghs.

To take the last point first: the tendencies to legislate for the burghs as a whole, and for the burghs to take concerted action together, appear all through Scots economic history. As Gross points out, they led to a certain uniformity of burgh organization in Scotland, whereas in England "each town council had a history of its own as regards the principle of self-election."[1] In the period before the Wars of Independence these tendencies had already shown themselves very markedly in the code of the Laws of the Four Burghs, in the powers of inspection that the Chamberlain exercised over all the burghs, in the institution of the Court of the Four Burghs, and in the burghs' own inclination to secure uniformity in the matter of laws of succession. During the fifteenth and sixteenth centuries they were carried very much further.[2] Not only were the burghs

[1] G. Gross, *Gild Merchant*, p. 200. He goes on to point out certain typical burghal organizations that England had and that Scotland had not, p. 201.

[2] See Section I, Chapter III.

constantly legislated for as a whole, but, through chosen representatives, they tended more and more to act together in concert, and such concerted action was encouraged or, at least, recognized by the central authority. Inter-burghal organization culminated, in the second half of the sixteenth century, in the uniquely Scots institution of the Convention of the Royal Burghs. The activities of this body, formed of representatives of all the royal burghs, permeated the whole burghal life of the country. Perforce it will constantly be alluded to in the course of the descriptions of every single one of the aspects of urban life of our period, and it will be more convenient to describe its constitution and activities in more detail after the various institutions that it supervised have been dealt with.

The second of the most characteristic features of Scots burghal organization, the economic monopolies that the royal burghs exercised over wide districts, was the direct result of the deliberate legislation of the Scots kings of the twelfth and thirteenth centuries, especially William the Lyon. By the laws and charters granted by this king a beginning was made in the parcelling out of the whole kingdom into districts, each of which was dominated by a royal burgh, which possessed the sole right of carrying on crafts, selling and buying commodities, and in which fairs and markets alone could be held. During the period now being dealt with, the system was still in force. David II, in 1364, gave a charter to "our burgesses throuwcht Scotland," which gave them liberty to buy and sell everywhere within the liberties of their own burgh, and discharged them from buying and selling within the bounds of another without obtaining a licence. Foreign merchants were forbidden to buy and sell to any but the burgesses of the king's burghs. No bishop, prior, kirkman, earl, baron, or secular person was to buy any merchandise whatsoever, or sell any, except to the merchants of the burgh within whose liberty he resided.[1] Right through our period, though adjustments were made, the main principles were observed. A charter granted to Peebles in 1621 included the privilege of using the trade of merchandise in all places within the bounds of the sheriffdom of Peebles, and forbade any non-burgesses from occupying any merchandise belonging to a

[1] Th. Keith, "Trading Privileges of the Royal Burghs of Scotland," *English Historical Review*, vol. 28, p. 298.

free royal burgh within their bounds.[1] The town treasurer of Edinburgh, in 1570, put the case in a nut-shell: "The chief liberty and fredome of ane fre burgh of royaltie consistis in twa thingis, the ane in vsing of merchandice, the other in vsing of crafts, resaving fremen thairto."

This curious arrangement, which the interested burghs did their utmost to enforce, had far-reaching effects upon the economic development of Scotland in the seventeenth and eighteenth centuries. Its importance cannot be overstressed. It was responsible for that lack of villages in Scotland which was so marked a feature of her social development until the very end of the eighteenth century, and it is therefore also the cause of the retarded development of the domestic type of industry (of which the Yorkshire wool trade is such a favourable example in England), which would necessarily flourish best where there was a fairly closely nucleated rural population. So stringent was the monopoly that until 1517 not a single legal fair or market was held outside a royal burgh. One was instituted between 1517 and 1570 and five more between 1571 and 1603. So very slowly did the old ideas break down.[2]

It is not very profitable to try to distinguish the enforcement of one particular part of the elaborate organization of monopoly that controlled and limited Scots trade. The monopoly against rural districts, however, had such far-reaching consequences that it is worth noting that even in the disorganization and tribulation of the Wars of Independence the royal burghs still clung to these rights. In 1303–7 they petitioned Edward I and his council that no markets be held in any sheriffdom except within "Les burks chivales noster siegnur le Roy." In the sixteenth century their attitude was rigorously set against the general economic development of the age and the rise of domestic industries. They still tried to enforce their rights against villages and the country-side, and in this they were strongly backed by the Crown, which was itself interested in the maintenance of burghal rights.[3]

[1] Th. Keith, "Trading Privileges of the Royal Burghs of Scotland," *English Historical Review*, vol. 28, p. 456.

[2] A. Ballard, *Scottish Historical Review*, vol. xiii, pp. 22 and 28.

[3] *Calendar of State Papers relating to Scotland* (First Series), vol. iv, No. 1834.

Act after act was passed by the Scots Parliament to enforce the rights of the burghs. In 1457, 1466, and 1488 laws were passed that " saylaris in merchandice be fre men of burowis and Induellaris with in the burgh," or else the " familiars, factors or servants " of such persons who were " with theme of household at mete and drink " ; that no man of craft use merchandise unless he renounce his craft; that ships must only come to free burghs, and that strangers must not buy fish or other goods except at free burghs. In 1503 a further act was passed " anent the fredomes and privileges of merchandis and burrowis," which confirmed these privileges, enacted that no one dwelling without the burghs was to use merchandise, nor buy (in order to sell again) nor sell wine, wax, silk, spicery, nor staple goods, and that no one was to "pack nor piel" in Leith, nor in other place without the king's burghs. During the sixteenth century the privileges of the burghs were again and again confirmed. At least thirty acts were passed by the Scots Parliament dealing with burghal monopolies—no less than thirteen in the parliament of 1567. During this century the royal burghs' monopoly of the fishing trade was specially emphasized and the other privileges were strengthened. In 1554, for instance, the Lords of Session were charged to give letters commanding that none of the lieges should violate these acts; and in 1572 they were confirmed, and it was stated that they had not been observed because no penalty was inflicted, and that therefore anyone exercising the traffic of merchandise "nocht being frie burgess thair haill guidis and geir sall becum escheat, the ane half to our souerane lord and the vther half to the burgh quhais commissioner or collector sall first apprehend the same." [1]

Not only did the central authority pass acts. It urged on the burghs to enforce their rights. In 1458, 1495, and 1511 the burgh authorities of Aberdeen were ordered to escheat wool, hides, and skins that were exported from the sheriffdom without

[1] Th. Keith, "Trading Privileges of the Royal Burghs," *English Historical Review*, vol. 28, p. 459 onwards, gives a summary of the legislation ; see also J. D. Marwick, *Edinburgh Gilds and Crafts*, where it is arranged chronologically.

For a royal burgh's own description of its privileges, see *Register, Privy Council*, vol. vi, p. 289 (Linlithgow in 1601).

A.P.S. vol. ii, pp. 49, 86-87, 178, 221, 224, 245, 246, 375, 488, 499; vol. iii, pp. 252, 348.

paying custom. At a later date Montrose, Stirling, and Peebles were also urged to greater diligence. All merchants were prohibited from using merchandise at any kirks within Cunningham, and were ordered to bring their goods to Irvine or other free burghs, because " in this trublous tyme sen the field of Flowdoun " merchants and chapmen had made markets on Sundays at the parish kirks of Kilmarnock, Largs, and other places, and " oure burgh is utirlie distroyit fer want of repaire and use of change and we gretumlie defraudit in our custums." [1]

The royal burghs were not backward in protecting their privileges. Edinburgh had a continuous struggle to maintain her monopolies against the adjacent towns, villages, or suburbs of Potterrow, the Canongate, and especially Leith. In 1489 the Edinburgh Town Council ordered that whensoever the town's freedom was usurped in Leith, all the neighbours and deacons, with their craftsmen, were to be ready to pass with the magistrates to Leith for the holding of the water court, to reform injuries done against their freedom. The town council minutes are full of the struggle, which continued intermittently all through our period and on into the next. The attention of the Privy Council was also constantly engaged by these rather sordid squabbles, and more than once Edinburgh was able to have a restrictive clause, specially directed against Leith, inserted in an act of parliament. As the sixteenth century wore on, relations seem to have become more and more embittered. The following is a good example of the painstaking pugnacity with which Edinburgh sought to enforce her rights to the uttermost stretch of the law. In 1574 she was prosecuting the men of the Canongate before the Lords of Session, and appointed a rota of persons who, month by month, were to expedite the case.[2]

Dundee and Perth and many of the lesser burghs also had passages-of-arms with suburbs or villages. For instance, the town council of the small burgh of Peebles, in 1555, passed a minute narrating that the burgh had the right to a weekly market day, with the power to sell wax, wine, woollen cloth,

[1] Th. Keith, "Trading Privileges of the Royal Burghs," *English Historical Review*, vol. 28, p. 298.

[2] J. D. Marwick, *Edinburgh Gilds and Crafts*, pp. 53, 81, 106, 109. *Register, Privy Council*, vol. ii, pp. 33-34 ; vol. vi, p. 81.

broad and narrow, and all other lawful merchandise, and to have within the burgh bakers, brewers, fishers, fleshers, preparers of fish and flesh, and all other craftsmen "belongand to ane burgh regale"; but that certain burgesses were trading outside the burgh and that "every landwart toun" in the country was trading daily in lint, tar, iron, wool, hides, skins, malt, and meal, so that the burgh itself was "depauperat and heriet." Rather later the town officials proceeded to the "usurpit mercat" of Brighouse and collected their dues there, and the town took action against certain other fairs and markets.[1]

In the second half of the sixteenth century the royal burghs were able to take collective action through their Convention. Not only were individual burghs incited to activity and given financial support,[2] but the agent of the Convention of the Royal Burghs sometimes undertook the work of pursuing unfree traders of individual burghs. In 1595, Stirling paid him £4 for the "persute" of "the werkmen in clachannis," and in 1592 he was to prosecute all persons whose names were sent in to him by the authorities of the different burghs, and £200 was raised for his expenses.[3]

The royal burghs waged war against individuals as well as communities who infringed their privileges. The number of cases in which "outland" men were complained about or proceeded against is legion. They are to be found in all printed collections of town council records, and in the records of the Convention of the Royal Burghs the subject takes up more space than any other. In many individual cases the prosecution is for the infringement of the special class monopolies of the merchants or the craftsmen. The monopoly of the burgh, however, was a more important factor in Scots history than were the individual rights of the types of burgesses who inhabited it.

In the first section of this book it has already been suggested that one of the original reasons for granting the royal burghs

[1] J. W. Buchan, *Peebles*, vol. ii, p. 188. See also *Records of the Convention of Royal Burghs*, vol. i, pp. 35, 69.

[2] Th. Pagan, *Convention of Royal Burghs*, p. 127.

[3] Th. Keith, "Trading Privileges of the Royal Burghs of Scotland," *English Historical Review*, vol. 28 (1913), p. 268.

their monopoly of foreign trade was the greater facility that such concentration offered for the collection of the customs. This is clearly admitted in an act of 1567 passed against the resorting of strangers to unfree ports, and ordering them only to load coal, lime, and stone at such places, on account of the "great scaith and damage [done] to the Kings majesty in defraude of the great customs" by trading there.[1] The royal burghs, however, during the fourteenth, fifteenth, and sixteenth centuries, in return for their special privileges, bore a special share in the national burdens: in especial they paid a definite proportion of the levies that were from time to time required to eke out the national revenue, and individually were stented according to their relative wealth. The recognition of the connection between privileges and burdens was tacitly understood or was definitely stated in all the acts granting or confirming the monopolies of the royal burghs and those of the two classes of freemen who inhabited them.

In addition to their economic monopoly the royal burghs enjoyed the privilege of parliamentary representation in return for bearing their share of the national burdens. Professor Rait has traced out the close connection that existed between the appearance of the names of new royal burghs upon the stent roll and their sending of representatives to parliament. Except for a very small number of unusual cases, which were explained by special circumstances, the payment of taxation and parliamentary representation "invariably" went together.[2]

The remaining outstanding feature of Scots burgh organization was the classification of the towns of the country into the two different grades of royal burghs and of burghs of regality and of barony. A. Ballard has pointed out that the erection of the latter was brought about by the royal burghs' monopolies over wide districts. He argues that although it was necessary, for financial reasons, to maintain the royal burghs' monopoly, it was impossible to deprive wide districts of all craftsmen, shops, and markets: "The solution of the problem was found in the establishment of burghs, with powers of holding markets

[1] *A.P.S.* vol. iii, p. 42.

[2] R. S. Rait, *Scottish Historical Review*, vol. xii, p. 130.

For the more complex subject of the appearance of the representatives of the burghs at Conventions when taxes used to be voted, see *ibid.* p. 247.

and fairs, whose inhabitants had the right of trading only within their own burghs. In this way new markets could be set up as required, and the burgesses of the Royal Burghs suffered the least possible interference with their monopolies."[1] Perhaps, however, the actual institution of such burghs, which became known as burghs of regality and barony, was in most cases due to the power of the feudal lord, who obtained the charter of erection, was the superior of the burgh, and no doubt benefited financially by the possession of such town property. The power of the nobles has already been stressed, and as a rule the right to hold such burghs was granted to one of them as a personal benefit. The privileges of Glasgow, for instance, can only have been served by the interest of the bishop—there was no economic need, such as A. Ballard suggests, for a lesser town so close to the royal burgh of Rutherglen.[2]

Between 1450 and 1516 fifty-one burghs of barony were erected. The catalogues of privileges granted to them in their charters were all very much alike. They were granted the right of having bakers, brewers, butchers, and other craftsmen. They might buy and sell certain articles within their bounds. They might set up a market cross and hold weekly markets and annual fairs. These privileges, as Ballard points out, made them little "oases in the districts of monopoly of the older burghs." But they, in their turn, were sheltered behind a wall of privilege against the country round. They all held of a mesne lord and not of the king, but the method of electing their town officers varied. Sometimes the burgesses had the right of doing this themselves; sometimes they might only do so with the advice of their lord. Sometimes absolute power was vested with the latter. The *Register of Cupar Abbey* shows the building up of such a little burgh. About 1495 the abbey, having secured a grant of the right to erect a burgh of barony from the king, formed the burgh of Keithock out of a "cottery" of craftsmen and others holding a few acres of land. Life

[1] A. Ballard, "Theory of the Scottish Burghs," *Scottish Hist. Review*, vol. xiii, p. 20.

[2] For an example of the "erection" of burghs at the instance of powerful nobles, see G. Law, "Earlsferry," *Scottish Hist. Review*, vol. ii, p. 22. See also the attempt of Arran to make Blackness a burgh of barony, *Register, Privy Council*, vol. vi, p. 289 (1601).

leases were given to the new burgesses of building ground and agricultural land. Their privileged position was secured by the order " that nane hant nor crave the office of brewing, selling, baking, wine selling, or ony other merchandis " outside the burgh. The burgesses had the right to build as much as they chose. They might have sub-tenants " to put out and in " as they might think speedful. " And thai and thare tennandes sal be obedient to vs, and correkit of al faltes be our successouris and ministeres, spirituale and temporale."[1] Of the constitution of the little burgh we learn nothing.

A word may be said about the five principal church burghs, which acquired an equal status with the royal burghs. It was only by degrees that they secured this position. Renfrew and Rutherglen did their utmost to repress Glasgow in the twelfth century, and in the fourteenth and fifteenth centuries the royal burgh of Cupar complained of the growing privileges of St Andrews, and those of Montrose, Forfar, and Dundee opposed Brechin. The ecclesiastical burgh of St Andrews obtained parliamentary representation in 1456, Brechin and Glasgow in 1558, Arbroath and Dunfermline a little later. Meanwhile they had all acquired the commercial privileges of royal burghs, and also appeared upon the stent roll and paid their quota of taxation. By 1555 they were all members of the Convention of Royal Burghs, and were obviously regarded as the equals of the royal burghs which composed the rest of that assemblage.[2]

The greater number of royal burghs had already been erected before the fourteenth century, but there were additions, notably on the Fifeshire coast and in outlying districts. There were, of course, a few cases where small burghs died out of existence or lapsed for years, but, considering what strenuous times they lived through, it is surprising how tenaciously the Scots burghs continued to exist. By the middle of the sixteenth

[1] A. Ballard, *Scottish Hist. Review*, vol. xiii, p. 2.

W. Chalmers, *Book of Scotland*, pp. 80-81.

Register of Cupar Abbey, vol. i, p. 246.

For an example of the subjection of the civic authorities of Glasgow to the archbishop, see *Diocesan Register of Glasgow*, vol. i, p. 20.

[2] Th. Keith, "Trading Privileges of the Royal Burghs," *English Historical Review*, vol. 28, p. 463.

R. S. Rait, "Parliamentary Representation in Scotland," *Scottish Hist. Review*, vol. xii, pp. 123-130.

century the royal burghs numbered thirty-five and they remained for many years at that number. It was only with difficulty, owing to the strenuous opposition of the existing burghs, that any new ones were created.[1] The following table taken from the data collected by A. Ballard shows the relative increase of the different types of burghs during our period:[2]

	Royal Burghs created.	Burghs of Regality and Barony created.
1450–1516 . .	4	51
1517–1570 . .	7	25
1572–1603 . .	7	36

Part II. The Constitutions of the Royal Burghs

The constitutions of the royal burghs were developed considerably during our period. The first great modification had already taken place, or at least had made considerable progress, in the period reviewed in Section I: for the leasing of certain of the royal revenues collected within the burghal boundaries—the rents, fines, and petty customs—had become usual by the end of the Wars of Succession. In the case of some burghs, such as Berwick in 1327, Roxburgh in 1329, and Cullen in 1342, there was an intermediate stage, during which their revenues were leased to a great man or courtier.[3]

The next step took place—in the case of the more important burghs—in the fourteenth century, when they obtained charters from the Crown, converting their tacks into perpetual feus. In 1319 Aberdeen obtained such a charter, and in 1329 Edinburgh did likewise. Between 1359 and 1396, Dundee, Inver-

[1] *Exchequer Rolls*, vol. xi, p. xxxii.

R. S. Rait, "Parliamentary Representation in Scotland," *Scottish Hist. Review*, vol. xii, p. 129.

The opposition of the other burghs was generally voiced by the Convention of Royal Burghs. For an example of their opposition, see G. Law, "Earlsferry," *Scottish Hist. Review*, vol. ii, p. 25.

[2] A. Ballard, "Theory of Scottish Burghs," *Scottish Hist. Review*, vol. xiii, extracted from table on p. 22 and figures on p. 28.

[3] *Exchequer Rolls*, vol. ii, pp. lxxxvii, lxxxviii, 273, for actual example of a lease and the payment of a "grassum" to acquire it (Linlithgow, 1330).

ness, Montrose, Perth, Rutherglen, Renfrew, Linlithgow, and Inverkeithing all secured feu-charters, and other burghs followed suit. In the case of some of the ecclesiastical burghs of regality similar feus were given. The Abbey of Dunfermline granted to the burgh of that name a feu of its fermes and petty customs in 1395, and to Kirkcaldy a similar feu in 1450. The possession of such a feu-charter was evidently of great moment to the burghs: they were ready to pay considerably more for it than had been extracted from them under the older régime. It is a matter of considerable importance to the student of economic history, for it definitely shows how greatly advanced the organization of the burghs had become. In the period preceding the Wars of Independence the town officials gradually changed from being employees of the king to being representatives of the people. Under the régime of feu-charters they must definitely and entirely have become the latter.[1]

The burghal elections seem to have given some thought to parliament during the fifteenth century. In 1455 an act was passed "for the common profet of all the burrowis of the realme, at that be viij or xij personis, efter the quantite of the towne, chosin of the secret consale, and suorne thairto, the quhilkeis sall decret all materis wrang and unlawe within the burghe to the avale of v li or within apone viij dais warnying." This was followed by the much better known act of 1469 anent the election of aldermen and bailies. It states that "because of gret truble and contensione zeirly for the chesing of the samyn throw multitude and clamour of comonis sympil personis it is thocht expedient that nain officiaris na consail be continuit eftir the Kingis lawis of burrowis forthir than a zeir. And at the chesing of the new officiaris be in this wise, that is to say that the Aulde counsale of the Toune sall cheise the New Counsale in sic noumyr as accordis to the toune. And the new cunsale and the aulde of the zeir before sall cheise all officiaris pertanyng to the toune as Alderman bailzies Dene of gild and vthris officiaris. And that ilka craft sall cheise a persone of the samyn craft that sall have voce in the said electioune of the officiaris for that tyme in like wise zeir by zeir."[2] An act of

[1] *Exchequer Rolls*, vol. ii, p. lxxxv.
D. Murray, *Early Scots Burgh Organization*, pp. 143-146.

[2] *A.P.S.* vol. ii, p. 95.

1472 enacted that four members of the old council should remain upon the new.[1]

The most important act in this group, that of 1469, had a deep and lasting effect upon the organization of the Scots burghs. The procedure laid down in it was not an innovation, for an act of the town council of 1456 shows that it was already the custom at elections in Edinburgh. The act, however, made it the recognized method of conducting burghal elections in Scotland. The Convention of Royal Burghs made every effort to enforce this. (In 1552, for instance, it enacted that the constitution of Edinburgh should be the standard upon which all royal burghs should form themselves, and the constitution of Edinburgh was closely modelled upon the act of 1469.) The burghal authorities were elected yearly at Michaelmas. The old council chose the new council, and, together, they prepared leets of names of the new officials, provost, bailies, etc. Then, acting together, but with the addition of the deacons, the actual officials were chosen.[2] The practice of choosing the new officials and town council by the old was, indeed, the universal method of conducting burghal elections in the royal burghs of Scotland until the electoral reforms of the nineteenth century.

The 1469 act has been stigmatized as a reactionary measure, but, bad as it undoubtedly was, it would be somewhat rash to say that it is retrograde, when so little is known about the methods that preceded it. The provision that the old town council should choose the new undoubtedly tended to throw the main power of the management of the burgh into the hands of an oligarchy or clique. It seems a thoroughly unsound method according to modern ideas, and, in the case of the Scots burghs, it undoubtedly worked very badly. Inferior as it may have been to modern ways of conducting elections, however, it seems to have followed, not a good system of popular election, but a state of extreme vagueness; for the only previous regulations regarding the burgh elections seem to have been those of the Laws of the Four Burghs and of the Merchant Gild of Berwick. According to one of these codes, it would appear that

[1] *A.P.S.* vol. ii, p. 107.

[2] *Records of the Convention of the Royal Burghs*, vol. i, p. 3.
M. Wood, *Edinburgh, 1329–1929*, p. 286.

the provost was to be selected or accepted by popular acclamation and was to choose twelve of the wisest of the burgesses to assist him. According to the other, both the provost and the bailies were to be chosen at the sight and by the consideration of the whole community—meaning, of course, the freemen only. In Aberdeen records there is an example of such an election actually taking place. In 1399 twenty persons were elected as common councillors—*Communis Consiliarius*—and the alderman and bailies were elected the same day, also apparently with the consent and assent of the whole community.[1] During the fifteenth century the whole body of citizens of Aberdeen seem to have retained specially wide powers. In 1454 "the hail community in Aberdeen being gadderit be public premunition of the belman and warning of the officers," imposed a new tax. In other entries the whole community is represented as being summoned by the handbell, but as upon one occasion it met in the Tolbooth, a vast assemblage cannot have responded. Perhaps the lesser folk knew when they were not wanted. In 1502 the formula is used of the aldermen, bailies, and council, *and divers of the community representing the town.*[2] What happened at elections in other burghs at this so early date is not recorded. It is rather significant that although many of the old burgh charters specify the burgesses' privileges and rights in other directions, none of them include a clause stating that the citizens are to have the right of free election of their officers, which either shows that the franchise was not a greatly esteemed privilege or that the citizens had not got it.[3]

It must be remembered that acclamation by the majority at a mass meeting of the citizens could only be workable in comparatively small communities, and it would not necessarily involve the election of democratic candidates—an example of such an election exists in the case of Ipswich, and, as a result, a limited number of persons, many of them with the aristocratic "de" or "fitz" in front of their names, monopolized nearly all the offices.[4] Fifteenth-century Scotland was certainly not a

[1] J. D. Marwick, *Edinburgh Gilds and Crafts*, p. 19.
[2] *Spalding Club Miscellany*, v, pp. 28-35.
[3] *Report of Municipal Corporations in Scotland, 1819*, vol. i, p. 4.
[4] G. Gross, *The Gild Merchant*, p. 23.

democratic country and it would be unlikely to find the burghs in any way exceptional. The lesser burghs of regality and barony certainly do not seem to have had electoral powers. The provosts and bailies of the church burghs of Paisley, Dunfermline, and Arbroath were chosen by their feudal superiors —the abbots of the monasteries to which they belonged.[1] In the case of Glasgow, we have a picturesque account of so late as 1553, narrating how the Bishop of Glasgow, according to custom, chose the two bailies of Glasgow from a list presented by the provost and council of the city, "in the inner flower-garden of the said most reverend father, within the stone walls surrounding his palace," the "canons of his chapter standing by him all the time." [2]

In any case, bad though the principle of election prescribed by this act appears to us moderns, it seems to have been well thought of by our forebears. When the Merchants and Guild Brethren of Edinburgh—by far the most powerful body of men within their town—obtained the Seal of Cause in 1518 which gave them their formal constitution, it was laid down that the retiring Master of Faculty and the other officers of the Guild were always to choose their successors.[3]

The act of 1469 probably represented a development in organization made necessary by the growth of the nation, but it has been suggested that it also was brought about by the increasing political power of the merchants and by their more rigid exclusiveness from the craftsmen. An entry of 1463 in the Burgh Records of Edinburgh shows that the distinction between the crafts and merchants was not yet drawn. It records the election of the "dozen" of the burgh, "quhair of everie ane stylit be his craft." [4] "The gret truble and contensione" complained of in the act may well have been caused by the craftsmen, angry at the growing exclusiveness of the merchants. But the intention of the act was to secure them a modicum of representation. In this case it is noteworthy that the craftsmen were to be represented by

[1] D. Murray, *Early Burgh Organization*, p. 165.

[2] J. Clelland, *Annals of Glasgow*, vol. i, p. 315. Quotation from a contemporary record.

[3] J. D. Marwick, *Edinburgh Gilds and Crafts*, p. 63.

[4] *Edinburgh, 1329–1929*, p. 268.

their *deacons*, the officers of the new craft organizations, just struggling into power, and by that they were to have a voice in the election of the *Dean of Gild*, the head of the merchants' especial organization.

The constitution of the royal burghs was certainly not a satisfactory achievement. Not only did the very limited powers assigned to the craftsmen cause serious trouble and the peculiar system of election lead to constant abuse of the franchise among the merchants themselves, but in all but the largest burghs there was a tendency for the provostship to pass away from the indwellers of the town altogether and to become vested in one of the families of local gentry. So early as 1503 an act was passed that neither craftsmen nor gentlemen indwellers again usurp the authority of the king's officers chosen in the burghs or make bands or leagues.[1] Throughout the sixteenth century there were further acts and constant complaints to the Privy Council. Inverkeithing stated that the Hendersons of Fordel had made themselves heritable provosts; Forres, that the Dunbars of Cumnock had usurped power; Renfrew was suffering in the same way in 1576. The smaller burghs were the most liable to this abuse; but at St Andrews, Sir Patrick Learmonth of Dairsie had himself constantly re-elected as provost, appropriated the common lands and their revenues, and feathered the nest of one of his sons. At Perth, during a period of prolonged trouble and of constant uproar, Lord Ruthven was provost.[2] As we shall see, the alienation of the "Common Good" of the burghs was the temptation which often led interested burgesses and needy lairds to secure office in the burghs, but it would be monstrous to suggest that landowners were invariably actuated by such motives. In those troublous times the protection of a feudal magnate must often have been most advantageous to the burghs, and the services which the burgesses gave were a legitimate return. In many cases the connection was no doubt a friendly one.[3] Nevertheless, on the whole, it was regarded as an evil, and the prohibi-

[1] *A.P.S.* vol. ii, p. 245.

[2] *Register, Privy Council,* vol. ii, pp. 15, 16, 19, 305, 784; vol. iv, pp. 42-44, 53-54.

E. Bain, *Merchant and Craft Gilds*, p. 85.

[3] Cf. Peebles. J. W. Buchan, *Peebles*, vol. ii, p. 36.

tions against "outland" interference with the burghs are frequent.

Town councils that were always elected by their predecessors could hardly fail to fall into the hands of a clique or faction. Their deliberations were carried on in secret in some burghs, and the community had no redress except the empty one of airing their grievances at the annual Head Court, unless they applied to the Privy Council. In 1567 one of many of such cases occurred. Certain merchants and inhabitants of the burgh of Cupar complained of the bad management of the town council, "quhilk abusioun and confusiouns hes now takin sic increment that the auld counsale having always facultie to elect the new, they cheis men of thair factioun and swa haldis the publict offices and counsale amongis a certane of particular men fra hand to hand, usand and disponand the common gude of the said burgh at thair plesour, to the griet skayth and detriment of the commoun weill thairof, and expres againe all justice and lovabill custum of the burrowis of this realme." The Privy Council took the part of the complainants and itself appointed new burgh magistrates and council to act until the proper election could take place.[1]

In common fairness, however, it must be admitted that at Aberdeen, where the more primitive method of election persisted, there was no happier state of affairs. The records of the burgh show that from the end of the fourteenth to the end of the sixteenth century the provost, four bailies, and four common sergeands were generally elected in the Head Court by the votes of the burgesses. The provostship, in spite of this, was monopolized for a hundred years by a family of local gentry, alluded to as "the race of Menzies." In 1590, in the course of a struggle between the craftsmen and the merchants of the burgh, the former appealed to the Privy Council, alleging very serious maladministration. At that time the same members of the town council had held office for years. The matter was referred to the Court of Session, and the burgh was ordered to

[1] J. W. Buchan, *Peebles*, vol. ii, pp. 172, 168.

Register, Privy Council, vol. i, p. 382.

H. T. Buckle, *History of Civilization in Scotland*, pp. 646-647, alludes to the protection given to Dunbar by the Earl of March, Elgin by the Earl of Moray, and even Aberdeen by the Huntly family.

conduct its elections according to the principles laid down in the act of 1469.[1]

The constitutions of all the Scots burghs are closely bound up with the Gild Merchants—the merchants' special organization in each town. It is therefore necessary to consider these organizations, and the particular privileges and monopolies that made of the merchants a favoured and distinct class in all the royal burghs.

PART III. THE GILD MERCHANT

Before considering the more debatable subject of the nature and organization of the Merchant Gild, it is helpful to consider the status and commercial privileges of the merchants themselves. The merchants were not a small, rich oligarchy in the burghs, but, in relation to the small size of these towns themselves, a fairly large proportion of the citizens. In 1558 the contingent that the merchants undertook to raise in defence of Edinburgh outnumbered those of all the crafts put together.

They were, moreover, men of greatly varying wealth and position. There were men of considerable substance, such as Mercer, the burgess of Perth, of the fifteenth century; some of the Douglas kinsmen; and, at the end of the sixteenth century, the goldsmith, Foulis (who lent King James over £25,000), Heriot, Arnott, Lowrie, and other Edinburgh merchants, who were creditors of the king. There were merchants who obtained licences for two or even three ships to trade, but others only used boats. The cargoes that they sent might be of considerable value: one worth 2299 nobles was plundered in 1406, another worth £2250 in 1370, but they might be owned by a few or by many merchants. Some were little more than packmen: such a one was an unfortunate merchant of Glasgow who, in the course of his vocation and trade of merchandise, was travelling in Mull and was set upon and robbed of his pack, worth 3000 merks, by a gentleman of the Macleans.[2] The

[1] Th. Keith, *Scottish Hist. Review*, vol. xiii, p. 111.
Register, Privy Council, vol. iv, p. 533.

[2] R. Chambers, *Domestic Annals of Scotland*, vol. i, p. 253.
State Papers relating to Scotland (First Series), vol. iv, Nos. 164, 720, 1340.
Register, Privy Council, vol. vi, p. 141 (see also *State Papers relating to Scotland*, vol. iv, No. 1558).
J. D. Marwick, *Edinburgh Gilds and Crafts*, p. 90.

quarrels between the craftsmen and the burghal authorities were often not class conflicts between craftsmen and merchants, but struggles against the small clique of the most influential merchants who had monopolized the burghal offices.

The merchants' special trading privileges were of old standing. As we have seen, when William the Lyon recognized and established the foundations of the burghal organizations of Scotland in the twelfth century, he granted or endorsed the special rights of the merchants. They had the monopoly of trading in the most important marketable commodities of Scotland, hides, skins, and wool, and all foreign imports. These privileges they continued to hold and even to amplify throughout the fourteenth, fifteenth, and sixteenth centuries. The whole trade in salmon and herrings also became their particular province, and, throughout our period, they received constant parliamentary confirmations of their rights. The regulations made by the different burghs also definitely recognized them. In Edinburgh, Aberdeen, Dundee, Arbroath, Ayr, Dunfermline, Dumbarton, etc., the merchants' monopoly of buying and selling of wool, hides, and foreign wares and the prohibition against all infringement of their rights is repeated.[1] In Dundee, in addition, they assumed the right to deal in coal.[2] Unlike so many of the constitutional rights and practices in the burghs, there was no indefiniteness about the scope of these trade monopolies, and in the merchants' struggle with the craftsmen, they are carefully specified. For instance, in Edinburgh, in an agreement with the craftsmen, besides the merchants' absolute rights in the wholesale trade, they alone were to " top or sell in smalls any manner of wine, as woad, spiceries of all sorts, cloth of silk, gold, silver, or any foreign or outlands cloth of wool (excepting always these cloths following, to wit, linen, fries, kelt, Yorkshire cloth, kerseys, and all sorts of shrinking cloth, which shall be common to all burgesses)."[3] Gradually the term " staple goods " became a convenient definition of the merchants' monopoly. In 1602 this term was defined as "all

[1] Cf. *A.P.S.* vol. ii, pp. 166-167 (1466), 178 (1487), 221 (1488), 264 (1503), 252 (1535), 348 (1555).

A.P.S. vol. iii, p. 578 (1567, 1578, 1579, 1592).

[2] A. Warden, *Burgh Laws of Dundee*, p. 115.

[3] J. D. Marwick, *Edinburgh Gilds and Crafts*, p. 133.

merchandice quhilk payis custome, alsweill brocht within the realm as transportit furth of the samyn."[1] Among the foreign wares they dealt in, wine seems to have been a specially valued monopoly.

Nor were these regulations vague and barren enactments. The acts of parliament are definite and carefully framed measures, and, in practice, the merchants were consulted by the central authority in matters appertaining to their monopolies. For instance, in 1566, when strangers applied to the Privy Council for licences to fish for herring in Loch Broom and other lochs of the North-West, where "it hes plesit God to oppin ane greit commoditie to the common weill of this realme," the council consulted the merchants, and, on their advice, refused such licences.[2] The records of the Convention of Royal Burghs abound with such instances, and, in fact, the very existence of this association seems partly to have grown out of the practice of the Government of consulting the merchants in matters concerning trade.

The burgh authorities, moreover, were most active in passing regulations to enforce the maintenance of the merchants' monopolies, and they constantly took active measures to see that they were obeyed. In this the individual burghs were urged on to greater diligence by the Convention as it gradually took form.

The merchants, however, only received their privileges in return for the specially heavy burdens that they bore. The goods in which they dealt, as we have seen, were the customs-paying commodities. It was probably convenient to collect these dues from a definite body of citizens, but, in addition, they contributed specially heavily to the burghal revenues. In Edinburgh their scale of entrance fees to the freedom of the city was one-third more than that of craft burgesses in 1507–8, and in 1550 it was double the amount.[3] Moreover, they were differently and more heavily assessed for the payment of taxes: in their case, taxation was levied on their property; in the case of the craftsmen, upon the craft as a whole.[4] This connection

[1] Davidson and Gray, *Scottish Staple at Veere*, p. 190. Quotation from *Convention of Royal Burghs*. [2] *Register, Privy Council*, vol. i, p. 482.

[3] J. D. Marwick, *Edinburgh Gilds and Crafts*, pp. 60-76.

[4] I am indebted to Dr M. Wood, Archivist to the City of Edinburgh, for this information. J. D. Marwick, *Edinburgh Gilds and Crafts*.

between privilege and extra burdens was quite clearly recognized. Thus an act of the Edinburgh town council declared that: In all times coming when any taxes, stents, or other portable charges shall happen to come upon this burgh, all manner of persons that haunts, uses, or exercises the liberty and privilege of merchants or free burgesses of the same, that is to say, the venting of wine or any other kind of merchandise, of " quhatsumever " state they be, men of law, scribes or other privileged persons, notwithstanding their said privileges, shall in all times coming " stent, scait, lott and beir chargis, walk and waird " with the said merchants so long as they use their liberty or any part thereof." [1] The act of 1592, confirming burghal privileges, says that everyone using merchandise must bear their share " in taxations, stents, watching and warding, because of the heavy burdens of the burghs." [2] Another act orders all sons of Gild brethren who trade upon their own account to become Gild brethren themselves, because "the great charges dailly falling upon them, intollerable to a few number, ought of all good equity to be borne of all that has their life and trade within the burgh." [3]

Besides their commercial privileges, the merchants had very special political rights. As we shall see, the organization of the Merchant Gild and of the burgh were in most cases curiously intertwined. But the favoured position of the merchants was not merely fortuitous. During the period at present under review it became clearly and definitely recognized that the whole or almost the whole political power of the burghs lay in the hands of the merchants. In the preceding period statutes had been made forbidding certain classes of craftsmen from holding office in the burghs, but, until the act of 1469 gave the craftsmen some voice in the elections, it is not easy to say, in the state of extreme vagueness that seems to have enveloped burghal constitutions, how far the craftsmen were debarred from holding office or sitting on the town council. An act of 1503 ordered

p. 88, says that in 1557 when the queen-regent ordered that burghs commuting their military service were to be stented on the wealth of their citizens, craftsmen and merchants alike, the craftsmen of Edinburgh, though they allowed themselves to be stented in this way, specially bargained that it was not to be made a precedent.

[1] J. D. Marwick, *Edinburgh Gilds and Crafts*, p. 89.

[2] *A.P.S.* vol. iii, p. 578.

[3] J. D. Marwick, *Edinburgh Gilds and Crafts*, p. 135.

that provosts, bailies, and all others having jurisdiction within the burghs were to be changed yearly, and that "nain have jurisdictioune within burgh but gif thai merchandice within the said burgh." Similar provisions were made in 1535 and 1555.[1] These acts seem to have been directed rather against encroachments by landed gentry than craftsmen, and, until after the sixteenth century, it was tacitly assumed that the bulk of the town councillors as well as the magistrates ought to be merchants. One of the great struggles between the merchants and the craftsmen was the latter's claim to even a modicum of representation on the councils. In one of the latest acts of James VI relating to the burghs it is laid down that no one is to be capable of holding the office of magistrate or any other office within the burghs except merchants and actual traffickers in merchandise within them.[2] In the case of individual burghs of some importance it was an actual fact that the merchants held all or nearly all the seats on the town council until nearly the end of our period. In Edinburgh, where the names of the members of the town council from year to year have been preserved, it can be seen from the town records that until the middle of the sixteenth century the town council generally included one or at most two craftsmen, and it is by no means clear whether even these were always full members or were deacons of the crafts. Later in the century there were nearly always one or two craftsmen upon the council, never more. So late as 1582 the Town Council of Dundee enacted that only members of the Gild Merchant were to be upon the town council.[3] The Convention of Royal Burghs many times repeated the rule that the representatives sent by the different burghs must always be merchants and not craftsmen, and, if this order were infringed, refused to receive such a representative.[4] In 1581, in a quarrel between Perth and Dundee with regard to precedence, Dundee based its claim upon its greater age, upon the fact that it was

[1] *A.P.S.* vol. ii, pp. 44, 252, 349. Like all Scots laws, these regulations were often ignored. The civic authorities of Banff, complaining to the Privy Council in 1660 of the interference of various gentry in burghal affairs, state that the magistrates of the town are all poor, mean men, fishers and craftsmen (*Register, Privy Council*, vol. vi, p. 125).

[2] *A.P.S.* James VI, parl. 20, cap. 8.

[3] A. Warden, *Burgh Laws of Dundee*, p. 42.

[4] G. Gross, *The Gild Merchant*, p. 216, has collected examples.

" mickle mair burdened in the service of our sovereign lord both in bodies and goods," and because " the estate of the said burgh being also governed by the merchants, excluding the craftsmen from all offices of government in the same." [1]

Often the merchants' special privileges were regarded as vested in their special organization, the Gild Merchant. The Gild Merchant was already in being in the period before the Wars of Independence. It was, in fact, in existence at the earliest time when we begin to learn anything of the existence of the burghs. It had acquired its especial privileges, *i.e.* the sole right to foreign trade ; it had shown itself from the first definitely an exclusive and aristocratic body; Gild brethren were obliged to keep a good horse, and all craftsmen working with their hands, which must have meant a very high proportion, were excluded. It was distinctly the organization to which the ruling classes of the burghs belonged, otherwise the clauses in the statutes about the proper care of the town and the election of the town authorities would hardly have appeared.

The Gild Merchant was a common feature in Scots burghs. In the following towns such an organization is definitely known to have existed :

First mentioned in the period before the Wars of Independence: Perth, Aberdeen, Berwick, Dundee, Elgin, Stirling.

First mentioned in the fourteenth century: Cupar, Dunfermline, Irvine, Montrose.

First mentioned in the fifteenth century: Ayr, Edinburgh.

First mentioned in the sixteenth century: Arbroath, Banff, Culross, St. Andrews, Wick.[2]

The institution, by the sixteenth century, seems to have come to be regarded as part of the make-up of a normal burgh. It appears in charters of incorporation relating to ten more burghs during that century—all of them, except the Anstruthers, very small burghs—and, in 1605, the Convention of Royal Burghs forced Glasgow to have a Gild Merchant.[3]

The relationship between the Gild Merchant and the burgh

[1] *A.P.S.* vol. iii, p. 233.

[2] G. Gross, *Gild Merchant*, vol. i, p. 207. See also R. Miller, *Edinburgh Dean of Gild Court*, p. 7.

[3] D. Murray, *Early Burgh Organization*, p. 484.

has been a matter of dispute.[1] It is important to remember that not only did England differ from Scotland, but that, in both countries, town differed from town.[2] In Scotland, at any rate, in earlier times, burghal constitutions were only being worked out and were very fluid. It was only in the sixteenth century that they tended to take more definitely, and in a more stereotyped form, the shapes that had gradually been evolved. In days that were largely illiterate and when life was in many ways much less organized than it is at present, things probably very largely just happened, and were arranged as they came along, according to what was most convenient at the moment. It is surely rather a fallacy to attribute a definiteness and tidiness of mind to our ancestors in regard to institutions and theories of government, that the untrained person of the present day most certainly does not possess.

In early times in Scotland variations certainly existed. In Aberdeen all burgesses appear to have belonged to the Gild Merchant.[3] In Glasgow, right through our period, there was no Gild Merchant at all.[4] In Edinburgh in the sixteenth century all burgesses were most definitely not members of the Gild Merchant, for the separate lists of admissions are preserved. That membership of the Gild Merchant was something additional to ordinary burgess-ship may, on the whole, be taken as the normal condition in Scotland.[5] The clearly stated differentiation between craftsmen and Gild brethren in the statutes of Berwick shows that this was the intention from the first. In the fourteenth-century directions for the chamberlain's visitations it is ordered that separate lists of the Gild brethren and of the burgesses be presented to him. In the sixteenth century examples abound. The whole rivalry between the craftsmen

[1] D. Murray, *Early Burgh Organization*, pp. 37, 78-79, gives a summary of the differing theories and their protagonists.

[2] G. Gross, *Gild Merchant*, vol. i, p. 43. Gross notes that there were "so many peculiarities that it is difficult to analyse the gild-laws in detail."

[3] D. Murray, *Early Burgh Organization*, p. 349.
Kennedy, *Annals of Aberdeen*, ii, p. 237, 449.

[4] D. Murray, *Early Burgh Organization*, 351.

[5] G. Gross, *Gild Merchant*, vol. i, p. 209, quotes a formidable list of references to prove this, including *A.P.S.* i, p. 693; *Commission on Municipal Corporations of Scotland*, 1835, pp. 11, 89, 90, 181, 127, 451; *ibid.* 1836, pp. 93, 113, 130, 190, 228, 295, 383, 409; *ibid.* 1819, pp. 104, 385.

and the merchants is proof positive. It is, however, far more difficult to say whether members of the Gild Merchant were always also burgesses. In practice perhaps it would be safe to assume that as a rule they were so; in Edinburgh this was certainly the case.[1] The mass of laws and of burghal regulations against persons who were non-resident in burghs and used merchandise shows that by the seventeenth century at least it was strongly held that merchants ought to be indwelling burgesses.

The connection between the Gild Merchant and the general government of the burgh in early times is very puzzling. It was certainly very close, as the Berwick statutes prove. But possibly some writers are too apt to regard as constitutional principles what was largely the result of fortuitous circumstances. The burghs were very small; the few men of ability, activity, and position would naturally fill most of the offices available—the people of mediaeval Scotland were quite unused to electoral institutions, and would naturally follow the leadership of their "betters." If one considers the closest parallel of the present day—women's organizations in rural districts—one finds that the small group of local great ladies practically monopolize the chairmanships and committee memberships of a strange variety of organizations, largely according to their social prestige; but no one can imagine that this is the result of any deliberate constitutional organization. The election at Ipswich, quoted by Gross, is a contemporary example of how the thing happened.[2]

However it came about, entirely of deliberate intent or partly by chance, the organization of the Gild Merchant and of the burgh were very much mixed up from the earliest times that we have track of. The statutes of the Gild Merchant of Berwick refer as much to matters affecting the general regulation of the burgh as to the affairs of the merchants themselves, and fines for certain offences against the whole community went to the Gild.[3] The passage of time did little or nothing to separate the spheres of influence of the two bodies.

In Edinburgh fragmentary records of the old Head Court of

[1] G. Gross, *Gild Merchant*, vol. i, pp. 66, 209.
J. D. Marwick, *Edinburgh Gilds and Crafts*, p. 51.
[2] G. Gross, *Gild Merchant*, vol. i, p. 22.
[3] J. D. Marwick, *Edinburgh Gilds and Crafts*, p. 33.

the Gild Merchant survive from the early fifteenth century, and the affairs of the burgh and of the Gild are both entered therein. In 1403, for instance, the Head Court of the Gild chose the provost, the Dean of Gild and keeper of the kirk wark, the bailie of Leith and the duzane or council. The provost and council of the burgh were therefore, as R. Miller points out, "simply an elective committee of the Merchant Gild." On the other hand, in 1500–1 an entry occurs that the provost, bailies, and council granted and consented that the Gild Court begin on Friday next coming, and that persons warned to compear by the officer and failing to do so were to pay 20s. to the Church work (of the burgh).[1]

At Aberdeen one finds the same domination of the organization of the burgh by the Gild, and the same tendency for the burgh to absorb the Gild. In 1437 the Aberdeen Dean of Gild was elected with the consent of the town council and of the Gild brethren. In 1450 we learn that he was elected by the whole community, and in later years sometimes by the "Curia Gildae" and sometimes by the "curia ballivorum." In 1442 the Gild brethren of Aberdeen made certain regulations "for the governance of merchandice," the fines that were imposed to go to the burgh. The accounts of the Dean of Gild during the fifteenth century have been preserved and they consist largely of purely burghal expenses, the payment of the dempster's fee, the mending of a bridge, the repair of the quay, much entertaining on behalf of the burgh. D. Murray calls the Aberdeen Gild "rather an adjunct or pendicle of the council than an independent body."[2]

The identification of the Gild and burgh organization was meanwhile proceeding to unexpected lengths. In 1469, in the well-known act regarding burghal elections, the representatives of the craftsmen were given a voice in the choice of the Dean of Gild, the head of the Merchant Gild, along with and as if he were

[1] R. Miller, *Edinburgh Dean of Gild Court*, p. 7.
J. D. Marwick, *Edinburgh Gilds and Crafts*, pp. 29-30, 60.
D. Robertson and M. Wood, *Castle and Town*, p. 58.
It must be noted that this old court was quite different to the Dean of Gild's Court appointed in 1584–85, and which merely carried out certain duties entrusted to it by the town council.

[2] D. Murray, *Early Burgh Organization*, p. 467.
Miscellany of the Spalding Club, v, p. 28.

one of the burgh officials. An act of 1502 ordered that no burgesses or Gild brethren should be created without the consent of the town council, and that their entrance fees should be paid into the Common Good of the burgh.[1] From this time onwards the Dean of Gild, who had already been doing a great deal of burgh work, became more and more exclusively an official of the burgh.

In Edinburgh he was responsible for the loading of ships, which might have been part of his province as an official of the Gild, which from earliest times had controlled shipping and merchandise (see statutes of the Gild). It was perhaps through his connection with shipping that he also became responsible for the fabric and upkeep of St Giles', for the fees paid for freighting were devoted to this purpose. In any case, his connection with the Church continued long after the Reformation, and the " tokens " which admitted communicants to the Sacrament were stamped on one side with his initials and upon the other with the city arms.[2] After the act of 1469 was passed, the Edinburgh Dean of Gild was elected by the town council like the other office-holders of the burgh.

In the sixteenth century the Edinburgh Dean of Gild presided over the Dean of Gild's Court. This was a judicial body, probably originally formed from the old court of the Gild, the general meeting of the members of the Gild Merchant, but towards the end of the sixteenth century it entirely changed its character. Its members were chosen from members of the town council, of three years' or longer standing, by the retiring Dean of Gild and the old members of the court, and its duties consisted of adjudicating in all cases of " neighbourhood," all disputes relating to buildings and amenities—boundary walls, building encroachments, etc. It dealt with unfreemen usurping the rights of burgesses and Gild brethren, supervised the weights and measures, regulated the freighting of ships, had jurisdiction in all cases affecting ships' captains, merchants and their sureties, etc. It also had the right to tax Gild brethren for the support of decayed brethren and their dependants.[3]

[1] D. Robertson and M. Wood, *Castle and Town*, p. 58.

J. Davidson and A. Gray, *Scottish Staple at Veere*, pp. 28-29, for example of regulations favouring the merchants' monopoly.

[2] R. Miller, *Edinburgh Dean of Gild Court*, pp. 16-20.

[3] *Ibid.* pp. 21-23, 26-28.

The Dean of Gild was an important official in all Scots burghs. In Aberdeen he seems to have been elected by the town council from early in the sixteenth century, and to have become purely a burgh official.[1] In Dundee he freighted ships, tested the weights and measures, and performed other public functions, but also prevented unfreemen from carrying on foreign trade. About 1570 he was for a time elected by the Gild Merchant, which at that time reasserted its powers, but twenty years later he was being chosen by the town council.[2] Parliament, in 1593, ratified the constitution of the Edinburgh Dean of Gild Court and made it the standard for all Dean of Gild Courts throughout Scotland. It was declared to be according to the lovable form of judgement used in all good towns of France and Flanders.[3]

The absorption of much of the Gild machinery by the burghs is not of such striking importance when one remembers that the control of the burghs was, even at the end of the sixteenth century, very largely in the hands of the merchants. Nevertheless, in some towns they also acquired an organization of their own. We have seen that an important act was passed in 1502 ordering that Gild brethren might only be made with consent of the town council, and that their entrance fees were to be paid into the Common Good of the burgh. In 1518, on the supplication of the "haill merchandis and gild brether of this burgh," the Edinburgh town council granted them a Seal of Cause, or charter of incorporation. They were given the right to have a Master of Faculty and other officers, the retiring officials to choose their successors. These officers had the right to punish "extranearis" who trespassed within the bounds of the burgh and tried to infringe the privileges of the burgh or of the Gild brethren. They had the right of holding a court, uplifting fines, and, if need were, of poinding and distraining. The Master of Faculty in office was not to be chosen to fill any office in the town. No one was to be made a burgess or Gild brother without the consent of the master and his councillors.[4] They also were granted an altar in St Giles' for

[1] D. Murray, *Early Burgh Organization*, p. 467.
[2] A. Warden, *Burgh Laws of Dundee*, pp. 103, 113, 115, 130.
[3] *A.P.S.*, James VI, parl. 13, cap. 180.
[4] J. D. Marwick, *Edinburgh Gilds and Crafts*, p. 63.

worship. The new organization of the merchants closely resembled that of the craft gilds which were already springing up.

The merchants of Dundee, three years previously, in 1515, had also secured a Seal of Cause on essentially similar lines. It would seem that the organization to some extent lapsed, for in 1570 a fresh set of rules were drawn up for the Gild Merchant of Dundee. The whole body of merchants and Gild brethren bound themselves and their heirs to defend their privileges against all "novations," and the Dean of Gild was specially entrusted with this duty. He was to be chosen by the merchants, and the whole Gildry bound themselves to obey him. The particular rights and privileges of the merchants were re-enacted, and, to make sure that no unfreeman infringed the monopoly of foreign trade, every Gild brother sailing to Flanders, France, or Danzig was to take a "testification" that he was a freeman of the burgh and a member of the Gild. Once a year all brethren were to convene to be examined as to whether they had associated in any way with unfreemen. The Gild also made itself responsible for the support of its decayed members and contributed towards the maintenance of the ministers of the Church.[1]

PART IV. THE FUNCTIONS OF THE BURGHAL AUTHORITIES

These very outstanding features, which clearly differentiate Scots burghs from English ones, were all the result of developments that had begun during the preceding period. In tracing out the modifications, developments, and adaptations of burghal institutions that took place during the fifteenth and sixteenth centuries, one of the most important points to bear in mind is that not only did older institutions and forms of government persist but that the actual spirit that had produced them still remained, an active and creative force, until the very end of our present period, and was to persist and continue on into the seventeenth century.[2]

The whole plan of civic life of the thirteenth century survived the cataclysm of the Wars of Independence intact. Two

[1] A. Warden, *Burgh Laws of Dundee*, pp. 53, 94, 111-127.

[2] See Section I, Chapter III, Part V.

fourteenth-century questionnaires have survived[1] which the chamberlain—who, it will be remembered, was the court official set over the burghs—was to use in his visits of inspection. Both these questionnaires closely follow the provisions laid down in the *Leges Quatuor Burgorum*. He was to enquire into the due administration of justice according to the procedure laid down in the Laws of the Four Burghs: if the regulations made to ensure that the necessaries of life were sold at fair prices and of proper quality were observed; into the timely payment of the royal revenues; whether the regulations made to secure the well-being of the burgh were properly carried out—the segregation of lepers, the control of disorderly persons, etc.; into the safeguarding of the rights of the burgesses, especially in regard to "stallangers" and outsiders and non-freemen of all kinds; and the due supervision of certain of the crafts—dyers, butchers, leather-workers. The years that followed were to see a considerable modification in regard to the authorities entrusted with carrying out these duties, but the duties themselves remained curiously unchanged.

It is not enough to say that the laws and customs of the burghs, which had been evolved during the period preceding the Wars of Independence, survived far on into the fourteenth, fifteenth, and sixteenth centuries and even beyond into the seventeenth. In certain cases, it is true, one simply finds established customs lasting on with tenacious conservatism—a case of trial by compurgation, for instance, is recorded at Peebles in 1475; the distinctive burgh laws, that inherited land might only be sold in cases of necessity and must be offered to the nearest of kin, were observed in Glasgow, Linlithgow, and Stirling, and possibly other burghs, in the fifteenth and sixteenth centuries. An instance of the observance of the ceremonious procedure enjoined in the Laws of the Four Burghs in the case of a landlord claiming his property on account of the non-payment of rent, with stones and earth formally brought to four successive courts, occurred in Glasgow in 1457.[2] These are instances of

[1] *Articuli Inquirendi* and *Itinere Camerarii*, attributed to the second half of the reign of Robert I.

Itinere Camerarii, attributed to the early fourteenth century. Printed in *A.P.S.* vol. i. See J. D. Marwick, *Edinburgh Gilds and Crafts*, p. 3, for date.

[2] D. Murray, *Early Burgh Organization*, pp. 199, 205, 234-238.

mere survival, and, as a matter of fact, the laws of the burghs were becoming merged in the law of the land.[1] What is far more noteworthy is that the principles underlying the Laws of the Four Burghs remained as living forces, actively developing and influencing the institutions and affairs of the Scots burghs.

Town life, indeed, went on in much the same way. Sanitation was almost as primitive. Folk still bought and sold their goods at the booths in the markets, although " chops " are mentioned fairly often in the sixteenth-century town records of Edinburgh. Fairs were still the occasions of the greatest commercial activity and of general jollity and festivity. In some places, at least, the peace of the fair was proclaimed and the *piepowder court* was held, as laid down in the old burgh laws. The *tron*, or public weigh-house, and the market cross were the centre of the life of the burgh. The market crosses were nearly all of the same pattern, with a gallery, from which proclamations were made, running round a central obelisk. In 1581 the Scots Parliament discussed whether proclamation at the crosses of all the royal burghs was essential for the promulgation of new laws, and enacted that, in future, proclamation at the market cross of Edinburgh should suffice.[2] The actual spirit, moreover, that inspired some of the most pleasing parts of the Laws of the Four Burghs and of the statutes of the Berwick Gild Merchant still lived on among the burgesses. The communal purchasing of goods was still common. So late as 1522–23 the bailies and town council of Edinburgh ordered that any freeman of the burgh should have the right of demanding a share in any bargain made by a fellow-burgess in his presence, if he could make immediate payment for his share of the price. The order made by the Convention of Royal Burghs that if a merchant lost his goods by storm or pillage his more fortunate fellow-travellers should share in the loss, is a later development of the old sharing spirit.[3] As we have seen, when the merchants formed new organizations in the sixteenth century they made

[1] W. Chambers, *Book of Scotland*, p. 68.

[2] G. M. Fraser, *Scottish Hist. Review*, vol. v, p. 177.

A. Warden, *Burgh Laws of Dundee*, p. 19.

[3] Cf. (for Glasgow) D. Murray, *Early Burgh Organization*, pp. 320-321, 327.

J. D. Marwick, *Edinburgh Gilds and Crafts*, p. 66.

themselves responsible for the maintenance of decayed brethren and their dependants, just as did their predecessors, who framed the old statutes of the Merchant Gild of Berwick, and the craft organizations of the fifteenth and sixteenth centuries made themselves responsible for the maintenance of the poor of their craft.

The actual running of the burghs was still carried on in the old way. Even in Edinburgh, until almost the end of our period, watching and warding was done by the burgesses themselves by rota, and in the other burghs the practice was carried on for long afterwards. The expenses of the burgh were shared, and " commoning " lay at the root of all ideas of burgess-ship. To extent, watch and ward and bear all portable charges was considered the plain duty of all those who claimed any share in the rights and privileges of the burghs. In the Laws of the Four Burghs a widow was allowed to continue to buy and sell if she "commoned" with her neighbours but not otherwise; but in practice, as the minutes of the town council of Edinburgh show, exemptions were often granted. After the terrible losses at Flodden, however, no exceptions could be made and the widows all had to supply a substitute to watch and ward in their place or else to find board and lodging for one at least of the town's armed men.[1]

The freedom of the burghs involved public duties and responsibilities as well as economic privileges, just as a freeholder, under the feudal system, meant very much more than someone possessing land. The burgesses were liable to be called up for military service, and it was one of the duties of the burgh authorities to see that they had proper equipment, and to inspect them at the annual wappenschawings. In 1588, for instance, it was ordered that anyone applying to be made a burgess of Edinburgh was to satisfy the town authorities that he had proper armour and accoutrements.[2] The burgesses were also expected, as part of their duties as freemen, to help to maintain the peace of the burgh. It was usual to order all merchants and craftsmen who had booths to keep axes, other

[1] *Leges Quatuor Burgorum*, civ.
D. Robertson and M. Wood, *Castle and Town*, p. 266.
[2] J. D. Marwick, *Edinburgh Gilds and Crafts*, pp. 101, 103, 104, 117, 152, 158.

weapons, and armour there, so that they might be ready to come to the assistance of the provost and bailies at a moment's notice. During the sixteenth century this order was repeated five times in Edinburgh, and it was also in force in Glasgow. The Privy Council, in 1597, complained of a " grite slawness " of the citizens of the burghs, and especially those of Edinburgh, in resorting to their weapons " fer redding and stopping of pairties quhilkes commounlie enteris in sudden tuilzies, quarelling and persute of utheris be way of died, upoun the publickt strietis of the saidis burrowis," and ordered them to support their burgh magistrates better in future.[1]

The powers of the burgh officials remained almost unimpaired right through the fourteenth, fifteenth, and sixteenth centuries and on into the seventeenth. Besides the barbarous punishments of the time, flogging, branding, ducking, etc., they could banish citizens from their burghs and inflict the death penalty.[2] The administration of justice in Edinburgh was carefully organized, in the sixteenth century, between three courts, held by different burgh authorities. The powers of interference in the daily lives of the burgesses possessed and busily exercised by the magistrates and town councils are almost incredible. The authorities of most burghs endeavoured to restrain the women from " flyting." They sought to enforce a rigid observance of Sunday. They assumed an inquisitorial supervision over the morals of the burgesses, and, for any lapses, obliged them to appear as defaulters in the parish kirks. Pages might be filled with examples of " village pump legislation." As became persons with such detailed albeit such strictly local powers, the magistrates of the city were treated with great respect, and citizens who failed in this important point were punished. In Dundee, for instance, a £10 fine was imposed upon persons drawing a whinger or cuffing anyone in the presence of the provost. Burgesses were not to state their cases before the burgh

[1] *Register, Privy Council*, vol. v, p. 403.
D. Murray, *Early Burgh Organization*, p. 329.
J. D. Marwick, *Edinburgh Gilds and Crafts*, pp. 68, 74, 78, 88.

[2] J. Mackintosh, *History of Civilization in Scotland*, vol. ii, pp. 23, 232.
M. Wood, *Transactions of the Old Edinburgh Club*, vol. xvi, p. 8.
D. Murray, *Early Burgh Organization in Scotland*, pp. 202, 282.
For a late example of the endorsement of full burghal powers, see Queen Mary's charter to Jedburgh, *Second Statistical Account*, vol. iii, p. 7.

magistrates till they were called upon, and were to speak becomingly. In Edinburgh there was considerable civic ceremonial. The magistrates were attended by halberdiers when holding their courts, and were ordered to wear "comlie and decent apparell," "whereby they may be discerned from other common burgesses and be mair reverenced by the people subject to their charge." [1]

One of the most important duties in the mediaeval idea of civic organization was the regulation of prices and the supervision of the quality of the necessaries of life of the people. Owing to the almost absolute dependence on local supplies, the whole situation in mediaeval Scotland was radically different to that of the present day. The fact is obvious, and yet, so colourful and robustly vivid are the details of life that have come down to us, that it is not always easy to remember the lurking presence of the fear of sheer starvation that must have been so often present with the picturesque, light-hearted, and violently emotional folk who lived and had their being in this land of ours three hundred years and more ago.

As we have seen, the central authorities were constantly occupied in regulating exports and imports so as to try to prevent dearth, but, with very few exceptions, the town authorities were definitely entrusted with regulation of actual prices and the supervision of the quality of the goods. Among the exceptions may be noted an act of 1535, during the struggle with the craftsmen, when the prices of their work were to be regulated by a commissioner in consultation with the Provost of Edinburgh, and the occasional regulation of the price of wine, salt, timber, and malt. There are, however, many more examples of the delegation of this duty to the town authorities. In 1551, for instance, the Lords of the Council especially ordered the Provost of Edinburgh to deal with maltsters,

[1] *Extracts from the Burgh Records of Edinburgh*, 1589–1603, pp. 39, 44, 47, 378.

J. Mackintosh, *History of Civilization in Scotland*, vol. ii, pp. 233-235, 247-249, 252-253.

J. W. Buchan, *Peebles*, vol. ii, pp. 75, 170, 173, 176.

A. Warden, *Burgh Laws of Dundee*, pp. 18, 19, 25, 38, 41.

R. Chambers, *Domestic Annals of Scotland*, vol. i, pp. 330-331.

G. Hay, *Story of Arbroath*, pp. 110, 112, 119, 130, 131.

Article by D. Robertson, *Edinburgh, 1329–1929*, p. 105.

bakers, and regraters. This system continued right on into the seventeenth century, and in this respect the development of Scotland was very much slower than that of England. Ashley points out that in England, by the sixteenth century, price-fixing had become vested in the central Government, and he cites it as a sign of the growth of centralized nationalism in that country.[1]

Throughout our period the control of the prices and quality of the essentials of life continued to be one of the main concerns of every one of the Scots burghs. In many burghs so late as the sixteenth century the old " assize of bread " still continued to function, and fish-pricers and ale-tasters did their work, as ordained in the Laws of the Four Burghs and the questionnaire of the chamberlain. They were not merely the survival of empty forms, for the actual price-fixing of grain, meal, and malt was carefully performed in the seventeenth century. Surviving records show that Edinburgh, Dundee, Glasgow, Stirling, Peebles, Aberdeen, and other burghs supervised the quality of the meat and other foodstuffs.[2] It must not be forgotten that it was partly in the performance of the public duty of regulating the prices and qualities of the necessaries of life that the burgh authorities came into collision with the craftsmen.

Not only the fixing of prices but the methods of sale were carefully regulated. Forestalling and regrating—in other words, buying up goods under advantageous conditions in order to sell them at an undue profit—were two most heinous mediaeval crimes. Five acts of parliament, the last one so late as 1592, were passed condemning such practices, and the Privy Council also inveighed against them. In 1436, when the fines inflicted

[1] *A.P.S.* vol. ii, pp. 36, 291, 349, 373, 451, 483. The wine-pricing policy of the Government appears most clearly in *Register, Privy Council*, vol. vi. On p. 291 it rather amusingly admits complete failure.

J. Mackintosh, *History of Civilization in Scotland*, vol. ii, p. 292.

W. Dickie, " Scottish Burghal Life in the 16th and 17th Centuries," *Transactions of the Dumfriesshire and Galloway Scientific Society*, vol. 17-18, p. 97.

W. Ashley, *Economic History of England*, vol. ii, p. 47.

[2] *Extracts from the Burgh Records of Edinburgh*, 1589–1603, cf. pp. 380-384.

D. Murray, *Early Burgh Organization*, pp. 199, 264, 314-315, 317.

A. Warden, *Burgh Laws of Dundee*, pp. 12, 30, 45, 337.

E. Bain, *Merchant and Craft Gilds*, p. 235.

upon regraters and forestallers happen to appear under a separate heading in the chamberlain's account, they amounted to £342 9s. The prevention and punishment of these crimes, however, mainly devolved upon the authorities of the burghs.[1] In Edinburgh, in 1495, twenty-two men were convicted of buying and regrating French flour, and it was one of the crimes most often punished by banishment in that burgh ; and, to turn to one of the lesser burghs, a merchant of Dumfries was tried and had his whole cargo of wine confiscated.[2]

In times of dearth or passing scarcity the burgh authorities were expected to take special action to deal with the situation. Edinburgh possessed special regulations during the famines of the sixteenth century, and incurred expenses in preventing the export of corn contrary to the orders of the Privy Council. In 1598 there is a circumstantial account of how Dumfries was "hardlie handillit fer want of necessar sustentation," and how the magistrates sent out into the country to buy cattle and have them brought to the town.[3]

The town authorities, of course, fulfilled many other public duties: the care of harbours, bridges, tolbooths, etc.; the proper regulation of markets; the maintenance of the means of defence of the burgh; regulations to prevent the infection by plague—a terrible menace in the sixteenth century. Among such duties was the care of the Common Good, a charge in which they by no means distinguished themselves.

The Common Good of the burghs consisted of fishings, mills, rights to levy tolls, etc., and, above all, of considerable portions of land. The revenue derived from these sources of

[1] *A.P.S.* vol. ii, pp. 347, 376, 488 ; vol. iii, pp. 452, 577.

Exchequer Rolls, vol. iv, p. xcvi.

Register, Privy Council, vol. i, pp. 115, 129, 140, 141-142. Similar regulations appear in following volume.

[2] For the Edinburgh example I am indebted to Dr Marguerite Wood, City Archivist.

W. Dickie, "Scottish Burghal Life in the 16th and 17th Centuries," *Transactions of Dumfries and Galloway Scientific Society*, vol. 17-18, p. 97.

A. Warden, *Burgh Laws of Dundee*, pp. 16, 51.

G. Hay, *Story of Arbroath*, pp. 112, 119, 130.

[3] *Extracts from the Burgh Records of Edinburgh*, 1589–1603, pp. xxi, 341.

Register, Privy Council, vol. v, p. 505.

income was spent in defraying the expenses of the burgh, but the land, whether it was divided among the citizens or let out to them in pieces, was also an important source of livelihood to many of them. One of the chamberlain's duties, in his annual visitations to the burghs, was to inquire into the proper administration of the Common Good, but it would seem that, as his powers declined, there was increasing maladministration. Two acts of parliament were passed at the very end of the fifteenth century that show that all was not well with the burghs. By an act of 1487 the election of the officers was to be "of the best and worthiest indwelleris of the toun, and nocht be parcialite nor masterschip quhilk is vndoing of the burrowis." Four years later, another act ordered that the Common Good of the burgh was to be kept for the common good of the citizens and spent in common and necessary things by the advice of the deacons of the crafts, and that it was not to be let on leases of more than three years. Inquisition into the matter was to be made yearly at the chamberlain's ayre—but this last provision can only have been a worn-out remedy.[1] So far, however, it was only possible for the burgh authorities to misuse the yearly revenue of the Common Good, for it was customary for burgh property to be let upon leases and never for more than five years.[2]

Unluckily, however, a new development took place. The introduction of feuing has already been described. The king was encouraged to feu his lands, and the nobles and freeholders were permitted to do so; and although the lands of the burghs were not included in this permission, they, unfortunately for themselves, managed to introduce what was to prove "an ill-omened system" (*Report of Commissioners on Burgh Reform*). In 1508, Edinburgh obtained a royal licence to feu her lands; Aberdeen and a few other burghs followed suit, but most of the burghs simply assumed that the former restraints of the law were relaxed, and that they possessed a

[1] For list of Common Good of Edinburgh, see M. Wood, Preface, *Extracts from Burgh Records of Edinburgh*, 1589–1603, p. xviii.

Th. Keith, "Municipal Elections in the Royal Burghs of Scotland," *Scottish Hist. Review*, vol. xiii, p. 113.

A.P.S. vol. ii, p. 227.

[2] *Report of Commission on Municipal Corporations in Scotland, 1819*, vol. i, p. 13.

general right to alienate.[1] The dilapidations that followed were both widespread and serious. They are the constant subject of complaint by the craftsmen, and by the burgesses in general, throughout the rest of the century.[2]

The peculiar methods of electing the burgh councils encouraged the government of the towns by a clique, and the facilities for alienating the town lands proved only too strong an incentive to dishonest persons to try to obtain control. Oliver Maxtoun managed to become Provost of Perth, and then declared " planelie he suld have his handis full of our commoun gudis." Fifty years later the treasurers of the same burgh were found to have distributed the Common Good to their own particular advancement.[3]

Against such forces the safeguards that were introduced from time to time were ineffective. By the act of 1491 some control was given to the chamberlain, whose powers were decaying, and to the deacons of the crafts. The craftsmen thus were given a definite voice in the disposal of the Common Good of their burgh, and from time to time, during the sixteenth century, instances are recorded where they tried to assert their powers. Sometimes they appealed to the central authority and were able to obtain some redress, but, left to themselves, they were not strong enough to do anything.[4]

In 1535 an act was passed stating that the burghs were becoming " waistit and destroyit in thair gudis and polecy and almaist Ruynous." This was attributed partly to the decay of trade, but also because outland men were becoming provosts and bailies " for thair awine wele in consuming of the commoun gudis of the burrowis." As a remedy, only merchants and burgesses were to be elected in future : the account books of

[1] *Report of Commission on Municipal Corporations in Scotland, 1819*, vol. i, pp. 13, 22, 23.
A.P.S. vol. ii, p. 253.

[2] *Register, Privy Council*, vol. vi, pp. 43 (St. Andrews), 494 (Renfrew), 532 (Perth).
D. Murray, *Early Burgh Organization*, pp. 276, 277, 278-279.
J. D. Marwick, *Edinburgh Gilds and Crafts*, p. 110.
E. Bain, *Merchants and Craft Gilds*, p. 66.

[3] *Proceedings, Lords of the Council*, vol. ii, quoted by Th. Keith, *Scottish Hist. Review*, vol. xiii, p. 114.
Register, Privy Council, vol. ii, p. 784.

[4] *A.P.S.* vol. ii, p. 227.

the burghs were to be submitted to the Lords of the Exchequer annually, to see that the Common Good of the town was spent upon the common weal: the authorities of the burghs were to give notice fifteen days before submitting the books, so that anyone might inspect them. By a second act, earls, lords, barons, and other men were prohibited from interfering with the freedom of the burgesses. It will be noticed that the Lords of the Exchequer are in this act substituted for the chamberlain as the supervising power over the burghs. So far as the letter of the law was concerned, the provision that the books were to be submitted was actually carried out. It was, however, an ineffectual one. Only the account books and not the rentals had to be submitted, so that it would be difficult to found a charge against the magistrates. Citizens who did inspect the books and wished to complain would have had to do so at their own charge, and no inducements or facilities were offered. As a matter of fact, no record survives of the Lords of the Exchequer taking action against any burgh. The order against the interference of the nobility and gentry was a dead letter, and the dilapidation continued.[1]

Towards the end of the century the Convention of Royal Burghs took a good deal of action in trying to check the abuse of the dilapidation of the Common Good of the burghs. In 1589, for instance, it passed a regulation that all the common property of the burghs, land, fishings, customs, etc., was to be rouped to the best avail, and that the representatives of every burgh were to report their diligence under this order. Not only was this order repeated and reports upon their Common Good required from all the royal burghs, but action was taken against certain defaulters.[2] The Convention, therefore, in some sort assumed the supervision that had been exercised at an earlier period by the chamberlain. It is impossible to say how much worse things might have been had the Convention not taken action. As it was, they were very bad. There are many examples of the grossest misuse of the Common Good. In 1551,

[1] *Report of Commission on Municipal Corporations in Scotland, 1836*, p. 23.
A.P.S. vol. ii, p. 349.
Th. Keith, "Municipal Elections in the Royal Burghs of Scotland," *Scottish Hist. Review*, vol. xiii, p. 114.

[2] Th. Pagan, *Convention of Royal Burghs*, pp. 107-109.

Aberdeen alienated her fishings, which in 1830 were worth £10,000, for an annual feu-duty of £27 7s. 8d.; in 1581, Banff got permission to feu the burgh land to the burgesses, but the whole of it passed into the hands of the noble families of Findlater, Fife, and Banff. Ayr had been regranted the whole of the parish of Ayr in 1507, and feued nearly the whole of it.[1]

About 1581 the magistrates of the burghs began to receive private acts authorizing them to levy tolls and customs for revenue, which seems to show that the income derived from the Common Good was no longer sufficient for the needs of the burghs. In that year an act was passed requiring the burghs to secure the consent of the Estates before they disposed of their possessions.[2]

The burghs, however, were now encountering a more insidious danger, in the extreme need of the Crown for money. It would appear that James VI had adopted the practice of selling commissions to persons which would enable them to get possession of burghal property. A rather ambiguous act of 1593 annuls and forbids the alienations made " under pretext of certaine commissionis purchest fra his hienes, with decreettis, sentencis and ordinances interponit thairto." [3]

Yet another set of activities fulfilled by the burgh authorities was the maintenance of the special privileges of the burgesses, both merchants and craftsmen. The monopolies enjoyed by the merchants have been indicated. The craftsmen burgesses also had their special rights. They alone, as freemen burgesses, might carry on their particular crafts, not only within the burgh of which they were members, but throughout the wide areas which, under the peculiar Scots system, were allotted to each of the royal burghs. Where their interests were so deeply concerned it is not wonderful to find that the authorities in all the burghs were most energetic in passing ordinances and trying to enforce them. These ordinances were sometimes directed against persons living outside the burgh, whether they were nominally burgesses or Gild brethren or not, because " they did not reside within the burgh, and did not scot, lot, extent, walk, or ward, nor yet bear portable charges within the

[1] Cf. *Register, Privy Council*, vol. ii, pp. 627-629, 556-557, 54-60, 279, etc.

[2] *Report of Commission on Municipal Corporations in Scotland, 1836*, pp. 30-31.

[3] *Ibid.* p. 24.

burgh as they ought to do, and as others, neighbours and freemen of the burgh, did." Nor were such orders an empty formality. In 1557 a burgess was deprived of his liberty for refusing to live in Edinburgh. The persons complained of were sometimes actual burgesses of the towns and sometimes wandering individuals that "passis throu the cuntre, foirstallis skyn, hyde, and other merchandice, and trafectis in selling, bying and saling, nocht withstanding the quhilks thai eschap fra and can nocht be appredit nor caussit to pay nor do the samyn be ressoun thai haif nother stob nor staik as said is. . . ." [1]

The Edinburgh town council was also much concerned to prevent non-freemen within the burgh or non-merchants from usurping the merchants' privileges. Constant orders were made forbidding them from doing so; the shops belonging to non-freemen were to be forcibly closed; apothecaries were specially forbidden to sell spices, and the wine-selling monopoly of the merchants was the subject of several special regulations. There were special orders forbidding merchants from "colouring" non-freemen's goods, and one of them was deprived of his burgess-ship because he had bought and sold with strangers. The Dean of Gild, who was specially responsible for the enforcement of these regulations, was constantly urged to greater diligence. In 1559 his court was ordered to meet twice weekly, especially in order to deal with the matter, and a scale of fines was laid down at another time. Other burghs, such as Dundee, Perth, Lanark, Aberdeen, Elgin, and Irvine, maintained the same attitude as Edinburgh, and the Convention of the Royal Burghs, the body representing the whole of the royal burghs of Scotland, was indefatigable in making regulations against infringement of any kind upon the burghal privileges and in urging individual burghs to greater diligence. The representatives of the burghs had constantly to report to the Convention how far they were observing the regulations.[2] The Convention was able to secure

[1] J. D. Marwick, *Edinburgh Gilds and Crafts*, p. 63. See also pp. 67, 73, 81, 87, 90, 94, 102, 116.

[2] J. D. Marwick, *Edinburgh Gilds and Crafts*, pp. 67, 87, 93, 94, 95, 151, 59, 60, 62, 91, 145.

A. Warden, *Burgh Laws of Dundee*, pp. 14, 27, 32, 40, 46.

Th. Pagan, *Convention of Royal Burghs*, p. 129.

J. D. Marwick, *Edinburgh Gilds and Crafts*, p. 123.

Such constantly reiterated regulations show that they were much in need the support of the central authority, both in the form of general acts confirming the burghs' privileges and in special action against individual defaulters.

The activities of the burghs in guarding their monopolies were, in fact, a part of the peculiar national system of recognized privileges granted in return for special services or payments. This is especially marked in the case of the merchants' sole right to carry on foreign trade. An act of parliament of 1457 ordered that anyone sailing in merchandise must be a freeman of the royal burgh, and this enactment was ratified over and over again throughout the rest of the fifteenth century and throughout the sixteenth.[1] In 1535 three acts were passed, making more stringent provisions to prevent non-free merchants from trading. The trade with the Low Countries, passing as it did through the staple port, could easily be regulated; and the conservator, an official in charge of the interests of the Scots merchants and answerable both to the Crown and to the Convention of Royal Burghs, was ordered to take careful precautions that only merchant burgesses of royal burghs came there to trade. Every merchant who came to the port was obliged to show him a written ticket from the Dean of Gild of his own burgh to show that he had the right to engage in foreign trade, and this had to be renewed every voyage; and the conservator, on his part, had to send each of the burghs a list of the merchants who had traded from them, so as to insure that there should be no leakage.[2]

The only staple port was in the Netherlands; in the case of traffic with other countries precautions could only be taken at the ports of embarkation. They were, however, very thorough. The coquet, or official notification that customs had been paid, might only be granted to freemen and to ships sailing from a free port, and the Dean of Gild, who was in charge of the freighting of ships, was ordered to see that no one except properly qualified persons sailed.[3]

of improvement. The records of Edinburgh abound with cases where they were ignored, even by those responsible for enforcing them, and specially heavy dues collected from the non-freemen.

[1] *A.P.S.* vol. ii, pp. 49, 348.

[2] The Convention of Royal Burghs passed acts enforcing these laws in 1555, 1578, 1579, 1591, 1593, 1594, 1595.

[3] A. Warden, *Burgh Laws of Dundee*, p. 115.

I am indebted to Dr Marguerite Wood for seeing a copy of the minute

It is not surprising that the burgh councils, which mainly consisted of merchants, should have been energetic in enforcing the rights of their own particular class. To do them justice, they also seem to have done their best to protect the rightful claims of the craftsmen, even when the two classes of burgesses were most at loggerheads over their respective shares in the government of the burgh. In 1559, at a time of great stress between the Edinburgh merchants and craftsmen, the town council ordered the Dean of Gild to show greater activity in preventing unfreemen from usurping the privileges of merchants and craftsmen, and the deacons of crafts were ordered to furnish him with a list of persons wrongfully occupying crafts, so that he might proceed against them. This order was repeated in the following year. In 1558 the town council made two decrees, one protecting the skinners and the other the bonnet-makers from unfreemen who sold "made work" in the High Street on non-market days, and similar instances abound both in the records of Edinburgh and of the other burghs.[1]

Such was the work of the busy office-bearers and town councils. It is rather amusing to find a good deal of evidence that their regulations, like most others that were made in contemporary Scotland, were often successfully evaded. The mere reiteration of the orders gives a strong suggestion that this was so, but it is almost ludicrous to find the town council of Edinburgh, in 1555, in the middle of its absolute prohibitions against non-free traders, tamely ordering that all ships lading for France or Flanders were to give the preference to freemen's goods.[2]

In spite of their theoretically sweeping powers, the burghal authorities were not able to maintain very good order in their burghs. An act of parliament of 1491 forbids leagues or bands to be made within the burghs, and also convocations and risings of the commons for hindering of the common law, under pain of confiscation and death; and that no man "Ride na Rout in fere of were" except with the lawful authorities. Burgesses

instructions regarding the lading of ships contained in the Burgh Council Records of Edinburgh.

[1] J. D. Marwick, *Edinburgh Gilds and Crafts*, pp. 91, 93, 89, 97, 115. A. Warden, *Burgh Laws of Dundee*, p. 385.

[2] I am indebted to Dr. Marguerite Wood for this information.

were ordered to live neighbourly and to support their officers in serving the king and enacting justice. The burgesses, however, were often very far from living neighbourly. A similar act was passed in 1503, followed by many others, and the records of all the burghs contain many details of tumults and tuilzies within the burghs. Thus in Edinburgh in 1583 there is a circumstantial account of how certain craftsmen and other wicked persons, under silence of night, convened themselves together in arms and, in a most treasonable, barbarous, and shameful manner, broke into the house of one of the bailies by means of forehammers, and with awful countenances and boasting words forced him to liberate a malefactor who was imprisoned in the Tolbooth. There was serious and frequent trouble in St Andrews, Aberdeen, Pittenweem, Perth, and many of the other burghs, and it was by no means confined to those of large size. In 1593 the little town of Cupar in Fife was said to be "accustumat" to "raging tumults, and to be full of disorderly persons who were never punished." The sheriff was ordered to interfere.[1]

In reading the old records, one is sometimes tempted to think that it was often lack of power rather than a merciful disposition that inclined the burgh authorities so often to make compromises or cry quits with individual offenders. Nevertheless, it is clear that, on the whole, they generally dealt tolerantly and humanely with merchants, craftsmen, and even unfreemen who transgressed their manifold rules.

Moreover, the burghs were subject to considerable regulation from outside bodies. The Convention of Royal Burghs, which represented the whole of the burghs, interfered constantly in the affairs of individual ones, had the power of fining them, and generally managed to make itself obeyed. The burghs were also subject to the orders of the Crown and of its instrument the Privy Council. As a rule, in Scots history, the executive powers

[1] *A.P.S.* vol. ii, p. 227.

Register, Privy Council, vol. ii, pp. 703-704, 731; vol. iii, p. 567; vol. v, pp. 16, 61-68, 56-57, 107, 224-225, 487-489; vol. vi, pp. 749-750.

R. Chambers, *Domestic Annals of Scotland*, pp. 89-90, quotes examples from Glasgow.

G. Hay, *Story of Arbroath*, p. 122, for many cases of "strublens" in that burgh.

of the central authority were so weak that it is difficult to realize how absolute they were in theory. In its dealings with the burghs, however, it carried its prerogative to very great lengths. It was able to dictate to Edinburgh with regard to the election of the provost. In 1519–20 the Regent Albany forbade the burgesses to elect either a Hamilton or a Douglas, and, much later on, in 1582, James VI sent directions to Edinburgh regarding the councillors whom he wished chosen; and when the burgesses ventured to object, he nominated the provost as well. James VI, moreover, on another more historic occasion was able to bring the " good town " to heel.

Sometimes the higher authority was exerted to prevent the town authorities from abusing their powers. In 1561 the baker craft of Dundee appealed to the Court of Session that the magistrates were fixing the price of bread regardless of the fluctuations in the cost of wheat, and a royal decree sternly ordered the magistrates of the town to compear before the royal presence. The Privy Council records abound with examples of such jurisdiction. The case of Cupar has been noticed already. Much about the same time Lanark was called upon to account for appropriations made from its Common Good. And within a few years the Privy Council was ordered to deal with Inverkeithing, Renfrew, Ayr, Forres, Haddington, and Perth. The Crown sometimes abused its powers. The Provost of Jedburgh is a case in point. In 1565 the town council of this burgh appealed to the Privy Council not to be obliged to choose Sir Nicholas Rutherford as provost, because there was " bluid " between him and them. It appears that Rutherford's ancestors had been provosts of Jedburgh for some generations, and that he himself had bought an order from Queen Mary commanding the town council to make him provost. In 1599 the burgh magistrates of Montrose were warded for disobeying a royal order and refusing to " elect " the Earl of Mar as their provost. Many other instances of royal interference occurred.[1]

[1] R. K. Hannay, *Old Edinburgh Club*, vol. ix, p. 152.
Th. Keith, *Scottish Hist. Review*, vol. xiii, p. 117.
A. Warden, *Burgh Laws of Dundee*, p. 337.
Register, Privy Council, vol. ii, pp. 15, 19, 59, 305, 472, 556, 734; vol. iii, pp. 36-37, 765; vol. vi, pp. 34, 39.

PART V. THE CRAFTSMEN

The description of the constitution of the burghs leads inevitably to that of the merchants and their privileges. It is now time to consider the merchants' relationships with the craftsmen and the political status of the latter. On the whole, the attitude of the Government was more favourable to the merchants than to the craftsmen. As we have seen, the merchants received royal endorsement of their privileges, and they were recognized and consulted. On the other hand, the craftsmen's organizations were frequently denounced, and they had no recognized channels for communicating their particular views to the central authority. It must, however, be remembered that in the stage of economic development in which Scotland remained throughout our period—in which the export of raw materials was the basis of her commerce, when she was very largely dependent on the importation of manufactured commodities, and when crafts were of comparatively little account—the merchants were really far more valuable citizens. It is surely not far-fetched to trace, in the organization of the towns, the working of the same theory that preserved feudalism in the country—the idea that service and privileges ought to be correlated.

Compared to the craftsmen, from first to last the merchants were rather aristocratic folk. In the statutes of the Berwick Gild each brother was obliged to keep a good horse, and craftsmen who became merchants were ordered to give up their trades. The prohibition against craftsmen entering the Gild Merchant, unless they renounced their crafts, was repeated in an act of parliament in the fifteenth century, and regulations to the same effect were made in the different burghs.[1] To some extent this was merely snobbish. The following example is by no means unique. In 1587, Robert Vernour, skinner, having

[1] *A.P.S.* vol. ii, p. 86.

D. Murray, *Early Burgh Organization*, p. 344. Cf. Aberdeen, 1498; Stirling, 1697.

See also Chapter III. of the present book.

G. Gross, *Gild Merchant*, p. 213.

been admitted a Gild brother, became bound: "to observe and keep the laws and consuetudes of burgh concerning the Gild brether thereof, and to desist and cease from all trade and occupation in his own person that is not comely and decent for the rank and honesty of a Gild brother; and that his wife and servants shall use and exercise no point of common cookery outwith his own home, and, namely, that they shall not sell nor carry meat dishes or courses through the town to private chambers, hostilare houses, or any other parts outwith his own house under whatsoever colour or pretence, nor pass to bridals nor banquets within or without this burgh to the occupation of common cookery, or yet to be seen in the streets with their aprons and serviettes as common cooks and their servants uses to do," under pain of losing the freedom of the city and of the Gild brotherhood for ever.[1] By act of parliament no one was to use merchandise abroad unless he had at least half a last of goods.[2]

The advantages, however, did not lie entirely on the side of the merchants. So heavy were their extra burdens that, so far from being exclusive, they were generally very anxious to induce other people to share both their rights and their burdens. In 1500 the Edinburgh town council ordered that the burgh should be searched for people who might be obliged to become burgesses or Gild brethren; and in 1560 two ordinances were made again ordering a search, so that all unfree men using staple wares be made to become burgesses and Gild brethren, and that their booths were to be closed until they did so.[3] There are cases where burgesses tried to pass as craftsmen instead of merchants, so as to escape the heavy dues. In 1579 a Gild brother even appeared before the town council of Edinburgh and announced that he wished to renounce his burgess-ship because he was "sa extraordinarly extented in all extentis bygane, and in speciall in this last extent maid to the kingis entry . . . as he culd nocht sustene the samyn," and asked that he should be excused from all portable charges

[1] J. D. Marwick, *Edinburgh Gilds and Crafts*, p. 151. See also p. 103 for an exactly similar case.

[2] *A.P.S.* vol. ii, pp. 86-87.

[3] J. D. Marwick, *Edinburgh Gilds and Crafts*, p. 95; for another example, p. 135.

in the future. The council, however, " altogether and halely disasented " from his request.[1]

Probably the separate status of the merchants was much more marked in those larger towns where their especial monopoly of foreign trade would naturally come into greater prominence. There are certainly instances, in the smaller towns, of craftsmen attaining to the highest rank; in 1330 one of the two prepositi of Linlithgow was a dyer, and, ten years later, the prepositus of Banff belonged to the same trade. Haddington, in 1575, had a craftsman provost, and he and the deacons outvoted the other members of the council. In Banff, in 1600, the magistrates of the town were said to be all poor men, fishers and poor craftsmen. Some small burghs, however, such as Brechin, had no craft organization—at least, until the seventeenth century.[2]

The craftsmen, however, did not acquiesce in the favoured position of the merchants, and a bitter struggle was fought out in the sixteenth and seventeenth centuries in practically every burgh in Scotland.

It is not easy to find information that gives the relative numbers of the merchants and the craftsmen. It is, however, evident that the merchants were a comparatively small body of men, and that the craftsmen were not very large sections of the community. The social organisation of Scotland of the fifteenth and sixteenth centuries was unlike that of the present day and did not consist of a small number of capitalists and a huge industrial population. In 1558, for instance, during a threatened invasion by the English, the merchants of Edinburgh undertook to provide 736 suitably armed men, and the craftsmen 717.[3] In 1604, in Glasgow the relative numbers of the merchants and craftsmen were 213 merchants and 361 craftsmen.[4]

The craftsmen formed, indeed, very small bodies of men. When the burgesses of Edinburgh in 1558 made their

[1] J. D. Marwick, *Edinburgh Gilds and Crafts*, p. 118.
[2] *Exchequer Rolls*, vol. i, pp. 273, 457.
D. Murray, *Early Burgh Organization*, p. 351.
Register, *Privy Council*, vol. vi, pp. 125, 391.
[3] J. D. Marwick, *Edinburgh Gilds and Crafts*, p. 90.
[4] D. Murray, *Early Burgh Organization*, p. 484.

offer of military service the crafts offered the following quota of men:

Tailors . . .	178 men	81 masters	21 servants	25 servants in merchants' houses
Hammermen .	151 ,,	66 ,,	85 ,,	..
Baxters . .	100 ,,	45 ,,	55 ,,	..
Skinners . .	63 ,,	42 ,,	21 ,,	..
Bonnetmakers .	53 ,,	14 ,,	39 ,,	..
Cordiners . .	49 ,,	..	24 servants within the town	
Waulkers . .	43 ,,	..	19 servants outwith the West Port	
Websters . .	26 ,,	13 masters	13 servants	..
Barbers . .	25 ,,	..	..	..
Goldsmiths . .	20 ,,	14 masters	6 servants	..
Furriers . .	9 ,,	..	..	..

In Glasgow, in 1604, the numbers of craftsmen were as follows:

Tailors . .	65	Bakers . .	27	Masons . .	11
Malsters . .	55	Coopers .	23	Bonnet-makers .	7
Cordiners . .	50	Skinners .	21	Dyers . . .	5
Weavers . .	30	Wrights. .	21	Surgeons . .	2
Hammermen .	27	Fleshers .	17		

In Dundee the membership of the Bakers' Gild, a very active one, varied between 52 and 60 in the sixteenth century, while the skinners, in 1516, numbered 34.[1]

The relative wealth of the crafts varied. In 1573–74 it was found that some of the Edinburgh crafts were so much decayed that they could not pay their old quota of taxation and a new roll was drawn up. For every £100 levied on the Edinburgh crafts—one-fifth of the whole extent—the different crafts were to pay a given proportion. Another similar roll for 1576 has also been published.[2]

These figures give an interesting indication of the industrial state of Scotland. The comparatively small number of the

[1] J. D. Marwick, *Edinburgh Gilds and Crafts*, p. 90.
D. Murray, *Early Burgh Organization*, p. 484.
A. Warden, *Burgh Laws of Dundee*, pp. 381, 408.
[2] J. D. Marwick, *Edinburgh Gilds and Crafts*, p. 109.
L. Smith, *Edinburgh Hammermen*, p. xci.

weavers and waulkers—the manufacturers of Scotland's one manufactured export—as well as their poverty, is significant. The comparative poverty of the goldsmiths, whom one would expect to find among the most wealthy of the crafts, is also an indication of the lack of capital in the burghs. In Glasgow, which at that time largely exported herrings, the coopers are only seventh in point of numbers. Taking the lists as a whole, it is striking to find how predominant are the crafts that ministered to the immediate needs of the citizens—tailors, bakers, fleshers, barbers, etc.

	Old Stent, Undated.	1574 Stent.	1576 Stent.
Skinners and furriers . .	£18 0 0	£20 1 6	£22 18 0
Bakers	17 12 6	13 0 4	13 3 0
Tailors	14 5 4	18 1 6	18 18 0
Hammermen	13 5 6	13 5 6	13 5 6
Fleshers	13 2 4	9 0 0	9 0 0
Wrights and masons . .	7 2 9	8 3 4	8 3 4
Cordiners	6 13 4	6 13 4	6 13 4
Goldsmiths	4 11 3	6 0 0	6 0 0
Barbers	3 1 3	3 1 3	3 15 0
Weavers, waulkers, bonnet-makers	2 13 4	2 13 4	0 4 4

On the other hand, the differentiation that existed among the crafts shows that the economic organization of the burghs was considerably more advanced than that of the countryside. A list of craftsmen mentioned in documents dating before 1400 has been compiled, and it includes: barbers, bakers, bowmakers, caldroners, carters, chapmen, coalmen, cooks, coopers, farriers, fishermen, fleshers, flesh-hewers, furbishers, girdlers, goldsmiths, hatters, locksmiths, masons, millers, napers, painters, porters, saddlers, skinners, shearers, souters, waulkers, wrights.[1] Such specialization must have been mainly confined to the burghs, for in country districts, until very much later, there was a great deal of homework and folk were largely their own craftsmen. (No doubt the curious system of burgh monopolies over the rural areas was largely responsible for the backwardness of the country.) On the other hand, although

[1] W. A. Craigie, "Earliest Rocords of the Scots Tongue," *Scottish Hist. Review*, vol. xxii, p. 60.

the presence of the merchants as a separate class postulates a state of society that has developed considerably, since in more primitive times the craftsman would do his own merchanting, in Scotland the differentiation between merchants and craftsmen arose from other causes. The merchants were mainly concerned in the export and import of goods to and from foreign countries, and the craftsmen did their own selling—their booths and market stances are frequently mentioned in the burgh records.

It is not surprising that, in the association-loving Middle Ages, fellow-craftworkers should have banded themselves together. Nothing is known about the commencement of the movement, but by the fifteenth century craft organizations were in existence in Scotland. The laws relating to them and their deacons prove this. In Edinburgh, at least, they had secured recognition from the burgh. Between 1456 and the end of the fifteenth century the bakers, hatmakers, masons and wrights, websters, hammermen, coopers, and fleshers had obtained Seals of Cause, i.e. charters of incorporation from the magistrates and town council. Between 1500 and 1533 the waulkers and shearers, tailors, surgeons and barbers, cordiners, candlemakers, bonnetmakers, and skinners and furriers had followed suit.[1] In Glasgow nine of the crafts were incorporated between the beginning of the sixteenth century and the Reformation, and five more after it.[2] In Aberdeen two deacons of the weavers were sworn in, in 1444. Seals of Cause were obtained in other burghs, but the number of the " incorporated trades " varied very much from town to town and also the seniority of the crafts among themselves. In Edinburgh there were by the end of the sixteenth century fourteen main crafts, with certain minor ones associated with them ; in Glasgow there were also fourteen ; in Aberdeen, seven incorporated crafts and three separate societies ; in Stirling, seven crafts and three tolerated communities ; in Perth eight, in Dundee nine, in Arbroath eight.[3]

[1] J. D. Marwick, *Edinburgh Gilds and Crafts*, pp. 43, 47, 50, 51, 53, 56, 59, 61, 62, 68, 70.

[2] D. Murray, *Early Burgh Organization*, pp. 361-363.
E. Bain, *Merchant and Craft Gilds*, p. 292.

[3] E. Bain, *Merchant and Craft Gilds*, p. 27.
G. Hay, *Story of Arbroath*, p. 284.

It is often suggested that the Scots craft gilds originated as religious associations. But we know too little to say definitely, and, by the time that they first come within our ken, they had already developed many lines of activity. The religious side, however, was very strongly stressed. Their funds were primarily devoted to the upkeep of their particular altar ; they held services for their dead fellow-craftsmen ; the representations that they performed at the great festivals of the Church are a bright and charming feature in the old records. Aberdeen, for instance, in 1531, revived its older customs and ordered that on the festivals of Candlemas and Corpus Christi the craftsmen of the burgh were to join in the processions, each man in his best array, and " every craft with their own banner, with the arms of the craft thereon, and they shall pass each craft by themselves, two by two. . . ." The crafts were also to produce pageants: the fleshers were to produce St Bastian and his tormentors; the barbers, St Lawrence and his tormentors ; the skinners, St Stephen and his tormentors ; the shoemakers, St Martin ; the tailors, the coronation of Our Lady; the litsters, St Nicholas ; the weavers, waulkers, and bonnetmakers, St John; the bakers, St George; and the hammermen, the Resurrection and the Cross.[1] With the Reformation the crafts still took their part in the maintenance of the Church. This had now become a civic responsibility within the burghs, and the crafts contributed their share of the expenses. In Edinburgh, in 1570, they contributed £75, the sums given by the individual crafts varying from under a pound to £16 or £20.[2] They also bore their part in the wappenschaws, almost the last vestige of pageantry left to the burghs; and, as the support of the poor became an increasing burden during the sixteenth century, the craft gilds of all the burghs accepted responsibility for those of their own members who were unable to support themselves or their dependants.[3]

[1] D. Murray, *Early Burgh Organization*, p. 368, and ch. xvii; *Burgh Records of Aberdeen*, vol. i, p. 449.

[2] J. D. Marwick, *Edinburgh Gilds and Crafts*, p. 107.

[3] A. Warden, *Burgh Laws of Dundee*, p. 249. In 1603 the Nine Incorporated Trades of Dundee arranged for the support of their poor.

A leaflet published by the Trades House of Glasgow upon the occasion of the visit of the British Association, 1925.

E. Bain, *Merchant and Craft Gilds*, p. 31.

It was, however, those activities of the gilds that were directly connected with their crafts that became increasingly the most important side of their work, and it is these which mainly concern us. The activities of the crafts may be classified under two very general headings: those which were primarily intended to benefit themselves, and those which fitted into the general framework of the organized social service of the times. Curiously enough—so mixed are human motives, and so slight is our knowledge of the cross-currents of policy that underlay the formal documents of the time—it is not easy to say how far much of what they did was social or anti-social in intention. Among the mainly self-regarding activities was their exclusive attitude towards unfreemen of the burgh, dwellers in country districts, and craftsmen of other burghs who encroached upon their own preserves.

Many careful regulations were made to prevent craftsmen from "colouring" unfreemen's goods and from entering into partnership with unfreemen, and the right to exclude nonfreemen from selling their goods, except on market days, was an important item among the privileges of nearly all the Edinburgh crafts. The craftsmen were well supported in their efforts. An act of 1592 forbids craftwork in the suburbs because of the inferiority of work and the hardship to the free craftsmen—"and als the frie craftismen resident within the said burrowis ar gritlie damnifiet seing thay beir ane greit pairt of the chargis of the burgh."[1] And the activities of the Convention of Royal Burghs also benefited the craftsmen. In fact, the repression of suburbs, clachans, and unfree towns that has already been noted was more often on account of the infringement of the monopolies of the craftsmen than of those of the merchants.

The town council also generally supported the craftsmen and enforced their rights for them. The records of Edinburgh are full of appeals by the craftsmen and of the responses made by the town council. They issued stringent ordinances, gave the craft organizations special power to punish delinquents, and sometimes took action themselves.[2] In 1584 the websters and

[1] *A.P.S.* vol. iii, p. 579.

[2] Cf. J. D. Marwick, *Edinburgh Gilds and Crafts*, pp. 60, 64, etc. A. Warden, *Burgh Laws of Dundee*, p. 385.

waulkers made pitiful complaint that although they were burgesses and freemen of their crafts and watched, warded, bore all portable charges, etc., yet: Nevertheless the whole inhabitants of this burgh, or at least the most part, moved by "solistation," acquaintance and divers other means and ways . . . daily puts their work in the hands of the unfreemen dwelling to the landward and in the suburbs of this burgh. These escape all burdens, increase in wealth and numbers, and even presume to appoint deacons and appoint apprentices, to the great damage of the craftsmen, who are utterly decayed and depauperated on account of these unfreemen "at thair veray durris eitting thair breid furth of thair mowthis." The town council ordered that no burgesses or indwellers of the burgh, neither themselves, their wives and children, nor their servants, should carry, send, or deliver their yarn, cloth, webs, or other stuffs to such unfreemen, under pain of forfeiting it.[1] The craftsmen also often complained of the inhabitants of the Canongate, of Potterrow, of the West Port, and of Leith, who came into the town and took back work to do at home. The burgh council generally seems to have supported them, and on one occasion its proceedings against the craftsmen of the Canongate involved it in trouble with the Privy Council.[2] The craftsmen were also occasionally faced with competition from other royal burghs. The skinners of Edinburgh complained that the men of St Johnstone sold "made work" on the High Street daily, and the town council prohibited the sale of such work except on market days and at fairs.[3]

The illustrations that have been quoted all refer to outside competition. There are many cases of unfreemen within the burgh who usurped the craftsmen's privileges and were forbidden to do so, but it will be more convenient to refer to them in connection with the vexed question of the proportion of non-free inhabitants who dwelt within the burgh.[4]

The craftsmen were thus able to secure outside support in their endeavours to suppress the competition of unfreemen, but

[1] J. D. Marwick, *Edinburgh Gilds and Crafts*, p. 140.
[2] *Ibid.* pp. 106, 135, etc.
[3] *Ibid.* p. 91.
[4] See Chapter VIII, Part VI.

they must have relied a great deal more on their own organizations, the gilds. Nearly all the gilds of Edinburgh—the websters, bonnetmakers, hammermen, fleshers, coopers, tailors, surgeons and barbers, cordiners, bakers, and skinners and furriers—had a clause in their Seal of Cause granting members of the gild the sole right of carrying on the craft within the town as master workers.[1] And one of the duties of the craft deacons was to prevent unfreemen from infringing this monopoly. In the case of the cordiners and of the waulkers and shearers the prohibition was not absolute, for the deacons were empowered to collect a penny a week from all members of their craft who dwelt "vtouth the fredome" of the burgh and took work out of the town.[2] The craft deacons also had the right of inspecting the work that non-free men were allowed to sell at special stances and times on market days and fairs, the only time at which real competition existed. In cases where they complained to the town council of the invasion of their privileges they were generally empowered to enforce their rights, so that their position was a very strong one.

In the two instances that have been quoted at some length it will be noticed that the craftsmen base their plea for special treatment upon the special burdens that they are called upon to bear within the burghs. This is the attitude that they invariably took up. It was not one of mere exclusiveness, for as they had to pay a considerable share of national and local taxation in return for their special rights, they naturally resented it when those who did not share in their burdens enjoyed their liberties. Their attitude is exactly on a par with that of the merchants and of the royal burghs themselves The insistence on apprenticeship was probably a bar to the enrolment of non-free craftsmen, but, as has been mentioned, the cordiners and the waulkers and shearers were willing to allow outsiders who paid special dues to work, and at one time the Dean of Gild was empowered to enrol non-free craftsmen of the suburbs if they would pay their entrance fee and live in the town. When the fleshers complained that the burgesses not of their craft were invading

[1] J. D. Marwick, *Edinburgh Gilds and Crafts*, pp. 47, 48, 30, 51, 53, 56, 59, 61, 62, 69, 66, 70.

[2] *Ibid.* p. 56.

their rights, the town council ordered that the interlopers should be examined to see if they were fit to join the craft, and stranger-hatmakers coming to the town were ordered to join the Hatmakers' Gild within a year. There are many other instances that show that the object of the craftsmen was rather to limit their privileges to those who were willing to pay for them than to exclude as many people as possible.[1]

In other respects the crafts were part of the social organization of the nation. It must be remembered that the mediaeval idea of proper civic administration included the careful supervision of the prices and quality of the necessaries of life. Markets were so local, means of transport so elementary in the case of many commodities, monopolies were so absolute, that regulation was probably very salutary. The importance of free competition in securing reasonable prices and goods of reasonable standard was not realized, and, after all, free competition can hardly be said to have existed at the time. Craftsmen and traders seem to have descended to the most puerile tricks and dishonesties when they wished to cheat—the axiom that honesty is the best policy was not a fact in the very limited conditions of sale that obtained in sixteenth-century Scotland.

As we have seen, one of the chief duties of the burgh authorities was the supervision of the prices and qualities of foodstuffs and of other necessary things, but these duties, especially in the case of "made-work" of different kinds, were gradually delegated by them to the craft organizations. In 1536, for instance, the Aberdeen town council ordained that the deacons were responsible for searching out and punishing any faults in their crafts, and that if they failed to do so they themselves were liable to punishment by the bailies. The powers of the deacons and other officials of crafts to see that only "good and sufficient workmen" were admitted to the liberties of their craft, to examine the craftsmen's work, to make regulations regarding materials, etc., and to punish craftsmen guilty of faulty workmanship are among the provisions of nearly all the Seals of Cause granted in the different

[1] J. D. Marwick, *Edinburgh Gilds and Crafts*, pp. 47, 56, 60, 72, 145.

burghs.[1] These duties were no empty sinecure; there are many examples of the punishment of craftsmen by their own deacons.[2]

The craft deacons were often remiss in seeing that the monopoly position of the crafts was not abused. This was especially the case with their powers of fixing prices, which was one of the main causes of quarrel with the authorities. It is important to remember that their authority was never absolute, and that they never seem to have made any claim that it was so. The central authorities, in the course of the disputes with the craftsmen, often gave the burgh magistrates and councils the right to override or abolish the privileges of the crafts, or ignored them. The ultimate responsibility for seeing that the necessaries of life were duly available to the people rested with the burghs and not with the crafts. For instance, in 1540, parliament ordered every burgh to appoint a "sealer" to examine and certify cloth, because of the "drawers" of cloth and the dyers of false colours.[3] The magistrates could and did interfere to force the deacons to do their work properly or to prevent the crafts from pushing their monopolies to undue lengths, and they were the court of appeal in disputes between the crafts. The magistrates of Edinburgh crushed an attempted strike by the bakers, settled a demarcation dispute between the tailors and furriers about the trimming of garments, fixed the price of shoes, and had many passages-of-arms with the masons and wrights. For instance, in 1577, these crafts had charged exorbitant prices, and had prevented unfree workmen from taking their place—as was specially allowed by act of parliament when these craftsmen would not finish their work. The town council passed an order enforcing the act, and declared that it was to remain in force in all time coming when wrights and masons became unreasonable in their prices. The power of the Edinburgh town council over the crafts was, indeed, always very great. They were able to interpose and prevent the

[1] E. Bain, *Merchant and Craft Gilds*, pp. 99, 199, 216, 239.

J. D. Marwick, *Edinburgh Gilds and Crafts*, pp. 43, 48, 50, 52, 56, 59, 61, 66, 146.

[2] Cf. *The Manuscript Minutes of the Town Council of Edinburgh*, iv pp. 57-62 (1562); iv, p. 497 (1569), etc., for the punishment of weavers by the weaver craft.

[3] *A.P.S.* vol. ii, p. 373.

fleshers from deposing their deacon and electing another; and even in 1579, after the crafts had considerably improved their political position, the whole body of deacons, after being reasoned with, agreed that it was "maist reasonabill" that all craftsmen seeking the freedom of the town must be presented to the burgh authorities "conforme to the auld ordour." In other burghs the relationship between the burgh and the crafts was much the same. One finds the Aberdeen magistrates themselves punishing the shoemakers for bad workmanship and high prices, because the deacons were negligent; and in Dundee the craftsmen had the right of appealing against the deacons of their crafts to the town council.[1]

The rules of the different crafts contain a good many provisions designed to ensure good workmanship. A period of apprenticeship was insisted upon: it varied from three years, in specially favoured cases, to five or seven, but it was generally for the latter period. There was usually a provision that applicants for entry were to be examined by the officials of the Gild to see that they were competent workmen, and in a good many crafts and burghs a "masterstick," or specimen of the candidate's work, had to be submitted.[2] It is, however, impossible to say how far these rules were due to a genuine pride in their craftsmanship among the handworkers, how far they undertook to enforce them because they preferred autonomy to

[1] The writer is indebted to Dr M. Wood for some of this information.

J. Mackintosh, *History of Civilization in Scotland*, vol. ii, p. 293.

J. D. Marwick, *Edinburgh Gilds and Crafts*, pp. 114, 115, 200; for further examples, see pp. 70, 113, 115, 117.

A. Warden, *Burgh Laws of Dundee*, p. 100.

[2] Apprenticeship, Edinburgh (J. D. Marwick, *Edinburgh Gilds and Crafts*), p. 45, masons and wrights, 7 years; p. 48, weavers, 5 years; p. 50, hammermen; p. 51, fleshers; p. 56, waulkers and shearers; p. 56, tailors, 7 years; p. 61, cordiners, 7 years; p. 66, bakers; p. 68, bonnetmakers. Good and sufficient workmanship (J. D. Marwick, *Edinburgh Gilds and Crafts*), p. 42, skinners; p. 47, hatters; p. 48, wrights and masons; p. 50, hammermen; p. 56, tailors; p. 57, surgeons and barbers; p. 61, cordiners; p. 70, skinners and furriers. The provisions of the cordiners, p. 46, were especially careful and seem to be designed to ensure thorough teaching.

The Dundee Seals of Cause were very similar. A. Warden, *Burgh Laws of Dundee*, p. 411.

Masterstick, A. Warden, *Burgh Laws of Dundee*, p. 411.

E. Bain, *Merchant and Craft Gilds*, pp. 100, 107.

J. D. Marwick, *Edinburgh Gilds and Crafts*, pp. 18, 68, 72.

supervision by the burgh authorities, and how far they were regarded as means for maintaining an exclusive monopoly. Apprenticeship has often been treated as a means of limiting entrance to a trade. Provisions such as that of the hatmakers of Edinburgh, which enjoined a seven-year apprenticeship for strangers and a three years' one for the son of a freeman of the craft, probably had this end in view. The power of examining candidates with regard to their workmanship would, of course, be capable of abuse, and the extraordinarily elaborate master-stick required of craftsmen in Aberdeen would be apt to limit entry into the craft to lads with enough capital to supply the materials, and might be a useful means of excluding unwanted candidates. Many of the crafts charged higher entrance fees to strangers than to the sons of freemen.[1]

The rise of the craft gilds is an advance in democratic government in so far as it represents an increase of power to a new and more humbly placed section of the community. Nevertheless, the craftsmen did not represent the "masses," but only a highly favoured section, and the emergence of the craft organization in Scotland at so comparatively late a period is definitely a sign of the backwardness of her development. Cunningham, writing of the breakdown of craft organization in England by the time of Elizabeth, says that "the crucial difference between mediaeval and modern industry lies in the fact that under the older system the necessary oversight was exercised by the officers of a gild over its members; while in modern times the employer is individually responsible for the organization of the business and supervision of the work carried on by his employees."[2] It is rather striking that that very astute observer of Scots affairs, James VI and I—one of the most thoroughgoing innovators and reformers in economic affairs that Scotland has ever known, though his motives were at least as mixed as those of the worst of the craftsmen—definitely considered that the craft organization was anti-social. He

[1] J. D. Marwick, *Edinburgh Gilds and Crafts*, p. 47.

The regulations of the tailors of Dundee show a similar tendency. A. Warden, *Burgh Laws of Dundee*, p. 428.

E. Bain, *Merchant and Craft Gilds*, pp. 100, 107, 230.

[2] W. Cunningham, *Growth of English Industry and Commerce, Modern Times*, Part I, p. 11.

wrote to his son Prince Henry: "The craftes-men thinke we should be content with their worke, how bad and dear soever it be, and if they in anything be controlled, up goeth the blew blanket" (the Edinburgh craftsmen's banner). "But for their part take example of England, how it hath flourished both in wealth and policie since the stranger craftsmen came in among them. Therefore not only permit but allure strangers to come here also; taking as straite order for repressing the mutining of ours at them, as was done in England at their first in-bringing there."[1]

The main matters of dispute between the craft gilds on the one side and the burgh authorities and the central authority on the other seem to have been three. Firstly, the desire of the crafts to have a larger share in the government of the burghs. This is the object of contention that most obtrudes itself in the minutes of the burgh councils that relate to the disputes. Secondly, the desire of the craftsmen to have a share in the merchants' monopoly of foreign trade. This cause of friction is not so evident in the burgh council records, but there is reason to think that it was an important one. Though there are not so many ordinances forbidding craftsmen from engaging in such trade as there are against unfreemen, the craftsmen were specifically and definitely excluded, both by act of parliament and by the regulations of the burghs. In 1500, for instance, the Parliament of the Four Burghs, with the chamberlain, his assessors, and the commissioners of the burghs, ordered that because all burghs had been greatly hurt in time bygone by craftsmen using merchandise within them, therefore the acts of parliament must be properly enforced and craftsmen be forced to confine themselves to their own crafts, under pain of a fine of £10; and that searchers, such as the provost, bailies, and custumars, be chosen in the burghs to search out all breakers of the acts. In the case of Dunfermline the craftsmen were strong enough openly to usurp the merchants' privileges about 1595.[2] In other burghs they evidently did so less openly, for many of the burgesses who were not members of the Gild

[1] Quoted, *Report on Municipal Corporations in Scotland, 1835*, p. 81.
[2] *A.P.S.* vol. i, pp. 86-87 (1466), 175 (1487).
Extracts from the *Burgh Records of Edinburgh*, p. 86.
Convention of Royal Burghs, vol. i, p. 448.

Merchant and were proceeded against for engaging in foreign trade were probably craftsmen. That the merchants' commercial privileges were among the causes of the dispute is, however, most convincingly shown in the careful delimitation of the rights of either party that almost invariably appears in the many compromises between the merchants and the craftsmen that were made in the second half of the sixteenth century. On the whole, it is evident that the craftsmen did advance their economic position to some extent.

The third cause of dispute was the price-fixing proclivity of the crafts.[1] Combination for the purpose of raising prices was repugnant to all mediaeval ideas of proper government, and the fear that the crafts would abuse their powers in this way seems to have been largely responsible for the attitude of parliament and of the central authority to the craft organizations. The whole struggle was, however, infinitely complicated by the political exigencies of a most unhappy period. At times during the sixteenth century the Crown was evidently obliged to make a bid for the support of the craftsmen. (It is possible that these sometimes took a different line with regard to the Reformation from that followed by the merchants, who were favourable to the reformers: this would certainly go far to explain the sudden *volte-face* of Mary of Lorraine that will presently be described.) It is interesting and significant that the restrictive acts against the craftsmen were all passed by parliament and are on the statute-book, whereas the four favouring ones seem to have been issued on the ruler's personal authority.[2]

The struggle of the craft gilds for recognition begins in the fifteenth century. In 1424, immediately after an act intended to prevent the undue raising of prices during the king's presence in any burgh, another was passed requiring each craft in every town to choose one of its " wise men," with the consent of the officers of the town, to be deacon or masterman, to assay and govern all work done by the men of his craft. Two years later, however, an act was passed permitting the deacons' appointments to stand until next parliament, but only to see that the workers were properly skilled and their work sufficient.

[1] D. Murray, *Early Burgh Organization*, pp. 481, 483.

[2] J. Smith, *The Edinburgh Hammermen*, p. lxxxviii.

In the same parliament an act was passed ordering the town councils to fix the prices of craft work.[1] In 1427, by one act the ordinances regarding deacons were declared to have tended to the hurt and common loss of the realm, and they were repealed and deacons were abolished. By a second act the town council of every burgh was ordered to appoint wardens, who were to fix prices and inspect the quality of all goods, and especially the work of masons, wrights, smiths, tailors, and websters.[2]

Forty years of silence follows. An act of 1457, forbidding leagues and bands, suggests that all was not peace in the burghs; but in 1469 the famous act relating to burgh government was passed, which gave the crafts the right to have a share in the burgh elections through two chosen representatives. In the same parliament an act was passed confirming the merchants' privileges and forbidding craftsmen from using merchandise unless they renounced their crafts without colour or dissimulation. Three years later an act was passed ordering that wardens and deacons be appointed to examine goldsmiths' work, but nothing is said about who was to appoint them. The act excluding craftsmen from the privileges of merchants was repeated in 1491, but three years later deacons' powers received recognition. The common good of the burghs was to be administered by the town councils and the deacons of the crafts.[3]

By 1493 they were in disgrace. Craftsmen, shoemakers especially, were forbidden from taking special and increased dues from non-freemen frequenting markets, and infringements of the rule were referred, not to the burgh courts, but to the justice ayres. All deacons were to cease for a year and were only to examine "the fynace of the stuffe and werk that hes bin wrocht with the remnant of his craft." Craftsmen, wrights and masons especially, were accused of communing together and making rules for their craft—as, for instance, that they must be paid for feast days as well as for work days, and that if one craftsman begin a piece of work no other one may finish it. The making of such rules was strictly forbidden, under pain of indictment as common oppressors of the lieges. In the preamble of the act, deacons were said to be right dangerous, and likely to be the cause of great trouble by making statutes contrary to

[1] *A.P.S.* vol. ii, pp. 7, 13.

[2] *Ibid.* vol. ii, pp. 14, 15.

[3] *Ibid.* vol. ii, pp. 105, 227.

the common profit and for their own profit and avail. The mind of parliament was evidently running upon prices, for the next act on the statute-book deals with the wrongful exaction of multures.[1] Three years later parliament passed an act complaining of the inordinate prices charged by workmen, and ordering all barons, provosts, and bailies to oversee the price and quality of all foodstuffs and necessary things wrought and brought by the lieges and to appoint examiners to enforce their regulations.[1]

The craft organizations would have been abolished over and over again had these laws been effective, but, as we have seen, during this period they were developing and receiving official recognition from the burghs. In the sixteenth century the struggle enters upon a new phase in so far as the relationship with the town authorities is concerned, but the price-fixing activity of the craftsmen was to remain one of their principal menaces, in the opinion of the Government. Gross, in his monumental work upon the Gild Merchant, has pointed out that the struggle between the merchant class and the craft gilds is not found in England and is a feature peculiar to Scotland. He has collected evidence of such a struggle in twenty of the Scots burghs : Edinburgh, Stirling, Perth, Dumbarton, Brechin, St Andrews, Inverness, Inverkeithing, Montrose, Banff, Burntisland, Haddington, Kirkcaldy, Elgin, Culross, Lanark, Dunbar, Cupar, Kirkcudbright, and Dunfermline.[2] Considering that the quarrel was so general, and taking into account the aptitude for working together displayed by the Scots burghs, it is a little strange that the craftsmen of the different burghs seem hardly at all to have co-operated together in their fight against the merchants and the burgh councils.[3] The affair was adjusted separately in each town, but the struggle that took place in Edinburgh directly influenced the attitude of the Crown, and the two are most easily described together.

In Edinburgh, during the second half of the fifteenth and

[1] *A.P.S.* vol. ii, pp. 243, 238.

[2] G. Gross, *The Gild Merchant*, p. 223. See also E. Bain, *Merchant and Craft Gilds*, p. 27, for a general summary.

[3] In 1581 the craftsmen of Edinburgh, Perth, Dundee, and Aberdeen combined to appeal to James VI for a new charter of their privileges. This seems to have been exceptional. E. Bain, *Merchant and Craft Gilds*, p. 79.

the first half of the sixteenth centuries, the crafts secured their Seals of Cause. There is no evidence to show how far the provisions of the act of 1469, which gave them a voice in the election of the burgh office-bearers, was carried into effect; but individual craftsmen, it is not stated whether as deacons or as ordinary members of the council, are constantly mentioned in the burgh records as voting at the meetings of the burgh council. In 1492, for instance, we learn that the provost, bailies, council, great duzane, and deacons gave formal assent to two acts. In all matters affecting the crafts, their representatives were consulted and had considerable power.[1]

The craftsmen, however, wished for more power. In 1508 some of them applied to the town council to have six or eight members of the crafts on the daily council of the town, and that some craftsmen should be appointed to the office of bailie and other offices. The rest of the craftsmen sided with the burgh authorities in contending that such an innovation was impossible without the consent of parliament.[2] A good deal seems to have happened of which we know nothing, for, in 1529, James V granted an edict under the Great Seal in which he declared that he had ratified certain articles to the "heavie damage and skaith of all craftsmen" without the consent of his council and upon some "vexious, sinister, and wrangus information" given by the merchants for their particular profit. He therefore restored all liberties and privileges previously granted to the craftsmen; annulled certain articles and statutes made by the merchants; and ordered that all the lieges cease from molesting the said craftsmen.[3] It will be remembered that James had but just emerged from the tutelage of the Douglases, and that that family had many links with the burgh authorities of Edinburgh. Beyond a slight clash over the election of some of the minor officials in Edinburgh and an annual protest at the burgh elections, nothing more of national importance seems to have happened until nearly the middle of the century.

In 1536 parliament again became alarmed at the price-

[1] Article by M. Wood, *Edinburgh, 1329–1929*, pp. 276, 278-9. (Published in celebration of sexcentenary of Edinburgh's Charter.)

[2] J. D. Marwick, *Edinburgh Gilds and Crafts*, p. 189.

[3] J. Smith, *The Hammermen of Edinburgh*, p. lxxxi.

fixing activities of the craftsmen, and a commission was appointed which, with the provost of Edinburgh, was to fix prices. The craftsmen, however, do not seem to have mended their ways. In 1540–41 an act was passed confirming the privileges of the burghs and of the merchants, and specially ordering that the provosts, bailies, and aldermen must be merchants, and which declared that: because it is heavily murmured that all craftsmen of this realm and especially within burghs uses such extortion upon others of our sovereign lord's lieges by reason of their crafts and of private acts and constitutions made amongst themselves contrary to the common weal, and in great hurt, prejudice, damage, and scaith to this realm, therefore anyone within or without burghs may employ whoever he likes, freemen or non-freemen, to build or repair. Another act regarding the exorbitant prices of craftsmen was passed in 1552. Prices were said to be sometimes doubled and trebled. All provosts were ordered to fix prices and to send up written lists of these to the Lords of the Articles (the executive committee of the Scots Parliament).[1] But in between these acts, during James V's estrangement from many of his subjects just before Solway Moss, another royal edict in favour of the craftsmen was passed.[2]

The craftsmen were not passive sufferers. There were many riots and disturbances. In 1543, for instance, several of the deacons of the Edinburgh crafts appeared before the provost, apparently about some grievance. In the course of the interview several of them drew their swords, were arrested, and were sent to the Castle. The craftsmen appealed to the governor (Arran), who ordered their release. This leniency may be accounted for by the English attack upon Edinburgh which was then impending. In any case, one of the insurgent craftsmen lost his life defending the city.[3]

The craftsmen, however, must have considerably consolidated their position, for, in 1552, the Convention of Royal Burghs passed an order that the constitutions of all the royal burghs were to be modelled upon that of Edinburgh. And the Edinburgh council, according to this edict, consisted of the

[1] J. D. Marwick, *Edinburgh Gilds and Crafts*, pp. 74, 77.

[2] J. Smith, *The Hammermen of Edinburgh*, p. lxxxviii.

[3] *Ibid.* p. lxxxv.

provost, of four bailies, of the Dean of Gild, and of the treasurer, all seven of these being merchants, and of three merchants and two craftsmen as ordinary town councillors. The old and new councils were to prepare leets of the names of the office-bearers at the annual election, and then these two bodies and the deacons of the crafts were to select the actual names.[1] The Convention of Royal Burghs consisted of merchant representatives of the burghs and was a most conservative body. The craftsmen had therefore achieved a very great advance. Yet within three years, in 1555, an act of parliament was passed ratifying all the privileges of the burghs and merchants, but stating that the choosing of deacons and men of craft within burghs had been right dangerous, and that the manner in which they had used themselves in times bygone had caused great trouble in burghs, commotions and rising of the lieges in divers parts, and the making of leagues and bands amongst themselves and between burgh and burgh, which deserved great punishment. That, therefore, in future, no deacons were to be elected, but that the burgh authorities were to choose men of craft, of good conscience, one of every craft, to " visie " their craft that they labour sufficiently. These persons were to be called " visitors " and were to be chosen yearly. At the same time the assembling of craftsmen in private conventions and the making by them of private acts and statutes were prohibited. The visitors were declared to have the same rights as the deacons had previously exercised in the choosing of officers and other things.[2] This severe act seems to have been put into some execution—probably the merchants saw to it that it was so. Visitors were appointed at Edinburgh, Stirling, and Perth.[3] The Edinburgh visitors, however, seem to have been no whit more satisfactory to the merchants than the deacons had been.

What followed can only be guessed at. To piece the fragments of information together it is necessary to consider the background of national history against which the lesser drama of the craftsmen's struggle was being waged. Mary of Lorraine, the queen-regent, was making her last stand for the French alliance and the Old Religion. In the middle of these harassments of

[1] *Records of the Convention of Royal Burghs*, vol. i, p. 3.
[2] J. D. Marwick, *Edinburgh Gilds and Crafts*, p. 81.
[3] D. Murray, *Early Burgh Organization*, p. 345.

greater issues she was perpetually in need of money. The nation was distracted by factions and general lawlessness and the rift of the Reformation was beginning to cleave society. The burghs were in a thoroughly dissatisfied state, for there were "debates and pleas" between the merchants and craftsmen, and the merchants were displeased with three ordinances lately promulgated by the queen: (*a*) that merchants were compelled to bring home bullion in exchange for goods, even from countries from which its export was prohibited; (*b*) that they were only allowed to export fish by licence, and (*c*) that the Privy Council had fixed prices, instead of the burghs.[1]

The queen-regent, perhaps because she was already playing for the support of the craftsmen, invited each of the burghs to send two commissioners, one a merchant and one a craftsman, to settle these matters. Edinburgh town council sent four commissioners, the provost, two merchants, and one craftsman, but protested that in sending the latter it did not wish to prejudice the burgh in time coming, inasmuch as craftsmen had never before been chosen as commissioners. The "visitors" meanwhile protested that they ought to have taken part in the choosing of the commissioners, and that two craftsmen as well as two merchants ought to have been sent.[2]

The burghs had their own way of setting right their grievances. A few days later the magistrates, council, and visitors agreed that Edinburgh should join with the other burghs in making a contribution and "propine" to the queen-mother, if she would repeal the ordinances that they objected to, and agree that such acts, affecting the interests of the burghs, should in future only be made in parliament. The share of the "propine" to be paid by the burghs was not to exceed 4000 merks.[3] The "visitors" (how heartily must the merchants have regretted having chosen them!) urged the provost and council to add to these conditions that the craftsmen's privileges should be given back to them, and added that otherwise they would do their best to get redress in their own way.

What followed is wrapped in mystery. Probably the crafts-

[1] *Extracts from the Burgh Records of Edinburgh*, (1528–1557), pp. 233-235.

[2] J. Smith, *The Hammermen of Edinburgh*, p. 161.

[3] *Extracts from the Records of Edinburgh*, pp. 235-236.

men bargained with the queen on their own account, offering her their support in return for the repeal of the obnoxious act of 1555. Whatever happened to change the policy of the queen, the results were dramatic. Early in 1556, Mary of Lorraine granted the craftsmen a charter, in which she stated that since the act of 1555 had not produced the effects for which it had been passed, " nay, that everything is done more carelessly among those craftsmen at this day than formerly "—therefore, being desirous that the privileges of the craftsmen should not be abridged without urgent and enduring cause, and being desirous also that dissensions and contentions among the merchants and tradesmen dwelling in her burghs should be prevented, she granted dispensation to all and sundry craftsmen of her burghs and cities in regard to that act of parliament, in so far as the same conflicted with the liberties and privileges which the craftsmen had previously enjoyed, either by royal grant or long and continued use. She further expressly restored to them the power to elect deacons of their several crafts, having votes in the election of officers of burghs, and being auditors of the common good; and empowered the craftsmen to meet and make ordinance to their several crafts, to the preservation of good order among the craftsmen and the maintenance of divine service. The craftsmen were further empowered to use merchandise of all sorts within the kingdom and beyond the same as might seem to them to be most advantageous. Every privilege, liberty, and custom they had ever enjoyed was to be restored to the craftsmen, notwithstanding the provisions of the said act. They were, however, made liable to pay up what they owed of past extents, a *quid pro quo* for the royal favour [1]

As we learn from the minutes of the hammermen, the queen's " dekrie " was solemnly proclaimed " with sound of trimpatts and ye heralds with yr coit arms. Ye mercat cross all hynging about with fyne Tapysstyr quhilk was ryt honest and pleasant to all ye craftismen." A month later the deacons were once more in office.[2]

The craftsmen were not slow in showing their support of

[1] J. D. Marwick, *Edinburgh Gilds and Crafts*, p. 85. M. Wood, *Edinburgh, 1326–1929*, p. 277.

[2] J. Smith, *The Hammermen of Edinburgh.*

the Crown. Later in the year there was a dispute between the town council and the queen over the election of the water bailie of Leith. The queen ordered the votes of the council for and against her nominee to be made in writing to her; but the council refused, saying that "thai wer ane counsale sworn to gif the best counsale thai culd, and consele the counsale schewn to thame." The queen, however, insisted upon the election of her nominee, and dismissed from office those councillors who opposed her. The craftsmen in this dispute supported her.[1] The story of the struggle, though it descends somewhat into a chronicle of small beer, is of considerable interest as showing how little constitutional privilege counted for in Scotland, and how absolute were the powers of the Crown—when they were not opposed to those exercised by the more formidable subjects. Not only was the capital city of the kingdom obliged to submit to the arbitrary exercise of the regent's will; parliament itself, as Murray points out, "took no exception to the setting aside of its statute, and tacitly accepted the election of deacons, although it had but just declared that this 'was rycht dangerous.'"[2] The 1556 charter in favour of the deacons was re-granted by Mary Queen of Scots in 1564 and by James VI in 1581.[3]

The alliance between the queen-regent and the deacons continued. The burgh authorities refused to accept the deacons' votes at the annual elections, and in 1559 the deacons appeared with a royal letter ordering the town council to do so. The council refused, upon the excuse that the deacons of Edinburgh had never had this privilege and that the charter of 1556 only gave them back the rights that they had enjoyed before 1555. Eventually a compromise was reached. The town council agreed to nominate two deacons to sit on the council, whom they were to select from a list of six names submitted to them by the crafts. They reserved, however, the right of refusing to nominate any of the names on the list and of requiring a new one to be presented to them.

During the next twenty years the struggle continued. The

[1] J. D. Marwick, *Edinburgh Gilds and Crafts*, p. 86.

[2] D. Murray, *Early Burgh Organization.*

[3] J. Smith, *Edinburgh Hammermen*, p. lxxxviii.
For text of James VI's charter to crafts, see E. Bain, *Merchant and Craft Gilds*, p. 79.

craftsmen, on the whole, seem to have confined themselves to the demand for greater political rights, and not to have attempted to make good the claims to economic equality that the 1556 charter gave them. They did not make this a point at issue in Edinburgh, Aberdeen, or Dundee, and in the compromises that were eventually reached in these towns, as we shall see, the monopolies of the merchants were carefully safeguarded. It was probably because the craftsmen thought that such demands were hopeless that they refrained from making them, for it must be remembered that although Mary and James VI confirmed the charter to the craftsmen, they and their parliament also continued to pass legislation endorsing the merchants' monopolies. Almost the only allusion to the grant of the very important trading privileges to the craftsmen comes from Stirling, where they complained that in spite of the royal order giving them liberty to use merchandise, the burgh authorities and the merchants prevented them from doing so.[1]

The quarrel over the political rights of the craftsmen, however, waxed violent at times. The craftsmen pressed for a generous interpretation of their rights and for their extension to the lesser crafts; the town council were consistently obstructionist.[2] That two acts of parliament against leagues and bands in the burghs had to be passed is not surprising.[3] In 1582 the quarrel came to a head in Edinburgh over one of the burgh elections and there was a serious riot,[4] and the Privy Council had to interfere. They ordered the disputed election to stand, but they required both parties to submit their differences to twenty-four arbiters, chosen by both sides, with the king as oversman. The arbitrators issued an award which the merchants accepted, but not so the craftsmen. Thereupon the king recommitted the whole subject of the dispute to the same arbitrators, with himself as umpire, and their finding was accepted by both parties, was ratified by parliament, and became known as the "set" of the city.[5]

[1] *Register, Privy Council*, vol. iii, p. 216 (1579).

[2] J. D. Marwick, *Edinburgh Gilds and Crafts*, pp. 96-117.

[3] *A.P.S.* vol. iii, p. 38.

[4] *Historical Notices of Scottish Affairs* (Bannatyne Club), vol. i, pp. 53-81—*Fountainhall.*

[5] J. D. Marwick, *Edinburgh Gilds and Crafts*, p. 126.

This agreement enacted that the magistrates and officemen—provost, bailies, Dean of Gild, and treasurers—were to be merchants. Any craftsman who might be specially elected must, with his servants, give up the exercise of his craft. The town council was to consist of twenty-four persons, ten of them merchants—seven of whom were to be members of the old council and three of whom were to be elected by it—and of eight craftsmen, six of them deacons and two of them persons selected by the burgh officemen and the rest of the council. The town council was to have control of the common good, but the whole of the fourteen deacons (not merely the six upon the council) were to share in its management. The merchants and the craftsmen were to have almost equal representation in such matters as the auditors, the council of the Dean of Gild, and the commissioners representing the city in parliament and upon the Convention of Royal Burghs. A most important provision enabled craftsmen to join the Gild Merchant, "the admission and tryall of qualificatioun to be in the power and hands of the Provost, Baillies, Tresaurer and council" together with the representatives of the gild. The admissions of candidates able to pay the high entrance fee and to pass this "selection board" cannot have been very extensive. The demarcation between the merchants and craftsmen, though it was evidently softened by the effect of the decreet, continued long after the end of our period. The merchants and the craftsmen, meanwhile, were to be assessed equally, and the custom of "devyding and setting of extents, quhairin the merchants payet four pairts, and the craftis the fyft pairt," was "abrogatt," and they were to share equally in all contributions, extents, imposts, and like subsidies imposed upon the burgh according to their individual ability and substance (an alteration in the assessment of the craftsmen).[1] The entrance fees, however, varied between merchants and the craftsmen.

This set is interesting, for it was to serve as the model for many similar agreements.[2] It shows that the craftsmen and deacons had to a considerable extent made good their position,

[1] J. D. Marwick, *Edinburgh Gilds and Crafts*, p. 126. Article by M. Wood in *Edinburgh, 1329–1929*, pp. 280-282, has an excellent summary of the agreement.

[2] J. Clelland, *Annals of Glasgow*, vol. i, p. 233, for text of agreement between merchants and craftsmen in Glasgow.

but it also illustrates the fact that to all intents and purposes practically no advance had been made in ideals of burgh government since the fifteenth century. The careful arrangement made by the burgh council for carrying out the award is also very interesting, for it defines the position of the merchants and craftsmen in the premier city of the kingdom at the very end of our period. The agreement runs as follows: First anent the article of the gildry, to bring and reduce the said gildry to the first institution thereof, so far as may be, after so long confusion of all things, and to make distinction between a gild and other simple burgesses who are not called to that estate and honour within burgh, it is declared, statute, and ordained that no manner of person but they that are received and admitted in the society of the gild brether, top or sell in smalls "retail" any manner of wine, wax, woad, spiceries of all sorts, cloth of silk, gold, silver, or any foreign or outlands cloth of wool (excepting only these cloths following, to wit, linen, fries, kelt, Yorkshire cloth, kerseys, and all sorts of shrinking cloth, which shall be common to all burgesses), discharging and inhibiting all persons simple burgesses and others which are not gild brothers to trade, occupy, exchange, top or sell in smalls from this day forth the wares and merchandise before written under the pain of escheat thereof, and that no gild brother use the trade of topping and selling in smalls of such gross wares as effiers not to the honesty of a gild brother but specially of these wares following, to wit, oil, soap, butter, fruit, figs, raisins, "plowmdames," eggs, fish, vinegar, or such like, under the pain of fine bound so oft as they fail.[1]

The struggle between the craftsmen and the merchants in Aberdeen was begun much about the same time. The immediate cause of the trouble there seems to have been the taking of unduly high entrance fees by the craftsmen, and their claims to exercise merchandise. After very serious and long-continued trouble and an ineffectual interference on behalf of the craftsmen by the king, an agreement, called the "Common Indenture," was reached in 1587. The craftsmen were to be accepted as burgesses before they were accepted by the crafts, and two-thirds of their entrance fees were to go to the burgh. Two of them were to be auditors, but they were not to hold the principal

[1] J. D. Marwick, *Edinburgh Gilds and Crafts*, p. 133.

burgh offices. They were to be allowed to buy and sell butter, sheep, raw cloth and cloth made in their own houses, but they were not to "meddle with na kind of forean nor oversea wares," nor deal in any staple goods, such as fish, hides, skin and wool, which, "sall properly appertain unto the merchant bretheren of gild allanerly." Fresh disputes broke out and were settled in 1595, when the Convention of Royal Burghs gave the craftsmen and deacons more power to vote in the burghal elections.[1] In Dundee there had been trouble between the crafts and Gild so early as 1527 and a decreet arbitral was pronounced. It, however, chiefly concerned the jurisdiction of the Dean of Gild and of the deacons in their own spheres. In 1590, however, the elaborate and rather aggressive reconstitution of the Merchants' Gild shows that there was considerable tension with the craftsmen. The selling rights of the merchants were defined and their monopoly in foreign trade. They were, however, forbidden to sell eggs, apples, onions, kail, or pears because it was below their dignity.[2] As developed by the end of the sixteenth century, the craft gilds in some burghs, such as Glasgow and Aberdeen, formed themselves into a body presided over by a deacon convener.[3] In Edinburgh, however, this further development was less complete.

Part VI. Non-free Town Dwellers

The position of the craftsman burgess in earlier times is uncertain. There is no information to tell us whether as a rule he worked on his own account, with the assistance of an apprentice, or whether he often employed labour. Servants are mentioned in the Laws of the Four Burghs, but they may have been exceptional. The craft ordinances, however, give a much clearer idea of what the master craftsman had become by the sixteenth century. He still made and sold his goods, for the craftsmen's booths, their particular stances in the market-places, etc., are many times mentioned. Only skinners and furriers

[1] E. Bain, *Merchant and Craft Gilds*, pp. 77-79, 82, 85.
D. Murray, *Early Burgh Organization*, p. 345.
G. Gross, *Gild Merchant*, pp. 219-220.

[2] A. Warden, *Burgh Laws of Dundee*, pp. 97, 115, 124.

[3] E. Bain, *Merchant and Craft Gilds*, p. 43.

and cordiners who were members of the craft gild might set up booths. The waulkers and shearers required four master craftsmen to vouch for the ability of every candidate to set up a booth, possess three pairs of shears, and provide " ane stick of hewit cloth," i.e. a bolt of shorn cloth, so that he might be able to satisfy anyone whose cloth he injured.[1] Weavers had to satisfy the craft that they had a sufficiency of graith and work looms, and hammermen also had to assure the craft authorities that they had a sufficiency of property ; fleshers who were too poor to set up for themselves were allowed to go into partnership with other freemen of the craft but not with unfreemen.[2] In the case of the waulkers, they worked upon commission, upon their customers' goods, and this was probably still usual in other crafts. We find, for instance, in a complaint by the deacons of the tailors and other trades in 1584 to the town council against the employment of unfreemen, that the tailors offered to bind themselves always to supply servants who would do the work of the public in their own houses—who should work from five in the morning till nine at night for twelve pennies and their meat; and that if disagreement arose with regard to price or workmanship, the matter should be dealt with by a committee formed of one of the bailies and two members of the town council, one a merchant and one a craftsman.[3]

By the sixteenth century the craftsmen had evidently become to some extent employers of labour. The Seal of Cause of the Edinburgh Hammermen, granted in 1483, enacts that no one shall work at this craft except freemen, apprentices, and employees of freemen. The bonnetmakers complained that other craftsmen, fleshers, wrights, cordiners, etc., had drawn away their apprentices and servants, and the town council supported them and ordered that no one else should employ a servant or apprentice who had started under the bonnetmakers. The Seal of Cause of the candlemakers gave to freemen of the craft the sole right of employing others and having booths ; non-freemen might work for them. In Dundee the regulations of the shoemakers also constantly allude to the master craftsmen's booths and servants as well as apprentices. The very interesting offer of military service made by the

[1] J. D. Marwick, *Edinburgh Gilds and Crafts*, pp. 56, 70, 73.
[2] *Ibid.* pp. 48, 50.
[3] *Ibid.* p. 138.

merchants and craftsmen in 1559 (see p. 382) gives us at least some idea of the proportion of servants in the different crafts.

The decreet which settled the differences between the Edinburgh merchants and craftsmen thus alludes to the non-free workers : The great multitude of journeymen or taskmen of the crafts are nothing else but idle, vagabond persons, bound to no master, troublers of the quiet estate of this common weal, polluting the same with all wickedness, and bears no burden with the town, but are very hurtful to the honest neighbours, burgesses, and free craftsmen of the same ; therefore the said provost, bailies, council, and deacons of crafts commands, in our sovereign lord's name and theirs, that no such persons remain within this burgh, but dispatch themselves forth thereof under the pain of punishing of their bodies as vagabonds, conform to the acts of parliament." No manner of person who was not a free burgess was to occupy any craft within the burgh " without they be bound to one master as a paid servant for meat and fee for a year or half-year, who shall answer for him to the magistrates." [1]

The craftsmen had reasonable excuse for their rancour against the non-freemen. As the deacons plaintively declared in 1584, the craftsmen were " heavelie hurt and damnifiet " by the number of unfreemen, dwelling in the town and under no master, and subject to no stenting, watching, warding, or other portable charges with the other freemen.[2] In the case of an English bookseller who came to Edinburgh the craftsmen complained that if non-freemen usurped their privileges " it wer nocht possibill to free burgesses to leif and beir chairgis." [3] The same connection between rights and special payments is present in almost all the craftsmen's complaints and was endorsed by an act of parliament.

The many ordinances and complaints of the sixteenth century certainly suggest that the free craftsmen were being subjected to increasing competition. In 1590 the weavers of Dundee, hearing that their brethren of Edinburgh had obtained a confirmation of their privileges from the town council, wrote to ask them for a copy. They complained of the " opressit

[1] J. D. Marwick, *Edinburgh Gilds and Crafts*, p. 133.
[2] *Ibid.* p. 138.
[3] *Ibid.* p. 125 (date 1582); for a similar case, see p. 122.

and sorrowfull present estait" of the freemen of the crafts everywhere in this realm by the "increasing of ye number of unfriemen of craft." This Dundee grievance, however, seems to have been directed very largely against the competition of outland weavers.[1]

It is difficult to say whether there were many burgesses who were neither merchants nor craftsmen. In Edinburgh, the burgess roll shows that practically all burgesses on admission were specified as merchants or as belonging to one of the crafts. A good many retired burgesses, however, lived in the country round. It was possibly these that the fleshers referred to when, in 1508, they complained that their privileges were being invaded by persons who were burgesses but who were "uncorporat in thair faculty and fredome."[2] It must be remembered that agriculture was still an important occupation in all but the largest burghs, and that, even in these, the lands were extensively cultivated by the burgesses. Although, as a matter of fact, many of the holders of shares in the burgh land were either merchants or craftsmen, a considerable class of non-industrial burgesses was quite possible, either as owners or workers upon the holdings of others. At a later date there is definite evidence that agricultural workers lived in and were employed in the smaller burghs.

Part VII. The Convention of Royal Burghs

The Convention of Royal Burghs has inevitably been mentioned from time to time, but the evolution of this institution deserves more than piecemeal attention. It was peculiar to Scotland; its enactments and activities embody the policy and tendencies of the Scots burghs; its development is a specially interesting example of the growth of ideas already manifested in the amazingly formative period that preceded the Wars of Independence and which were carried forward and

[1] A. Warden, *Burgh Laws of Dundee*, pp. 512-514, 517, 590.

[2] J. D. Marwick, *Edinburgh Gilds and Crafts*, p. 66. The Burgess Roll of Edinburgh has been printed by the Scottish Burgh Record Society.

At Arbroath, by a statute of 1563-4, the punishment for "mispersoning" the town's "flesh prisser" was to consist of a fine for a *freeman*, but of the stocks for an unfreeman. G. Hay, *Story of Arbroath*, p. 130.

made concrete, not merely formally but in the very spirit of the older period, during the fourteenth and fifteenth centuries. The code of the Four Burghs showed that in Scotland there was a considerable degree of uniformity among the burghs, and the deliberations of some of them with regard to the laws of succession, which are recorded in the first volume of the Scots Acts of Parliament, prove that it was the desire of the burghs themselves to work together. Their joint organization, moreover, had reached a further degree. They had a court of appeal from the sentence of the burgh courts, the cases being heard by the chamberlain and sixteen good men of the burghs of Berwick, Roxburgh, Stirling, and Edinburgh. During the struggle for Scots independence both the English invaders and the Scots defenders made makeshift arrangements to carry on this court.[1]

During the fifteenth century the Court of the Four Burghs continued to function. There are acts of parliament regarding its procedure, records of some of the cases that came before it have survived, and even the cost of sending representatives from the burghs has come down to us.[2] After the very early years of the seventeenth century no more is heard of it: with the decline of the powers and functions of the chamberlain and the reorganization of the administration of justice, its standing and work dwindled away, and the College of Justice, instituted in 1537, took its place as the court of appeal for the burghs as well as for the rest of the nation. It had, however, wider powers, which were exercised and developed at meetings held during the fifteenth century. For instance, in 1454, James II ordained that the court should meet in Edinburgh, and besides hearing appeals, amongst other duties entrusted to it was that it should give the correct measures of the ell, stoup, and stone to the lieges. The Four Burghs were responsible for the standard measures during the sixteenth century and later. Edinburgh had the custody of the ell, Stirling of the stoup, Lanark of the stone, and Linlithgow of the firlot. The court had also wider powers. In 1500 a record survives of a meeting of the Court of Parliament of the Four Burghs at which the following characteristic regulations were passed: the acts of parliament

[1] Th. Keith, "The Convention of Royal Burghs," *Scottish Hist. Review*, vol. x, p. 384.

[2] *Ibid.* pp. 387-389.

forbidding craftsmen from using merchandise were ordered to be enforced; no one who was not a burgess was to go to France or Flanders with merchandise; only persons resident within the burghs were to be freemen or "haunt merchandise." [1]

Meanwhile the official originally entrusted with the supervision of the burghs, the chamberlain, was waning in importance. As part of the reorganization of the national administration undertaken by James I when he returned from captivity, the powers of this official were reduced, and other offices to do some of his work were created—notably that of the Lord High Treasurer. The chamberlain's ayre is last mentioned in 1491, and after 1487 no receipts from these courts are recorded in the *Exchequer Rolls*. His connection with the burghs seems, gradually, to have died away. In 1486, for instance, he was still the authority appealed to by some of the citizens of Perth to adjudicate in a quarrel over the site of the fish market. In 1598–99, when similar trouble again arose, they applied to the Privy Council.[2]

The habit of acting together seems to have been innate among the Scots burghs, for even before the decline of the chamberlain's authority over them they were already creating the organization that eventually took his place. In 1357 seventeen burghs appointed the representatives of the four burghs of Edinburgh, Perth, Aberdeen, and Dundee to act for them in the negotiations regarding the payment of David II's ransom. The constant negotiations that were involved in the carrying on of the trade with the Low Countries were several times referred to the "quatres grosses villes" and once to "toutes les autres grosses villes du royaume d'Escoce,"[3] and the expenses of the embassies involved were met by the burghs. During the fifteenth century meetings of representatives of the Royal Burghs were summoned from time to time by the royal authority, to consider legislation that affected the commercial community. By an act of 1487 the commissioners of the burghs were even ordered to meet yearly, under pain of fine, to consider the "weilfare of merchandes, merchandice, guid rewle and statutis for the common profite of burrowis." The burghs

[1] Th. Keith, *Scottish Hist. Review*, vol. x, pp. 390-391.
[2] *A.P.S.* vol. ii, p. 227; *Register, Privy Council*, vol. v, p. 513.
[3] Th. Keith, *Scottish Hist. Review*, vol. x, pp. 393, 395.

also seem to have met sometimes on their own account.[1] But there was no formal annual gathering. During the sixteenth century the burghs continued to hold meetings, though the chamberlain was no longer present and the gatherings were no longer called the Court of the Four Burghs. These meetings exercised no judicial functions, but they carried on negotiations regarding foreign trade and made regulations concerning it, and gradually, from them, was evolved the unique Scots institution of the Convention of Royal Burghs.

In 1533 an important meeting was held at which the provost, bailies, and council of Edinburgh and the commissioners of Dundee, Perth, St Andrews, and Stirling decided that all royal burghs should send commissioners yearly to Edinburgh to: advise and decern anent all manner of things counter the common weal of burghs and of merchants, and to find remedy for taxation and stents that may happen to come against them, and that every burgh bring with them such articles and writings in what things they are hurt in, so that reformation and help may be put thereintil for the universal weal; and that any burgh not sending a representative be fined five pounds. This proposal to hold annual meetings did not materialize for some years, but the idea and the tendency towards organizing continued to grow. From 1552 regular records of the meetings that did take place have been preserved. The burghs continued to meet at irregular intervals—the state of the country was, of course, at the time very troubled—till 1578, when regular meetings began to be held.[2]

The Convention of Royal Burghs was a body composed of representatives of all the royal and free burghs; no royal officer presided over their meetings, and they met upon their own initiative to consult about the affairs of the burghs and of trade and commerce, and to defend the privileges of their members, although they received some endorsement from parliament. In 1578, some time after they had become fully formed, an act of parliament that ratified the privileges of the burghs also enacted that commissioners from the burghs might meet four times a year, in what burgh they pleased, "for sic matters as concerns thair estait." Three years later, in 1581,

[1] *A.P.S.* vol. ii, pp. 179, 224.

[2] Th. Pagan, *Convention of Royal Burghs*, pp. 21-22.

another act stated that, " for as much as it was found necessary to the king and his predecessors that the commissioners of burghs should convene at such time as they think good, in what burgh they thought most expedient, with full commission to treat upon the welfare of merchants, merchandise, good rule and statutes for the common profit of the burghs" . . . therefore these privileges were ratified, and, in addition, burghs not sending representatives to the Convention were to be fined £20.[1] They appear to have grown up without a charter or any other formal authorization from the state. Yet, on the other hand, they fulfilled public functions. The management of the Scots staple at Campveere was in their hands; the conservator who was in charge there was their servant, although he also acted as the king's ambassador. They were also responsible for the assessment of the individual burgh's share of the lump sum of taxation imposed upon them as a whole by parliament.[2] The position seems a little strange to modern eyes; it was, however, evolved to meet sixteenth-century needs and not those of the present day.

The Convention was made up of one commissioner from each of the royal burghs, except Edinburgh, which sent two. In nearly all the burghs these commissioners were selected by the town council, but in Aberdeen he was " chosin by sound of bell, and consent of the community "—Aberdeen, it will be remembered, had not adopted the constitution prescribed in the act of 1469. The Convention made its own regulations with regard to the commissioners, and rigidly insisted upon their being merchants (1574, 1578). It had, however, as we have seen, statutory powers to punish burghs that did not send representatives. It met annually, at different burghs, but constantly exercised the right of having emergency meetings or meetings of only some of the commissioners in between whiles, and these less formally constituted assemblages were often, though not always, held in Edinburgh. The meetings were not always harmonious. Once the commissioner for Anstruther Easter signed himself " Iohne Alexander submitt him under yok of oppressioun." This was stigmatized as a " horiable and schamfull offense," and he was punished. The Convention

[1] *A.P.S.* vol. iii, pp. 102, 224.

[2] Th. Keith, *Scottish Hist. Review*, vol. x, p. 395.

had an "Agent," who was responsible for collecting dues, fines, etc., and acted as a sort of secretary.[1]

Of the public duties undertaken by the Convention, the assessment of the individual burghs is perhaps the most surprising. The precedent for such action occurred at the very outset of the tentative association of the burghs. In 1357, at the council which made arrangements for the payment of the ransom of David II, the four burghs who were delegated to represent the rest were entrusted with the duty of assessing them for their individual shares of the payments; again, in 1483, the taxation of the burghs north of the Forth was to be modified by a Convention of Burghs. The first occasion upon which the Convention of the Royal Burghs actually made the assessment was in 1555.[2]

The arrangements made under the Convention of Royal Burghs are important and interesting, not only as a part of the activities of the institution itself, but as an illustration of that strongly-felt connection between privileges and burdens which is such a marked feature of Scots social life during our period. The earliest stent roll (taxation roll) that is extant contains the names of thirty-six royal burghs and of five church burghs. All these appear at later meetings of the Convention without any formal admission, while the twenty-six which were admitted later each had to apply for admission and to produce its charter as a royal burgh before becoming members. After being admitted, the burgh seems to have become liable to taxation and its name appears on the stent roll, and, as a rule, it was only after its name had been put on the stent roll that it gained parliamentary representation.[3] All the members of the Convention had the trading rights of royal burghs, including the five church burghs who appeared upon the stent roll. A few of the burghs which were admitted later, such as Annan and Kirkwall, were ancient though small royal burghs, but they do not appear upon the stent roll until after the exhibition of their charters to the Convention. When burghs of barony or of regality were promoted to be royal burghs, they generally applied to the Convention for admission soon after they had

[1] Th. Pagan, *Convention of Royal Burghs*, pp. 32, 38, 45, 46, 47.

[2] *Ibid.* pp. 8, 15.

[3] R. S. Rait, *Scottish Hist. Review*, xii, p. 131.

received their charters. Such applications were generally opposed by the neighbouring royal burghs, who feared encroachment on their privileges over economically subject districts and monopoly of foreign trade.[1] This opposition was especially marked in the case of the Fifeshire towns, where the royal burghs, during the sixteenth century, became strung along the coast, almost like beads upon a string. Pittenweem was made a royal burgh, and, after some delay, applied for admission in 1563, but Crail opposed this by bringing an action before the Lords of Session, declaring that Pittenweem was within its bounds and liberties. Pittenweem, however, was admitted. Crail also unsuccessfully opposed the admission of Anstruther Easter and Anstruther Wester and of Kilrenny (1587 and 1592). Culross opposed the admission of Inverkeithing, but the latter was admitted after the matter had been submitted to arbitration.[2]

The assessment was drawn up by a committee of the Convention and was then approved by the whole body, and the same one was used both for national taxation and for that raised by the Convention itself for the service of the burghs. The stent roll of 1555 had to be made because some of the burghs were impoverished, owing to " weir, pest and utheris cummeris " (it was indeed a most troublous time), and thereafter constant changes were made in the relative proportion of taxation payable by the different burghs.[3]

The work of the Convention of Royal Burghs in connection with the foreign trading relations of Scotland was even more important. It was, as Th. Pagan says, " one of the chief duties of the commissioners." " Until the latter part of the seventeenth century no trade of any importance was carried on except under the auspices and control of the Convention, whether organized, as was the trade of the Low Countries, or carried on by individual members, without any highly organized system, as were the trades of England, France, and the Baltic countries." [4]

[1] Th. Pagan, *Convention of Royal Burghs*, p. 28.

[2] *Ibid.* p. 29. Another example is the opposition of Sanquhar to the admission of Lochmaben.

[3] Th. Pagan, *Convention of Royal Burghs*, p. 57 (in 1582, 1587, 1591, 1594, 1597).

[4] *Ibid.* p. 150.

Scotland, largely owing to its backwardness and poverty, was without the regulated and joint-stock companies which were beginning to appear in England, and the services of the Convention, as the representative of the individual merchants, must have been of great value. An agent sent to the English court was described as "the gentleman appertayninge to the merchantes of Scotland."[1] Apart from the Low Countries, where the Convention was greatly concerned in the administration of the staple, it undertook its most important negotiations with France. It was many times called upon to repeal the duties levied on Scots goods in contravention of existing commercial treaties. Sometimes the Convention sent representatives of its own to negotiate. For instance, Ninian Cockburn was despatched there to obtain the repeal of a French ordinance that no Scot was to trade with France without the permission of the queen-regent or of her lieutenant, and was promised 300 crowns if he succeeded (he apparently got the reward). At other times the burghs specially employed—and paid—the Scots ambassador for such work.[2]

The Convention, however, was even more concerned in the arrangements and negotiations concerning trade in the Low Countries. During the fourteenth and fifteenth centuries a body referred to as the Commissioners of the Burghs played an important part in such transactions, but it is not clear whether they were the members of a less developed form of organization such as the Convention itself or were the parliamentary representatives of the burghs acting together. During the earlier part of the sixteenth century, in the tortuous negotiations regarding the establishment of the staple, there was a good deal of uncertainty and the burghs did not always act together. They were divided in their opinions as to which town would be most convenient for the establishment of the staple and even as to whether it were desirable to have a staple port at all.

Eventually, in 1577, the burghs were summoned, as they had been summoned many times before, to discuss the establishment of a fixed staple port, and the Convention of Royal Burghs was now established and was the organization through

[1] Th. Pagan, *Convention of Royal Burghs*, p. 159.

[2] *Ibid.* pp. 200, 201, 198.

which the burghs were consulted. Burghal opinion had by this time changed, and it was generally felt that a fixed staple was desirable, as it would prevent the transportation of forbidden goods. It was decided that the staple should be established at Campveere; and after long negotiations regarding the advantages that the Scots merchants should enjoy there, this was arranged. It remained almost continuously the staple port, although proposals were made, from time to time, to change it. In such negotiations the king and the Convention of Royal Burghs both took part, and " it is impossible to assign to either one particular sphere and it is difficult to estimate their respective influences. On the whole, the Convention appears to have had its own way, unless the king was specially anxious to enforce his wishes, and, generally speaking, the Convention attended to all the details of regulation and arrangement " (Pagan).

The Convention was pertinacious in gaining more and more privileges for the Scots at Campveere. It " appointed the factors, the minister, and the keeper of the Conciergerie House; made regulations for their conduct, and exercised a general supervision over the whole settlement. And also, an important and difficult work, they endeavoured to secure that the Scots merchants should keep their side of the contract: that is, that they should restrict their trade to the staple port " (Pagan).

There was, however, considerable difference of opinion between the Convention of Royal Burghs and the Crown with regard to the right of appointing the conservator at the staple port. This official is first mentioned in a treaty of 1407 between Scotland and the Duke of Burgundy regarding the staple at Bruges. He was to be appointed by the Duke. All successive conservators were appointed by the king ; but towards the end of the sixteenth century, as the Convention of Royal Burghs gradually took form, it began to claim that it ought to be consulted in such appointments and that officers to whom it objected ought to be removed.

It must be remembered that from the very first the conservator was subject to the merchants as well as to the king. An act of the Scots Parliament of 1503 had ordered that he should either appear himself or send a representative to appear before the merchants every year. It is not clear what body of merchants was meant at that time, but from the very beginning of the records of the Convention of Royal Burghs he is found appearing before them from time to time, and they often exercised the right of summoning him. The conservator had to serve many masters. He was the agent of the king for Scots affairs in the Low Countries. He sometimes received instruction from parliament. But far more often he got orders from the Convention of Royal Burghs, in the course of their supervision of Scots trade. For instance, in 1529, they laid down the composition of the court for dealing with the disputes and crimes of Scots merchants in the Low Countries, over which he presided. Any merchant who wished to complain of his conduct had the right of appealing to the Convention of Royal Burghs. In 1575 the Convention drew up a list of his duties. It also regulated the amount which the merchants were to pay as his fees.

The Convention made its first effort to obtain some say in his appointment in 1565, when the old conservator was dying. The commissioners then asked that one of the factors at Campveere should be appointed to the post, but dutifully added that the king should appoint a more qualified person if he pleased. The king gave the post to a favourite, Sir Robert Dennistoun, and the Convention refused to acknowledge him, forbade the merchants to pay the duties which had been granted to him, and ordered him to appear before it. Dennistoun obeyed, and explained that when he had accepted office he had not known that the burghs objected so strongly to him. After he had made ample apologies, the Convention accepted him as conservator; but he did not give satisfaction, and after sundry complaints against him, the burghs, acting through the Convention, decided to get the appointment of conservator into their own hands: for whose behoof only he is created and constituted, and of whom he has his living for the service to be done to them in the Low Countries. Dennistoun again managed to smooth things over. He promised to appear before the Convention every year to receive instructions. The matter, however, had not reached any finality and there was some difficulty over the appointment of almost every one of his successors during the seventeenth century.[1]

The Convention, moreover, interested itself in Scots trade

[1] Th. Pagan, *Convention of Royal Burghs*, pp. 161-179.

generally. It made regulations about the proper barrelling of fish. Barrels were to be of a uniform size and stamped by an inspector. Coopers were to be sworn in and their barrels marked with their name and that of their burgh (1550 and 1579). In thus regulating the fisheries, the Convention was not only carrying out the policy of the Scots Parliament, but was copying the methods of the Dutch, who were outstandingly successful in their fisheries at this time.

It also endeavoured to deal with the pirate nuisance, though without much success. At one time it proposed to fit out a ship to purge the seas of pirates and wicked persons, but apparently nothing was done; on another occasion 1000 merks were to be paid to someone to provide such a ship, but nothing is known of the result (1574, 1587). In 1577 a representative was sent to England to try to get redress, but he achieved no permanent abatement although he remained there two years. Petitions were also sent to the King of Denmark and the Prince of Orange in this matter.[1]

The Convention was the mouthpiece of the trading community in all national legislation affecting these interests. It has been already stated that the main policy of the central authority in Scotland was to ensure abundance of home supplies of necessaries. On the whole, the desires of the merchants (which were voiced by the Convention) were in accord with this attitude. They wanted plenty of coal, victual, and wool. Their attitude towards the export of wool is, however, rather puzzling from another point of view, because this article was one of the main exports of the kingdom and formed one of their monopolies. It is most conveniently considered in relation to the new industries.

Quite naturally, the Convention strongly disapproved of the new import duties imposed by act of parliament in 1597. It stigmatized them as "ane new and intollerabill custom," and ordered its members to "lament thair caus to the king and the lords of the exchequer," and advised the burghs to obstruct trade so that the people generally might be sensible of the hurt this innovation would do them. All this, however, met with no success.[2]

[1] Th. Pagan, *Convention of Royal Burghs*, pp. 158-160.
[2] *Ibid.* p. 152.

A rather curious enterprise undertaken by the Convention of Royal Burghs was the leasing of the customs in 1582. When James VI assumed control of affairs it will be remembered that the state of the national finances was deplorable. A much stricter administration of the customs was instituted, and, owing to friction and complaints, both by the king's comptroller and by the merchants, the Convention of Royal Burghs resolved to take a tack of the customs and to administer them itself. A sum of £4000 was to be paid and also 30 tuns of wine, and the lease was to last for four years, but was eventually extended for three more. The burghs appointed custumars to collect the customs at all ports, and Edinburgh, Perth, Dundee, and Aberdeen became sureties for the payment of the rent. The undertaking was not at all successful. It was not lucrative to the burghs, and, although an act of parliament had been passed to safeguard the lieges from undue exactions, there was discontent with the way that the customs were collected, and in 1587 a dearth was attributed to this cause.[1]

Another enterprise in which the Convention regulated the communal activities of the burghs was the development of the making of cloth of better quality. This enterprise, so ineffective in itself and yet so significant of a great change in the whole fiscal and economic policy of Scotland, is, however, more easily described as a whole.

Besides such external activities, the Convention of Royal Burghs was very active in supervising the affairs of the individual burghs, over which it had considerable power. In this it was acting thoroughly in accordance with the old spirit of unification of the earlier period. Upon occasion it acted on their behalf in negotiations with the Crown—as, for instance, in arranging the amount of composition they should pay if they wished to obtain exemption from their military service. Besides assessing the share to be paid by individual burghs in their contribution towards the burghs' quota of the national taxation, it had the right of levying private taxes upon them, for money to be spent upon the service of the burghs—embassies, etc.—and it could also exact fines from them. It constantly ordered individual burghs to report their diligence in carrying out its regulations

[1] Th. Pagan, *Convention of Royal Burghs*, p. 56.
See also *Exchequer Rolls*, vol. xxi, pp. liii, lix, lxi.

—whether they observed its prohibition against trading with unfree towns, conducted their elections in the manner prescribed, administered their Common Good properly, etc. It also granted special help to burghs who required assistance in carrying out works of public utility or because they were specially afflicted. An example occurs in 1587.

The Convention strongly inculcated uniformity in the methods of conducting burghal elections. It appears to have been entirely satisfied with the strange and oligarchical procedure enjoined in the act of 1469 and the other parliamentary statutes. Its energies were bent upon making all the burghs observe these acts. In 1552—one would think at a singularly unfortunate moment, for the quarrel between the Edinburgh merchants and craftsmen was entering upon an acute phase and affairs in the burgh cannot have been very happy—the Convention enacted that because there was so much variation in the methods of conducting their elections, all the burghs were in future to follow the procedure of Edinburgh.[1] It was constantly making rules that the acts of parliament in this matter must be obeyed, and it took action in the case of individual burghs. In 1595, for instance, it tried to make the burgh of Glasgow have a Dean of Gild like all royal burghs. Glasgow was unwilling, but eventually, in 1605, as the result of further pressure by the Convention, a new burghal constitution was drawn up very much in conformity with those of the royal burghs.[2] In regulating the elections of the burghs it was acting in accordance with the wishes of parliament. For instance, in Aberdeen, the craftsmen were dissatisfied by the corrupt and oligarchic government of the burgh, and in 1590 they applied to the Convention to have the proper constitution of the burgh observed. The Convention at first refused to interfere, but the matter was also referred to it by parliament, and, in 1592, it gave directions as to the proper carrying out of the elections.[3]

[1] Th. Pagan, *Convention of Royal Burghs*, p. 77.

[2] *Ibid.* p. 80. Some authorities describe this transaction as due to the initiative of the Convention. Others suggest that the merchants of Glasgow, desiring a stronger position, " inspired " the action of the Convention. In any case, the results were not very happy, for trouble between the merchants and craftsmen followed.

[3] *Ibid.* p. 80.

It also endeavoured to supervise the administration of the Common Good of the burghs. This had been one of the duties of the chamberlain, and probably the gradual dying away of his supervision of burghal affairs, at the end of the fifteenth century, encouraged the alienation and dilapidation that set in. The facilities for alienating burgh lands were certainly increased in the sixteenth century, for although the acts allowing the feuing of land did not originally apply to burghal property, "the burghs began to get licences from the king allowing them to convert common property let under short leases into heritable estates to be held in feu-farm" (Pagan). Parliament passed acts to try to prevent the alienation of the Common Good, but the Convention of Royal Burghs was the authority mainly responsible for trying to check the abuse—a very serious one, when it is remembered how dependent were the burghs upon agriculture. Considering that the commissioners of which it was composed were the nominees of the burghal authorities who had to be called to book, the arrangement, like so many others made in sixteenth-century Scotland, seems to be a strange one. Yet the Convention displayed considerable activity. Until far on into the second half of the seventeenth century, it was the policy of the Convention to make the burghs submit all the leases of their property to its scrutiny. In 1589 it passed regulations that all the common property of the burghs, lands, fishings, customs, etc., were to be rouped to the best avail, and that every burgh was to report to the Convention their diligence under this order. In 1591 it again considered the matter, and found that some burghs had obeyed and that others had been slothful. The order was repeated, with the further provision that lands should not be let to gentlemen outwith the burghs. Further discussions took place in 1598, 1599, and 1600, but the Convention did not merely confine itself to words. Action was taken against individual burghs: in 1594, for instance, against Inverkeithing.[1]

It was, however, as the guardians of the ancient privileges of the royal burghs, of the merchants, and of the burgesses, that the Convention was most active, and in which it shows how innately it was a conservative development of the ancient urban and industrial organization of Scotland. The burghal authorities,

[1] Th. Pagan, *Convention of Royal Burghs*, pp. 102-108.

whom the commissioners of the Convention of Royal Burghs represented, were mainly dominated by the merchants, and it was expressly laid down that the commissioners themselves should be "merchantis and trafficquaris, haifand thair remanying and dwelling within burgh and beris bourdene with the nychbouris and inhabitants thairof." In 1574—very early in the career of the Convention—Haddington sent a commissioner who was a cordwainer, but the other commissioners insisted that he should leave, because " na craftisman hes evir had, noder aucht or suld haif, voit or commission amangis thame." [1]

Such was the composition of the Convention, and it is not surprising to find that its attitude towards the privileges of the merchants and of the royal burghs was consistent and active. It is, however, worth noticing that in defending their privileges the commissioners did not take the narrowest view of all, and that they strongly supported the craftsmen when the latter were struggling against unprivileged persons. In 1587 the Dundee tailors, apparently finding their own magistrates lax in defending them, appealed to the Convention that they were suffering from the competition of unfree workers, and that all craftsmen ought to be under the supervision of a craft deacon and to pay their fair share of the burdens. In reply, it ordered that all provosts and bailies " scharplie attend to all vnfriemen " who were usurping freemen's privileges.[2] In 1595 the craftsmen of St Andrews appealed to the Convention of Royal Burghs against the misuse of the Common Good by the burgh authorities.[3]

The strenuous efforts of the commissioners to maintain their privileges took up much of their time at their meetings and occupied a great deal of space in the records of their meetings. It was a continuous striving, begun under those tentative meetings of the representatives of the burghs during the fifteenth and early sixteenth centuries. But, for convenience, the objects of the jealous attention of the burghs may be classified under several headings. One of their principal objects " was to prevent the infringement of their trading privileges by the erection

[1] Th. Pagan, *Convention of Royal Burghs*, pp. 33, 34.

[2] A. Warden, *Burgh Laws of Dundee*, p. 423.

[3] *Records of the Convention of Royal Burghs*, vol. i, p. 460.

of new royal burghs, which would share in foreign trade; and by the erection of "burghs of regality and barony, which had the right of holding markets and fairs, while their inhabitants could trade within their own burghs." In 1584 the Convention ordained that if a new royal burgh was created within the limits of an existing one the whole of the burghs should interpose their powers in contrair thereof. Ayr opposed the erection of Maybole and the Convention helped to pay her legal expenses and ordered all the royal burghs to refuse to recognize Maybole until she actually became a member of the Convention. It also assisted Wigtown against Stranraer and Aberdeen against Fraserburgh. Individual royal burghs were stimulated to try to stop burghs of barony within their boundaries from infringing their monopolies. Forfar went to law with Kirriemuir, Perth was ordered to proceed against Clackmannan. In 1582, Edinburgh received orders to pursue all unfree towns usurping the privileges of burghs. The proceeding of several royal burghs against Minniegaff, in Kirkcudbrightshire, lasted until well into the seventeenth century.[1]

The struggle, however, was also waged against individuals; against non-freemen living outside the royal burghs; against actual burgesses and merchants of these burghs who chose to live outside, and who thus escaped many of the burdens attached to their freedom; and against non-freemen within the burghs themselves. The representatives of the burghs, from almost the first, had exerted themselves to obtain statutory protection. The act of 1488, for instance, ordering that sailors in merchandise be freemen of the burghs and indwellers, was the ratification of a former act granted at the desire of the whole of the commissioners of the burghs (the latter may have been the parliamentary representatives or members of an incidental meeting). In 1500 the Court of the Parliament of the Four Burghs ordained that none but burgesses who were dwellers within the royal burghs should take merchandise to Flanders or to France, and that all who "haunted" merchandise should make continuous residence within the burghs and pay duties there. In 1529 the commissioners of the burghs repeated this prohibition. All persons disobeying it were to forfeit the

[1] Th. Pagan, *Convention of Royal Burghs*, pp. 123, 126-127.

goods, and no merchant was to act on behalf of a craftsman or unfree person.[1]

After the beginning of the regular records of the Convention of Royal Burghs, as Th. Keith points out, few of the annual meetings passed without the making of some regulations against the multitude of " unfriemen saillaris " who engaged in foreign trade and thus reaped the benefit of the merchants' monopoly without helping to bear their charges ; or invaded the exclusive trade and manufacturing rights that the royal burghs enjoyed within their districts but did not share in their burdens. To achieve this object the Convention adopted many methods. They petitioned the king, the Privy Council, parliament, to strengthen the laws that protected them, pointing out that the royal burghs were " subject to all taxationis, impositiounis, and chairgis for the commoun weill of the realm, quhairof the saidis vnfrie townis ar frie and delyverit." Some of the acts of parliament supporting the burghal privileges were passed in response to such petitions.

The most detailed instructions were issued. Merchants were forbidden to " colour " the goods of non-freemen upon any pretext. All who wished to trade abroad were to obtain a ticket certifying that they were entitled to do so from the Dean of Gild or magistrates of their burgh, which was to be renewed every voyage, and, if they went to the Low Countries, had to be handed to the conservator. The most stringent orders were issued that no skipper was to ship anyone without a ticket. The conservator was to send home a list of all merchants who visited the staple port to their own burghs, so that unfreemen might be detected and punished. No " coquets," the official notification that customs had been paid and without which a ship might not sail, were to be granted to unfreemen or to ships loaded at an unfree port. Again and again all merchants were ordered to live within their burghs. The Convention also tried to make the burghs themselves prosecute unfreemen within their bounds, or merchants and burgesses who lived outside them. This was the most usual method, and " in the records for each meeting during the sixteenth and early seventeenth centuries, and especially at the beginning of the seventeenth century, there are continual and rather wearisome reports from

[1] Th. Pagan, *Convention of Royal Burghs*, pp. 120-122.

different burghs of their diligence in pursuing some unfreemen or non-resident burgesses, and making them cease trading or reside in the burgh and bear the burden with the inhabitants."[1]

It is noteworthy that the Convention of Royal Burghs grew up during our period from more ancient tendencies, and that at the end of the sixteenth century it was not only still largely imbued with the same ideas but was just attaining to the time of its greatest power and vigour.

Part VIII. The Stirring of New Ideas

The close of the sixteenth century and of the period under review saw the ancient burgh organization, with its peculiar privileges, still firmly established and full of vigour ; the exports of the country were mainly the same as at the beginning of the period, the only exceptions being a considerable manufacture of leatherwork and the weaving of more plaiding ; the balance of importance between the country and the towns had not been materially altered ; there was no scope for a large industrial class, and there is no evidence that such a one existed ; the economic life of the country must have been very largely as it had been in the fourteenth century. The Union with England was destined to bring great changes to Scotland, the evolution of new economic ambitions and changed forms of social organization. Nevertheless it is interesting to notice that the beginnings of these changes were faintly stirring before the Union of the Crowns. How far the country would have developed upon the newer lines, had this Union never taken place, is, however, merely a matter of conjecture.

All the Stewart kings were very accessible to new ideas, and all of them were hard up and eager to add to their revenues. They nearly all introduced new projects to increase the productivity of their kingdom : the gold-mining enterprises of James IV are but an example. It is not, therefore, at all wonderful that they should have wished to improve the craftsmanship of their country by introducing foreign workmen. The famous swordmaker Andrea de Ferrara, whose sword-blades were heirlooms in many a Scots family, is supposed to have come to Scotland from Italy in the reign of James IV or V. According

[1] Th. Pagan, *Convention of Royal Burghs*, pp. 122, 123, 125.

to Pitscottie, James V imported craftsmen—gunners, wrights, carvers, painters, masons, smiths, harness-makers, embroiderers, tailors—from France, Spain, Holland, and England. The advantages of such a course were obvious. Henderson, an Englishman, in his *Godly and Golden Book*, urges that the Scots should "gar draw the weste and easte sees togither" (by a canal ?), should improve their mines, and should import a hundred craftsmen to teach their craft workers to improve their "commotities of myndes, wull, skynns, and hide" before exporting them, and "as myners, cutters of mosses for makinge of menns landes of thos that be but maresse, makers of iron mylls, saw mylls and others, collyerdes, dighters of woll, websters, walkers, tappischers, makers of worsates and serges, workers in the scols, diers of skynnes and hides, as bowers, thatchers and such other." Although they were extremely jealous of any infringement of their privileges, the burgesses themselves were sometimes not averse to profiting by the skill of the foreigners. In Edinburgh, in 1564–65, an English arrowsmith was received as a burgess upon the condition that he would teach his craft to others.[1]

James VI, to whom far greater innovations were due, was no doubt influenced by the same considerations as his predecessors : the hope of adding to the riches of his kingdom, the desire to curb the exclusive and turbulent craftsmen. The king himself attributes his introduction of foreigners to the latter reason, in his advice to his son : "The craftes-men thinke we should be content with their worke, how bad and dear soever it be, and if they in anything be controlled, up goeth the blew blanket. But for their part take example of England, how it hath flourished both in wealth and policie since the stranger craftsmen came in among them. Therefore not only permit but allure strangers to come here also ; taking as straite order for repressing the mutining of ours at them, as was done in England at their first inbringing there." In this passage James shows that he was keenly alive to economic developments to the south of the Border, and, indeed, the

[1] S. Smiles, *Industrial Biographies*, p. 23.

J. D. Marwick, *Edinburgh Gilds and Crafts*, p. 101.

James Henderson, *The Godly and Golden Book*, printed in *Calendar of Scottish Papers*, vol. i (1547–1563), p. 144.

stirring of the new ideas that are now to be described must be attributed to the outside influences from the South and not to native developments.[1] The king's motives, moreover, were very mixed ones, and were largely inspired by his desire to plenish his ever-empty treasury.

It will be remembered that in England, unlike Scotland, the sixteenth century was an age of great economic advance.[2] After the middle of the century the court and the men of affairs of Scotland were brought into increasingly close touch with the South and would naturally be familiar with conditions there. Scotland, poor and with little maritime power or ambition, could not hope to copy England in her chartered companies or her overseas enterprises, although at least one company was formed even during this period. In 1575–76 a company with fifty shares was formed to work the gold and silver, lead and copper mines of Scotland, and was given certain privileges. There was, however, another institution which was only too congenial to the needy king and courtiers: the practice of giving special privileges, generally monopoly rights, to encourage individuals to introduce some improved method of manufacture or useful invention. Such benefits came to be conferred in return for a money payment, or as a reward to a favourite or person whose support had to be secured. About the same time the same methods were applied to the fiscal arrangements and the export of goods was forbidden, and then licences to do so were granted or sold to individuals. It is needless to enlarge upon the wide possibilities for royal money-making and for public abuses that such a system opened up, but in individual cases it is impossible to tell whether such grants were made mainly in the public interest, to encourage a genuine improvement or really to develop home trade, or mainly for the benefit of the sovereign. In the case of licences to export forbidden goods free of custom, a further development of the system, the harm done was double, for not only was a monopoly created, but the national revenue derived from the customs was diminished.

[1] Quoted, vol. i, *Report of Commission on Municipal Corporations in Scotland*, 1836, p. 81.

[2] Cf. H. Meredith Williams, *Outlines of the Economic Development of England*, p. 185.

Salt was a favourite subject for such grants. In 1563 an act of parliament was passed stating that, in order to encourage a new process of salt-making by certain foreigners, no native was to make this particular kind for fifty years except by special licence, and two years later Queen Mary "contractit" with a Florentine and his English partner "anent the making of greit salt within our realm of ane new sort and fassioun." In 1587, Lady Burleigh was given a seven-year monopoly of a process for making Scots salt that would cure fish. In 1599 a Fleming had certain monopolies in the making of great salt granted in reward for inventions he had introduced. Meanwhile, in 1573, owing to a shortage of salt, its export was forbidden except in the case of ships bringing timber, that most necessary commodity, from Norway and the Eastland, who were to be allowed to carry away salt on their return journey. In 1574 the export of salt was again forbidden, but by this act the licensing system was introduced. No one was "to transport or cary ony maner of salt out of this realm without oure soverane lordis licence in writt first obtenit to that effect under the signet and subscription of the regentis grace." In all of these instances the motives may have been good or, at least, mixed. There can be little excuse for the following: in 1598–99 the comptroller of artillery complained that the office of collector of the duties on salt, which he had enjoyed for fourteen years, had been purchased by a burgess of Edinburgh "be sum sinister moyen maid with his majesty." [1]

Salt was only one item among the goods that might not be exported. The export of live stock, tallow, and corn had been forbidden from time to time when home supplies ran low, but in 1573 (the same year as that in which the export of salt was prohibited) an act was passed ordaining that linen cloth and yarn, lintseed, candles, tallow, butter, cheese, barked hides, and made shoes were not to be taken out of the country. The reasons for this measure can only be guessed at. Some of

[1] *Register, Privy Council*, vol. iii, pp. 510-511.
A.P.S. vol. ii, pp. 538, 495; vol. iii, p. 82.
Register, Privy Council, vol. v, p. 512; vol. xiv, p. 249 (1565–66).
Ibid. vol. vi, pp. 17-18.
See also J. Davidson and A. Gray, *The Scottish Staple at Veere*, p. 65.

the items may have been prohibited to ensure home supplies; hides were the raw material of native manufacturers. In other instances one can only wonder. In any case, the "forbidden goods" were to figure very often in the acts of parliament and the proceedings of the Privy Council. In 1578 parliament enacted that no licence should be given for transporting forbidden goods, and in 1581 a special act was passed dealing with the export of wool and another forbidding the export of live stock. In 1585, in a further act, it was stated that under colour of the king's licences, wool, tallow, and victuals were being daily transported out of the kingdom. In this case, as Professor Gray points out, "the issue of licences was not forbidden; parliament merely restricted itself to a measure which aimed at preventing a dishonest use of the system of licences, by requiring that licences should be signed by His Majesty's Comptroller, and without this signature they were to be invalid and to have no effect." In 1587 the Privy Council had decided that no licence to export forbidden goods should be valid unless signed by the Treasurer and Comptroller "sittand togedder in chekker." In 1597 wool once more received special attention. In 1600 a final act was passed discharging all licences already given, and imposing safeguards for their future issue.[1]

Such legislation gives an indication not only of the magnitude of the abuse of licence-giving, but of the struggle that the Privy Council waged against it. It is characteristic of the Scots mentality that in 1589–90 books were imported duty-free into Scotland by the special order of the Privy Council, which prevented the farmer of customs from levying taxes on them. In consequence English and foreign books sold as cheaply in Scotland as in England.[2]

Some of the manufacturing licences may be quoted, because of the sidelights that they throw on the life of the times. In 1593 a twenty-one years' tack of mining rights was given to an Edinburgh goldsmith on advantageous terms, because of the great expenses that he would incur, and because the king could not repay him money he had borrowed, the royal "fynanceis being swa exhaustit and sparpallit." In 1599 a

[1] *A.P.S.* vol. iii, pp. 83, 353, 379; vol. iv, p. 231.

[2] R. Chambers, *Domestic Annals of Scotland*, vol. i, p. 195.

burgess of Edinburgh complained that he had been granted by letters patent the sole right of painting the arms of the nobility at the times of their belting, promotion, forfeitures, and funerals, and that another burgess, by some privy moyen, had purchased a gift of the office over his head. Unfortunately for him, the lords of the Privy Council took the view that both gifts had been "inconsiderately granted," and gave leave to all persons to make choice of their own craftsmen as they might be had best and cheapest. One of the most ingenious of these royal attempts to raise the wind was the grant, in 1601, of sundry commissions against regraters, forestallers, and usurers. It was not, however, a success. For the purchasers made use of it to acquit any of their friends who had committed such crimes, to revenge themselves against any "innocents" against whom they bore any quarrel, and to make their own private gain and advantage by keeping the whole of the fines and escheats that they collected and by not paying over an agreed proportion to the treasury. The commissions were therefore abolished. More conventional monopolies were given for the making of copper, paper, glass, and iron, and in such cases, especially a nine-year paper-making monopoly which was granted to a German whilst the king was in Denmark, the object may have been largely disinterested.[1]

Weaving was one of the crafts in which the king gave monopolies, or rights to work in, to foreigners. Gilliam Van Narsone, a Fleming, had letters of gift granting him a twenty-one years' monopoly of the making of "amedone called stiffing," but he complained of a Scot who had learnt the secret. A Dutchman named Cornelius Draggie had a royal licence granted him to weave fustians and other stuffs. The weaver craft of Edinburgh, supported by the burgh authorities, interfered with the Dutchman; were ordered to cease doing so; and in consequence they complained to the Privy Council. The report of the proceedings throws a good deal of light upon the granting of such licences. The craftsmen complained of the invasion of their old privileges and narrated the laws under which they

[1] *Register, Privy Council,* vol. iv, pp. 452 (1589–90), 36, 291; vol. v, pp. 305, 117 (1593).

R. W. Cochran-Patrick, *Mediaeval Scotland,* pp. 54, 60.

Register, Privy Council, vol. iv, p. 159.

enjoyed them ; they declared that weaving was their only source of livelihood and that they were subject to watching, warding, and such other impositions that occurred. They also pointed out that Draggie was a " gross ignorant " of the craft, as well as an unfree person ; that he was a lapidary by trade, and that he merely employed the servants of Edinburgh weavers, trained up by them in the craft ; and that the licence was granted to him upon " sinistruos narration," because it was given upon the understanding that he was an apt and experienced weaver, whereas he was not present in this country at the time and was not called upon to prove his skill, as should have been done before the licence was granted. The granting of such a licence imported only the daily " preparative " to others to obtain the like, to the utter " domage," undoing, and detriment of the webster craft, who were the free lieges of His Majesty. Apparently there was foundation for the weavers' complaint, for the Privy Council suspended the licence, although, eventually, Draggie managed to have his privileges continued.[1]

These isolated licences to foreign wool-workers must be considered in relation to the plans for the improvement of the woollen industry—a complicated subject, for there are many currents and cross-currents of policy and interest which can only be guessed at. In 1580 the Convention of Royal Burghs proposed that the export of wool should be prohibited for three years. The reasons given were that the desolate craftsmen and poor labourers which are now put to extreme poverty for fault of labour and handwork be helped and supplied and also our sovereign's customs greatly advanced. (These admirable sentiments come strangely from the merchant-ridden Convention, for the export of wool was one of the valuable privileges of the merchants. It was far greater than that of cloth, and much of the cloth itself was of rural or suburban make. Early in the seventeenth century the burghs admitted that this was so, and said that their main interest was in " negotiating " it.) In the following year, in accordance with this resolution, an act of parliament was passed forbidding the export of wool. The preamble of this act states that it was passed so that the poor might be set to work and money increased. At the same

[1] *Register, Privy Council*, vol. vi, pp. 288, 107, 306-307.

time the holding of licences to export wool was categorically and most strictly prohibited. The improvement of the native woollen manufacture was, moreover, an important object in the eyes of the authorities. In 1582 an act was passed in favour of three Flemings who were to come to Scotland to instruct the people in cloth-making, and were to bring thirty companions. They were to teach the making of serges, grograms, fustians, "bombesies," stemmings, seys, "covertours of beds," and other fabrics. They were to take only Scotch apprentices, and were to be free of all taxes and services. These weavers are supposed to have settled at Bonnington, near Edinburgh. Nothing more, however, is heard of this enterprise, which seems to have achieved no permanent results. The Convention, however, still desired to prevent the export of wood. In 1578 and 1594 it passed resolutions ordering the burghs to punish anyone severely who made use of the royal licences and exported it.[1]

About 1597 there was renewed interest in industrial matters in parliament and the Privy Council. The import of English cloth was forbidden except under licence and upon payment of custom. This was perhaps to encourage home manufactures, but it also had the ulterior motive of increasing the royal revenue. An ordinance by the Privy Council of the following year, which provided for its proper enforcement, quite frankly states that it had been passed for the augmentation of the king's income. In future all such cloth, after paying duty, was to be stamped. The proper administration of this act was the matter of constant attention during the rest of the century, and there is evidence that it was really enforced and that merchants who infringed it were punished. At the same time, probably influenced by a fourth and more emphatic resolution of the Convention of the Royal Burghs, the Privy Council, and parliament, absolutely forbade the export of wool and the granting of licences. They therefore acted against the interests of the Crown. The sale of licences was a valuable source of income, and the tacksman of the customs had to be let off £700 on account of this act. The entrance of foreign craftsmen into the realm was at the same time forbidden. In this the Privy Council was

[1] *A.P.S.* vol. iii, p. 507.
Records of the Convention of Royal Burghs, vol. i, pp. 22, 75, 264-265; vol. ii, p. 203.

stultifying the efforts of 1587, but its action was no doubt pleasing to the craftsmen.[1]

The Convention of Royal Burghs, meanwhile, seems to have persisted in its attitude toward the export of wool, and, in the same year, passed another act forbidding its export. In 1598, however, there was a complete change in the royal policy. The Lords Auditors of the Exchequer, for the better advancement of the king's customs, had licensed the export of wool upon monthly payment of 5s. a stone, and the Privy Council, in spite of its own order of 1597, passed an act in 1598 annulling that of the Convention of the Royal Burghs, as a "pretendit act" and one that they had no right to pass, and declared that it had prevented many of the lieges from exporting wool and had "verrie far prejugiet his Heines in his custumes." In the following year the Privy Council again alluded to the effects of the action of the Convention of Royal Burghs in preventing the export of wool and hurting the custom receipts. The prohibition of the import of English cloth (it was sometimes forbidden and sometimes imported under licence) had led to a dearth of cloth, "thair being na present ordour tane for working of the country wool fer the use of the people," and an order was therefore made allowing merchants to export wool or import cloth for the benefit of the customs—as the act specially says. It was evidently the intention to continue the licence system for wool and the imposition of import duty for cloth. In 1600 these provisions were repeated. The entry of foreign craftsmen had again been prohibited in 1599, perhaps as a sop to vested interests. During the next few years the duty on imported cloth seems to have been fairly strictly collected.[2]

Meanwhile the king and his advisers turned to the improvement of native cloth. In 1600 they considered the petition of John Sutherland, clothworker, anent "the grite abuisses and imperfectiounes of the claith maid ordinarly within this realm, and the remedies thairof." A committee formed of six influential men of the realm and three burgesses of Edinburgh

[1] *Register, Privy Council*, vol. iv, p. 461; vol. v, pp. 385, 386, 471-472; vol. vi, p. 230.

Records of the Convention of Royal Burghs, vol. ii, pp. 26-29.

[2] *Register, Privy Council*, vol. v, p. 477; vol. vi, pp. 32, 77, 135-136, 320, 358, 602.

was appointed to consider Sutherland's proposals. At this time the Convention of the Royal Burghs was also favourable to the proposal to improve the woollen industry. It was proposed to bring in twenty labourers in wool and to raise money to pay the expenses of those who were to go abroad to secure them. The Privy Council (still in 1600) granted licence for a hundred foreign clothworkers to be brought into the country. The very long preamble gives a reasoned statement of the general position, and is worth paraphrasing: Forasmuch as one of the great causes that has procured the poverty of the country and the increase of so many sturdy and idle beggars has been that heretofore there has never any care or diligence been taken upon such commodities as the country itself yields, but, by the contrary, whereas the country has offered many good occasions for entertainment of the poor, with a particular benefit besides to every subject, yet the same has been in times bygone so far rejected that other realms and countries having our commodities transported to them have forced us to buy the same back from them, and they, having but a little bestowed their pain and labours, have reaped thereby inestimable profit. This inconvenience is most evident in the transporting of wool forth of the country, by the which, not only might the whole beggars, if the same were restrained, be put to work, but also the commonwealth might reap such benefit as others our neighbour countries do by the like, and every subject might have the buying of it at a far lower price nor the same has heretofore given, besides His Majesty's custom in great quantity in manner after specified. And because that the unskilfulness of our own people hithertofore, together with the unwillingness to suffer any strangers to come amongst them, has been one of the causes that has hindered this good work, they (the people) being unable, without the help of strangers, who are better acquaint with that trade, to attain to any perfection in that work: therefore our sovereign lord, to the effect that the said purpose, so oft hithertofore intended and as yet having no good success, may at the last have a prosperous beginning, has given and granted full power and liberty for a hundred families of strangers, being clothworkers of their trade, to transport themselves within this country. Owing to their ignorance of the language they might have a minister to teach them the word of God in their own tongue, provided he nowise "expones" himself to any point of discipline of the present Kirk. And the more to induce the strangers to repair hither, the master of every one of the said hundred families shall be, immediately after his coming within the country, naturalized and made free denizen of the same, and shall be made a free burgess of whatever burgh he takes up his abode in, and shall enjoy and bruik all the privileges of other burgesses, native-born subjects within this realm. And because the said hundred families, by their hither transporting, will be drawn to great and exorbitant charges, besides the loss of time before they be well settled, therefore our said sovereign lord and his council has "exemit" the said families during the space of ten years after their repairing to this country of all taxations, impositions, watching, warding, skatting, lotting, or any other burden that may be laid upon them during the said space.[1]

The king also wrote in 1601 to the burghs offering the management of a wool-making enterprise to the eight burghs of Edinburgh, Dundee, Perth, Aberdeen, Stirling, Glasgow, Ayr, and Cupar, with any others they might care to co-opt. To assist the scheme, he undertook that the next parliament should prohibit the export of wool and the import of cloth, and, if the burghs would not accept the enterprise or were dilatory, he threatened to put the matter into the hands of the country gentlemen. The burghs seem to have accepted, and the Privy Council was emphatic in hurrying them on. Edinburgh, to which the other burghs referred the arrangements, seems to have been energetic over the matter of fetching home foreign workmen. The correspondence between the town council and Sutherland and Hunter, the two representatives of the burghs who were sent to find the foreigners, survives. They were to secure people capable of all the processes of cloth manufacture and especially of the making of mixed colours, and they were to bring back a combmaker and a dyer, also a press and everything that the workers might think needful. Unmarried men were to be preferred, and they were not to buy tools unless they could get workers. They first went to Norwich, and careful arrangements were made with a Flemish weaver there, a cardmaker and a dyer. Matters, however, did not go very satis-

[1] *Register, Privy Council*, vol. vi, pp. 98, 123. *Convention of Royal Burghs*, vol. ii, pp. 98-99.

factorily, and Sutherland complains that the workers there could do little and thought no shame to ask much.

The agents went on to Holland, and described their experiences. They went round the workshops at Veere, and had their business announced in the kirk, bidding all those who were willing to go to Scotland to come to the sign of the Half-Moon, near the market-place, resolved upon what conditions they were to ask. Workers in broadcloth were hard to secure and their terms were unduly high. They would not agree to separate, but insisted upon working together in one burgh. Other weavers were not so hard to come by. Particulars about the making of combs and the growing of teazle follow. One of the agents went on to Amsterdam, where he secured four young men, and to Leyden, whence the people were very willing to come, but the magistrates, who did not wish to further the setting up of a rival industry in Scotland, refused to let them go. The Scots agent managed to send off several workmen secretly from the town, and, after receiving a present of wine from the magistrates, followed them. A list survives of the ten men and the two women that he induced to come with him, and of the advances that he was obliged to make to them. Unfortunately, one of them never sailed. Against his name is the entry: "quha past away without gud-nycht from the camphier." As well as the workers—shearing boards, implements for scraping the cloth, cards, shears, gloves for holding the shears, needles, presses, and vices, were brought over. Looms were difficult to get. Along with the correspondence of the agents are the written offers of the foreign workmen, the statement of their requirements in wages, and of the houses and cauldrons that they would need. The terms that were agreed upon with the three Flemings from Norwich were that they should be paid £3000 Scots, half within a month of their arrival and half within a year, and that they should remain in Edinburgh and instruct the master weavers of the city as directed by the authorities of the burgh. The workers brought from the Low Countries were to be distributed among Edinburgh, Perth, Ayr, and Dundee. Meanwhile the Government approved certain "articles" regarding the making of cloth which the bailies of Edinburgh and representatives of the Convention of the Royal Burghs produced, and gave them the force of acts passed by the Privy Council, viz., that the acts forbidding the export of wool should be enforced; that no duty should be imposed upon stuff made within the realm; that the visiting, trying, comptrolling, and selling of cloth should be entrusted to the magistrates of the burghs concerned only, notwithstanding any gift made to the contrary (we have here evidence of the insidious practice of the royal sale of privileges and offices).[1]

Unfortunately all did not go smoothly with the scheme. By July there were recriminations upon both sides. The Provost of Ayr wrote complaining that two of the Flemings who had been ordered to go to that burgh had refused to do so, and the foreigners declared that it was impossible for them to work without more craftsmen—dyers, fullers, card and comb makers and the like. The Privy Council considered the complaints of the foreigners that they were "not entertaneit nor putt to the work," and that they were "sinderit—quhilk wald be a grit hinder to the perfectioun of the said werk." The Council decided that instead of the Convention of Royal Burghs' plan to "plant them severallie," the strangers should "be haldin togidder within the burgh of Edinburgh," and that Edinburgh should be empowered to entertain them in meat and drink and recoup itself from the other burghs. By another act of the Privy Council, Edinburgh was threatened with the loss of its privileges in cloth-making if it did not comply with this order. A letter was also sent to the Convention saying that the cloth-making enterprise was "nocht so cairfullie and dewtyfulle haldin hand to as we hoipit for." The Convention acquiesced in the royal plan for keeping the Flemings in Edinburgh, and among the archives of that city there still survive the accounts for the entertainment of the strangers, including a collation that was given them. With the cost of wool, dyestuffs, and skins supplied to them as working material, the total sum was £1333 6s. 8d. It is a most orderly and business-like document and was audited by five individuals.[2]

[1] *Register, Privy Council,* vol. vi, pp. 250, 269.

The writer is indebted to Dr Marguerite Wood for the information regarding the weavers in reports of the agents.

[2] *Register, Privy Council,* vol. vi, pp. 274, 285.

The writer is indebted to Dr Marguerite Wood for information regarding the settlement of the weavers in Edinburgh.

Unfortunately, the enterprise did not prosper. By the end of 1601 four of the strangers had returned home "because the Council will not grant a reward." And the Privy Council had to consider further complaints, and again tried to urge on the burghs to activity. In 1605 the Government once more resolved to make an effort to introduce the "airt of clotherie" into Scotland, and offered the enterprise to the burghs. These latter, however, replied that the work was not really suitable for them, as more workers lived in the country than in the towns, and that some of their number had already sustained great loss through their own inability and the iniquity of strangers; that they would willingly assist others but could not undertake the whole burden on themselves.

In 1609 we learn "that the few number of strangearis that hes remanit heir" of the Flemings imported at such cost in 1601, had settled in the Canongate, and according to their own account were carrying on their craft and giving "grite licht and knawledg" to the country-people. The bailies of the Canongate were endeavouring to force them to become freemen of the burgh, but this the Privy Council peremptorily forbade. About four years later two of them wished to go back to Flanders. As they petitioned for £300 to indemnify them for loss of time and goods, their stay does not seem to have been profitable. A petition by the websters, weavers, and clothmakers of the country, in 1603, asking that the export of linen yarn as well as of wool should be forbidden rather suggests the idea that the protectionist policy of the Government may have stimulated the native workers.[1]

The failure of the first attempt to introduce an improved cloth-working industry into Scotland has been told in some detail because it is of general importance in showing how unfit was Scotland for the development of a great handicraft industry. There is, however, nothing to show whether sheer inertia, or the lack of craft skill, or the peculiar system of organised privileges that obtained, or the opposition of some of the vested interests involved were most to blame. Time has calmed the ripples that might have exposed the swirl of cross-currents. We shall never know the inner history of the movement and what really happened.

[1] *Register, Privy Council*, vol. vi, pp. 309, 373; vol. viii, p. 366. The writer is also indebted to Dr Marguerite Wood.

The improvement of the cloth industry seems to have absorbed the attention of the Government almost exclusively. Nevertheless, the country was developing certain other industries, notably leatherwork, which made little further growth—no doubt the cattle trade eclipsed it—and the very important linen industry. A table of Scots products, in 1614, has the following list, arranged under the heading " Manufactured Goods: "

Small salt	£39,780
Cloth and plaiding	59,374
Linen cloth	11,550
Harden cloth	155
Linen yarn	33,331
Prick hose	10,758
Almeit leather	1,143
Gloves (£5 per doz.)	12,300
Leather points	288
Sewed cushions	172
Ticking for beds	20
Shoes (40 pairs)	26

It is quoted here in full to show that, in spite of the preponderance of rural exports, Scotland had very definitely an industrial section of the community by the early years of the seventeenth century.[1]

[1] P. Hume Brown, *Scotland in the Time of Queen Mary*, p. 227.

CHAPTER IX[1]

PART I. THE EVOLUTION OF THE HIGHLANDER

THE period of history previous to the Wars of Independence saw the emergence of all the most characteristic features of modern Scotland. From a kingdom mainly dominated by a Gaelic form of culture, but with the important appendage of the Anglian Lothians, was evolved the Lowlands of Scotland—which contained elements of the culture and the institutions of the Angle, the Norman, and, to a very much lesser extent, of the Gael—and, sharply demarcated from them, the Highlands. It was the development of the Lowlands that increasingly marked their differentiation from the Gaelic North-west. In the description of the Battle of the Standard, which has already been quoted, many different sections of the fighting men of the Kingdom of Scotland are enumerated, but no distinction is drawn between the Highlanders and the Lowlanders. The accounts of the Battle of Bannockburn, fought less than two hundred years later, make it clear that by that time a distinction was fully realized, and we hear of Highlanders and Lowlanders with their different weapons. Fordoun, writing between 1363 and 1383, says: " The Highlanders and people of the Islands are a savage and untamed nation, rude and independent, given to rapine, ease-loving, of a docile and warm disposition, comely in person but unsightly in dress, hostile to the Anglic people and language, and, owing to diversity of speech, even to their own nation, and exceedingly cruel. They are, however, faithful and obedient to their king

[1] *Highland family titles show so much variation that it is difficult for any outsider to recognize the identity of a particular branch. For convenience' sake the same title has so far as possible been used throughout this chapter for the outstanding families.*

and country, and easily made to submit to law, if properly governed." [1]

During the fifteenth and sixteenth centuries, as the Lowlands continued to develop, the utter difference between the two sections of the country was clearly recognized, and it became even a matter of pride, upon either side of the Highland line, to accentuate it. For instance, John Major, writing in the first half of the sixteenth century, draws a careful distinction between the "Wild Scots" and the "Householding Scots." The former, he says, speak Irish, and "in dress, in the manner of their outward life, and in good morals" they "come behind the householding Scots—yet they are not less but rather much more prompt to fight." "It is with the householding Scots that the government and direction of the kingdom is to be found, inasmuch as they understand better, or at least less ill than the others, the nature of civil polity. One part of the wild Scots have a wealth of cattle, sheep, and horses, and these, with a thought for the possible loss of their possessions, yield more willing obedience to the courts of the law and the king. The other part of these people delight in the chase and a life of indolence; their chiefs largely follow bad men, if only they may not have the need to labour; taking no pains to earn their own livelihood, they live upon others, and follow their own worthless and savage chief in all evil courses sooner than they will pursue an honest industry. They are full of mutual dissensions, and war rather than peace is their normal condition." Major goes on to describe the distinctive dress of the Highlanders. "From the mid-leg to the foot they go uncovered; their dress is, for an over-garment, a loose plaid and a shirt saffron dyed." In his time they were armed with bows and arrows and wore chain mail. "The common folk among the wild Scots go out to battle with the whole body clad in a linen garment sewed together in patchwork, well daubed with wax or with pitch, and with an overcoat of deerskin. But the common people among our domestic Scots and the English fight in a woollen garment." [2] In the foregoing description, Major notes not only the more picturesque elements of difference, the High-

[1] Fordoun, *Chronicle*, vol. ii, p. 38, translation by W. F. Skene.

[2] Quotation from John Major, *History of Greater Britain*; the translation is that of the *Collectanea Rebus Albanicis* (Iona Club), Appendix.

landers' distinctive dress and warlike propensities, but also the important economic difference that they were mainly a pastoral people. Pride in their own side of the Highland line was not confined to the Lowlanders. John Elder, who also lived in the first half of the sixteenth century, wrote a racy account of the North-west of Scotland from the point of view of the Highlander.[1]

It would not, however, be correct to make the sweeping generalization that the difference between the Highlands and the Lowlands was merely due to the fact that the latter went on developing while the former remained in the condition in which they had been previous to the reign of Malcolm Canmore, in the eleventh century. As we have seen, the Lowlands themselves were rather consolidating and elaborating their social institutions during the fifteenth and sixteenth centuries than making great innovations. On the other hand, the Highlands, in spite of the fact that their social organization remained very primitive, yet made very significant and fundamental advances during the period we are dealing with.

Thus, the dress of the Highlanders was altered. During the fifteenth and sixteenth centuries the old pleated, saffron-dyed, linen shirt, the *leiné chroich*, the characteristic dress of Gaeldom both in Ireland and in Scotland, was gradually giving place to the *feileadh-mor*, or belted plaid—the ancestor of the kilt—and to the tartan trews. The fashions for wearing these garments seem to have overlapped. The tartan trews were part of the Highland dress supplied to James V when he went to visit the Isles in 1538, yet the linen shirt, or yellow war coat, was still worn by the son of the chief of Mackintosh so late as 1591.[2]

The literature of the Highlands was also developing. From very early times the Irish bards had freely passed over to the Western Highlands and their compositions were widely known there. In the sixteenth-century collection of contemporary Gaelic poetry made in Central Perthshire by the Dean of Lis-

[1] Printed in the *Collectanea Rebus Albanicis*.

[2] Highland dress has been extensively described. All the original contemporary documents dealing with the subject are collected in an Appendix to *Collectanea Rebus Albanicis*, p. 25.

more there were a large number of Irish pieces, and the subject-matter of those that were of Scots origin, when they were not concerned with contemporary affairs, mainly dealt with the incidents of the old Irish saga-cycles, such as the story of Cuchullin, the Feiné, etc. It may be noted that this Gaelic poetry was still a living and developing art, both in Scotland and Ireland. The forms and metres underwent a fundamental change at the end of the sixteenth century, and, according to so great an authority as Douglas Hyde, the earliest or one of the very earliest bards to introduce some of these innovations was a Highland woman, Mary Macleod. The interlaced patterns so characteristic of the seventh and eighth-century Gaels, also underwent considerable modification, and foliated designs were introduced (in this case, however, the influence probably came from outside sources, and it was rather a case of native adaptation than of original inspiration).[1]

It is important for the student of economic history to remember that in dealing with the conditions of the Highlands, at least as late as the end of the sixteenth century, he is studying something not in a stage of disintegrating survival but of living development. The subject-matter of the contemporary epics and folk-tales of Scotland, however, are valuable from another point of view, for they give us an insight into the social ideals of the people. Certain themes were the subject of songs and stories which were sung or told all over the Highlands with an individualized and localized setting, although they most abounded on the West Coast and in the nearer islands. Stories of Deirdre and Cuchullin are among them, but the greater number concern Finn MacCoul and his near kinsmen, Caolte, Diarmid, Oisin, and others, who were collectively known as the Feiné, and who were the originals of the Fingal and Ossian of Macpherson's poems. To the isolated and imaginative Highlanders these mythical personages were extraordinarily real. It has been pointed out that the people gossiped about them as if they were neighbours and intimate friends ; that in all the stories the main characteristics of the different personages are accurately preserved ; that their attributes, the strength of Finn, the minstrelsy of Caolte and Oisin, the bravery of Oscar, etc.,

[1] D. Hyde, *Literary History of Ireland*, p. 543.
J. Anderson, *Scotland in Early Christian Times*, vol. i, pp. 81-83.

have become enshrined in many of the proverbs and forms of speech of the people.[1]

In the more elaborate works into which the *Irish* cycles developed we have a good deal of quasi-historical matter. The dynastic affairs of the High King and provincial kings of Ireland are touched upon. Moreover, the Feiné are clearly described as a kind of national or, rather, racial militia, organized for the defence of Gaeldom in Ireland and Scotland. It was the law that the people of Ireland were to maintain them during the winter, in return for their services, but that in the summer they were to live by hunting; and a good deal of information about the imaginary organization can be culled. In the songs and stories of *Scotland*, however, little or nothing is said about such matters. The stories mainly concern the personal experiences of Finn himself and his kinsfolk, Oscar, Diarmid, and the rest, and his more distant connection and rival, Gol MacMorna, and his family. All these persons were Feiné, but the nature of the organization is not explained. *The* connecting link between them, that is constantly stressed, is the nature of their blood relationship. In most of the stories, they are represented as engaged in hunting in the intervals of their battles with the Lochlannach and other enemies, but occasionally they are occupied in agriculture. The connection with the land, however, is very slight. The surviving relics of these old stories do not show that Finn and his fellows were supposed to have any claim to it by tribal custom, right of conquest, or other tie. The essential status of all the others seems to rest upon their blood relationship to Finn, the leader of the band. And it is very significant to find how exactly this corresponds with one of the aspects of the clan system, as evolved in Scotland in the fifteenth and the sixteenth centuries.

In the complex situation with regard to the holding and possession of the land, which so greatly complicates the economic history of the Highlands during the period at present being dealt with, and, indeed, that of the land question right down to

[1] For transcripts of the Scots versions of the tales, see the five volumes of *Waifs and Strays of Celtic Tradition*, edited by Lord Archibald Campbell; *Leaber na Feiné*, by J. F. Campbell of Islay; *The Book of the Dean of Lismore*, translated by T. McLauchlan; also Report upon the Poetry of Ossian by the Highland Society.

the present day, it is helpful to trace out the existence of four distinct and largely conflicting sets of ideas or theories. In the first place, there was this clan idea, the theory of a social group united by close blood ties to the leader or chief. In the second place, there was a strongly felt right to the possession of the land that was occupied. This may have been dimly connected with some very ancient tribal ideas, but it is, after all, only a natural impulse, especially in simple communities where the observation of any elaborated system of law has little or no effect. Thirdly, there were traditions of the Gaelic laws with regard to landholding, partly derived from Ireland, where such laws had been codified, partly perhaps from the laws of Scotland of the period before Malcolm Canmore: one finds, for instance, the use of the word *tanister* (i.e. the *chosen* successor among the kinsfolk) for the next heir, although the fully elaborated system of alternate succession by two branches of the leading family, which seems to have been a feature in early Scotland, had died out. Fourthly, there were the conventional feudal ideas of primogeniture, landholding of the king, and charter rights, which were not only the law of the whole kingdom of Scotland but were accepted to a certain extent by the Highlanders themselves.

The Highlanders, however, were living in a state of constant turmoil and of great simplicity. Their immediate necessities were land to support them and a chief to defend them, and under stress of circumstances they resorted to many expedients to procure these two things. It is very striking that similar social conditions produced a society upon the Borders that, in sixteenth-century legislation, is stated to be analogous to the clan system of the Highlands. One finds a mass of conflicting practices dictated by the exigences of the moment, for the people's ideas with regard to landholding and succession had not the elaboration or the clear-cut definiteness of a legal code. Nevertheless they were strongly held and fundamental ideals, profoundly affecting the desires and actions of the Highlanders in their makeshift, hand-to-mouth, precarious way of life.

As we have already seen, a considerable part of the Highlands fell under Norman influence during the period previous to the Wars of Independence. Feudal practices, moreover, were largely adapted by the Gaelic possessors and occupiers of the land. In an earlier chapter it has been shown that where the ancient lines of mormaers persisted into the feudal period, as, for instance, in the case of the rulers of Menteith, they adopted feudal usages and gave charters to their own vassals. Much the same sort of thing took place in the Highlands, and the great magnates, such as the Lord of the Isles, gave charters in the conventional form to their followers.[1]

In yet another way the feudalizing process in the Highlands was carried considerably further. So far as the central authority had any power at all in Gaelic Scotland, its influence was a feudalizing one. Crown charters were exactly the same in all parts of the country; the law of the land, so greatly affecting landholding and succession, was the same in the Highlands and the Lowlands; the two districts where there had been separate codes of laws were the Lothians and Galloway, but by the end of the fourteenth century all differences had been obliterated. The custom of giving wadsets, for instance, was usual both in the Highlands and Lowlands and was identical in both parts of Scotland.[2] These influences, backed by the policy of the Crown, had already come into play before the Wars of Independence, and they continued in operation throughout the period we are at present considering. They were, however, at variance with the theories underlying the indigenous clan system, which during the fifteenth and sixteenth centuries was not merely holding its own but was reaching its highest form of development.

Part II. The Development of the Clan System

Unfortunately, the early pedigrees of the clans cannot be accepted as they stand. W. F. Skene, in *Celtic Scotland*, has made an interesting analysis of the clan pedigrees and of the influences that brought about certain "manipulations," and

[1] Cf. charter by the Lord of the Isles to his Armour-Bearer, 1456, C. Innes, *Scotland in the Middle Ages*; charters from Lord of Isles to Mackintosh, *Mackintosh Muniments*, pp. 1, 3, 8.

[2] The Duke of Argyle, *Scotland as it was and is*, much stresses this point. See, for instance, pp. 58-59, 138. See also *Calendar of Documents relating to Scotland*, vol. iv, No. 1815. For an instance of the grant of the feudal casualty of ward, see A. M. Mackintosh, *Mackintoshes and Clan Chattan*, p. 107.

although most of his theories regarding the actual descent of the clans is open to serious dispute, his generalizations about the influences that affected clan traditions are not thereby invalidated. The narratives of all Scots chroniclers from the eleventh century onwards, down to the more ambitious historians of the fourteenth century, were much perverted by their desire to enhance the ancient origin of their country's institutions in comparison with those of England. The myth that Scotland had been originally colonized by an Egyptian princess named Scota, long before the Christian era, and that it was mainly inhabited by her descendants, was generally accepted. According to Elder, who wrote in the sixteenth century, the Highlanders were less influenced by this story than the Lowlanders. Nevertheless, the historical background was vitiated.

In the second place, during the fourteenth and fifteenth centuries, there was a very close connection between the West Coast of Scotland, the greatest stronghold of Gaeldom, and Ireland. Irish seannachies were frequently employed in Scotland, and Highland genealogies were primarily derived from Ireland. "The latter portions of these pedigrees, as far back as the eponymus or common ancestor from which the clan takes its name, are in general tolerably well vouched, and may be held to be authentic. The older part of the pedigree will be found to be partly historical and partly mythic. So far as these links in the genealogical chain connect the clans with each other within what may be termed the historic period, the pedigree may be genuine ; but the links which connect them with the mythic genealogies of the elaborate system of early Irish history, when analysed, prove to be entirely artificial and untrustworthy."

Another influence tending to vitiate the stories of the clan origins was introduced in 1597, when an act was passed ordering all landholders in the Highlands and Islands to compear before the Lords of the Exchequer and bring and produce with them all their infeftments, rights, and titles whatsoever whereby they claim right and title to any part of the lands and fishings within the bounds foresaid. Many of the chiefs merely occupied their lands by force. Others depended upon grants made by the forfeited Lord of the Isles, or that were in other ways invalid by the letter of the law. There must have been a very powerful temptation to invent titles to the land where such did not exist, and to manufacture spurious pedigrees "better calculated to maintain their position when a native descent had lost its value and was too weak to serve their purpose." From this period MS. histories of the leading Highland families began to be compiled, in which these pretensions were advanced and spurious charters inserted, and the fashion spread to chiefs whose legal position was unequivocal: they usually made the eponymus or male ancestor the cadet of some distinguished family, or a Norwegian, Dane, or Norman, who married the daughter and heiress of the last of the old Gaelic line. The Grants, the Camerons, the Campbells, the Mackenzies, and many other clans, all have such pedigrees, and, where both exist, they conflict with earlier genealogies of the semi-Irish type.[1]

Tradition therefore gives little aid in forming a picture of the early growth of the clans. But, in any case, the general history of the country shows that the inhabitants of the Highlands must have suffered constant disorganization. There is nothing to suggest that the North of Scotland, before it was known to history, was a peaceful country; the probability is otherwise. During the twilight period there was the invasion of Dalriada by the Scots, the conquest of the Picts by this people, and the ravages of the Norsemen, who made permanent settlements on the coastland of the North and the West. Apart from the Macdonalds and Campbells, the Irish genealogists do not trace the links in the descent of the clans dwelling in historic times in Dalriada from the stock of the old Scots *colonists*. The connection with the past was evidently completely broken by the Norse invasions and the interlude of the Gall-Gadheal. On the East, the penetration by the feudal forces of the Scoto-Norman nobility must have once more upset whatever organization had been built up upon the Scots conquest of the Picts.

Political events combined to favour a period of Gaelic revival. The waning of the power of the Scandinavians, as we have seen, gave the Gaels upon the West Coast and in the Islands an opportunity for reorganization, and, all over the Highlands, the period of weakness and disorganization of the authority of the Crown, brought about by the Wars of Inde-

[1] W. F. Skene, *Celtic Scotland*, vol. iii, pp. 336, 338, 347, 348.

pendence and the indifferent kingship of David II, Robert II, and Robert III, largely arrested the process of unification of the kingdom, which had been going on in the preceding period. It is upon the East Coast that the word clan first reappears, as the direct result of the second of these causes.

The end of the fourteenth century saw a time of great lawlessness and unrest in the North-East. The power of the Crown was very weak in the reigns of Robert II and III, but, bad as was the state of the whole kingdom, that of the Highlands seems to have been considerably worse. In 1385 an act of parliament alludes to the many malefactors and "Ketherani" in the North, and empowers Carrick, the king's son, to take action. He does not appear to have achieved much; and, indeed, among the unfortunate king's foes were the members of his own household: for, in 1389, he was obliged to dismiss Alexander, the "Wolf of Badenoch," the son on whom he had heaped such rich grants of land, for his negligence in performing the duties to which he had been appointed.[1]

The Wolf of Badenoch was, indeed, one of the main causes of the troubles. With the help of "wild, wikkid hielandmen" he burnt down Elgin Cathedral in the course of a quarrel with the Bishop of Moray; and about the same time, under the leadership of one of his sons, there was an incursion of Highlanders "to the number of three hundred and more" into Angus, and, in a pitched battle with the sheriff of that county, the Highlanders were victorious and the sheriff and some other gentlemen were killed. The cause of the quarrel is supposed to have been a dispute between the sheriff and the Wolf over the succession of some land in Strathnairn. As a result, in 1390, the king issued a brief ordering the sheriff and bailies of Aberdeen to put to the horn as outlaws the following persons: Duncan and Robert Stewart, Patrick and Thomas Duncanson, Robert de Athale, Andrew Macnayr, and John Ayson, junior, and all others their adherents; and, as taking part with them in the slaughter, Slurach and his brothers, with the whole Clanqwhevil; William Mowat, John de Cowts, Donald de Cowts, with their adherents; David de Rose, Alexander M'Kintalyhur, John M'Kintalyhur, Adam Rolson, John Rolson, with their adherents; Duncan Neteraulde, John

[1] *A.P.S.* vol. i, pp. 183, 188, 192, 208, 209, 210.

Mathyson, with their adherents; Morgownde Ruryson and Michael Mathowson, with their adherents.

This document is of great importance. It is the first instance of the Letters of Horning that were to become so common a feature in the struggle of the central authority to maintain law and order, and it contains the first mention of the word clan for several hundred years. It is in many ways a landmark, showing that a new phase in the social life of the district was beginning, and the list of persons who were implicated in the raid is therefore of considerable value. W. F. Skene analyses them very suggestively. They fall into five groups. The first one includes the two Stewarts, the Wolf's illegitimate sons, and otherwise consists of persons belonging to Athole, where he had much property; "the Duncansons, with Robert de Athale, were the heads of the Clan Donnachie, descended from the old earls who possessed the north-western district bordering upon that of Badenoch; the Macnairs possessed Foss, in Strathtummel, and the Aysons, Tullimet, in Strathtay." The second group consisted of Slurach and his brothers, who, with their followers, formed Clanqwhevil. The identity of this clan has been the subject of much dispute. It is, however, probable that the scribe who wrote the Letters of Horning had got rather perplexed over the intricacies of Gaelic nomenclature, and that, in this brief, Clan Chattan is meant, under the leadership of Shaw, who lived in Rothiemurchus (at the lower end of Badenoch) and who led the clan at the battle on the Inches of Perth. The third group, consisting of the Mowats and Cowts, Skene places in Buchan, of which district the Wolf of Badenoch was earl; and the fourth, the Roses, came from Strathnairn. Skene does not attempt to identify the fifth group, but, as the Wolf also had land in the lower valley of the Spey and in the strath of its tributary, the Avon, they may very possibly have come from there.[1]

The list of the component parts of the body of raiders therefore shows the effect of a distorted feudal influence, for the force that brought them into the field was apparently their territorial connection with Alexander Stewart, the feudal superior of their lands. On the other hand, another type of organization is in evidence, for one clan is specifically mentioned, and Skene identifies the Duncansons with the Clan Donnachie. An

[1] W. F. Skene, *Celtic Scotland*, vol. iii, p. 309.

event which took place in 1396, the battle of the clans on the Inches at Perth, shows, more convincingly, that the clan system was in existence. Four fifteenth-century writers describe the fight. The old-standing feuds of two clans had so vexed the country that it was agreed that they should each send thirty champions, all armed alike, to fight out their difference in specially prepared lists before the king and his court at Perth. The names of the clans are very variously spelt, and there is some contradiction in the details of the fight as given by the different chroniclers. Moreover, later historians have disagreed in their attempts to identify the two clans, although it is now very generally accepted that they were Clan Chattan and the Camerons. These clans were certainly at feud in the succeeding century, for the story of the struggle between the Lord of the Isles and the Crown, which brought the Highlands into considerable historical prominence, contains several allusions to their bickerings.

It is interesting to find that the favourable conditions that encouraged the development of the Highland clans also produced the beginnings of the similar type of organization on the Borders. In 1498 an order was made that all of the *surname* of Rede in Tyndale were to be forfeited as resetters of outlaws, and also the Hoggs, Robsons, Hunters, Wilkinsons, and men of about eight other *names*.[1]

During the fifteenth century by far the most important factor in the political history of the Highlands, deeply influencing the whole development of the clans, was that of the relations between the Lord of the Isles and the Crown. It is essential, therefore, that we now turn to the clans of the West Coast. Something has already been said about the rise of certain great families there, especially those descended from Somerled. The descendants of Somerled had shown two marked tendencies: (*a*) Their land had been again and again divided among the sons in each generation; (*b*) there was a strong dynastic feeling, so that, by means of the marriages of heiresses, the offshoot families that resulted were several times reunited with the principal ones. During Bruce's struggle for Scots independence the heads of two of the then principal families that had survived, the house of Islay and the house of Garmoran, supported Bruce,

[1] *Calendar of Documents relating to Scotland*, vol. IV, No. 1649.

whilst the Lord of Lorn was attached to the Comyn and Baliol party. As a result, Islay and Garmoran were enriched by most of the possessions of Lorn. There were further complicated adjustments, but, about 1337, John, the head of the family of Islay, married Amie Macruari, heiress of the Garmoran branch, and, by right of the great estates that he now held, began to term himself Lord of the Isles. The earliest surviving document in which he thus styles himself is dated 1354. The adjustments of the dynastic arrangements during the period before the lordship of the Isles was formed involved much fighting. The papal dispensation for the marriage of John of Islay and Amie Macruari alludes to the constant quarrels, "on which account murders, fire raisings, plunderings, pillagings and very many other evils happened and still do not cease to happen, and, moreover, many churches of those parts have suffered and do not cease to suffer no slight damage thereby."[1]

The story of the lordship of the Isles can only be briefly indicated here. John, the first Lord, divorced his first wife, with whom he had secured so important an accession of territory, married King Robert II's daughter, and secured a royal charter confirming the whole lordship of the Isles to himself and his children by this second marriage. The lordship was held successively by four generations and lasted nearly a hundred and fifty years. During part of this time, by another fortunate marriage, the Lords of the Isles claimed, and finally secured, the earldom of Ross. During the rule of each of the Lords in turn, there was trouble with the Crown, and, to a varying degree, they nearly all made some claim to sovereign independence and even to the suzerainty of the North of Scotland. As a result, the earldom of Ross was forfeited in 1476 and the lordship of the Isles in 1493. Clan Donald and its allied clans, however, made repeated attempts to revive the lordship of the Isles, and rallied again and again to claimants who, with more or less right, represented themselves as the rightful successors of the last forfeited Lord.[2]

The importance of the story of the lordship of the Isles to the student of Scots social and economic history lies in the

[1] See *Scottish Historical Review*, vol. viii, p. 248.

[2] D. Gregory, *History of the Western Highlands of Scotland*, pp. 23-30.

illustration that it affords of the building up of a clan. After the assumption of the title of Lord of the Isles, the principal family continued to throw off offshoot branches, though it was now the custom to establish these younger sons or brothers upon lands to be held of the head of the house as their feudal superior. After the forfeiture of 1493 all the possessions of the lordship of the Isles were annexed to the Crown, and the history of the sixteenth century is largely taken up with the question of how far the collateral branches of the Clan Donald could make good a permanent title to these Crown lands, which they continued to occupy.

The table on p. 486 shows the origin of the different branches which were formed. The information on which the table is founded is taken from D. Gregory's *History of the Western Highlands of Scotland*, pp. 59 and 412. It contains only the families who existed as vassals of the Lord of the Isles in the fifteenth century. Most of the independent branches formed previously to the thirteenth century were either re-absorbed or had died out. There were, however, the survivors of the house of Lorn, the descendants of Dugall, one of the sons of Somerled. Lorn, it will be remembered, was forfeited, but it was restored to the old family. Much of the land passed by very devious means, and through an heiress, to the Stewarts, but the old line was continued by the Macdougals of Dunolly and their cadets.

If the first column of this table is examined it will be seen that the founders of the different branches or septs were all the near relations of the reigning Lord of the Isles, who were planted out by their father or elder brother upon portions of his territory. This is typical of clan organization. The connecting link that entitled them to a share in the land was their blood relationship to the chief. It was not a tribal arrangement, for the Lords of the Isles held their land in their own right as individuals and by no tribal law or custom, and they granted portions of their estates to their near kinsmen by their own authority and according to their pleasure. The relationship between the Lord of the Isles and the followers who occupied his lands and those of the heads of the offshoot branches and the retainers whom they also possessed is not known at this so early period; one can only imagine that it was very similar to those existing in other clans

Name of Family and its Connection with that of the Lord of the Isles.	Lands at the Time of the Forfeiture of the Lord of the Isles.	Position in the Time of Charles I.	Cadet Branches surviving till the Seventeenth Century.
Clan Allaster of Kintyre, descended from Allaster, s. of Donald of Islay (the g.-son of Somerled). Head of family, Macallister of Loup.	In Kintyre, not extensive.	Still there.	Tarbert.
Clan Ian of Ardnamurchan, descended from John, younger s. of Angus Mor of Islay (who was g.-father to 1st L. of Isles).	Ardnamurchan, *Sunart, Islay, Jura, Mull.	†Destroyed early 17th century. Most of its lands passed to Campbells.	..
Clan Ian Abrach of Glencoe, descended from John, n. son of Angus Og of Islay (who was father of 1st L. of Isles).	*Glencoe.	Still existed.	..
Siol Gorrie, descended from Godfry, 1st son 1st marriage John, 1st L. of Isles.	†Had already lost lands.	..	..
Clan Ranald of Garmoran, descended from Ranald, 2nd s. 1st marriage John, 1st L. of Isles.	Had already split up into 3 branches of *Moydert*, *Knoydert*, Glengarry. Occupied *Benbecula, *Garmoran, *N.W. of Lochalsh, *Sunart.	*Moydert* still existed. †*Knoydert* had died out. Lands had gone from Lochiel to Macdonald of Keppoch. Argyle had secured the superiority. *Glengarry*. Flourishing.	Macdonalds of *Boisdale*, *Staffa*, *Kinloch Moidert*, *Glenalladale*. Macdonnells of *Barrisdale*, *Greenfield*, *Lundie*.
Clan Ian Vor, descended from John, 2nd son 2nd marriage of John, 1st L. of Isles. Also known as Clan Donald South (from Donald Balloch, s. of founder), Macdonald of Islay, Lords of Dunyveg.	Islay (*part claimed by Macleans), Kintyre (forfeited but still occupied), *Sunart. The family also gained extensive lands in Antrim.	†Had lost all lands in Scotland in early 16th century. Had been re-established and then forfeited early 17th century. †Lands in Islay and Kintyre passed to Campbells.	*Largie*, *Sanda*, reacquired *Colonsay* occupied by Campbells.
Clan Ranald of Lochaber, descended from 3rd s. 2nd marriage L. of Isles. Also known as the Macranalds of Keppoch.	Received lands in Lochaber, but forfeited them. Continued to occupy them as tenants or by force.	Maintained and improved position.	Many cadets.
House of Loch Alsh, descended from Celestin, 2nd s. 3rd L. of Isles.	Lochalsh, Loch Carron, Loch Broom, lands in Sutherland and Lochiel.	†Had been forfeited. Lands held by Mackenzie.	..
House of Sleat, descended from Hugh, 3rd s. of 3rd L. of Isles. Known as Clan Huistean or Clan Donald North.	Sleat, *Uist, *Benbecula, *Garmoran.	In a flourishing condition after many vicissitudes.	..

* Denotes that the ownership of the land was disputed, † that the branch had died out.

at a later date. By the sixteenth century most of the branches had grown into considerable clans, able to put several hundreds of fighting men into the field, and it is therefore obvious that these clans were not entirely composed of the descendants of their original founders in the fourteenth and fifteenth centuries. But it is also certain that their lands were originally granted to these founders as individuals; that in the eyes of the law and in all charters or forfeitures relating to them they were always treated as the private and personal holdings of the heirs of these persons. We have here an example of the clash between different systems of land occupation, and also one of the exceedingly rapid growth of clan ideas.

The race of Somerled and the retainers that were attached to it, however, never occupied the whole of the great dominions claimed by the Lord of the Isles. A considerable number of other clans acknowledged him as their superior. Their origins are so shadowy, and to trace them out would be so controversial, that they are better left undefined. What is striking is to find how completely they had been knit up into a group of allies or vassals, and that in every case a real or fictitious connection with the Lord of the Isles was accepted as accounting for the alliance.

The table on p. 488 will give some idea of their position at the time of the forfeiture.[1]

There are certain interesting points about the organization of these clans. When they secured legal title to their lands, it was bestowed, like any other feudal grant, upon the chief as an individual. The law gave no recognition to "clan territories." This point may be carried even further. The Lord of the Isles, when he granted lands, also bestowed them upon individuals. There was no formally constituted "tribal land."

Nevertheless, there was a very definite instinct towards clan organization. In the case of Clan Ranald of Moydert, and also in that of Clan Ranald of Lochaber, the clansmen deposed an unpopular chief. An extraordinary instance of the tenacity with which a clan survived is furnished by the Camerons. It has been suggested that the bitter feud between this clan and the Mackintoshes (whose chief was captain of Clan Chattan) was due to some ancient tribal connection between Clan Cameron and Clan Chattan, which led to conflicting claims to the district

[1] D. Gregory, *History of the Western Highlands*, pp. 59 onwards, 418.

Name.	Lands held at the Time of the Forfeiture.	Position at the Time of Charles I.	Cadet Branches surviving till Seventeenth Century.
Macleans = *Clan Gillian*. 4 branches:			
Dowart (most powerful but perhaps not senior branch), chief m. daughter by 1st marriage of 1st L. of Isles.	Mull, Tiree, Islay, Jura, Scarba, Morven, Lochaber, Knapdale.	After great prosperity much declined. Argyle now has superiority of lands.	Torlusk, Kinlochaline, Ardtornish, Drimin, Tapul, Scallasdale, Muck, Borrera, Tressinish, etc.: many of these cadets held directly of Argyle.
Lochbuy (claims to be senior branch)	Mull, Tiree, Jura, Scarba, Morven, *Lochaber, *Duror, *Glencoe.	Lands retained but now held of Argyle.	..
Coll (offshoot of Dowart) . . .	Coll, Mull, *Lochaber.	ditto.	..
Ardgour (offshoot of Dowart) .	Ardgour.	ditto.	..
MacLeods. 2 branches:			
Siol Torquil (Macleods of Lewis).	Lewis, Raasay, Assint, Cogeach, Gairloch.	† Lost all lands to the Mackenzies except Raasay, which was held by a cadet branch that survived.	Cambuscarry, Cadbol.
Siol Tormod (Macleods of Harris).	Harris, Glenelg (always held of Crown), Dunvegan, Duirinish, Bracadale, Lyndale, Trouterness, Minganish.	Lands retained.	Bernera, Talisker, Gresernish, Hamer, Luskinder.
Camerons. Branches probably adopted into clan: *Macsorlies* of Glen-nevis. *Macgillories* of Strone. *Macmartins* of Letterfinlay.	*Lochaber. Before forfeiture connection with Lord of Isles broken.	During 17th century made good its claim to the disputed lands, but held them of Argyle.	..
Mackintoshes as representative of *Clan Chattan*.	*Lochaber. Before forfeiture connection with Lord of Isles broken. Mainly an East Coast clan.	..	..
MacNeils:			
Clan Neil of *Barra*. . . .	Barra, *South Uist.	Barra retained.	
Clan Neil of *Gigha*. . . .	Gigha.	Gigha sold to Macdonald of Islay. Repurchased about this time.	Gallochelly, Carskeay, Tirfergus, Arichonan.
Mackinnons = Clan Fingon . . .	Skye and Mull.	Still held land.	..
Macquarries = Clan Guarie . . .	Ulva.	There in 1609 †.	Ormaig.
Macfies = Clan Duffie	Colonsay.	There in 1615 †.	..
Maceachern	Kintyre.	Line of chiefs died out; land still occupied by lesser clansmen under Campbells.	..
Mackays of Ugadale	Kintyre.	† End of 17th century passed, with heiress, to cadet branch of Macneils.	..

* Denotes that the ownership of the land was disputed, † that the branch had died out.

round Loch Arkaig. But setting aside such suppositions, in historic times, in the first half of the fifteenth century, we find the Camerons as vassals of the Lord of the Isles—the connection dated from the days of Bruce. When the Lord of the Isles rebelled in 1429, the Camerons went over to the Crown, and, in revenge, when the Lord of the Isles was restored to power, he granted their lands to the Macleans of Coll and of Lochbuy, and then to Celestin of Lochalsh, brother of the fourth and last Lord of the Isles, and also ratified the Mackintoshes' claims to the lands on Loch Arkaig. Nevertheless, the clan managed to maintain itself, by fighting the Macleans and by accepting the overlordship of the house of Lochalsh, and, in later years, by alternately accepting and defying the overlordship of the great rivals, Huntly and Argyle. Only by the extraordinarily strong support and tenacity of his followers could this chief have continued to occupy these much-disputed lands.

The Macleods of Harris, or Siol Tormod, furnish another illustration of the emergence of clan ideas that ran contrary to the laws and customs of the land. This family held the lands of Dunvegan in Skye, the island of Harris, and the district of Glenelg, upon the mainland, of the Crown after the forfeiture of the Lord of the Isles. They also had a legal title to the lands of Trouterness and Sleat in Skye and to the island of North Uist, which were occupied, by right of the sword, by the Macdonalds of Sleat. In the middle of the sixteenth century, the owner of the heritage of the Siol Tormod, according to feudal ideas, was the only child of the late chief, Mary Macleod, a girl and a minor, who, like any other vassal of the Crown, was liable to the casualties of wardship and marriage. It is not necessary to trace out the cross-currents of intrigue that affected the disposal of the heiress. For reasons of policy, she passed from Arran (the Regent) to Huntly, from Huntly to Argyle, from Argyle to Macdonald of Islay, from whom her person was somehow secured by Mackenzie of Kintail. Eventually the queen forced Mackenzie to give her up, and, after being a maid of honour at court, Argyle once more secured the gift of her marriage. Meanwhile her clan had not accepted the succession of the heiress, and had supported the nearest male heir, the brother of the late chief, in his assumption of the chiefship and the occupation of the lands. He was, as a matter of fact, murdered by a cousin, who continued to occupy the lands until his death, when the next male heir, Tormod Macleod, the uncle of the heiress, obtained possession of the estates and was in occupation of them when Argyle arranged the marriage of Mary Macleod, the feudal heiress, with his own kinsman, Duncan Campbell, younger of Auchinbreck. Argyle evidently did not feel able or willing to force the feudal heiress upon her clan, and arranged the following agreements: Tormod Macleod had already given Argyle a bond of manrent for himself and his clan. He now agreed to resign to Argyle all claim to the Macleod lands occupied by Macdonald of Sleat—Sleat, Trouterness, and North Uist—and to pay the sum of one thousand merks towards the dowry of his niece. In return, Argyle engaged that the heiress and her husband should renounce all claim to the lands actually occupied by Tormod and the clan, i.e. Harris, Dunvegan, and Glenelg, and that he would obtain a Crown charter to the estate for Tormod. With Donald Macdonald Gorme of Sleat, Argyle made the following arrangement: That chief was to pay five hundred merks towards the dowry of Mary Macleod and was to give his bond of manrent and service for himself and his clan to Argyle, and, in return, Argyle undertook to make him his vassal in the lands of Sleat, Trouterness, and North Uist, which the Macdonalds occupied, but the legal title to which had rested with the Macleod of Harris and had now been resigned to Argyle. As Gregory points out, " It is evident . . . that, although in the case of the Siol Tormod, at this time, ancient custom prevented the feudal law from being carried into effect in its full extent, yet the Earl of Argyle did not surrender his legal claims without indemnifying himself amply for the sacrifice."[1] This example of compromise and adaptation is very typical of the Highlands. Among other illustrations of the clash between the feudal and the clan ideas may be quoted a quarrel which broke out in 1561 between Maclean of Dowart and his cadet, Maclean of Coll. Dowart claimed that Coll should follow him in his quarrels, like the other gentlemen of his clan. Coll refused, because he held his lands directly of the Crown. Dowart ravaged his lands, and although the Privy Council, who supported Coll, forced

[1] D. Gregory, *History of the Western Highlands*, p. 207.

the senior chief to make reparation, the feud was only patched up.[1]

Referring to the lists of clans that were offshoots or associates of the original stock of the Lords of the Isles, it will be noticed that some branches achieved complete independence and that others remained vassals of the parent stock; that they sometimes increased and sometimes died out, according to force of circumstance. On the whole, however, the establishment of independent branches was an early feature. This is certainly the case with the race of Somerled, and the same process seems to have been going on in some of the other clans, for when they first appear they had already split into separate organizations having little or no connection with each other. There has been serious conflict of opinion over the seniority of the Macleans of Dowart and Lochbuy; the former was the more powerful clan, but the latter claims to be descended from an elder brother. In any case, they were separate clans when they first became known to authentic history during the period of the lordship of the Isles. The Macleods of Lewis and of Harris were separate clans, and so were the Macneils of Barra and of Gigha.

The chiefs, moreover, had very much scattered possessions. This was especially the case in earlier times before they were able to do much to consolidate them. Perhaps the fact is worth some elaboration, for the maps of "clan territories" that are sometimes published are apt to be misleading, for they suggest a hard-and-fastness of boundary like that of a modern state, such as certainly did not exist. The table of clans gives the names of the districts in which they each had their possessions, and shows to some extent how mixed up together they were. But if a list of the chiefs holding land in the different districts is made, the fact emerges more convincingly. In Kintyre, in 1493, there were the Macalisters, who had held their lands of Macdonald of Islay (*Clan Ian Vor*); the Macdonalds of Islay themselves, who, although forfeited, continued to occupy lands in the district; and also a cadet branch, Macdonald of Largie. The MacEacherns were also there, and the Mackays of Ugadale, who obtained a grant from Robert the Bruce. In the centuries that followed, the Macdonalds founded one more cadet branch.

[1] D. Gregory, *History of the Western Highlands*, p. 190.

By the middle of the seventeenth century the Macalisters were still there and had acquired heritable rights to their lands. The lands of Mackay of Ugadale had passed, with an heiress, to a cadet branch of the Macneils; the MacEacherns still continued to occupy some of the land, and the two cadet branches founded by Macdonald of Islay had also survived. The Macdonalds of Islay, however, had disappeared and their place had been taken by the Campbells.

Islay was occupied by the Macdonalds of Islay, the Macleans, and the MacIans—clans that were often at feud with each other—and there was considerable fighting over certain "debatable lands." By the seventeenth century both the MacIans and the Macdonalds had been driven out and the Campbells were in possession.

In Lochaber, in 1493, there were the Clanranald of Lochaber (who were forfeited, but continued to occupy land there), the Camerons, and two branches of Macleans. Clan Ranald of Garmoran had also just obtained a footing there, and the Mackintoshes had claims which they were never able to make good with any permanency. Most of these clans were more or less inimical to each other. By the middle of the seventeenth century the Camerons and the Macdonalds of Keppoch, the descendants of the Clanranald of Lochaber, were left in possession. Maclean of Dowart had a large share of the island of Mull in 1493, and two other branches of the Macleans, the MacIans, the Mackinnons, and the Macquarries also had land there. In Skye, at the time of the forfeiture of the Lord of the Isles, the district of Sleat was owned by the Macdonalds of Sleat; Dunvegan by the Macleods of Harris; Trouterness was occupied or claimed by the Macdonalds of Sleat, the Macdonalds of Garmoran, and the Macleods of Harris. The district of Waternish was owned by the Macleods of Waternish, and that of Strathordill by the Mackinnons.

The foregoing summary of the clans occupying some of the main islands and districts of the West Coast not only shows how greatly intermingled were their territories, but how largely they changed hands. The clan system, though it is founded upon very ancient ideas, was most elastic in adapting itself to the changing conditions of the moment. We have seen how the lordship of the Isles was built up upon the wreck of the Norse occupation of the West Coast and Isles. The lordship itself only lasted for about a hundred and fifty years, and the whole of the sixteenth century was occupied with feuds and struggles that were largely the result of the confusion caused by its fall. Immediately after the forfeiture, the chief of the Macdonalds of Lochalsh took the lead, but about 1565 the chief of the Macdonalds of Islay was the most powerful chief of the North-West. He met, however, with reverses, and from this time onwards the power of the clan largely declined. By 1608 the leading chiefs in the lands of the old lordship of the Isles seem to have been ten—Macdonald of Islay, Macdonald of Sleat, the captain of Clanranald, Macleod of Harris, Maclean of Dowart, Maclean of Coll, Maclean of Lochbuy, Mackinnon, Macquarrie, and Macfie. At this time the Macleans of Dowart, under an able and vigorous chief, were at the zenith of their prosperity.[1] Meanwhile, not only were others of the older clans rising into greater power, but new clans were being built up and were attaining to prominence.

In order to realize the changes that were constantly going on, it is helpful to turn to the estimated strength of the clans at the very end of their existence as fighting organizations. Just before the Jacobite Rising of 1745, President Duncan Forbes of Culloden compiled a list of the man-power that the chiefs of the different clans of the Highlands would be able to put into the field.[2] This document shows most convincingly that the most powerful clans were of comparatively recent growth. The strength of the various chiefs of the Macdonalds he estimates as follows:

Macdonald of Sleat, 700 men.
Macdonald of Clanranald, 700 men.
Macdonald of Glengarry, 500 men.
Macdonell of Keppoch, 300 men (holding of Huntly and Mackintosh).
Macdonald of Glencoe, 150 men (holds his lands of Stewart of Appin).

The strength of many of the chiefs of the clans that were originally the vassals of the Lord of the Isles are also quoted separately:

[1] D. Gregory, *History of the Western Highlands*, pp. 192, 330. *Collectanea Rebus Albanicis*, p. 115.

[2] D. Stewart of Garth, *Manners and Customs of the Highlanders*, Appendix.

Maclean (Forbes does not state if this is only Maclean of Dowart or of all the separate branches of the clan), 500 men (he notes that these largely come from Campbell estates, and that 200 years previously the following of the clan had been estimated at 800 men).
Macleod of Dunvegan, 700 men (the old Macleods of Harris).
Mackinnon, 200 men.
Cameron of Lochiel, 800 men (he held of Huntly and Argyle).

The Macneils he mentions further on, but does not specify their man-power. It will be noted that the Macdonalds of Islay and of Lochalsh and several branches of Clan Ranald of Garmoran, besides other lesser septs bearing the patronymic Macdonald, have disappeared. So have the MacIans, the Macleods of Lewis, and some of the lesser septs of the allied clans. The other West Coast clans that he mentions are the Maclauchlans, with 300 men; the Stewarts of Appin, 300 men—descendants of the last Stewart Lord of Lorn, whose main properties had been carried by an heiress into the family of Argyle; and the Macdougalls, 200 men, descendants of the old Macdougalls of Lorn, who were the descendants of Dugall, son of Somerled, who from various causes had lost a very large part of their lands.

The Campbells he estimates at 5000 men, exclusive of branches in Nairnshire, Dumbartonshire, Perthshire, and other districts, and he says that they are the richest clan in the Highlands.

He estimates that 5400 Highlanders were the followers of the Duke of Montrose, the Earl of Moray, Macneil of Barra, Macnab of Macnab, the laird of Buchanan, Colquhoun of Luss, Lamont of Lamont, and among the Macnaughtons, in districts of Argyleshire, Dumbartonshire, Stirlingshire, and Perthshire.

He estimated that of the Robertsons 200 followed their own chief and 500 the Duke of Athole. The Laird of Menzies had 300 men, Stewart of Grantully 300 men, and Clan Gregor 700 men.

Of the following of the Duke of Athole he wrote that "Murray is no clan family, though the Duke of Atholl is chief, and head of a number of barons and gentlemen of the name of Murray in the Lowlands; but he is deservedly placed here on account of his extensive following of about 3000 Highlanders, a good many out of his own property, but most of them from the estates of the barons and gentlemen who hold their land of him on account of his great superiorities in Athole, Glenalmond, and Balquhidder. The most numerous of these, and the readiest of them, out on all occasions, are the Stewarts of Athole, in number more than 1000 men; as also 500 Robertsons, who do not follow their chief; likewise the Fergussons, Smalls, Spaldings, Rattrays, Mackintoshes in Athole, and Maclarens of Balquhidder."

The other clans and families that he mentions are:

The Farquharsons, 500 men.
The tenants upon the Duke of Gordon's estates in Strathavon and Glenlivet, 300 men.
The Grants, 700 men in Strathspey and 150 men in Urquhart.
The Mackintoshes, 800 men, including the Macbeans, Macgillivrays, Macqueens, and other septs of Clan Chattan.
The Macphersons, 400 men (holding of the Duke of Gordon).
The Mackenzies, 1000 men following Seaforth, the chief, and 1500 more men following Lord Cromarty, Mackenzie of Gairloch, Mackenzie of Redcastle, and other lairds, all chieftains of the clan.
The Chisholms, 200 men.
The Frasers, 900 men.
The Monroes, 300 men.
The Rosses, 500 men.
The followers of the Earl of Sutherland, 2000 men.
The Mackays from Strathnaver, 800 men.
The Sinclairs, 1000 men.

This estimate places the man-power of the Highlands at 30,600 men. Of these, more than one-third (nearly 10,700 men) were largely followers of the holders of the great superiorities. Huntly had 300 followers from his Strathavon and Glenlivet estates. Athole had 3000 men, Sutherland had 2000 men. Of the 5400 men whom Forbes groups together, a large number were of this category. The force bringing these men into the field was the feudal authority of their superiors, but, no doubt, they fought in septs, many of these very ancient; and, superficially at least, there is some resemblance to the older condition of the Highlands, in which the mormaers had large and devoted followings, but in which the clan organization, though it existed, had not attained to much prominence. All through the history of the Highlands the territorial connection was a strong one, and there was no hard-and-fast line between a clan and a "name," or laird's family. In the legislation of parliament and of the Privy Council dealing with clans towards the end of the sixteenth century there are lists in which some of the Highland families appear, sometimes under one heading and sometimes under the other.[1]

Among those that were definitely clans at the end of the sixteenth century, some of the more important were not of ancient Gaelic extraction. Such were several branches of Stewarts (Appin, Athole, Grantully, and others), the Frasers, the Grants, the Sinclairs, the Chisholms. At least six or seven thousand men belonged to clans whose very names prove that they were built up after feudalizing influences had attacked the Highlands.

The descendants of the Macdonalds numbered over 2300 fighting men, and the origin of this clan has already been dealt with. Without even querying the origin of any of the clans whose claims to antiquity may be more considerable, it can be seen that the clan system of the Highlands, in the form in which we usually think of it, was largely a comparatively modern development (though many of the ideas underlying its social relationships were, no doubt, very ancient), and that the territorial type of organization was very important in the Highlands.

The list, moreover, was very helpful in showing how certain clans were rising and others declining during the fifteenth and sixteenth centuries. Of the rising clans there were two outstanding examples: the Campbells and the Mackenzies. In the tables showing the composition of the following of the lordship of the Isles it can be seen how the different families of the Campbells absorbed the lands of the old Macdonalds of Islay and several other branches of Clan Macdonald, and how Argyle, the chief, secured wide superiorities over lands occupied by clans farther north. In the same way the Mackenzies ousted the Macleods from Lewis, absorbed the lands once held by the Macdonalds of Lochalsh, and in other directions also greatly increased their possessions. Both these clans were ancient, but in both cases they were of comparative unimportance till the fourteenth century or later.

The Campbells (if the Campbello derivation be dismissed) were of ancient Gaelic stock, but comparatively early they became recognized as feudal landholders. Their earliest charter is dated 1315, and in the conventional feudal formula it grants

[1] *Register, Privy Council*, vol. iv, pp. 781-782.

to Sir Neil Campbell "the whole land of Lochow, in one free barony, by all its righteous metes and marches, in wood and plain, meadows and pastures, muirs and marshes, petaries, ways, paths, and waters, stanks, fishponds and mills, and with the patronage of the churches, in huntings and hawkings, and in all its other liberties, privileges and just pertinents, as well named as not named." A charter of 1368, however, confirmed the lands of Craignish, Melfert, Strachur, Over Cowall, and others in Argyleshire to Archibald Campbell, with all the liberties of these lands as freely as Duncan McDuine did enjoy them in the barony of Lochow. The date of McDuine is uncertain—family history places him about 1200—and also the extent of the rights he was supposed to exercise in Lochow. A descendant appears in the thirteenth century who was connected with Stirlingshire, and the rise of the family may be said to begin with this man's son, Sir Colin Campbell, from whom, very significantly, is derived the patronymic of his descendants—*MacCailein Mor*: that is, Son of Big Colin. He was one of the signatories to the elder Bruce's claim to the crown of Scotland. His son, who succeeded at the end of the thirteenth century, was the faithful adherent of Robert the Bruce. He received great rewards from the forfeited estates, married the king's sister, and is mentioned as one of the barons of Argyle. In the succeeding generations the Campbells were steady supporters of the Crown. They were used again and again against the turbulent house of the Isles, its lesser branches and adherent clans, and they profited from the forfeitures that constantly took place. In the sixteenth century the head of the Campbells had become the Earl of Argyle, with many powerful barons of his name to support him, and was the most formidable and most used instrument that the Crown employed against the wilder clans of the North-West.[1]

The origin of the Mackenzies is the subject of conflicting stories. They have been derived from the Irish family of Fitzgerald and from the progenitors of the Earls of Ross. The first chief regarding whom there is a more definite tradition is said to have married a Macdougall of Lorne and to have died in 1304. The clan pedigree gives his descendants with full details, but the first of them who appears in a surviving con-

[1] See article on Argyle in the *Scots Peerage*.

temporary document was a youth in 1427. The chief of the Mackenzies at this time held his lands of the Earl of Ross (who was also the Lord of the Isles), and they were situated in Central Ross-shire and probably were not of great value. Later on, he supported the Crown and helped to crush one of the rebellions of the Lord of the Isles, and, when the latter forfeited the earldom of Ross, he received a Crown charter for Strathconon, Strathgarve, Strathbraan, and other lands in Ross-shire. His successors served the Crown upon many occasions; like the Campbells, they took a considerable share in the administrative work of the State, and were often in touch with their sovereigns. As time went on; they gradually extended their dominions. Forbes of Culloden's memorandum shows how important were the followings of the branches of their name that they had established.[1]

The foregoing summary tells of how the chiefs of these clans acquired greater and greater territories in return for their services, just as any Lowland feudal baron might receive them. It is highly significant that as their territories increased they were able to extend the clan spirit. The nimble Gaelic wit was fertile in creating traditions that should develop the idea that underlay the clan system—the bond of blood relationship or of some other close personal connection. One amusing illustration of the habit must suffice. When the Lord of the Isles in the fifteenth century secured the earldom of Ross through his mother, Countess of Ross in her own right, a tradition became current that the Irish wife of his ancestor Angus Og, the Lord of Islay, who supported Robert the Bruce and secured such large accessions of territory, had brought some of her adherents with her from Ireland, and that they became the heads of five Highland clans, the vassals of the Lord of the Isles. Among these clans were mentioned the Roses, the Scoto-Norman family settled in Morayshire, and the Monroes, who held their lands in Ross-shire of the Earls of Ross, but who, according to

[1] See article in the *Scots Peerage* on Seaforth. A. Mackenzie's history of the clan is very full and quotes abundant references. Sir Robert Gordon, in his History of Sutherlandshire, says: "From the ruins of the family of Clan Donald and some of the neighbouring Highlanders, and also by their own vertue, the surname of the Clan Kenzie, from small beginnings, began to flourish in these bounds." Quoted by W. F. Skene, *Highlanders of Scotland*, edited by Macbain, p. 328.

their own tradition, had been there at least since the time of Alexander II, and perhaps (according to W. F. Skene) were descended from some of the rebellious subjects of the old province of Moray.[1]

The Grants, who in the eighteenth century were a powerful race, furnish an interesting illustration of the forming of a clan. There are various conflicting theories with regard to their origin, although the probability is that they were originally of Norman extraction and came up from England to Morayshire as connections of the Bissets. The name first appears in a charter of 1258. In 1357 a Grant held the lands of Boleskin and Abertarf (to the south-east of Loch Ness). But by 1420 these lands were held by Fraser as a vassal of the Earl of Moray, and they remained in the possession of the Frasers, though the septs who actually occupied them altered considerably.[2]

Meanwhile, several Grant landowners appear in Strathspey, the first of these who can be definitely proved to be the ancestor of the chiefs of Grant, in 1434.

The table on p. 500 gives the earlier owners of the lands finally possessed by the Grants—showing that they had already been feudalized; the date at which they came into possession of the lairds of Grant, and the method of holding them. The information has been taken from Sir William Fraser's *Chiefs of Grant*, vol. i. The table only refers to the Grant lands in Strathspey. The barony of Urquhart (to the north of Loch Ness) was acquired in 1509.

This carefully built up estate shows the territorial ambition of a long line of lairds, and the same spirit was consistently shown in the succeeding centuries. But they were also very much more than mere landlords. In 1704 the son of the chief ordered the whole of the tenantry to wear Grant tartan when they attended him.[3] The creation of a clan with a fighting power of nearly 1000 men upon such slowly acquired estates is an extraordinary tribute to the innate clannishness of the Highlanders. It is obvious that they could not all be the descendants of the chiefs, who only acquired much of their land in the fifteenth and sixteenth centuries.

[1] A. Mackenzie, *History of the Monroes*, p. 3.

[2] *First Statistical Account*, vol. xx, p. 20.

[3] Sir William Fraser, *Chiefs of Grant*, vol. i, p. lxxv.

Property.	Original Owners.	Subsequent History.	Acquired by Grant.	Subsequent History.	Consolidation.
Glencarnie .	1180–1391. Held by descendants of a younger son of 3rd Earl of Fife.	Passed to Earls of Moray; after forfeiture of Douglas Earl of Moray, 1455, held by Crown and let.	1478. Let by Crown to laird of Grant.	1490. Grant secures a feu.	In 1694 all these lands and other outlying portions, the estates of Urquhart and Corrymonie, to the north of Loch Ness, were formed into the *Regality of Grant*. Some of these lands held of a subject superior, but most of them of the Crown.
Inverallan .	1223–42. Apparently in the hands of the de Moravia family.	1288–1316 In hands of a certain Augustin who termed himself Lord of Inverallan in Strath Spey.	1316. Augustin disposed of lands to Grant, who disposed of half of them to Pilch, burgess of Inverness. Passed into hands of ten persons, involving much litigation.	1583–87. Grant bought lands outright from other claimants.	
Barony of *Cromdale* (Boundaries of Barony much changed at different periods)	1226–1389. Owned by Earls of Fife, then resigned into hands of Crown.	1431. In possession of John of Nairn.	. .	1609. Nairns sold land to Grants	
Barony of Abernethy	1226. Owned by James, son of Morgund. Then by Comyns.	1381. Resigned into King's hands by Comyn. 1384. Granted to Alex. Stewart, E. of Buchan (Wolf of Badenoch), and erected into a lordship. Interregnum. 1501. James granted it to E. of Moray (Stewart).	1516. By this date Grant had got a feu of it from Moray.	. .	
Freuchy . .	Late 13th cent. in hands of Gilbert of Glencarnie (des. of E. of Fife).	. .	1453. Grant acquired half through marriage with Gilbert's daughter.	1493. Grant's share made into a separate barony with some additions. 1586. Grant bought in more of old lands of Freuchie.	
Strathspey—Barony	1364. Bp. of Moray given powers of justiciary in Strathspey and Badenoch, and apparently great landholder there.	. .	By 1539 Grant was renting greater part of Strathspey from Bp. on terminable leases.	1540. Laird of Grant and seven clansmen feued Barony of Strathspey.	
Tullochgorm—with other lands	From 1379, John of Inverpeffer. 1379. Granted to Alexander, E. of Buchan (Wolf of Badenoch).	Later it was held by Huntly.	1491. Huntly exchanged it for other lands with Grant of Freuchie.	. .	

It is true that from the beginning the laird of Grant was supported by his kinsfolk in consolidating his property. The barony of Strathspey was feued by himself, his three sons (one illegitimate), and his kinsmen, Grant of Culcabock, Grant of Ballindalloch, the latter's brother, and another Grant. As time went on, the reigning lairds wadsetted and, more rarely, feued out their land to younger sons and other relations. Many families of the stock of the laird or chief were thus established, but these did not amount to the bulk of the clan, and it must be remembered that the fertile strath of the Spey was not empty when they came there.[1] There is evidence that the custom of taking their landlord's surname, which was fairly common in the Highlands, was adopted by the other inhabitants. A document of 1537 gives the names of fifty-nine parishioners of Duthil, and Sir William Fraser, who unfortunately does not quote them, says that they were none of them Grant but all " Celtic." In 1569 a remission contains forty-seven names, all of them Grant and all but three from Duthil. This is not conclusive in itself, for it was customary for Highlanders to use patronymics and not surnames; but as Grant only acquired Duthil in 1475 (as part of Glencarny), and as he had a good deal of other property, to have established so many descendants in this one parish would premise a more than rodent-like fecundity. Fraser quotes another document of 1537 which refers to " John M'Conquhy in Garthrynbeg," but an endorsement dated 1581 concerns " Duncane Grant in Gartinbeg, sone and air to vmquhill John Makconachie Grant in Gartinbeg." In 1538 " lye clan de Grantis " is mentioned for the first time. It occurs in an agreement with the Farquharsons.[2] The rapidly built up clan was a staunch one. The fulminations of the Privy Council during the sixteenth century bear tribute to the efficiency of the forces that the chief of Grant had at his command.

The Frasers furnish another example of the rapid manufacture of a clan. They also were of Norman origin, and succeeded to lands in the North that had been largely feudalized by other Normans. Yet when the reigning chief died, away

[1] Sir William Fraser, *Chiefs of Grant*, p. 97.

[2] *Ibid.* pp. 97, 99. Examples of Highlanders taking their landlord's name have occurred within the last fifty years to the personal knowledge of persons known to the writer.

from home, in 1576, the "tutor" of the heir trysted the "whole numerous name of Fraser" at Tomnahurich, and out of eight to nine hundred men who gathered there, chose five hundred, with twenty-four gentlemen to act as officers, to bring the body home.[1]

In the case of these clans the original source of the connection was the holding of the land; in other words, it was a feudal connection that gradually developed into one that was partly clannish. Sometimes the relationship between the chief, who was also feudal superior, and the inhabitants of the land was differently achieved. The rise of the Campbells has been alluded to. In this case a Gaelic family, originally settled in one district of Argyleshire, gradually extended its influence and possessions over a great part of the Western Highlands and Islands, till the clan of Campbell was the richest in Scotland. As was the case with most of the successful clans, the head of the name established many offshoot branches, and the charter chests of two of these families furnish examples of another type of clan construction.

The founder of the Campbells of Glenurchy (from whom is descended the Earl of Breadalbane) was a younger son of the head of the great name of Campbell, and his father granted him the lands of Glenurchy in 1432. The successive heads of the house were able men, active servants of the Crown, and by means of wealth and influence, and in reward for services, they steadily extended their possessions. They absorbed a considerable portion of the old Crown lands of that district, and the feuing and sale of the great Church territories in Perthshire furnished Glenurchy with a further opportunity for increasing his territories. The head of the house established many cadet branches. In all this there is little to differentiate him from a Lowland baron. He was, however, also definitely a Highland chief, and the documents that have been left behind show the curious mixture of feudal charters and such purely Highland arrangements as deeds of fosterage and, most important of all, of bands of manrent from dependent Highland septs, dwelling upon his land and acknowledging him to be their chief.[2]

1 *Wardlaw MS.* by Master James Fraser (Scottish History Society).

2 For acquisition of lands, see *Scots Peerage* under "Breadalbane." See also D. Campbell, *Memoirs of an Octogenarian Highlander*, p. 92. C. Innes, *Sketches of Early Scotch History*, pp. 365, 366-374; *Black*

These dependent septs, families, or clans termed themselves Glenurchy's "native men," undertook to give him the "caulp of Kenkynie," i.e. the calp of the head of the kin (the Highland calp due to the chief was the equivalent of the Lowland heriot due to the landlord, and was the best beast, which had to be given to the superior upon the death of a vassal); to visit the chief's house with "sufficient" presents twice in the year; to serve him in hosting and hunting, and to be ready at all times "to ride and go" on their lord's affairs. The term native man does not necessarily imply a very ancient race. Mackintosh of Strone, whose forebear, born about 1500, was an illegitimate son of the chief of Mackintosh and who held wadsets of Mackintosh and Huntly, in 1597 acknowledged Huntly as his "native lord," and was received by him, with his sons, as Huntly's "proper native tenant." The charter chest of the Campbells of Craignish, another cadet branch of the Campbells, contains very similar agreements. The head of the house in 1592 had restored the family fortunes, and a curious collection of notarial instruments record that he was formally accepted as chief by seven different septs or families. For example, a father and three sons named "Makesais," "of thair awin frie motive and will" for themselves and their successors, gave to Ronald Campbell McEan VcDonald of Barrichibyan (Campbell of Craignish) and his heirs, "all and hail thair band of manred and calpis for evir, and sall follow and obey him and his airis in quhatsumevir place he and his foirsaidis transportis thameselffis in the cuntrey or without, and sall obey thame as native men aucht and sould do to thair chieff in tyme coming." In return, Craignish, on behalf of himself and his heirs, "bindis and oblisses him and thame to be ane guid chieff and maister to the saidis personis and thair successioun of men and wemen aucht to haiff eftir calpis, conform to the use of the cuntrey." A notarial instrument of 1612 records another similar bond of manrent. The head of the McCoshems states that: "Forasmuch as I understand of gude memorie that the surname of Clantyre VcCoshem wer of auld native men, servandis and dependaris of the house

Book of Taymouth, p. 405 onwards, for charters setting kinsmen on the land, especially p. 411.

Further details are given in *Miscellany Scottish History Society*, vol. iv (Third Series), pp. 215, 282.

of Clandule Cregnis alias Campbell in Cregnis," he wishes to renew the bond in all " lawliness and subjecioun " to Craignish, and to serve him according to the custom of his ancestors and of those of the other native men of Argyleshire. He undertakes to serve him by sea and land and as need be, and against all persons, the " auctoritie " only being excepted. He also binds himself to give Craignish the customary calp. But these services were to be rendered " provyding " that Craignish and his heirs " do the dewtie of ane chief and master to me and my airis male and female as the use is." [1] Certain points may be specially noticed in connection with these agreements. In the first place, the use of a notarial instrument to record the clan relationship is very significant of the mixture of forms of the time. Secondly, it is very noteworthy that the arrangements were entirely non-feudal; no grant or gift of land took place—in fact, this is stressed when the " Makesais " promise to follow and obey Craignish in whatsoever place he and his heirs should transport themselves in the country or without. Thirdly, the connection between the landowning chief and dependent native men was evidently a usual relationship. McCoshem several times alludes to customs used and wont among the native men of Argyleshire.

The Stewarts of Appin, of Scoto-Norman stock, had a dependent sept of the name of McColl, and it has been pointed out that every Stewart chieftain belonging to the cadet branch of Auchnacone was buried with the grave of a McColl upon either side of him. It would be tempting to trace out the connection between this custom and ancient paganish ideas. In long after years, when the Stewart of Appin of the middle of the eighteenth century formed his men into a regiment in support of Prince Charlie, the names of the killed and wounded furnish something of an index of the structure of the clan. The regiment numbered three hundred men at the least, often considerably more. The casualties among the kin of the chief and of the five cadet families of the name of Stewart numbered 47, but 109 men bearing nineteen other names were also killed and wounded; of these, the McColls lost 33, the Maclarens 27, the

[1] *Collectanea Rebus Albanicis*, published by the Iona Club, pp. 197, 206.

A. M. Mackintosh, *The Mackintoshes and Clan Chattan*, p. 393.

Mackintyres 10, and the Carmichaels and the McCombichs 8 each.[1]

In all the clans whose structure has been mentioned, Macdonalds, Campbells, and the others, the existence of cadet families, the descendants of the sons and near kinsfolk of the successive chiefs, has been alluded to. The genealogies of every one of the greater clans show that where their leaders were in a position to do so, they invariably provided for their immediate families in this way. These lesser gentlemen of the clan, who acted as the chief's lieutenants when the clan aspect of the organization was uppermost, and as his principal tenants and vassals if the landholding side was in question, were an integral part of the organization of the Highlands. Probably the Mackenzies form one of the most striking illustrations of the growth of these offshoot branches. As we have seen, in Culloden's estimate, the chief of this clan was able to put 1000 men into the field, but the other lairds of his name had a following of 1500 men. The status of these kinsmen varied very greatly. It depended upon the position of the head of the family—a powerful chief or landholder could, of course, do more for his relations; upon the degree of relationship—legitimate sons, for instance, would generally, but not always, receive better grants than those who were illegitimate; and upon the fortune, good or bad, of the individual cadets. These branches varied from such important personages as Campbell of Glenurchy, Mackenzie of Cromarty, Grant of Rothiemurchus, etc., to men who occupied holdings now rented by average working farmers. Graham of Gartmore, whom Scott cited as an authority upon the Highlands, wrote: "The property of these Highlanders belongs to a great many different persons, who are more or less considerable in proportion to the extent of their estates, and to the command of the men who live upon them, or follow them, on account of this clanship, out of the estates of others.

[1] A contract of 1628 with regard to the preservation of deer mentions a considerable number of the Mackenzie and Fraser cadets. *Collectanea Rebus Albanicis*, p. 193.

Quotation from *Graham of Gartmore Manuscript.*

W. F. Skene, *Celtic Scotland*, vol. iii, p. 318.

C. Fraser Mackintosh, *Antiquarian Notes*, p. 183, quotes a 1678 proclamation regarding the state of the Highlands that in the list of names shows the great development of cadet branches that had taken place.

These lands are set by the landlord during pleasure, or on short tack, to people whom they call Goodmen (Duine Uasail), and who are of a superior station to the commonality. These are generally the sons, brothers, cousins, or nearest relations of the landlord (or chief). This, by means of a small portion and the liberality of their relations, they are able to stock, and which they, their children and grandchildren, possess at an easy rent, till a nearer descendant be again preferred to it. As the propinquity removes, they become less considered, till at last they degenerate to be of the common people, unless some accidental acquisition of wealth supports them above their station. As this hath been an ancient custom, most of the farmers and cotters are of the name and clan of the proprietor."[1]

The existence of these lesser gentlemen of the clans was a factor of great importance. The Lord Lovat of 1632 granted many wadsets. "There was no earthly thing he put in ballance" with his kindred, whom he would still keep by him within the country, nor would he ever suffer any of them to settle among neighbouring clans. He justified his policy of thus reducing his estates by declaring that his men were "his ammunition, his guard, his glory and honour, and few could compare with them."[2]

In the case of the Grants and of the spreading branches of the Campbells we have seen how the landholding connection was combined with the clan system. It is obvious in such cases that the clan system itself must have had considerable practical uses, which made it worth while incorporating into the feudal system. There are, however, many instances where the clan organization itself was the main connection, and the territorial possessions of the chief were due to his position as a leader of men. Indeed, sometimes, as with the Camerons, the clan existed and held its own for centuries without a legal title to any of the lands occupied. Under the clan system *the* supreme function of a chief was to act as the leader of the fighting forces of the clan, and *the* main value of the members of the clan was as warriors. This fact is of great and increasing importance in the social and economic history of the Highlands. It explains why the chiefs encouraged

[1] Mrs Smith, *Memoirs of a Highland Lady*, gives the most vivid account of the social position of the lesser Duine Uasails in the eighteenth century.

[2] *Wardlaw MS.*, Scottish History Society.

"broken men" to settle upon their lands, a practice which brought them into collision with the central authority and perpetuated the lawless elements in the Highlands, and which clearly shows that these lands were not in the strict sense "tribal." Moreover, in later times the fact that this incentive to crowd their lands with retainers had existed, and that it suddenly came to an end, explains the most tragic features of the "Clearances," the most distressing episodes in the whole history of the Highlands. But, besides his services as a leader of the offensive and defensive forces of the clan, the chief fulfilled other useful functions. Bishop Leslie, writing of Clan Mackintosh in his own times—that is, in the middle of the sixteenth century—says that the custom of the clan, "as of many others in the Irish country, has been at all times to acknowledge one principal for their chief captain, to whom they are obedient in time of war and peace, for he is mediator between them and the prince. He defends them against the invasions of their enemies, their neighbours, and he causes minister justice to them all in the manner of the country, so that none should be suffered to make spoil or go in sorning, as they call it, or as vagabonds in the country."[1] In fact, even where the chief had not feudal claims to his lands, he fulfilled duties which in other parts of Scotland were largely performed by the feudal superiors of the land.

There were, however, other aspects of the functions of a clan. An act of parliament of 1581 speaks of them as "clans of thieves" that were "for the most part copartners of wicked men, coupled in fellowship by occasion of their surnames, or near dwelling together, or through keeping society in theft, or reset of theft; not subject to the ordinary courts of justice, nor to any landlord that will make them amenable to the laws, but commonly dwelling upon sundry men's lands against the goodwill of their landlords, whereby true men injured by them can have no remedy." Membership of a clan was of very real advantage. An unfortunate laird, who was being held responsible under the General Band for the presence of certain obstinate malefactors upon his lands, and who declared to the Privy Council that, they being clannit gentlemen, their arrest was

[1] Bishop Leslie, *History of Scotland*, vol. ii, p. 210 (Early English Text Society).

altogether impossible to him,[1] was only one sufferer among many.

In a considerable number of clans, the chief had little or no feudal status, and the clan relationship was the only connection or was the primary one through which lands were eventually acquired. Clan Mackintosh is an example of clan organization that originally owed nothing to the feudal system. According to the traditional clan histories, the Mackintoshes are the descendants of a younger son of the Earl of Fife who came to Morayshire in the twelfth century and whose descendant, in 1291, married the heiress of the chief of Clan Chattan. Some nineteenth-century historians have suggested other origins. In any case, in the fourteenth century, when the Mackintoshes emerged into the noontide of documented history, there is a wealth of tradition showing that they were already established in Badenoch—the upper valley of the Spey; round about Petty, in the rich coast lands between Inverness and Nairn; and in the upper valley of the Findhorn. They had also some claim to the lands of Glenlui and Loch Arkaig, territories occupied by the Camerons in Lochaber, upon the West Coast. The confederacy of clans which made up Clan Chattan had also begun to take form. In a charter of 1442, Malcolm, chief of Mackintosh, is alluded to as the captain of Clan Chattan.[2] In the fifteenth century, according to Major the historian's account, the Mackintoshes were already a powerful clan. The story of the different lands that they occupied gives an interesting picture of clan tenacity. In none of them were they exclusive occupiers. They held no compact territories. In the coastal land they occupied several large holdings, and, according to their own tradition, the founder of the race, the son of an Earl of Fife, had received these from the king in 1163. From time to time, when the earldom of Moray lapsed into the hands of the Crown, rentals of the estates appear in the *Exchequer Rolls*, and the head of the Mackintoshes and sometimes some of his kinsmen are mentioned among the tenants. They were thus tenants in 1464, and in 1545 they

[1] Quoted by the Duke of Argyle, *Scotland as it was and is*, p. 176. *Register*, *Privy Council*, vol. iv, p. 443 (1589).

[2] A. M. Mackintosh, *The Mackintoshes and Clan Chattan*, pp. 13-27, for sketch of early Mackintosh traditions.

secured an eleven years' lease. But although in the meantime they obtained heritable possession of a neighbouring property and afterwards lost this again, they did not secure permanent title to Connage, Petty, Brachly, or any of the lands, though they managed to continue to occupy them under five successive families of Earls of Moray, with interludes of Crown possession—and even during periods when a lesser superiority was interposed between themselves and their lord. During this time some of the Mackintosh holdings were occupied by successive branches of the family; and upon two occasions when their superior ejected them, they were able to turn out the intruding occupiers put in their place, and to regain their lands with the help of the rest of the clan.[1]

Moy, which was one of the principal dwellings of the chief, and the lands round it, fared differently. According to clan tradition, Mackintosh was in possession there at the time of the forfeiture of the Comyns at the end of the Wars of Independence, and he secured a lease of the lands in 1437 from the Bishop of Moray, who was the superior. In 1545 he obtained a feu from the bishop.[2] The valley of the Findhorn, of which Moray and Huntly held the superiorities, in the sixteenth century was held on lease by tenants with many different surnames, but by the eighteenth century Mackintosh and some of the leading families of his own clan and of other septs of Clan Chattan had secured feus for nearly the whole of it. In Badenoch the clan had a traditional connection with Rothiemurchus, and in the fifteenth century Mackintosh had a lease of it from the bishop. But in 1464 the cousin of the chief, a leading man in the clan, managed to obtain a heritable lease of it from the bishop, against the wishes of the chief. Eventually, in 1539, the descendant of this cousin disposed of his rights to Huntly, who sold Rothiemurchus to the laird of Grant. Farther up the river, and not adjoining Rothiemurchus, the chief of Mackintosh had a considerable amount of land; the most important part of it was acquired by marriage in 1502, and Mackintosh obtained a charter consolidating his possessions

[1] A. M. Mackintosh, *The Mackintoshes and Clan Chattan*, pp. 71, 79, 82, 99, 109, 111, 128, 157, 218, 220.

One of the cadet branches secured heritable possession of Petty in 1609.

[2] *Ibid.* pp. 73, 79, 82, 139.

from Huntly in 1568 [1] (largely in compensation for the latter's wrongful execution of a chief of Mackintosh).

By an irony of fate, the only lands which Mackintosh held of the Crown, and where he was therefore entitled to exercise the feudal rights of a superior, were in Lochaber—where he had obtained considerable extensions of the traditional lands of Clan Chattan from the Lord of the Isles, and, after his forfeiture, held them of the Crown—but which were all in almost continuous occupation by the Camerons and the Macdonalds of Keppoch, who, in spite of Mackintosh's many attempts to drive them out or to force them to acknowledge his superiority, continued to occupy the lands. A settlement was at last reached with the Camerons in 1665, when Lochiel, the captain of that clan, bought the disputed territories for 72,500 merks. As he was not able to produce this large sum, Argyle paid it for him, and Lochiel held the lands in feu of Argyle. A settlement was reached with Macdonald of Keppoch in 1690, who acknowledged himself to be Mackintosh's tenant.[2] In addition to these possessions, the chief of Mackintosh, whenever he was in a position to do so, bought certain isolated properties, but he was not able to retain permanent possession of them.

Not only were the chief's possessions scattered, and some of them but insecurely held. A good many of the cadet branches of his name secured heritable rights to lands that they held independently of him from Huntly, Moray, or Campbell of Cawdor. Moreover, many of the septs that made up Clan Chattan were territorially quite independent of their captain. The Farquharsons occupied Deeside, the MacCombies moved to Glenshee, and both these clans for a long time co-operated with the main body of the confederation. The Macgillivrays, the Macbeans, and the Macqueens occupied estates that were adjoined to or intermixed with the lands of the captain, but they held them quite independently of him, and yet the relationship was extraordinarily close and friendly. Many other septs of the confederacy had no territory, sometimes even no chieftain of their own. The bond connecting these allied septs and clans was in some cases a real or traditional descent from Clan Mackintosh or from the ancient Clan Chattan; in others, circumstances

[1] A. M. Mackintosh, *The Mackintoshes and Clan Chattan*, pp. 88-89, 150-152, 161, 148.
[2] *Ibid.* ch. x, p. 241, ch. xi, p. 269.

formed or were said to form a connecting link—the Gows were said to be the descendants of the Smiths who fought for the clan on the Inches at Perth. In other cases the original connection is unknown. The mutual adherence of the component parts of the Clan Chattan, however, was a very real thing. In 1578–79 Mackintosh was described as the chieftain of a Highland clan whose followers were "the tenentis and servandis of sindrie landlordis," but who gave "litill gude obeydience to any ordinar law and justice." A few years later, in 1603, Mackintosh was denounced by the Privy Council because he had not restrained the broken men living in Petty, Brachly, Strathnairn, Strathdearn, etc., and their misrule and insolence, "although had they understood that he was offended with them, they durst not have oppressed the meanest subject in the country."[1] No doubt the condition of the country and the paramount need for maintenance and protection by a powerful leader was the main factor in the cohesion of Clan Mackintosh and of the confederacy of Clan Chattan. Certain other clans, for the same reason, occupied their lands in defiance of the law. The Macgregors are a case in point.

An extreme example of the triumph of the clan occurs in the history of the Macdonalds of Moydart. Moydart had legal title to his estates, but Ranald Bane, the ruling chief in 1513, fell foul of the Government and, for unknown reasons, was executed. He was succeeded by his eldest son, who was detested by the clan for his cruelties, and was killed by them; and they then passed over this chief's sons and elected Alister Allanson, the brother of Ranald Bane. Alister Allanson also secured possession of a great part of the family estates and remained in occupation of them till his death. He was succeeded by his illegitimate son, John Moydertach, who secured a royal charter granting him the family possessions. Nevertheless, there were several individuals with better rights than his own. There were the two sons of the murdered chief, the elder of whom had received the lands of Morar, and who seem to have made no further claim. There was also a half-brother of Ranald Bane, the executed chief, who was also named Ranald and was known as Galda or Stranger. This man was not only legitimate, but had the advantage, through his mother, of being

[1] *Register, Privy Council,* vol. vi, p. 435.

the grandson of Fraser of Lovat, who was head of a rising clan and enjoyed the favour of the king.

In 1540, when James V had made a progress through the Western Isles, and when John Moydertach, the *de facto* chief, had been apprehended and put in ward as a dangerous subject, Fraser bestirred himself on behalf of his kinsman Ranald Galda. He persuaded the king to revoke the charter to John Moydertach and to grant the lands to Galda. Galda, being legitimate, had, of course, a better title, but the sons of the assassinated chief had a better one still. Their existence, however, is not alluded to. Galda secured possession of the lands, but his clansmen disliked him, and, when Moydertach was set at liberty, the whole clan, including the sons of the assassinated chief, acknowledged him as their chief and expelled Galda. Shortly afterwards, Scotland was plunged into the troublous minority of Mary Queen of Scots, and, in spite of the efforts of the regents and of the lieutenants of the Crown entrusted with the administration of justice in the North, John Moydertach continued to act as chief. On the few occasions when the royal forces penetrated as far as Moydart, he slipped away into inaccessible regions, and at other times enjoyed the family estates and was accepted by the clan as their leader. Once, during her brief supremacy, Mary of Lorraine was too strong for him, and forced him to surrender; but, in the words of the old annalist, the queen-regent did not hold the Highland fox firmly enough by the ear, and he escaped. Eventually his eldest son succeeded to his lands and another son founded a cadet branch, and they both received Government recognition.[1]

In trying to build up some sort of a mental picture of the Highlands in the old days, it is important to remember that usually the lands occupied by the clans were not clearly demarcated blocks of land—very few chiefs were able to achieve complete consolidation of their estates, like that attained by Argyle and the neighbouring barons of the name of Campbell. In most cases the lands of the chiefs were scattered, and there was in addition a considerable movement among the Highlanders. The clans raided and fought far and wide. A famous clan story concerns a raid undertaken by the Monroes, a Ross-shire clan, to Strathardle, in Southern Perthshire. The Mackin-

[1] D. Gregory, *History of the Western Highlands*, pp. 157-163.

toshes were the allies of the Mackays, who dwelt in the extreme North, and often sent men up to help them. The "thieves and limmers" of the Camerons and Clan Ranald constantly raided in Morayshire, and the lairds of Lovat, Grant, Kilravock, and Cawdor were told by the Privy Council, in 1602, that they would be held responsible for the acts of those whom they allowed to pass through their lands. In 1602, in order to harass some of their neighbours, certain Morayshire lairds brought Alaster MacIan Og of Glencoe with members of his clan and other broken men to Morayshire, gave him a bond of maintenance, and sustained them there for two months by means of a stent raised from their kin and friends. Moreover, landless and "broken" men were constantly on the move and ready to attach themselves to any turbulent chief who wanted men. In 1602, Glengarry raided in Glenisla (in Forfarshire) with two hundred followers, but many of these were Macgregors and members of Clan Chattan, and therefore, as chief and landlord respectively, Mackintosh and Huntly were considered responsible.[1]

Moreover, in many parts of the country, there was no dominant clan or "name," and the population was a very mixed one. This was especially the case in Central Perthshire. In Glenlyon the population "was at no time composed of the members of one clan only. Even from the earliest recorded times it consisted of a mixture of different clans, and at no time in its history did the clan to which the proprietor belonged form the majority of the inhabitants. After the time of Sir William Olifant [a Scoto-Norman], Macdougals, Stewarts, Campbells, Murrays, and Menzies successively owned the greater part of the glen, but none of these clans ever formed more than a comparatively small part of the population." Before the modern changes, the following names were found well established in the glen, with long traditions of their occupation of their lands. The Macarthurs, Maccalums, Macgregors, Stewarts, Campbells, and Macnaughtons all claimed originally to have come from Argyleshire. The Menzies came from Weem, the Mackerchars came from Braemar, and the Robertsons from Athole. There were also a few Maclellans, Camerons, and Macdonalds, but the latter were mostly of later arrival,

[1] *Register, Privy Council,* vol. xiv, p. 454.

having moved to Glenlyon after the Jacobite risings of the '15 and the '45. In Fortingall there was a similar mixture of names, but the Macgregors were more numerous, and there were Macdougals, supposed to have come from Lorne in the fourteenth century, when a Stewart of Lorne owned the glen; Dewars from Glendochart, Andersons, and Scotts and Irvines, the latter supposed to have come from Aberdeenshire when the Huntly family owned the glen for a short time. The population of Rannoch was equally mixed.[1] The existence of these mixed populations explains the great followings of those feudal magnates having land in the Highlands—Huntly, Athole, etc.; and they also furnished the material from which the growing clans of the fifteenth and sixteenth century were built up.

Though the theories of landholding that underlay the rival systems were so different, in practice feudalism and the clan system were very much alike. The holding of land was the main connection under the feudal system, but it secured protection and the provision of those social services essential even to rather primitive communities. The clan also provided the individual with protection and formed a kind of social organization for him, and, "either be or by the law," it enabled the clansman, through his chief, to occupy land. Sometimes the two systems worked together, but at other times they were at variance. The whole tenor of legislation, much of which has been quoted, seems to show that in the opinion of the authorities the power of the clans was a disturbing force, cutting across the system of territorial organization that they were trying to perfect. The important act of 1587, and the legislation of 1593 and 1594, in which landlords and bailies were ordered to arrest rebels and outlaws dwelling on their lands, enacts that chiefs, captains, and chieftains were also responsible for the good behaviour of their followers, and orders them to furnish pledges for this and to produce any offenders if required to do so. This differentiation in wording is slight in itself, but it seems to bring out how very grudging was the admission of the power of the chiefs and captains. The list contains separate lists of captains and of chiefs. Among the list of landlords appear the

[1] A. Stewart, *A Highland Parish*, pp. 79, 109, 126.

D. Campbell, *Memoirs of an Octogenarian Highlander*, p. 88, endorses this. He quotes several other examples.

names of heads of almost all the greater clans: Argyle and more than half a dozen lairds of his name, Chisholm, Grant, Mackintosh, Fraser, Mackenzie, Munro, half a dozen branches of the Macdonalds, Macleods, Macneils, MacIans, Macleans, Macfies, Macfarlanes, Stewarts of Appin, etc., generally under their territorial designation and often with several cadet landholding branches, are also given. There were also a large number of unclanned names—the Earls of Athole, Menteith, etc.: in all, the names of 111 persons appear. The list of chiefs and captains on whom broken men depended, " oftymes agains the willis of thair landlordis," includes 35 names; but of these, 21 had already appeared in the other list. Probably in such cases the chiefs were the landholders of only a part of the territory occupied by their followers. Among the entirely landless clans were the Camerons, the Macnabs, the Macgregors, and the Clan Ranald of Moydart.[1]

The conflicting claim of chief and landlord must have been a disturbing factor in the lives of many Highlanders. Generally they were known definitely to have thrown in their lot either with one or the other, but sometimes dramatic incidents occurred. For instance, when Queen Mary came to Inverness in 1562, at the beginning of her quarrel with Huntly, there were rumours that the latter meant to carry her off. The chief of Mackintosh had raised his nearest clansmen for the queen, but meanwhile the Mackintosh tenants on the Gordon estates were being called out for Huntly. The old clan history tells how the young chief hastened over the hills, met his men on their march to join Huntly, and brought them all to the queen in spite of the " raging " of Huntly's son.[2] The complications in the ordinary management of estates under such conditions can easily be imagined.

The institution of the feudal custom of landholding by charter and the subsequent development of feu-farm tenure, though it placed those chiefs whose title to their lands was precarious in a position of great disadvantage,[3] seems to have tended on the whole to the stabilization of the clan system. The little that

[1] *Register, Privy Council,* vol. iv, p. 783.

[2] *Macfarlane's Genealogical Collection* (Scottish History Society), vol. i, p. 336.

[3] Cf. D. Gregory, *History of the Western Highlands of Scotland*, p. 122.

we know of the Highlands during the period *preceding* the Wars of Independence shows how dependent upon propitious circumstances was the survival of a family in the days when land was held by no definite title and was constantly subdivided among sons, and when there was no arrangement whereby the senior branch retained superiority over lands that were bestowed upon cadets. During the period at present under review it was by means of feudal institutions that the rising clans made good their position, and especially by means of feu-farm; and this process was continued during the seventeenth century.

In the case of cadet branches of most clans, the enormous importance of the possession of a heritable title to land is more obvious, because the ups and downs of political circumstances are not so much in evidence. It was only in very rare cases that these junior branches managed to maintain themselves if they did not secure the right to transmit the possession of land from one generation to another. The proportion of the lesser Highland gentry whose families were founded upon the grant of a feu must be extraordinarily high.[1]

PART III. ECONOMIC ASPECTS OF THE CLAN SYSTEM

The relationship between chief and clansman was a very beautiful one. The traditions of the clans abound with stories of selfless devotion in the hour of danger and of loyalty unto the death, and in the less heroic times of peace the intercourse between them was a very close one. Among their own people the greatest of the Highland chiefs were never known by any feudal title they might possess, but by the patronymic which proclaimed their relationship to the founder and ancestor of the clan, from whom all, whether correctly or incorrectly, claimed to be descended. There could be little class feeling when the link that bound the whole fabric of the little society together was that of kinship. Moreover, whatever his claim to his lands, the Highland chief was dependent upon his people for their

[1] No summary of figures is available. The fact is apparent from the notices of individual cadet branches given in most histories of individual clans.

support, as well as they upon him. The Highlanders were never slavish in their allegiance. In most clans there are instances where the clansmen refused to follow a chief whom they disliked and despised, in which event he was deposed, and even killed, by his clan or a section of it.

In the case of the chief, as in that of the ordinary feudal landlord, besides other things, there was a definite economic connection. The clan largely supported the chief, but the payments that they made varied. Sometimes he was actually the landlord or the principal tenant and they paid him rent. But, at least on the West Coast, he also received the ancient Gaelic dues of calpe (the equivalent of the feudal herezelde), even from clansmen who were not upon his land, and " cuddiche," i.e. a given amount of hospitality when he visited them. By means of the Gaelic institution of fosterage he not only provided for his children, but drew the bands of clanship closer.[1]

On the other hand, the clan system was built up upon certain very definite services performed by the chief to the clansmen. In the first place, it was in his name that the lands occupied by his followers were held. The clansmen as such had no individual rights to the land. Perhaps this has already been sufficiently stressed, but an interesting example may be quoted. In 1599, when Macdonald of Islay was trying to make his peace with the Government, he offered to remove " his whole clan and dependaris " from their lands in Kintyre, so that the Crown should let these to new tenants.[2] The chiefs constantly settled broken men upon their lands in order to increase the strength of their following—this habit was a perennial source of quarrel with the Government. Thus a Privy Council minute of 1602 records that Glengarry, " with all glaidness of hairt," had received certain broken and disordered Highlandmen upon his lands. Under the command of his son and other gentry of the clan, and armed with weapons provided by the chief, they had committed a particularly lurid murder.[3] So far as the present writer can

[1] W. F. Skene, *Celtic Scotland*, vol. iii, p. 426, prints a report upon the revenue of the Isles, *circ.* 1577–95. Several rentals have been printed in the *Scottish Hist. Review*. See also W. F. Skene, *Highlanders of Scotland*, p. 111.

[2] D. Gregory, *History of the Western Highlands of Scotland*, p. 288. Duke of Argyle, *Scotland as it was and is*, p. 169.

[3] *Register, Privy Council*, vol. iii, p. 87.

discover, in no instance did the other members of the clan object to sharing with the newcomers.

A curious letter to the laird of Balnagown, the chief of the Rosses, shows the attitude of the clansmen towards their chief as the landholder for the clan. The letter is directed to the laird by his kin and friends, viz. fourteen of the principal gentry of the clan, and it advises him that of late they have seen an appearance of a fall and utter wreck falling upon the house and of the "tinsal of the riggis" (loss of the lands): they therefore urge him to serve God, desist from rebelling against the Government (which he was doing at the moment), and to fix a tryst at which his friends and kin may come to confer with him upon the lasting weal of his house. The letter once more earnestly desires him to change his ways, rather than to perish with his house, kin, and friends, and "tyne the riggs yat his elders wan," for his kin and friends fear a stranger will come in his room, which will be his and their utter "wrak."[1] In this case the chief went his own way and ignored the wishes of the clan.

The chief was evidently held responsible for providing for his followers. A letter from the laird of Glenurchy to the keeper of his castle of Kilchurn, dated 1570, is a good example of what an efficient chief would do for his followers. It runs: "Gregor M'Ane, I commend me hartlie to you. McCallum Dow hes schawin me quhow the Clangregour hes tain vp your geir and your poor tenants' geir, the quhilk I pray yow tak na thoucht of, for albeit I haue na ky to recompanss yow instantlie, I sall, God willinge, mak yow and youres sour of rowmis" (holdings) "that sall mak yow mair profeit nor the gear that ye haue tint at this tyme, ye beand trew faythfull seruand to me. And gif the puir men that wantis geir duellinge onder yow be trew to yow, tak thame into the place vpoun my expensis, and gif to thair wyifis and bairnis sum of my victuall to sustein tham as ye think expediant. I pray yow haue the place weill provydid with sic furnesing as ye ma get, and spare nowther my geir nor yit your awin, for God levuinge ws our healthes, we will get geir enewche."[2] Glenurchy was upon the right side of the law; the protection of a chief was even more useful in cases where a clan occupied their lands "by" the law. The analogous organiza-

[1] W. Macgill, *Old Ross-shire*, part 2, p. 2.

[2] *Black Book of Taymouth*, p. 387.

tions upon the Borders furnish one example among many that might be quoted. In 1578–79 Walter Scott of Tushielaw had seized some land belonging to the sheriff of Selkirk " be plane force." The sheriff and the king's lieutenant on the Borders tried to remove him and failed, and they appealed to the Privy Council to prevent Scott from establishing himself on the lands, because " the said Walter being a clannit man on the Bordour, qhais possession ane yeir will be comptit a kyndnis gif it be sufferit." [1]

The chief also defended the goods and persons of his clansmen, and administered law and order within his territories; [2] there is, however, but little evidence to show whether the laws and regulations were mainly based upon the laws and customs evolved in the Lowlands or how far they were survivals of the ancient laws of the Gael, such as were codified in Ireland. According to the traditional history of the Macdonalds, the Lord of the Isles had organized the making and administering of the laws of their great dominions. A council of sixteen persons, representing the great men and the lesser gentry among their followers, used to meet at Islay, and a judge was placed in every island. As a matter of history, the Breve, the Gaelic title for a judge, is mentioned several times in sixteenth-century documents. Nevertheless, in 1613, in Islay, where old customs might well be expected to linger longest and to be reinforced by Macdonald of Islay's close connection with Ireland, where he had much property, the people sent a bitter complaint to the king that an Irish cousin of the last Macdonald of Islay, who had obtained a lease of the old patrimony of the line, was oppressing them by introducing additional dues and by endeavouring to astrict and subject them to the forms and laws of Ireland, " which is a matter of great grief, that they being His Majesty's native-born subjects should be ruled and governed by foreign and strange laws." An interesting survival was an ancient weight, the *lapidis M'Coul*, which had been in use in Mull, Coll, Jura, Tiree, and Lorn, and was still used in Mull in 1587.[3]

[1] *Register, Privy Council*, vol. vi, p. 127.

[2] *Wardlaw MS.*, printed by Scottish History Society, gives some excellent examples of the duties fulfilled by a chief, cf. pp. 171, 184, 255.

[3] *Collectanea Rebus Albanicis*, pp. 296-297, 160, 172.

D. Gregory, *History of the Western Highlands*, pp. 210, 213, 271, 291.

The possession of an efficient chief was all-important to the Highlanders. In order to procure one, the Highlanders upon occasion departed from the feudal law of primogeniture. The succession of the eldest son had not been a Gaelic custom. In ancient Alban the strange practice of alternate succession by the two leading branches of a family had to some extent prevailed. Another Gaelic practice, known as tanistry, was the selection of the most suitable male among the kindred to succeed. Somerled and his descendants divided their possessions among their sons. In the fifteenth and sixteenth centuries the eldest son of a Highland chief generally succeeded his father, according to the law of the land, but not invariably. John, first Lord of the Isles, married the heiress of Garmoran, and thus secured great additional estates. He had three sons by this lady, but he had his marriage with her annulled and married the daughter of the king; and by his will, and in the royal charter granting him his lands, the son of this royal second wife was made to succeed to the whole estates, those of the first wife as well as those of John himself. The clan is said at first to have wished to follow the eldest son of the first marriage, but they eventually became reconciled to this strange arrangement. One of the elder brothers accepted the position from the first and looked after his younger brother's estates till he grew up. The other was irreconcilable. In after years the descendants of these brothers quarrelled bitterly over the possessions that had been the portion of the pliant brother, but they never, even in its most critical years, made claim to the lordship of the Isles. Curiously enough, the new lord's full brother, his heir-presumptive, was known as the Tanister, the name of the chosen heir under the old Gaelic elective system.[1] According to the traditional history of the Macleans, a somewhat similar arrangement was made in that clan. The chief was captured at the battle of Harlaw (fought in 1411), and, apparently to regain his liberty, "took to his second lady a daughter of the Earl of Mar. In his contract with this lady he was obliged to make the heirs male of that marriage his successors, in prejudice to the sons of the first marriage, which he did accordingly, for Neill, the eldest, renounced his right to the estate and superiority, so

[1] D. Gregory, *History of the Western Highlands*, pp. 29, 30, 32.

that [to the old chief] succeeded Lachlan Og, his son by Mar's daughter."[1]

Succession by co-heiresses was a feudal custom. It was generally held that under Gaelic clan custom a woman could not succeed. This was the reason why the Macleods of Dunvegan would not accept the heiress, Mary Macleod. Yet, upon occasion, the Highlanders ignored their own customs. In a certain type of Highland tradition the founder of the new clan is often made to marry the heiress of an older race—the marriage of Mackintosh and the daughter of the chief of Clan Chattan is a case in point. In actual history the transference of land with heiresses took place three times, at least, in the early history of Somerled's descendants, the progenitors of the Lords of the Isles. Stern necessity rather than old tradition seems to have influenced the Highlanders when they departed from the accepted laws and customs of Scotland.

The case of John Moydertach is an example of the election of a chief who was not the legal heir and the deposition of the heir-male.[2] There are other examples of the Highlanders deposing a chief whom they disliked or despised;[3] and when a chief was incapable of leading his clan, owing to his youth, infirmity, or other causes, the leading men of the clan itself—details of the methods of election are not given—chose the most suitable of the kinsmen to act as the captain of the clan in his place. In some cases the captain gave up his duties as soon as there was a rightful chief able to fulfil them, but in others he and his successors became the permanent leaders of the clan. Many of the laws relating to the Highlands of the late sixteenth century allude to chiefs, chieftains, and captains of clans.[4]

A subject that has been but little explored is the degree of democracy that existed within the clans. Probably it varied in different clans and at different times. There was always a distinction between the gentle-men, the duine-uasail, who were generally the kinsmen of the chief, and the lesser folk, but in some cases it was far more sweeping and arbitrary than in

[1] *Macfarlane's Genealogical Collection* (Scottish History Society), vol. i, p. 126.

[2] See p. 512.

[3] Cf. *Sixth Report, Commission on Historic Manuscripts*, p. 716.

[4] Cf. A. M. Mackintosh, *The Mackintoshes and Clan Chattan*, pp. 100, 116, 141.

others. In a report on the Isles, dated between 1577 and 1595, we learn that the chiefs could bring out 6000 men, of which 2000 carried armour, but that "in raising or furth bringing of thair men ony time of yier to quhat somiver cuntrie or weires, na labourers of the ground are permitted to stir forth of the countrie whatever their master have ado, except only gentlemen which labour not, that the labour belonging to the tilling of the ground and winning of their corns may not be left undone." [1]

Members of the clan, as we have seen, sometimes exerted considerable control over the chief, but in all the more circumstantial accounts it is not the clan as a whole but the leading men who do so. The letter to Ross of Balnagown is a case in point.[2] Another instance is the story of the choosing of a "tutor" to act during the minority of a Fraser of Lovat who succeeded in 1576. We learn that there was "a generall meeting of the leading men of Fraser." It consisted of five country-gentlemen (named) and "some of the houses of Farrelin and Relick." [3] In other, more general accounts, the clan at large is alluded to, and mass action may possibly have taken place.

The relation of the chief, the clan, and the land clearly shows how adaptable and changeable an institution was a fifteenth- or sixteenth-century clan. Its organization was shaped rather by present needs than by ancient tradition. This is clearly brought out by the fact that, during the period that we are considering, the organization spread into districts far outside the Highlands. The social conditions of the Borders and of the North of Scotland were, indeed, dealt with by contemporary authorities as if they were exactly the same. The names of the clans and of the broken men inhabiting both are intermingled in the lists drawn up by parliament and by the Privy Council, and at the end of the sixteenth century the same special committee was entrusted with dealing with them both.

Moreover, in the north-eastern Lowlands and in the south-east, families such as Arbuthnot, Innes, etc., are often spoken of as clans, and references to "clannit men" appear. For instance, Leckie of that Ilk in 1593 had to find caution for the

[1] Printed in W. F. Skene, *Celtic Scotland*, vol. iii, p. 429.

[2] See p. 518.

[3] *Wardlaw MS.*, published by the Scottish History Society, p. 176.

good behaviour of himself, his tenants, servants, and whole clan dwelling in Stirlingshire. In 1598, Gardyne of that Ilk (of an old Forfarshire family) had been ordered to subscribe an assurance and to find caution that he and his kin and friends would not quarrel with his neighbour, Guthrie of that Ilk. He protested to the Privy Council that he could not do this, because some of the cadet branches of his house, "having shaikin of that dewitie which thai aucht to him, thair chief," had banded themselves together against him, disowned his authority, and drawn the whole friendship of his house from him.[1]

The fifteenth- and sixteenth-century clan system, in which this type of organization reached its fullest development, does not account for the average Highlander's attitude to the possession of the land that he occupies. There is no direct connection between the lands held by any chief of that period (and occupied by his clansmen) and any more ancient tribal system, either in fact or theory. The chief owned lands an an individual, and he allocated them as he chose. Nevertheless and in spite of this, in the agrarian troubles of the eighteenth century and on to the present time many Highlanders have shown that they strongly believe that they have definite rights to the lands that they occupy. It is impossible to say whether this theory originated in an older form of social order, in times beyond the ken of history, or if it is instinctive. So far as historical records are concerned, the lesser folk in the Highlands were inarticulate during the troublous times that we are dealing with. Nothing survives to tell us what they thought upon the matter, when the clan system interfered, as it very often did, with any prescriptive rights that they may have claimed to ownership of the land that they lived upon. There is, however, an illustration of strong feeling in some instructions that the laird of Mackintosh gave to an emissary entrusted to buy back Rothiemurchus, which had passed into the hands of the laird of Grant. It will be remembered that, according to accepted clan tradition, the ancestor of Mackintosh was a younger son of the Earl of Fife, who came up to Moray in the twelfth century. His descendants soon moved up into Badenoch. One of them was, according to the same traditional

[1] *Register, Privy Council*, vol. v, pp. 39, 452.
A. J. Warden, *Angus or Forfarshire*, p. 69.

history, a leader of the men of Badenoch. Certainly in the fourteenth century, and very possibly earlier, Mackintosh had a lease of Rothiemurchus from the Bishop of Moray, who had received the superiority of great stretches of land in the valley of the Spey from the king. Later on, a collateral of Mackintosh obtained possession of Rothiemurchus from the bishop, quite independently of the chief. He sold it to Huntly, who sold it to Grant. In the instructions to the emissary, Mackintosh begs that the laird of Grant will " let me have my own native country of Rothiemurchus for such sum of money as he gave for the same or as he and I may goodly agree, and that because it is not unknown to the laird and his wise council that it is my native country as said is."[1] The laird of Grant would not give up the land, and for twenty years there was a feud between the clans. The history of the Highlands abounds with examples of the tenacity with which clans clung to lands that they had once occupied. The feeling is stressed here because it explains the bitterness of the people when the clearances took place after the break-up of clan ties in the eighteenth century. It still survives and is a serious factor in the Scots land problem. It is a legacy from the past, but it is not a relic of the fifteenth- and sixteenth-century clan system, and it happens (for quite other reasons) to survive most strongly in certain districts that have changed hands several times and where clan sentiment has had a lesser chance of developing.

Part IV. Relations of the Government and the Highlands

It must be admitted that the clan system did not work at all smoothly. Probably there is little need to emphasize this fact, for clan feuds and clan raids are among those picturesque incidents that help to make up the general impression that most people have of the condition of ancient Scotland. Nevertheless they are of special interest in a sketch of the economic history of Scotland, not only because they were so largely brought about by economic causes, or that they exercised a

[1] Sir William Fraser, *Chiefs of Grant*, vol. iii, p. 285. See also p. 500 of the present book.

considerable effect in retarding the possible development of the country, but because they were blamed for preventing a development of resources that she, in fact, never possessed. It is perhaps some excuse for James VI's treatment of the Highlanders that he honestly believed that the North of Scotland held great sources of wealth that might be tapped, and that he blamed the turbulence of the natives for preventing the realization of these mythical assets.

The clan system, having been built up fortuitously, did not parcel out the available land very successfully. Even during the period of the lordship of the Isles there were territorial disputes among the clans who adhered to it. These were intensified after its forfeiture, and disputed land was at the bottom of a very large number of the troubles between the clans of the Highlands. It was the cause of the feuds between the Macdonalds and the Macleans, the Mackintoshes and the Camerons, the Macleods and the Mackenzies, and many more. When a whole clan, as was the case with the Macgregors, or a leading family, became landless, there was inevitably trouble, for then their only other source of livelihood was by raiding. The "broken men," who rallied to any aggressive chief, and were a constant source of concern to the Privy Council, were desperate because they were landless.[1] It is only fair to add that the land difficulties were largely increased by the clash between the clan and the feudal systems, and by the grant of lands to more than one person, which occurred several times.[2] The most lawless conditions undoubtedly existed on the West Coast, but, from time to time, all parts of the Highlands were liable to crises in which the slumbering hostilities, that always existed, burst into flame, the network of bonds of manrent widened the scope of the quarrel, and there was general trouble. Such a conflagration, in 1590, involved Huntly, Moray, the Grants, Mackintoshes, Camerons, Campbell of Cawdor, and the Lowland

[1] D. Gregory, *History of the Western Highlands of Scotland*, gives many examples of the restlessness and lawlessness of chiefs or leaders who were landless (cf. p. 187).

[2] A particularly glaring example is furnished by the conflicting grants to claimants of lands in Moidart, which caused disputes in the clan itself and disorders that Huntly and all his forces could not quell, and which culminated in the murderous battle of *Blàr na Leine*. D. Gregory, *History of the Western Highlands*, pp. 147, 161, etc.

family of Dunbar. The burgh of Inverness also took a side.[1]

The internal structure of the clans tended to produce constantly recurring minor troubles as well as serious feuds. The gentlemen of the clan, and especially the heir to the chief, had to make good their position of leaders in the eyes of the clan, and often did so by raiding. Unless the chief had great personal ascendancy, there was generally a good deal of intermittent raiding by this irresponsible younger element. The position of the duine-uasail—who, unless they could acquire heritable rights to their lands, were liable to be dispossessed as new generations of chiefs, with their nearer kindred to provide for, arose—was another source of unsettlement.

In addition to all else, there was probably in the sixteenth century, as there certainly was in the seventeenth and eighteenth centuries, the strong economic incentive that the land was often insufficient to maintain the people. In any case, the economic effects, not only upon the Highlands themselves, but upon the adjacent districts (some of them, like Morayshire, very fertile lands), were deplorable. In Kintyre, in 1596, out of 344 rent-paying merklands, 81½ were lying waste. By 1605 the number of wasted merklands had increased to 113.[2] It was one of the crimes of the Highlanders that not only were the rents of any Crown lands that they occupied often unpaid, but that neighbouring and more peaceful royal estates were made unprofitable by raids and counter-raids. In Aberdeenshire a long line of strong castles had to be built and maintained for the purpose of guarding the passes into the hills and preventing the descents of the Highlanders—but this expensive measure was often quite ineffective. Many incidents bear out the complaint of " the hevy wrak and daylie oppressioun that the true and peceble

[1] D. Gregory, *History of the Western Highlands of Scotland*, gives an excellent account of the feuds of the West Coast.

Vol. iv of the *Privy Council Register* is full of an East Coast feud that has already been alluded to, pp. 569, 571, etc. This was only one feud among a good many in one of the most orderly districts of the Highlands.

[2] J. R. N. Macphail, *Highland Papers* (Third Series), Scottish History Society, vol. iii, p. 72.

The Duke of Argyle, *Scotland as it was and is*, p. 217.

For examples of unruly young men, see *Register*, *Privy Council*, vol. vi, p. 169 (1600).

subjects inhabitantis the cuntreyis west the Bordouries and hielandis sufferis throw the struff and reiff of their guidis be the theivis and brokin men inhabiting the same bordouris and Highlandis."[1]

Even the Northern burghs suffered, Elgin, Forres, and the others. So late as 1580, Robert Dunbar of Durris, burgess of Inverness, was ordered to come and live within the burgh, in the course of the campaign against "outland" burgesses. He offered as excuse that it was "notoriouslie knawin" that he could not "repair, hant, and make his residence" there "without the great hazard of his lyfe, because of the deidlie feid standing and as yit vnreconsalit betwix him and some of the clannis ewous to this burgh." This reason was accepted.[2] In earlier and wilder times, during the struggle between the Lords of the Isles and the Crown, the burgh of Inverness was seven times occupied by the Islesmen, and upon most of these occasions was sacked, and the royal revenue drawn from the town (and incidentally those of the unfortunate burgesses) suffered accordingly.[3]

In reading the political history of the Highlanders it must be admitted that sympathy, pity, and admiration are blended to some extent with a sense of horror. In considering the economic effects of their internal fightings and raids upon the Lowlands, besides feeling the hopelessness of such a state of society, one cannot but be struck with a somewhat sordid element in the pettiness of many of the depredations. The Privy Council Records are full of the complaints of very humble folk, whose two or three beasts and small stores of corn—the little all that they possessed—had been lifted by the Highlanders.

The Highlanders, however, had no sense of sin. They honestly believed that they had been deprived of the richer lands of Scotland by the Lowlanders, and that they were entitled to get their own back so far as they could. A letter of the

[1] *Register, Privy Council*, vol. iv, p. 298 (1588). Preamble of an important act.

Cf. *Exchequer Rolls*, vol. xvi, p. 200; W. Douglas Simpson, "The Watch on the Celts," *Scottish Notes and Queries*, vol. iii (Third Series), p. 43.

[2] Th. Keith, "Trading Privileges of the Royal Burghs of Scotland," *English Historical Review*, vol. 28, p. 471.

[3] E. M. Barron, *Inverness in the Fifteenth Century*, pp. 49, 55, 67, 96, 97, 103, 107.

middle of the seventeenth century from Cameron of Lochiel to the laird of Grant is worth quoting. The Camerons had lifted cattle from the lands of a Grant, and the captain of Clan Cameron thus makes his excuses :

"Respd. and Lowing Cousin—My heartly commendations being mentioned to you. I have received your letter concerning this misfortunate accident that never fell out the like between our houses, the like before in no man's days; but praised be God I am inocent of the same, and my friends, both in respect that they were not in your bounds, but to Murray lands where all men taken their prey, nor knew not that Moynes was ane Graunt but thought he was ane Murrayman, and if they knew him they would not stor his lands more than the rest of your bounds in Strathspey; and, sir, I have gotten such a loss of my friends, which I hape you shall consider, for I have aucht dead already, and I have 12 or 13 under cure quhilk I know not who shall die or who shall live of the samen. . . ."

It is satisfactory for a Grant to record how this long-dead Grant of Moyness was a man whose hands could keep his head, even if he had the bad taste to live among the Moraymen. At times the Highlanders raided swiftly, furtively, under cloud of night; such were their tactics, but they felt no more sense of shame than the two hundred lads who spuilzied the lands of Drumquhassil, and repaired there with "twa bagpypis blawand befoir thame."[1]

In truth, the inefficiency of the Government was largely to blame for the lawlessness of the Highlands. In many cases the wild deeds of the Highlandmen were merely their attempts to redress wrongs that had been done them, or to carry out personal reprisals, when there was little or no hope of obtaining justice in any other way. A sixteenth-century manuscript history of the Mackenzies illustrates their very natural attitude of mind. It relates that in the days of Murdo, fifth laird of Kintail, the king (James I) was prisoner in England and "at that time all this north parts were wtout order of Law so as the strongest usurped ag^t^ ye weaker." So the Earl of Ross [at that time the Lord of the Isles] took the opportunity of seizing the laird, of executing him, and of giving his estate to Leod

[1] *Northern Rural Life in the Eighteenth Century*, Anonymous, p. 67. *Register, Privy Council*, vol. v, p. 27.

M'Gilleandris, " till God gave opportunies to this Murdo's son to kill Leod M'Gilleandris and possess himself w^{t} his just heritage." [1] A most business-like agreement between two members of Clan Mackintosh for the seizing and holding of Kilravock Castle arranged their respective shares " als lang as it may be brukyt and joyssit be ony maner off way, other be the law or by the law." [2] It is from the details of such practical arrangements made by the Highlanders for carrying on their daily life, rather than from the stories of the wild ebullitions of clan warfare, that we get a picture of the curious state of the Highlands in the fifteenth and sixteenth centuries.

With all their wildness went the sense of ancient civilization and the pride of race of a people that had in some respects developed very far, in spite of the state of almost barbarous simplicity in which they lived. A Highlander can best convey the curious duality of aspect with which one is obliged to view the people of the North at this time. Fraser, the author of the *Wardlaw Manuscript*, describes the men of the Lewis as "the stoutest and prettiest men, but a wicked bloody crew whom neither law nor reason could guide nor moddell."

In commenting upon the weakness of the Government in administering law and order in the Highlands, it must be remembered that this was rather the result of inefficient machinery than of absolute impotence. At times of emergency, such as the more serious risings by the Lords of the Isles and of those of the claimants to that dignity, when the Crown was obliged to call out the feudal levies of the country, it could always eventually force the Islesmen to submission. Often the mere threat of such serious measures brought about the surrender of the rebels. But such measures could only be resorted to occasionally, and, even as it was, the lieges of the south-west were heartily tired of such service and only took the field with reluctance.[3] The Government was quite incapable of maintaining permanent executive forces that could keep good rule in the Highlands ; and in these circumstances it was obliged

[1] Printed in *Highland Papers*, Scottish History Society, vol. ii, p. 8.

[2] C. Innes. *Family of Rose of Kilravock*, p. 147. Exactly the same phrase is used in an agreement, Macfie and Campbell of Craignish, 1605. *Collectanea Rebus Albanicis*, p. 203.

[3] Cf. D. Gregory, *History of the Western Highlands*, pp. 266-267.

to employ other means for attaining that end. Among the most usual of these were the appointment of one or more of the greater nobles to enforce law and order with special powers, especially Huntly and Argyle; the granting of commissions to neighbouring chiefs or landholders to restore order or exact reprisals, generally with "letters of Fire and Sword." Examples of these letters of fire and sword and of their inefficiency have already been given. The most complete illustration of their harmfulness and lack of direct effect is that of the Clan Gregor. The Macgregors begin to be in disgrace at the end of the fifteenth century. It has been suggested that they originally came into opposition with the Government because they had occupied royal forest land in Central Scotland and had been dispossessed when these territories were feued. In any case, the records of the sixteenth century teem with entries recording the ferocious measures of the Government and the desperate retaliations of the landless, nameless clan. For instance, an order of the Privy Council of 1563 declares that Clan Gregor, already at the horn, have not only massed themselves in great companies, but also have drawn to them the most part of the broken men of the whole country, who at their pleasure burn and slay the poor lieges of this realm, reive and take their goods, sorn and oppress them in such sort that they are able to lay waste the whole bounds where they haunt and to bring the same to be uninhabitable. Certain noblemen and lairds were therefore made responsible for capturing them or expelling them and were given ample powers, and in this way the Central Highlands were systematically divided up. The Earl of Moray was made responsible for the districts of Braemar, Badenoch, Lochaber, Braes of Moray, Strathdearn, and Strathnairn; the Earl of Argyle, for Argyle, Lorn, Levenax, and Menteith; the Earl of Athole, for Athole, Strathardle, Glenshee, and Dunkeld; the Earl of Errol, for Logie-Almond; Lord Ogilvie for the Braes of Angus; Lord Ruthven for Strathbraan; Lord Drummond for Strathearn; Campbell of Glenurchy for Breadalbane and Balquhidder; and the Laird of Grant for Strathspey, Strathavon, and the Braes of Bogie. All through the sixteenth and seventeenth centuries such mandates continued to be issued. Nor were they an empty form. Many of the great men were interested in exterminating the outlaw clan; especially so were the Campbells of Glenurchy. As an illustration of how the work was carried on, an extraordinary sixteenth-century document may be quoted, in which two individuals bind themselves to make continual slaughter upon Clan Gregor, as sole return for the heritable grant of certain lands by the laird of Glenurchy. In other cases, chiefs, lairds, and lesser individuals were punished for not executing the orders against the Macgregors or for allowing them to remain upon their lands.[1] Nevertheless, in spite of persecution that lasted with little intermission until the eighteenth century, it was estimated that the Macgregors were able to put 700 fighting men into the field in 1745.

The Government finally tried yet another method of endeavouring to maintain law and order in the Highlands—that of making the chiefs of the different clans responsible for their followers. Historically, this was a development of the feudal principle of making landlords responsible for the conduct of their tenants, for it appears about the same time as the systematic application of this principle all over Scotland. On the other hand, it also implies an acknowledgement, by the central authority, of the existence of the clans as social institutions. There were, however, a succession of definite phases of treatment of the Highlands by the rulers of Scotland, and as they have some connection with the economic development of the country they may be alluded to here. It must, however, be remembered that besides these more general phases there were considerable variations due to the personalities of the actual kings and regents. During their too brief periods of personal rule all the abler rulers of Scotland brought their personal influence to bear upon the Highlands. Nearly all of them

[1] *Register, Privy Council*, vol. ii, pp. 448-450.
Black Book of Taymouth, p. 416.
Sir William Fraser, *Chiefs of Grant*, vol. i, p. 518.
Early in the seventeenth century, Argyle, by a gross breach of faith, secured the chief and many of the leading men of the Macgregors, and delivered them up to execution. An act of parliament thankfully acknowledges his services conducing to the surrender of the insolent and wicked race and name of Macgregor, notorious, common malefactors, who were worthily executed to death for their offences, and he is rewarded by a grant of 20 chalders out of the lands of Kintyre.—Quoted by Scott in his Preface to *Rob Roy*.

visited the northern parts of the kingdom, not once, but several times. On the whole, the Highlanders were responsive to the royal authority, and still more so to the royal kindness; but again and again, during the disastrous minorities, the work was undone, and had to be begun all over again when the next king took the reins of authority into his own hands.

The first phase may be said to extend till the fall of the lordship of the Isles in 1493. The fourteenth and fifteenth centuries saw the development of the clan system in its final form and of the lordship of the Isles. As Lord of the Isles and Earl of Ross, the chief of the great Clan Donald took his place as one of the great feudatories of the kingdom. There was, however, constant trouble caused by his[1] assumption of powers greater than those of a subject and by his intrigues with England, and the most effective national forces of the moment had to be again and again employed to bring him to submission. Eventually, first the earldom of Ross and then the lordship of the Isles were forfeited during the later part of the fifteenth century.

The sixteenth century was a period of great turmoil. Clan feuds were incessant; there were serious risings to restore the Lord of the Isles. During this second phase, some of the great nobles of the North, such as Moray and Athole, but most often Huntly and Argyle,[2] were employed to "daunton" the wilder Highlanders, and to endeavour to administer the great estates that had fallen to the Crown with the forfeiture of the Lord of the Isles. James IV began this practice when he became absorbed in European affairs, and it was continued. It is not easy to see what else could have been done, considering the general condition of the kingdom, but it was not a successful form of government. The great nobles were themselves sometimes in opposition to the Crown.[3] Their administration of their trust over the Highlanders was by no means always a

[1] The title of Lord of the Isles was self-assumed, but was afterwards conferred by the Crown. The acts of aggression during the rule of the last Lord of the Isles were carried out by his turbulent relatives, who seized his powers.

[2] For examples of such commissions see Argyle Papers, *Historical Manuscripts Commission*, 4th Report, Part I, p. 487.

[3] Cf. 1577, when the inhabitants of Ross, Moray, Badenoch, and Balquhidder were ordered to support Glengarry in resisting invasion by Argyle. —*Register, Privy Council*, vol. ii, p. 674.

disinterested one. Argyle, especially, seems to have well deserved the accusations made against him of using the misdeeds of the Highlanders for his own aggrandisement and even of deliberately stirring up trouble for this reason.[1] The attitude of these lieutenants towards the Highlanders, and sometimes that of the Government who entrusted them with their great powers, seems an extraordinarily hard one. In 1531, Argyle and Moray were entrusted with the pacification of the Islands, then in a state of rebellion. Argyle made certain proposals for the reduction of the rising and offered to try to induce the inhabitants of the southern islands to take their lands from the king's commissioners and to pay their yearly rents, but, if they would not do so, he pledged himself with his own kinsmen, friends, and followers to compel them to obedience, or else to destroy them, root and branch, and quiet the Isles in that way, without creating any burden upon the rest of the country. He suggested, however, that two of the king's household should accompany him, to see that he did not unnecessarily proceed to extremities. Moray made similar proposals for dealing with the northern isles.[2] It was Argyle's constant policy to try to make the Government bind itself to conduct all dealings with the Islanders through himself, as an expert in "the danting of the Ilis." When the Crown was strong enough, however, negotiations were as far as possible carried on directly with the chiefs themselves; and the policy was adopted by James V, who was very successful in dealing with the Islanders, and by Mary of Lorraine, of systematically making them give hostages of their sons or near kinsfolk for their good behaviour.[3] These hostages, who were brought under Lowland influences, would, it was no doubt hoped, be a civilizing influence when they returned home.

The policy of James VI and of his advisers marks certain new departures in the dominant lines of policy pursued. They did not make complete innovations, for the two special features

[1] D. Gregory, *History of the Western Highlands*, pp. 216-201, 183, and especially p. 132. The chief of Clan Mackintosh was illegally executed by Huntly, and the laird of Grant at one time complained that Huntly had "maist awfullie" oppressed his tenants.—*Register, Privy Council*, vol. iv, p. 646. The line of policy pursued by successive Earls of Argyle was so uniform that a generalization regarding this house is justified.

[2] D. Gregory, *History of the Western Highlands*, p. 136.

[3] *Ibid.* pp. 182-183.

of their policy, that of making the superior responsible for his followers, and that of trying to utilize the economic resources of the Highlands, had already existed. In a land so completely feudal as Scotland, it may have been theoretically an innovation, but, in practice, it was quite natural that the chief should be made responsible for his followers, especially when in very many cases he was, if not the superior of the land that they occupied, at least its tenant. So early as 1496, when a considerable number of civil actions against the Islesmen were pending, an act was passed by the Lords of the Council ordering that the chief of every clan should be answerable for the due execution of summonses and other writs against his own clansmen, under the penalty of being made liable himself to the party bringing the action.[1] It is probably significant of the extreme suspicion with which the Government regarded the organization of the clans that the latter received no further recognition for almost exactly a hundred years, although, as feudal superiors, a considerable number of chiefs were expected to exercise jurisdiction over their followers.

The other object of James VI, that of trying to extract some revenue from the Highlands, had also been in the minds of his predecessors, though in a much simpler form. It will be remembered that when the lordship of the Isles was forfeited the lands were annexed to the Crown. The chiefs who actually occupied these lands, Macdonalds, Macleans and the rest, except in the cases where they were able to obtain heritable rights, were Crown tenants, often upon short leases, and liable for the payment of the rents of themselves and their sub-tenants. In the troublous history of the West Coast it is not surprising that these rents were very often not paid. The Crown made many attempts to make the local chiefs do so, and in the commissions to Argyle and other lords there was generally a clause ordering them to secure the payment of the Crown rents, either by the old inhabitants or by " true men " who were to be brought in.[2] The threat of being removed, more than once brought about a rising among the inhabitants. Moreover, the fishings in the lochs of the north-west were becoming of increasing import-

[1] D. Gregory, *History of the Western Highlands*, p. 91.

[2] *Ibid.* pp. 95, 165, 169, etc.; *Register, Privy Council*, vol. vi, p. 255, for a similar proclamation in 1601.

ance. The herring fisheries were the monopoly of the royal burghs, but the Highland chiefs tried to make as much money as they could by means of heavy charges for the use of their land for drying the nets, salting the fish, etc. Both James V and Mary of Lorraine fixed the charges that the chiefs who owned or occupied land on their shores were to make from the fishermen from the south who followed the herring shoals there, and about the middle of the sixteenth century the Privy Council interfered several times to protect these men from the violence of the Highlanders.[1]

When James VI, that busy monarch, and his later advisers came into power, he devoted much time and energy to the taming of the Highlands. No doubt his activities were largely due to his desire to establish an ordered government all over the kingdom. This was probably the main reason for his operations against the Borderers, and, as a matter of fact, he legislated for the Highlands and the Borders together in several acts that had this object. In the case of the Highlands, however, he also had the strong economic motives of securing his rents and of opening up the resources of the country. And in tracing out the story of James' attempts to obtain these objects it must be remembered how desperately poor he was, and that he tried to exploit not only the Highlands but many aspects of Lowland life. The harsh measures that he used towards the Highlanders were, in the preambles to the various acts and ordinances, excused, not only by highly-coloured accounts of the barbarity and lawlessness of the people, but by the fact that they were preventing the development of rich economic resources and the raising of the Crown revenues. In a most sweeping order of 1599 to Huntly and Lennox to help the Lowland company that was at that time trying to colonize Lewis, after retailing the evil deeds of the Islesmen, it states that: besides all their other crimes, they rebelliously withhold from His Majesty great part of the patrimony and proper rent of the Crown; deprive the country of the benefit which might redound thereto, by the trade of fishing, and of other commodities which these bounds render; and now, at last, a great part of them have banded, conspired, and daily practise, by force and policy, in their barbarous and

[1] *Register, Privy Council*, vol. iv, pp. 121-123. *Collectanea Rebus Albanicis*, pp. 99-102.

rebellious form to disappoint His Majesty's service in the Lewis. At a rather later date (in 1608), James quite frankly recorded the "ayme and drift" of his policy with regard to the Highlanders. "First in the cair we haif of planting of the Gospell amang these rude, barbarous, and uncivill people, the want whairof these yeiris past no doubt has bene to the grite hazard of mony poore soullis being ignorant of thair awne salvatioun. Nixt we desire to remove all such scandalous reproaches aganis that state, in suffering a pairt of it to be possessed with such wilde savageis voide of Godis feare and our obedience, *and heirwith the losse we have in nocht ressaving the dew rentis addebtit to us furth of those Yllis, being of the patrimonie of that our crowne*." [1]

Acts were passed, notably in 1581 and 1585, condemning the lawlessness of the Highlandmen, and also the clan system, when it clashed with the feudal jurisdiction of the landlords. These latter were ordered to eject broken men and to burn their houses, and were made responsible for their conduct whilst they remained upon their lands. In 1587 a more systematic and sweeping series of acts was passed, which were to be specifically applied to the Highlands and the Borders. In the most important of these acts the chiefs who harboured broken men against the will of their feudal superiors were strongly condemned. The landlords were ordered to arrest all rebels and malefactors dwelling on their lands, and the chiefs and captains of the Borders and the Highlands were ordered to give pledges (i.e. hostages) and were declared responsible for the behaviour of their followers. The clan organization was therefore acknowledged by the Government. Attached to the act are two separate lists of the landlords or feudal superiors on whose lands the broken men resided and of the chiefs and captains on whom they depended. The lists show that in some cases the same person was landlord and chief; in others they were separate individuals. Both lists include the names of Borderers and of Highlanders. In spite of the thoroughness of the legislation, and of the serious efforts that were made to enforce it, these acts were of little avail.[2]

[1] *Collectanea Rebus Albanicis*, p. 115.

D. Gregory, *History of the Western Highlands*, p. 287.

[2] Duke of Argyle, *Scotland as it was and is*, p. 176.

J. Stewart, *Index to the Acts of the Scottish Parliament*, shows a large

In 1590, during a period of very energetic rule by the Chancellor Maitland, further attempts were made to introduce law and order. By an ordinance which only specifically mentioned the Borders a special committee of the Privy Council was appointed, consisting of seven persons, including the chancellor, justice-clerk, and other officers of state, to give their special attention to the good rule in these districts. It was evidently intended, however, that this committee should also deal with the Highlands, for their minute book was entitled " Book of Acts appertaining to the rule of the Highlands, the Isles, and the Marches of the Kingdom." The first entry is, very significantly, a copy of the act of 1587 and of the lists of the landlords and of the chiefs and captains of clans, and the committee proceeded to make strenuous efforts to enforce its provisions. A large number of orders were made to individuals named in the lists that they should find caution that they would deliver up or expel the broken men upon their lands.[1]

The Privy Council continued to make repeated efforts to bring order into the Highlands. In 1593 copies of the acts passed for this purpose were before it, and a systematic attempt was made to force the landlords and chiefs to obey them.[2] In 1594 the ordinances were once more repeated and further orders for their enforcement were given.[3] Nor were these proceedings an empty form. The *Register* abounds with cases in which the provisions of the acts were really put into force, and landlords and chiefs were compelled to find caution or give pledges that they would make their men observe the law and expel or deliver up all broken men, or were punished for not doing so. For instance, Macdougal of Dunolly tried to evade the provisions of the act by declaring that certain men were not his

number of acts dealing with the Highlands. See also *A.P.S.* vol. iii, pp. 379, 461, 466; *Register, Privy Council,* vol. iv, pp. lii, 298, 825 (two acts admitting failure of the previous legislation), pp. 151-152, 264 for an example of enforcement. The 1587 act, though it recognized chiefs of clans, was only a part of a general policy of making landlords responsible for their tenants. A more striking example of the Government recognition of clan organization is the act of the Privy Council of 1602, ordering wappenshawings to be held in the Highlands and the dependants to muster under their " maisters, chiefs, and chieftains." See *Collectanea Rebus Albanicis*, p. 46.

[1] *Register, Privy Council*, vol. iv, pp. lii, liii, liv, 781-782, 807, 812-814.

[2] *Ibid.* vol. v, p. 95.

[3] *Ibid.* vol. v, p. 95.

tenants, and a most pertinacious inquiry was made into the matter. Stewart of Appin was held responsible for a theft committed by his men and was imprisoned till he made restitution. The younger son of Mackintosh, with thirty broken Highlandmen, "all bodin with armour, swords and habergions," had raided some of the tenants of Campbell of Cawdor; and Monro of Foulis and Sir Robert Innes, who had become surety for the good behaviour of the Mackintoshes, together with the chief, had to pay 10,000 merks as penalty.[1]

This policy had certain indirect effects. The king seems to have exacted considerable fines from chiefs that he pardoned, though the actual amounts are not known,[2] and, by acting as sureties for their more turbulent neighbours, Argyle and certain other great men largely increased their political influence.[3] The Privy Council meanwhile continued to tighten up its enactments regarding the maintenance of order in the Highlands. An act of 1599 declared that the giving of hostages had been useless, because they sometimes escaped and sometimes the clans were not restrained by their fate, and that, in future, Highland landlords, chiefs, and captains must make good the damage caused by their men, and must also find Lowlandmen to be cautioners for them. The latter provision must have proved far from easy for many of the poorer and remoter chiefs. It seems, however, to have been enforced. As a matter of fact, in the administration of the earlier regulations, these provisions had already been carried out in practice.[4]

Meanwhile the king was pursuing other means for opening up the Highlands. In 1595 there was a rising of the Catholic earls, Huntly and Erroll. The heather was quickly in a blaze, and almost all the North took sides with Huntly or Argyle, who opposed him, and the battle of Glenlivat was fought, and won by the insurgent forces. The rising, which was entirely political, petered out, but James seems to have been concerned at the unsettlement that it left behind it in the North, and he evidently

[1] *Register, Privy Council*, vol. v, pp. 101, 229, 269.
A. M. Mackintosh, *The Mackintoshes and Clan Chattan*, p. 183.

[2] D. Gregory, *History of the Western Highlands*, p. 241.

[3] *Ibid.* p. 244.
Register, Privy Council, vol. v, p. 741.

[4] *Ibid.* vol. vi, pp. 45, 175, 415, 417, 442 (on this page five are dealt with, including Argyle).

felt himself strong enough, after its suppression, to force on his economic projects in the North-West. In 1596 he planned a military expedition to the Isles, which, however, did not come off. In 1597, an act of parliament was passed, which clearly shows that in the dealings of the Crown and Privy Council with the Highlanders, there were strong motives of interest as well as a desire to maintain law and order. By this act the landlords, heritors, and leaders of clans in the Highlands and Islands were ordered to produce their title-deeds to the lands which they possessed before the Lords of the Exchequer and within a given space of time. They were also ordered to find security for the regular payment of His Majesty's rents, and for their orderly and peaceable behaviour and for that of their men, tenants, servants, and dependants, under pain of the forfeiture of their lands. In the preamble it is stated that the inhabitants of the Highlands and Islands of this realm, which are for the most part of His Majesty's annexed property, have "not only frustrated His Majesty of the yearly payment of his proper rents and due service properly addebtit by them to His Majesty forth of the said lands, but that they have likewise through their barbarous inhumanity made and presently make the said Highlands and Islands, which are most commodious in themselves as well by the fertility of the ground as by the rich fishings by sea, altogether unprofitable both to themselves and all others His Highness' lieges within this realm, they neither entertaining any civility or honest society among themselves neither yet admitted others His Highness' lieges to traffic within their bounds with safety of their lives and goods." As Gregory points out, the penal clause, the forfeiture of the lands, is a very important one. The loss of title-deeds must have been a common occurrence in the wild state of the country, and it cannot have been easy for even the more powerful chiefs to find security for their peaceful behaviour and that of their followers; and "it is evident that this act was prepared with a view to place at the disposal of the Crown, in a summary manner, many large tracts of land—affording thus an immediate opportunity to the king to commence his favourite plans for the improvement of the Highlands and Isles." The loss of the records prevents us knowing how many chiefs or proprietors lost their lands through failing to satisfy the provisions of this act. It is known that the lands of Lewis, Harris, Glenelg, and Dunvegan were declared forfeit, although the three latter were eventually, and with much difficulty, saved by the able chief of the Siol Tormod. Lewis, however, and the district of Trouterness in Skye were granted to a company of Lowland adventurers, formed in order to colonize and improve lands in the Hebrides.[1]

In 1597, also, an act was passed ordaining that "for the better entertaining and continuing of civilitie and policie within the Highlands and Isles" three royal burghs were to be erected in Kintyre, Lochaber, and Lewis, with as much land and fishings as might sustain them. This act never came into force, but eventually, and many years later, Stornoway in the Lewis, Fort-William in Lochaber, and Campbeltown in Argyle were erected, the last of which only was a royal burgh. In addition, to carrying out the founding of the burghs and of the king's other schemes, a council of ten was appointed to consider Highland affairs and to advise the king. Unfortunately, they were no more successful than have been most of the other people who in after years have tried to improve the economic condition of the Highlands.[2]

The story of the Fife adventurers in Lewis may briefly be told here. They consisted of eleven Lowland gentlemen, some of them also members of the committee that the king had appointed to advise him in regard to Highland affairs. By an agreement ratified by parliament they were to occupy the island of Lewis and the lands of Trouterness for seven years free of all payments, and were then to pay a rent of one hundred and forty chalders of bere for Lewis and four hundred merks for Trouterness. About the same time Harris, Glenelg, and Dunvegan were also granted to them. The island of Lewis, to

[1] *A.P.S.* vol. iv, p. 138.

D. Gregory, *History of the Western Highlands*, pp. 277-278.

See also whole tenure of proceedings in *Register of Privy Council*, vol. v, p. 467 (1598). Another example of confiscation under the 1597 act was the loss of Mackintosh's lands in Lochaber, through loss of charters that he had possessed. The lands were gifted to the Clerk-Register and Mackintosh had to buy them back for 10,000 merks.—A. M. Mackintosh, *Mackintoshes and Clan Chattan*, p. 183.

[2] *A.P.S.* vol. iv, p. 139.

Register, Privy Council, vol. v, p. 455.

D. Gregory, *History of the Western Highlands*, p. 277.

which they first turned their attention, offered a favourable opportunity for colonization, for the Macleods of the Siol Torquil, who occupied it, were distracted by a savage internecine feud, and were scarcely in a position to offer effectual resistance. Trouterness, however, had only lately been granted upon lease to Macdonald of Sleat. Harris, Dunvegan, and Glenelg belonged to the able chief of the Siol Tormod branch of the Macleods. Moreover, in attempting to colonize the isles of the north-west, the Lowland adventurers rendered themselves obnoxious to the laird of Kintail, the powerful chief of the Mackenzies, who was already extending his influence in Lewis. The company of adventurers therefore had three powerful enemies to contend with, and their failure was largely brought about by the influence of these great chiefs. The adventurers sailed for Lewis in 1599, with four or five hundred hired soldiers, artificers of all sorts, and many gentlemen volunteers. The story of their sojourn on the island is like that of the colonization of some savage land. They suffered through inclement seasons, managed to build for themselves a town, were vexed by the hostility of the natives, but finally, taking advantage of the rival parties among the Macleods who claimed the chieftainship, they managed to secure the alliance of one party against the other. For a time their affairs prospered, but eventually in 1602 they quarrelled with those Macleods who had supported them, and eventually the latter attacked and captured their camp, killed many of the soldiers, and took the principal adventurers prisoner. They were released upon promising that they would obtain from the king a pardon for the Macleods, and that they would leave Lewis and never return to it; but no sooner were their hostages released than this agreement was ignored. A royal proclamation summoned the lieges of the northern shires to proceed against the rebels in the Lewis, but, owing to various circumstances, nothing was done for two years. At last, armed with despotically wide powers from the king, the adventurers again occupied Lewis in 1605. They remained there for two years, but eventually gave up the enterprise in despair, and the king granted it to Lord Balmerino, secretary of state, with two companions. Balmerino was disgraced, but his partners tried to colonise the island. They were, however, quite unsuccessful, and, eventually, in 1610 they sold Lewis to Mackenzie of

Kintail.[1] The story of the Fife adventurers is a complicated one, and it carries us beyond our allotted period. To the student of Scots economic history its importance lies in the fact that it is a practical illustration of how valuable and how full of possibilities the lands of the Highlands were considered, and of the difficulty of their development. As a matter of fact, the Highlands were really of considerable economic value at this time, and it is now time to consider this aspect.

Part V. Economic Position of the Highlands

Much has been said about the so different social life of the Highlands, and perhaps it is necessary to stress the fact that great as was the gulf between the Highlands and the Lowlands there was yet considerable intercommunication between them. In spite of occasional intrigues between the Lord of the Isles, or the claimants who tried to revive that dignity and the chiefs who supported them, with the English, the Highlanders took their share in the wars with the Auld Enemy; many of them fought at Flodden, Pinkie, and other battles; when Argyle was Warden of the Marches, Highlandmen served under him there and seem to have struck cold horror into an English agent, who described their barbaric appearance and manners. Many of the chiefs were only too familiar with Edinburgh, for their fairly frequent appearances before the Privy Council and their acquaintance with Edinburgh Castle can have left no happy memories. Probably their sons and other relations, who were often sent to the Lowlands as hostages for the good behaviour of their clans, had pleasanter associations. By the sixteenth century it had become quite usual for the leading men of the Highlands to send their sons to one of the Scots universities, and there is an entry in the Register of the Great Seal that in 1508 a certain Kanoch Williamson received a grant of some of the crown land in Trouterness to enable him to study law so that he might administer it in the Isles. During the manhood of James II, IV, and V, and during the earlier part of Mary of Lorraine's regency, the connection

[1] D. Gregory, *History of the Western Highlands*, pp. 279, 280, 290, 291. *Register, Privy Council*, vol. vi, pp. 420-421 (1602). King James made the Fife adventurers find caution that they would pay their rent.

between the Crown and its Highland subjects was often a very happy one. James IV had many Highland servants and employed Highland harpers, and there was considerable coming and going between the court and the North. Elder ("Clerke and Redshanke"), in his letter to Henry VIII, said that when the Highlanders appeared at court "we have as good garments as some of our fellows."[1] It was therefore natural that the Highlanders and Lowlanders should also trade with each other to a considerable extent.

An act of the Privy Council of 1566 states that since it is not only needful that good neighbourhood and abstinence from all displeasure and invasion be observed amongst the whole lieges, but that they must sustain and relieve each other's necessities by interchange of the excrescence and superfluous fruits growing in the Highlands and the Lowlands, and that therefore it is necessary that markets be kept so that all men indifferently without exception may repair thereto for selling of their goods and buying again of such necessaries as are unto them needful and requisite, it orders, therefore, that letters be sent to be read at the market crosses of Perth, Stirling, Dumbarton, Renfrew, Glasgow, Irvine, Ayr, and other places, ordering that the lieges none of them take upon hand to invade or pursue others, whether they be Highlandmen or Lowland, or to make provocation or "tuilzie" to others, notwithstanding any offence, quarrel, or question. All provosts, bailies, sheriffs, and other officials are ordered to stop and stay trouble and impediment-making to the said Highlandmen, in bodies or goods, in their coming to the said markets, remaining therein, or departing therefrom. The *Register of the Privy Council* is not a happy record of Scots affairs, for it deals mainly with the problems and difficulties that arose, but it is clear that Highlanders did resort to many of the burghs named in the act, sailing up the Firth of Clyde in their boats with bestial and

[1] D. Gregory, *History of the Western Highlands*, pp. 112, 180, 208.
Hamilton Papers, vol. i, No. lxxiii.
Chiefs were often summoned to Edinburgh or warded in the castle; cf. *Register, Privy Council*, vol. vi, p. 213 (1542).
Exchequer Rolls, vol. xiii, p. l (1494).
Accounts of the Lord High Treasurer, vol. i, pp. cxcviii, ccxliv.
Collectanea Rebus Albanicis, p. 29.
W. Macgill, *Old Ross-shire*, Part II, p. 2.

herrings, and driving their cattle from the outermost bounds of the Highlands to the East Coast fairs—even although the avoidance of trouble so earnestly enjoined in the act was not always obeyed. On the other hand, the merchants of the burghs not only sailed to the Highland fisheries, but with their packs penetrated into out-of-the-way and unsettled districts, like an unfortunate burgess of Glasgow, who in his vocation and trade of merchandise was travelling in Mull with his pack of goods and was robbed and assaulted.[1]

The Highlanders, moreover, sometimes went farther afield. The number of " Macs " that appear in all the collections of English State Papers relating to Scotland is quite surprising, and we learn of transactions such as the following: In 1350 and 1398 respectively, Macobyn, a merchant, and Makelar of Argyle get licences to trade. Rather earlier the Scots king asks for the release of Alexander de Argadia and his crew, who had touched at Bristol and been arrested on suspicion of piracy. In the sixteenth century, Chisholm (the chief ?) sends salmon to Cromwell.[2]

The relative wealth of the different parts of Scotland in the sixteenth and in the preceding centuries was very different to what it is now. The great industrial belt from the Forth to the Clyde did not, of course, exist, and the importance of the individual burghs varied very greatly from that of the present day. The Northern burghs, many of which drew part of their trade from Highland districts, were relatively far richer. A special tax, raised in 1526, was levied as follows: burghs north of the Forth, £876 15s. 2d.; burghs south of the Forth (not including Edinburgh), £507 15s.[3]

The privileges of the royal burghs, however, must have hampered Highland trade and made it peculiarly liable to exploitation. On the West Coast there was no royal burgh farther north than Dumbarton on the Firth of Clyde; on the

[1] *Register, Privy Council*, vol. ii, pp. 470-471 (1566); vol. iii, p. 125 (1579); vol. iv, p. 535 (1590); vol. v, pp. 305 (1596), 87, 301; vol. vi, p. 141.

[2] *Documents relating to Scotland*, vol. iv, Nos. 1398, 1689; vol. ii, No. 74.

State Papers relating to Scotland, 1509–1589, p. 33.

[3] *Exchequer Rolls*, vol. xv, p. lxxi.

For examples of trade of Northern burghs, see *Documents relating to Scotland*, vol. iv, Nos. 23, 116, etc.

East, the district over which Inverness, as a royal burgh, exercised monopolies of trade and of manufactures, included the modern counties of Inverness, Sutherland, Caithness, and Ross. From the fifteenth century onwards, Inverness was frequently trying to inhibit the inhabitants of Tain, Dingwall, Dornoch, and Wick from infringing on her privileges. Her rights were upheld by the king and the courts of law, although she does not seem to have been able to achieve great practical success in suppressing the trade of these burghs.[1] Therefore, although the motives of James VI in his dealings with the Highlands were not high ones, and although many of his actions were much to be reprobated, his policy, in wishing to establish three more royal burghs upon the West Coast and on the Long Island, was a sound one.

No doubt the principal import into the Highlands, besides manufactured goods, was grain and its products. (This was certainly the case in the seventeenth century.) In 1555, at a time of dearth, when exports of victual from the burghs were prohibited, the Western burghs were allowed to send to the Isles " bacin bread, ale, and aqua vitae." The sending of victual into the Highlands was, however, several times specially forbidden.[2] In return for what they received from the South, the Highlands had several valuable exports. Already in the period preceding the Wars of Independence a map made by Matthew Paris shows that the Highlands were well known as a cattle- and skin-producing country.[3] During the fifteenth and sixteenth centuries, the main exports consisted of cattle, herrings and other fish, hides and skins, and timber.

The cattle trade was extensive, and it is strange, considering the unsettled state of the country, to find how far the animals were brought. In 1502 the marts (the beasts destined for killing at Martinmas for salting for use during the winter), from the Crown lands of Trouterness in Skye, were conveyed to Inverness and from thence to the Lowlands. In 1600, Mackenzie of Kintail complained that several of his men and servants from Kintail and Lochalsh had been robbed by men

[1] E. M. Barron, *Inverness in the Fifteenth Century*, pp. 111, 112.

[2] *Collectanea Rebus Albanicis*, p. 151.

[3] This map is published as the frontispiece to P. Hume Brown, *Early Travellers to Scotland*: Matthew Paris d. 1259.

dwelling in Glenshee, while they were driving their cattle to the Lowland fairs, and he points out that such practices discouraged the lieges from sending goods to the incountry. The cattle of the Islands were sometimes ferried across to the mainland and driven thence to the South, and sometimes were taken by sea to Glasgow. Sometimes the Highlandmen drove their own cattle to the markets, but certain Lowlanders seem to have made a trade of driving cattle from Argyle. The owners of such beasts may well have been somewhat suspect in the eyes of the law, but Mary Queen of Scots made a regulation that cattle and other goods brought forth of Argyle by her good and true subjects, and sold in the Lowlands for the sustentation of the lieges, were not to be escheated as the goods of rebels and enemies, provided that those who brought them out took no victual into the Highlands.

The cattle trade was of great importance to the Highlanders. Some of the leading chiefs of the West, appealing against a proclamation that interfered with it, declared that on this account they could not pay their mails and duties: "The saidis yllismen having no utheris meanes nor possibilitie to pay his Majesties dewyteis bot be the sale of thair mairtis and horsses, and the buying of such commoditeis being in all tymes bygane a free, constant and peccable trade to the merchandis alsweill of Ergyll as of the incuntrey, without any restrent, trouble, questioun or impediment moved or intended to the contrair at ony tyme heirtofoir." On another occasion the inhabitants of Mull pleaded that the cattle trade was the only means whereby they could pay their duties.[1] The herds of cattle in the Highlands must, indeed, have been considerable. The frequent appeals for damages for spuilzie contain many lists of the live stock possessed by Highland lairds. The laird of Grant had two hundred and fifty head of cattle on his Glenmoriston property, and his tenants had also considerable stocks. In one raid Ramsay of Bamff lost sixty-three beasts. Mackenzie of Kintail appears to have sent eighty beasts yearly to the Southern markets. In 1602, Rose of Kilravock lost twelve score kye and twenty-four score sheep and goats. Nevertheless,

[1] *Exchequer Rolls*, vol. xii, p. lxviii.
Register, Privy Council, vol. vi, p. 184.
Collectanea Rebus Albanicis, pp. 151, 154, 158

in the long list of spuilzie, the three or four head of stock, often said to be all they had, of the lesser men, make most pathetic reading.[1]

The herring fisheries were not of equal importance to the Highlanders. It is but seldom that allusion is made to their engaging in these fisheries; and the other source of income that they derived, viz., the levying of charges upon the Lowland fishermen who came to their lochs, was also carefully limited by the Crown. On the other hand, the fisheries were of considerable importance to the burghs. As we know, the selling of herrings for export was one of the treasured privileges of the merchants of the Royal Burghs, and it was also a considerable item of Scots foreign trade; and the Highland fisheries were an important source of the herring industry.

The herring shoals seem to have begun to repair to the north-western sea lochs in great abundance sometime in the middle of the sixteenth century. A minute of the Privy Council, dated 1566, states that "it hes plesit God to oppin ane greit commoditie to the commoun weall of this realm throw the fisching of Loch Brume and utheris lochis of the north seyis," it goes on to say that various strangers had asked for licences to fish there, but that the Privy Council, thinking that the matter concerned the merchants, consulted some of them and now forbids all strangers from doing so. Later legislation refers to regulations of the amount of the dues that the Highlanders might demand, that had been made in the reign of James II and in the regency of Mary of Lorraine. By the end of the century, and probably much earlier, the fisheries off Shetland and the Orkneys were also valuable, and brought great commodities to these islands.[2]

The burghs of the South-west were the most accessible for this fishery. Ayr, Irvine, Renfrew, and Dumbarton were in the habit of "packing and peiling" their herrings in the lochs opening off the Firth of Clyde—Loch Goil, Loch Long, the Gareloch, etc.; and these burghs, and also Glasgow, carried on a considerable export trade in salted and barrelled herring.

[1] Sir William Fraser, *Chiefs of Grant*, vol. i, p. 112 (1544).
Register, Privy Council, vol. vi, pp. 443, 459, 431.

[2] *Register, Privy Council*, vol. i, p. 482; vol. iv, pp. 303, 121-123, 739.

But the East Coast burghs also had a valuable trade in exporting herring from the Western Highlands and Isles. Herrings from the North-west are mentioned several times in the late sixteenth century accounts of Wedderburn, the Dundee merchant whose ledger has fortunately been preserved, and in other documents. For instance, a proclamation that the herrings from Loch Broom were not to be exported for a year, owing to the need of them for food in Scotland, was ordered to be read at the market crosses of Edinburgh, Leith, Burntisland, Kinghorn, Dysart, Pittenweem, Anstruther, Crail, and St Andrews.[1]

It is evident that the merchants of the burghs sent fishing busses up to the lochs of the North-west, and that the fishermen remained up there for some time, living in houses upon the land and preparing the fish as they were caught.[2] But the Highland fisheries were rather hazardous enterprises, judging by the complaints of ill-treatment of the fishermen and of extortionate dues. At one time the chiefs demanded 20s. for each last of herrings caught in their waters and 4s. in addition for their bailies, with a payment of meal and of ale. They also charged anchor dues and required a rent for the houses the fishermen put up, and even charged for the seaweed that was used for covering the fish. The authorities, however, did all that they could to protect the fishermen: in 1574, for instance, when some fishermen of Kirkcaldy had been beaten and killed on Loch Strone by some of Glengarry's men, that chief was ordered to see that the culprits were tried by a jury composed of the crews of the next fishing boats that came there. The fact that they interfered with the fisheries was one of the crimes most often imputed to the Western chiefs by the Government and they were constantly ordered to amend their ways. In 1576 the Macleods of Harris and Lewis had to bind themselves for their kin, friends, servants, tenants, and part-takers as dutiful and obedient servants of the king, to keep the peace and in no ways molest, trouble, or make impediment to any of His Majesty's subjects in their lawful trade of fishing in the lochs of Lewis and other islands, nor to raise any "towist," extortion,

[1] *Register, Privy Council*, vol. iv, pp. 16, 123; vol. vi, p. 277 (1601). See also vol. iii, p. 247 (1579). In this reference, salmon as well as herring were brought.

[2] *Register, Privy Council*, vol. iv, p. 16.

or imposition upon them, and to supply them with meat and drink at reasonable prices.[1]

The herring fisheries were no doubt important, but in the eyes of King James VI they came to assume potential values that were never to be realized. It was these fisheries that more than anything else furnished the economic incentive which led the king to use such relentless measures to bring the Western Highlands and Isles into subjection. In one of his merciless proclamations he declares that the Isles of old had been the most constant and sure source of rental for the Crown, but were now inhabited by a number of rebellious and insolent persons, void of the fear and knowledge of God and of all obedience to the king, and delighting in blood, theft, reiving, and oppression; and that the Isles, being enriched with an incredible fertility of corns and plenty of fishes, would render inestimable commodities to this country if the barbarity of the savage inhabitants thereof would suffer and permit a peaceable trade and traffic among them.[2] No doubt the king hoped to enrich the realm in general as well as his depleted treasury by exploiting these great resources. Several of the proclamations ordering the lieges to render service in military expeditions against the Islanders and Highlanders during this reign alluded to the barbarity of the Islesmen, which defrauded the whole realm, and especially the burghs, of the great commodity of traffic in the Isles. But the burghs themselves were not lacking in extravagant ideas of the value of the West Highland fisheries, could they be properly exploited, as a petition of 1586 clearly shows. It was, no doubt, the same unduly optimistic view of the resources of the Highlands that led to the insertion of a clause in a Crown charter of 1578–79, of some lands in Mull, obliging the tenant to provide a certain amount of coal every year.[3]

The other exports of the Highlands may be alluded to briefly. Salmon was a valuable commodity. We have seen that the salmon teinds formed the main income of Ardchattan and Beauly Priory. The scarcity of timber in the Lowlands

[1] *Register, Privy Council,* vol. ii, pp. xxv (1574), 534.

[2] *Ibid.* vol. vi, p. 255 (1601).

[3] *Ibid.* vol. iv, pp. 121-123; vol. vi, pp. 306 (1596), 130. *Collectanea Rebus Albanicis,* p. 161.

was a serious weakness, but a certain amount seems to have been imported from the Highlands. An order from the Privy Council to Lovat, of 1575–76, ordering him not to take dues from Glengarry when he brought timber down Loch Ness, or to interfere with him, his friends, or the commons upon his lands, alludes to the Highlanders' practice of floating down timber to the neighbouring burghs, such as Perth and Inverness, by rivers and lochs.[1] Skins and hides, especially the hides of red deer and of roes, which, as we have seen, were among the most important exports of Scotland, must originally have come from the Highlands, although there is hardly any record of their doing so.

The Highlanders were not great flockmasters, and their sheep were very small and had scanty though fine fleeces. Wool was not an important export. A certain amount of plaiding, however, seems to have been sent to the Lowlands. We learn, quite incidentally, that in 1592 certain tenants in the Isles paid their rent by sending to Glasgow 190 ells of plaiding, 22 hides, and 11 otter skins.[2] It may also be noted that the Highlanders seem to have made a good deal of iron, by primitive processes, from bog-iron. Perhaps they were self-supporting. There is nothing to say that they imported or exported iron.[3] One of their later-day most characteristic beverages they did not make, for, from an act of parliament already quoted from, we know that they imported aqua vitae, the ancestor of whisky.

[1] *Register, Privy Council*, vol. ii, pp. 500-501.

[2] *Ibid.* vol. v, p. 10.

Cosmo Innes, Preface to *Ledger of Andrew Haliburton*, p. lxvi.

[3] W. Ivison Macadam, *Proceedings Society of Antiquaries*, 1886–7, "Ancient Iron Industry of Scotland," p. 89. He gives a list of the old smelting places in the Highlands: 17 in Argyleshire, 15 in Inverness-shire, 14 in Ross-shire, 12 in Perthshire, etc., and it is noteworthy that the neighbouring Gaelic place-names often have reference to the smiths, showing that these places were, many of them, not prehistoric, but dated from after the Scots invasion of Alban.

For aqua vitae, see R. Scott Moncrieff, "Early Use of Aqua Vitae in Scotland," *Proc. Soc. Antiquaries*, 1915–16.

CHAPTER X

General Social Conditions

THE general life of the people in Scotland can scarcely be dealt with in a single book, and yet, so far more vital is the actual way of living of a nation than the formal institutions that it builds up and bends to its use, that the matter cannot be ignored. During the fifteenth and sixteenth centuries, a determining factor that can never be forgotten in Scots economic history is the extreme poverty of the country, and the fact that its resources were inadequate to maintain its people, according to the standard of life of neighbouring countries. There was a ribald saying that when the Devil showed all the countries of the world to our Lord, he kept his mickle thoomb upon Scotland.[1] Nearly all the travellers who visited Scotland, and who left an account of their wanderings there, comment upon the poverty of the country; Froissart in the fourteenth century, Eneas Sylvius and Pedro de Ayala in the fifteenth, Nicander Nucius and Estienne Perlin in the sixteenth. The latter says that in Scotland a merchant with 400 livres is esteemed rich, whereas in England, Spain, Portugal, Germany, and Flanders twelve to fifteen hundred livres would represent the income of a rich man.[2] The careful legislation about the disposal of the victual of the country, contained in so many of the acts of the Scots Parliament and of the Privy Council, shows how precious was the food of the people.[3]

There were many reasons to account for the poverty of the country. The sixteenth century was visited by many dearths. During the whole of the period under review greater or lesser

[1] Quoted in Warrack, *Domestic Life in Scotland*, p. 2.

[2] P. Hume Brown, *Early Travellers to Scotland*, pp. 11, 27, 43, 57, 76.

[3] Cf. *A.P.S.* vol. iii, p. 452.

outbreaks of the plague again and again visited Western Europe —these were of course general misfortunes, but a land peculiarly liable to suffer bad weather and almost entirely dependent upon agriculture, as was Scotland, would naturally suffer from the former in an intensified degree. The political condition of Scotland, its constant wars and internal dissensions, would also, of course, intensify her natural poverty. The main reason, however, for this poverty, was the economic condition of the country: the fact that the population was almost entirely dependent upon a far from bountiful supply of raw products, and that there was a constant drain of resources abroad, to supply the manufactured luxury-goods which the Scots required.

Sumptuary laws give very contradictory evidence. On the one hand, they show that the rulers of the country thought that it was too poor to support the style of living of the people, but, on the other hand, they show that the people did actually indulge in the forbidden style. Such acts occur in the much richer country of England as well as in Scotland; in the latter they abound all through the fifteenth and sixteenth centuries. Certain sections, in all ranks of the community, seem always to have indulged a very pretty taste in clothing and food.[1]

The general picture of poverty, which can be drawn from those more solid sources of information, the *Exchequer Rolls*, as well as from the observations of passing travellers, was lightened by the strong recuperative powers of the Scots. There are several passages, probably far too widely quoted, which describe how the circumstances of the people improved during the few interludes of stable Government. Pedro de Ayala, who visited Scotland during the hey-day of James IV's power, remarked that the revenue of the country was increasing. Etienne Perlin, who came to Scotland in 1551, and who was magnifying the help that the French were giving at that time, said that the Scots revenue doubled and was worth six times its former value. Bishop Leslie, writing a few years later, during the earlier and happier years of Mary of Lorraine's regency, declared that at last, when the country was at rest,

[1] Sumptuary and kindred enactments, *A.P.S.* vol. ii, p. 18 (1429), 49 (1457), 100 (1471); vol. ii, pp. 487-488; vol. iii, p. 78 (1550).

R. Chambers, *Domestic Annals of Scotland*, vol. i, p. 370, quotes an amusing description of a fine lady's life from a sixteenth-century poet.

the burgesses and landward men began to mend and repair those houses that in time of war the enemy had raised fire in, or furiously cast down, and to till the ground in like manner, and began with diligence to put their house in order. In 1572, after the country had profited by the strong regencies of Moray and of Morton, Killigrew was able to write of greatly increased trade and shipping.[1] These brighter intervals were probably greater in appearance than in reality. There was no permanent relief of the financial stringency. They mark no radical change in the very unfortunate economic position. Like Froissart's account of the recovery of the Scots countryside after an English raid, they merely show the spirit and energy of the people.[2]

It is impossible to read the lists of the cargoes of goods brought to Scotland—the acts of the Scots Parliament—the regulations of the crafts—the household inventories of the times—without carrying away an impression of the vividness of the people's tastes and surroundings. The glorious clothing of the king and his court has been referred to. From the sumptuary laws we gather that mere merchants and their wives longed to wear scarlet and silks and rich furs, and the latter sweeping trains, furred under, an unpleasantly unhygienic fashion; that labourers and husbandmen had to be ordered only to wear gray and white (viz. made of undyed wool) clothes on work days, and might only appear in light-blue, green, or red on Sundays and holidays.[3]

The pageantry of the old church festivals, combined as it was with the craft organization, is one of the most attractive features of the civic life of the fifteenth and early sixteenth century burghs, although various craft organizations seem to have found their shares in the ceremonies a heavy burden. The revels that accompanied May Day, the playing of *Robin Hood* and of the *Abbot of Unreason*, were probably more congenial to the popular taste. These saturnalia took place

[1] P. Hume Brown, *Early Travellers to Scotland*, p. 74.
Bishop Leslie's *History*, vol. ii, p. 344.
Quoted by W. L. Mathieson, *Politics and Religion in Scotland, 1550–1695*, p. 202.

[2] For Froissart, see P. Hume Brown, *Early Travellers to Scotland*, p. 7.

[3] *A.P.S.* vol. ii, p. 49 (1457).

all over the Lowlands of Scotland. They were democratic, for not only were they the delight of the rascal multitude, but the court and the great nobles indulged in such ploys in their own halls, and the king, at least, encouraged the amusements of his lieges—James IV and V made many payments to such individuals as "Robin Hood of Perth," "Bishop Nicolas and his Diablattis," etc. Unfortunately, Robin Hood and his confrères had fallen out of official favour by the middle of the sixteenth century. In 1555 he was put down in Aberdeen, though the craftsmen rioted in protest. With the Reformation the authorities became increasingly discouraging to banqueting, feast days, May Day celebrations, and the like.[1]

Among the pleasures of the people were the games of golf and football, which were strictly prohibited by James I, II, III, and IV, but which in later years seem to have been freely indulged in. It is rather striking to find, in 1598, in the austere period following the Reformation, that the Privy Council passed an act ordering that Monday should be a weekly holiday for pastimes and exercise in place of Sunday, which the lieges break because no day in the week is granted them for their relief from labour except the said Sabbath. The Courts were not to sit. No household labour was to be required from servants. Scholars and students were to stop work at noon. Cottars, tenants, and farmers astricted to shear their landlord's corn, were to be exempted from this service upon Mondays. There is no evidence that the act was put into force. But the intention and attitude of mind are significant.

Musicians and bards abounded. The acts for the suppression of beggars and vagrants describe a motley crew of bards, players upon musical instruments, and fortune-tellers. The successive kings all had a considerable number of musicians and players in their permanent employ, and, in the course of their constant wanderings, they did not scorn to share in the music of the people. The Lord High Treasurer's accounts are full of payments to such folk as "Hob the tale-teller," the "fiddler

[1] For a good account of the well-known church pageants see W. Cunningham, *Church History*, p. 496.

E. Bain, *Merchant and Craft Gilds*, pp. 49, 51, 61, 62.

Accounts of the Lord High Treasurer, vol. i, pp. ccxxxix, xxxii, xxxviii.

W. L. Mathieson, *Politics and Religion in Scotland, 1550–1695*, p. 190.

who played to the King," a lutist, a minstrel, the Highland harpers of Strathfillan.[1] The burghs all over Scotland catered for their play-loving citizens. They arranged magnificent pageants for such occasions as the state entries of royalty. Abbots of Unreason were officially appointed to take the lead in popular frolics. There were the craft representations in religious processions, and the towns subsidised clerk-plays and interludes. They organised folk-games and ridings of the marches, and they paid for the upkeep of playing fields out of public funds. Traces of some or all of these activities are preserved in the records relating to Aberdeen, Arbroath, Ayr, Dalkeith, Dumfries, Dundee, Dunfermline, Edinburgh, Elgin, Errol, Glasgow, Haddington, Inverness, Kelso, Lanark, Peebles, Perth, St Andrews, Stirling. The lieges also liked to enjoy the pleasures of the chase. Many enactments were made declaring that the hunting proclivities of the people spoilt the sport of the nobles and even of the King himself. Nevertheless, in spite of heavy penalties, including the loss of the right hand, the commons seem to have continued to indulge this taste.[2]

Primitive as was contemporary life in many ways, even the burgesses used considerable elegance, at least on great occasions. The expenses for several Edinburgh banquets have survived, which include the cost of providing flowers to strew about the room, arras to hang the walls, and napery, besides abundance of good cheer. In 1589 the Edinburgh authorities spent 50s. upon food for the swans on the Nor' Loch. A burgess who had shot one of the birds was summoned, and was made to promise never to do so again.[3]

The eighteenth-century descriptions of the Scots (when the droving trade was at its height) as a nation that lived upon oatmeal, have so much captured the popular fancy that it is quite surprising to remember that until the seventeenth century

[1] *Account of the Lord High Treasurer*, vol. i, pp. cxcviii, clxi, cxcix, xxxi, xxxix.
Register, Privy Council, vol. vi, p. 462.
A. F. Mill, *Mediaeval Plays in Scotland*, pp. 40, 50, 60, 104.

[2] See, for instance, *A.P.S.* vol. ii, p. 487; *Register, Privy Council*, vi, p. 353.

[3] *Extracts from the Burgh Records of Edinburgh*, 1589–1603, pp. 10, 19.
R. Chambers, *Domestic Annals of Scotland*, p. 130 (1579), etc.

the people were probably largely meat-eaters. Corn and other grains were often very scarce. From the nature of trading conditions, the export of live stock cannot have been large, and it does not appear at all in the 1614 estimate of Scots trade. But the export of hides and skins was one of the principal industries of the country. According to the 1614 list, 1944 skins of cattle, 1092 skins of deer, 238,666 skins of sheep, 162,243 lamb-skins of several varieties, 16,321 goat-skins were exported annually, although the export of £300 worth of beef must be set against this. When it is remembered that the population was certainly a comparatively sparse one—Hume Brown thinks that it was not more than 500,000 persons about 1560—it is clear that the canny Scot, who is scarcely likely to have wasted the carcases of these animals, must have indulged in a good deal of meat, though no doubt the distribution of this meat was very unequal.[1]

Apart from the times of the dearths of cereal food, the people's diet seems to have been a liberal one. University folk are not usually held to be very affluent, and an amusing dietary of the professors and of that of the students upon the foundation of Glasgow University survives for the year 1602. The professors on meat days had soup with wheaten bread in it, ale, and cold meat, over from the previous day, for breakfast. For dinner they had white bread, a roast of beef or mutton, and, for a second course, a cunyng (rabbit), fowl, or pair of pigeons or chickens, washed down by a better sort of ale. For supper they were to have something equivalent. The students had soup and oaten bread for breakfast, with ale; for dinner, oaten bread, a dish of kail or of brose, one kind of meat, and ale; and something similar for supper. There were a good many non-meat days, but both tables seem to have been provided with bountiful supplies of fish and eggs. This dietary is very different to that of the eighteenth-century student, who lived largely upon the poke of meal he brought from home with him.[2] In Edinburgh, at least, by the end of the sixteenth century, even the common artizans and the rascal multitude drank a good deal of wine, and the people chose to indulge this taste even when

[1] See P. Hume Brown, *Scotland in the Time of Queen Mary*, p. 227, for this table. See also p. 52.

[2] *Register, Privy Council*, vol. vi, pp. 408, 552-556.

prices rose considerably. The price of wine increased by nearly eight times its original cost between 1556 and 1599, and yet the demand for it continued.[1]

Something has been said about the exceedingly primitive sanitary conditions of the towns. In many of them the middens stood in the streets and animals were slaughtered there. It is not surprising to find that a writer of the middle of the sixteenth century noticed that town dwellers were " subiect tyl al sortis of sicknes, be rason of the corrupit infectione and euyl ayr that is generit in ane cite quhar maist confluens of pepil assortis," and that " the maist part of them endis ther dais in there grene zouthed." [2] The hours of work were long, but perhaps leisurely. In Edinburgh, in summer, at the end of the fifteenth century, work was started at 5 A.M. and went on till 7 P.M., with breaks amounting to three hours. In Aberdeen, at the end of the sixteenth century, they worked from 4 A.M. till 8 P.M. Most burghs employed musicians to play round the streets to let the people know when it was time to start and to knock off work. In Aberdeen they consisted of a man with an " Almany quhissil " and an assistant with a tabroun.[3]

Probably enough has been said of the people's quarrelsomeness and lawlessness. It seems to have struck most of the visitors who came to Scotland. Pedro de Ayala said that the Scots were poor and not industrious; that they preferred to fight. When no war was going on, they fought one another. He goes on to describe the Scots as follows : " The people are handsome. . . . They are vain and ostentatious by nature. They spend all they have to keep up appearances. They are as well dressed as it is possible to be in such a country as that in which they live. They are courageous, strong, quick and agile. They are envious to excess." Major, the sixteenth-century historian, who after long residence abroad knew so well how to sum up

[1] *Register, Privy Council*, vol. vi, p. 205.

I am indebted to Dr Marguerite Wood, City Archivist, for the information regarding the price of wine.

[2] Anon., *Complaynt of Scotland* (1549), p. 45.

R. Chambers, *Domestic Annals of Scotland*, vol. i, quotes some examples of regulations regarding middens ; cf. p. 91. C. Rogers, *Social Life in Scotland*, vol. i, p. 304, quotes the primitive sanitary arrangements of Dundee.

[3] D. Murray, *Early Burgh Organization*, p. 367.

his countrymen, notices their boastfulness of high birth and their pride. He says that there was a French proverb, "Il est fier comme un Écossais."[1]

This craving for fine clothes and appurtenances appears again and again in contemporary descriptions. It had its most important bearing upon the economic life of the nation, for it was in order to gratify such tastes that the produce of the country was exchanged for foreign luxuries. It was perhaps a kind of national "inferiority complex." Several historians greatly praised the first Stewart Earl of Moray (the illegitimate son of James IV) for the following piece of ostentation. A papal legate was visiting Scotland and Moray invited him to a banquet. Wishing to make the visitor understand that there was a great abundance thereof in Scotland, he caused a cupboard of fine crystal glass to be overturned, as if by accident, and had another one carried in. The patriarch praised as well the magnificence of the Earl as the fineness of the crystal.[2] There are other similar stories. The authorities were most anxious that when Scots went abroad they should not disgrace their countrymen by their slovenly apparel. By an act of parliament of 1466, no one might use merchandise unless he had at least half a last of goods. This enactment was many times repeated, but the authorities went very much further. In the sixteenth century the conservator at the staple town was to see that the merchants there were properly dressed, and, if necessary, to seize the goods of anyone whose clothing was discreditable and have proper clothes made for him. A dignified manner of selling their goods was strictly enjoined on the merchants in another order. Moreover, the individual towns were jealous of the appearance of their traders. Aberdeen, in 1484, ordered a burgess named Robert Buchan to have a new gown and doublet made for himself within four days of his arrival in Flanders; and, in 1551, the Edinburgh records state that the governor (Arran) had been informed of "the evill bruit and lichtling" of Scotland in Flanders and France owing to the "passing of certain sempill persouns thair in merchandice cled

[1] P. Hume Brown, *Early Scotch Travellers*, p. 43.
John Major, *History of Greater Britain.*, pp. 43-45.

[2] This account is paraphrased from Bishop Leslie's *History*, vol. ii, p. 276.

in vyle array." The provost and baillies were ordered to see that no one should sail to these countries without at least half a last of goods.[1]

The character of the Scots, was, indeed, very far from impeccable. Not only was their pride and vanity a byword, but their rashness and self-confidence lost them the battles of Dupplin, Halidon Hill, Neville's Cross, Hamildon Hill, Flodden, and Pinkie. The term "perfervid Scot" was for long accepted as a description of the national character and was derived from the sixteenth-century George Buchanan's uncomplimentary estimate of his fellow-countrymen: "*ne Scotorum praefervida ingenia in errorem inemendabilem universam rem praecipitarent.*"[2]

Allied to this ostentation went what would now appear a very snobbish spirit among the merchants and the magistrates of the burghs.[3] The exclusion of the craftsmen from office has been dealt with. It was strictly forbidden to merchants to engage in manual labour. An Edinburgh burgess was censured because he removed stones from before his door with his own hands. By an act of the Convention of Royal Burghs of 1529 no chapman might be made a burgess unless he had £100 worth of goods."[4]

It is the more striking to find, with this exclusive spirit of the burghs, a marked lack of class feeling between the burgesses of the towns and the landed gentry. The two classes intermarried—a burgess of Edinburgh married a lady whom the king styled "our cousin," and who was the illegitimate daughter of his aunt; and many of the great nobles had kinsmen who were in trade. It was quite usual for the younger sons of the nobility and gentry to become burgesses and, on the other hand, for substantious burgesses to acquire land and become lairds.[5]

[1] Roseboom, *Staple at Veere*, p. 52.
Davidson and Gray, *Staple at Veere*, pp. 34-35.

[2] Quoted, P. Hume Brown, *Life of George Buchanan*, p. 3.

[3] *A.P.S.* vol. ii, pp. 86-87.

[4] J. D. Marwick, *Edinburgh Gilds and Crafts*, p. 67.

[5] *Exchequer Rolls*, vol. xii, p. xxxi (1502–1507).
The Earl of Arran (Stuart), the cousin of the king, had an uncle who was Provost of Dumfries.—Sir Herbert Maxwell, *Dumfries and Galloway*, p. 206.
C. Innes, Introduction to the *Ledger of Andrew Haliburton*, p. xxviii, comments on this lack of class feeling.

It is interesting to compare the relative wealth of the average laird and burgess. An act of 1579 that ordered householders to have a Bible and a Psalm book was to be applied to all gentlemen householders worth 300 merks a year, and to all substantious burgesses and yeomen householders who had £500 worth of goods or land. An act of 1429, which specified the kind of armour to be worn at the king's host, alludes to two classes of gentlemen. Those who had £200 yearly or £100 worth of goods were to be mounted. Those with £10 yearly or goods worth £50 were to be heavily armed in plate. There were two classes of burgesses. Those with £50 in goods were to be armed as gentlemen ought to be. A lower class had £20 worth of goods. There were several classes of yeomen: the two richest had £20 and £10 in goods or land respectively.[1] The smallness of the sums quoted is very remarkable. Unfortunately, owing to the change in the value of the coinage, it would not be safe to draw any parallel between the wealth of the same classes at different periods.

Something has been said of the high spirit of the country-folk. The townspeople were no whit behind them. In the regency of Mary of Lorraine the burgesses of Edinburgh upon one occasion "refused to condescend to sic unreasonable desyres," and the insubordination of Perth at that time is part of the general history of Scotland. The Scots mob was a formidable one, not easily amenable to royal authority. An unfortunate messenger who had been sent, in 1601, to read an unwelcome proclamation at Dundee, bitterly complained that during the reading the crowd, hounded on by the bailies, called him *knave*, *lowne*, and *deboschit swingeour*, and threw snow-balls at him, and that when he came down from the cross there "was shouting and hoying of him with loud cries throw the gait as gif he had bene a thief or malefactour."[2] The people, however, were able to rise, at least by the sixteenth century, to a most determined stand for the independence of their country. When Henry VIII was trying to secure the crown of

[1] *A.P.S.* vol. ii, p. 18; vol. iii, p. 130.
The word yeoman did not have the meaning attached to it in eighteenth-century England.

[2] A. Cameron, *Scottish Correspondence of Mary of Lorraine*, p. xi.
Register, Privy Council, vol. vi, p. 254.

Scotland by a marriage between Edward, his son, and the little Queen of Scots, and many of the nobles proved themselves to be so lacking in patriotism, the burgesses of Edinburgh, even to regain some ships that had been captured by Henry VIII, refused to lend themselves to his schemes. Sadler, the English ambassador, declared that if their little queen were carried off to England "there was not a little boy but he would hurl stones against it, the wives would handle their distaffs, and the commons would universally rather die than submit to it." The limited influence of the burgesses upon the Reformation and Killigrew's dictum regarding the decay of the noblemen's power and the rise of that of the lesser barons and the burgesses have been indicated already. As a matter of fact, the noblemen's great credit was destined to sway the destinies of Scotland for the rest of her existence as a separate state, but it is rather remarkable that any rise in middle-class influence at all should have taken place, seeing that there was no great economic change to bring this class into prominence during the whole period.[1]

Nevertheless, if the Scots of the time showed little political aptitude, they certainly displayed a magnificent fortitude under adversity. Examples abound of their courage. When rumours of the defeat at Flodden reached Edinburgh, proclamation was made that all men were to have their weapons ready, and to appear before the provost at the tolling of the common bell for the defence of the town against them that would invade the same. The women were ordered not to be seen upon the street clamouring and crying, but to pass to the kirk to pray for the king and his army and the townsmen with the army, or to hold themselves at their private labours within their houses, as becometh.[2] In 1572, whilst Edinburgh Castle was undergoing a siege, and the country was being vexed by civil war between the supporters of James VI and of Mary, the deposed queen, the *Diurnal of Occurrents* records that "thair wes in this moneth greit penuritie and scant of vivaris within the burgh of Edinburgh, sua that all wes at ane exceiding darth. Noch-

[1] *Calendar of State Papers*, vol. i, p. 70.
Hamilton Papers, vol. ii, No. 5, 1543.
Foreign Calendar, *1572–74*, p. 634.
W. L. Mathieson, *Politics and Religion in Scotland*, *1550–1695*, p. 201.

[2] Quoted by T. A. Taylor, *Life of James V*, p. 293.

theles the remaneris thairin abaid, patientlie, and wer of good comfort, and vsit all plesouris quhilkis wer wont to be vsit in the said moneth of Maij in ald tymes, viz. : Robin Hude and Litill Johne " (which as a matter of fact had been illegal since Mary Queen of Scots had suppressed them in 1562).[1]

Certain social institutions of Scotland during the period call for at least a passing allusion. A care for education characterized the old as well as the new Faith. In spite of her poverty, Scotland, during the period under review, founded most of her universities and made great advances in the provision of schools. The town council minutes of Edinburgh, which have been published for the 16th century, show how genuine was the care of the city fathers for the schools of the burgh.[2]

The rise of a pauper class and the beginning of poor law legislation and administration in Scotland is a more purely economic matter. Scotland, like England and other countries of Western Europe, suffered from a very large increase in the number of destitute persons during the fifteenth and sixteenth centuries. Their actual number and the proportion that they bore to the total population cannot be estimated, but, judging by the continuous stream of measures that were required to cope with them, they must have been very numerous. There seems to have been a good deal of unemployment in the burghs. The acts ordering burgh authorities, nobles, and barons to provide new fishing busses, empowered them to put unemployed persons to work upon the building and manning of these, and Henderson, in the *Godly and Golden Book*, published 1548, also alluded to much unemployment in the towns. There is nothing to show whether these unemployed persons were burgesses or were dependent non-freemen, but, from the wording of the Vagrancy Acts that were passed, it is evident that there was a comparatively large class of impotent persons, beggars, and wanderers who had no place in the social structure of the burghs.

During the fifteenth and the sixteenth centuries the burgh organization was able to cope with the poor who actually were part of it. This is an important feature of the Scots Poor Law

[1] *Book of the Old Edinburgh Club*, xvi, p. 5.

[2] See Hill Burton, *History of Scotland*, vol. iii, p. 400.

W. L. Mathieson, *Politics and Religion in Scotland, 1550–1695*, pp. 32, 207.

administration of the age. In the burghs of Scotland the Merchant and Craft Gilds assumed full responsibility for the support of the aged, disabled and unfortunate members of their organization and for that of their dependants. In 1603 the Nine Incorporated Trades of Dundee arranged for the support of their poor. In Glasgow it was also well organized. In Edinburgh, though the crafts showed less joint organization, the matter was dealt with systematically. In 1564-65 the deacons of the crafts obliged themselves to maintain their own poor so that the good town should not be troubled with them. In 1580 the deacons of the craftsmen held a meeting among themselves and then appeared before the magistrates and undertook to sustain their own poor and their dependants. At the same time, however, they disassented from all contributions to be universally uplifted of all the neighbours of this burgh overhead for sustaining of the whole poor thereof in general, and to any other order to be taken for their part except as before rehearsed and offered by them.[1]

The support of such poor folk, however, only touched the fringe of the problem. The trouble seems to have become serious about 1424. In that year two acts were passed forbidding companies of people from traversing the country begging and harbouring on kirkmen and husbandmen. All able-bodied folk between the ages of fourteen and seventy were forbidden to beg. In the next ninety years nearly a dozen acts followed: ordering the able-bodied poor to find themselves masters and to cease begging; commanding the burgh and county authorities, under pain of fine for negligence, to use diligence in enforcing the acts; enjoining such punishments as imprisonment, cutting-off of the ear, branding, banishment, and, for a second offence, death upon the beggars. (The penal clauses of the Scots Acts were not so severe as those of the contemporary English ones.) The acts allowed "cruiked folk, blind folk, impotent folk, and weak folk" to beg.[2]

[1] Henderson's book is printed in *Calendar of Scottish Papers*, vol. i (1547–1563), p. 144.

A. Warden, *Burgh Laws of Dundee*, p. 249.

Sketch of the activities of the Trades House of Glasgow, issued at the time of the visit of the British Association, 1928.

J. D. Marwick, *Edinburgh Gilds and Crafts*, pp. 101, 121.

[2] G. Nicholls, *History of the Scotch Poor Law*, pp. 6-9, summarizes this legislation.

In 1535 there was an important innovation, and every parish was made liable for the support of its own aged and infirm poor, who alone were allowed to beg within it. The headman of the parish was required to make collections for this purpose. During the next forty years the provisions of this act were several times recapitulated. Some attempt was made to put them into force: the town council of Edinburgh, for instance, was energetic in carrying out its obligations. Such legislation, however, was not constructive, and it seems to have done little to suppress the abuse. In spite of previous acts, we are told that beggars daily and continually multiply and resort in all places where my Lord-Governor and other nobility are convened, so that none of them may pass through the streets for raming and crying upon them.

During this period, which, it will be remembered, covered the great changes involved in the Reformation, a new theory of Poor Law administration was introduced. In 1561 the Protestant ministers, who had been entrusted with drawing up a constitution for the new Church, presented to the Estates the famous First Book of Discipline. Hume Brown points out that although the primary intention of this " extraordinary book " was the scheme of an ecclesiastical polity, " it was in fact the draft of a ' republic ' under which a nation should live its life on earth and prepare itself for heaven. It not only prescribes a creed and supplies a complete system of church government; it suggests a scheme of national education, defines the relation of Church and State, it provides for the poor and unable, it regulates the life of households, it even determines the career of such as by their natural gifts were specially fitted to be of service to Church or State. As we shall see, the suggestions of the Book of Discipline were to be but imperfectly realized; yet, by defining the ideals and moulding the temper and culture of the population, of the prevailing majority of the Scottish people, it has been one of the great formative influences in the national development."[1]

The educational provisions of the First Book of Discipline

[1] G. Nicholls, *History of the Scotch Poor Law*, pp. 9, 13, 14, 15.
A.P.S. vol. ii, p. 487.
J. Mackintosh, *History of Civilization in Scotland*, vol. ii, pp. 288-289.
P. Hume Brown, *History of Scotland*, vol. ii, p. 75.

are far more elaborate than those dealing with the poor. Nevertheless, the principles that underlie the proposed organization for the relief of the latter are of great historical importance. The axiom is laid down that " Every several kirk must provide for the poor within itself." " Stubborn and idle beggars, who, running from place to place, make a craft of their begging," were to be referred to the civil magistrates for punishment; but the Book insisted that the widow and fatherless, the aged, impotent or lamed, and persons of honesty who were fallen into decay and poverty ought to be supported as a Christian duty. The able-bodied were not to beg but were to be made to work, but those who could not work were to repair to their birthplace " unless of long continuance they have remained in one place," and reasonable provision was to be made for them as the kirk should appoint. In these provisions we have the germ of the idea of parochial relief collected and administered by the kirk authorities.

In 1579, in complete opposition to the type of organization proposed in the First Book of Discipline, an act was passed that was closely modelled upon contemporary English legislation. As in all other acts, strong and idle persons were to be punished, but special officials were entrusted with the duty of apprehending them. A sad commentary upon the state of the country is furnished by the list of persons liable to be arrested. Besides the usual motley crew of beggars, jugglers, Egyptians, fortune-tellers, minstrels, and masterless men, were persons " alleging themselves to have been heryit or burnt in some far part of the realm, or alleging themselves to be banished on account of others' wicked deeds." The infirm and aged were to be provided for in the parishes of their birth, but this was to be entrusted to the burgh authorities in the towns and to the justices of the peace—a typically English office—in the country. These officials were to have power to tax and stent all inhabitants for the support of the poor, and the machinery of administration was worked out in considerable detail. Two more acts followed. In one it was provided that should the authorities prove remiss, the ministers, elders, and deacons were to have power to appoint persons to carry out their duties. In 1579, by another act of parliament, the whole duty of dealing with the poor was entrusted to the parochial kirk-sessions. And this was endorsed

in 1600. The theory advocated in the First Book of Discipline had therefore triumphed.[1] As Nicholls points out, there had formerly been considerable resemblance between the Scots and English laws dealing with the treatment of the poor. These last two acts mark a parting of the ways. Almost contemporary with these Scots acts, which merely handed the poor over to the care of the kirk-sessions, were two elaborate English ones, making state provision for the relief of the destitute and ordering the punishment of the able-bodied.

It must be admitted that the kirk-sessions were called upon to deal with a tough proposition. The act of 1593 states that lymmers and sorners are so multiplied and grown to such boldness that they spare not to pass and wander over all parts of the realm singly and in companies, armed with swords, hacquebuts, pistols and other weapons, sometimes alleging themselves to be banished for slaughter or burnt or herried in the Borders or Highlands, sometimes disguised with false beards, or in linen clothes, or in fools' garments, hagging and extorting not only meat, drink, and victuals, but money, and in case of refusal awaiting privately until they may steal and rob the same in the night, compelling both gentlemen and yeomen after their daily labours to stand on their feet all night for safety of their own gear.[2]

In this sketchy and discursive summary of general conditions, one other point may be touched upon—the influence of continental countries, especially France and the Netherlands, upon Scotland. In the period before the Wars of Independence, Scotland was deeply influenced by England. After the break with the "Auld Enemy," when friendship between the two countries ceased, the main outside influences that affected her came from the Continent. The introduction of French words is a well-known fact. As we have seen, the trade connection with France was not so great as with the Low Countries, but socially the bond was a close one. The connection with the Low Countries was primarily an economic one. The foreign influence can be traced in the architecture, the manners and customs of the age, the institutions of Scots law: but here it is only possible to indicate a few of the more purely economic

[1] G. Nicholls, *History of the Scotch Poor Law*, pp. 16-24, 27, 29, 31-32, 33.

[2] *A.P.S.* vol. iii, p. 576.

effects. The masterstick required when a craftsman applied for admission to a Gild was usual in Scotland and abroad, but not in England. Continental precedents were often quoted in the arrangement of Scots municipal matters. In the Seal of Cause—itself a word of foreign derivation—granted to the Edinburgh wrights and masons in 1475, the overseers were to have their places in the procession like as they have in Bruges and such-like good towns. The other burghs of Scotland were ordered to have their Dean of Gild and his court as they were in Edinburgh and according to the forms used in Paris, Rouen, or other towns in France and Flanders. By another act of parliament, passed in 1489–90, the standard of silver was to be the same as that of Bruges.[1]

Such is an outline of the main features in the economic and social life of Scotland before 1600. In describing them the writer has tried to show that she is portraying, not merely the background against which the vivid, turbulent episodes of Scots political history were staged, but the all-important circumstances to whose inexorable influences these episodes were, largely, merely constantly repeated reactions. Nevertheless, in an even deeper sense, the significance of Scots economic history may be said to lie in its negative character: in the fact that the backwardness of Scotland's industrial development, the archaic social conditions under which her people continued to live, her hampering poverty, could not frustrate the evolution of the proud and vigorous race that has grown up in the grey, bleak, beloved land.

[1] J. H. Burton, *The Scot Abroad*, pp. 238, 240.
G. Gross, *Gild Merchant*, p. 190.
W. Ashley, *Economic History*, vol. ii, p. 105.
J. D. Marwick, *Edinburgh Gilds and Crafts*, pp. 48-53.
Scottish Hist. Review, vol. v, p. 515.
A.P.S. vol. iii, p. 221.
A. J. Warden, *Burgh Laws of Dundee*, p. 27.

INDEX